PATTON'S WAR

PATTON'S WAR

AN AMERICAN GENERAL'S COMBAT LEADERSHIP

VOLUME 1

November 1942–July 1944

KEVIN M. HYMEL

UNIVERSITY OF MISSOURI PRESS
Columbia

Copyright © 2021 by
The Curators of the University of Missouri
University of Missouri Press, Columbia, Missouri 65211
Printed and bound in the United States of America
All rights reserved. First printing, 2021.

Library of Congress Cataloging-in-Publication Data

Names: Hymel, Kevin M., 1966- author.
Title: Patton's war : an American general's combat leadership / Kevin M. Hymel.
Other titles: American general's combat leadership
Description: Columbia : University of Missouri Press, [2021] | Series: American military experience | Includes bibliographical references and index. | Contents: v. 1. November 1942-July 1944 --
Identifiers: LCCN 2021018747 (print) | LCCN 2021018748 (ebook) | ISBN 9780826222459 (v. 1 ; hardcover) | ISBN 9780826274632 (v. 1 ; ebook)
Subjects: LCSH: Patton, George S. (George Smith), 1885-1945. | Patton, George S. (George Smith), 1885-1945--Military leadership. | Generals--United States--Biography. | United States. Army--Biography. | World War, 1939-1945--Campaigns.
Classification: LCC E745.P3 H96 2021 (print) | LCC E745.P3 (ebook) | DDC 940.54/1273092 [B]--dc23
LC record available at https://lccn.loc.gov/2021018747
LC ebook record available at https://lccn.loc.gov/2021018748

Jacket image: Patton examines Fedala beach. He wrote his wife that he thought this photograph would made a good book cover. Library of Congress.

∞™ This paper meets the requirements of the American National Standard for Permanence of Paper for Printed Library Materials, Z39.48, 1984.

Typefaces: Minion and Museo Sans

THE AMERICAN MILITARY EXPERIENCE SERIES
JOHN C. MCMANUS, SERIES EDITOR

The books in this series portray and analyze the experience of Americans in military service during war and peacetime from the onset of the twentieth century to the present. The series emphasizes the profound impact wars have had on nearly every aspect of recent American history and considers the significant effects of modern conflict on combatants and noncombatants alike. Titles in the series include accounts of battles, campaigns, and wars; unit histories; biographical and autobiographical narratives; investigations of technology and warfare; studies of the social and economic consequences of war; and in general, the best recent scholarship on Americans in the modern armed forces. The books in the series are written and designed for a diverse audience that encompasses nonspecialists as well as expert readers.

Selected titles from this series:

Loss and Redemption at St. Vith: The 7th Armored Division in the Battle of the Bulge
Gregory Fontenot

Military Realism: The Logic and Limits of Force and Innovation in the US Army
Peter Campbell

Omar Nelson Bradley: America's GI General, 1893–1981
Steven L. Ossad

The First Infantry Division and the US Army Transformed: Road to Victory in Desert Storm, 1970–1991
Gregory Fontenot

Bataan Survivor: A POW's Account of Japanese Captivity in World War II
Frank A. Blazich

Dick Cole's War: Doolittle Raider, Hump Pilot, Air Commando
Dennis R. Okerstrom

*To my Mom and Pop, Alice "Winkie" and Gary Hymel,
without whom this book never would have been written.
My Mom didn't live to see this book, but she was my biggest fan.*

Contents

List of Photographs and Maps   xi

Preface   xv

Introduction   3

PART I: NORTH AFRICAN CORPS COMMANDER

Chapter One
    First Day of Battle   15

Chapter Two
    TORCH: Planning and Execution   31

Chapter Three
    The Restless Lion of Morocco   47

Chapter Four
    Rejuvenating II Corps in Twelve Days   67

Chapter Five
    The Battle of El Guettar   87

Chapter Six
    The Drive East   107

PART II: ARMY COMMANDER IN SICILY

Chapter Seven
    Planning the Invasion of Sicily   127

Chapter Eight
> Fighting from Gela to Palermo   153

Chapter Nine
> Victory at Messina   181

PART III: LIMBO

Chapter Ten
> The Slapping Incidents and Italy   219

Chapter Eleven
> Spiraling Down and a Chance for Redemption   245

Chapter Twelve
> A New Country, a New Army, and the Ghosts of Sicily   269

Chapter Thirteen
> FORTITUDE and Knutsford   297

Chapter Fourteen
> D-Day and the Dawn of Third Army   319

Acknowledgments   347

Notes   353

Bibliography   399

Index   413

Photographs and Maps

Photographs

1.	Patton enjoys a laugh with Rear Admiral Kent Hewitt.	22
2.	Patton, Hewitt, and others head to Fedala beach in a small boat.	24
3.	Robert Henriques poses with "Charlie," Patton's war god lava statue.	25
4.	Smashed landing craft and equipment litter Fedala beach.	27
5.	Patton surveys Fedala beach on November 8, 1942.	29
6.	Patton and Hewitt dine with Vichy French officers.	45
7.	An American M3 Grant tank rolls through Casablanca.	48
8.	The sultan of Morocco and his son greet Patton in Rabat.	52
9.	Patton, dressed in Moroccan robes, meets with the sultan and General Noguès.	54
10.	Patton's son-in-law, Lieutenant Colonel John K. Waters.	59
11.	Lieutenant General Lloyd Ralston Fredendall.	69
12.	Brigadier General Hugh Gaffey discusses the attack on Gafsa with Patton.	71
13.	Eisenhower pins Patton's third star.	84
14.	Patton visits El Guettar battlefield with Terry Allen and Teddy Roosevelt Jr.	97

15.	Major General Orlando Ward, commander of the 1st Armored Division.	99
16.	Patton inspects the Tunisian front in his personalized scout car.	101
17.	Patton watches Allied tanks advancing.	104
18.	Patton's picture of his aide, Dick Jenson.	111
19.	Al Stiller stands in the crater left by the bomb that killed Dick Jenson.	112
20.	Patton stands beneath the Arch of Trajan in Timgad.	123
21.	Montgomery and Patton inspect a map of Sicily.	133
22.	Omar N. Bradley talks with his aide, Chet Hansen.	138
23.	Patton and Hap Gay unfurl the new Seventh Army flag while Geoffrey Keyes folds the II Corps flag.	150
24.	Patton climbs over the *Monrovia*'s side to a landing craft.	155
25.	Patton gives direction on Gela beach.	156
26.	Patton puffs on a cigar in the streets of Gela.	158
27.	Truscott regails Patton with the capture of Palermo.	182
28.	Patton confers with Cardinal Luigi Lavitrano.	183
29.	Patton escorts Montgomery to his Palermo headquarters.	189
30.	Eisenhower visits General Patton at the Palermo airport.	192
31.	Patton talks to Lyne W. Bernard about his amphibious attack at Brolo.	196
32.	Sant'Agata beach on the northern side of Sicily.	200
33.	Patton visits with wounded soldiers in Sicily.	204
34.	Patton holds an informal conference with General Sir Harold Alexander.	208
35.	Patton addresses soldiers from the 82nd Airborne Division.	229
36.	Patton visits a cemetery for tankers of the 2nd Armored Division.	250

37.	Patton cuts his birthday cake with Geoffrey Keyes and Paddy Flint.	251
38.	Patton's dog Willie resting in a jeep.	280
39.	Patton addresses his troops in England.	289
40.	Patton speaks at Knutsford Hall on April 25, 1944.	299

Maps

1. Operation TORCH, November 8, 1942.	17
2. The capture of Casablanca, November 8–11, 1942.	41
3. The Tunisian campaign, March 17–April 13, 1943.	90
4. Plan for Sicily, 1943.	144
5. From Gela to Palermo, July 11–23, 1943.	167
6. From Palermo to Messina, July 24–August 17, 1943.	199
7. Early plans for the invasion of Italy.	221
8. The eve of Third Army, Normandy, July 31, 1944.	340

Preface

THERE ARE TWO General George S. Pattons. There's the man remembered from his own diaries and letters and from biographies written about him and the autobiographies of his peers. Then there's the man mentioned in the letters and memoirs of the many soldiers he led into battle. The first Patton is readily available, easily found in published books, archived documents, and films, including the Academy Award–winning Hollywood blockbuster *Patton*; the second Patton is much harder to find. This one shows up in a few paragraphs scattered among thousands of veterans' and reporters' memoirs, oral history collections, and veterans' surveys.

When I wrote my first book on Patton, *Patton's Photographs: War as He Saw It* (2006), I had considered myself lucky to find a niche of Patton's life that had not yet been explored. Specifically, I had discovered his photo albums, packed with pictures the camera-toting general personally took as well as with, in some cases, his commentary—documents that no other author had used. Still, I could not help but ask if there was anywhere to go from there. Patton's life had already been recorded in great detail by a number of fine historians, including most prominently Martin Blumenson, Carlo D'Este, and Stanley Hirshon. Other authors had already traced his family tree, researching and writing about his wife and children. Was there more left to uncover?

Although my first book is a collection of Patton's photography, in talking to veterans and other historians in the course of my research, I realized there was much more to add about the general outside of the context of a man and his camera. Having focused my research, I found myself accumulating a pile of never-before-revealed stories. This book is a result of that work.

Yet as I embarked on this book, I still had a fundamental decision to make: should I just list the new information in a short treatise, or should I take up the far greater challenge and present the general's combat experiences from day one of World War II to the last day of battle? In order to do the latter, I needed to contextualize the new revelations I had compiled in order to better understand Patton's thinking and actions during the momentous conflict. This led me to examine all of Patton's diaries and letters at the Library of Congress. While Martin Blumenson's *The Patton Papers* is considered the Bible for anyone wishing to form an understanding of the iconic American general, space limitations forced Blumenson to edit out a portion of Patton's WWII material. But I wanted it all. I also studied the works of the people surrounding Patton during the fighting—staffers, corps commanders, and division commanders. If, for example, Patton wrote his wife that he was feeling sick, or even just blue, I wanted to know what affected him. Again, I wanted the whole story. The result is a thorough examination of Patton's growth in some areas and his deterioration in others during the zenith of his military career.

This book originated in a comment made by my friend John McManus, professor of military history at the University of Missouri of Science and Technology and the editor of the University of Missouri Press's series *The American Military Experience*. John pressed me to find a new perspective on Patton. Upon reflection, I decided to focus exclusively on Patton's experiences in World War II. My hope was that in doing so I could illuminate his actions, eradicate a few myths, and possibly discover some of his motivations. I also had access to information that had not been available to either Blumenson or D'Este: published memoirs and letters from WWII veterans who served under Patton; firsthand accounts of meetings with Patton that found their way into museums and library special collections; and newly created digital maps, all of which helped put his exploits into sharper focus. By combining well-known sources with this new vein of information, I hope to present a more thorough examination of one of the United States' best-known military leaders.

Every soldier who met Patton remembered the moment distinctly. In each case it was a high point, or at least a memorable experience. For many, it became a badge of honor to be chewed out by him, and for some even to be accosted by him. Not only was Patton already famous by the time he arrived on the coast of Morocco, where this story begins, but both his ire and occasional manifestations of humor in these encounters left distinct marks worth remembering. Most important, each encounter with a soldier presented yet another example of Patton's frontline presence.

This first volume of *Patton's War* focuses on the general's life from November 8, 1942, when he landed on the shore of Fedala beach in Morocco, until July 31, 1944, the day before his Third Army went to war on the European continent. Both this volume, appearing in the American Military Experience series, and its sequels analyze Patton's leadership on the battlefield and his actions between campaigns. The book is written for both the serious student and the casual reader. Because I did not set out to write anything like a full biography, I only address Patton's previous education and experience when they affected his battlefield decision making.

While I have been to almost all of Patton's WWII battlefields, from Morocco and Sicily to England and the continent of Europe, and have poured through some twenty-five hundred soldiers' memoirs in the Library of Congress and other repositories around the United States and England, I am confident I did not find every story about him. Logistical challenges, complicated further by the coronavirus pandemic, got in the way of some of my research. Nevertheless, I have endeavored to present a much more layered portrait of one of America's iconic generals than previously existed.

All opinions and interpretations expressed in this book are mine alone and all errors, both of omission and commission, are my responsibility.

Kevin M. Hymel
Arlington, VA

PATTON'S WAR

Introduction

ONE OF THE best stories this historian ever heard about General George S. Patton Jr.'s generalship did not qualify for the subsequent chapters of this book—but I will tell it here. An American soldier sat alone in a foxhole, exhausted and disheveled, in the Tunisian desert. He hadn't eaten or bathed in days. Then, behind him, a U.S. Army command car rolled up and out popped Patton, impeccably dressed in his battle uniform. The general marched up to the soldier and berated him for his appearance, calling him a disgrace. As Patton turned and walked away, the soldier raised his rifle and took aim at his back. Thinking better of it, he lowered the rifle. It took twenty years for the soldier, by then a civilian, to realize that Patton had done the right thing. Before his brief but enraging encounter with the general, the soldier said, he would have readily surrendered to the first German soldier who showed up. But Patton left him angry, so angry that he was more than ready to kill anyone who dared to approach his foxhole.

The curator of France's Brittany American Cemetery related this story to me in 2005. He had met the veteran years before at the North African American Cemetery in Carthage, Tunisia. Unfortunately, the story was not documented and so cannot be verified, but it exemplifies Patton's leadership, highlighting his use of aggressiveness and brusqueness to get his soldiers to fight. This scenario would be repeated across the battlefields of North Africa, Sicily, England, and the European continent. Patton's was a unique style of leadership, one which got results but sometimes bordered on the tyrannical. It was his leadership and temper that Patton worked hard though not always successfully—to balance.

This book examines Patton's leadership as a general during World War II. The U.S. Army defines a leader as someone who serves as a role model through strong intellect, physical presence, professional competence, and moral character. In addition, a leader is someone willing and able to act decisively, within a superior leader's intent and purpose, in the Army's best interest, as well as being someone who recognizes that organizations (not individuals) accomplish the mission.[1] Throughout the war, Patton strove to live up to this ideal. At times he surpassed it, at other times he fell woefully short.

While Patton had fought before—in Mexico as a lieutenant in the cavalry and in World War I as a lieutenant colonel in the tank corps—in World War II, from the first day of battle to the last, he fought as a general. The stars on his shoulders, collar, and helmet meant that he now controlled and coordinated different branches of the service—the infantry, armor, and the artillery, as well as engineers, doctors, and the military police—and in Patton's case, the U.S. Navy and Army Air Forces. Patton the general understood how each separate entity functioned alone and with one another—the mark of a generalist. He spent the war perfecting his style of generalship, rising through the ranks from a two-star to a four-star general by the time the guns fell silent.[2]

An emotional man, he was prone to a short temper that could explode at any time. He could equally be brought to tears, usually in front of battlefield wounded. At times, the temper and tears manifested together. He could be abrupt to the point of driving people away and suffered bouts of depression. He also enthralled people with his knowledge of poetry and history. One of the keys to Patton's leadership was his love of reading history, especially military history. All his life, and throughout World War II, he consumed volumes of history, always learning through examples of victory and defeat. An extrovert, he relished public speaking, motivating and teaching soldiers how to attack, adapt, and win on the battlefield.

From the training camps of the United States to battlefields across the Atlantic, there was no mistaking George S. Patton or his effect on those he commanded. When he entered a room or stepped onto the battlefield, the men around him changed. Salutes became sharp and spines stiff. He brought a sense of urgency wherever he went, and that energy brought results. Whether the men around him feared him, loved him, or hated him, the effect was the same: action.

Throughout World War II, Patton fought bravely and brilliantly. He took calculated risks and could often be found near the front, where the bullets flew and the artillery exploded. He stood as a warrior example to his men in the field, encouraging those he commanded, although sometimes resorting to irrational verbal abuse and inflicting corporal punishment upon those who did not live up to his standards. His personal judgements also, at times, lapsed.

In Morocco Patton pushed landing craft back into the water, ordered his men to return fire at strafing enemy aircraft, and helped retrieve dead bodies from the sea. He also fired his sidearm when needed. The Vichy French surrendered to him before he could prove his mettle at the gates of Casablanca. In Tunisia, he resuscitated a defeated corps through discipline (that at time seemed excessive) and improved conditions. He pushed and prodded his divisions forward, on occasion personally leading them through minefields. He constantly exposed himself to enemy fire. He also fired ineffective commanders and supported those who fought well.

In Sicily, he personally helped repel an enemy armored attack that threatened to throw his troops back into the sea. When denied roads by British general Bernard Law Montgomery, and any meaningful objective by British general Harold Alexander, Patton created his own extra corps and sent it north to Palermo, effectively cutting the island in half. He followed up that victory by hopscotching along Sicily's north coast to beat Montgomery to Messina, Montgomery's objective for the entire campaign. During this operation, Patton's decision to remove the 1st Infantry Division commander and deputy commander—Terry Allen and Teddy Roosevelt Jr.—proved incredibly unpopular, but his reasons for doing so were sound. Oddly enough, Patton's corps commander, Omar Bradley, took credit for the removal, calling it a relief.

Patton made mistakes, some of them horrible. In Tunisia, he possibly caused, and covered up, the death of his aide, Captain Richard Jenson. He also killed a Sicilian civilian who blocked his route on a mountain road. Patton's draconian discipline angered his subordinates and sometimes turned soldiers against him. His penchant for berating soldiers and delivering corporal punishment culminated in episodes at two different hospital tents in Sicily, in which Patton slapped soldiers suffering from what we now recognize as post-traumatic stress disorder. Both incidents had far-reaching effects, as Patton's commander, General Dwight D. Eisenhower, decided his fate. Patton spent months in semi-exile as Eisenhower weighed his usefulness. But even after Eisenhower decided to keep Patton as an active commander, the latter still had to wait to be called back to the war. In the meantime he busied himself by planning his own army's invasion of the Italian mainland. During that wait, two more incidents surfaced, involving men under his command who had killed prisoners of war, actions which, they claimed, had been committed under Patton's order. While both cases would eventually be resolved, they haunted Patton.

Finally called back into the war at the start of 1944, Patton arrived in England to take command of Third Army as part of the battle for France and the invasion of Germany. He attended training demonstrations and often interjected when he saw soldiers or tankers committing minor mistakes that could cost lives on the battlefield. He also lectured units, providing them with practical instruction, mixed with stories and anecdotes to improve their fighting spirit, with curses liberally added to get the men's attention. While Patton honed his army, the Allies used his name to trick the Germans into believing he would lead an amphibious assault at the French port of Calais, northeast of Normandy. As part of the deception, he was ordered to keep a low profile while in Britain.

But Patton could not seem to keep himself out of trouble. A speech he gave to a group of British civilians in Knutsford appeared in the local papers. Worse, some accounts had him insulting one of the Allied countries. Patton's exposure to the press enraged Eisenhower while the gaff caused an uproar in the United States. Despite the minor crisis, Eisenhower decided that Patton's value to the war effort outweighed the embarrassments. He kept Patton in command of Third Army, albeit after berating him for his behavior and eliciting a promise to keep quiet.

The invasion of France, D-Day, June 6, 1944, occurred without Patton. Despite his knowledge of the area (he had visited it as a young officer), his experience with both amphibious combat assaults and fighting the Germans on an army level, Patton remained behind while other, less-experienced and less-creative leaders planned and executed the assault. Patton, no doubt, would have done things differently. He waited a month in England before finally flying across the English Channel to Normandy, where he waited another month as enough troops and tanks arrived. Finally, on August 1, 1944, he took the reins of Third Army. Volume 1 of this book ends here.

Throughout the fighting in North Africa and Sicily and in the aftermath of each campaign, Patton constantly frustrated, embarrassed, and impressed Eisenhower. Early in the fighting, Patton respected his superior and his seemingly impossible job as Allied commander. As the campaigns ground across Tunisia and Sicily, however, Patton grew sour on Eisenhower, feeling his commander was more interested in politics than combat (he was not) and more concerned with holding together an alliance than promoting the U.S. Army (he was). On the personal level, Patton continually worried that Eisenhower would send him home. While most of these fears swelled between campaigns, they remained in the back of Patton's mind as he led combat operations. When Patton felt Eisenhower was ignoring him, or worse, shunning him, he resorted to drinking and sulking. He would also vent to his staff or disparage Eisenhower in his diaries and letters to his wife. He accused Eisenhower of short-sightedness on the battlefield, of cozying up to British allies—if not entirely caving to their ideas—and favoring weak American generals.

Patton's relationship with General Omar Bradley was more complex. Patton was Bradley's superior in North Africa and Sicily, yet Bradley went on to command Patton as an army group commander as Patton prepared Third Army for combat. While Bradley got along well with Patton in North Africa, in Sicily he felt Patton caved to British demands without a fight. By the time Patton arrived in England, Bradley wanted little to do with him. And if Patton's relationship with Bradley was complicated, his relationship with British general Bernard Montgomery was a simple combination of hatred and envy. Although Patton started the war respecting the British officer, by the planning stage of the invasion of Sicily, his distrust of Montgomery had taken root—and would only grow over the next three years. He judged Montgomery to be a pompous, arrogant, and overly cautious general who openly worked against him during most of the Sicilian campaign. Patton could tolerate pompousness, but only if backed up with battlefield success.

The Patton who first stepped onto Moroccan sands on November 8, 1942, was well-educated and experienced at his profession. He had a keen sense of humor and sharp temper, but he also had an energy about him. As a young officer, he had constantly tested his own courage, often sticking his head out on rifle ranges to face his fear. He believed in his own reincarnation and that he had lived all previous lives as a warrior. He wrote poetry about war and combat. He knew how to fly planes. He wore his own special pistols on the battlefield, yet also carried a camera. He steeled himself most of his life to be a perfect warrior, waiting and hoping for the chance to prove it on a large scale.[3]

Born in California on November 11, 1885, and named after his father, George S. Patton, the young Patton grew up on Bible stories, the classics, and heroic tales of the Confederate Army. His grandfather and uncles—Virginians all—had fought and died for the Confederacy, forcing his grandmother to leave the blighted state and head west to join her more prosperous family in California. Patton's father had attended the Virginia Military Institute (VMI), like his father before him, but became a lawyer. Young George had one sister, Nita, who never married.[4]

Patton held a strong belief in the social class system, hesitating to socialize with people below his perceived class. "It is too much work with people out of ones [sic] own class who are not dressed up," he once wrote his wife.[5] He grew up in a world where institutional racism and anti-Semitism permeated American society. Jim Crow laws kept blacks from enjoying any kind of equality, while people of the Jewish faith experienced less prejudice—but not by much. Patton's father admitted that blacks were treated poorly but refused to consider reparations because they might "imperil the continued supremacy of our own race, or threaten the pollution of its Aryan blood." Patton's world, including his schools and the U.S. Army, were mostly all white, overwhelmingly Anglo-Saxon Protestant, politically conservative, and racially segregated. Patton constantly used the word "nigger" when referring to African Americans, and "Jew" when writing about anyone of the Jewish faith. Paradoxically, during the war, he was close to his aide Sergeant George Meeks, an African American, and Colonel Oscar Koch, a Jewish officer. Patton got along with both men, yet continued to make derogatory comments about both groups. His prejudices would pop up from time to time on the battlefields of the Mediterranean and Europe, tainting his leadership role, as a general is supposed to look past such distinctions.[6]

Patton often displayed traits of his specific leadership style throughout his youth and young adulthood. As a child, he played with toy soldiers and wooden swords and reenacted ancient battles. He started attending a private academy at age eleven, where he experienced reading and writing difficulties—probably the result of dyslexia, an unknown disability at the time. After high school, he attended VMI for a year before transferring to the U.S. Military Academy at West Point. While he excelled at VMI, earning good grades and high marks for his military bearing, West Point proved more challenging. He excelled in history and military comportment, but his grades suffered in other classes, forcing him to repeat his first, or "plebe" year. It was at West Point that Patton's fierce temper emerged. Promoted to second corporal, he harassed plebes, angering almost everyone around him in the process. Infractions, however slight, literally made him see red. He admitted that just looking at a plebe angered him, a rage that could last for days. He graduated in 1909 and went to serve in the U.S. Army's cavalry.[7]

Patton married his childhood sweetheart, Beatrice Ayer, on May 26, 1910. She would be his companion, lover, muse, confidant, and confessor, as well as his greatest cheerleader, for the rest of his life. Born to a rich Boston family, Beatrice accepted George's marriage proposal minutes after their first kiss. She bore him three children: Beatrice, whom they called "Little Bea," Ruth Ellen, and George. Army life kept the couple apart for long periods, and, while World War II kept them separated for three years, he wrote her almost every day.[8]

Patton was also an accomplished athlete, so much so that, three years into his Army career, he participated in the 1912 summer Olympics in Stockholm. He competed in the modern pentathlon, which included a pistol shoot, a three-hundred-meter swim, fencing, a steeple-chase ride, and a two-and-a-half-mile run. In so doing, Patton displayed to the world his strength, skill, determination, and passion for winning. He pushed himself so hard during the swim portion that he had to be drawn from the pool with a boat hook. He did well in the shoot, only missing the target twice. He pushed himself too hard again during the run, holding the lead until he neared the finish line, slowing to a walk and collapsing after crossing it. He finished third in fencing and earned a perfect score in the steeplechase. Overall, he finished fifth out of forty-two athletes.[9]

After the Olympics, Patton learned about a new design for the sword, modeled after the French cavalry sword, and brought it back to the United States. The Army soon adopted it as the M1913 Patton Saber. He traveled to France, where he attended the French cavalry school in Saumur and studied fencing under Europe's champion, Lieutenant Mas de la Tree, whom he had bested in Stockholm. He and Bea visited locations in Cherbourg and Normandy, including Vanes, St. Malo, St. Lo, and Caen, making friends with French officers and improving his French language skills along the way.[10]

Determined to take advantage of any opportunity to prove himself a fighter, Patton served on Brigadier General John Pershing's staff during the Army's punitive expedition to hunt down the Mexican revolutionary Pancho Villa in 1916. At his own request, Patton was transferred to the cavalry, as part of which he tracked down one of Villa's lieutenants, General Julio Cardenas, at Rubio Ranch. Using automobiles in combat for the first time in American military history, Lieutenant Patton and a handful of soldiers encircled the ranch and gunned down Cardenas and two other banditos on horseback in a wild shootout. The Americans strapped the corpses to the hoods of their cars and proudly brought them back to Pershing.[11]

When the United States entered World War I on April 2, 1917, Patton first served as an assistant to General Pershing before leaving for the newest branch of the U.S. Army—the Tank Corps. He established a tank school, created a tank training ground, and wrote the first manual for tank operations. He brought discipline and intelligence to the fledgling unit, and made it one of the most efficient in the Army. So impressive was this young tanker that he also lectured on tank tactics at the French Army General Staff College before he had even led the iron beasts into battle.[12]

He brought that same drive to the battlefield. At the Battle of St.-Mihiel, on September 12, 1918, he followed his tanks on foot and helped dig some out of the mud. He stood in the face of an artillery barrage that forced almost everyone else to the ground and walked over a bridge to prove it was not mined. He climbed onto a tank and led it forward, leaping off when he noticed machine-gun bullets chipping away the paint on the turret. About nine days later, he led his tanks again in the Meuse-Argonne offensive. Again, he followed his tanks into battle and again helped dig them out of the mud. This time, with his tanks out of gas, he led an impromptu infantry attack until a German bullet struck him in the upper thigh. The war ended two months later, on November 11, 1918, his thirty-third birthday. As a result of his battlefield actions, the name Patton would forever be associated with tanks.[13]

The conclusion of World War I meant the end of combat exhilaration for Patton. Worse yet, he now found himself in a shrinking peacetime army. When it cut its armor budget in 1920, he returned to the cavalry. He attended the Command and General Staff College at Fort Leavenworth, Kansas, and the Army War College in Carlisle, Pennsylvania, served in Massachusetts and Washington, D.C., and spent two tours in Hawaii.[14]

The first tour of Hawai'i, from 1925 to 1928, began well. Patton served as both the head of intelligence and personnel, earning a promotion to head of war plans and training. However, his abrasive nature, impatience with others' mistakes, including the brash denunciation of his superiors' errors, cost him his job. Transferred to the Chief of Cavalry Office at Fort Myer near Washington, D.C., he served as executive officer. When Depression-era WWI veterans who wanted their promised pay bonus sooner rather than later—the Bonus Army—converged on Washington and were eventually ordered out of the capital, Patton, on horseback, scouted ahead for the cavalry, then joined the main force in driving the bedraggled and shocked marchers back across the Anacostia River.[15]

Transferred again to Hawai'i, this time from 1935 to 1937, Patton felt his usefulness to the Army had come to an end. He grew bored with his intelligence duties, drank too often, and cursed too much. His aimlessness led him to an affair with his wife's niece, twenty-one-year-old Jean Gordon (he was forty-two at the time), for which he later apologized. When his Hawai'ian tour ended in 1937, he sailed the family back to the United States in his own yacht.[16]

Patton returned to a world unraveling. The Japanese had invaded China and Spain was fighting a civil war, mostly with weapons from Nazi Germany and the Soviet Union. Italy, which had invaded Ethiopia the year before, entered into a supportive pact with both Germany and Japan. Just as the world around him was becoming interesting, Patton's army career almost ended. A horse kicked him, double fracturing his leg. It took him six months to recover, all the while bed ridden. While working himself back to health, he taught cavalry tactics to the soldiers of the 9th Cavalry Regiment at Fort Riley, Kansas.[17]

Promoted to colonel, Patton commanded the 5th Cavalry Regiment at Fort Clark, Texas, for only four months, before being called to Washington to take command of the 3rd Cavalry Regiment at Fort Myer on December 10, 1938. He found the assignment disappointing, even though it led to a close relationship with the Army's new chief of staff, General George C. Marshall. While Patton was at Fort Myer, on September 1, 1939, Germany invaded Poland. For the next two years, Patton's star would rise as the war crept closer to the United States. Olympic athlete, motorized and armored warfare pioneer, cavalry officer, pilot, sailor, tanker, war hero—Patton could point to an exciting and diverse career that seemed to align him perfectly for the challenges ahead.[18]

This is the man who stepped onto the sand of Fedala beach in Morocco on November 8, 1942, and would go on to spend the next thirty months spearheading the destruction of the Axis Powers, until he stood in Pilsen, Czechoslovakia, on May 7, 1945, and learned the war in Europe was over. While Patton led a unique life of military opportunity, his exploits in World War II specifically made him an icon of American history, military study, and even international pop culture. The accumulation of Patton's experience, hard work, and unique personality paid off on the battlefields of North Africa, Sicily, and the European continent. Everything he had strived for in his life seemed to benefit him and his soldiers during the war. It was as if the path of George Patton's life intersected with world events when the world most needed someone like him.

As much as World War II saw the culmination of his career, so too did it symbolize the global ascendancy of the United States military, which had long been in the shadow of Europe's professional armies. This was no coincidence. Patton's accomplishments helped make the United States a superpower. While Patton did not live to see it, so too would his exploits grow to legendary status. His image will forever be associated with World War II—Patton's War.

PART I
North African Corps Commander

CHAPTER ONE

First Day of Battle

MAJOR GENERAL GEORGE S. Patton Jr. unholstered his ivory-handled Smith and Wesson .357 Magnum revolver, aimed, and fired. The bullet whizzed past the head of his intended target. He missed, but he achieved his goal just the same. His target, a local Moroccan man picking up an American rifle on Fedala beach, got the message, dropping the rifle and darting off. American soldiers nearby popped their heads above their sandy foxholes to investigate what had disturbed the relative quiet. Patton had announced his presence on the battlefield his way, with his first shot fired in World War II.[1]

Sunday, November 8, 1942, was a long day for Patton. It started at 2:00 a.m. when he awoke, fully clothed in khaki trousers, shirt, and tie, in the captain's cabin aboard the USS *Augusta*, the flagship of the American Western Task Force. After only five hours of sleep, he got out of bed and put on a pair of regular Army buckle boots instead of his flashier cavalry ones. He tucked his pants into his boots and pulled on a simple button-up infantryman's jacket with the triangular I Armored Corps patch on the breast, identifying his command prior to taking on the mantle of the Western Task Force. He hung a pair of binoculars around his neck, a camera case over one shoulder, and donned his war helmet. He chose not to strap on his two ivory-handled pistols, instead having them packed on a landing craft that would take him to shore. The double-starred rank of a major general gleamed from his helmet, his collar, and shoulders. There would be no mistaking him on the battlefield.[2]

The face that greeted Patton in the mirror reflected almost fifty-seven years of adventurous living. His silver-white hair had receded to his temples, but a few strands still graced his crown. Crow's feet spread from the corners of his eyes, and skin hung slightly from his jowls on either side of thin lips. His teeth were stained brown from a lifetime of smoking cigarettes, cigars, and pipes. Despite an outdoor life of horseback riding, sailing, and soldiering, a small paunch had developed in his midsection. He explained his weight gain in 1945 thus: "My weight is due to more brains." Scars from horse-riding accidents, competitive sports, and bullets speckled his body, but his uniform provided ample cover.[3] Dressed for battle and fully awake, he went on deck to see the lights of the Moroccan city of Fedala. The sea, predicted to be pitching and turbulent, lay perfectly still, a dead calm. "God is with us," he thought.[4]

Patton stood at the tip of the spear of thirty-five thousand men ready to storm three Moroccan beaches. His Western Task Force comprised 106 large naval vessels and numerous small landing craft. He commanded soldiers from the 3rd Infantry Division and elements of the 9th Infantry Division. He had 252 tanks from both the 70th Tank Battalion and the 2nd Armored Division. His air force claimed 229 Navy and Army aircraft. Naval guns would handle any sustained heavy fire beyond his soldiers' reach. The task force was split into three groups: the Northern Attack Group, consisting of the 9th Infantry Division's 60th Combat Team under Brigadier General Lucian Truscott attacking Mehdia and Port Lyautey; the Center Attack Group, consisting of the 3rd Infantry Division, under Major General Jonathan W. Anderson, taking Fedala, sixteen miles north of Casablanca; and the Southern Attack Group, consisting of the 2nd Armored Division and the 9th Infantry's 47th Combat Team under Major General Earnest (Ernie) Harmon, attacking the port of Safi, 150 miles south of Casablanca. Patton would go ashore with Anderson's troops.[5]

Patton's attack was just one part of Operation TORCH, which brought western Allied forces onto North African shores in three separate amphibious assaults. Two task forces of combined American and British troops departed from England to simultaneously attack the cities of Algiers and Oran, both in Algeria. Only Patton's all-American Western Task Force journeyed across the Atlantic Ocean for Morocco's shores. TORCH was the United States' first offensive in the war against the Axis powers and came almost a year after the Japanese attack on Pearl Harbor. However, the Allies would not be fighting the Germans or Italians during TORCH. Instead, they faced the Vichy French.

As Patton waited to begin his first attack of the war, Europe had been ablaze for the last four years. Adolf Hitler's invasion of Poland on

CHAPTER ONE ★ FIRST DAY OF BATTLE

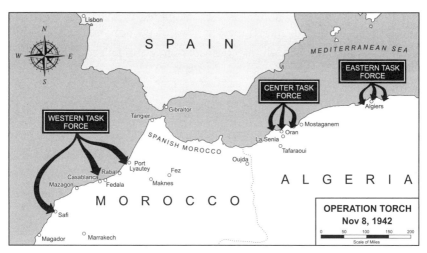

Map 1. Operation TORCH, November 8, 1942

September 1, 1939, signaled the official opening of World War II. The Soviet Union's Joseph Stalin soon joined him in dividing up Poland. Stalin next invaded Finland while Hitler attacked Norway, ejecting British and French forces. Then, on May 10, 1940, Hitler attacked France and the bordering Low Countries, driving the Allies west. British prime minister Winston Churchill saved a portion of his army from the beaches of Dunkirk, but Great Britain stood alone until the next year, when Hitler invaded the Soviet Union on June 22, 1941. While war raged in Eastern Europe, the western Allies fought the Germans in the seas and skies and faraway battlefields. German forces invaded Yugoslavia and Greece. They also dropped paratroopers onto Crete. In North Africa fighting seesawed across the Egyptian and Libyan deserts after the British defeated an attacking Italian force. To contain the British gains, the Germans sent a corps commanded by General Erwin Rommel to help their whipped partner.[6]

Rommel soon went on the offensive and drove the British back to Egypt. Attacks and counterattacks raged across the desert, with Rommel constantly fooling or overwhelming the British. A worried Churchill continued to replace his desert commanders until he landed on General Bernard Law Montgomery, who restored morale and, after an intense battle at El Alamein, overwhelmed and drove Rommel west in early November 1942. Operation TORCH was meant to help Montgomery by getting men and arms behind Rommel, shutting off his retreat to Tunisia, surrounding him, and eventually destroying his army. This was the world that Patton entered the morning of November 8.

Patton's mission was almost the operation that wasn't. During the TORCH planning sessions in Washington, D.C., in which Patton took part, the British protested that his assault on Morocco was unnecessary. They argued that the port at Casablanca was too distant—thirteen hundred miles—from the Tunisian battlefield where the British hoped to fight the Axis. They also contended that the Atlas Mountains made travel between the two locations difficult. But the Americans wanted possession of Africa's closest port to the United States and argued vehemently for the operation. After one particularly heated debate, an infuriated Patton stormed home, picked up a foot-tall Hawai'ian war statue, marched out to the backyard, and threw it into the pond. The statue, nicknamed "Charlie," had been a good-luck gift from Patton's wife. But with the Moroccan landings stymied by politics, Patton felt the war gods had turned on him and took his wrath out on Charlie. Still, the British eventually bent to the Americans' desire to attack Morocco and Patton's Western Task Force set sail for North Africa.[7]

Patton spent the fifteen-day voyage to Morocco exercising, attending religious services, and shooting an M1 carbine rifle off the ship's fantail. He exercised by walking around the ship, using a rowing machine, or holding onto his dresser and running in place; by his calculations, 480 steps equaled a quarter mile. He took pictures of his staff and enjoyed the *Augusta*'s amenities: a private bathtub in his room and well-prepared meals: "I have to watch eating too much," he confessed. Everywhere he went on the ship a Marine guard shadowed him, to Patton's irritation. He filled his daily lulls by writing letters and diary entries and reading books, including the Koran. Emotionally, he oscillated between worrying about the coming battle and trusting in fate.[8]

As the task force neared the North African shore, Patton's war speech played over each ship's public address system. "Soldiers and sailors," his voice barked, "We are to be congratulated because we have been chosen as the units of the United States Army best trained to take part in this great American effort." In a booming, though high-pitched tone, Patton explained the operation's objectives, described the enemy, and offered encouragement: "When the great day of battle comes, remember your training, and remember above all that speed and vigor of attack are the sure roads to success, and you must succeed—for to retreat is as cowardly as it is fatal. Indeed, once landed, retreat is impossible. Americans do not surrender." He stressed that a pint of sweat saved a gallon of blood and concluded, "On our victory depends the freedom or slavery of the human race. We shall surely win."[9] The men were issued the password of the day to prevent friendly fire incidents once ashore. To the challenge "George," a soldier would answer, "Patton."[10]

Patton steeled himself for whatever lay ahead. "My whole life has been pointed at this moment," he wrote his wife. "All I want to do right now is my full duty. If I do that, the rest will take care of itself." To a friend he wrote, "We shall be completely successful." But a small quiver of doubt was palpable: "If we are not, it is not my intention to live to make excuses; however, I feel very healthy for a dead man."[11] Patton had done everything possible to ensure success, from training his troops to requesting all needed equipment, in only a few months' time. Only hours before the landings were to take place, he spotted an imperfection that he felt might hinder the operation. Shown a French-language pamphlet intended to be dropped by the thousands over Moroccan cities, he noticed it lacked accents on certain French words. He quickly gathered his staff and ordered them to add the accents. "Or do you expect me to land on French soil introduced by such illiterate calling cards—Goddam it?"[12]

If the poorly worded pamphlet irritated Patton, a message from the president infuriated him. As the fleet arrived off Morocco well before sunrise on November 8, a BBC broadcast from Franklin D. Roosevelt to all of North Africa asked the Vichy regime not to obstruct the assaulting forces. The broadcast had been timed to coordinate with the assaults on Oran and Algiers, which took place hours earlier than Patton's landing. Patton worried that the broadcast blew his cover before a single landing craft had headed to shore.[13]

Somewhere in the darkness, Patton's troops clambered down rope nets into those landing craft. Some overloaded soldiers fell into the water, never to reemerge. H-hour, the time for the assault, approached—4:00 a.m.—and passed without action. The Navy kept delaying as coxswains struggled to get their landing craft into formation for the push toward the shore. Patton anxiously watched the transports line up, visible only by their colored lights. Over the radio, he heard the naval commanders speaking in code, organizing the fleet: "All my chickens are here, am holding them." Then an American submarine cruised up and guided in the destroyers. All was quiet.[14]

The Navy had delivered Patton's force to the battlefield on time and in the right spot, despite his doubts. A month before, he had predicted that the Navy would break down in the first five minutes and the Army would have to provide the victory. "Never in history," he had told his Navy comrades, "has the Navy landed an army at the planned time and place. If you land us anywhere within fifty miles of Fedhala [sic] and within one week of D-day, I'll go ahead and win." When poor weather threatened his landing, he radioed Eisenhower that if he could not land on the west coast of Africa, he would land somewhere else, even neutral Spain. But the weather held, and the Navy had done its job. Now it was Patton's turn.[15]

The general gathered a group of Army officers together for one last pep talk. "All I can promise you is that we will attack for sixty hours, after that, we will attack for sixty hours more." He told them if the French fought back, they would do so at their own peril. If they chose not to, his men should kiss them on their cheeks and move on. He explained that soldiers could walk faster forward than backward, alluding to his disdain of retreat. "Gentlemen," he concluded, "the weather is delightful and so are our prospects. Prepare at once for action."[16]

The speech revealed the single question that dogged Patton, as it did all the men in landing crafts and every commander as far away as the War Department in Washington: Would the Vichy French fight? Would there be an exchange of wine and chocolate bars on the beaches or of hot lead? The French held no love for the Germans, but since France's surrender to Germany in 1940 they were subject to German orders. In exchange for Hitler giving the French a portion of their own country to police—Vichy France, which included French territories like Morocco—the Vichy regime swore to defend their country from Germany's enemies. The Americans hoped the French would join them in the fight against the Axis, but as the soldiers and sailors headed ashore, no one, not even Patton, knew what would happen once the boats touched sand.

The radio crackled and Patton heard from General Harmon at Safi: "Batter up." Bad news: his troops were under fire. An hour later Patton eyed a single searchlight on shore shoot into the sky—the prearranged signal for no opposition—then turn to the beach. The sun rose as the destroyers opened fire, providing covering fire for the men spilling out of their landing craft. To Patton, their tracer fire looked like fireflies. Four French ships steamed in to challenge the U.S. Navy, commencing a duel. General Lucien Truscott radioed in: "Play ball." He needed naval firepower to knock out a coastal battery on Mehdia beach. Patton's watch showed 7:13 a.m.[17]

Patton prepared himself to go ashore at for 8:00 a.m., but his favorite pistols were missing, waiting for him on his landing craft, which had just been swung out over the water by two davits. Not wanting to wait until he was bobbing toward the African shore to strap on his weapons, Patton ordered Staff Sergeant George Meeks, his African American orderly, to retrieve the pistols. He had purchased his .45 caliber automatic Colt "Peacemaker" in 1916, just before departing for Mexico to take part in General John J. Pershing's hunt for Pancho Villa. Patton had an eagle carved into one of the ivory grips. After a shootout at Rubio Ranch in which Patton helped kill one of Villa's commanders, Julio Cardenas, and two of his men, he cut two notches into the grip, denoting the two bandits he helped kill. Patton kept an empty shell in the chamber under the hammer after accidentally wounding himself when a holstered Colt discharged as he stomped his feet, searing his thigh. He wanted a second pistol after having to reload his Peacemaker in the middle of the Rubio Ranch shootout, purchasing the Magnum, which he called his "killing gun," in late 1935. Patton wore the pistols, both with ivory grips and his initials carved onto them, on a belt that included a compass in a handcuff case and an extra cartridge in a rectangular case.[18]

As soon as Meeks brought Patton the holstered pistols, three French warships appeared, driving hard for the fleet. The *Augusta* accelerated and opened fire with its rear gun. The subsequent blast bent Patton's empty landing craft in half, and it had to be dropped overboard.[19] Patton lost all his personal items except his pistols. Barely batting an eye, he remarked to his bodyguard, "Such are the fortunes of war. . . . Let's go to the beach!"[20] But he wasn't going anywhere.

For the next three-and-a-half hours the French and American fleets exchanged fire. Geysers erupted on either side of the *Augusta*. One, containing a French yellow dye marker, drenched Patton as he leaned over the side. He witnessed an even closer near miss while on the bridge, but this geyser could not reach him atop his high perch. He considered naval warfare impersonal. Gone were the days of cutlass-wielding sailors clashing between wooden sailing ships. When the French fleet retreated around 11:30, Patton and some officers sat down for lunch. "Naval war is nice and comfortable," he remarked. Lunch complete, Patton prepared

Figure 1. Patton enjoys a laugh with Rear Admiral Kent Hewitt, the officer in charge of the naval portion of TORCH. Hewitt originally wanted Patton fired, but they eventually resolved their differences and worked well together. Hewitt amazed Patton by arriving off Fedala beach on time. Catalog number: 80-G AFA 56, National Archives and Records Administration.

to go ashore when he got another message from Harmon: his force had captured a battalion of the French Foreign Legion infantry, three tanks, and a large cache of guns. Patton was pleased.[21]

Six members of Patton's staff joined him on the landing craft: his chief of staff, Hobart Gay; his amphibious force commander, Colonel E. Johnson; his aides, Colonel L. Ely, Captain Richard Jensen, and Lieutenant Al Stiller; and his orderly, Staff Sergeant Meeks. Admiral H. Kent Hewitt, the Western Task Force's naval commander was also on board, wearing his helmet backward. Most of the men accompanying Patton would be with him for the rest of the war. Hobart Gay, nicknamed "Hap" for always being happy, excelled at horsemanship and spent most of his career in the cavalry. He was also an expert logistician who served with Patton in the 2nd Armored Division and the I Armored Corps. He had lost an eye in the 1920s, but, as another staffer commented, "He saw more with his one good eye than most people saw with their two." Along with his assigned duties as chief of staff, Gay was also Patton's closest confidant.[22]

Twenty-six-year-old Richard "Dick" Jensen also served with Patton in the 2nd Armored Division. Jensen's father had been a naval commander, and the Jensen and Patton families had been close back in California. Patton treated the young, bespectacled captain like a son and wrote Jensen's parents constant updates.[23] Texan Al Stiller had served as a tanker with Patton in World War I. As a "retread"—the term for a war veteran who returned to the service, often filling staff positions to free younger men for combat—he began World War II as a lieutenant and Patton's unofficial bodyguard. An expert marksman, rumored to be a better shot than even Patton, Stiller would accompany his commander to almost every battlefront.[24]

Staff Sergeant Meeks had served as Patton's orderly for five years. Quiet and unobtrusive, he ensured that Patton's uniforms were immaculate. Despite serving in World War I (where he claimed to have "seen Patton a lot") and the 1919 American intervention in the Russian Civil War, Meeks had remained a private until 1937, when he began working for Patton at Fort Riley, Kansas, cooking meals for the 10th Cavalry Regiment—the famed Buffalo Soldiers. Meeks could neither read nor write and shaved his head, as he said, "so that the gray wool wouldn't show." He developed a reputation as the only man who could give Patton orders. When asked by reporters about this, the sergeant replied, "Sure he takes it from me, I just tell him to sit down and be quiet for a while."[25]

If Patton's staff wanted to serve with him and admired his leadership, the same could not be said for Admiral Hewitt. Still, even though the naval commander tried to have Patton replaced soon after their first meeting, Hewitt would eventually grow to appreciate the foul-mouthed general and work well with him. A graduate of the Naval Academy, Hewitt had served with the Great White Fleet that circumnavigated the globe in 1907 and commanded a destroyer in World War I. At the beginning of World War II, he commanded the Atlantic Fleet Task Groups before taking command of the Amphibious Force, Atlantic Fleet, which became the Western Task Force.[26]

As the small craft pulled away, a cheer went up from the sailors aboard the *Augusta*. Patton took off his helmet and held it out so they could all see his bright smile. He was finally off to war. After a brief trip inland, the landing craft approached the crescent-shaped shore and Patton and

Figure 2. Patton bids farewell before heading to Fedala beach, north of Casablanca. Behind him is Admiral Hewitt (with helmet on backward). Patton's African American orderly, Sergeant George Meeks, holds up a Thompson machinegun, while Brigadier General Hap Gay does the same in the upper right corner. The captain (with the two bars of his rank showing on his helmet) is probably Richard "Dick" Jenson. Catalog number: 80-G-30122, National Archives and Records Administration.

crew jumped out, splashing into the thigh-high water. Patton waded over to a landing craft stuck on a sandbar. "Come back here!" he roared to a line of soldiers carrying ammunition from the flailing craft. "Yes, I mean all of you. *All of you*. Drop that stuff and come back here." The men began dropping their loads on the sand and returned. Patton, knowing how few landing craft the Navy had, ordered the men to assist him in pushing the craft off the sandbar. They waited for a wave to raise the craft slightly, then heaved as the craft's propeller chopped the water, refloated, and slowly backed away. Patton berated the men again: "Don't you realize that boat has other trips to make?" The men were stunned to see a general doing their work. "How do you expect to fight a war without ammunition?" he asked them, before ordering them to hurry their equipment to a depot.[27]

Patton strode up the beach only to see that the war had moved inland. American equipment littered the sand while rear echelon soldiers milled about with little sense of urgency. Major Robert Henriques, Patton's British liaison officer, approached and handed Patton his Hawai'ian war statue—Charlie. Patton did not even notice it: "Goddammit, Robert, didn't I tell you to stay on your goddamn ship?" Henriques held up the statue: "Mrs. Patton made me promise to bring Charlie ashore with the assault." Beatrice, ever the thoughtful wife, had dutifully fished Charlie out of the pond back home and entrusted it to Henriques to bring her husband luck during the assault. "So she did," the general quipped.

Figure 3. British major Robert Henriques poses with "Charlie," Patton's war god lava statue, which he presented to Patton on Fedala beach. Catalog number: 111-SC 51976, National Archives and Records Administration.

As Patton surveyed his surroundings, he noted listless GIs standing or sitting around, smoking, talking, and arguing. Some had even stopped digging foxholes. A lone Arab wandered the beach with his donkey, picking up discarded equipment and storing it in sacks on the braying animal's back. "Jesus, I wish I were a corporal!" Patton said to Henriques.

When a naval officer walked by, Patton insisted they have their picture taken together, to prove he was coordinating with the Navy. As they spoke, Patton eyed the Arab picking up a discarded rifle and sticking it into one of the donkey's sacks. That's when Patton unholstered his pistol and fired. The man dropped the rifle and scurried off, while the troops popped their heads out of their shallow foxholes.[28]

Patton walked up to a small bathing cabana overlooking the beach where a field telephone had been rigged. Here he made his first combat decision of the war, ordering the incoming boats to stop landing on the rough beach and start docking at Fedala's harbor. As he received reports, a French Dewointine fighter plane peeled out of the sky and headed for the beach, guns blazing. Some men returned fire while others dropped prone on the beach. Patton dashed over to the men. "On your feet!" he stormed. "What the hell's the matter with you men anyways? What do you think you've got guns for?" The men looked up sheepishly at their commander. "You heard me; you've got guns. Use them." As he marched back to the cabana, he concluded his diatribe: "If I see another American soldier lying down on this beach, I'll court-martial him!" Above, the fighter banked and headed down the beach again, this time higher. A staccato of fire met it—this time, everyone stayed on their feet. The plane turned away and waggled its wings. "Should have come in sooner," Patton lamented.[29]

As the day progressed, General Anderson, the 3rd Infantry Division commander, delivered a French army colonel who told Patton that the French did not want to fight and that he should send a surrender demand to the commanders in Casablanca. Patton sent Gay and Lieutenant Colonel William Wilbur to see the French naval commander, Admiral François Michelier. As the two Americans headed off to Casablanca, Anderson updated Patton on the day's progress. Shore batteries and antiaircraft guns had caused the most damage, but overall resistance had been light. The Americans had crossed two rivers and taken the high ground before noon. They also captured the last gun by 2:30 p.m., along with at least one hundred French sailors and eight German soldiers. The Germans admitted to not hearing about the Allied landings until 6:00 a.m. "So it was a complete surprise," Patton later cheered in his diary, adding "Anderson is good but lacks drive—however, he did well."[30]

Patton spent the rest of the day inspecting Fedala and its port. French sailors and soldiers saluted him, but not the French marines. As the sun went down, he dined on fish and cheese in the partially damaged Hotel

CHAPTER ONE ★ FIRST DAY OF BATTLE

Figure 4. Smashed landing craft and equipment litter Fedala beach where Patton came ashore on November 8, 1942, beginning his war. Catalog number: 208-AA-4JJ-10, National Archives and Records Administration.

Miramar, which would become his temporary home and headquarters. The unfriendly manager declined to offer Patton and his staff anything to drink until Stiller threatened to shoot the lock off of his wine cellar. Champagne appeared and everyone imbibed. After dinner Patton returned to his inspection, his staff in tow. He stopped outside a café packed with American soldiers. Standing on the sidewalk, he glared at them through a glass wall. He could see the blue and white patch on their shoulders, identifying them as men from the 3rd Infantry. The men stared back. They had survived their first day of battle and were celebrating. "I wish I was a corporal," Patton said for the second time.

Turning away from the party in the café, Patton noticed for the first time that Colonel Henriques was wearing his British rank. "Goddammit, Robert, didn't I tell you to wear an American uniform?" Henriques replied that he was, but Patton was not buying it. "Those goddamn crowns!" he shouted as he pointed at Henriques's shoulders and helmet. "There haven't been any goddamn crowns in the American army since the

Declaration of Independence." He then launched into a humorous comparison of American and British rank, but never cracked a smile. Patton told one of his officers to give Henriques some American army colonel eagles, which he immediately pinned on the colonel's shoulders. "Get that helmet fixed likewise," he ordered. "I'll have it entered into orders." And with that, Patton headed back to the hotel to sleep.[31] Only Meeks followed him to his room, where the staff sergeant would slump to the floor outside the door, a Thompson machinegun clutched in his hands.[32]

It had been a long day, but it had also been a successful one. Patton had capably gotten his troops ashore under trying circumstances. He understood the importance of supply and personal leadership. He never passed up an opportunity to set an example or teach men under fire to do their job. And he did not hesitate to let his pistols do the talking. "God had been very good to me today," he confided in his diary before going to sleep.

Yet Patton had failed to take one critical action that day: he never contacted his superior, Lieutenant General Dwight D. Eisenhower, the overall commander of TORCH, who waited in his headquarters at the Rock of Gibraltar, some 260 miles away, for word of Patton's success or failure on Morocco's shores. Eisenhower had repeatedly radioed Patton, asking where he was setting up his headquarters, the condition of the port, and whether he needed a squadron of fighter planes. Silence had been the only response. Eisenhower's staff, bombarded by the British with questions about resupply timetables, referred to Patton's command as the "lost Western Task Force." Captain Harry Butcher, Eisenhower's naval aide, wondered in his diary why Patton had not contacted Eisenhower's headquarters, since "Patton has planes that could fly couriers with complete dope to Gib[ralter]." To Butcher, Patton's silence was the second greatest failure of TORCH, right after the communications problems between the U.S. and Royal navies. Eisenhower even sent several reconnaissance aircraft to monitor Patton's progress, but French fighter planes and unwitting Navy gunners shot them down.[33] Eisenhower eventually resorted to sending the HMS *Welshman*, a fast minelayer, to rendezvous with Hewitt on the USS *Augusta* to deliver dispatches and collect information. It was later discovered that Patton had used the wrong codebooks in sending communications to Eisenhower. The correct ones were stowed in the bottom of one of his ships.[34] When Eisenhower later rebuked Patton for his lack of communication, Patton wrote him: "I regret you are mad with me over my failure to communicate, however, I cannot control interstellar space and our radio simply would not work."[35]

CHAPTER ONE ★ FIRST DAY OF BATTLE 29

Figure 5. Wearing his two ivory-handled pistols, Patton stands on Morocco's Fedala beach on November 8, 1942, his first day of battle in World War II. Reading College, UK.

November 8 would not be the last time Patton would taint his battlefield success by failing Eisenhower. In fact, it almost set the precedent for the remainder of their relationship. Patton knew his battlefield success was no guarantee that he would keep his command, and he worried constantly that his boss would send him home for such perceived slights. It would haunt him for the rest of the war. Still, Patton had reason to be proud. His untested force had crossed an ocean and successfully defeated an enemy in the field, even if that enemy fought merely to save its honor. Patton would have 884 more days of war to prove himself, to lead men into battle, to be a great general. It was now his war.

CHAPTER TWO

TORCH
Planning and Execution

ALLIED PLANNERS INITIALLY conceptualized Operation TORCH, in early 1942, as a single amphibious attack upon Dakar, West Africa, to be led by Major General Joseph Stillwell. Dakar, as the closest African port to the United States, made sense, but the logistics, manpower, and equipment proved too overwhelming for a country that had just entered World War II and whose main battle fleet lay battered at Pearl Harbor. The U.S. military would need nine months, and help from the British army and Royal Navy, before it could make a serious concerted effort to join the fray in the Western Hemisphere. The destination would also change from Dakar to North Africa, where the British needed help to defeat German general Erwin Rommel.[1]

But who should lead TORCH? General George C. Marshall, the Army chief of staff, picked Lieutenant General Dwight D. Eisenhower, his former chief of war plans, whom Marshall had sent to England to oversee the buildup of American forces there. Originally from Abilene, Kansas, Eisenhower had missed out on the fighting in World War I but had impressed his superiors as a staff officer during Army-sized maneuvers held in the United States before the war broke out. A long-time friend of Patton's and impressed with the latter's tank and leadership skills, Eisenhower picked him, Major General Lloyd Fredendall, and Major General Charles Ryder to command TORCH's three separate task forces.[2] Patton was an obvious choice. His star had been on the rise as America drew closer to war. Germany's invasion of Poland in 1939 found Colonel Patton commanding the 3rd Cavalry Regiment at Fort Myer, Virginia, where he had obtained a roommate, General Marshall, whose house was under construction. Earlier that summer, in corps-sized maneuvers at nearby Fort Belvoir and Manassas, Patton showed particular élan and dash. He stressed flanking the enemy with his horses and suggested that troops ignore designated boundary lines, which inhibited maneuver schemes. He was already thinking outside the box.[3]

During this anxious period, as the war clouds over Europe and Japan encroached on the United States, Patton remained on the cusp of an ever-expanding U.S. Army. In 1940 he served as an umpire in Fort Benning's spring maneuvers and as a control officer in the corps-level Louisiana maneuvers, during which he revisited the potential of the use of tanks. Considered one of the fathers of the tank from his experiences in World War I, Patton had abandoned his beloved machines when the army disbanded the tank corps soon after that war's end (although he privately pushed for better tanks even after the war).[4] A few diehard tank pioneers continued to work on tactics at a little-known camp in Kentucky called Knox. Now, as German tanks overran Western Europe, Patton realized they were the tools of the future. On the last day of the Louisiana maneuvers, May 25, Patton attended an important meeting in the cafeteria of Alexandria's Bolton High School, where he and other tank visionaries agreed the Army needed a separate tank corps, free of the infantry and cavalry, to develop its own doctrine and tactics.[5]

On July 26 he took command of the 2nd Armored Division's 2nd Brigade at Fort Benning, Georgia.[6] Promoted to brigadier general three months later, Patton did not remain a brigade commander for long. With the rapid expansion of the armored force, new divisions were being forged, armored corps created, and leaders promoted. He soon found himself commanding the entire 2nd Armored Division, where he proceeded to whip his men into shape with a combination of discipline and personal example, insisting on perfect comportment and driving his troops hard. In a major test of his division's strength and maneuverability, he led his men on a four-hundred-mile march from Columbus, Georgia, to Panama City, Florida. The trip not only trained the men, it instilled in them immense pride. It also captured the public's imagination, as news reports about it appeared in newspapers around the country and made the march a national phenomenon. Patton later designed a new tanker uniform (which the Army never adopted) and incorporated light planes into his division to serve as couriers and observers. His efforts earned him a promotion to major general on April 4, 1941, eight months before Japanese bombs fell on Pearl Harbor.

One of Patton's first orders of business was to invite his old friend, then-Lieutenant Colonel Eisenhower, to join the division as a regimental commander. The two men had known each other ever since Eisenhower had impressed Patton with his energy, intelligence, and enthusiasm at Fort Meade after World War I. The two commanded tanks at the fort and quickly became friends, as did their wives. They dined together, cruised the countryside, and debated tank tactics. When the Army dissolved the corps in 1920, they went their separate ways but continued to correspond. Eisenhower, "Ike" to his friends, wanted to join Patton when he took command of the 2nd Armored Division but was instead assigned elsewhere.[7]

During large-scale Army maneuvers in Tennessee, Louisiana, and the Carolinas in 1941, Patton's efforts bore fruit. At another corps-level exercise in Tennessee, the 2nd Armored stole the show. After a disappointing start, the division slashed through the opposition force in a night attack, cutting lines of communications along the way. Twice, Patton's force captured the "enemy's" headquarters. In another demonstration of his speed, Patton completed a two-day combat maneuver in nine hours. Popular acclamation followed: As the colorful commander of this new and dashing form of warfare, Patton's face appeared on the July 7 cover of *LIFE* magazine.[8]

Following the corps-level Tennessee maneuvers came Army-level maneuvers in Louisiana and the Carolinas. For Patton, Louisiana was a repeat of Tennessee. During the first phase of mock battles in September of 1941, his 2nd Armored was quickly detected and bottled up. Patton tried to break his division loose, but failed. During the second phase, however, he spearheaded a flanking attack aimed at capturing the city of Shreveport. As his tanks closed in for the kill, however, the maneuver leaders prematurely cancelled the exercise. Despite being prevented from completing his mission, Patton's leadership and tactical sense were displayed for everyone to see. He pushed his tankers with his usual combination of enthusiasm and whip cracking. When his tanks ran low on gas, the men refueled at local filing stations, paying cash (rumored to be from Patton's own pocket). To thoroughly befuddle the opposition force, Patton personally guided his tanks out of the designated maneuver area. Officers complained, but Patton showed he was willing to do whatever it took to reach his goal. He would repeat his "going off the map" tactic later, during the war, also frustrating the actual enemy.[9]

The Carolina maneuvers proved to be 2nd Armored's capstone. Long marches and flank attacks were the order of the day. Even though antitank units initially stopped them, Patton's tankers again captured the opposition force headquarters, this time capturing Lieutenant General Hugh Drum. The press closely watched Patton's performance, as always finding him to be excellent copy, but this time someone much more important watched as well. General Marshall had flown down from Washington to witness the final days of the maneuver and came away impressed with the division commander's performance. Marshall decided Patton would have a wider role in the coming war.[10]

The maneuvers ended on December 4, three days before the Japanese attacked Pearl Harbor. With the nation now at war, Patton received orders on January 15, 1942, to command the I Armored Corps at Fort Benning. He now commanded two armored divisions, but, again, he did not last long at the post. The War Department needed a tank training area to prepare the U.S. Army for the war in North Africa, and Patton was selected to organize and command it. Retaining his I Armored Corps designation, he flew all over southern California, Nevada, and Arizona over the course of three days in March, determining the borders of the new Desert Training Center.

With the camp's multistate parameters decided, Patton went to work training new recruits while the center was completed, sharing his men's plight in the harsh desert environs, as they lived in tents, ate canned rations, and collected rainwater to drink. The troops conducted marches and ran ten miles at a time hauling full field packs and rifles. In mock battles, Patton stressed radio communications, accuracy in shooting, air support, and mobility. A visiting British tank officer considered the center's terrain tougher than Libya's and the troops more competent than any in the British army. But the actual fighting front was exactly where Patton wanted to be, battling Rommel. When one of his officers asked him about his favorite pistols, he energetically responded, "I am going to shoot that SOB Rommel and throw these pistols in his face!"[11]

On June 21 Patton's training duties were interrupted when he was ordered to report to Washington. He arrived at the War Department and met with Eisenhower, now a brigadier general in Marshall's operations office, who asked him if he would take command of an armored force headed for North Africa to help stem Rommel's offensive against the British Eighth Army in Egypt. The situation was becoming desperate: Rommel had captured the British-held town of Tobruk, which had resisted a seven-month siege the year before. The defeated and demoralized British lost up to 140 tanks and retreated east to the Egyptian border.[12] Patton immediately agreed. His response pleased Eisenhower, especially after another general had refused an assignment in the Pacific because he did not want to serve "under an Australian 'amateur' soldier."[13] For three days Patton worked on the plan, suggesting to General Marshall that two armored divisions would be appropriate for the mission. However, the relief mission evaporated just as quickly as it had begun. Marshall, realizing an American force would take too long to organize and that he lacked enough ships for the tank crews, decided instead to send the British three hundred tanks and one hundred howitzers. Not knowing why he had lost his first wartime assignment, Patton returned to the West Coast dejected, swearing he would take whatever job came his way without complaint. He would hold tightly to that vow throughout the war.[14]

Two weeks after his return to the Desert Training Center, Patton received a letter from Eisenhower, who had traveled to London to plan the next stage of the war, suggesting that he would need Patton's services very soon. The need came on July 30, when Patton was assigned command of one of the task forces headed to North Africa. With a few members of his Armored Corps staff, he flew to Washington, set up an office in the War Department's Munitions Building, and began familiarizing himself with Operation TORCH. He learned his I Armored Corps would be redesignated the Western Task Force, the only all-American invasion element. He had less than three months to prepare his force for an amphibious assault and combat.

Patton, now a wartime commander, flew to England with Brigadier General James Doolittle, who had famously bombed Tokyo four months earlier, for two weeks of planning. Once there, he reunited with Eisenhower. Patton was happy to see his old friend but resented the younger Major General Mark Clark, Eisenhower's deputy, who Patton thought had been promoted without having proved himself. He may also have felt slighted by Eisenhower's trust of and friendship with the younger general. Nevertheless, the four men worked on the details of TORCH with their British allies, who vigorously opposed Patton's mission. The American generals all agreed that the poorly planned invasion was more political than strategic—President Roosevelt wanted to get the Americans into the war, and quickly. They also worried about potential French resistance and that Patton's landings in Morocco might compel neutral Spain to join the war on the side of the Axis. While most of Morocco came under French rule, Spain controlled northern Morocco as a colony. During the Spanish Civil War, Hitler had supplied tanks, aircraft, and other equipment to the fascist forces under Francisco Franco. Since then,

Hitler had been pressing Franco to ally himself with the Axis Powers, or at least let the Germans use Spain as a base of operations to capture the British-controlled Gibraltar, which overlooked the western entrance to the Mediterranean Sea. The Spanish leader maintained cordial relations with the Fuehrer but did not commit his country to war.[15] If he were to do so, his troops in northern Morocco could overwhelm and flank Patton's forces, guaranteeing a disastrous start to the fighting against the Axis and an enormous embarrassment to the Americans. Still, despite all the misgivings and the potential for disaster, the Americans remained committed to the mission.

During the negotiations in London, Patton irked Brigadier General Walter Bedell "Beetle" Smith, Eisenhower's poker-faced and cantankerous chief of staff. At a dinner attended by American and British generals, a Marine Corps colonel, William Eddy, with the Office of Strategic Services (OSS)—the precursor to today's Central Intelligence Agency—limped into the room with a chest full of war medals. "The son of a bitch's been shot at enough, hasn't he?" Patton laughed. Eddy, who had been conducting clandestine operations in Morocco, briefed the group, adding that the resistance there needed arms. He and Patton hit it off. Eddy soon began reporting his Moroccan activities to Patton, who passed the information to Eisenhower, bypassing Smith. Suddenly, accusations flew around London that the OSS was conducting rogue missions without guidance, until the problem was traced back to Patton. His wartime relationship with Smith would not improve.[16]

Upon his return to the States, Patton prepared for his task force's departure date, set for October 23, thirty-seven days away. For his deputy commander, he picked Major General Geoffrey Keyes, a fellow cavalryman who had served as Patton's operations officer in the 2nd Armored Division. Patton considered Keyes firm in character and levelheaded. He would be the perfect person to replace Patton if he fell on the battlefield: "There will be someone to carry on," Patton wrote a fellow general.[17] Keyes would serve with Patton throughout most of the Mediterranean campaign.

While the choice of Keyes pleased Patton, elsewhere things were not going well. The Navy and Army had almost never worked together on such a large scale, and preparing to do so exposed their philosophical differences. Patton frequently clashed with his Navy peers, whom he thought were disenchanted, unenthusiastic, and would rather be fighting in the Pacific. His first meeting with his naval counterpart, Admiral Kent

CHAPTER TWO ★ TORCH: PLANNING AND EXECUTION

Hewitt, was a disaster. Perceiving Hewitt as less than helpful, Patton lost his temper and let loose with his usual profanities. Hewitt and his staff, unfamiliar with Patton's personality, simply walked away from the ranting general. Patton exacerbated the problems with Hewitt by establishing his headquarters in the War Department's Old Munitions Building on Washington's Constitution Avenue, while Hewitt commanded from Norfolk, Virginia, where the fleet would set sail. While the distance between the two HQs reduced clashes between the two commanders, it created numerous communications problems. Hewitt repeatedly asked Patton to relocate, but he refused, leaving the respective staffs to rush between the two cities relaying important information. Hewitt requested a new army commander, but Marshall insisted that Patton was indispensable to TORCH.[18]

The problems with the amphibious assault were countless. With all the naval experts in the Pacific focused on Guadalcanal, Patton and Hewitt had to make their best guesses on how to stow equipment and develop priorities—another source of conflict. When Brigadier General John Reed Kilpatrick, the commander of the Newport News Port of Embarkation, reported that there was not enough room for both equipment and food, Patton told him, "I will take all the guns and tanks. Cut the subsistence to enough for five days." Patton reasoned that if the invasion were a success, his men could live off the land after five days. If not successful, his men would be casualties. "You see, General Kilpatrick," Patton explained, "corpses don't eat." Despite his request, deep down Patton believed equipment was actually secondary for his task force. To win, he would need only four things: leadership, speed, drive, and sound tactics.[19] But he also knew his limits, telling his logistics officer, Colonel Walter J. Muller, "I don't know anything about logistics. You keep me out of trouble." It would not work out well. Not knowing what to expect in a first-ever amphibious landing across an ocean, Patton and his staff ordered too much equipment for the voyage, resulting in half the requested equipment being left on the docks as the task force departed.[20]

As the two branches trained at performing amphibious landings, Patton wrestled with both the Navy and Army to guarantee success. Some arguments stemmed from a simple lack of resources, others from different views of warfare. A week before departure, Admiral Royal Ingersoll discovered that Patton intended to use a mine-laying ship to carry ammunition and aviation fuel. Patton needed the mine-layer's shallow draft to carry Lucian Truscott's Northern Attack Group up the Sebou

River's shallow waters for an attack on Port Lyautey. They had already loaded the ship when Ingersoll denied them its use, insisting that Patton only use ships for their intended purpose. A frustrated Patton added a merchant ship to his fleet for the task. To make matters worse, on that same day, Eisenhower cancelled planned airborne support and denied Patton's request for five light-draft craft. "In general," he penned in his diary that night, "it has been a bad day."[21]

As the date of disembarkation neared, Patton flew up to West Point, New York, to bid farewell to his son George. Back in D.C., to stay in General Marshall's good graces, he lent him some air conditioners for his Leesburg, Virginia, home. Patton also visited troops preparing for TORCH. In front of his beloved 2nd Armored, he broke down, crying, unable to speak. He did much better with the 9th Infantry Division, delivering a diatribe on making the enemy suffer. The purpose for his speech, he told them, "was to let you know that you are not going in to take casualties, but to kill the enemy. Attack them, cut their guts out with your bayonets."[22] He left the troops chanting, "More! More!" He also sent out a bevy of letters to friends and family, in case the gods of fate called on him. He wrote his Irish-Catholic family nurse that, by the time she received his letter, "I will either be dead or not. If I am, please put on a good Irish wake; if I am not, get busy with the Pope."[23]

Patton's last personal visit was to Walter Reed Army Hospital, where eighty-one-year-old General John J. Pershing resided. Patton's old commander, friend, and mentor did not recognize Patton when he entered his personal room until he spoke. It was an emotional scene, the two men reminiscing about their time together in Mexico and France. Patton, realizing this would probably be their last time together, asked, "General, I can't tell you where I'm going, but I couldn't go without coming to ask you for your blessing." Pershing did not hesitate. "Then you shall have it," he told his former aide. "Kneel down." Patton dropped to one knee and kissed the old general's hand. Pershing gripped Patton's hand and told him, "Goodbye George, God bless and keep you, and give you victory." Patton put on his hat to leave and snapped a salute, Pershing returned it "just like he used to," Patton later wrote, "and 25 years seemed to drop from him." Before Patton left, Pershing reminded him that he had been Patton's age—fifty-six—when he left the United States to serve in World War I.[24]

With mere days left before departure, Patton made the rounds to the White House and War Department, bidding farewell and receiving

CHAPTER TWO ★ TORCH: PLANNING AND EXECUTION

good wishes. He told a group of general staff officers, "I want to fight the champ [meaning Rommel]. If you lose, you've lost to the champ, and it's no disgrace. If you win, you're the champ." On October 22, he flew down to Norfolk for the last time, to watch the men of the 3rd Infantry Division walk up their ships' ramps. He was in good spirits and full of confidence. Despite all the stress and strain, the worrying about preparations was behind him. The next day, his last in the United States before embarkation, he watched his 2nd Armored Division load up, "men and officers in fine spirits," he noted. Noticing some Army and Navy officers on a pier, he called them together. "We shall attack and attack until we are exhausted," he told them, "and then we shall attack again." Later, to his staff, he was more pragmatic. "The newspapers call me 'Blood and Guts.' That's all right, it serves its purpose. It makes good reading. But it takes more than blood and guts to win battles. It takes brains and guts. Remember that: brains and guts." He then explained how brains and guts led to victory. "I expect you to use both in your utmost capacity at all times," he concluded. "That is all gentlemen."[25] The next morning, at 8:10 a.m., October 24, the fleet set sail. Destination: Morocco.

★ ★ ★ ★ ★

By November 9, the second day of TORCH, General Harmon had captured Safi but Patton's other two objectives, Casablanca and Medhia, held out. That morning, Patton rose before sunrise and found General Anderson, the 3rd Infantry Division commander, still asleep. Worried that Anderson was not taking his responsibilities seriously, Patton headed down to the docks only to discover chaos. Equipment was strewn everywhere and landing craft lay beached and abandoned. The docked French battleship *Jean Bart* still burned furiously from the previous day's action. The weather was horrible. Seven-foot swells tossed ships around as they tried to approach the beach. His order to use the harbor had not been followed, leaving landing craft stranded on the beach. He immediately ordered a launch to guide the follow-up ships to the port, but as the launch headed out, one of the boats heading to shore flipped over and drowned sixteen men, leaving Patton to help pull a "nasty blue" corpse from the surf. He blamed Anderson for the mess, for not showing "proper push." Just as Patton finished dragging the body ashore, French bombers flew over and dropped bombs, followed by strafing fighters. Again, men scattered and Patton lost his temper. When he saw a man drop into the fetal position, Patton "kicked him in the arse with all my might." The man returned to duty.[26] Patton continued his rampage, chewing out a lieutenant for hesitating to jump into the water, hitting a soldier for failing to push out a boat, and kicking a lot of local beachcombers. When soldiers were not doing their job and Patton's anger spiked, he became physically aggressive. It was a dangerous reaction.

Souring Patton's mood even more, Hap Gay showed up from his attempted surrender negotiations the day before to report that the Vichy French had stood Lieutenant Colonel Wilbur against a wall and shot him. They had led Gay to a basement to repeat the action but decided at the last second to let him live. Exacerbated by his sluggish troops, transport captains who refused to head closer to the shore, and Gay's revelation, Patton headed back to the *Augustus*, where he hoped communications would be better.[27]

While Patton sailed off, two regiments of 3rd Infantry pushed south toward Casablanca, encountering only small arms fire. Each time an enemy gun fired, the men dispersed, coordinated with each other, laid down covering fire, and advanced. Despite the rushed training schedule, the men were performing well, not going to ground. There was at least one friendly-fire casualty to the American rear: a Navy salvo demolished Patton's kitchen.[28]

Patton reached the *Augusta* and climbed up a rope net. Exhausted from the morning's events and weighed down by his equipment, he struggled. As he reached the top, Hewitt and one of his officers dropped to their knees, grabbed Patton's arms and hauled him onto the deck. Hewitt later wrote of the incident, "If he had ever let go, he would have sunk like a stone."[29] Concerned for Patton's well-being, Hewitt ordered a doctor to prescribe Patton a shot of liquor. "I needed it," Patton later confessed. By the afternoon, he ordered the rest of his staff ashore. Truscott reported in from Mehdia, asking for an additional battalion of men. "There was none to send," Patton lamented. The French then attacked Truscott with World War I-era Renault tanks and the Americans scattered. Truscott, with the help of a few light tanks and some naval shelling, personally lead a counterattack, pushing his men inland. Patton debated going back ashore, but when he learned that the "Goddam Navy" had destroyed his kitchen, he spent the night on board.[30]

The next morning, November 10, Patton heard again from Truscott, this time reporting he needed help. No word came from General Harmon. The afternoon brought good news. Truscott had captured the Fedala airfield while a tank battalion under Lieutenant Colonel Harry Semmes

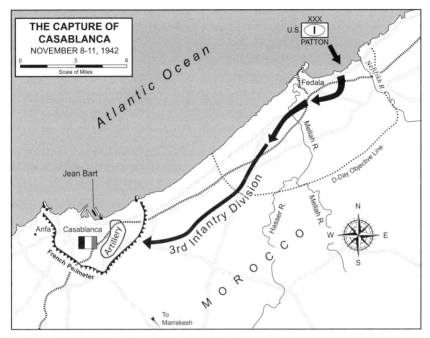

Map 2. The capture of Casablanca, November 8–11, 1942.

had bagged fifteen French tanks. "Semmes must have had a good time," Patton mused. When Harmon reported capturing Safi's airport, Patton sent him some fighter aircraft. That left Casablanca, with its population of two hundred fifty thousand, directly in front of Patton. He decided to assault the city with Anderson's 7th and 15th Infantry regiments and the 67th Tank Battalion. He told Hewitt he wanted a naval bombardment and fighter aircraft added to the attack. He also wired Harmon to race his tanks north and attack the city from the south. He would squeeze Casablanca like a vise.[31]

Eisenhower cabled Patton, asking about his progress. The other landings in Oran and Algiers had already succeeded. "The only tough nut left is in your hands," Eisenhower wrote. "Crack it open quickly." With a renewed sense of urgency, Patton returned to the beach, only to learn that Anderson's attack had been driven back. His men had panicked, but Geoffrey Keyes, Patton's deputy commander, had stepped in and restored order. "Men simply got scared," Patton reasoned. He reached the battle line north of a French fort and examined it through a pair of high-powered binoculars. Before leaving, he ordered a captain to act as a spotter, watching the troops assault the fort. "When it happens," he told the captain, "I expect to pin some medals on 'em."[32]

Patton's hands were full, preparing the assault while seeking peace with the French. He sent a letter to the sultan of Morocco, Muhammad V, the country's official ruler and Muslim spiritual leader, promising the American army was only there to fight Nazis and would leave as soon as the task was complete. He also sent more officers through the lines to negotiate a surrender. The French, likewise, were sending emissaries, but they expressed a serious concern: A British army officer had released convicted communists from their prisons. Patton knew of only one British officer within his task force, Colonel Robert Henriques, and he ordered him arrested.[33]

As Patton prepared for the coming battle, Henriques showed up at his headquarters in the Miramar building. After a long wait, the colonel burst into Patton's office. "Get out!" Patton roared in his high-pitched voice. Henriques tried to explain himself, but Patton merely repeated the arrest order and stood up behind his desk. "I am a British officer sir," Henriques argued, adding that as such he had the right to see Patton when necessary to make his report. Patton, cooled by the officer's logic, sat down and explained the fragile peace he was trying to build. "All this you have prejudiced by letting loose a bunch of dangerous convicts." Henriques explained that the men were some six hundred British soldiers, sailors, airmen, and merchant mariners who had been imprisoned as criminals. Henriques had gone to the prison, where he accepted the French commandant's unloaded pistol, then pointed it at him and demanded the surrender of the camp. Patton did not entirely buy Henriques's story. "Are they, or are they not, communists?" he demanded. Now Henriques lost his temper. "I don't know and I don't care," he declared. "If His Majesty doesn't care what political opinions are held by members of his forces, what business of it is mine? And what business is it of any American general?" Patton stared at Henriques for a long minute, then blinked, smiled and said, "I guess that's right." He put his arm around Henriques, and led him to a room where two French officers waited. "I've just got to buy this Goddam, son-of-a-bitch a big drink, and I'll be right back," he told his staff.[34]

His political problem dealt with, Patton returned to military matters. He received more good news from Truscott, who had accomplished his mission. After capturing the airfield, Truscott ran up against a fortress the Americans called the "Kasbah," where the French refused to surrender, repulsing numerous American attacks, including an attempt to blow the fort's main gate with two 105mm howitzers firing at point blank range. Finally, eight Navy dive bombers swooped in and dropped bombs inside the fort, after which American infantrymen charged the gate and forced a French surrender. When the French attacked a nearby lighthouse, a single soldier kept them at bay with repeated bazooka blasts.[35]

By the end of the third day, Casablanca remained the only objective outside of Patton's grasp, and even now his dusty and dirty soldiers and tankers were surrounding it. He went to bed that night determined to crush the French the next morning, only to be awakened at 4:20 a.m. to learn that a French general and a major were waiting for him downstairs with a ceasefire order from the French army commander. His staff begged him to call off the attack. With no word from the French navy, Patton delayed the attack until 7:30, allowing Anderson to organize his attack in daylight. Patton sent the French major, escorted by Colonel John Ratay, back to the city to inquire about the French navy. As the two officers departed, Patton, recalling what had happened to Gay and Wilbur, called to Ratay, "And don't get yourself shot." He then shook hands with the French general and told him, "I wish you the best of luck." Before going back to bed, Patton radioed Hewitt to prepare to call off his aerial support and gunfire on his order.[36]

At 6:15 a.m., Patton showed up at Anderson's headquarters to watch the attack on Casablanca. The troops were poised and ready, battleships stood in firing position, and fighters circled above. At 6:40 the French surrendered. Patton, who had turned fifty-seven that morning, faced Anderson and smiled, saying, "Thanks for the birthday present, Andy!" He then called off the attack. Some tanks had already assaulted a machinegun nest and a few of the supporting artillery had registered their guns, but that was it. With minutes to spare, Patton's Navy liaison officer contacted the pilots and the aircraft gracefully broke away.[37] Patton ordered Anderson to advance into Casablanca and to fire only if fired upon. The infantrymen set off for the city, marching in columns down the streets as curious residents looked on. Patton waited tensely for news of their reception. It could be a trap. "The hours from 7:30 to 11:00," he later wrote, "were the longest in my life." The troops peacefully occupied the city—there was no resistance.[38]

Patton returned to Hotel Miramar, where he prepared to meet the French delegates. There, he ran into a dust-covered Ernie Harmon, who had just led his tankers through Casablanca. "Where in hell have you been all this time?" Patton barked. Harmon was taken aback. With almost no knowledge of the bigger picture, he had driven all night and day to reach Patton from Safi. His only guidance had been a single communiqué, which had arrived twenty-four hours late, ordering him to attack Casablanca, followed by another, calling off the attack. Harmon was expecting a pat on the back from Patton, not a reprimand. But when Patton winked at him and smiled, Harmon understood, and the two men relaxed and reviewed the situation.[39]

Soon, General August Noguès and Admiral François Michelier, the Vichy commanders of the French army and navy in Morocco, respectively, arrived at Patton's headquarters to discuss surrender terms. Patton had placed an honor guard outside the building to greet them, complete with American and Western Task Force flags. He was unimpressed with Noguès, calling him "a crook—and a handsome one." Michelier, on the other hand, was "a man, and a very mad one at the moment." The American fleet had sunk all his ships, but Patton respected Michelier, whose navy had gone down fighting. The French army, on the other hand, had simply quit. When Patton entered the room to join the talks, he immediately apologized to Michelier. "I am sorry we had to fire on you." Michelier replied, "You did your duty; we did ours."[40]

Patton had brought with him two treaties for the occasion. The first presupposed that the French had only offered token resistance, while the other assumed a protracted battle. Neither had happened and only Eisenhower had the authority to approve a new armistice. Patton opened the meeting by praising the French courage and skill in three days of battle. "We are now met to come to terms," he concluded. "Here they are." With that, one of Patton's officers read the one of the treaties aloud. The French were uneasy with the terms. "Permit me to point out," Noguès finally said, "that if these terms are enforced, it means the end of the French Protectorate in Morocco." Patton did not want that, he needed the French to enforce law and order and, more important, to keep an eye on Spanish Morocco, so he could fight the Germans and Italians.[41]

Taking the initiative, Patton stood up, took the treaty from its reader, and tore it up. "Gentlemen," he addressed his former enemy, "I had the pleasure of serving with your armed forces throughout two years of World War I." He then told them of his faith in the French officers' word of honor. "If each of you in this room gives me their word of honor that there will be no further firing on American troops and ships, you may retain your arms and carry on as before—but under my orders. You will do thus and so. We will do this and that. Agreed?" They did.[42]

Figure 6. With negotiations completed with the Vichy French, Patton enjoys dinner with his new allies. Patton laughs heartily. Hewitt sits to his right at the head of the table. French admiral Frix Michelier sits to Hewitt's right. National Archives and Records Administration.

Before the French could enjoy their good fortune, Patton spoke up again. "There is, however, an additional condition upon which I must insist." The Frenchmen's faces tightened as they contemplated just what kind of bomb this American general was about to drop now that they had agreed to his rule. "It is this," Patton continued, signaling to one of his aides, "that you join me in a glass of champagne." The tension immediately subsided as the glasses were passed around. Patton had concluded his battle successfully, negotiated a peace on his own terms, and brought the Vichy French in Morocco over to the Allies—all in three days.[43]

As Patton exited his headquarters, a young Frenchman, covered in blood, pedaled up to him on a bicycle and pleaded for help. He was a doctor and explained in broken English that he had a great many wounded in his hospital and not enough medicine, bandages, or assistance, drawing pictures in the air with his blood-soaked hands as he tried to relay his crisis. Patton immediately arranged for aid to the French medical corps.⁴⁴ That night, he received another stark reminder that the war had not ended when he heard a ship explode in the harbor, the victim of a German U-boat. Morocco was still a violent place.⁴⁵ For all that, a few days later, when asked to hold a press conference to explain conditions in his sector, he issued a one-sentence report: "Everything is godammed [*sic*] quiet in Casablanca."⁴⁶

Historian and Patton biographer Martin Blumenson claimed that Patton's TORCH victory confirmed his "military brilliance." It did not. For most of the campaign, Patton was out of touch with his three attack units. He spent the first day commanding only the soldiers within his field of vision. He spent the second day entirely with his center force, and he never had a chance to test his skills in a set-piece battle before the French surrendered Casablanca. In addition, Patton fought an enemy that was more interested in honorably surrendering than fighting. While Patton had performed competently and chalked up a victory in his first operation, it would not be until he faced a truly motivated, well-armed enemy that he would test his leadership in battle, and that would not be for a while.⁴⁷

CHAPTER THREE

The Restless Lion of Morocco

THE SUCCESS OF Operation TORCH left Morocco in an uneasy peace as the war passed Patton by. While the soldiers of the Eastern and Central task forces pushed east toward Tunisia, the general and his troops remained in the west. About all there was to do for the moment was to monitor Spanish Morocco and make sure Francisco Franco didn't move south. Patton set up his headquarters in Casablanca's Shell Building, previously home to German and Italian troops. The walls of almost every room in the building were adorned with portraits of Hitler, Mussolini, and Vichy marshal Philippe Pétain, all of which had been looted during the battle. When Patton first entered the building, the manager presented him a bouquet of roses.[1]

Casablanca impressed Patton, who described it as a combination of "Hollywood and the Bible" or "a cross between the ultra-modern and the Arabian Knights but […] quite clean." Outside the city he could still find traces of the battle: destroyed vehicles and shell holes. He marveled at the trees and shoreline, which reminded him of Hawai'i. But his thoughts never strayed far from his profession: "The finest tank country I have ever seen."[2]

The day after the surrender, Patton called his staff together for a review of the three-day campaign. "Gentlemen, you have done well," he began. "Mistakes were made. We should not have fallen into ambushes. Some of the troops were too slow." He proceeded to pick apart his task force's performance and warned the men that just because the shooting had stopped, it did not mean their job was over. Spanish Morocco was still a threat. He implored them to continue working hard. He wanted them to remain proficient in rifle training and to get out of their offices and check on the troops: "I don't want a lot of officers who get varicose veins and

Figure 7. An American M3 Grant tank rolls through Casablanca, after the Vichy French surrendered. Catalog number: 80-G 30480, National Archives and Records Administration.

waffle-tails from sitting in their chairs all day." With that, he dismissed them.³

The general busied himself with problems with the Navy, the French, and the Spanish. When Admiral Hewitt pointed out that the huge stacks of supplies sitting on Casablanca's docks—including ammunition and aviation fuel—were an inviting target for the Luftwaffe, Patton assigned three battalions to help with moving the supplies inland and asked Eisenhower to supply him with night fighter aircraft to protect the docks. The French again groused about British colonel Henriques, who had confiscated a German safe filled with lists of French communists. Patton had a good laugh when he learned that Henriques burned the lists, which included members of the French Resistance, against whom the Vichy would undoubtedly seek retribution.⁴

Back in Washington, in his newly established headquarters in the Pentagon, Secretary of War Henry L. Stimson worried that the Germans might try to attack Patton through Spain. When the Spanish threatened to expand their territory into the American zone, Patton invited the Spanish military commander, General Luis Orgaz Yoldi, to a demonstration of American tank power. On this occasion, Harmon's tanks and motorized infantry under fighter escort paraded by Orgaz Yoldi as Patton boasted about American strength. Orgaz Yoldi, whose forces had no tanks, backed down.[5]

Despite its success, Operation TORCH triggered a political crisis. With the Vichy French in North Africa now an ally, who would be their leader? The British asserted that it should be Charles de Gaulle, the self-appointed, cantankerous leader of the French government-in-exile in England. But de Gaulle and the Vichy leadership hated each other. To de Gaulle, the Vichy were no better than the Nazis; they had allied themselves with Hitler and applied Nazi law to their subjects, particularly toward Jews. To the Vichy officers, de Gaulle was a rogue two-star general who had fled France at its dire hour. Eisenhower chose Vichy leader Admiral François Darlan. The British were furious over the selection, feeling that allying with Darlan equaled supporting fascism. But Eisenhower, Supreme Commander Allied Force, had decided the matter on pragmatic, not political, grounds. The French in North Africa respected Darlan, and his new position allowed for the French to maintain control of the region, fully freeing American forces for combat against the Axis. Darlan, a naval commander, could guarantee keeping the French fleet at Toulon and out of German hands, something Churchill had asserted was "worth crawling on my hands and knees to get." Patton, too, would turn a blind eye to the Vichy's troubled past to get them onboard.[6]

Patton also worked to normalize America's relationship with the French and Moroccans. If they could be made to remain cooperative, he figured, he could keep his force ready for the call to battle. But the Vichy had been following Germany's anti-Semitic policies, forcing Patton to walk a fine line to appease his new allies without denouncing them for their criminal deeds. Kenneth Pendar, the U.S. vice-consul in Marrakech and Casablanca, brought Patton a letter from President Roosevelt for the sultan of Morocco. Vichy general Noguès was supposed to have delivered it to the sultan before the Americans landed, but had refused to do so. Now Pendar asked Patton to deliver it. Patton read the letter and looked up, saying "I don't like it. . . . There's not enough mention of the French in it." With that, he began inserting new sentences, asking Pendar if his changes made it sounded better. Shocked at Patton's brazenness, Pendar mumbled that no one should edit a presidential letter. "Goddammit!" Patton stormed as he pounded his desk, "I take full responsibility for this letter." Pendar relented and said he would call Robert Murphy, the ambassador to Vichy France, about it. "Goddammit!" Patton repeated, "I won't have you or any other God-dammed fool talking about this letter on the phone. Don't you know the wires are tapped?" "Yes sir, I do," replied the experienced diplomat, "they have been tapped for the last year and a half." The quip broke the tension.

But when Pendar probed Patton about the anti-Semitic Vichy policies under Noguès, Patton defended the French general, saying, "Morocco is a difficult country to manage. Now, the Jewish problem. . . ." Again, Pendar was shocked. He knew that Vichy policies mirrored the Nazi policies that had enslaved the Jews and wondered if Patton was encouraging the same practices as the Nazis. Patton, no enlightened thinker on race or religion, was more concerned with letting the Vichy continue with business as usual than with repealing the regime's anti-Semitic policies, which included forcing Jewish people in North Africa to wear a yellow Star of David patch and barring them from many jobs.[7] Pendar wanted to stop the practices, lest the United States be seen as condoning Nazi policy. Still, the anti-Jewish laws would not be repealed for another four months, after Patton had left Morocco.[8] The next day Pendar reported again to Patton, explaining that he had spoken to Murphy on the phone and that the latter wanted to know if the letter had been delivered. Patton raged, "I told you I didn't want this discussed on the phone," and vowed again that he would take full responsibility for the matter—with a few extra "goddamn-its" tossed in for good measure. Pendar had had enough: "Then communicate with my superior, Ambassador Murphy, and tell him as much." Patton immediately cooled, "You know Pendar," he said calmly, "my bark is worse than my bite."[9]

Keeping the Vichy content was difficult. When OSS agent Carleton S. Coon submitted a report on the French regime's poor treatment of the locals, one of Patton's staffers compared their behavior to that of the Nazis and asked, "How long has this been going on?" "Twenty years," said Coon, "too long for us to do anything about it at this point." Patton asserted that he would not have his men police North Africa and would, however unjust it might be, leave it to the French. "Our job is simply to kick the Axis out of North Africa with the men at our disposal," he explained, to which Coon warned that his plan might backfire and spark

CHAPTER THREE ★ THE RESTLESS LION OF MOROCCO

a native revolt. Patton shot back that he had his instructions, adding that a dangerously small number of soldiers were actually fighting the war.[10] These kinds of run-ins prompted Eisenhower to write Patton, "I have a definite feeling that you are not making as full use of the various civilian agencies of the government as could be done with profit."[11]

In yet another instance with political implications, Patton refused to intervene in a case of imprisoned Vichy soldiers who, after hearing President Franklin D. Roosevelt's liberation broadcast, cut the communications wires to their own officers' quarters and dismantled their artillery pieces. The men were found guilty of treason. When the White House urged Patton to look into the matter, he wrote back, "They got what they deserved. It was treason, wasn't it?"[12] To appease the defeated French, Patton issued a statement in the local newspapers, hailing the French as "gallant fighters." He praised Noguès for his collaboration and explained, "We want political as well as economic normalcy to return as soon as possible."[13]

Coon's reports elevated concerns that the Arab population might revolt against the French now that the Americans were in power. By Patton's estimation, it would take sixty thousand fully equipped Americans—twice as many troops than he had—to put down any rebellion.[14] To keep relations smooth, five days after the French surrender, on November 16, Patton and Noguès headed for Rabat, Morocco's capital, to meet with the sultan. General Ernie Harmon had arranged an escort of scout cars and tanks, but Patton dismissed them, not wanting to seem threatening. Before leaving Noguès's residence, the two generals inspected a battalion of Moroccan cavalry and the governor general's bodyguard while bands played. Patton commended the men on their appearance, but thought, "It was rather pathetic to think that one of the light tanks in the escort could have easily destroyed all of the splendid creatures standing to salute."

Once inside the sultan's palace, Patton again inspected the guards. The sultan's grand vizier, with a long gray beard and a set of gold teeth, escorted Patton and his party up to the palace's third floor to a room with thick carpets and gold chairs lining the walls. The sultan sat on a raised platform at the far end of the room. Patton judged him "a very handsome young man, extremely fragile, with a highly sensitive face." Patton bowed several times as he approached the platform. The sultan stood up and shook hands with Patton and Noguès before the three sat down. Patton expressed his contentment that the French, Arabs, and Americans were reunited and assured him the United States only desired to fight the Germans. For his part, the sultan told Patton he hoped the Americans would respect Arab institutions, and Patton insisted that he had already ordered his men to do so. He concluded by telling the sultan how he admired Morocco's beauty. At some point, Patton handed over Roosevelt's embellished letter but never recorded the sultan's reaction to the missive.[15]

Figure 8. The sultan of Morocco, Mohammed V, greets Patton at his Rabat palace during the festival of Id el Kabir. To the sultan's right is his oldest son, Prince Moulay Hassan. Catalog number: 208-PU-153 F-3, National Archives and Records Administration.

The next day, Patton flew to Gibraltar to meet with Eisenhower. He found his headquarters deep in a mountainside cave, which Eisenhower called his dungeon—"in great danger," Patton sarcastically noted.[16] Eisenhower asked him to send a contingent of tanks to Tunisia in support of British general Kenneth Anderson, who was leading American, French, and British forces, now designated First Army. Patton considered the request "the most foolish instructions I have ever read," but agreed. He told Eisenhower about Roosevelt's letter, and Eisenhower supported his decision to edit it. Patton came away disappointed by what he had perceived as the British influence on his commander, who had spent the previous five months in England: Eisenhower had called lunch "tiffin," gasoline "petrol," and anti-aircraft fire "flack," all British terms: "I truly fear that London had conquered Abilene." Ironically, the British referred to Eisenhower's headquarters as the "American Empire." On Patton's flight back, Spanish anti-aircraft guns fired at his aircraft but missed.[17]

The next day, November 18, Patton attended the anniversary of the sultan's coronation. A squadron of Moroccan cavalry on white stallions escorted the general to the palace. Trumpeters blew horns the whole way. After listening to a long rendition of the national anthem, Patton entered the palace, where he spied the sultan's harem through a wooden screen, surprised to see many of the women wearing glasses.[18] Noguès stood before the Moroccan ruler and delivered a lengthy oration, followed by the sultan giving a speech of his own. Realizing he had prepared nothing for the occasion, but not wanting to embarrass the United States with his silence, Patton stepped forward and spoke extemporaneously.

"Your Majesty," Patton began, "as a humble representative of the Great President whom I had the honor of representing as the commander of a huge military force in Morocco, I wish to present the compliments of the U.S. on this the anniversary of your accession to the throne." He assured the sultan that as long as Morocco cooperated, the Allies would win. He ended with a historical note connecting the United States and Morocco. "One of your Majesty's great predecessors established friendship with our great president, George Washington, when he gave the beautiful building which houses the American mission in Tangier to General Washington as a token of friendship and respect."[19] The sultan thanked Patton for his remarks and assured him his presence at the anniversary would have a profound and salutary influence on the entire Muslim world. "Apparently," Patton wrote his wife, "I should have been a statesman."[20]

Patton enjoyed the rest of the day by walking General Truscott's battlefield at Lyautey. Truscott presented Patton a bronze cannon from the Kasbah, forged in 1521, and told him stories about his tank battles, sieges, and attacks. Later, when Patton awarded Second Lieutenant Stephen Sprindis the Silver Star for single-handedly having fended off the French tank attack with a bazooka, he asked the young man his rank. "Second lieutenant, sir," Sprindis replied, "You are a liar," Patton declared. "You are now a first lieutenant."[21]

Patton's life in Morocco took on an almost surreal aspect. Noguès bedazzled him with his horsemanship, fine meals, militarism, and colonial glamor. Patton grew to enjoy Noguès's company, despite word from

Figure 9. Patton dressed in Moroccan robes when he met with the Sultan and Vichy French General August Nogués. He later wrote, "I should have been a statesman." Library of Congress.

Eisenhower's headquarters that the French general would soon be sacked. Eisenhower worried about reports of Noguès's corruption and feared the Frenchman would quickly switch sides should the Germans take the offensive. Patton responded that the sultan and the Muslims respected Noguès and that he should be left alone.[22] In that spirit, Patton attended extravagant parties mixing Vichy French officers with Americans, affairs which he often attended in full regalia, his two holstered pistols clearly visible. At all times, however, he kept a sidearm and asked Beatrice to send him his small .22-caliber "Banker's Special" revolver, considering it lighter to wear and easier to conceal. "One has to go armed here," he wrote her.[23] He sometimes clashed with the French over local protocol. When they learned that Patton had accepted an invitation to dinner from a powerful tribal leader outside Rabat, the French officials advised him not to attend, but he went anyway. The meal lasted three hours and included music and dancing girls.[24]

His willingness to socialize notwithstanding, Patton much preferred military matters to diplomatic work. He created a receiving center for men and equipment in Casablanca. Nearby Marrakech became the most important airport in North Africa, with B-17 bombers and C-47 cargo aircraft arriving daily from the United States. The city swarmed with American soldiers, sailors, and airmen.[25] Patton went on numerous inspections, instilling strict military protocol. He banned officers not wearing dress uniforms from the officers' mess.[26] At first, he hollered at anyone who failed to salute but eventually resorted to getting their names and reporting them to their commanding officers. He even developed a system to enforce saluting and proper dress, carried out by military police (MPs). When American servicemen became wise to MPs looking for violators, Patton ordered off-duty doctors of the 95th Evacuation Hospital to walk the streets of Casablanca, followed by two MPs several yards behind. The doctors acted as decoys for soldiers out of uniform so the MPs could catch the offenders. When the doctors spotted the offenders, who quickly tidied themselves up before the MPs arrived, the doctors would identify them to the MPs.[27] Most of the violators were pilots. Patton often came across drunken soldiers who either threatened to punch him or accused him of hitting them. Nothing ever came of the incidents. One day, he passed a sergeant who did not salute. Patton stopped and asked the man why he failed to salute, and the man told him, "I don't salute generals, they don't need it." A furious Patton screamed, "Lock the son-of-a-bitch up!"[28] Within a month, he would boast, "This is the only place in Africa where anyone salutes at all."[29]

Patton also displayed his keen eye for detail. Going over the 1st Armored Division's manifests, he learned that the static unit consumed about five hundred gallons of fuel a week. He ordered Harmon to get to the bottom of it. Harmon reported that men were using the fuel for cooking fires, adding that these were a good morale booster. Patton cursed for a few moments, then he said brusquely, "Okay, let's continue it. I guess it's a good idea."[30]

Yet Patton craved action. News that Mark Clark was being considered for the Medal of Honor for leading a secret peace negotiation mission prior to TORCH depressed him. He had wanted the same award as far back as World War I. Worse, on November 22, Eisenhower sent him a letter chastising him for not delivering Anderson the twenty-five tanks he had requested at Gibraltar. "I am disappointed that this movement was not ready as promised," scolded the Allied commander. The letter put Patton into a funk, leading him to complain about a stomachache to Beatrice: "I have the most awful blues all day."[31] The war in the east frustrated him: "[Major General Lloyd] Fredendall [commanding the U.S. II corps against the Germans] seems perfectly happy to just sit but I think I will go mad if we don't get some more battles."[32]

On November 24, Patton flew to Oran to visit a very depressed Fredendall. Patton had spent the trip in the nose of his B-25, enjoying the view. Upon landing, he learned Fredendall was worried that American units were being parceled out to the British, a sore spot with American generals who remembered the British and French attempting the same tactic in World War I, which had diluted American strength and leadership. General Pershing had resisted efforts to break up the American army in France, but Eisenhower, trying to get the Allies to work together and not willing to intercede with a commander in the field, was not doing the same in North Africa. "I seem to be the only one beating my wings against the cage of inaction," Patton confided to his diary.

The visit with Fredendall left Patton, if anything, even more depressed. He wanted to be back in command, leading men from the front and tearing through the enemy. "I want to be top dog and only battle can give me that," he wrote in his diary. Beatrice sent him several sets of lieutenant-general stars in anticipation of his promotion, but he feared it would never come. Only his belief in a higher calling seemed to cheer him, "but the waiting is hard. Perhaps I am being made perfect through suffering, for I do suffer when I cannot move."[33]

Thanksgiving morning found Patton watching two 3rd Infantry Division regiments march to Rabat. When he saw three men riding in a truck, he marched over and chewed them out for laziness until he realized that one of the three was wounded and decorated for bravery. Thereafter, he gave the men a ride in his own vehicle. He ate Thanksgiving dinner at the American Consulate and issued an order comparing his troops' voyage to North Africa to that of the Pilgrims and thanking God for "bringing us safely to shore, in providing us with ample food and supplies, and in placing us in the midst of a smiling land whose people are again united with us in the battle for human freedom."[34]

December started with a surprise. Called to a meeting with Eisenhower and Clark, Patton flew to Algiers, where he hoped to get a fighting command. Instead, Eisenhower took a call, and when he hung up, said "Well Wayne," using Clark's middle name, "you get Fifth Army." Shocked, Patton offered his congratulations, even though he inwardly seethed that a younger officer, one who had not yet led men in combat, was getting promoted while he remained a corps commander, under Clark no less. He convinced himself that he would pass them all, but the incident kept him up all night. The next morning, one of Eisenhower's aides went to wake Patton at 5 a.m. but found the general already up and shaving by flashlight. The sergeant offered to pull back the blackout curtains, but Patton scoffed, "Hell, Sergeant, I'm used to this sort of stuff," and went on shaving. Clark's promotion bothered him so much that he fantasized about being shot through the heart in battle, considering it "the easiest way out."[35] He spent the rest of the day touring Algiers' TORCH battlefields before flying back to Casablanca. His pilot entertained him by flying only seventy-five feet off the ground, buzzing sheep, camels, and Arabs along the way. The ride cheered up Patton, who now chalked up Clark's promotion to "an additional act of God to temper me, so I feel fine."

With little else to do, Patton went wild boar hunting with some local French officials. With approximately 250 natives beating the woods and driving the animals toward his party, Patton shot two boars and a jackal with an over-under 12-gage shotgun, which fired a solid slug from one barrel and buckshot with the other. First, he hit a charging boar at ninety yards with a head shot. Then he nailed another at fifty yards with a bullet through the heart. He caught the jackal with buckshot. The animals were strapped to the hood of his command car for the ride back to camp. He enjoyed himself, but it was hardly the kind of hunt for which a warrior longed. Patton was bored.[36]

While the restless general waited in Morocco, things were not going well in the east. Incessant rains in Algeria and Tunisia, which turned the terrain to mud, had slowed Anderson's First Army. Anderson worked to keep the offensive going but sudden German counterattacks, starting on December 1 and continuing for ten days, brought the offensive to a stop. What was to have been a quick thrust to Rommel's rear had now turned into a slog. In short, the war in North Africa would last longer than the Allies had expected.[37]

A chance at some excitement came Patton's way when Eisenhower ordered him to look into the Army's high rate of tank losses. Eisenhower needed a professional he trusted to assess the situation. Patton leapt at the opportunity. The excitement started early on December 9, when his plane came under friendly fire as he was flying to Algiers. Anti-aircraft fire rocked the craft as shrapnel tore a hole in a wing. Once Patton was safely on the ground, Eisenhower sent him off to inspect the front.[38]

In the desert on December 11, Patton encountered the 1st Armored Division's Combat Command B, whose men had just come off the front with heavy losses in equipment. He jumped out of his car and shouted to the men, "Where are the damned Germans, I want to get shot at!" He then regaled the tankers with stories, anecdotes, and details of the Casablanca operation.[39] Next he traveled to Mediez-el-Bab, cruising along a road strewn with wrecked vehicles and blackened shell holes. He came across his son-in-law, Major John Waters, husband to his oldest daughter, Little Bea. Waters, a battalion commander in the 1st Armored Division, visited with Patton long enough for Patton to notice a bullet hole in his overcoat. They would not see each other again for almost three years.

Close to the front, Patton found a drunken British brigadier who, in Patton's estimation, had incorrectly deployed his armor. Patton did not record his name. Things looked up, however, when he reached Waters's battalion. The men were in good spirits but told Patton that he was the only general officer they had seen at the front. "A sad commentary on our idea of leadership," he later wrote. On December 13, after four days at the front, he reported back to Eisenhower and Clark and explained that British tactics were the root of the problem. The British favored holding the low ground and ceding the high ground to the enemy; they set up positions in front of, instead of behind, rivers; they viewed the tank as a defensive weapon, refusing to support their tanks with infantry; and they only used about 10 percent of their communications capacity.[40] Patton was disappointed to learn that neither Eisenhower nor Clark had yet been to the front. It would be another month before Eisenhower got there. Flying back to his headquarters in Casablanca, Patton's plane encountered a violent storm. His pilot circled the city for an hour, but when fuel became low, they decided to either attempt a belly landing or parachute out. Fortunately, the rain let up, and they touched down. Patton treated the flight crew to dinner and a night's sleep at his headquarters.[41]

CHAPTER THREE ★ THE RESTLESS LION OF MOROCCO

Figure 10. Patton saw his son-in-law, Lieutenant Colonel John K. Waters, in the Tunisian desert before Waters became a prisoner of war, captured by the Germans. U.S. Army.

Safely back in Morocco, Patton began to spend more and more time with the sultan: visiting his palace, hosting military displays, and sharing meals, sometimes even donning a traditional African robe for the occasion. On December 20 he attended a joint American and French parade in Rabat. The French brought out their light Renault tanks. American artillery batteries, a company of light tanks, and a platoon of medium tanks followed. As Patton left the event, crowds cheered him, shouting "Vive l'Amérique!" He responded by blowing kisses to the crowd. "If the worst comes I shall run for Sultan," he wrote Beatrice.[42]

To soak up the local culture, Patton toured Marrakesh with some of the sultan's family. He cruised the market, enjoying the sights and smells, but was startled when an Arab woman in flowing robes propositioned him. Stiller shouted at her to get away, but the woman retorted: "Whattsa matta? No like fuckee Arab women?" Patton managed to keep a poker face but, once she left, burst out laughing. He concluded his visit with a ten-course lunch with the sultan.[43]

Things turned serious on Christmas Eve when Eisenhower sent word to "alert your command." Patton put extra guards around the gas and ammunition dumps. But the alert had nothing to do with the enemy. Admiral Darlan had been gunned down by a soldier supporting Charles de Gaulle. Eisenhower's pick to lead the French had just assumed the mantle when he was killed. Fortunately, there were no repercussions in Morocco. Patton spent the next day celebrating a subdued Christmas, passing out candy at church to soldiers and French children. Ever the diplomat, he also sent Eisenhower two "liberated" turkeys to enjoy for a traditional holiday dinner.[44]

On New Year's Eve 1943, the Germans bombed Casablanca. When explosions awakened Patton around 3:15 a.m., he ran to the roof to watch the action. Searchlights crisscrossed the sky as anti-aircraft guns fired wildly into the rainy night. A tremendous flash lit the sky—a flare. Patton heard the bombers long before they arrived but one flying in low behind him still surprised him. The searchlights caught the bomber in their beams. "Apparently every anti-aircraft gun in the vicinity opened fire," Patton remarked. Anti-aircraft tracer rounds swept the aircraft as explosive rounds created white clouds. One round found its mark and the plane exploded in a black cloud. Patton remained on the roof, dispatching officers over the phone to collect information. The raid lasted about an hour and a half. He went back to bed, only to be roused by a second raid. Upon his return to the roof he noticed that this time, the Navy was contributing to the return fire. "It was better than the greatest Fourth-of-July demonstration possible to image," he beamed. He watched a bomber take a hit, drop about two thousand feet, right itself, then fly over the ocean, disappearing into the mist before crashing into the water. As the last bomber flew off, Sergeant Meeks turned to Patton. "If I had my saddle," he told the general, "I could throw it on him and ride him." As the sun rose, Patton toured the area, inspecting the damage, before meeting with his aviators and anti-aircraft crews to review and correct their defenses.[45]

With the excitement over, Patton returned to his diplomatic duties, writing apologies to the sultan (whom at times Patton referred to as the Pasha) and Noguès for the damage done by the raid. He also lost his designation as the Western Task Force commander, when the command was redesignated as I Armored Corps. He met again with General Luis Orgaz Yoldi, the head of Spanish Morocco, who now put on a military demonstration for Patton. The two got along splendidly and Patton, impressed with the Spanish Honor Guard, admitted that they "were the best looking and best drilled troops I have ever seen." He came away convinced that the Spanish posed no threat to the American army.[46]

The most significant event of Patton's tenure in Morocco was the Anfa Conference, also known as the Casablanca Conference, at which President Roosevelt and Prime Minister Winston Churchill met to forge a future strategy: where would the Allies fight next once the Germans and Italians were ejected from North Africa? Who would represent the French? What would be the overall strategy? Under the code name "Symbol," the two leaders brought their staffs to Morocco and convened in Casablanca's Anfa district on January 14, 1943, for ten days of meetings. Patton oversaw security, housing, and any other creature comforts that the parties might require. Although in this capacity he saw himself as a "two-star manservant," he knew this would be his best chance to show his leaders that he was ready for more.

As the planning for Anfa went forward, the U.S. Army prepared to stand up a new command. The North African Theater of Operations, U.S. Army (NATOUSA) would deal with purely American, as opposed to Allied, matters. Eisenhower was slated to assume command of NATOUSA and, with Marshall's urging, considered making Patton his deputy commander of ground forces, a position that would put Patton in charge of all military matters, except naval and air. Marshall had become concerned over Eisenhower's dual military and political jobs and felt Patton could fill the gap. Eisenhower worried the other services would resent Patton, but ultimately agreed, writing Marshal that he wanted Patton's "great mental and physical energy in helping me through a critical period."[47]

Patton knew none of this. He was too busy preparing for the conference: inspecting honor guards, arranging security, and preparing military displays. Before his guests arrived, he gave the sultan a tour of Casablanca's airfield. It paid off when the sultan insisted that Patton sit next to him in Patton's command car, the first time the honor ever had gone to a foreigner. Patton got another boost when the sultan presented him with the Grand Cross Order of the Ouissam Alaouite: an elaborate medal with an orange sash that stretched diagonally across the chest. The French inscription on the back translated as "The lions in their dens tremble at his approach." Patton's new assistant deputy chief of staff, Captain Charles Codman, added, "And so does everyone else." Patton joked with

Brigadier General Everett Hughes, an old friend and Eisenhower's chief of services and supply, that instead of signing his title as "Major General," he would now use "Lion Tamer."[48]

Eisenhower arrived for the conference looking sick and weak. He had developed an undiagnosed respiratory ailment in the damp cliffside offices of Gibraltar back in November. Once in Algeria, the stress of the Tunisian campaign and Allied politics had further compromised his health. His blood pressure skyrocketed, forcing him to spend four days confined to quarters. He worried that his inability to drive into Tunisia had soured Marshall on him and that he would be sent home. Adding to Eisenhower's stress, on his flight to the conference, his bomber lost two engines and he had to strap on a parachute and prepare to jump from the stricken plane. Fortunately, the pilot made it in without error.[49] Patton had heard the rumors of Eisenhower's relief of duty and chalked it up to deceitful maneuvering by Clark, who would later demean Eisenhower in front of Patton. The two generals, Patton and Eisenhower, stood in stark contrast to each other: Patton, hale and hardy, battle wise and rested, ready for a new assignment; and Eisenhower, ailing, overworked, stressed, and worried about his future.[50]

While Roosevelt and Churchill debated the course of the war, Patton enjoyed himself by showing his friends and colleagues his version of Casablanca. He wined and dined his visitors, took them shopping, toured them around his battlefields, and held inspections so they could see firsthand the fruits of his labors. "George's troops were by far the best disciplined and best trained looking group of soldiers I ever saw in all of my travel," General Jacob Devers later wrote. "Not only all the soldiers saluted you, but all the Arabs and civilians did likewise." When Patton led dignitaries on tours of the Fedala harbor, with its sunken ships, he would have his driver quickly pass the damaged French battleship *Jean Bart*, not wanting the French to think he was gloating about the American victory.[51]

Patton also began to spend more and more time with the president, moderating meetings with Roosevelt, Noguès, and the sultan and escorting FDR on troop reviews. He considered the president a great statesman, affable, and interested in his views.[52] The 2nd Armored and 3rd Infantry divisions paraded for FDR while Patton stood by, stone faced but proud of his smart-looking troops. Cameramen clicked photos of the president and his entourage, all but ignoring the passing troops. "It was

CHAPTER THREE ★ THE RESTLESS LION OF MOROCCO   63

very disgusting," Patton later wrote. True to form, Patton repeatedly told the president that he wanted to die with his boots on.[53]

Whenever Patton spoke to Eisenhower alone, he encouraged him to visit the front, but Eisenhower declined, explaining that politics prevented it. Eisenhower tried to cheer Patton by telling him of the possible ground forces job, but Patton wasn't buying it, noting, "Am not sure I want the job." The president's advisor Harry Hopkins also presented him a potentially new vocation. Impressed with Patton's job in Morocco, Hopkins offered to make him an ambassador, twice pressing him about it. "I still said I would resign and go fishing rather than take such a job," Patton wrote. Yet, somehow he knew he would get a fighting command: "It looks to me as if pretty soon they will have to put in a second team."[54]

The Anfa Conference answered all the Allies questions for the immediate future. There would be no cross-channel invasion of France in 1943; the war after the African campaign would continue into Sicily; French generals Charles de Gaulle and Henri Giraud agreed to work as co-presidents of the Free French; and the Allies crafted a policy of unconditional surrender. For his part, Patton had put on an impressive show for his guests. And for ten days the eager general had access to the top leaders of the United States, England, and France, including their generals. His assessment: "The more I see of the so-called great, the less they impress me—I am better." When it came to Clark, spending time with him only increased Patton's disdain: "It makes my flesh creep to be with him."[55]

The new arrangement on the Tunisian front infuriated Patton. British general Harold Alexander would serve as an army group commander over General Montgomery's Eighth Army, pursuing Rommel's Afrika Korps in the eastern desert, and British general Anderson's First Army, which would attack German general Hans-Jürgen Von Arnim's recently arrived Fifth Panzer Army from the west. First Army consisted of the British V Corps, a French corps, and Fredendall's American II Corps, made up of the 1st Infantry and 1st Armored Divisions. To strengthen the French forces, Eisenhower loaned them the American 34th Infantry Division. Patton deplored the idea of a British general commanding the combined force. "Shades of J. J. Pershing!" he grumbled in his diary, seeing American forces under British command instead of an independent command. "We have sold our birthright . . . I am shocked and distressed." But however poorly he viewed the situation, he still wanted in. "God, I wish I could really command and lead as well as just fight."[56] A few days later, Eisenhower activated Mark Clark's Fifth U.S. Army, composed of Patton's I Armored Corps and Fredendall's II Corps. The news wasn't all bad. Eisenhower had chosen Patton to plan the invasion of Sicily.[57]

With the conference over, Patton returned to diplomatic duties, spending time with the sultan, dining, fishing, and hunting. All were elaborate affairs. In one hunt, more than one thousand beaters forced packs of boars, foxes, and jackals from the brush, all of the creatures charging towards Patton, the sultan, and other guests. There were almost too many to shoot. Patton fired his weapon three times, hitting nothing. A huge black boar charged him. As it rapidly closed the distance, Patton, his heart racing, leveled his gun and fired. The slug ripped into the beast's right eye, killing it instantly and splashing blood from the animal's mouth onto Patton's boots. "It is fortunate I killed him instantly," he later reflected. He sent its teeth to Beatrice.[58]

The next day, at a meeting with Eisenhower and Clark, Eisenhower surprised Patton by declaring, "George, you are my oldest friend, but if you or anyone else criticizes the British, by God I will reduce him to his permanent grade and send him home." He told Patton his promotion to lieutenant general, as well as that of Fredendall and Carl "Tooey" Spaatz, was being held up because Fredendall had recently criticized the British. Patton was shaken. Had he done something wrong? Later, Eisenhower wrote him, explaining that he was not angry with him but had just wanted to warn him to keep his opinions about the Allied partners to himself. Eisenhower wanted Patton for the future, but he worried that Patton's mouth might get the better of him before he could prove himself again in combat. Patton saw it as Eisenhower trying to cover himself against criticism. "Cromwell beware ambition," he quoted Shakespeare, "by it the angels fell." Ever the good soldier, however, Patton held a staff meeting the next day and warned everyone to watch their language.[59]

On February 15 Patton flew to Tripoli to attend a four-day, after-action conference hosted by Montgomery on the British Eighth Army's successful campaign at El Alamein and the pursuit of Rommel. Only a few American officers were invited. Patton found the conference enlightening. He came away from it impressed with Montgomery: "He is small, very alert and wonderfully conceited and the best soldier." He later compared him to the American Civil War general Thomas "Stonewall" Jackson, famous for his rapid movement on the battlefield. A British officer warned

CHAPTER THREE ★ THE RESTLESS LION OF MOROCCO 65

Patton, however, that Montgomery was the most disagreeable general he knew.[60] Patton soon learned why.

Montgomery banned smoking from his lectures. Patton chaffed at this, and at one point reached for a cigarette. Beetle Smith, who was sitting next to Patton, quickly offered him a piece of gum, which he accepted. Later in the day, British lieutenant general Oliver Leese asked Patton over lunch what he thought of not being allowed to smoke during the lecture. Patton puffed on a cigarette and said, with a twinkle in his eye, "Well, I may be slow, and I may be stupid, but it just didn't mean a durn thing to me." Unfortunately, British officers embellished Patton's harmless comment. By the time it reached Montgomery's ears, it had grown to Patton considering himself "old and deaf," and that it was Montgomery's speech—not his smoking ban—that Patton considered as not meaning "a durn thing." The misquote insulted both men and may have explained Montgomery's cool attitude toward Patton.[61]

Back in Morocco, Major General Jonathan Anderson's 3rd Infantry Division disappointed Patton during a training exercise as the men froze whenever they heard fire. The 3rd had performed well during TORCH, but to Patton, Anderson was not sufficiently aggressive. Three months earlier, Patton wrote that Anderson was "just good enough not to be relieved," but now Patton worried that Anderson had lost so much weight he was down to just skin and bones. After watching the exercise, Patton called Eisenhower to have Truscott take over the division. It was one of Patton's most significant decisions.[62]

Things were going poorly over the horizon to the west. There was news of a German breakthrough against II Corps. On February 19, Fredendall requested all the mines Patton could supply. On March 2 Ernie Harmon reported to Patton that John Waters, Patton's son-in-law, had been missing for two weeks. The Germans had slammed into Fredendall's II Corps and Waters had been captured while defending the high ground near an area called Dj Lassouda. Helplessly outnumbered, Waters had left his headquarters in a halftrack and raced to a frontline observation post to help his men escape. In one of his last radio transmissions he said, "Don't worry about me, just kill these bastards at the bottom of the hill." Waters' fate dogged Patton: "I fear John is dead." Waters would spend the rest of the war in German POW camps, but the tragedy that befell the II Corps was about to bring Patton the combat he craved.[63]

CHAPTER FOUR

Rejuvenating II Corps in Twelve Days

THE DESERT WAR revealed Lloyd Fredendall as a poor leader. He entered the conflict as one of "Marshall's Boys," the officers who had impressed the chief of staff enough that they were slotted to the most important commands and expected to rise through the ranks. Marshall described him as "one of the best" and once remarked, "I like that man. You can see determination all over his face." Despite Fredendall's successful landing at Oran as commander of the Central Task Force, he rarely left his command ship during the three days of fighting. Given a position within the British First Army's front, he did not impress his British allies, barely communicating with his superiors and openly grousing about the Brits. "Surely," British general Harold Alexander told Eisenhower, "you have better men than that."[1] Eisenhower did, but he did not want to pull a "Marshall's Boy."

Fredendall's relations with his own subordinates were no better. He constantly meddled with General Orlando Ward's 1st Armored Division, often bypassing him and issuing orders to his combat commanders. Fredendall, forced to give up parts of Ward's division to his Army commander, as well as cover a wide front, scattered Ward's units, weakening the division commander's command and control. Fredendall mixed infantry, armor, and artillery units together in "penny packets," the same kind of formations that had led to British defeats early in the desert war.[2] Eisenhower considered his attacks piecemeal and sloppy. Major General Terry de la Masa Allen, the 1st Infantry Division's commander, also found Fredendall's leadership lacking. After Fredendall leapt into a foxhole during a German shelling, Allen disdained him for cowardness.

Fredendall did not inspire confidence in his lower-ranking officers either. While touring Oran in Major John Waters's tank, he never left the vehicle, fearful of being shot. "He wouldn't stand up in the turret and look around," Waters later reported. "The people were welcoming us with open arms. He would only peek over the turret."[3] Fredendall's speech impediment also compounded his inability to inspire his troops. Men had trouble understanding him over the radio, since he spoke in slang. He rarely visited the front, and, almost worst of all, he set up headquarters sixty-five miles behind the line, in an Algerian cave that took extra engineers three weeks to blast out of a canyon. Omar Bradley considered it an embarrassment to every American soldier.[4]

The Germans took full advantage of Fredendall's weaknesses. To counter Operation TORCH, Hitler had sent more troops and tanks to Algeria and Tunisia, eventually creating the Fifth Panzer Army under General Jürgen von Arnim. By February of 1943 von Armin commanded four divisions and assorted other units, including two hundred tanks.[5] On February 14 he smashed into Fredendall's II Corps with his 10th and 21st Panzer divisions. The corps faced east, spread out north-to-south along the Eastern Dorsal chain of the Atlas Mountains about 150 miles from the Tunisian coast. The Germans, utilizing two passes through the mountains, struck the 1st Armored at Sidi Bou Zid, knocking it back about fifty miles in a two-day fight. The German offensive turned into an ugly rout, with Americans throwing down their weapons and surrendering to the onrushing Germans. Those who retreated often left their equipment behind. Rommel, who had recently arrived in Tunisia and stopped Montgomery at a series of defenses known as the Mareth Line, followed up von Arnim's attack two days later, splitting his forces in two. The first headed twenty miles north for the town of Sbiba, while the other plowed through the Kasserine Pass, dividing itself again, with one column heading as far as Thala, thirty miles away, and the other to Dj El Hamra, roughly the same distance. The Germans mauled Fredendall for five days. When the dust cleared, the II Corps had lost three hundred men killed, almost three thousand wounded, and nearly three thousand missing in action, for a total of almost sixty-three hundred men. The corps also lost 183 tanks, 194 half-tracks, 208 artillery pieces, 512 trucks and jeeps, and more materiel than could be found in the stocks of Morocco and Algeria combined. The Germans lost only 201 men for their efforts. It was the worst American defeat since the surrender of Bataan and Corregidor in the Philippines, where fifteen thousand American troops surrendered to the Japanese.[6]

CHAPTER FOUR ★ REJUVENATING II CORPS IN TWELVE DAYS

Figure 11. Lieutenant General Lloyd Ralston Fredendall, from whom Patton took command of the II Corps. National Archives and Records Administration.

The defeat at Kasserine Pass not only shook the confidence of the American army, it also spurred British disdain for the United States' unpreparedness for harsh, modern combat. But British leadership did not place blame on Fredendall. "They simply do not know their job as soldiers and this is the case from the highest to the lowest, from the general to the private soldier," British general Alexander explained to General Sir Alan Brooke, the chief of the Imperial General Staff. "Perhaps the weakest link of all is the junior leader, who just does not lead, with the result that their men do not really fight."[7] To the British, the Americans were the green army that couldn't shoot straight or hold its ground against the Germans. More than just American morale would have to be improved if they were going to shoulder a larger responsibility in the war. The Allies had to believe that the Americans would fight and win on the battlefield.

Although Fredendall made several trips to the front, lobbied for the return of the 1st Armored's separated units back from Anderson, and moved his headquarters to Djebel Kouif closer to the front, Rommel's forces drove his corps back, with all of Fredendall's counteroffensives ending in disaster and resulting in men killed, tanks destroyed, and ground lost. Eisenhower sent Major General Harmon to II Corps headquarters to assess Fredendall, who immediately handed over his command to Harmon and took to his bed. Harmon spent the next few days shoring up the battlefront, reporting to Eisenhower that Fredendall was "no damned good" and needed to be relieved of command. Eisenhower offered Harmon the command, but he declined, since he could not accept the position after having recommended the relief of its commander. Eisenhower next offered the job to Mark Clark, who also refused, considering a corps command a demotion for an army commander, even if it was the only part of the U.S. Army currently battling the enemy. Eisenhower toyed with calling Patton, but he did not want to distract him from planning the Sicily invasion. When General Marshall explicitly told Eisenhower to replace Fredendall with Patton, the call went out on March 4.[8]

Patton had been spending that day reviewing replacements for the 3rd Infantry Division and enjoying some horseback riding when he received Eisenhower's message to pack up for extended field service. Curious, Patton called Beetle Smith and asked him what was going on. Smith told him he was replacing Fredendall. Patton, already aware of Fredendall's shortcomings from what his son-in-law had told him, knew he would be taking over a dysfunctional command, but he later reflected, "I will make a go of it." Harmon had told Patton he considered Fredendall a physical and moral coward. Later, once Patton took the reins of II Corps, he noted that Fredendall "merely existed—he did not command."[9] Yet Patton predicted he would have more trouble with the British than with the Germans. Before going to bed that night, he wrote in his diary, "God favors the brave, victory to the audacious!"[10]

The next day Patton received the official word from Eisenhower, in the form of a hand-written note: "You will assume command of the Corps, relieving Maj-Gen-Fredendall, who has been relieved." Patton took his new chief of staff, Brigadier General Hugh Gaffey, with him to the airfield. Also accompanying him were Colonel Kent Lambert, his operations officer, and Colonel Oscar Koch, his intelligence officer. Keyes remained behind to take over as the temporary commander of the I Armored Corps until Patton returned. On the way to the airfield, soldiers lined to the street to bid him farewell. An honor guard and band greeted him at the airfield, where he stood ramrod straight in a pilot's leather jacket, clutching a riding crop in one hand and saluting the troops with the other before boarding his C-47. Patton was heading to war again, this time to rejuvenate a defeated unit.[11]

CHAPTER FOUR ★ REJUVENATING II CORPS IN TWELVE DAYS   71

Figure 12. Brigadier General Hugh Gaffey discusses the attack on Gafsa with Patton at his headquarters in Feriana, Tunisia, on March 17, 1943. Gaffey served on Patton's staff and commanded the 2nd Armored Division during the Sicily campaign. Catalog number: 111-SC 179178, National Archives and Records Administration.

When Patton's plane landed at Algiers, Eisenhower, Smith, and Lieutenant Commander Harry Butcher, Eisenhower's naval aide, greeted him. When he noticed the Navy man was unarmed, he handed him a sawed off .45 Colt revolver and shoulder holster. Butcher delighted in his new weapon. No ceremony, parades, or ruffles and flourishes accompanied Patton's assumption of command. Eisenhower simply explained II Corps' mission: Help to squeeze the Germans between the British Eighth Army, approaching from the south, and the British First Army, attacking from the west. Patton's two objectives were to tie up as many German units as possible until Montgomery's Eighth Army pushed through Rommel's Mareth Line, and to capture the port town of Gabés, which Montgomery could then use as a supply base.

Eisenhower warned Patton not to plow forward, for fear of cutting across Montgomery's line of advance, and not to criticize the British. He wanted Patton to foster a feeling of partnership. Even though II Corps was part of Anderson's First Army, Patton would be taking orders from General Harold Alexander, the British 18th Army Group commander, who also commanded Montgomery's Eighth Army. Patton thought it was a nice way of saying "we are pulling the chestnuts [out of the fire] for our noble allies."[12] Eisenhower knew of Patton's proclivity to get up close to the action from his exploits in World War I. While it was the opposite of Fredendall's approach, Eisenhower did not want Patton under enemy fire again, since it had ended his World War I career. Eisenhower preached personal caution— "We need a corps commander, not a casualty"—and reminded Patton to stay at his headquarters, where he could better communicate with higher headquarters. Eisenhower also wanted every II Corps soldier to learn mine removal, not just the engineers. He was not preaching, however, to Patton, but to the ghost of Fredendall.

To bolster Patton, Eisenhower told him to fire poor commanders with cold-blooded precision. All Patton had to do was send them to him, and he would take care of them. To encourage Patton, Eisenhower incorrectly told him that the Army's 37mm cannon could effectively penetrate a German Tiger tank at four hundred yards. The Tiger, the heaviest armored and gunned tank of the war, could fire effectively at twice that distance. When Eisenhower finished his instructions, Patton formally assumed command. He then damned the Germans so violently in front of the group that tears welled up in his eyes. As Patton strutted off, Butcher worried about Patton's mental state, but Eisenhower waved it off. "Patton hates the Hun," Eisenhower told Butcher, "like the devil hates holy water."[13]

Indeed, he did. Just two days before, Patton had told NBC reporter Robert St. John that he wanted to square off with Rommel in a duel to the death: "It would be like combat between two knights, in the old days. The two armies could watch. I'd shoot at him. He'd shoot at me. If I killed him, I'd be the champ. America would win the war. If he killed me . . . well . . . he wouldn't." Patton knew how to make headlines while promoting himself, and the "Rommel duel" was a perfect example of his desire to capture the public's imagination. Eventually the tale morphed into a tank duel, much more to Patton's liking.[14]

In retrospect, Patton's long sojourn in Morocco may have benefitted him. After the three days of fighting in Operation TORCH he was relieved of combat duties and turned his energies to instilling discipline and conducting diplomatic missions. He had time to analyze his combat performance and relax, going on hunts and attending ceremonies. In contrast, Eisenhower and his staff, as well as Fredendall, continued under the strain of wartime command, a position for which none of them were prepared. Eisenhower had not yet recovered from his ailments, while Beetle Smith suffered bleeding ulcers. Fredendall, of course, had taken to shying away from the battlefield. With all the strain of new commands, details slipped through cracks and military priorities and control systems broke down. Within II Corps, poor communications, lack of transport, absent leadership, and green troops exposed the Americans' inability to lock horns with the enemy. Kasserine Pass was a disaster waiting to happen. All this Patton missed while staying fresh in Morocco.[15]

It was this fresh Patton who arrived at his new headquarters in warrior style on the morning of March 6. A line of armored scout cars and half-tracks, bristling with machine guns and whipping antenna wires, roared into the II Corps headquarters in Djebel Kouif, splashing mud and scaring civilians off the streets. Patton stood in the lead car, a tight scowl on his face. His scout car had been fashioned to carry a .50 caliber machinegun to defend against air attack—a testament to the Allies' lack of air cover. On either side of the hood stood two metal flags, one bearing Patton's two-star rank, the other the letters "WTF" for his Western Task Force.[16]

Tunisia's atmosphere shocked Patton. The terrain consisted of valleys, dry riverbeds (called wadies), and sharp rows of mountain ridges, perfect for enemy defenses. After surveying the ridges, Patton understood what the Americans would be up against. "A man in a track suit could make only about two miles a day," he wrote. Tunisia's harsh climate contrasted with Morocco's mild temperatures. When the men weren't getting soaked in heavy rain, they were being pelted by hail. Mud was everywhere. Patton later described it as "blue clay so thick that it sticks like cement and won't brush off." Vistas of metropolitan cities like Rabat and Casablanca were replaced with Roman ruins. While Patton enjoyed viewing Tunisia's ruins, evidence of bygone empires, he never got over the elements, often returning to his headquarters from long days shivering and covered from head to foot in mud. To help him ward off the cold, Jimmy Doolittle sent him a fleece-lined bomber's jacket that he wore for the rest of the war.[17]

Inside his headquarters, an unheated French schoolhouse, Patton found Major General Omar Bradley, whom Eisenhower had sent to monitor Fredendall and now Patton. The two had known each other from their days serving in Hawai'i, where they played polo together. Bradley was the antithesis of Patton. A poor kid from rural Missouri, he entered West Point in hopes of a better life. Bradley played baseball while Patton enjoyed football and fencing. He relaxed by solving math problems, a trait he picked up while teaching math at West Point, whereas Patton loved to read military history and biographies. Bradley was also more even tempered, though, at times, he appreciated Patton's passion and strictness (other times he despised it). Neither Patton nor Bradley was satisfied with Bradley's status, so Patton called Beetle Smith and requested a change. "We're awfully hard up for a good Number Two man as a deputy commander," he told Smith, "Bradley can fill the bill perfectly." The word came back quickly that Bradley would be with Patton for his tenure with II Corps.[18]

With Bradley now on board, Patton next met with Fredendall's staff and came away appalled at just how poorly they functioned. "Worthless," he confided in his diary. The rest of the troops around headquarters were equally unprofessional. Patton followed up the staff meeting by meeting with his two division commanders, Ward and Allen, to review plans for the corps's next movement. Patton knew both of them, having served with them in Mexico and World War I. Both men had performed well during Operation TORCH, and their troops held them in high regard. During the Battle of Kasserine Pass, Ward had taken the brunt of the German offensive, yet Fredendall blamed him for almost everything that went wrong. Allen had fared better, but under Fredendall neither man had commanded their entire division. Patton changed that, eliminating the penny packets and restoring division unity of command. During the meeting, Patton was in no mood for exchanging pleasantries with his old friends. He berated their troops, called them undisciplined and too cowardly to fight, and accused them of looking more like a mob than a smart, soldierly unit.[19] None of those characteristics would be tolerated in a force commanded by George S. Patton. Once the meeting ended, Patton issued orders on dress, saluting, and general military comportment. "It is absurd to believe that soldiers who cannot be made to wear the proper uniform," he later wrote in his diary, "can be induced to move forward in battle."[20]

Ward and Allen were somewhat a study in contrasts. While both attended West Point (Allen dropped out his second year), and both had served in the Mexican Punitive Expedition and World War I, Allen served in the cavalry and infantry whereas Ward had spent his time as an artilleryman. At age fifty, Ward was four years younger than Allen but did not look it. His hair had gone completely grey, while Allen only had grey temples. Ward also looked heavier than the lean-bodied Allen. During Operation TORCH, Allen led his men in successfully capturing Oran, while Ward cooled his heels in England, waiting for the city to be taken before taking command of his division. Once the fighting commenced in Tunisia, Ward faced the harsh desert conditions against a stubborn enemy. The constant plucking of units from his division further drove down his spirit. While Allen faced the same conditions, he had Oran under his belt, endearing him to his men, mostly for embracing an austere existence. General Marshall referred to Allen "the firebrand," but he earned the name "Terrible" Terry Allen from the rest of the Army. Newspaper reporter William Frye summed up Allen in a 1943 bio: "Maj. Gen. Terry de la Mesa Allen. Even his name swaggers."[21]

While Patton may not have impressed Ward with his speech, Allen came away pleased. Fredendall's tactic of splitting up divisions infuriated him. Now Patton held the reigns and he had specifically told Allen that his 1st Infantry, known as the Big Red One for its red division patch, would fight as a whole again. He shot off a memorandum to his units, telling them that their next mission was unknown, however, "WE WILL FIGHT AS A UNIT." Patton's style of leadership already was having direct effects.[22] Allen's chief of staff was also excited about Patton's presence. Brigadier General Teddy Roosevelt, Jr., the eldest son of the twenty-sixth president, cousin to President Franklin Roosevelt, and a World War I veteran, wrote his wife Elenore (whom he called Bunny) that he considered Patton the right man for the job and who would make "all the difference in the world," adding that he had "lived with troops, lead them and fought with them."[23]

The next day, March 6, Patton went to work. He sent out word to his combat leaders that he wanted citations written for men who had performed exceptionally well during Kasserine Pass. Later, he hosted an awards ceremony, praising the men who had stood toe-to-toe with the enemy, stressing that they had covered themselves in glory. His voice choked with emotion as he delivered his conclusion: "Give me a corps of men like you, and I'll take it straight to Berlin!" After he left, the men relaxed and began discussing their medals, unaware that he had secretly returned. "Lieutenant," he said into the ear of a young officer. "You can be pleased with that medal. Those things go over well with the girls back home." Without thinking, the lieutenant responded: "Hell yes, but when will we get to see those girls?" Realizing he was talking to a major general, the lieutenant quickly followed up with "Sir." Patton laughed and said, "Don't worry, you'll see them soon enough. God be with you."[24]

Next, Patton traveled to the front to visit elements of the Major General Manton Eddy's 9th Infantry Division, in front of whom he declared, "We'll beat the sons of bitches!" The men cheered. Fredendall had never bothered to speak to them. Patton's address to the tankers of the 1st Armored Division was so laden with expletives they could not report it: "It would be unprintable." To them, he radiated action, glamor, and determination. All over the corps, he improved living conditions, expediting the arrival of new equipment, clothing, and mail. He insisted on better food and well-cooked meals. Finally, he issued an order to II Corps, laying out their mission and the enemy's capabilities. By explaining the enemy's strengths, he zeroed in on the American problem: "We are not ruthless, not vicious, not aggressive, therein lies our weakness." Patton then applied the solution: "Of course we are willing to die, but that is not enough, we must be eager to kill, to inflict on the enemy—the hated enemy—wounds, death, and destruction. If we die killing, well and good, but if we fight hard enough, vicious enough, we will kill and live. Live to return to our family and our girl as conquering heroes—Men of Mars."[25] He never missed an opportunity to motivate, even rehashing old speeches from his World War I tanker days. He told one group of soldiers, "Go forward, always go forward. You must not fail. Go until the last shots are fired and the last drop of gasoline is gone. Then go forward on foot."[26]

While visiting a corps hospital, he told the medical staff, "If you have two wounded soldiers, one with a gunshot wound of the lung and the other with an arm or a leg blown off, you save the son-of-a-bitch with the lung wound and let the other goddamn son-of-a-bitch with an amputated arm or leg go to hell. He is no goddamn use to us anymore."[27] He then walked through the recovery ward, speaking to every soldier, asking their names and how they were wounded. When one sergeant explained that he had been captured and shot before escaping, Patton exploded. "Damn you sergeant! We're over here to fight a war and win and not to get shot and lay in the hospital. You understand that?" The sergeant responded, "Yes sir!" and Patton moved on. The next day he returned and worked his way down the aisle again, this time calling every soldier by name and rank. He came across the sergeant and asked him how he was progressing. After the sergeant explained, Patton said, "Good, I hope to see you hopping around the next time I come in." Patton not only controlled his temper, he also showed his knack for remembering names.[28]

With inspiration came discipline. Patton knew that, with so little time to get the corps moving, he would have to shock II Corps into the "fighting pitch" Eisenhower desired. When he found one of his staff officers eating breakfast alone in the mess hall at 7:00 a.m., he ordered the mess closed at 7:30 from then on. He did not want men lingering. He instituted speed limits on all vehicles to save gas, even under fire.[29] He insisted every soldier button up his shirt and wear leggings and a tie, even on the battlefield. Woolen uniforms of olive drab—not the summer khakis—were to be worn. By his logic, men sweating during the day froze at night in khakis. While the wool uniforms might be uncomfortable, they were better suited for the nights.[30] Soldiers were also ordered to wear their helmet chin straps—especially if they were wearing the olive drab wool cap (the chin strap order would later prove to be a deadly mistake). Patton loathed the Army-issued wool cap, which the men referred to as a derby. He thought it made soldiers look slovenly and insisted it be hidden. Steel helmets became a must, from the soldier on the frontline to doctors and nurses in the rear. When asked if motor pool mechanics were included, he said, "You're Goddamn right—they're soldiers aren't they?" Woe to the lowly private caught in a rear area with his wool cap on sans helmet.[31]

To enforce his new rules, Patton instituted a system of fines: $25 for a lost pistol belt or for wearing a wool cap, $15 for failing to wear leggings, and $10 for a missing tie. Men were threatened with a court martial if they did not pay up. Of course, these amounts were subject to change upon Patton's mood. "When you hit their pocketbooks," he said, "you get a quick response." He patrolled the area, looking for offenders. In one day, he fined thirty five enlisted men and a handful of officers for being out of uniform. He fined so many soldiers for wearing the wool cap that it became known as "the $25 derby."[32] When a soldier told Patton something to the effect of "go screw yourself," one of Patton's aides fined him $15.[33] It was rumored that Patton found one of his staff officers in the latrine without a helmet and promptly fined him $25. A week later he made eight soldiers and two lieutenants fall in behind him and led them to the MP station to pay their fines. Some men defied the order: "I heard a couple tried to see if he was serious," recalled one 1st Infantry Division officer, "and were picked up and promptly fined." However trivial his new rules might have been, they had the desired effect, as Bradley later explained: "Each time a soldier knotted his necktie, threaded his leggings, and buckled on his heavy steel helmet, he was forcibly reminded that Patton had come to command the II Corps, that the pre-Kasserine days had ended, and that a tough new era had begun."[34]

Not everyone agreed with Patton's instructions to wear wool uniforms. Terry Allen visited his headquarters and insisted that Patton issue khaki uniforms since the desert weather had turned humid. "The yellow bellies of the 1st Division don't need khakis," Patton shot back in his high-pitched voice. "Tell you what I'll do, if you get a third of your sons of bitches across the sands, I'll see that those that are left get some khaki uniforms." A furious Allen stormed out of the headquarters, angry more about Patton's insult to his men's bravery than the loss of better uniforms.[35]

Patton also put out an order that all officers wear their ranks on their helmets, something frowned upon by frontline troops because it gave the enemy a perfect target for a headshot. The order, however, did not reached Major General "Doc" Ryder and his 34th Infantry Division. When Patton paid Ryder a visit to see an anti-tank demonstration, he took one look at the gathered men, with no ranks on their helmets, and declared, "Worst disciplined troops I've ever seen in my life." He was so disgusted that he climbed back into his jeep and rode off without seeing the demonstration.[36]

Patton's brand of discipline bordered on tyrannical, if not just plain insulting. In one case, he noticed a soldier wearing a British jacket and ordered the man take it off and hand it to him. Then he used the jacket to slap the man in the face several times. Next, he gave the man a shovel and ordered him to bury the jacket. As the man completed the task, Patton shouted to a cluster of nearby officers, "This soldier is fined $25.00! Make sure it is taken care of, and if I find any other soldiers out of uniform, I'll fine and demote all of you. I'll be back!"[37] In another, better known case,

CHAPTER FOUR ★ REJUVENATING II CORPS IN TWELVE DAYS   79

Patton arrived at Allen's headquarters and woke him up, rapping on his tent with his riding crop and shouting, "Terry! Terry! You SOB, come out of there!" When Allen emerged, Patton asked him about a row of trenches outside the command tents. Allen explained that they were for the men's protection during air raids. Patton, promoting offensive fighting, wanted to show Allen and his troops his poor opinion of trenches. He promptly walked over to Allen's trench and urinated into it. "There," he told Allen, "now try to use it." Allen walked by his commander and murmured an angry "You SOB." Patton's lesson was ill received. Allen's guards, enraged by Patton's insult, audibly clicked off the safeties on their Thompson machineguns. Patton, to his credit, realized he had crossed the line and quickly departed.[38]

In another case, Patton ordered his jeep stop when he spotted an officer wearing a derby without a helmet. Patton got out of the jeep, grabbed the officer by the neck, and "shook him like a rabbit," a witness recalled. He then took off the man's cap, threw it to the ground and fined him ten cents. When his driver asked him if he had been a bit rough with the officer, Patton replied, "It'll be all round the corps tonight and you'll never see one of them goddamn caps again." He was correct.[39] Patton's harsh methods contained a certain logic: he wanted the men fighting mad, and if that meant getting them mad at him, so be it. When the time came, he intended to turn that hatred toward the enemy and let his warriors loose. At times, men challenged Patton's philosophy of authority. When he came up to a group of men filling in a road crater and shouted, "Who's in charge here?" The men pointed at their sergeant, who was not wearing any rank. Patton reprimanded the NCO for not delegating the work to the enlisted men. Surprisingly, the sergeant snapped back that he always worked with his men and that's how he earned their respect. Patton let the insignificant insubordination slide.[40]

Patton also confronted a sergeant who had removed his rank chevrons to avoid detection from the enemy. "You look like a Goddamned private to me!" Patton roared to the sergeant before storming off to the division headquarters, where word went out that night that all officers and men were to put on exposed insignia and sew on stripes.[41]

The doctors were the most rebellious against Patton's disciplinary actions. While visiting the 34th Infantry Division, Patton eyed a lieutenant marching with his chin strap unclasped. "Lieutenant, button that chin strap!" He ordered. "Yes," the lieutenant responded. "I'll button it. But when you leave, sir, I'll unbutton it." Patton repeated the order two more times, only to receive the same answer each time. Finally, he told the lieutenant, "I'm going to fine you a-hundred dollars for insubordination." The officer explained that he was a surgeon, and secondly, "Don't you know that if I have my chin strap buttoned and a shell hits up here pretty close to us, it will break my neck?" Patton did not say a word and left.[42]

With the corps now feeling Patton's bootprint, he began preparing its advance. On his third day at the helm, he ordered all his patrols to make contact with the enemy. Eisenhower had wired him that day, complaining about "normal patrolling but no contact with the enemy." Within days, Patton boasted eighty-nine enemy soldiers captured, as well as two pilots, and a spy. To make sure the corps was keeping contact with the enemy, Patton began riding to the front, standing up in a jeep or armored command car, with helmet and brass glistening in the sunlight and ivory handled pistols on his hips. A blaring siren announced his presence to both his troops and to the enemy. Sometimes, in the open desert, he would have his driver stop, after which Patton would fire his vehicle's .50 caliber machinegun at a tree, just for practice. Once, when Patton and Al Stiller stopped to relieve themselves against a large rock, a local Arab popped up from the other side of the rock and took a shot at them with an ancient flintlock. Patton and Stiller drew pistols and blasted away as the man ran off. They both emptied their weapons without scoring a hit.[43]

When Patton finished the day's frontline inspections, he often returned to the rear either by plane or huddled down in a jeep. He wanted his men to see him ever advancing and never retreating.[44] With his visits to the front came an unexpected—and to Patton, an inexcusable—fact of life: visits from the Luftwaffe. While he was returning from the front one day, a German plane strafed his column, forcing Patton to hit the ground. The second attack came when he was standing in his command car, addressing the troops near Sened Station. As three Messerschmitts strafed, Patton hit the ground again. He would do it again two more times before the Battle of El Guettar. He hated the humiliation of ducking under fire, "but all do it."[45]

As a combat commander, Patton received a briefing from Royal Air Force Wing Commander Frederick Winterbotham about Ultra, Britain's amazing cryptology breakthrough, which enabled the Allies to read most German wireless communiqués. Patton had first learned about it in England and was told to stay away from the front, for fear of being

CHAPTER FOUR ★ REJUVENATING II CORPS IN TWELVE DAYS   81

captured and revealing Ultra's existence. Patton bristled at the idea of restricting his movements, but now he was upbeat about the transcripts. When Winterbotham stressed the importance of security, Patton cut him off, saying, "You know young man, I think you had better tell all this to my intelligence staff, I don't go much on this sort of thing myself. You see, I just like fighting."[46] Patton would become a strong proponent and frequent user of this new weapon.

Three thoughts gnawed at Patton: that his troops simply were not ready; that Rommel would attack him first; and that his son-in-law was still missing in action. He checked with graves registration to see if Waters was listed as buried. He was not.[47] He also traveled out to where Waters had disappeared and searched for his remains, finding nothing save a spent ammunition clip, which he had sent to his daughter's sons as a memento.[48] He then called for Major Robert Moore, the commander of 2nd Battalion, 168th Infantry Regiment, 34th Infantry Division, who had managed to survive the German encirclement at Faïd Pass back on February 14, near where Waters had been captured. Moore showed up at Patton's headquarters while the general was still sleeping. When Patton woke up, he jumped out of his bed and shouted at Moore, "What the hell happened to my son-in-law, John Waters?" Moore, who had lost many men during the Kasserine fight, responded, "What the hell happened to my regiment?" Patton was unmoved. "I don't give a damn about your regiment, what happened to Waters?" Moore was equally unmoved by Patton's anger. "My interest is in my regiment," he told a fuming Patton, then turned and left the headquarters. To Patton's credit, he did not sack Moore, as he was just venting his frustrations at the loss of his son-in-law.[49]

As Patton prepared for the renewed offensive, he worried again that the Germans would be first to launch an attack. On March 14, he rode to the front and got a look at the Kasserine Pass. If the Germans were going to attack, he wanted to be there. Nothing happened, so he inspected the 1st Armored Division in the pouring rain, getting plastered with mud in the process. "Kasserine Pass is fierce and a sea of mud," he lamented in his diary that night.[50]

Patton's primary mission was straight forward enough: drawing off enemy forces facing Montgomery's Eighth Army by capturing Gafsa, some forty-five miles southeast, and the Maknassy Pass, more than one hundred miles southeast. Patton was to launch his attack on March 15 but delayed it for two days due to heavy rains. The order for attack included airbases to capture and supply dumps to build up, but everything boiled down to one simple command: Get going! Nothing more was expected of Patton. No one was looking for a brilliant end run or a feint to fool the enemy. If he could just get his corps moving and keep pressure on the enemy, that would be a victory enough. Everything the corps did was in the shadow of Montgomery's Eighth Army, and anything it accomplished would support the British general's efforts against Rommel.

But simply advancing was not enough for Patton. He envisioned restaging the American Civil War's Battle of Second Manassas, wherein Confederate General Robert E. Lee's two corps commanders, Thomas "Stonewall" Jackson and James Longstreet, took turns flanking and hammering Union general John Pope's Army of Virginia, while the other held defense.[51] Patton saw his corps imitating Jackson's flanking attack while the British, in the role of General Longstreet's corps, broke through. He liked using Civil War analogies. When he learned that German general Juergen von Arnim had overreached at Kasserine Pass, he said, "Von Arnim should have read about Lee's attack at Fort Steadman," referring to the Confederate general's last, desperate failed attack outside of Petersburg in the last month of the war.[52]

Patton reviewed Ward's and Allen's attack plans, both of which had their divisions pushing southeast before splitting, with the 1st Armored Division heading east to Maknassy and the 1st Infantry turning southeast, pushing towards El Guettar. During the meeting, he found out that the German 10th Panzer Division was headed near El Guettar. Now he really worried that Rommel would attack him first. To prepare for any such eventuality, Patton, thinking that the Germans might capture his artillery guns and use them on his troops, ordered that no artillery ammunition would be dumped at artillery batteries, limiting the allotment of shells per gun. The officers of Allen's division considered this a foolhardy decision and ignored it.[53]

On March 10 Alexander visited Patton. The British general had started World War I as a lieutenant and finished the war as a brigadier. Twice wounded, he went on to serve two years fighting communist forces in Russia. Alexander was the quintessential soldier of the British empire: suave, relaxed, and confident. Patton really like him, especially after Alexander, seeing an Arab man load a barrel on a woman's back, offered, "Let's kick his ass." The two of them thought better of it, but Patton enjoyed Alexander's brand of chivalry. Alexander told Patton that he

CHAPTER FOUR ★ REJUVENATING II CORPS IN TWELVE DAYS   83

had asked for the best corps commander the Americans had and was assured that Patton was the man. For his part, Patton preferred answering to General Alexander's 18th Army Group than to Anderson's First Army. By bypassing Anderson, Patton had a more prominent position in the chain of command and on the battlefront, something important as the American role in the war expanded.[54] But while Patton considered Alexander one of the best British field commanders, the latter's visit was not for enjoyment. He needed to know that Patton was whipping the soldiers of II Corps into shape. Although still worried about the American soldiers' greenness, Alexander did see immediate improvements in the men's morale. As one of his staffers commented, "Georgie Patton was not only an inspirational leader, he was a consummate trainer of men and had a wealth of experience." Alexander and his staff departed feeling confident about II Corps.[55]

On March 12 Patton got an unexpected boost. He found out that President Roosevelt had recommended his promotion to the temporary rank of lieutenant general to the U.S. Senate. Captain Dick Jenson presented Patton with a three-starred flag he had been carrying for a year. When his staff presented him with various sets of the collar insignia, an amazed Bradley thought that if Patton "had been named admiral of the Turkish navy, his aides could probably dip into their haversacks and come up with the appropriate rank." He jokingly warned Patton that the Senate had not yet approved the promotion, to which Patton retorted, "I've waited long enough for this one." He wasn't kidding. He had waited since childhood for this extra star: "When I was a little boy," he wrote in his diary, "I used to wear a wooden sword and say to myself, 'George S. Patton, Jr., Lieutenant General.' At that time, I did not know there were full generals. Now I want, and will get, four."[56]

To help kick off the drive, Eisenhower arrived at Patton's headquarter in Le Kouif and officially pinned the lieutenant general's rank on Patton's shoulders and collar. It was an upbeat occasion, yet Patton found a way to make it memorable—at least for one of Eisenhower's staffers. With his new stars on, Patton called Eisenhower's aide, Sgt. Michael McKeogh, over, looked him up and down, and asked him if he had $25 to throw away. When McKeogh explained he did not, Patton told him he had then better get himself a helmet. When Eisenhower heard what had happened, he told McKeogh to get one for him, too. From that date on, Eisenhower always wore a helmet in the II Corps operations area.[57]

Figure 13. Eisenhower pins Patton's third star, making him a lieutenant general. Catalog number: 208-PU-1536-17, National Archives and Records Administration.

The ceremony over, Patton moved his headquarters to Feriana, about twenty miles south of Kasserine Pass. Never again would an American combat commander whose troops were fighting in Tunisia command them from Algeria. Nor would Patton ever command from a cave or some other form of a protected, isolated sanctuary. The Feriana headquarters consisted of small one- and two-story buildings across from a Roman column that dominated the town center, all surrounded with barbed wire. The atmosphere was deliberately subdued. There was no motor pool and no messengers coming and going. Three MPs stood at the main gate and shooed away any visiting vehicles, keeping the place as innocuous to German observation planes as possible.[58] Inside his new headquarters, Patton radiated confidence as he monitored the 1st Armored and 1st Infantry divisions. He wrote his wife that "the hardest thing a General has to do is to wait for the battle after all the orders have been given" and admitted to her that "I hope that I do my full duty and show the necessary guts." He had sworn off smoking and drinking for the campaign, telling the press, "I hope that when I enter Tunis somebody meets me with a cigar and a bottle of whiskey."[59]

Certainly, Patton's achievements with II Corps were nothing short of amazing. In only twelve days he had pieced together a defeated unit and got it moving. His harsh discipline and fighting spirit had shocked his soldiers, shaken off their rust, and put fire in their bellies. The men sharpened their discipline, tightened their appearance, and felt like soldiers again. They had received Patton's new rules with derision, thinking he was out of touch with reality, but those rules commenced a transformation. Within a week, the II Corp was a new outfit. The men looked better, felt better, and were better. But now they had to prove Patton's methods worked. They did not have long to wait for the chance to do so.[60]

CHAPTER FIVE

The Battle of El Guettar

PATTON LOOKED FORWARD to fighting Rommel, his North African nemesis. But it would not be Rommel who faced Patton. The famous field marshal had departed North Africa on March 9, eight days before Patton attacked the German line. Rommel had been promoted to commander of Army Group Africa, but the new position was merely a charade. In the previous weeks and months, he had clashed with his superiors and his Italian allies, his negative assessments of the situation having displeased Hitler. In addition, Rommel's heart, nerves, and rheumatism were dragging him down. That morning he boarded a plane and flew to Rome to assume his new command. General von Arnim, who had been instrumental in the Sidi Bou Zid and Kasserine attacks, took command of all forces in Tunisia, now called Army Group Afrika.[1] Rommel or no, there was still a German army fighting in North Africa. Neither Patton nor any of the Allies realized Rommel had left for good, and all of them believed that they were still fighting the Desert Fox. Either way, Patton appreciated his new task. "I suppose it is an honor to be given all the tough nuts to crack," he boasted to Beatrice. "I hope my teeth hold out."[2]

With Montgomery's offensive stalled at Rommel's Mareth Line, Patton hoped his offensive in Tunisia would draw off German reserves, creating a weakened force for Montgomery to overwhelm and continue his northern drive. If things went well, Patton might even drive to Gabès, splitting the enemy in two in the process.[3] As II Corps prepared to renew its offensive, one thought still nagged Patton: was his captured son-in-law alive? "Did General Eisenhower speak about Johnnie Waters?" he asked visiting reporters who had recently interviewed Eisenhower. They told him he had, and even described Waters's heroism. Patton then told the reporters he could not speak about the upcoming attack, saying,

"Fewer people know about it, less chance the Germans have of getting information out of people they capture." He sent the reporters on their way, promising to tell them something more when the time was near.[4]

For the offensive, Patton planned to send Allen's 1st Infantry Division south from Feriana to attack and hold Gafsa, some forty-five miles away. Once completed, Ward's 1st Armored Division, supported by elements of Manton Eddy's 9th Infantry Division, would head out of the Kasserine Pass and attack southeast past Gafsa, driving approximately twenty-five miles east to Maknassy. Defending the passes to Patton's rear would be other elements of the 9th and Major General Charles Ryder's 34th Infantry Division. It was a simple plan, but Patton knew there was nothing simple about combat. The day before he got II Corps rolling, he assessed his divisions. Of the four, he considered Allen's 1st Infantry as ready for battle, Ward's 1st Armored too "timid," and Ryder's 34th Infantry too defensive minded. He reserved judgment about Eddy's 9th Infantry, which had yet to experience any real fighting but was still blessed with, in Patton's words, the "valor of ignorance." Patton considered Eddy, a World War I veteran, an excellent tactician but too cautious.[5]

Patton wanted to start forward on March 15, but heavy rains forced him to delay until March 17. He fancied a whimsical idea to control the moving parts of the offensive: he wished he were triplets so he could command the two attacking divisions and the corps himself.[6] He visited Allen on March 16 to make final preparations before the offensive. Allen's troops would be up against the Italian Centauro Division, which defended Gafsa, but Patton worried that the German 21st Panzer Division might join the fight. When he noticed that one of Allen's infantry regiments lacked anti-tank support, he ordered Allen to remedy the situation. Allen tapped the 601st Tank Destroyer Battalion, composed of thirty-four lightly armored M3 half-tracks armed mostly with 37mm guns, with a few 75mm guns, as opposed to thicker-armored M10 tank destroyers, which ran on a tank chassis and sported a 76.2mm gun. It proved an important decision.[7]

Later that day, Patton addressed his staff. "Gentleman, tomorrow we attack. If we are not victorious, let no one come back alive." Then he retired to his bedroom to pray. That evening, as the troops of II Corps moved to their assembly areas, Patton hosted Eisenhower and Alexander and their staffs at his Feriana headquarters for what he dubbed Operation WOP, a politically incorrect name since the Americans were facing Italian troops.[8] Tension hung in the air as the commanders worried that the

Germans might strike first, before the Allies made their move. Alexander paced back and forth in front of Patton's fireplace, still concerned about the Americans' fighting prowess. "We might get in trouble," he stressed, if II Corps found itself in a pitched, indecisive battle.[9] At the designated hour, the troops started forward. Whenever Patton received a battlefield update, he would whisper it to Eisenhower, who listened intently with his hands behind his back, and then Alexander, who continued to pace. A large map on the wall depicted Allied and enemy positions, but the generals ignored it. Outside, soldiers shoveled sand through a window to set up a sand table map. Patton later wrote that he "radiated confidence," despite one genuine worry: "The only trouble I have is a cold-sore on my lip." That night, as Patton prepared for bed, he received reports that there was fighting north of Gafsa. "Well," he wrote, "the battle is on."[10]

As the sun rose on March 17, Patton went out to observe the 1st Infantry Division enter Gafsa. When he saw no movement on the battlefield, he stormed up to Allen and asked, "What the hell is this? When are you going to move?" Allen surprised him with, "General, we are already on our first objective," adding that he had not been given permission to make a night attack. In fact, he had been told expressly not to launch a night attack. When Allen tried to explain his actions by mentioning Knute Rockne, the renowned Notre Dame football coach from the 1920s who popularized the forward pass, Patton asked, "What the hell does a Swede football coach have to do with night attacks?" Allen answered, "Why beat your brains out for a yard and a half when you can throw for forty yards?" Allen's attack had been a forward pass for the infantry. Patton now knew he had a creative, aggressive commander in charge of 1st Infantry.[11]

Later in the day, Patton drove to the front, where he climbed a large rock outside Gafsa and uneasily surveyed the town, not yet convinced it was in American hands. He watched as artillery shells burst in the distance and American troops advanced. "Go down that track until you get blown up," he told his aide, Dick Jenson, "then come back and report." Jenson took off in his jeep, with a bevy of curious reporters following. The town was deserted; the Italian Centauro Division, which had been defending the city, had pulled out and the 21st Panzer Division never showed itself. It was a bloodless victory.[12]

Patton climbed into the back of his command car. As he neared the Gafsa, he ordered his driver to stop next to a reporter-filled jeep. He smiled, pointed at his command car and, wanting to defend his warrior image, explained, "I'm using that because the tank I usually move around in hasn't caught up with me yet." Then he looked through his binoculars at some soldiers walking up a hill towards the town. He handed the binoculars to a reporter. "That's the 16th Infantry [Regiment] going up that hill ahead. Looks as though they're going right into Gafsa." When a

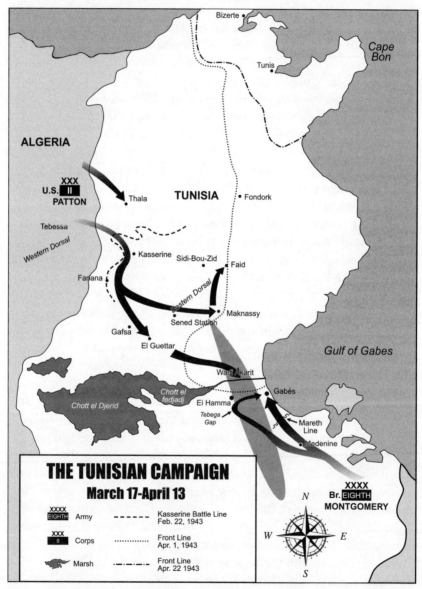

Map 3. The Tunisian campaign, March 17–April 13, 1943.

reporter asked him how the battle was going, Patton told him, "Oh, fine, fine. But I'd feel happier if I knew where the Germans were. As long as I know where they are, I don't mind how hard they fight. But I'd like to know where they are." With that, he climbed back into his vehicle and sped into the city.[13] That night, in a letter to his wife, Patton admitted his feelings about the advance. "When I started forward, I was really scared of an air attack but soon got used to it and stopped worrying."[14]

Patton had won his first victory as II Corps commander. More important, his attack had forced Von Arnim to commit two-thirds of his mobile reserve to his western front on the eve of Montgomery's offensive.[15] Both Eisenhower and Alexander visited Patton to tell him they were pleased with his progress, albeit against nothing. Eisenhower later informed George Marshall, "The officers and men of both divisions are in fine shape and eager to fight. Patton, assisted by Bradley, has done a splendid job in a very short time."[16] Eisenhower was right: II Corps had come a far way since the Kasserine Pass debacle. Despite Patton's success, he chaffed at remaining in his headquarters during a battle, even if it was the right thing to do: "When one is fighting Erwin [Rommel] one has to be near the radio."[17] But his advance was about to slow. For the next two days it rained incessantly, bogging down everything in a sea of mud. Alexander ordered Patton to halt while Montgomery pressed north. Patton had little choice. He still worried that Rommel would hit II Corps before he could continue his attack or before Montgomery assaulted the enemy's Mareth Line, scheduled for the next day.[18] "I feel that if I strike first Erwin will have to parry," he wrote.[19]

Patton hated to pause and give the enemy time to regroup. With nothing else to do, he checked on the 1st Armored Division, visiting Brigadier General Paul Robinett, commanding Ward's Combat Command A. An English-speaking German prisoner was with Robinett when Patton found him. "The poor son-of-a-bitch must be up to some trickery," Patton told him. Once Robinett updated him on the situation, Patton began laying scorn on the Germans, finally exploding with, "We will kick the bastards out of Africa!" As Patton left, Robinett told him it was an honor to have the corps commander visit. Patton slapped him on the back, saying, "By God, it will not be the last time you see me."[20] Yet, Patton's mood changed when he wrote in his diary that night: "He is defensive and lacks confidence." Patton next visited General Ward, who complained that his tanks could not advance in the rainy conditions. Patton told him to use infantry and move their weapons in half-tracks. One good thing came out of Patton's visit: he noticed that the Germans signaled each other with colored smoke. He immediately requested colored smoke grenades and artillery from Eisenhower.[21]

Patton returned to his headquarters to find Alexander, who explained II Corps' follow-up objectives, telling him his 9th Infantry Division would be transferred to the British. Worse, as Montgomery pushed up from the south, Patton was to stay at Gafsa and Maknassy and let Montgomery pass in front of him, leaving the American forces out for the rest of the campaign and negating Patton's scheme to drive the Germans to the sea. "I kept my temper and agreed," Patton recorded in his diary. "I hope I will be back in Morocco on another job before we get pinched out." Before he went to bed that night, he got some relief when Bradley gave him the good news that John Waters had been reported as a prisoner of war and was fine. Bradley's words lifted a heavy burden off the corps commander's shoulders.[22]

The next day, Dick Jenson wrote Mrs. Patton, updating her on her husband's well-being. His recent promotion to lieutenant general and new command had changed him, Jenson reported. "He is years younger in feeling and appearance." The news that Waters was alive and well "tops the picture. If he gets any more good news, we will have to sit on him to keep him down."[23] But Patton was far from happy. Over the next two days he stewed about the halt order. His fear of seeing II Corps left behind while Montgomery pursued the Germans even made it into the II Corps Operation Report: "This plan apparently envisaged pinching out the II Corps after the capture of FONDOUK heights."[24] Patton sent Bradley to Alexander to argue against the plan.

Alexander's staff told Bradley that the slight was not intentional, just that their logisticians calculated that II Corps could not be resupplied over the existing roads. Bradley then visited Eisenhower, who had no idea of Alexander's plans. Bradley recommended moving II Corps north, to attack Bizerte, the last key city of the campaign. Eisenhower studied Bradley's recommendation on a map, then called Alexander, telling him he wanted to keep II Corps in the fight. He followed it up with a letter insisting that the unit should remain on the line "right up the bitter end of the campaign." Patton's plan worked. II Corps would remain on the battlefield, with all of its units intact.[25]

Meanwhile, Patton continued pushing east. On March 21 Ward's 1st Armored Division captured Sened Station, the halfway mark between

Gafsa and Maknassy, while Allen's 1st Infantry Division pushed east from Gafsa. The forces they attacked were mostly Italian infantry supported by German reconnaissance and artillery. Patton visited Allen at a company command post set up in a farmhouse. Along the way there, he spotted an infantryman walking without his leggings. "Stop and have this sergeant take that man's name," Patton ordered, "and see that he is demoted to private."[26] Once at the farmhouse, the two generals, accompanied by a captain, watched Allen's infantrymen maneuver deftly over rocky terrain and punch into the Italians following a heavy artillery barrage. After watching several hundred prisoners pour through the American lines (one of his aides called them "additional Roman ruins"), Patton, Allen, and the captain walked forward until they found a hill to perch on and watch the action close-up. Suddenly, a salvo of enemy artillery screeched in. The captain, Allen, and Patton all jumped into a foxhole on top of each other. "It's too damn hot," said Patton. "Let's get the hell out of here." As Patton left, he noticed an enemy barrage explode right where he had been sitting.[27]

Things were not going as well for the 1st Armored Division. Patton visited Sened Station, where he determined Ward was moving too slowly—a sin for the branch that was supposed to slash into the enemy. He ordered Ward to drive harder and move his command post closer to the action. When that did not work, he sent General Gaffey to prod Ward, again without result. When Ward mentioned in a phone call to Patton that he had the good fortune of not losing any officers that day, Patton exploded: "Goddammit Ward, that's not fortunate. That's bad for the morale of the enlisted men. I want you to get more officers killed." When a stunned Ward asked Patton if he was serious, Patton shot back, "Yes, Goddammit, I'm serious I want you to put some officers out as observers well up front and keep them there until a couple get killed."[28]

The next day, March 22, Patton received word that the Germans and Italians were slugging it out with Montgomery along the Mareth Line. He was not drawing enough enemy troops away from Montgomery. Alexander now wanted Patton to make an armored thrust through Maknassy and head for the sea between Sfax and Gabès.[29] But Ward called to say he had captured Maknassy but failed to assault the enemy-occupied heights east of the town. While Ward's lack of aggressiveness angered Patton, he blamed himself: "If I had led First Armored Division we would have taken the heights."[30] Patton ordered Ward to capture the heights immediately, since intelligence reported the German 10th Panzer heading toward him. Ward obeyed the order but failed in the mission. A furious Patton then called Allen to check on his progress. When Allen's intelligence officer told him they had not yet captured a hill named Djebel Berda to their right, Patton exploded, "Well goddamn it, get moving, and get there right away!" and hung up the phone. It took Allen's men most of the day to capture the objective, but they got it done.[31]

Patton went to bed that night convinced the Germans would attack Ward. He slept fully clothed, ready to jump into action, but the attack on Maknassy never materialized. Instead, the 10th Panzer smashed into Allen's 1st Infantry at El Guettar the next morning. Allen reported the attack to Patton at 6:30 a.m. and Patton immediately pushed infantry, artillery, and tank destroyer battalions to him. Allen ordered the 601st Tank Destroyer Battalion, the unit he had picked after Patton told him to bolster his anti-tank capability, forward to defend his artillery units. The lightly armored halftracks slugged it out with the German tanks until what was left of them were forced to pull back. The Germans cut through one regiment, captured two artillery batteries, and penetrated to within two miles of Allen's headquarters, but in the process the enemy lost a host of tanks and infantry. Allied air forces took more than an hour to reach the battlefield, but once they did, they flew 340 sorties, hitting the German supply lines. The Germans attacked again five hours later, but this time the Americans intercepted the attack order and the men of the Big Red One were ready. While the Americans sacrificed many of their anti-tank guns, trading space for time, the Germans sent in their infantry in front of their tanks, only to be cut down by American artillery airbursts. The Germans suffered more than three hundred casualties. Allen's men knocked out thirty-seven enemy tanks, much of the tank killing done by the 601st Tank Destroyer Battalion. While the Germans were unable to capture Djebel Berda, they did cut off the regiment defending it and kept their distance so the Americans could not knock out their tanks. When it was over, Allen's troops had held their ground and the Germans had retreated. It marked the first clear American victory against the Nazi war machine.[32]

During the battle, Patton worried about his lack of artillery pieces and shells. The Germans overran two artillery battalions once they ran out of ammunition. An opportunity to smash a German tank unit had been lost when another U.S. artillery unit ran low and had to conserve ammunition. Patton rushed the 7th Field Artillery Battalion, then supporting the 1st Armored, to the battlefield, arriving in the nick of time to turn back the German's morning assault. According to Brigadier General Clift Andrus, the 1st Infantry Division's artillery commander, who witnessed the 7th in action, its rounds hammered into the German unit until "the battalion broke from cover and started to run for another wadi in the rear. But none ever reached it." As for ammunition, Brigadier General Reese Howell, the artillery commander for the 9th Infantry, trucked shells to the front from Tebessa, some sixty-five miles away, despite a lack of air cover. The shells, like the 7th Field Artillery, reached the front in the nick of time. Months after the campaign ended, Patton told Andrus, "You know, Andrus, you really made a God-damned horse's ass out of me? But you also taught me something." Patton then explained he had almost lost El Guettar because of his artillery ammunition shortage. Andrus explained about Howell's actions and Patton, ever the student of war, had Andrus write up a report on artillery resupply ideas. According to Andrus, "We always had ammunition after that."[33] During the day's fighting, Patton got one break from the tension. When he saw a soldier sporting a green beret walking down the street outside his headquarters, he asked Lieutenant Colonel William O. Darby, the head of the 1st Ranger Battalion, "What the hell is that?" Darby explained he was a British chaplain assigned to the Rangers, "and about the only man I know who can get away with not wearing a helmet." Patton laughed uncontrollably at the situation.[34]

While Patton oversaw the El Guettar battle, it was really Allen's victory. Patton gave Allen everything he could spare, but it was Allen who expertly positioned his men and weapons on the battlefield and fought aggressively. When the Germans closed in on his headquarters and a staff officer suggested Allen withdraw, he snapped back, "I will like hell pull out, and I'll shoot the first bastard that does."[35] Patton considered Allen a fighter and gave him enough of a free hand to exchange blows with the enemy. One of Allen's officers later commented that after Patton took command of II Corps, "we knew he was there to win even if he had us killed doing it."

Patton spent part of the battle watching from an observation post. As the enemy lines thinned and wavered under American artillery and anti-tank fire, he shook his head. "They're murdering good infantry," he said to no one in particular. "What a helluva way to expend good infantry troops." He only called Allen once during the battle. When Allen complained about the lack of air support, Patton changed the subject and wondered, "I don't understand the loss of so many tank destroyers," not appreciating how vulnerable half-tracks were to tank fire. When Allen explained their contribution to the battle, Patton merely hung up.[36] Despite their differences, Patton's and Allen's fighting spirit filtered down to the soldiers in the trenches. A half-written letter written by one of Allen's soldiers, penned during a lull in the battle, opened, "Well folks, we stopped the best they had."[37] But El Guettar was a defensive battle, not the slashing, flanking pursuit of victory Patton sought. In other words, it was no Second Manassas. Patton had spent the battle working the phones from his headquarters, just like Eisenhower had ordered. That night, before going to bed, he penned in his diary, "I hate fighting from the rear."[38]

The next day, March 24, Patton visited the battlefield. On the way, his column passed a group of 1st Infantry soldiers, one of whom was not wearing leggings. Patton stopped his vehicle and ordered the man to put them on, despite the man's nasty leg sore.[39] As he approached Allen's headquarters, a German shell exploded nearby, pelting his vehicle with metal shards. The Germans had retreated but were still firing at the Americans. The shelling continued as Patton climbed a rocky hill to Allen's command post, using a silver-tipped cane to keep his balance. At the top, he dropped into a foxhole to discuss the situation with Allen and Brigadier General Teddy Roosevelt Jr., Allen's deputy commander, who explained the various phases of the battle. When Patton learned that Allen's men had sent a message to the Germans daring them to attack, he asked Allen, "When are you going to take this damned war seriously?" Patton took in the battlefield's devastation: crippled enemy tanks, ruined American tank destroyers, and the corpses of the German infantrymen cut down by artillery fire.[40] The tank destroyer losses disappointed him. Only ten of the thirty-four howitzer-armed M-3 half-tracks survived, in addition to four of the twelve M-10 tank destroyers. Instead of exercising cover and concealment, the various tank destroyer crews maneuvered, exposing their inferior armor protection and guaranteeing their destruction. The crews had little choice, as they rushed to engage the enemy tanks. Although the Germans had lost thirty-one tanks, they managed to retrieve sixteen of them that night. Their bravery in tank removal impressed Patton.[41]

While Patton watched the action in Allen's foxhole, an enemy artillery round exploded nearby and everyone ducked. When Patton spied another soldier without leggings far below the hill, he dispatched a runner to order the soldier to put them on.[42] His conference over, Patton climbed

CHAPTER FIVE ★ THE BATTLE OF EL GUETTAR

Figure 14. Patton visits El Guettar battlefield with 1st Infantry Division commander Major General Terry Allen (center), and the assistant division commander, Brigadier General Teddy Roosevelt Jr. (left). Catalog number: 208-AA, National Archives and Records Administration.

out of the foxhole and started down the hill, amid the shelling. As he passed a private, the soldier told him, "Pretty heavy artillery barrage they're putting up." Patton answered, "That's not a real barrage. That's just some German gunners ranging their guns." Unimpressed, the private snapped back, "Well General, all I can say is if those Germans are just ranging, they are certainly ranging like hell." The two men laughed.⁴³ Patton then stopped to tell a group of soldiers they had done an exceptionally good job.⁴⁴ He later wrote a letter of appreciation to the American XII Air Support Command, in which he said, "We feel that each day mutual understanding between air and ground improves, with great benefit to ourselves, and greater and greater unhappiness and destruction to the enemy."⁴⁵

A group of soldiers brought in an Arab and a donkey. In the donkey's saddlebags were German Teller mines, which the man had planned to plant behind the Americans. Patton asked why the GIs hadn't just "buried" him. When the men explained that he was still alive, Patton replied, "Obviously, you can't bury him while he is alive, now do what I told you." Patton later called the Arabs "dirty bastards" to Beatrice. The incident made Patton look forward to Sicily, where there would be no neutrals or people playing allies while working for the enemy. Everyone would be considered the enemy.[46]

Before returning to his headquarters, Patton visited a hospital. Striding through the post operation ward, he conversed with the wounded and swapped stories about El Guettar. When he learned that one soldier had been shot while trying to surrender, Patton stopped at the suspected soldier's cot and read the chart. Looking up, he asked the young soldier if he was the man on the chart. The man whispered that he was, and Patton lit into him. "No soldier would surrender. The Germans did exactly what they should have done—shot you." With that, he turned on his heel and left.[47] An Army Ranger, unimpressed with Patton's presence, grumbled, "Blood and guts! We supply the blood and he supplies the guts. To hell with that."[48]

At dinner that night Patton learned that Orlando Ward had failed once again to capture the heights east of Maknassy. Now Patton was furious at his armor commander, especially after his infantry commander, without a single tank, had stopped a German panzer division. Worse, during the fight for Maknassy, American fighter aircraft supporting the attack had hit several American tanks.[49] Patton called Ward on the phone, demanding, "I don't want any Goddamned excuses, I want you to go out there and get that hill. You lead the attack personally. Don't come back till you've got it!"[50] When he hung up the phone, Patton worried that he had just ordered Ward to his death but reassured himself that he was doing his duty. "Vigorous leadership would have taken the hill the day before yesterday," he wrote in his diary. "I hope it comes out alright."[51] Ward followed orders and led one of his battalions up the eastern ridges the next morning, temporarily capturing the high ground until German mortars, machine guns, and artillery forced him off. Ward suffered bloody wounds to his nose and one of his eyes during the engagement. To Patton, he had shown "good personal courage" but had not made sufficient progress.[52] While Patton pushed Ward forward, the Germans made one last attack on Allen at El Guettar, driving a 1st Infantry battalion and a Ranger force off Djebel Berta before artillery put a stop to the attack. At times, both sides resorted to fighting with bayonets.[53]

Patton received good news the next day, March 25, when General Alexander told him he could keep his 34th and 9th Infantry Divisions. With the extra divisions, Alexander told Patton, the II Corps would take over more of the battle front. He wanted Patton to abandon the attacks

CHAPTER FIVE ★ THE BATTLE OF EL GUETTAR

Figure 15. Major General Orlando Ward, the commander of the 1st Armored Division, whom Patton fired. U.S. Army.

east of Maknassy and focus on the 1st Infantry's success east of El Guettar, with the help of the 9th. Despite the good news, Patton complained that, if allowed, he would have driven past Gafsa a week earlier when there were no enemy forces amassed. By holding up Patton's forces, Alexander had enabled the 10th Panzer Division to attack. But Alexander had held up Patton for a simple reason: the British had lost confidence in the Americans after the Kasserine debacle and would not risk another one by giving Patton a free hand to advance.[54] To Alexander, the Americans would be simply getting in the way of Montgomery's northern drive from the Mareth Line. After their meeting, Patton gave Alexander a tour of American equipment. When the two came across a group of soldiers working on a half-track, Patton boasted of the vehicle's mobility, firepower, and armor protection. "Isn't that right, sergeant?" Patton asked. "No, sir," the sergeant replied. "One bullet pierced the armor here, rattled around inside and killed Private Torgerson. The men call it a 'Purple Heart Box,' sir." An embarrassed Patton escorted Alexander away.[55]

The next day, Eisenhower presented Patton with a telegram from Prime Minister Churchill stating, "Many congratulations on your fine advance and capture of prisoners." More important was a note scratched on the bottom from Alexander, adding, "I have complete confidence in him." The British faith in Patton was at least growing.[56] The following morning, the two generals toured the battlefront. As they walked by soldiers in their foxholes and slit trenches, Patton told Eisenhower, "I'm going to drive right to the sea and we'll separate Rommel's forces, then we can mop him up between us and Montgomery." Eisenhower, who had personally urged Alexander to keep II Corps in the fight but did not want Patton to supersede Alexander's orders, was having no part of it. "You move one step from this spot, and I'll relieve you." The remark dumbfounded Patton. Rumors of tensions between Patton and Eisenhower spread among the troops. When a demolition charge exploded near some soldiers, one suggested, "That's General Patton telling General Eisenhower something—in confidence."[57]

Once Alexander approved of Patton remaining on the front, Patton could now focus his drive east to the coast. He planned to launch a four-division attack on March 28, using, from north to south, the 34th, 1st, and 9th infantry divisions to engage the enemy and elements of the 1st Armored to break through the line. He wanted Ryder's 34th to draw off Axis forces while the 1st and 9th made the main push. Patton specifically told Ryder to make a lot of noise but not to gain ground if it meant taking great risks. Patton then wrote a note to Alexander's headquarters, asking if he himself could order the armored exploitation once he breached the line or if it was Alexander who needed to make the call. Alexander got word to Patton that the decision was his to make and encouraged him to establish a forward command post to get a better understanding of the ground situation. Again, Patton was pleased. The British were finally giving him the leeway he needed to maneuver. Now if only the Germans would behave to the same way.[58]

On March 27, Patton went to General Manton Eddy's 9th Infantry headquarters to brief him on the plan. He wanted Eddy's infantrymen to engage the enemy with a bayonet charge. To ensure surprise, there

CHAPTER FIVE ★ THE BATTLE OF EL GUETTAR

Figure 16. Patton inspects the Tunisian front in his personalized scout car as the new II Corps commander. Catalog number: 111-SC 171647, National Archives and Records Administration.

would be no preparatory fires. He assured Eddy that only small numbers of Germans held the hills in his sector and stressed the importance of getting the green division bloodied.[59]

Patton then visited Ward and presented him with a Silver Star even as he reprimanded him for lacking drive and relying too much on his staff. Ward agreed with the criticism and Patton warned him if he failed in the next offensive, he would be relieved. He later admitted that he had wanted to give Ward the Distinguished Service Cross for leading his tanks up the ridge, "except for the fact that it was necessary for me to order him to do it."[60] Ward's star was already dimming in Patton's eyes. "I have little confidence in Ward or in the 1st Armored Division," he penned. "Ward lacks confidence. The Division has lost its nerve and is lazy." Unless Ward did something spectacular, Patton would have to find a new armor commander.[61] Patton then wanted to see the division's forward elements. A jeep escorted his command car to the front until they came upon engineers removing anti-tank mines from the road. The jeep driver, Lieutenant Colonel Hamilton "Ham" Howze, dismounted and told Patton they could not go further without being blown up. "The hell with that," he shouted. "Let's go! Ham, lead the way!" Howze climbed in and drove forward as the astonished engineers looked on. Patton's driver, although in a wider vehicle, made certain that he kept his left wheel in line with Howe's left track. A light tank then joined the small caravan and traveled fifty feet before it rolled over a mine. When Patton heard the explosion, he ordered a halt and the other two vehicles backed out, following their own tracks.[62]

Patton's renewed attack kicked off the next day, with poor results. Although the 1st Infantry Division made progress pushing east, the 9th Infantry attacked the wrong hill and lost contact with two of its battalions in the rugged, and confusing, high terrain. They would fight isolated for the rest of the day, losing an entire company, some one hundred men, to the Germans. When Eddy tried to correct the confusion by ordering another battalion forward, it took heavy casualties and retreated to its starting position. The Germans were too well dug into the high ground to be quickly pried out by a green division.[63]

To help the infantry, Patton ordered Ward to send a reconnaissance and an artillery battalion south overnight to hide them from German detection. Patton planned to use the two battalions to help with an eventual armor breakthrough. He next drove through an artillery barrage to visit Eddy's troubled 9th Infantry. Using foul language, Patton criticized him for being too far from the front. The meeting shook Eddy so badly that he later told one of his commanders, "In all my career I've never been talked to as Patton talked to me this morning. I may be relieved of command."[64] Later that night Patton wrote, "I fear that all our troops want to fight without getting killed."[65]

More bad news greeted Patton the next morning. Ward delivered the reconnaissance and artillery units after sunrise, ruining Patton's stealthy efforts. Reports also came in that the Germans had pushed back a company of the 1st Infantry, further darkening Patton's mood until he learned that it had only been one platoon. Eddy's 9th Infantry had made some progress but still could not take the ridges from which the Germans

CHAPTER FIVE ★ THE BATTLE OF EL GUETTAR   103

rained down mortar fire. The 1st Armored repeatedly beat off enemy armor and infantry attacks. Ryder's 34th Infantry had also been repulsed, but Patton did not mind as much since its attack had only been a diversion. As he monitored the situation and prepared his breakthrough, British general McCreery, Alexander's chief of staff, called and told him exactly where to place his units for the upcoming attack. A frustrated Patton called Alexander and told him, "As my commander, you can order me to march my army [sic] into the sea, and I will. But no one, including the Lord Almighty, has the right to tell a commander of an Army how he shall dispose his divisions." Alexander agreed.⁶⁶

Despite all the setbacks, Patton kept his soldierly bearing. One day he watched as four American soldiers marched a group of German prisoners past him. Suddenly, local Arabs rushed over to the Germans and began stealing their personal items. Patton stormed the Arabs, kicking one of them in the rear and chasing the others off. "These are prisoners of war!" he yelled at the guards. "They're military people! They're honorable people! Don't let them pick on them like that!"⁶⁷

To finally break through the German lines, Patton created a special tank task force from the units Ward had sent south and put Colonel Clarence C. "Chauncy" Benson, a trusted subordinate from Patton's WWI tank brigade, in charge. The task force comprised two tank battalions, a reconnaissance battalion, two armored field artillery battalions, a tank destroyer battalion, a company of engineers, a motorized infantry battalion borrowed from the 9th Infantry Division, and sixteen anti-aircraft guns. If Ward was too timid to lead an armored breakthrough, maybe Benson could. Patton removed Benson Force from the 1st Armored's zone of operation and sent it south to El Guettar, slotting it between Allen's 1st Infantry and Eddy's 9th. Patton optimistically supplied Benson with enough gasoline to advance 160 miles. Despite his optimism, Patton worried that the Germans would simply close the breach behind Benson, isolating and destroying his unit. For his orders to Benson, Patton tore a piece of paper out of a notebook and jotted down, "Attack and destroy the enemy; act aggressively. G.S.P. Jr."⁶⁸

On the morning of March 30, corps and division artillery, supported by dive-bombers, pounded the enemy line. The 1st and 9th Infantries attacked at sunrise, with the 1st making better progress than the 9th. Patton left his headquarters to see Benson off. When he finally found him, he learned that Alexander had delayed the task force. The decision to launch the armored thrust should have been Patton's, but Alexander had made the call, too early in the campaign and too late in the day. Still, Patton desperately wanted to break the German line, so he remained silent about the breach of protocol.

As Benson's tanks pushed forward, Patton refused to take cover and instead stood in the middle of the advancing infantry, watching with binoculars as German tanks roared up the valley. The Americans responded with their M-3 half-tracks.[69] Patton told some 9th Infantry men, "You boys have done a good job. Now just sit back and watch my killers go to work."[70] Patton then climbed a hill and watched as Benson's tanks drove into murderous fire. The Germans quickly destroyed three tanks and two tank destroyers, stopping Benson cold. Patton's grand breakthrough came to an abrupt end. To add insult to injury that day, *Stars and Stripes*, the newspaper for the American military, referred to Patton as "Blood-and-Thunder."[71] Yet, the setback did not phase Patton. "The life of a General

Figure 17. Patton watches tanks advancing against the Axis forces in Tunisia. National Archives and Records Administration.

is certainly full of thrills," he confided that night. "But I am not worried, only cold all over."[72] That night, when the Luftwaffe raided Patton's headquarters, he ran outside clutching a pistol, his adrenaline pumping from "the old lust of close battle hot as ever."[73]

The next day, Patton felt stuck. He went to Benson's headquarters and told him to break through, even if it cost him an entire tank company. Around noon, Manton Eddy radioed, asking Patton to hold Benson off until his infantry could capture a hill. Patton refused, explaining that Benson was achieving the long-awaited breakthrough. But Patton was wrong. Benson lost another five tanks and three tank destroyers with little progress to show for his losses. Patton then ordered Ward to attack to relieve the pressure on both Benson and Ryder, whose diversionary attacks up north had bogged down. When Ward said he could not, Patton told him to attack even if he lost a quarter of his division. "It is disgusting," he later penned. When Beetle Smith visited later in the day, Patton requested the 3rd Infantry Division, a unit he trusted, but Smith refused, explaining that there was not enough room in the line for an additional division. Unable to get the results he wanted from anyone, Patton decided to move his headquarters closer to the action.[74]

CHAPTER SIX

The Drive East

ON APRIL 1, 1943, Patton lost his trusted aide and friend Captain Richard "Dick" Jenson. Patton, Bradley, and Bradley's aide, Captain Chester "Chet" Hansen, all claimed that a Luftwaffe bomb killed Jenson in the Tunisian desert while he supported Benson Force—miles away from Patton's headquarters. Supposedly, he had been out there with Hansen and Bradley because the unit was short of officers. Another of Patton's aides, driver Private First-Class Jack Copeland, however, told a different story. According to Copeland, Patton moved his headquarters on April 1 in order to be closer to the front, despite Eisenhower's specific orders not to do so. As part of the move, he had earlier ordered engineers to clear out an area about five miles east of El Guettar, where he would place his new headquarters.

That day, Copeland led the way to the new location in a scout car, accompanied by Bradley. Patton followed in his command car, Jenson in Patton's jeep, and Hansen in Bradley's jeep. Other jeeps, trucks, and light tanks followed. Copeland recalled they were an obvious target because "any child could see such a concentration of antennas and vehicles."[1]

Along the way, Patton pulled ahead to lead the column and picked up an engineer. Upon arriving at the designated area, Patton jumped out of his vehicle and began directing traffic. A low ridge running north to south blocked the view of the eastern battlefield. Once everyone had parked, around 8:00 a.m., Patton ordered Copeland to reconnoiter the ridge. Copeland had started his way up when an enemy artillery shell whizzed over his head and exploded on the road leading to the front. Several more followed. "Copeland!" Patton shouted, "Get down here, the enemy are shooting at you on top of that ridge!"[2] Copeland worked his way back to Patton and reported that he had never made it to the top, because the Germans were already atop the ridge. "It's flat trajectory and they cannot get to us," Copeland reassured the general.³ Patton did not respond but instead turned and headed for his communications truck.

The artillery rounds were a bad omen. Two hours later, Copeland saw a flight of German JU-88 twin-engine bombers flying north along the eastern ridgeline at about three thousand feet. They turned to their left and came out of the sun, heading for the command post. "I am sure the German soldiers on the range were watching the whole show and telling them by radio of our concentration of vehicles and the importance of the mass of vehicles," Copeland wrote.⁴ Copeland jumped to the .50 caliber machine gun mounted to the back of the scout car and began firing. Again, according to Copeland, "Patton and Bradley both jumped into the same large foxhole about 70 feet from the side of my vehicle. They both yelled at me to get into a foxhole, but I ignored them."⁵

Copeland continued to fire. He had trouble seeing the bombers coming out of the sun and could not swivel his machinegun fast enough, so he swung around, waited for them to pass, and fired as they flew away. Copeland wrote, "Both Patton and Jenson yelled at me again to get into a slit trench, but I knew if I tried this other way, I might have a better chance." His plan worked. He knocked down one of the last bombers. "Kid," Patton shouted at Copeland, "you'll get a silver star for this action today."⁶ Bradley also said something about the excellent shooting, seeing the tracer bullets going through the aircraft.

During the attack, Lieutenant James Craig, serving as General Gaffey's aide, huddled in a slit trench. Jensen, whose slit trench was about five feet away, pointed out a radioman in a halftrack and shouted, "That guy's telling the Germans where the artillery's going!" Craig ran over to the radioman and told him to shut up. The short run saved his life.⁷

Copeland revealed what happened to Jenson. "One bomb had hit within 30 feet of the rear of the scout car leaving a hole in the sand five feet deep and twenty-five feet across. Why I was not killed, God only knows. Captain Jenson was in a trench about 50 feet from me, when he was killed by concussion. I felt the concussion of this one but was again saved. General Patton was very upset on the discovery of the death of his aide. General Bradley helped Patton over to his jeep, where he sat down in grief. Within a few minutes he left the CP area in his command car for Gafsa."⁸ Copeland suspected that Jenson had died because his chinstrap was fastened, which snapped his neck when the bomb's concussion forced his helmet upward. Copeland and Hansen lifted Jenson's body

CHAPTER SIX ★ THE DRIVE EAST

out of the trench and placed it in Hansen's jeep for the trip to a collection point in Gafsa.[9] The day before, Patton had taken a picture of Jenson. "I hope this is not a final picture," Jenson joked. Patton reminded him he had taken pictures of all his staff before they left the *Monrovia* at Casablanca.[10]

Hansen, Bradley's aide, had been caught in the blast that killed Jenson. It tore back his helmet. As Hansen dropped into a slit trench, he thought he had been hit in the neck but was greatly relieved when he realized he was not bleeding. Shrapnel riddled his rifle. When it was over, he helped treat the wounded. He took Jenson's body to a cemetery, then retrieved Patton to examine the body. According to Hansen, "He cried, kneeled, cut off lock of hair."[11]

The drivers, according to Copeland, were forbidden to talk about the incident: "The press tried at different times, but our lips were sealed, they had to be."[12] Back on March 6, the day Eisenhower had told Patton to stay away from the front, the supreme commander also issued Patton a memorandum listing Patton's tasks, the chain of command, information on equipment, and personal advice. It included the following instructions:

> I spoke to you about personal recklessness. Your personal courage is something you do not have to prove to me, and I want you as a Corps Commander—not as a casualty. I am quite well aware that in getting ready for the tasks to come, you must see every portion of your troops and of the positions they occupy; but don't forget that in actual battle under present conditions a Commander can really handle his outfit only from his Command Post, where he can be in touch both with his Commander and with his subordinates.[13]

Patton never mentioned Eisenhower's warning in his diaries, and the only reference he made to his wife was to write, "D[wight] met me at the airport and gave me some verbal instruction."[14] But according to Copeland, "All the staff knew about this order. It was no secret in the II Corps Headquarters."[15] Copeland believed that Patton worried that since he had only commanded II Corps for a few weeks, Eisenhower would send him home for having recklessly disregarded his orders, or even question his judgment and ability to lead a corps, much less a field army.[16] Although Patton thought he demonstrated leadership by moving his headquarters to the front, it violated the intent and spirit of Eisenhower's orders.[17]

The night of Jenson's death, Patton wrote to Beatrice, confessing that "it was my fault in a way."[18] He also revealed that he had written to Jenson's mother, Echo, about his death. In the letter to Echo, which included the lock of Jenson's hair, he did not mention any details of her son's death, only that it was the will of providence. "Truly God's doings are beyond our understanding."[19]

There is evidence that supports Copeland's claims. While Chet Hansen's diary relates the story of Jenson's death on April 1, the day the two captains were supposedly sent to support a force short of officers that was grappling with the enemy, Hansen's entry for the next day, April 2, reveals that he visited friends in a hospital, picked up his pay "in rear echelon and mailed it home," and bought flowers and candy for the staff; hardly the chores of a man sent the previous day to a frontline unit in desperate need of officers. The following day he returned to his duty as Bradley's aide, never returning to Benson Force.[20] In addition, Lieutenant Craig, who was present during the attack, was serving as Gaffey's aide, not assigned to Benson Force. Craig later served as a pallbearer at Jenson's funeral. Recalling Jenson decades later, Craig claimed, "Jenson was the best friend I had."[21]

Patton may have left a clue about his aide's whereabouts on April 1. He took numerous pictures during his visit to Benson's command post on March 30, including one of Jenson, with his helmet on with goggles, and chinstrap clasped. In one of Patton's photo albums (part of the Patton papers collection in the Library of Congress) he wrote underneath the picture, "Captain Jenson A. D. C. killed on April 1, 1943." The second picture shows Jenson talking with some other officers. Patton wrote, "Just before the start," referring to Benson Force's jump off, timed for noon.[22]

There is one photograph in the collection that Patton could not have taken on March 30. It shows Jenson's slit trench, the bomb crater, and aide Al Stiller, standing in the crater. Patton never claimed to have visited the location of Jenson's death in his detailed diary, only that he visited Jenson's grave the next day "and put some flowers on it."[23] Two days later, he visited Benson's headquarters again, but there was no mention of traveling to the location of Jenson's death. It is possible, however, that Patton took this photograph on April 1, the day Jenson was killed.

Copeland later reflected that he considered Jenson "a father to me."[24] Jenson had given Copeland some clothes after Copeland's ship was torpedoed during Operation TORCH. He also kept Copeland out of trouble

CHAPTER SIX ★ THE DRIVE EAST

Figure 18. Patton took this picture of his aide, Dick Jenson, the day before German bombers killed him in the Tunisian desert. Library of Congress.

with higher-ups and assisted him with some of Patton's more demanding requests. As such, Copeland felt duty-bound to make sure his version of Jenson's death saw the light of day. "Patton concocted the story that he assigned Captain Jenson temporarily to Benson Force," he wrote. "This military force (group) was in the process of advancing to contact General Montgomery's infantry progressing up from southern Tunisia, and that it was here that Jenson was killed. THIS IS NOT TRUE. I was there."[25] Copeland never received his promised Silver Star, but his account now lies in the Army War College in Carlisle, Pennsylvania.

For his part, here is how Patton described Jenson's death in his diary that day: "Generals Bradley, 'Pink' Bull, Crane, and Dunphie went to Benson's command post at 10. 12 Junker 88s bombed them with 500-pound bombs with instantaneous fuses. They fell right in the command post. All jumped into slit trenches, of which there were plenty. One bomb hit right at edge of trench Jenson was in, killing him instantly. His watch stopped at 10:12."[26] The "Pink" that Patton referred to was Major General Harold

R. "Pink" Bull, Eisenhower's head of Operations; "Crane" was Brigadier General Carey Crane, a staff officer with II Corps, and "Dunphie" was British brigadier Charles A. M. Dunphie, Patton's assistant chief of staff and a veteran of the battles of El Almain and Kasserine Pass. None were assigned to Benson Force.[27]

Figure 19. Lieutenant Al Stiller stands in the crater left by the bomb that killed Dick Jenson. Patton took this picture, yet never claimed to be in the area where the bombing took place. Library of Congress.

Bradley corroborated Patton's story in more detail in his 1951 memoir, *A Soldier's Story*, explaining that he was standing against a half-track studying the plan of attack when "three shrill blasts of a whistle signaled an air attack," adding, "I saw a flight of 12 JU-87 [sic.] twin-engine bombers headed toward our position at almost 8,000 feet." He recounted that after the raid, he "climbed from my trench to find Dunphie bleeding from a wound in his thigh. . . . A bomb had fallen between two trenches one of which was occupied by Hansen, the other by Patton's aide, Captain Richard Jenson of Pasadena, California. Jenson had been killed and his watch shattered by the concussion."[28] If Copeland's story is true, it might explain Bradley's resentment of Patton, having to cover up his commanding officer's deadly mistake.

A few days after Jenson's death, Patton brought on Lieutenant Colonel Charles Codman, a Bostonian and former World War I bomber pilot who had been shot down twice by the Germans but escaped. Between wars he had made a living as a wine selector, dividing his time between the United States and France. While Patton enjoyed Codman's company and his ability to speak fluent French, the staff, especially the enlisted men, considered him an elitist. Patton secretly hoped Codman would someday write a biography about him, since he managed all of the general's files, orders, and diaries.[29]

While Patton grieved Jenson's death, the 1st Armored Division pushed east; however, the offensive did not last long. The Germans counterattacked with their 21st Panzer Division, forcing the tankers to fight defensively the rest of the day. In addition to the air attack that cost Jenson his life, the Luftwaffe pounded the American lines, launching fifty-one different raids. With little to show for the armored thrusts in the northern and central parts of the line, General Alexander called a halt to II Corps' armor assaults and ordered that tanks support the infantry, something anathema to Patton. He felt Alexander committed the armor too early, ensuring defeat.[30]

Patton spent the next day helping repel a German armored attack in the 1st Infantry Division zone using artillery. The first barrage knocked out five tanks, a nice revenge for Benson Force. Subsequent barrages kept them at bay. Patton interjected and ordered a round of phosphorous shells, hoping to set some tanks on fire. He quickly followed up with a concentration of high explosives to kill the men escaping from their tanks. He called Alexander for air support to finish off the Germans but was told the aircraft could not take off in high winds. "Our air cannot fly at night, nor in wind, nor support troops," he vented in his diary. "The Germans do all three." Patton did not appreciate that the Americans were flying from unpaved airstrips while the enemy flew from large, all-weather airports.[31]

The next day, April 3, Patton was up at the front again, visiting the 1st and 9th Infantry Divisions. Allen boasted the most progress in the corps. The 9th was different. Patton yelled at Eddy's regimental and battalion commanders, telling the former that his troops were not advancing fast enough and the latter that he should be up front with his troops. Patton's language shocked a soldier who witnessed the encounter: "When I say cussed, I mean he used every bit of invective in his expansive vocabulary."³² Patton then proceeded to the front line, where he pulled out his map but quickly put it away when the Germans dropped mortars on his position. Spotting an enemy tank advancing, he told a lieutenant, "I want you to take your company and knock out that tank, right now!" The officer led his men to engage the tank, but it fired first, and they retreated to their foxholes.³³

Adding to the frustration of enemy resistance and what Patton felt was high command indifference came another insult: a humiliating letter from Air Marshal Sir Arthur Coningham, sent to all Army and corps commanders, dismissing Patton's claims of constant enemy air raids and criticizing Patton and II Corps. In the letter, Coningham brushed off Patton's complaint of constant enemy air raids, explaining, "It was assumed to be a seasonal first April joke." Coningham also downplayed the number of ground casualties inflicted by the Germans, directly undermining Patton's claims. He accused Patton of "using air force as an alibi for lack of success on the ground," claiming that the soldiers of II Corps "are not battle worthy in terms of present operation." He requested that "such inaccurate and exaggerated reports should cease," and that he would not let his pilots be affected "by this false cry of wolf." Coningham could not have been more insulting had he tried.

This was not the first time Coningham insulted American commanders who he felt were too green at war to teach the British anything. In an even bigger insult to Lieutenant General Carl "Tooey" Spaatz, the commander of the Northwest African Air Force, Coningham had stood up in the middle of a briefing at Spaatz's headquarters, went out to the garden where he picked some flowers, and returned, dropping to one knee and offering the flowers to Spaatz, saying "Master, I bring you these."³⁴

"He accused me of being a fool and a liar," Patton fumed in his diary. He hit the phones in a fury, calling Alexander and Eisenhower to defend his actions and complain about Coningham. Eisenhower, wanting no national friction, warned Patton to back off. If there was a problem, it was to be handled face-to-face, in "a friendly and personal conference with the man responsible."³⁵ The incident so frustrated Eisenhower that he drafted a resignation letter to General Marshall, explaining that he had failed to control his own commanders and therefore could no longer remain as the Allied supreme commander. Only Beetle Smith's urging that the situation could be salvaged prevented Eisenhower from submitting it.³⁶

That afternoon, three air generals—Chief Air Marshal Arthur Tedder, the commander of the Mediterranean Air Command, Lieutenant General Carl "Tooey" Spaatz, the commander of the Northwest African Air Force, and Major General Laurence Kuter, who served under Coningham—visited Patton to discuss the flap. Patton said he would take the matter up through official channels, making his visitors visibly uncomfortable. In an effort to convince him that the matter did not need to go higher, one general assured Patton, "We have it." Just then, four German fighter planes flew down the street outside, bombing and strafing. One bomb exploded a block away. Tedder told Patton, "I always knew you were a good stage manager, but this takes the cake!" Spaatz asked, "Now how in the hell did you manage to stage that?" Patton answered, "I'll be damned if I know, but if I could find the sonsabitches who flew those planes, I'd mail them each a medal!" The visitors rushed from Patton's headquarters as one shouted over his shoulder, "We'll get some support for you right away!" With the generals gone, Patton mused to no one in particular, "I would have paid that pilot to drop that bomb closer to this building."[37]

The matter finally cleared when Coningham called Patton the next day, April 4, requesting a meeting. At their encounter, Patton did not shake his hand and made sure to eat early in case Coningham requested lunch. Coningham immediately apologized for his telegram and asked how to remedy the situation. Patton told him an oral apology would not suffice for insulting an entire army corps. Coningham raised his voice, defending his pilots. Patton also raised his voice, telling Coningham, "Pardon my also shouting, but I too have pride and will not stand for having Americans called cowards!" Patton explained that he had called for an official investigation and that if he had used half the language Coningham used, he would have been demoted to colonel and sent home. That appeased Coningham, who apologized again. "What can I do to make amends?" he asked. Patton told him to send another message to everyone who received the first one, retracting his remarks about II Corps. Coningham did as Patton asked and Patton sent a follow-up letter to everyone, praising the coordination between air and ground forces. Later, Patton would call the meeting his greatest diplomatic feat of the war.[38]

Yet, the same day on which Patton received Coningham's offending telegram, he received more bad news. Alexander again planned to take the 9th and 34th Infantries away from II Corps and incorporate them into the British army for a push north of II Corps. Both Patton and

Bradley complained to Eisenhower, who said he would look into it. The two events—Coningham's telegram and Alexander's directive—enraged Patton. "I am fed up with being treated like a moron by the British," he complained in his diary. "There is no national honor nor prestige left to us." And he placed most of the blame on his American commander and friend, Eisenhower, who he felt had sold out to the British. "Ike must go." He later penned, "How I wish John J. Pershing were twins."[39]

In the event, however, Eisenhower supported Patton in the blowup with Coningham. He even wrote Patton, reemphasizing his support, noting, "The great purpose of complete Allied teamwork must be achieved in this theater." Eisenhower then railed against Coningham's distribution of Patton's original complaint and his criticism "couched along nationalistic lines." Eisenhower demanded cooperation among his commanders—not sniping—and he did not want Patton sinking to Coningham's level. Patton and his staff "are at the moment carrying the burden of battle command for the American side of the house," Eisenhower wrote. As a postscript, he informed Patton that the II Corps would remain in the fight after Montgomery's Eighth Army drove north.[40] It would not be the last time Patton blamed Eisenhower for his ills, despite Eisenhower's efforts to the contrary.

Patton may have been reacting to Coningham's reference to a lack of success on the ground when he finally dropped the axe on Orlando Ward on April 4. Fed up with his lack of daring and drive, Patton sent Bradley to do the dirty work. "You're a friend of Pink Ward's," he told Bradley. "Go up there and tell him why I've got to let him go."[41] Patton replaced Ward with Ernie Harmon, the 2nd Armored Division commander, one of Patton's better decisions. Still, even though Patton respected Harmon, the promotion began with a rocky start. Patton, in a foul mood over Coningham and Alexander, greeted Harmon at his headquarters and immediately ordered him to Maknassy to take over 1st Armored. When Harmon asked Patton if he wanted him to attack or defend, Patton lost his temper. "What have you come here for, asking me a lot of goddamned stupid questions?" he roared. Harmon didn't know the sources of Patton's rage and responded accordingly, saying, "I simply asked you a fundamental question, whether I am to attack or defend?" Patton snapped. "Get the hell out of here and get on with what I told you to do, or I'll send you back to Morocco!" Harmon left. A few hours later Patton's phone rang. It was Harmon, asking if Ward could remain at 1st Armored headquarters to fill him in on the situation. Patton shouted that he didn't give a damn what happened to Ward as long as he knew who was in charge, and slammed down the phone.⁴²

For the next few days, fighting continued along the line in typical fashion. The 1st Infantry made progress while the 9th struggled. Patton visited Eddy's headquarters to encourage an advance, but it did not go well. When his convoy pulled up to Eddy's headquarters, Eddy ran out to greet his commander. "Manton, Goddamn it," Patton screeched in his high-pitched voice, "I want you to get these staff officers out front and get them shot at!" Patton's words set off one of Eddy's young personnel officers, who broke down and had to be evacuated.⁴³

Later that day, Harmon sent 1st Armored on the attack, surprising Patton since this had never happened before without his having ordered it. Patton called Harmon. "What the hell are you doing out there?" "Nothing," replied Harmon. "We are just attacking here." Patton was not satisfied. "I told you to stay on the defensive," he shouted. "No, you didn't," Harmon replied. "I told you to stay on the defensive," Patton repeated. "You didn't tell me a damn thing," Harmon snapped. "You just told me to get the hell out." When Harmon explained that it was a limited attack, designed to keep the Germans off balance, Patton approved.⁴⁴

Pleased with Harmon's progress, Patton then ordered Benson to move his force back into the line. With the Germans now retreating, Patton saw this as the perfect opportunity, but Benson was slow getting into position and his attack seemed halfhearted. The Germans counterattacked, seeking to turn Patton's left flank. Bradley suggested that Patton withdraw his headquarters back to Ferina. "I refused to move," Patton later wrote. "When things looked bad yesterday, I decided not to leave Gafsa alive." Instead, he focused support on the 9th Infantry's 47th Infantry Regiment, which had taken heavy casualties while assaulting a hill five times. He got the idea to fire phosphorous shells at the hill, hoping the Germans would flee their shelters to avoid suffocation. He followed with high explosive rounds. The plan worked; the hill was taken without a loss. Hap Gay visited the area and found only enemy body parts.⁴⁵

Patton woke up the next morning, April 7, nauseous from the antimalaria medicine he had taken the day before. To add to his rancor, he received a note from General Richard McCreery, Alexander's chief of staff, noting that his American tankers were "timid." This was too much. For the last twenty-one days, his corps had been in constant contact with the enemy, drawing troops away from Montgomery's front. He had pushed, pulled, and fired commanders in order to keep II Corps moving. He was even conciliatory to the air commander who had insulted him, and now the British were criticizing Patton's most beloved asset: his tanks. He drove to Benson's headquarters and viciously reprimanded him for his lack of progress. He ordered him to push forward until he either got into a fight or reached the sea. Patton knew the Germans were retreating in front of Montgomery and the Americans might lose their chance of catching them. He berated Benson so severely that he woke up a nearby sleeping soldier who heard "the screeching and crackling of a shrill human voice hurling curses at someone named Benson."[46]

With Benson properly motivated, Patton drove up to an observation post to watch his subordinate's armor. But again, Benson's tanks moved too slowly for Patton's liking, so the general relayed messages to him to speed up. When that didn't work, he drove back down the hill and was proceeding east to catch up with the force when he came across Benson eating lunch on the side of the road. Patton exploded and ordered Benson to attack. When the tanks stopped in front of a mine field, Patton again ordered his driver forward into it. Fortunately, a jeep and a scout car preceded Patton's jeep. The three-vehicle spearhead rumbled forward for an entire mile before Benson, in his turretless Grant tank, caught up to Patton's caravan. Patton ordered him to "keep pushing for a fight or a bath." Patton turned back while Benson and his tankers continued east until contacting the advance elements of Montgomery's Eighth Army at Wadi Akarit, only ten minutes after Patton's departure. Patton was glad he missed the link up. It would have been too embarrassing for the British to see an American corps commander, in a jeep, leading a tank column. His tankers would have appeared timid.[47] More important, the Americans and British had united. The Germans, faced with a shrinking front line, pulled out of Maknassy's passes and fled north.[48]

As he was on his way back to corps headquarters, a pair of 1st Armored Division soldiers returning from a recon patrol were surprised to spot Patton at a frontline crossroads.[49] As Patton continued west, he came across a soldier guarding a stack of bedrolls. "What are you doing out here?" Patton asked. "You're twenty miles in front of our lines." The soldier explained that he was waiting for a truck to pick him up. Satisfied with the soldier's answer, Patton sped on, leaving the soldier to wonder, in turn, what a general was doing so far to the front.[50]

Benson's task force never found a real fight, much less took a bath in the Mediterranean Sea, but it did capture more than a thousand prisoners. With Montgomery's Eighth Army racing north, there was, contrary to Patton's ideas, no more mission for Benson. "After having spent thousands of casualties making a breakthrough, we are not allowed to exploit it," Patton wrote. But there was no real breakthrough. No enemy now stood before Benson, only Montgomery's Eighth Army. Patton now wanted to pivot north and relieve Maknassy from the rear. Actually, he wanted to go anywhere there was fighting. He was furious that his corps had been used to make progress easier for Montgomery: "We are to halt, so as not to take any glory." While the British seemed less than generous with the Americans, Patton was proving himself to be a fierce ally.[51]

With the main campaign at an end, Patton issued an order of the day, thanking his troops for their fine work: "After 22 days of relentless combat in mountains whose ruggedness beggars description, you have won the battle of El Guettar. Each one of you in his own sphere has done his duty magnificently." He singled out different support units that contributed to victory, including the Twelfth Air Support Command: "Due to your united efforts and manifest assistance of Almighty God, the splendid record of the American Army has attained added luster."[52]

Patton still longed for a fight. On April 8, the day the campaign ended, British general McCreery, who had called Patton's tankers timid, told Patton to send some of his forces north to Faïd Pass, where the 1st Armored Division had suffered losses during Kasserine Pass two months earlier. As Patton dispatched the 1st Armored, hoping to put it on the attack, he learned the fate of II Corps. Instead of being permanently pinched out of the line, as Patton had feared, it was to head north for the drive into Bizerte. The 1st Infantry Division would be pulled from the battlefield so it could prepare for the invasion of Sicily, while the 9th and 34th Infantry Divisions would take over the current fight. Patton was pleased with the arrangement. "It is not a bad set up," he penned in his diary.[53] But if he was now happy with his British allies, he was furious with the American press. The cover photograph of the April 9 issue of YANK magazine featured an unshaven, tieless corporal eating his lunch at an advance base in the desert, with his sleeves rolled up for all the world to see. It ran counter to everything Patton had instilled in the II Corps. He fired off a cable to the War Department, complaining that YANK was "encouraging dirt and disorder among the troops and needed strict censorship." His protest came to nothing.[54]

The next day, April 10, Patton led his last attack as commander of II Corps. The 1st Armored pressed east through the Faïd Pass and linked up with the 34th Infantry Division, trying to cut off any escaping

Germans. Patton drove out to witness the operation and was disappointed to find Harmon in his headquarters, having just issued orders. After lunch, the two generals drove to see Brigadier General Raymond E. McQuillan, who was supposed to lead the attack. "When we got there, nothing had been done," Patton later wrote. He asked McQuillan where his lead element was and when the commander said he did not know, Patton took Harmon forward. They approached a minefield where the soldiers implored Patton to turn back, but he saw fresh tracks on the ground and ordered his driver forward. For a third time in the campaign, Patton's vehicle made it through a minefield unscathed, but a half-track behind him rolled over a mine and exploded. Patton and his driver continued until they came upon engineers removing mines from the road. When a reconnaissance unit approached, Patton ordered them to continue off the road. "We lost two half-tracks but saved hours of time," he later wrote.[55]

But Patton wasn't finished leading from the front. As his jeep approached a pass through the mountains, he came across a soldier posted on a road in front of a hill. Patton ordered the man to fire at anything coming toward him on the road, then roared off. Patton then came to another minefield, and he and Harmon proceeded on foot to encourage the troops behind them. "I think my walking through the minefield saved about three hours," Patton wrote. He could not find McQuillan, so he sent a runner to find him. As Patton started heading back, he was infuriated to see two reconnaissance companies slowly approach, searching for mines. Tanks should lead the assault, not a reconnaissance unit, and certainly not a three-star general. Harmon tried to calm him, explaining that the troops were responding appropriately, but Patton would have none of it. When he finally found McQuillan, he fired him on the spot.[56] On the way back, Patton approached the sentry he had encountered previously. The soldier leveled his rifle at Patton's jeep but finally recognized him. "If I had not recognized him," the soldier later confessed, "I would have blown his tail off!"[57]

The next day, Patton attended a meeting at Alexander's headquarters to hammer out the final phase of the North Africa campaign. He saw Air Marshal Coningham, who thanked Patton for a letter he had sent out after Coningham's apology, exhorting the good relations between II Corps and its tactical air cover. "I think I will get plenty of air cover now," Patton mused. Called to a private meeting in Alexander's trailer, Patton learned that British general John Crocker, a corps commander who commanded Ryder's 34th Infantry Division at Fondouk Pass, said the division was "no good" and accused its soldiers of failing to clear a path for British armor at Fondouk, thus allowing Axis forces to retreat.[58] His desire to keep it out of the final push for Bizerte did not surprise Patton. Crocker, who already harbored prejudice against the Americans, had complained to the press about the 34th's lack of leadership and recommended it for retraining under British officers, failing to mention that he had sent it into the jaws of a German force he mistakenly believed had retreated. Alexander also told Patton that II Corps would come under direct command of the Anderson, even though Patton wanted to continue reporting directly to Alexander.[59]

A frustrated Patton left the meeting but later penned two letters to Alexander, imploring him to keep the II Corps under army group control and allowing the 34th to prove itself. He wanted II Corps under Alexander for prestige reasons, arguing that if it even appeared that part of U.S. Army was serving a minor role in the war, "the repercussions might be unfortunate." The letter regarding the 34th Infantry was even more emphatic. If Alexander agreed to put it back in the line, Patton would provide plenty of artillery to ensure its success, "and thereby restore its soul." In addition, the U.S. Army needed all the veteran divisions it could muster for future battles. "If we deny the 34th a chance, we will so besmirch its reputation as to render its future utilization of dubious value," he wrote. Finally, he argued, the division was a National Guard unit, whose "activities assume local interest of great political significance."[60] The whole incident embittered Patton. "Goddam[n] all British and all so-called Americans who have their legs pulled by them," he groused that night. The American he was referring to was, of course, Eisenhower. "Ike is more British than the British," he later wrote. "He is putty in their hands. Oh, for a John J. Pershing!"[61] Patton's letter-writing campaign, however, succeeded. The 34th remained with II Corps and proved itself in the battles for Bizerte, and the corps remained under 18th Army Group.[62]

In one of his last acts as II Corps commander, Patton visited a forward hospital. He walked the aisles and addressed men suffering with brutal head wounds and missing limbs. He asked a man with only one leg how he was doing, and the man said fine, now that Patton had seen him. "I suppose I do some good," he wrote Beatrice, "but it always makes me choke up." But Patton admitted he did not feel responsible for their injuries since he took the same frontline risks as they did.[63]

Patton's job in Tunisia was finally finished. He was needed to plan and lead the Army's operation to capture Sicily. In forty-three days, he had restored a defeated corps, fought and won several battles, advanced one hundred miles, diverted some thirty-seven thousand enemy troops from engaging Montgomery, proved his personal bravery, gained a third star, and, to his own delight, lost ten pounds. Despite his success, he never achieved the "Second Manassas" victory he craved. While the Confederates flanked the Union army and delivered a crushing blow, Patton never flanked the Germans. Where Union commanders were slow and at times hapless, the Germans responded quickly to Patton's thrusts, and further, Second Manassas was fought on the rolling hills of Virginia, not the jagged mountainous and cliff-filled deserts of Tunisia. Finally, while the Confederate army had a string of victories under its belt, II Corps was recovering from the humiliation of Kasserine Pass. While history would always be a guide for Patton, he was learning he would have to rely on his own battlefield experience and intuition to succeed. Many of his soldiers, who had performed well in training, lacked aggressiveness on the battlefield and it was up to him, personally, to push and prod his men forward. "As I gain in experience," he wrote, "I do not think more of myself, but less of others."[64]

On April 14 Patton passed the II Corps baton to Bradley. The event was kept from the press since Eisenhower did not want the enemy to know about the change of command, just as the Germans kept Rommel's absence hidden from the Allies. Eisenhower also did not want to create any sense that Patton had been removed from command. In fact, two days before Patton departed, *Time* magazine published an article about his generalship at the head of II Corps. Patton looked forward to leading the attack into Sicily but worried II Corps would lose its edge without him. When he visited Bradley's new headquarters, he realized none of the units had advanced. Why are we sitting around doing nothing? He roared at Bradley, "We must do something!" Bradley tried to calm him down and asked him exactly what it was he should do. "Anything rather than just sitting on our backsides!" Bradley was a very different commander from Patton.[65]

Eisenhower sent Patton a letter of appreciation, offering him his "sincere congratulations upon the outstanding example of leadership you have given us all."⁶⁶ Before he departed, Patton returned to Dick Jenson's grave, where he, Gay, and Meeks knelt hand-in-hand. Patton, with tears in his eyes, placed flowers on the mound.⁶⁷ The next day he began his journey west to Morocco to begin planning Operation HUSKY, the capture of Sicily.

Figure 20. Patton stands beneath the Arch of Trajan in Timgad, Algeria, where he hailed himself as a greater commander than the Roman emperor. Library of Congress.

Along the way, his caravan stopped at the ancient Roman city of Timgad, founded by Emperor Trajan in 100 AD. Patton walked through the ruins until he came to Trajan's Arch, a forty-foot-high sandstone columned structure. "I was tremendously impressed with this monument," he admitted. "Yet I have fought and won a bigger battle than Trajan has ever heard of." To commemorate the moment, and to celebrate his successful command of II Corps, Patton had his picture taken underneath the towering arch. When he later developed the photograph, he wrote on the back of it, "Trajan's arch, old and new conqueror."⁶⁸

PART II
Army Commander in Sicily

CHAPTER SEVEN

Planning the Invasion of Sicily

ON APRIL 16, 1943, Patton flew to Eisenhower's headquarters in Algiers to discuss closing out the war in North Africa and planning the invasion of Sicily, Operation HUSKY, scheduled for July 9. Patton would have less than three months to prepare HUSKY, less time than he had for TORCH, but this time he was an experienced amphibious assault commander and combat leader. Naval personnel and soldiers were also experienced, salty, and ready to continue the fight.

Things did not, however, start off well. No escort vehicles awaited Patton and his staff at the airport. Patton stomped into a hanger, where he saw a slovenly looking pilot. The pilot, Major Philip Cochran, just back from flying several combat missions, stood up and saluted. "Get your ass out of here," Patton yelled at him, "and get me some cars!" Cochran tried to explain that he had just landed and was not part of any unit. Patton wasn't having it. "I don't care what establishment you belong to, you go in there and get me some cars." Cochran walked toward the office. "I said run!" Patton hollered. Cochran kept walking. When the cars did arrive, Patton was still in a foul mood.[1]

But he had cooled off by the time he reached Eisenhower's headquarters in the Hotel St.-George, which overlooked the city. The two generals got straight to business. They agreed to fire ineffective leaders, even those who were old friends. When Eisenhower's aide, Captain Harry Butcher, quipped that Eisenhower and Patton both had a tough exterior but were actually chicken-hearted down deep, Patton admitted that before leaving II Corps, he had put flowers on Dick Jenson's grave. Then he blurted out, "I really guess I am a Goddamn old fool," as grief overwhelmed him and tears streamed down his cheeks. Patton stayed up late talking to Butcher, who suggested that he had opened himself up for criticism by not driving

II Corps all the way to the coast. Patton disagreed, saying that so long as he was doing his job, he could take any criticism or censure. If Eisenhower was satisfied, then he had accomplished his mission.[2]

As pleasantly as the meeting went, Patton still raged at British arrogance and at Eisenhower's acceptance of British ideas and protocol. In his diary, Patton called Eisenhower a Benedict Arnold, a popinjay, and a stuffed doll. In his mind, the British were playing the Americans for suckers. "The British dictate what troops come, what quantity and type of supplies we give the French and how and where our troops are used," he wrote. Patton saw the war merely as a fight for the Brits' empire and their postwar ambitions. He considered resigning to protest British dominance in all things operational, tactical, and strategic. "I feel like Judas," he confessed.[3]

The next morning, Patton vented his frustrations to Eisenhower, who received his protests coolly. When Patton accused him of acting as the opposite of John J. Pershing, Eisenhower cited Pershing's decision to put every American at the disposal of the French during a major German offensive in the spring of 1918. The two went back and forth, with Patton never getting Eisenhower to budge.[4] The tension finally broke when an aide passed Patton a wire from Marshall, reading, "You have done a fine job and have justified our confidence in you." Patton turned to Eisenhower: "I owe this one to you, Ike." Eisenhower shot back, "The hell you do."[5] Patton was still sore with Eisenhower when he lunched with his old friend, Major General Everett Hughes, to whom Patton said that Eisenhower was crazy and too pro-British.[6]

Hughes marveled at Patton's prowess. "He out Nazis the fiercest Nazi general," he wrote his wife, adding that Patton was "Old Blood and Guts" with the troops yet receptive to any advice from a staffer like himself. Hughes considered it his duty to keep Patton's spirits up between campaigns, knowing that once Patton saw Germans, he would immediately click into combat mode. "He certainly is a fighter," Hughes added in his letter. "I'd like to turn him loose in Germany with 500,000 men."[7]

Patton failed to realize that Eisenhower held a fundamentally different view of the Allies than he did. While Patton saw them as insufferable, Eisenhower knew that to win the war, the Allies had to cooperate with one another and see past national affiliations. Eisenhower also knew that the United States was on the rise as a world power and would eventually eclipse Great Britain. He was magnanimous, though, and appreciated what the British had endured alone at the hands of Nazi Germany. He also knew the British had to save face as the United States slowly took control of the war. Therefore, Eisenhower tolerated British outbursts against Americans but lacked patience for the same behavior from Americans toward the British. For his part, Patton saw the British as feckless fighters who looked down their noses at their American cousins and scorned their fighting ability.

With the North African campaign winding down, Sicily was the logical next step in keeping the western Allies fighting the Axis. It would relieve pressure on the Soviet Union, secure Mediterranean sea lanes for the Allies, and provide air bases closer to Italy, Romania, and Germany. Winston Churchill believed that if Sicily fell, Italy, with its population and army souring on Mussolini's war, would surrender. Yet, for all the benefits capturing Sicily would bring, General Marshall worried that the British would want to use Sicily as a springboard into Italy, further delaying the cross-channel attack into France. He wanted the island taken quickly so that sufficient quantities of men and naval craft could be diverted to England to prepare the main continental invasion.[8]

The mountainous island of Sicily, shaped like a jagged arrowhead pointing west with its tip broken off, lay off the extreme southwestern end of the Italian boot, just three miles from the mainland. The closest Sicilian city to continental Italy, and key to the campaign, was Messina. To capture the port city before large numbers of enemy troops could retreat back to it would deny Axis soldiers transport back to the safety of Italy. War planners in London envisioned an attack with two invading forces: a British one landing on the eastern waist of the island, at Catania, and an American one landing in the northwest, at Palermo. The two landings would gain two major airports and block the two main escape routes to Messina. Eisenhower picked Montgomery to land at Catania in command of Eighth Army, while Patton would attack Palermo with the I Armored Corps. Alexander would oversee the entire campaign as the 18th Army Group commander.[9]

While Patton fought in Tunisia, Eisenhower and Alexander worked on HUSKY. Eisenhower considered the capture of the port city of Palermo crucial, although he envisioned capturing it from the south, following the initial landings in Gela and once enough airfields had been captured. "No fixed date for the Palermo attack would be set," Eisenhower wrote his superiors, "and this attack would take place at such time as this fighter support could be insured [sic]." As far as Patton was concerned, Palermo was where his force would land.[10]

While Eisenhower and Alexander worked out the landings, Patton flew to Morocco to work on amphibious assault problems and solutions. He did not stay long. He visited old friends and toured Casablanca, before flying back to Algeria.[11] On April 12 he learned what Hughes meant about opening himself up to criticism. A *Time* magazine article portrayed Patton as a frustrated corps commander, in charge of ill-trained troops and unable to break through the German line. While the article complimented his leadership and drive, it hinted that he did not visit the front frequently and that the war had drained him of his fire: "Here his high-pitched voice was not 'the voice you can hear all over North Africa.' His bright blue eyes were not now the eyes of 'that disciplinary sonofabitch.' Here his two pistols were in their holsters to stay, his bloodthirsty boasts lay doggo in his throat." The article admitted that Patton had contained some of Rommel's strength, "but not effectively harassing it." It also portrayed Patton as uncertain of victory: "He must have his doubts as to who was winning the first round of the Rommel-v.-Patton match." The article, which Patton considered "nasty," caused him problems. After reading it, General Terry Allen accused him of criticizing the troops, which Patton emphatically denied. For two weeks, the article distracted him from his work.[12]

Patton established his Algerian headquarters in a four-story building in downtown Oran, but he also set up a fake headquarters in nearby Relizane to confuse German spies. Inside the faux headquarters, a map of Sardinia hung from the wall opposite an open window, where it could be seen by anyone passing by.[13] When not in his headquarters, Patton stayed in the resort town of Mostaganem, thirty miles away. He always arrived at the headquarters in an old car and entered through the back basement. MPs were posted outside the war room. A large map of southern Sicily hung on one wall, and on the other side behind a curtain hung a plastic-covered invasion force map. Only Patton—and those he approved—were allowed to see it. Every day an officer visited, handcuffed to a briefcase. Inside were the latest Ultra transcripts, which Patton read and then either burned or locked in a safe.[14]

Patton spent hours standing in front of the invasion map with his division commanders, theorizing invasion tactics while enlisted men drew unit positions on the map with grease pencils. If Patton did not like what he was seeing, everything would come down and an orderly would wipe the map clean with a towel. Then Patton would start anew, with the generals and colonels calling out recommendations and suggestions. If Patton thought a commander was overestimating his own progress, the plan would be scrapped and a new one begun. Sometimes arguments over tactics degenerated into arguments about who beat whom during the 1941 Louisiana maneuvers, forcing Patton to resort to meeting with division commanders one at a time.[15]

Patton knew from Ultra intercepts that he would be facing two German divisions: the 15th Panzer Grenadier and the Hermann Goering. Italian units were also in the area. The Germans defended the island with about three hundred fighter craft.[16] Patton planned for a nighttime amphibious assault by the 3rd, 45th, and 36th Infantry Divisions, but the 45th and 36th were both green National Guard units and he wanted at least one division experienced in combat as part of his amphibious landings. "I want those [1st Division] sons of bitches," he told Eisenhower. "I won't go without them." The request went to Marshall, who agreed to give Patton what he needed to ensure success. Patton also brought back General Keyes to serve again as his deputy commander.[17]

To achieve surprise, Patton planned for no prelanding naval or air bombardment on the assault beaches. General Spaatz intended to use his fighters and bombers to attack the enemy further inland to seal off the beachhead, yet, for flexibility reasons, he refused to tell Patton, or any of the other planners, how many aircraft he planned to use. His secrecy frustrated Patton, who pleaded with Hewitt to use his carrier-based aircraft to support his landings, admitting, "You can get your Navy planes to do anything you want, but we can't get the Air Force to do a Goddamn thing!" But there were no aircraft carriers available, as all of them were on anti-submarine duty.[18]

On April 29 Alexander held a high-level meeting on Sicily, at which he announced that General Montgomery had also requested changes to the attack plan. Montgomery wanted his army to attack Syracuse instead of Catania, and Patton's force to land in Gela, where the two forces could support each other. Patton did not like the change and chimed in that his force would be forty-five miles from Montgomery. British admiral Andrew Cunningham suggested that Montgomery's plan would cause too much congestion in the sea lanes, inviting disaster. Air Marshal Arthur Tedder, the commander of the Mediterranean Air Command, stressed the need to capture numerous airports to support the landings, something Montgomery's plan ignored. The participants finally agreed to send Air Marshal Coningham to Montgomery to discuss the plan. When Tedder heard the suggestion, he chided, "Fine, it will be good for Monty to hear his master's voice."[19]

Patton blamed the impasse on Alexander's indecisiveness. He considered him a fence straddler, "who cut a sorry figure at all times." Tedder took Patton to lunch, where he accused Montgomery of being only of average ability, someone who "thinks of himself as Napoleon—He is not." The indecisive meeting and Tedder's own assessment of Montgomery gave Patton hope that a change of command was on the horizon. "I am sure that such a change must eventually take place," he wrote in his diary.[20]

Montgomery viewed the invasion plan as too optimistic, based on the assumption that resistance would be light and the island easily captured. To him, such assumptions led to disaster. He had learned through painful experience that the British were usually defeated when they split their forces. "We must plan for fierce resistance, by the Germans at any rate, and for the real dog fight battle to follow," he wrote Alexander. He flew to Algiers to meet with Alexander, only to discover that he was not there yet. Looking for someone else to whom he could explain his ideas, Montgomery cornered Beetle Smith in a men's room and told him that if the Americans landed in the Gulf of Gela, they could capture the airfields that were so important to the campaign. Montgomery thought the two forces would also support each other, "giving cohesion to the whole invasion." Smith brought the plan to Eisenhower, who saw in it his own original ideas and signed off on it.[21]

On May 3 Patton attended another meeting, this one with Eisenhower and Montgomery present. He planned to get there early and argue for the Palermo assault, but heavy rain grounded his plane, forcing him to drive. Arriving late, he missed almost everyone. Eisenhower, Alexander, and Hewitt ushered Patton into a room where they unveiled the new invasion plan. Montgomery would land at Augusta and Syracuse, some twelve miles south of Catania, while Patton would land at Gela—on the southwestern coast, fifty-eight miles from Palermo. To make matters worse, Gela was not a port city but a coastal town. Supplies would have to come over its beaches until Patton's force linked up with Montgomery's, at which time he would receive supplies from Syracuse. There had been no change of leadership, only a radical change in the plan, and the whole thing had been settled while Patton was still on the road. Patton hid whatever shock he felt and immediately told his small audience that he

CHAPTER SEVEN ★ PLANNING THE INVASION OF SICILY

Figure 21. Montgomery and Patton inspect a map of Sicily. National Archives and Records Administration.

would land four divisions and two parachute regiments and turn west to capture Licata, the only nearby port city. Later, Beetle Smith told Patton that Montgomery always got his way because he was a national hero who corresponded directly with Churchill and because he previously taught Alexander at the British army staff college. Patton noted in his dairy that his supply officers claimed that Montgomery's plan was "logistically impossible." Churchill may have had a personal relationship with Montgomery, but he held both Patton and Montgomery alike in one regard: in a message to Roosevelt, Churchill referred to the generals as "two prima donnas."[22]

When a group of naval officers later urged Patton to protest the new plan, he refused, explaining, "I've been in this army thirty years and when my superior gives me an order I say, 'Yes sir!' and then do my Goddamndest to carry it out." It was the direct opposite of Montgomery's relationship with Alexander. Instead, Patton went to see General Charles Gairdner, Alexander's new chief of staff. Armed with a report listing all the problems with Montgomery's plan, Patton read off a laundry list of things he wanted changed in his assault, including more paratroopers and a promise of adequate supplies.[23] His assertiveness paid off. Alexander sent Major General Freddie de Guingand, Montgomery's chief of staff, to Algiers to coordinate with Patton.

Patton finally met Montgomery at Eisenhower's headquarters on May 7 to work out the invasion plan, but he could not get Montgomery to agree to either army boundaries or phase lines and came away from the meeting thinking that Montgomery was a forcefully selfish man. However, he noted, "I think he is a far better leader than Alexander and that he will just do what he pleases." He wrote Beatrice, "I should hate to be married to him."[24] A few days later at another lunch with Hughes, he confessed that he didn't like either Alexander or Montgomery. Hughes made a note of Patton's feelings in his dairy: "How he hates the British."[25] As for his own amphibious attack, Patton worried that only divine intervention would get enough supplies across Gela beach. "I have to exude confidence I don't feel, every minute," he confessed in his diary. Yet, for all his disgust with the new invasion plan, he accepted it. He even began to see its merits, believing it to be an easier attack plan that the previous one.[26]

Regardless of which set of plans may have been the better one, no plans were made beyond the amphibious assault. Alexander wanted to get his two armies ashore before worrying about any maneuvering. With Messina—the ultimate objective—closer to Montgomery's landing site, he foresaw Montgomery leading the main effort, the sword jabbing for Messina, with Patton as the shield, guarding Montgomery's flank.[27] For his part, Patton focused on his own performance and the dangers of the coming campaign. He worried that several officers, in warning him about taking risks, were "making a woman out of me." He wrote Beatrice that if he were killed, he hoped it would be "a nice clean job." He told her he felt like he was on a ship on the river of destiny. "My chief concern," he wrote, "is to do my duty, retain my self-confidence and follow my star."[28]

As Patton wrestled with his new role, back in Tunisia, Bizerte fell to Bradley's II Corps on May 8, ending German opposition in North Africa. When Patton learned of Bradley's success, he told Eisenhower, "Hail Caesar!" When Bradley arrived in Algiers eight days later to learn about his role in HUSKY, Patton greeted him with an honor guard. He then treated Bradley and his staff to a champagne lunch, at which he toasted Bradley as the "Conqueror of Bizerte." Later, the two generals considered their chances of surviving HUSKY, putting their odds at no better than fifty-fifty.[29]

Patton penned a letter to Marshall equating the North Africa victory with Eisenhower's moral courage, self-confidence, and driving energy, as well as his ability to add starch "to the somewhat flexible spines of most of the Allied commanders." Patton was being less than honest. "I lied in good cause," he later wrote, but in the same line he admitted that no one, except himself, could do a better job than Eisenhower, "and God knows I don't want his job." Later, at a press conference on the North African victory, reporters repeatedly asked Eisenhower what had happened to Patton. He explained that a tank expert was needed at El Guettar and an infantry expert at Bizerte. No one believed it and kept asking until finally Eisenhower admitted that he had pulled Patton out to plan a bigger operation, adding, "please lay off mentioning him." When Patton heard that, it reminded him of a quote from Civil War general William T. Sherman, when Ulysses S. Grant told him he wanted to use his corps for a feint at Vicksburg. Sherman responded, "Don't let my personal reputation interfere with winning the war."[30]

As the deadline drew near, Patton oversaw combat rehearsals to work out problems with the upcoming invasion. He was initially unimpressed with the amphibious landing drills. Landing craft hit the wrong beaches or landed in the incorrect sequences. The ramps on Landing Ship Tanks (LSTs) were too short, preventing tanks from disembarking. Soldiers and sailors moved too slowly, and officers showed a lack of drive.[31] As time went on and the men became more proficient, the exercises became smoother. Under Patton, infantrymen were uniformly equipped and alert, while tankers fired their cannons from LSTs at floating targets. To defeat enemy obstacles on the assault beaches, Patton's ordinance officer, Colonel Thomas Nixon, invented a grappling hook that could be fired from an 81mm mortar on a landing craft. Once the hook imbedded itself into an obstacle, the craft would reverse, yanking it out of the way. At a demonstration, Patton watched a hook fire and land so far away that Nixon ran to see where it had landed. After he left, Patton turned to an enlisted man manning the mortar and asked, "Do you think you could hit Nixon in the ass?"[32] Patton displayed his sense of humor during a later demonstration of Bangalore torpedoes used to explode mines. When a mine exploded, he tapped an unsuspecting Colonel Paddy Flint's helmet. "He thought he was a casualty," Patton wrote Beatrice.[33]

To perfect street fighting, Patton created mock towns in which live ammunition fired over his men's heads. He enjoyed watching knife fighting drills and loading exercises. "All left nothing to be desired," he wrote. Soldiers blasted pillboxes with machineguns, flamethrowers, bazookas, and artillery, trying to see which worked best. When a Bangalore torpedo failed to detonate an enemy Teller mine, Patton suspected it was too old, so he shouldered a rifle and fired on the detonator from one hundred yards. It failed to explode. He also rode in a tank during an armored advance while artillery exploded around him. Shrapnel hit the tank and tore up the ground. "I took the ride because some of the men felt it was dangerous," he later wrote. Harry Semmes, who witnessed the drill, said that Patton "had a wonderful time shooting the cannon of the tank," even though the artillery tore off his antenna and smashed his gunsights.[34] Patton also attended an armor-bottomed car demonstration. Mines were placed beneath the vehicle, right below the armor plating. To ensure the proper results, a live goat was put inside the car. Patton gave the signal and the men detonated the mines. Boom! The armor plating shot skyward, almost out of sight. Car and goat parts littered the ground. Without a word Patton got in his vehicle and drove away.[35]

Patton also spent time with Bradley's troops in Bizerte, who were scheduled to come under his command for Sicily. He strutted among the disheveled men, who had recently been in combat, and pointed out men who were either unshaven or had dirty uniforms. His sergeant wrote down names and assigned fines, then demonstrated how to bathe with only a canteen of water. The thirsty men were unimpressed, and some asked Patton why they had received no rations. Patton's answer: "They don't have enough refrigerator trucks!"[36] When inspecting bayonet drills, he told his soldiers they did not hate the Germans enough: "Just because you have been brought up not to kick your grandmother in the ass, don't think he hasn't." He then went into a tirade against the Germans, saying the only thing lower than them on the Earth were the Japanese. "For the present," he implored, "just keep hating the Germans. . . . After all, your outfit comes from a part of the country that has produced fighters." When Patton's new aide, Charles Codman, later asked him where the unit came from, Patton told him, "I haven't the slightest idea, that was just speech thirty-three." On the way back from the drill, Patton ordered Codman to stop a truck driver and find out why he was missing his tie. "Take his name," Patton told Codman. "Have him court-martialed."[37]

While the troops trained, Patton kept himself fit by running, doing calisthenics, walking up hills, swimming in the sea, and practicing at rifle and pistol ranges. Often impressed with his own feelings of confidence, he chalked it up to divine intervention. "I pray daily and do my duty. . . . No one can live under the awful responsibility I have without divine help." While he wrote Beatrice that he was eating well and getting to bed by 10:30 every night, he did admit to getting bombed once. He was reading in his room when the Luftwaffe struck. A scared Sergeant Meeks ran into his room "to see if the general needed anything."[38]

On May 17 Eisenhower upgraded Patton's I Armored Corps to a field army. He had already hinted it to Patton two weeks earlier, but Patton misinterpreted Eisenhower's musings as a suggestion that he would be placed under Clark's Fifth Army. Marshall had decided that if the British had an army in Sicily, so should the Americans, as a matter of prestige. Marshall designated it the Seventh Army, but he stressed that the Army designation would receive no publicity and would only be used in official planning papers. When Patton learned Eisenhower was giving him a field army, he penned in his diary, "I never asked him to do this but am glad he is going to." Seventh Army had a strange makeup. Instead of commanding two corps, Patton would command one: Bradley's II Corps, comprised of the 1st and 45th Infantry Divisions, while the 82nd Airborne, 3rd Infantry, and 2nd Armored Division would all report directly to Patton. Subsequently, Alexander's army group changed its designation from 18th to 15th, to represent the combination of Patton's Seventh Army and Montgomery's Eighth.[39]

With a newly minted army on his hands, Patton wanted a shoulder patch to go with it. He assigned his staff to come up with something that utilized an "A," with seven steps, and the color red "for the blood that has been spilled." The final design consisted of a red triangle inside of a yellow "A" with seven steps notched into each side of the "A." A blue

Figure 22. Lieutenant General Omar N. Bradley (right) talks with his aide, Captain Chester "Chet" Hansen, in Sicily. Omar N. Bradley Papers, Army War College, Carlisle, Pennsylvania.

triangle outlined the patch; thus the army's branch colors were represented: yellow for cavalry, red for artillery, and blue for infantry, all within the triangular shape of the armored corps. Each step represented a part of Patton's WWII career: (1) his creation of the Armored Tank Training School in California; (2) his planning future invasion tactics in Washington and London; (3) his creating the Western Task Force; (4) planning the convoy that crossed the Atlantic to invade Morocco; (5) the invasion of Morocco and establishment of successful civilian control; (6) his successful extermination of the Axis in Tunisia; and (7) his planning the invasion of Sicily. The patch would come to be known as the "Seven Steps to Hell."[40]

On May 20 Eisenhower, Patton, and Bradley attended a victory parade in Tunis. Patton and Bradley sat in a stand with French civilians and minor officers, or as Patton called them, "middle class frogs." Across from them in the main reviewing stand were Eisenhower and other high-ranking Allies. Patton watched as British Highlanders, French Foreign Legion soldiers, and French colonial troops marched by. Their marching ability and their military bearing impressed him. When soldiers of the 34th Infantry Division passed, Patton thought they looked sharp, but lamented, "Our men do not put up a good show in reviews. I think we still lack pride in being soldiers, and we must develop it." While he was pleased with the parade and the victory, he still worried about the soldiers' performance before he took command, particularly in places like Kasserine Pass, where so many men surrendered without a fight. "This surrender business must stop," he wrote Beatrice the next day. "I am going to do a little shooting next time I get hold of some surrenderers."[41]

When Eisenhower called Patton to tell him "my American boss will visit you in the morning," Patton snapped back, "When did Mamie arrive?" referring to Eisenhower's wife. Eisenhower was of course talking about Marshall. On June 2 Patton welcomed the chief of staff into his headquarters and briefed him on HUSKY. He even went out of his way to praise Clark, who was there. "I think that if you treat a skunk nicely," Patton confided to his diary, "he will not piss on you—as often."[42] He then brought Marshall, along with Eisenhower and Bradley, to watch Terry Allen's 1st Infantry Division conduct a practice landing. As the soldiers poured out of their landing craft and stormed the beach, Patton noticed some of the men's rifles lacked bayonets. He left the group, walked down to the water's edge, and shouted at the soldiers, "And just where in the hell are your goddamned bayonets?" Pink Bull, Eisenhower's operations officer, who was reviewing the demonstration with the generals, nodded at Marshall and whispered to Bradley, "Well, there goes George's chance for a crack at higher command. That temper of his will finish him yet." Even though Bradley and Eisenhower were familiar with Patton's outbursts, neither they nor Marshall said anything.[43]

Despite his busy planning and training schedule, for some reason Patton felt compelled to write an eleven-page essay on "The Arab," an extremely racist view of the typical North African male. He opened by calling them "bath-robed beggars," explaining that the famous Arab dignity was really just "pure dumbness . . . the eyes have no depth." He credited the dumbness to a life of leading slow-moving donkeys around the countryside, which "has reduced his mental reactions to a similar pace." Adding to this slowness was his penchant for wrapping his head "with a bandage and then pulls on a hood," thereby reducing his hearing and vision. Patton did compliment their ability to relax, to lie down and sleep anywhere between the hours of noon and two.

It got worse. "In common with so many so-called backward races," Patton started one paragraph, "the Arab has no fixed meal hours." He delved into a long diatribe about the North Africans' inability to plow fields in groups because everyone wanted to go a different way. He associated the locals with the animals they tended, be they sheep, camels, or burros, since all of them were equally illiterate, sitting for hours, gazing vacantly into space. He criticized the treatment of women as a "factor tending to retard the racial development," since they were degraded, uneducated, and ugly. "Arab women are prettier when you do not see their faces." He also claimed that they did not use toilets, since he had never seen one doing so, concluding that not doing so attracted flies as well as invited the plague, cholera, and dysentery. He ended the essay asking if Arabs would be so backwards if they became Christians. "Here I think is a text for some eloquent sermon on the virtues of Christianity."[44]

Patton held many of the same prejudices felt by many other American and European whites of his time: that white men ruled the world and that Jews, Blacks, and Hispanics were of lesser breeding. He could get along with people of different races and religions as individuals, as long as they knew their place, but as groups, they fell into generally accepted stereotypes. Whereas most whites possessed what historian Martin Blumenson referred to as "Gentleman's Club prejudices," Patton was open about those he harbored, expressing them outrightly in his essays, verbal outbursts, diary entries, and letters. He often used offensive racial slurs in his letters to Beatrice.[45]

Yet, when Patton wrote on military topics, his mind focused on practical matters. Here he was in his element, accepting no other views but his own. This world he understood from training and hard experience. He filled a June 5 letter of instruction to his corps and divisions with wisdom obtained from the battlefield and inspirational maxims. "There is only one sort of discipline," the letter opened, "perfect discipline." He scorned officers who failed to correct errors or praise excellence, proclaiming them "valueless in peace and dangerous misfits in war." He implored officers to "assert themselves by example and by voice" and believed that those soldiers who did not salute "will fall easy victim to the enemy."

The tactics he promoted were, according to Patton, "as old as war. Catch the enemy by the nose with fire and kick him in the pants with fire emplaced through movement." He called the M1 rifle "the most deadly small arm in the word" and praised American artillery and mortars. "When silent they are junk—see that they fire!" He stressed fear as an important factor on the battlefield and urged that it be used as a weapon: "Fear is induced by inflicting death and wounds. . . . Death and wounds are produced by fire. Fire from the rear is more deadly and three times more effective than fire from the front." To press that fear, he ordered all soldiers to keep their bayonets sharpened. To his own troops he preached, "Never take counsel of your fears. The enemy is more worried than you are." He called soldiers who surrendered with a weapon in their hands fools and cowards. "If they fight on, they will conquer. If they surrender, they will starve. . . . Cowardice must be ruthlessly eliminated." He boiled down the advice to a few sentences: "A good solution applied with vigor *now* is better than a perfect solution ten minutes later[. . .] In case of doubt, attack! [. . .] Oral orders will be repeated back [. . .]," and "Minefields, while dangerous, are not impassable."

He included fourteen points on amphibious landings, learned from Operation TORCH. They included such insights as: "Speed and ruthless violence on the beach is vital. [. . .] To linger on the beach is fatal. [. . .] In landing operations, retreat is impossible," and "Above all else, the assault must push on relentlessly to its objective. You know where you are going; the enemy does not." No detail was too minute for Patton. He ordered that all vehicles should cross the beach in second gear and that all vehicles going ashore should have their tire pressure recorded, since low pressure was best for dealing with sand dunes. He concluded the letter by stating, "We can conquer only by attacking."[46]

He preferred well-disciplined troops to well-trained ones. He wrote General Leslie McNair, the commander of Army Ground Forces responsible for the training standards, stressing his favorite topic: discipline. "We must have more discipline, and soldiers and officers must be required to practice it from the first day." He added, "Well-disciplined troops can be easily trained; well-trained troops cannot be so easily disciplined, and without discipline they are worthless in battle."[47]

Despite Patton's intensive training, and the troops' experience gained in North Africa, the British still had their doubts about the Americans in combat. When England's King George VI visited Oran with War Minister Sir Percy James Grigg to inspect the troops, Grigg told Patton that Alexander had told him that "American troops will shortly be the best soldiers in the world." Patton snapped back that, "at present the American soldiers *are* the best soldiers in the world." An embarrassed Grigg replied, "That is what I meant." Patton later wrote of the incident, "Although this may sound impolite, it is the only way to talk to an Englishman." After watching training exercises, Grigg admitted to Patton that the American troops learned quicker than their British counterparts.[48]

The British were not the only ones doubtful of the American army's fighting prowess. A German psychological study of the Western Allies at the time showed Americans to be poor fighters. "The American soldiers, too, are considered by our troops to be the worst possible," German propaganda minister Joseph Goebbels penned in his diary after reading the report. "Not only because of the fact that the American soldiers have had no combat experience but also that they are not cut out to be soldiers." Patton would have to prove the minister wrong.[49]

In mid-June, Brigadier General Albert Wedemeyer, from Marshall's War Plans Division, arrived to observe Patton's command. Patton welcomed Wedemeyer and handed him the plan for Sicily. An impressed Wedemeyer later wrote of Patton: "Emotional, and with a tremendous capacity for dynamic action, Patton was an unusual type of military man who was not only physically courageous but also possessed the rare quality which Germans call 'civil courage.' He dared to speak his mind and act according to his convictions. . . . He had a scholarly bent and a profound knowledge of strategy, tactics and military and political techniques. He had studied the campaigns of von Schlieffen and Frederick the Great and was more interested in them than in Napoleon's campaigns, which were far more familiar to most American staff officers."[50] Wedemeyer would later describe Patton as impetuous and vitriolic, but he was pleased Patton had picked Geoffrey Keyes as his deputy commander to balance his own wilder personality. Wedemeyer considered Keyes calm, deliberate, and circumspect. "The latter appears to have good judgment and is certainly an anecdote to Patton's impulsive tendencies."[51]

The Allied commanders held a review of operations aimed at the Gulf of Gela on June 21. As usual, Patton came away distrustful of his superiors. He felt Alexander's attitude toward preventing friendly fire deaths too casual; that Eisenhower's airborne advisor, British major general Frederick Browning, would deny him using the entire 82nd Airborne Division in the initial assault; and that no one would provide a definite plan for the airborne division's flight route and altitude. "I still feel sure we will get double crossed," he wrote in his diary. After lunch, the major commanders presented their plans. Not all of them did well. Admiral Hewitt, who would again deliver Patton to the battlefield, forgot his maps. Tedder fell asleep during one of the presentations. Air Marshal Coningham droned on without making any definitive statements. Then it was Patton's turn. Accepting a recommendation by Keyes, Patton only spoke for only six minutes. Four of his staff officers followed and went into detail. The entire presentation lasted only twenty-two minutes and thirty seconds, only thirty seconds longer than rehearsal. "We stole the show by using the War College method," Patton wrote. "Ike was pleased, and, for a change, said so."[52]

While the review may have made Patton distrustful of his superiors, he upheld his standing with the Allied forces. A few days earlier, a French colonel named Chauvin made Patton an honorary member of the 2ème Règiment de Marche Tirailleurs Algèriens. The colonel offered to bequeath the same honor on two other officers of Patton's choosing. Patton picked Bradley and Gaffey and asked if he could add Dick Jenson posthumously, which they granted. After a parade and inspection, they were all issued a Legion of Honor, with the French referring to Jenson as "dead on the field of honor."[53]

The final plan for Seventh Army's initial assault involved an airborne drop followed by a three-division amphibious assault. Colonel James Gavin's 505th Parachute Infantry Regiment, reinforced by a battalion

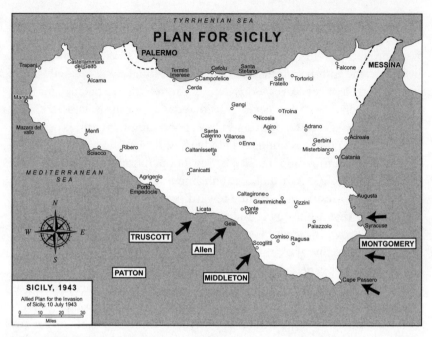

Map 4. Plan for Sicily, 1943.

of Colonel Reuben Tucker's 504th, both from Major General Matthew Ridgway's 82nd Airborne Division, would drop between 11:30 p.m. and midnight of July 9. Without enough C-47 cargo planes, Patton, as predicted, would not get the entire division to drop together. Once on the ground, the paratroopers would capture the high ground of Piano Lupo to block enemy forces headed south against the 1st Infantry Division. Their secondary mission was to cover the Ponte Olivo airfield, to make it easier for capture by the amphibious forces.[54]

The amphibious landings would hit the beaches at 2:45 a.m. and would be, from north to south: Truscott's 3rd Infantry Division, supported by Army Rangers and some tanks from Gaffey's 2nd Armored Division around the town of Licata; Allen's 1st Infantry Division, also supported by Rangers, around the town of Gela; and Major General Troy Middleton's 45th Infantry Division near the town of Scoglitti. Patton hoped to capture the three coastal towns and airfields and link up with the British in three days. D-Day was set for July 10. Combined with Montgomery's four-division assault and a single airborne brigade drop on the southeastern side of the island, Operation HUSKY would be the largest and most dispersed amphibious assault of the war.[55] Patton was proud of the plan, yet remained humble about the complex operation. When General Alexander asked him if he was satisfied with the plans, Patton clicked his heels, saluted, and responded: "General, I don't plan—I only obey orders."[56]

Follow-up forces included the rest of Gaffey's 2nd Armored Division, Eddy's 9th Infantry Division, and the 4th Moroccan Tabor of Goums, a French battalion commanded by French officers and noncommissioned officers with Berber Goumiers (indigenous Moroccans) as the fighting troops. Ironically, Patton had specifically requested the Goums from Eisenhower, despite his critical essay about Arabs. They had fought in Tunisia, possibly impressing Patton. Eisenhower quickly approved the Goum battalion, allowing them to train with Seventh Army.[57]

While Patton would lead four veteran divisions, he would also command two new ones: the 82nd Airborne Division and 45th Infantry Division. Major General Matthew Ridgway commanded the 82nd, which would be making the Army's first large-scale airborne assault. A West Point graduate of 1917, Ridgway had served as a Spanish instructor at his alma mater instead of overseas in World War I. During the interwar years he had served in China, Nicaragua, and the Philippines. He was working in the War Plans Division when the war broke out and later became the 82nd's deputy commander, then commander in August of 1942 when the division commander, Omar Bradley, departed. The 45th was a National Guard unit commanded by Troy Middleton, who enlisted in the U.S. Army and had served in both the Punitive Expedition against Pancho Villa and World War I, where he fought as the youngest colonel in the American army. He had retired in 1935 and became the dean of administration, as well as comptroller and acting vice president of Louisiana State University. After Pearl Harbor he was recalled to duty.[58]

Patton visited his green divisions to offer support and advice. He told the paratroopers, "Now, I want you to remember that no son of a bitch ever won a war by dying for his country. He did it by making the other poor, dumb son of a bitch die for his country." He told them to avoid direct assaults on the Germans and Italians and instead envelop their flanks, likening the tactic to sex. He warned the men that as they approached the enemy's rear, the enemy would try to change positions to protect itself. Some of the men loved it, while others were quite embarrassed. He may have missed the mark when he tried to use historical examples to inspire, telling the men "You're pissing through the same straw as Caesar." The men interpreted "straw" as a sipping straw, whereas Patton—the old cavalryman—was referring to hay.[59] After the speech, a paratrooper asked Patton his secret for leading American soldiers. With a twinkle in his eye, he replied, "I have a surefire formula. First, I take the American soldiers and dress him up till he's proud of being a soldier. Then I get behind him and give him a swift kick."[60]

The next day, he visited the 45th Infantry Division and had the men gather around him. He told them he wanted them to be tough: "If the enemy can go one day without water, you go two. If he can go two days without food, you go three. Kill all you can."[61] He cautioned them not to fall for the German trick of throwing down their weapons and surrendering, waiting for Americans to reveal themselves, thereby cueing other, concealed Germans to spring up and fire at the exposed Americans. He warned the men to be alert and, if the Germans employed this tactic, to show no mercy.[62] He also told them to continue advancing, even if the enemy brought them under fire and comrades fell. The only important thing was to keep on advancing. If the men could get within two hundred yards of the enemy, "he shall not live." If the enemy sniped at them from the rear, "you must kill him if you can." Patton then went into detail: "Stick him between the third and fourth ribs. You will tell your men that. They must have the killer instinct. Tell them to stick him. He can do no good then. Stick them in the liver. We will get the name of killers and killers are immortal. When word reaches him that he is being faced by a killer battalion, a killer outfit, he will fight less. Particularly, we must build up that name as killers and you will get that down to your troops in time for the invasion."[63] During an inspection, Middleton asked Patton if he would rather invade Europe with more experienced troops. Patton, ever the motivator, told Middleton, "I would rather be into Europe with these troops than to be Jesus Christ himself."[64]

Patton's voice carried a different tone when visiting his veteran units. Standing on the back of a tank carrier, with General Manton Eddy at his side, he told the officers of the 9th Infantry Division that because they were so experienced, he had nothing to tell them and then went into an explanation of the importance of shooting, killing, and using the bayonet. He told them that Americans were the most adventurous people of all races and compared war to a giant athletic competition, in which, he assured them, "the Americans will live up to their reputation for always winning when the going gets hard. Don't sell America short!" When he told the men not to take prisoners, Eddy tugged him on the sleeve and said, "General, I think you should rethink what you just said." Patton looked up: "Forget what I just said." The men would not. The many 9th Infantry soldiers wearing Purple Hearts impressed him. "That is a great division," he later wrote Beatrice.⁶⁵

Even when his troops were not at war, he wanted them to act as if they were. When he pulled up to a 3rd Infantry tent and beckoned an officer to come over, the man started walking to Patton's command car. Suddenly Patton exploded. "You son-of-a-bitch! When I tell you to come, I want you to run." When the officer told Patton he resented being called a son-of-a-bitch and felt he was owed an apology, Patton quickly acquiesced and apologized.⁶⁶ Later, while observing a 3rd Infantry Division night assault, he managed to spot in the darkness a group of lieutenant colonels and colonels gathered behind a large dune. "What the hell are you doing!?" he yelled in his high-pitched voice as he thrust his face right up the helmet visor of one of the colonels. "Why . . . why, I'm an observer, sir." The colonel stammered. "Well, then goddammit, get off your big fat ass and observe!"⁶⁷ Still, the visit was better than what the 1st Infantry experienced. Taking a break from their village infiltration drills, the men assembled in formation as Patton's command car rolled up with sirens wailing. Patton's riding boots and britches and his three-starred helmet impressed the men. But Patton's vehicle never stopped. Without a word, Patton's vehicle rolled on, leaving one of the men to crack, "Yeah, your guts and our blood." Patton may have been reacting to reports that the soldiers in the unit spent their off hours drinking hard and destroying villages in drunken rages.⁶⁸

Having done everything in his power to hone the soldiers into shape to yield a victory, Patton then turned to the Navy. To ensure the American fleet arrived at the correct beaches, the Royal Navy assigned three British S-class submarines to act as surface markers, providing the assault forces a final check on their run into shore. Patton personally addressed the commander the HMS *Seraph*, Captain Norman Jewell, ordering him in brusque terms that the submarines had to hold their positions throughout the period of darkness, until the American fleet came into view. Patton was taking no chances.⁶⁹

With the planning completed, Colonel Henriques, Patton's British liaison officer, suggested reloading the transports to make their assault more efficient. Patton gave the idea serious consideration but decided against it on the grounds that it would have changed the way his force had been training for months. Henriques later admitted his plan had been overly pessimistic.[70]

As the date of the invasion drew near, Patton penned "God of Battles," a sort of warrior's prayer for combat.

> From pride and foolish confidence,
> From every waking creed,
> From the dread fear of fearing
> Protect us, Lord, and lead.
>
> Great God, who through the ages
> Hast braced the bloodstained hand
> As Saturn, Jove, or Woden
> Hast led our warrior band.
>
> Again we seek Thy counsel,
> But not in cringing guise.
> We whine not for Thy mercy—
> To slay: God make us wise.
>
> For slaves who shun the issue
> We do not ask Thy aid.
> To Thee we trust our spirits,
> Our bodies unafraid.
>
> From doubt and fearsome 'boding.
> Still Thou our spirits guard,
> Make strong our souls to conquer,
> Give us the victory, Lord.[71]

Patton began his final staff meeting in Oran with a pep talk. He explained that the Navy, Air Force, and corps commanders all knew their exact missions, and that Montgomery and his Eighth Army were coordinating things in Algiers, because "I didn't want them down here messing things up!" Everyone laughed. Then he grabbed his invasion maps and headed for the attack transport *Monrovia*. On board, he bet Rear Admiral Alan Kirk a quart of Scotch that it would take the Navy eight days to completely unload all their transport ships. Kirk said he could do it quicker than that.[72]

With the plan set and his forces assembling, Patton exercised and went to the movies. On July 4, he flew to his old headquarters at Mostaganem and met with some of his commanders in nearby Oran. Flying back to Algiers, a storm closed in, so he sent word to the pilot that if it got worse, to turn back. "This is, as far as I know," he later admitted in his diary, "the only time I have ever publicly showed timidity." He rationalized by explaining he did not want to miss out on the next battle.[73] Eisenhower worried that Patton, in his aggressive mindset, would personally try to land with the first wave going ashore. To prevent this, he had Hughes talk to General John P. Lucas, who would accompany Patton for the journey to Sicily and tell him to keep Patton off the beach. Lucas agreed, but Hughes, knowing how stubborn Patton could be, stressed that if he tried to go ashore before control was established, Lucas should invoke Eisenhower's name to keep him onboard ship.[74]

On July 5, only four days before the invasion, Patton, Ridgway, and Gay went to say a final word to Eisenhower. It did not go well. Eisenhower, obviously stressed over the upcoming campaign, as well as a *LIFE* magazine article critical of his leadership in North Africa, criticized Patton for the 1st Infantry Division's poor discipline. Patton told him it was wrong to whip a dog just before putting him into a fight. When Eisenhower told Patton he was a great leader but a poor planner, Patton told him that, besides Operation TORCH, he had never been given a chance to plan anything. They discussed the *LIFE* article and its accusation that American troops had moved too slowly. Patton later wrote, "At no time did Ike wish us luck or say he was [in] back of us—fool."[75]

The next day, Patton boarded the *Monrovia*. At 8:10 that morning the word went out: "Let go all lines," and the fleet began to pull out of the harbor. Patton was relieved because he worried that the enemy could easily attack the moored fleet. "Why the Boche don't bomb this place is a mystery to me as the ships are five and six feet deep."[76] The 590-ship fleet was in fact so large that the *Monrovia* did not slip out of the harbor until sunset.[77] Patton was off to his second invasion, but this time he was an experienced commander in charge of mostly veteran units. "Only God and the Navy can do anything until we hit the shore," he confided in his diary. Admiral Hewitt conducted a brief ceremony for Patton, presenting him with a Seventh Army flag. The fire in Patton's eyes impressed one sailor. "It was to him not a ship's deck he stood upon," explained the sailor, "but a peak of glory." Back in his cabin, Patton worried that the invasion would somehow be halted now that it was underway, but he had made up his mind: "We will not be stopped."[78]

Figure 23. Aboard the USS *Monrovia*, bound for Sicily, Patton and Brigadier General Hap Gay unfurl the new Seventh Army flag while Major General Geoffrey Keyes folds the II Corps flag. Catalog number: 111-SC 189376, National Archives and Records Administration.

Patton sought out one of the ship's famous crew members, movie-star-turned-lieutenant-commander Douglas Fairbanks Jr., and asked him to read over his message to the assault troops to see if it would "play." Fairbanks studied the script with a critical eye while Patton fidgeted. Fairbanks finally gave the script his approval with no changes.[79] On board the other 589 ships, officers read aloud Patton's order: "We are indeed honored in having been selected by Gen. Dwight D. Eisenhower as the American component on this new and greater attack against the Axis." He praised the British Eighth Army and Alexander (somehow, he omitted General Montgomery). "When we land," he continued, "we will meet German and Italian soldiers whom it is our honor and privilege to attack and destroy." He acknowledged the European heritage of many of the soldiers but warned that "the ancestors of the people we shall kill lacked the courage to make such a sacrifice and continued as slaves." He closed by stressing the importance of staying on the offensive: "Remember that we as attackers have the initiative. We must retain this tremendous advantage by always attacking: rapidly, ruthlessly, viciously, without rest. However tired and hungry you may be, the enemy will be more tired, more hungry, keep punching. God is with us. We shall win."

With that, the word went out about the destination: Sicily! Soldiers were relieved to at least know where they were going. Maps and plans and aerial photographs were issued, and the men began studying their new battleground. Once the destination was known, reporters tried to get interviews with Patton, but he refused. He wanted the attention on the men going ashore.[80] To his staff, he explained that other officers might prefer fishing, farming, or other pursuits, but "I don't—I look forward to fighting, here, in Japan, or at home, for there rest of my days." He admitted to being a bit anxious, but "I would not change places with anyone I know right now."[81]

The four-day voyage to Sicily's southern coast was uneventful. Patton spent the time reading novels, praying, taking photographs, and discussing strategies with his staff. He penned a letter to Hughes, thanking him for "meals, drinks and night landings." Indeed, Patton had spent many a day at Hughes's office, drinking his gin and bitters, "the supply of which," Hughes complained to his wife, "is getting low due to George's repeated visits."[82] Patton had written a letter to Beatrice, to be mailed to her after the invasion commenced, predicting the invasion would be "a pretty bloody show especially on the ships." Along with the sunken ships, he foresaw a German counterattack. He doubted he would be killed and radiated the confidence of a veteran fighter, writing, "We have licked better and more numerous troops than those we will incounter [sic]." He concluded by telling her, "When you get this you will either be a widow or a radio fan, I trust the latter. In either case I love you."[83]

As the fleet completed its journey a storm rose in the Mediterranean on July 9, threatening to scatter the initial assault craft and delay the invasion until daylight hours. Would the airborne be able to jump in the high winds? Would the landing craft be launched and loaded in heavy swells? Would the invasion be delayed?[84] Patton worried that the rough weather would at least make his men seasick. He called for a chaplain and the two prayed together. The fleet stayed on course through the storm, but the Luftwaffe detected it and sent word of the approaching armada. The Italian high command placed Sicily on high alert. As the fleet approached in the darkness, Allied bombers struck Italian command installations.[85]

That night, Patton called his staff and other officers into his room for a brief ceremony. The I Armored Corps flag was taken down and replaced with the Seventh Army flag. "We become the Seventh Army at one minute after midnight," reported Gay. Before the sun rose the next day, Patton would again be commanding Americans in battle.[86]

CHAPTER EIGHT

Fighting from Gela to Palermo

GAVIN'S PARATROOPERS SPEARHEADED the invasion. All thirty-four hundred of them had loaded onto 226 C-47 transports at sundown and taken off at 8:30 p.m., July 9, bound for the island of Malta, where they were to turn north for the run to Sicily. But the pilots could not find Malta in the misty clouds and were forced to fly blind for part of their journey. Some of the pilots gave up on trying to find Sicily and returned their planes to base with full loads. The planes that did make it encountered enemy ground fire. In the confusion, they dropped their paratroopers wherever possible, widely dispersing them along the southern coast. Once on the ground, the paratroopers gathered themselves up, searched for comrades, and headed for bridges, high ground, or anywhere they heard gunfire.[1]

Patton stayed up that night on the *Monrovia*, sitting at a small table in his underwear, reading the Bible by flashlight. At 3:30 a.m. General Wedemeyer, in full battle gear, knocked on his door. He bid farewell to Patton and thanked him for his hospitality as he prepared to depart with the first assault wave. Patton teared up and told him he appreciated his help. He shook Wedemeyer's hand and told him to be very careful. "If anything happens to you," Patton said, "General Marshall will give me hell." With that, Patton went to bed for a few hours.[2]

The planes flying over the *Monrovia* on July 10 did not wake Patton, but a broken davit banging against the ship did. He donned a khaki uniform and leather bomber jacket and made his way to the bridge. The shoreline burned brightly as landing boats churned into the darkness. Searchlights in the distance pierced the night sky as mortars and rockets smashed into targets. Sicily and uncertainty lay ahead. "We may feel anxious," Patton reasoned, "but I trust the Italians are scared to death." Just as in

153

Operation TORCH, Patton would be virtually powerless until his troops made it ashore and his officers set up communications with the flagship. It would again be Hewitt's war until Patton stepped foot on Gela beach.[3]

The Luftwaffe bombed the fleet around 5:00 a.m., sinking the destroyer USS *Maddox*. American fighter planes soon arrived and tangled with the enemy. Despite difficulties caused by the weather and a shifting sandbar off the beach, the 1st and 45th Infantry Divisions landed and captured their objectives before sunrise, the 3rd Infantry following soon thereafter. Navy destroyers sailed to within a mile of the beaches, firing on enemy targets. Army Rangers overcame enemy machinegun nests and pill boxes in Gela so quickly that they ran into Navy covering fire. At 6:00 a.m. Lieutenant Colonel William O. Darby radioed Patton that Gela had been taken. Three hours later, Patton heard over the radio that thirty enemy tanks were attacking Allen's 1st Infantry. The paratroopers had failed to capture the Piano Lupo heights, allowing the Germans a route of attack. The Navy cruiser USS *Boise* shelled the enemy lines. Patton also wanted fighter planes to strafe the area, but they were not yet over the battlefield. Throughout the day, Navy anti-aircraft gunners fired wildly into the air at both friend and foe. By the afternoon, Patton ordered Gaffey to land most of his 2nd Armored Division at Gela and await further orders. He postponed a second airborne drop scheduled for later that day to the following night, so that he could focus on getting his armor ashore.[4] Communications with troops soon broke down. Much of the communication equipment was insufficiently waterproofed for the rough weather; only two of II Corps' hourly reports reached the *Monrovia*. While communications would improve, Patton initially relied on messengers going from ship to shore during his opening moves on Gela.[5]

Before the sun went down, the Luftwaffe attacked again, this time sinking an empty LST. But the news of the day was mostly positive. The beaches had been taken, objectives had been secured, casualties were low, and Patton's men had captured more than one thousand prisoners. There was no word from the paratroopers except from one unit that had linked up with 1st Infantry. Patton was so busy coordinating armor, naval, and air support that he never left the *Monrovia*. "I feel like a cur," he lamented in his diary, "but I probably did better here."[6] That night the Luftwaffe returned a third time. A series of bombs exploded in the water near the *Monrovia* as Patton entered his cabin. "Let's get off this damn ship the first thing in the morning," he told his staff. Another

CHAPTER EIGHT ★ FIGHTING FROM GELA TO PALERMO

succession of bombs burst nearby. "If this thing is still afloat." With that, he went to bed.⁷

The next morning, with Luftwaffe bombs still falling around his ship, Patton put on a khaki uniform with puffy, Jodhpur trousers and polished cavalry boots, strapped on his Colt revolver, binoculars, and camera, and grabbed his riding crop. To get more troops onto the beach, he ordered the 82nd Airborne's 504th Parachute Infantry Regiment to drop behind the 1st Division's zone. He then warned his principal commanders that paratroopers would jump about 11:30 that night.⁸

Figure 24. A cigar clenched in his teeth, Patton climbs over the *Monrovia*'s side to a waiting landing craft. Catalog number: 208-PU-153H-26, National Archives and Records Administration.

Patton boarded his landing craft with his staff and Ridgway for the half-hour trip to the beach. He waded ashore, chomping on a cigar. Equipment cluttered the beach as soldiers and seamen wrestled to free beached landing craft. Patton could hear machinegun and heavy weapons fire and saw a row of dead soldiers, attesting to the previous day's intense fighting. Geysers from enemy shells erupted in the water and artillery exploded on the beach, impeding unloading operations and killing civilians. "It's all right, Hap," Patton told Hap Gay. "The bastards can't hit us on account of the defilade afforded by the town."⁹ At the sight of Patton, some men climbed out of their foxholes and charged across the dunes at the Germans. A reporter later wrote, "I saw, for the first time, just how a brave general can turn the tide of battle by sheer leadership."¹⁰ General Ridgway took off on foot to find his paratroopers while Patton waited for his vehicle to be de-waterproofed. While he waited, an African American soldier greeted him and reminded him that they first met when Patton was a lieutenant at Fort Riley, Kansas. The soldier had gone AWOL just to take part in Patton's invasion.

Figure 25. Patton gives direction on Gela beach. The African American soldier had gone AWOL from his unit to be with Patton during the invasion. Catalog number: 208-PU-15YE-1, National Archives and Records Administration.

Patton drove down the coast road, looking for General Allen's headquarters. Propaganda slogans covered building walls, for example, "The sacrifice faced by the Italian people in Africa is an immense service rendered to civilization and world peace." When Patton spotted a flag on the side of the road designating a Ranger command post, he ordered his driver to pull over. It was a fortuitous move—if he had continued, he would have driven smack into seven advancing enemy tanks. The Italian 4th Infantry Livorno and the German Hermann Goering divisions were counterattacking to drive Patton's army into the sea. While the Italians were equipped with early-war French and Italian light tanks, the Germans possessed modern Mark IVs and Tiger tanks.[11] Patton found Lieutenant Colonel Darby just as the attack commenced, cutting off his Rangers from Allen's 1st Infantry Division. As Darby and his men placed their 4.2mm mortars, Patton asked from which direction was the enemy attacking. Darby quickly responded, "Which one do you want to see, General Patton?"[12] The enemy was all around. Patton helped place the mortars and even fired one. The phosphorous shells devastated the attackers, who rushed forward with their hands over their heads. "I was scared as hell," Patton later admitted.[13]

Patton then climbed the stairs of an apartment from which he could see Italian soldiers advancing across open ground toward Gela. "Can I help you sir?" asked a young naval ensign who was busy directing fire from the USS *Savanna*. "Sure," responded Patton, "if you can connect with your Goddamn Navy, tell them for God's sake to drop some shellfire on that road." The ensign went back to work as Patton grabbed his field glasses and stepped out onto the veranda, where German and Italian soldiers fired at him, forcing the ensign to temporarily evacuate the observation post. American naval and mortar fire, combined with two captured Italian artillery pieces and the Rangers' stout defense, repelled the Axis attack. As the fighting died down, Patton looked down to see a group of American MPs marching a handful of slovenly looking Italian prisoners to the rear. "Make it double time!" He shouted from his perch. "Kick 'em in the ass! Make it double-time!" The men broke into a trot. When Patton noticed a Ranger captain with his chin strap dangling, he pointed it out, and the officer quickly buckled it. Before he departed, he implored the captain, "Kill every one of the goddamn bastards."[14]

Patton and Darby returned to the latter's headquarters. As they spoke, two German artillery rounds punched a hole in the building across the street, injuring some civilians. "I have never heard so much screaming," Patton recalled later. He contacted the naval commander responsible for the landing force and ordered his tank reserves to land immediately, but the officer refused, explaining he needed orders from Admiral Hewitt. Patton eventually reached Hewitt and secured permission, but the delay caused confusion and stress. Patton's need for armor was finally satisfied when ten tanks arrived from Truscott's 3rd Division in Licata, some twenty miles away, at which point he ordered them to pursue the retreating enemy.[15] He then ordered a pontoon causeway rammed over a series of sandbars, allowing more tanks to race ashore. The rest of the reserve force finally arrived once an LST captain forced his way over several sandbars. Patton directed the tanks to close the gap between the 1st Infantry and the Rangers.

Figure 26. Patton puffs on a cigar outside of Lieutenant Colonel William Darby's Ranger headquarters in Gela. National Archives and Records Administration.

The enemy attack had almost achieved success, as the Germans and Italians pressed their tanks within two thousands yards of the beach. So close was the fighting that the ships had to stop shelling, for fear of killing Americans. The Axis forces had punched holes in both the 1st Infantry and 82nd Airborne lines but were finally halted at Allen's last defensive lines around noon. The attack had cost the Germans heavily. Ten tanks lay in smoking ruins. Once the Germans realized they could not push the Americans into the sea, they withdrew, giving the Navy even more targets. With shells raining down as they retreated, by the end of the day, the Germans had lost one-third of their tanks and some six hundred men. Additionally, Darby counted five hundred Italian prisoners.[16] When the Americans began feeding them, Patton put a stop to it, telling the men that rations would be limited until more supplies arrived.[17]

During the fight for Gela, some local children, chased by adults, had dashed to the enemy lines and begun climbing on their weapons, preventing the Americans from returning fire. While planning the campaign, higher headquarters had asked Patton how many military government officers he wanted. He responded, "Not a God damn one of those civilian sissies!" Now he radioed a request to immediately send twenty-five MPs and twenty-five military government officers competent in handling children. He also radioed for air support to bomb the advancing tanks, but the planes did not arrive until five hours after the action.[18]

Before noon during the fighting, the Italians had intercepted a message from Patton ordering his troops on the beach to bury their equipment and to be ready to re-embark. While several Italian officers after the war attested to seeing the message, several people who were with Patton that day had no recollection of him sending any such communique. "I am quite certain Patton did not personally send the message," explained British Colonel Robert Henriques, "but it is quite likely that someone, either in 1st Division or Seventh Army Headquarters, may have sent it when the battle was at its height." Allen did not recall Patton making the decision either: "At no time during his visit did General Patton ever make any mention whatsoever of any re-embarkation plans for the 1st Infantry Division or of any other unit in the U.S. Seventh Army."[19]

According to Bradley, Patton's decision to use Allen's 1st Infantry Division to replace the 36th Infantry Division had paid dividends; indeed, Bradley wondered if any other division could have repelled an enemy attack so quickly. "A greener division might easily have panicked and seriously embarrassed the landing," he later wrote.[20] After briefly meeting with General Roosevelt, Patton went to find Gaffey and Allen. Meanwhile, fourteen German bombers roared in and strafed the area. Nearby anti-aircraft batteries opened up and shrapnel rained down on the convoy, one piece of shrapnel landing ten yards from Patton. Two enemy aircraft were shot down. At Allen's headquarters, Patton declared his displeasure that the Ponte Olivo airfield—Allen's objective for the day—remained in enemy hands. Allen reassured him that the day was not over and that he was planning a night attack, "Come hell or high water." Mollified yet skeptical, Patton departed.[21]

Bradley would later angrily confront Patton about the attack on the airfield. He had specifically ordered the attacking unit to hold fast until a pocket of German resistance had been eliminated. Patton's order to Allen directly contradicted Bradley's, thereby violating the chain of command. Worse, Patton had neglected to inform him about it. Patton later apologized, but Bradley still considered Patton's move reckless. Bradley's poor health may have contributed to his sour mood. On the journey from Tunisia, he had undergone hemorrhoid surgery and had to use a flotation device as a pillow when driving around Sicily's rough terrain.[22]

On the way back to Gela, Patton marveled that he could drive parallel to the front without coming under fire. While it made him feel lonely, it still boosted his confidence: "It is good for self-esteem," he later wrote. Looking out to sea, he saw the Liberty ship *Robert Rowan* explode and split in two from a Luftwaffe attack. Upon reaching the beach, he gathered some of his staff and asked them to bet on how many days it would take to capture the island. He said eighty, Keyes reckoned ninety, Gay thought one hundred, while Harkins guessed forty-five. Suddenly, Patton noticed some soldiers digging a foxhole between two huge stacks of bombs and high-explosive shells. "I told them if they wanted to save the Graves Registration burials, that was a fine thing to do," he later wrote in his diary, "but otherwise they better dig somewhere else." Just then, two enemy bombers strafed the beach, and the men jumped into their foxhole. The bombers circled and came in for another run. As Patton watched, men unloading landing craft picked up weapons and returned fire. Naval gunfire helped break up the attack. The whole time, Patton strode up and down the beach, ignoring the strafing and barking orders. When a panicked signal officer destroyed a box of signal equipment, Patton ordered him arrested. When he later learned that the officer had been ordered to do so rather than have it fall into enemy hands, he had him released.[23]

Patton made it back to the *Monrovia* soaking wet from the turbulent waves. General Lucas was both happy to see him alive and worried for his health. He thought Patton stood up well under the terrific strain of command. "I would be more irritable than he is," Lucas later wrote.[24] After seeing the Luftwaffe's dominance over the battlefield, the accuracy of anti-aircraft weapons, and the Navy's willingness to fire at anything in the air, Patton cancelled the second airdrop. Unfortunately, the *Monrovia's* radios could not reach Ridgway's headquarters. Worsening matters, the Luftwaffe attacked the fleet around 10:00 p.m., an hour and a half before the 504th was scheduled to fly over. Allied and enemy fighter planes crisscrossed the night sky, dogfighting while dodging anti-aircraft fire from the ships and on the beach. Before he went to bed, Patton penned in his diary, "Am terribly worried."[25]

Patton's apprehension proved prescient. Although the 504th flew into peaceful skies above Sicily, tension and anxiety gripped the Americans on the ground. The first group of paratroopers landed without incident. The second drew fire from a single machine gun on the beach. Soon numerous American anti-aircraft guns on land and sea opened fire. Six aircraft crashed before their paratroopers had a chance to jump. Out of 144 planes, twenty-three never returned and thirty-seven were badly damaged. Eight planes returned to North Africa without having dispatched their loads. The 504th lost 229 men; 81 dead, 132 wounded, and 16 missing, all at the hands of their fellow countrymen.[26] It had been a disaster.

The next morning, July 12, Eisenhower visited Patton onboard the *Monrovia*, where Patton proudly showed him a map of Seventh Army's progress. All his divisions save Allen's 1st, which had blunted the Axis attack, had advanced beyond their objectives, while Middleton's 45th Infantry Division was expected to meet up with a Canadian Division at any moment. In fact, the 1st Infantry may have again saved the beachhead. At midnight, Terry Allen had launched his promised attack, supported by artillery and naval gunfire. The Germans, preparing to attack at dawn, were caught completely by surprise as Allen's division rolled up their lines and captured the Ponte Olivo airfield.[27]

Despite the rosy news, Eisenhower fumed. He scolded Patton about his progress reports, which did not adequately address the help needed, particularly in terms of air cover. Eisenhower did not realize communiqués were running seven hours behind, nor did he know yet about the airdrop disaster. His lecturing done, Eisenhower and his party headed to his launch, escorted by Patton. As Eisenhower motored away, reporter John Gunther, who was with Eisenhower, noticed Patton standing on deck, "looking like a Roman emperor carved in brown stone."[28] The meeting had left Patton embittered. Lucas, who did not hear Eisenhower's words, commented, "He must have given Patton hell because George was much upset."[29] Patton agreed: "It is most upsetting to get only piddling criticism when one knows one has done a good job." Butcher later summed up the tense meeting in his diary: "Ike had stepped on him pretty hard."[30]

Patton resumed leading his army from onboard the *Monrovia* until he departed the ship for good later that afternoon. He headed ashore aboard an LCT, while enemy fighter planes strafed the area. Two were shot down. On shore, as he had done the day before, he checked in with the Rangers and was pleased to learn that they had captured 250 Italian prisoners. He had reason to be proud. The Gela beaches had been taken, and all the American assaults had been successful. Patton then went to his headquarters, which his staff had established in the middle of town in an eight-room house with a backyard patio. It had been owned by a doctor who fled so quickly there were still toothbrushes in the bathroom. Patton's first order was for his staff to clean themselves up. Most had been unable to shave in the pitching seas. They had, almost to a man, lost all their equipment when their landing craft disgorged them in deep water and heavy surf, and they had failed to dig latrines for fear of hitting a landmine. As naval shells rumbled over the house, Patton tried to organize his units. He plugged gaps in the line and sent lost units to their commanders. Keyes called from Truscott's headquarters, and explained that after several running battles with the enemy, the 3rd Infantry Division had spread out. Keyes offered that Truscott could attack Agrigento, on the west coast, or Caltanissetta, directly north, but Patton refused to approve either attack until he heard from Alexander.

But before Patton could contact his British commander, he clashed with his British peer. A British lieutenant showed up at Patton's headquarters carrying a suitcase tied with a string. His presence infuriated Patton, who had earlier sent a liaison team consisting of a colonel, a major, and a communications section in two half-tracks to Montgomery's headquarters. In exchange, Montgomery had sent a single lieutenant. Patton sent the officer back to Montgomery, with a note explaining that he could not permit boys in his headquarters. Instead, Patton requested Colonel Robert Henriques, with whom he had worked so well in Morocco. Henriques arrived and summed up Patton's successful attack: "The Seventh Army plan was straightforward, simple and as ambitious as circumstances of

CHAPTER EIGHT ★ FIGHTING FROM GELA TO PALERMO

craft and shipping allowed. Within the limits of the Allied plan, General Patton had few, if any, alternatives to the course which he adopted."[31] That night, after a dinner of canned cheese and champagne, Patton discovered his bed filled with bedbugs, forcing him to sleep in his bedding roll on the ground.[32]

The next morning, July 13, Patton went to a 1st Infantry Division forward operating post, stomped up to the balcony, and demanded to see what was going on. Just then an artillery shell hit near the building and some forward observers ducked for cover. He bawled the men out for cowering and threatened to arrest them. He then left the building to watch supply ships arriving on the beach below. Colonel James Gavin, the commander of the 505th Parachute Infantry Regiment, who had been fighting nonstop since parachuting in on D-Day, rolled up in a jeep. Patton whipped out his flask. "Gavin, you look like you need a drink. Have one." To Gavin, Patton exuded confidence, and he was proud to see an army commander "in the midst of things." When a German Messerschmitt 109 strafed the beach, Major Stiller opened up with a .50 caliber machine gun, knocking it out of the sky. Patton immediately awarded him a Silver Star for setting an example, encouraging other soldiers and—most important—engaging the enemy and not diving into the sand.[33]

Consistent with his character, Patton continued shaming the soldiers of the 1st Infantry Division throughout the day. When he came across an artilleryman loading a round without his leggings, Patton fined him fifty dollars, even after learning the man's ankles were too swollen to wear them and that he had refused sick call that morning. By that evening, the story made it around the division.[34] Patton had less luck shaming a sergeant he found atop a telephone pole, stringing wire. When Patton asked him if the circling Luftwaffe fighters bothered him, the man snapped back, "Hell, no—but you do." Patton, uncharacteristically, held his tongue.[35]

The Rangers fared better. Patton pinned a Distinguished Service Cross to Lieutenant Colonel Darby's chest for repelling an enemy armored attack on July 11, during which Darby had raced to the beach in a jeep, confiscated a 37mm cannon, returned, and destroyed several tanks. Patton shook Darby's hand and offered him a regiment in the 45th Infantry Division with an immediate promotion to full colonel. "You mean I get a choice, General?" asked Darby. "I'm not used to choices in the army." Patton encouraged him, "There are a thousand colonels in this man's army who would give their right arm for this chance!" Darby's response surprised Patton: "General, thanks anyhow, but I think I better stick with my boys." Patton marveled at the kind of men he had in his army.[36]

With the American beachheads secure and growing, American newspapers praised Patton, claiming him "the first American soldier in Africa under Gen. Dwight D. Eisenhower" and noting that Eisenhower had great confidence in him.[37] That image of two tightly bound generals changed when Eisenhower sent Patton a scorching message about the airborne disaster, reminding him that he had personally requested the airborne drop. Eisenhower raged about the "inexcusable carelessness and negligence on the part of someone." He then ordered Patton to launch an immediate investigation and find the guilty party. He also wanted to know what disciplinary action Patton planned for the culprit. The message rocked Patton. "If anyone is blamable, it must be myself," he wrote in his diary. Yet some anxiety creeped into his writing. "Perhaps Ike is looking for an excuse to relieve me." He launched the investigation, already knowing the culprit: the fog of war. "There were 160 planes over us the day of the 11th and many more during the night," Patton wrote. "Men who have been bombed all day get itchy fingers." Still, he was ready to fall on his sword if the occasion called for it, writing, "If they want a goat, I am it."[38] In Patton's defense, the same thing happened with the second British airdrop. While flying to a bridge over the Simeto River, 124 transport planes encountered friendly fire. Of that number, eleven transports were shot down, twenty-seven returned to base, and twenty-four scattered across the area. Only fifty-six aircraft reached their drop zones. Friendly fire incidents were simply a tragic element of combat.[39]

That afternoon Alexander, Conningham, and their staffs showed up to discuss the situation. Patton took note that the Allied group commander had no Americans on his staff. "What fools we are," he wrote in his diary. When the two British generals laid out the plan of operations, Patton realized that his army had been cut off from any possibility of directly capturing Messina. He requested instead for permission to capture Agrigento with its port—Porto Empedocle. If he took it, he could supply his entire army through the port, no longer relying on the British port at Syracuse. It would also open the door to Palermo in the north. Alexander agreed, so long as Patton could take it with a reconnaissance unit and did not get drawn into a larger battle in the west. With that, Alexander left to see Montgomery.[40]

That night, the Germans weakened their defense in front of Patton when the Hermann Goering Division headed east to halt Montgomery, leaving the 15th Panzer Grenadier Division exposed. Alexander saw this and could have ordered Patton to exploit the gap and possibly drive for the sea, but he made no mention of it to the American general, judging that the Americans could not conduct a bold move of exploitation. He sent a message to General Alan Brooke, the chief of the imperial general staff, that while one of Montgomery's two corps would move to the north coast at San Stefano, the other would drive for Messina. "When the island is spilt in two [by Montgomery]," he concluded, "from north to south American 7th Army will be directed towards Palermo and Trapani [in the west].[41]

Alexander surprised Patton that night with a directive taking away Highway 124, which approached the town of Vizzini from the west, from Seventh Army and making it "all-inclusive to Eighth Army." Montgomery had shifted his own area of responsibility west into Patton's zone and had taken control of the road. Just as Patton had predicted, Montgomery went his own way without regard for Alexander. Stymied south of Catania, Montgomery decided to flank the enemy, despite American forces already occupying the area. In his communiqué to Alexander, Montgomery suggested the American army hold a defensive line facing west, while he swung west from his area, promising "the enemy opposing the Americans will never get away."[42] Patton shook with rage at the slight and pointed out that the move would slow the advance of Middleton's 45th Infantry Division, which would have to retrace its tracks almost to the landing beach. Alexander, understanding all of this, asked Patton if it would be alright. A defeated Patton replied: "Yes, sir." When Henriques told Patton that he should have argued more, Patton shrugged him off, mumbling, "I do what I'm told." One of Patton's officers later complained that the Americans "can sit comfortably on out prats [sic] while Monty finishes the goddamn war."[43]

Suppressing his anger, Patton went to work on a new plan, creating a provisional corps under Keyes consisting of 3rd Infantry, the 82nd Airborne, and a regiment of the 9th Infantry division. He designated the 2nd Armored Division as the corps reserve, which he could use as a breakthrough force once the opportunity arrived. He shifted the 45th

Infantry, which the British had blocked from any advancement, from the right flank of the 1st Infantry to its left. When he explained the plan to Bradley on the morning of July 14, Bradley correctly complained that it was a waste of effort to have a division that was pursuing the enemy pull out of the line, travel behind the front, and realign itself elsewhere. He asked if he could at least use the road to move the 45th. "Sorry Brad," Patton explained, "but the changeover takes place immediately. Monty really wants that road." He then handed Bradley Alexander's communiqué. There was nothing left to discuss.[44] Yet Patton worried that his lack of fortitude with Alexander would cost him his job. "Patton thinks he will be relieved," Lucas wrote as he headed off to report to Eisenhower, "but that is silly of course."[45]

Bradley later wrote that Patton readily accepted Alexander's orders without protest, "like a lamb," but Patton rued the decision. After the Sicilian campaign he complained to Beatrice that Alexander's order was "a fool change of plan" without which he could have taken Messina in ten days, then turned west and captured Palermo, instead of the other way around, which allowed the bulk of the German army to escape.[46] Bradley also suspected that Patton had not protested the order because he did not want to give Eisenhower further reason to relieve him after Eisenhower's criticism of his poor communiqués and the friendly fire incident. Disobeying Alexander would have been Patton's third strike.

Later that day, Patton sailed up to Licata on board the USS *Biscayne*, where he told Truscott to take Agrigento, coordinating with the Navy for heavy fire support. Although Patton had already told Alexander he would capture Agrigento with only a reconnaissance in force, he didn't follow through. Instead, he told Truscott not to push west and risk weakening support of the British. Truscott reassured him that he could take Agrigento without too much trouble if Patton gave him the word, proposing a reconnaissance in force, which, he insisted, Alexander would not care about. Patton had Truscott thinking the way he wanted. He reminded Truscott that the attack had to remain small but insisted that he was "extremely anxious to have that port." Truscott asked Patton's intelligence officer, Colonel Oscar Koch, if the attack on Agrigento would bring on a major engagement. When the officer responded, "No sir," Patton turned to his operations officer and said, "Issue the order."[47] Truscott concluded that Patton was impressed with his idea. "With a cat-that-just-ate-the-canary look," he later wrote, "Patton agreed."[48] Truscott

CHAPTER EIGHT ★ FIGHTING FROM GELA TO PALERMO

then presented Patton with an Italian flag his men had captured in Licata. The two generals unfurled it and admired it. Truscott had done well and accomplished his mission practically alone, while Patton was distracted by the Axis counterattack in Terry Allen's zone. "General Truscott has done a splendid job," Patton later enthused in his diary. He hoped that Truscott's advance, combined with Bradley's, would unite the two forces within five days, allowing him to point the 3rd Infantry and the 2nd Armored toward Palermo. He vowed to bring the idea to Alexander, "when the time is ripe."[49]

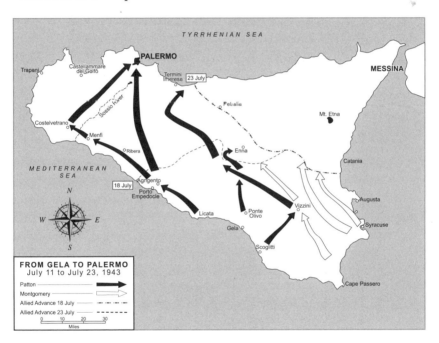

Map 5. From Gela to Palermo, July 11–23, 1943.

Despite the heavy fighting and Patton's seriousness about capturing Agrigento, he kept his sense of humor. The next day, July 15, he visited Darby, who had borrowed some 2nd Armored Division tanks and artillery to support his Rangers' capture the mountain-top town of Butera the day before. Patton was so impressed with Darby's accomplishment that he promised him, "If any dam fool in the 2nd Armored Division will follow you, you can have them in the Rangers." But then he added, "If any one of those guys joins the Rangers, I'm gonna charge them with desertion and insubordination."[50] He later lunched on K-Rations with Brigadier General "Wild" Bill Donovan, the head of the OSS. "You know Bill," Patton told him, "there are two things in life that I love to do—fucking and fighting!" To which Donovan replied, "Yes, George, and in that order too." The two men laughed.[51]

The mood quickly changed when Bradley reported that a captain in the 45th Infantry Division had killed between fifty and seventy prisoners. The captain had claimed he did it because of Patton's order to kill anyone within twenty yards of their positions—Patton's attempt to thwart the German practice of fake surrendering to kill Americans. Feeling the number was exaggerated, he told Bradley to "tell the officer to certify that the dead men were snipers or had attempted to escape, or something like that." Patton worried that the story would reach reporters and make civilians back home angry. "Anyhow, they are dead so nothing can be done about it." He later learned that many of the Germans had indeed been snipers, and that the action could be further justified by the fact that the Germans had been booby trapping their dead by putting live grenades beneath them. It was around this time that Patton began taking pictures of dead Germans. He usually wrote on the back of the photo, "Good Hun" or "Good German." Eventually, he took so many such pictures that he simply labeled them "G. G."[52]

The officer accused of shooting prisoners was Captain John T. Compton, from the 45th Infantry Division's 180th Infantry Regiment. This was his not first incident—he had earlier killed forty-five Italian prisoners on July 14. The Germans had indeed been sniping at the Americans and five of them had been captured wearing civilian clothes. Soon after, Patton would learn of a similar incident. Sergeant Horace T. West, a member of the same regiment, had also killed thirty-six prisoners, mostly Italians and a few Germans, along a road outside of the battle zone. Troy Middleton had already contacted witnesses and asked Bradley and Patton for permission for a trial. Patton approved.[53]

Meanwhile, that same day, Colonel Henriques visited Eighth Army headquarters, where Montgomery derisively told him, "Tell Patton, that when he gets to the north coast, he's not to go towards Palermo, but is to face east—better say 'right,' then he'll understand." Montgomery could not have been more condescending had he tried. "He's not to get in my way but is to make faces and draw off the Germans from my front." Henriques used more diplomatic terms when he relayed Montgomery's message to Patton.[54]

Despite Henriques's careful wording, the idea that he could not take Palermo bothered Patton so much that he could not sleep that night. He woke up Henriques at 3:00 a.m. and asked him about the chances of being officially denied Palermo. Henriques let his guard down and recited Montgomery's exact message. Patton flew into a rage. Henriques tried to appease him by explaining that Montgomery's chief of staff, General Frederick de Guingand, recommended that Patton follow Montgomery's policy of ignoring any orders from Alexander. "Whether this is in good faith or as a bait I do not know," Patton noted in his diary. "Nice people."[55] In retaliation, Patton ordered the rest of Eddy's 9th Infantry Division to head for Sicily. In addition, he sent Lucas to see Alexander to make sure he could still aim for Palermo and not remain "pinned down to the tails of the Eighth Army." As long as Alexander did not forbid Patton taking Palermo, that's where he would go. He planned to meet with Alexander the next day, June 17.[56]

When General Lucas later brought Alexander's decision to Eisenhower and explained that the Americans were being put in a secondary role, Eisenhower defended Alexander's assessment of American inexperience, telling Lucas, "Alexander should not be blamed for being too cautious" with two new inexperienced American divisions. Then Eisenhower turned around and ordered Lucas "to see that Patton was made to realize that he must stand up to Alexander," adding, "He would not hesitate to relieve him from command if he did not do so."[57] Patton's intuition proved right. Eisenhower's leadership here was lacking. He had reprimanded Patton before the invasion and on its second day. Now he refused to step into a critical situation that would cost lives. He was ordering Patton to do something he himself refused to do, something that Eisenhower, with his rank and position, would have accomplished more readily than Patton, an army commander subordinate to an army group commander. When Eisenhower and Smith praised Bradley and Truscott for their performance, Lucas admitted, "I don't see what this is based on" and concluded, "I think many people are jealous of Patton."[58]

While Patton prepared for his meeting with Alexander, he still had a war to fight. Near Comiso, Patton claimed that he "smelled the dead men for some ten miles, it is a very strong and disgusting odor."[59] Yet his men were still having trouble receiving air support. He personally complained to Air Marshal Philip Wigglesworth, the deputy air commander-in-chief at Mediterranean Air Command, that air support during enemy counterattacks was too slow. On average, it took sixty to eighty minutes for a fighter plane to respond to a request for support. By the time it did, any ground element could be overrun. Patton wanted an aircraft carrier available for his operations, like the marines had in the Pacific, to shorten the flight time. As Wigglesworth left, Patton bet him a bottle of whiskey that he would be in Palermo before midnight on July 23.[60]

As the day wore on, Bradley reported that the Germans were counterattacking the 1st Division. Patton could hear gunfire but noticed it was not intensifying. Believing the crisis could be handled, Patton sent Keyes and promised Bradley he would reinforce him with the 3rd Infantry and 2nd Armored, even though he knew the 3rd was on its rogue mission to capture Agrigento. When Keyes radioed back, "Fire out; damage not over $10.00," Patton knew he could shift his focus back to Agrigento and Palermo.[61] That night, Alexander made Montgomery's desires official when he radioed Patton specific orders that Montgomery was to "drive the enemy into the Messina Peninsula" and that "Seventh Army will protect the rear of Eighth Army."[62] It was a humiliating order.

The next day, July 17, before Patton could fly to Alexander's headquarters in Tunis, Alexander wired him, reiterating the new plan for Seventh Army to protect Montgomery's rear, but he assured Patton that he could seize Agrigento, "if it entails no heavy fighting."[63] Patton was furious about supporting Eighth Army, or as he saw it, "putting the Americans in a secondary role." Soon, he received word that Truscott had taken Agrigento and Port Empedocle in light combat. The Navy cruisers *Philadelphia* and *Brooklyn* had bombarded the hills around the town, resulting in hundreds of white sheets and pillowcases billowing from people's homes and businesses as signs of surrender.[64] Patton now had a port to supply his drive. He flew to Alexander's headquarters to discuss strategic ideas, later noting, "A general sitting in Tunis certainly cannot judge the reactions of an Italian on a mountain in Sicily."

At the meeting, a furious Patton told Alexander the American people would not understand why the victorious Seventh Army should be suddenly stopped cold and relegated to playing second fiddle to Montgomery.[65] But Alexander held firm. Lucas, who was present at the meeting, considered Alexander's attempt to belittle the Americans' efforts "an act of deep discourtesy." Yet, Alexander failed to mention Palermo. Patton, with the right flank of his army blocked by his own ally, focused on his left. He laid out his plan to envelope Palermo from the west and south. Alexander said that he had already sent word for him to take

Palermo but the messenger, his chief of staff, never delivered it. Patton didn't buy it, calling the excuse a weak one in his diary. In the event, Alexander told Patton if he could guarantee that the roads between the Seventh and Eighth Armies would be held, he could drive on to Palermo. Patton knew that if he took the city, the road net would be irrelevant; still, all he had to do at the moment was to make the promise and Palermo was his. "It's a mean man who won't promise," he later wrote.[66] Patton left the meeting and gathered some American officers together to tell them, "if the Goddammed Limeys" were going to beat him to Palermo, "they've got to pay for it."[67]

Before leaving, Patton received two letters drafted by the review board that had examined the airborne friendly fire incident. Both claimed that the incident resulted from five culminating factors: insufficient planning, troop carriers veering off course, the Navy's firing at all aircraft, the Luftwaffe attack just before the troop carriers arrived, and the failure of some ground commanders to spread the word of the paratroopers' approach. As Patton had predicted, the incident was deemed the result of the fog of war.[68]

With his plan to take Palermo approved and the friendly fire incident behind him, Patton flew back to Sicily and promptly fell ill with sand-fly fever, common for soldiers in Sicily. He spent the next day in bed with a fever of 104, unable to eat or read. He had a nightmare that the Luftwaffe had bombed him, his wife, and oldest daughter, but they escaped with Patton's driver to a lumberyard. "I suppose it caught fire, but I woke up before we fried," he wrote Beatrice.[69]

Once Patton had recovered, on July 19, he trekked out to visit II Corps in Enna, which Bradley had taken that day. Bradley informed him that the Canadians had failed to capture the town, leaving a dangerous gap between the Seventh and Eighth Armies. Although Enna was a Canadian objective, Bradley took it with elements of Allen's 1st Infantry, ensuring the safety of the strategic road net. Leaving the meeting, Patton drove past destroyed tanks and vehicles from earlier battles, finishing the day with his face and hair gray from Sicilian road dust. He was pleased with his army's progress. While the British had gained only four hundred yards south of Catania and the Canadians had lost five hundred men while failing to take the town of Enna, his troops were advancing. Patton credited the Americans' success with constantly attacking, as opposed to the British method of attacking, stopping, building up forces, and attacking again, which Patton believed gave the enemy time to dig in. "Alexander has no idea of either the power or speed of the American armies," he boasted in his diary. "We can go twice as fast as the British and hit harder."[70]

Yet, Alexander must have had some idea. On July 19 he signaled Montgomery that "if the Germans are too then too strong for you, Seventh Army can take over a sector in the north from S. Stefano to Troina." Alexander's shift to Patton must have shocked Montgomery, who described his troubles as "a dog fight of great intensity against determined Germans." All four of his assaults had been blunted: his attack along the coast had completely stalled; his attack on the right center was struggling south of Mount Etna; his attack on the center left was making progress but was also still south of Mount Etna; and his attack on the left was pretty much in line with his other thrusts. The Germans, aware of Montgomery's habit of building up forces, preceding attacks with artillery barrages, and sending his troops forward—as he had done in North Africa—were constantly parrying his thrusts. He was forced to bring up the 78th "Battleaxe" Infantry Division from North Africa, where the unit had fought with General Anderson's First Army. The men, resentful of having to rescue Montgomery again, chalked onto their vehicles, beneath their division symbol, the phrase "Nothing to do with the Eighth Army."[71] Not amused, Montgomery contacted Alexander that day, stating that once Patton captured the roads north of Petralia, which stood some fifteen miles southeast of Palermo, he wanted Patton to use one of his divisions to "develop a strong thrust eastward towards MESSINA," hoping to use Patton's forces to envelope the Germans. Montgomery was too late. Patton was headed north to Palermo. Messina would be next.[72]

Alexander promptly sent a coded message to Patton, ordering him not to head west, but encountered an unexpected obstacle: Hap Gay received the order but kept it from Patton. If Patton seized Palermo, he would have one of the best ports on the island, plus modern, concrete airstrips. Not only could he supply his army through Palermo, he could also coordinate amphibious attacks, bypassing the unforgiving Sicilian terrain bogging down Bradley and Montgomery. Gay had the staff slowly decipher the message, waited twelve hours, and then replied to Alexander that the message was unreadable and requested a retransmission. By the time the message finally made it into Patton's hands, he was already on his way into Palermo.[73]

CHAPTER EIGHT ★ FIGHTING FROM GELA TO PALERMO 173

Indeed, while Patton was visiting with Bradley in Enna, General Keyes's provisional corps jumped off to capture Palermo. Truscott's 3rd Infantry crossed its line of departure in the west, while Ridgway's 82nd Airborne, with elements of Eddy's 9th Infantry, attacked on the 3rd's right flank. The tankers of Gaffey's 2nd Armored waited in the rear to exploit a breakthrough. "If I succeed," Patton wrote his wife, "Attila will have to take a back seat."[74] He wanted his armor to steal the show. "Patton made no secret of the fact that he was not only desirous of emulating Rommel's reputation as a leader of armor," Truscott later wrote, "he wanted to exceed it."[75] By nightfall, Keyes's corps had advanced twenty-five miles.[76]

The next day, July 20, Allen's 1st Infantry Division mopped up Enna while Keyes's Provisional Corps advanced another twenty miles. Patton had enough time in his day to hold a ceremony for soldiers who earned awards during Operation TORCH. It had taken him eight months to get the awards approved. He also held a concert where the locals joined in, dancing and asking for food. "I could have been elected Pope right after the concert," Patton mused. Still, he worried about the specter of death. After eyeing the locals at the concert, he wrote, "I often wonder when one of them will try to kill me." He believed his bravery prevented any assassination attempts, adding, "it is good for the troops to see my flags flying all over the front. One dies but once, and I am on a high spot. A victorious memory may be better than to achieve success and be forgotten." He felt he would survive because he still had much to do, "but I do hate to be shot just as much as I ever did."[77]

Later in the day, he took a drive to Priolo with his staff and came across some of Germany's most powerful tanks, the Panzerkampfwagen IV Tiger Ausf. Es, better known as Tigers. Despite the tank's size and power (its frontal armor was four inches thick compared to two inches on the American Sherman tank, and it fired an 88mm cannon compared with the Sherman's 75 mm), Patton found the tank "a flop." He wrote Beatrice that they were too slow, but he was wrong. The Tiger, a heavy tank, had a maximum speed of twenty-eight miles an hour, only two miles an hour slower than the Sherman medium tank. Near Priolo, Patton found one Tiger in a roadside ditch, and another with its turret blown off. Patton posed his staff officers around the tanks and took pictures. The ditched tank showed signs of battle: two shallow divots on the turret Patton called "scars of battle," and a miniscule hole from a bazooka round. Later, Patton made it a habit to photograph both enemy and American tanks and circle with a pen any enemy innovations, while placing "Xs" where the American tanks had been hit. He would send the pictures to the U.S. Army's Aberdeen Proving Grounds in Maryland for study.[78]

That night, Patton wrote his wife a cryptic message, possibly about Seventh Army's Goum troops: "Some of George Meeks cousins did a little of their usual stunt and will wear rope ties." By invoking Meeks's name, Patton was telling his wife they were black, and writing that they were his "cousins," he probably meant the Goums, who were rumored to engage in raping and pillaging after a battle. The "rope ties" referenced hanging. The message was clear: Some Goums would be hanged for raping women. He made no other such reference in his diaries or other letters, and never mentioned if any charges were made or sentences carried out.[79]

The next day, American Major General Clarence Huebner, Alexander's American deputy chief of staff, visited Patton at his new headquarters in Agrigento to outline Montgomery's attack on Messina. Patton had other plans. With his Provisional Corps on its way north, the days of surviving on the beaches of Gela were over. He wanted Palermo. As the two spoke on Patton's front porch, Patton eyed a truck rolling by, filled with helmetless soldiers with their sleeves rolled up. He barked to one of his staffers to take care of it, one of whom promptly called over the sergeant in charge of the truck. With Patton watching, the interrogation began. "Do you have an excuse for letting your men be out of uniform?" "No," the sergeant replied. "What is your unit?" "7th Infantry [one of Truscott's regiments]," answered the sergeant. Patton asked, "Do you understand why you are busted to private, as of now?" "Yes sir," said the sergeant. "Alright, private," Patton admonished. "Dismissed."[80]

Patton soon took off for the front, passing through the 3rd Infantry to get to the 2nd Armored. His escort consisted of two motorcycles, a jeep, Patton's command car, a half-track, and two motorcycles in the rear. The siren on Patton's command car wailed as he stood in the vehicle. The convoy drove past a watering hole, kicking up dust clouds that choked the men. Patton looked at none of them, keeping his mask of command firmly in place.[81] Along the clogged, hilly roads, his convoy rolled up behind a local Sicilian in a horse-drawn cart. The two jeeps preceding Patton made it past the cart, but the half-track was too big. Instead of waiting for the driver to get out of the way, the half-tracks pushed the cart, horse, and man off the road and down a steep slope to the right. The soldiers who witnessed it were appalled at the sight.[82] Rumors swirled about the incident. Patton had been involved in a similar incident back in

Licata, where he spotted a mule-pulled cart stopped on a one-way bridge, holding up a column of Gaffey's 2nd Armored tanks. An enraged Patton had smacked the cart driver over his head so forcefully with his riding crop that he broke it in half. "That bridge is for military use only," he told an aide. "Shoot the mule." The aide obeyed. When Patton later heard complaints over his actions he wrote, "Human rights are being exalted over victory."[83]

South of Menfi, Patton's entourage roared up the road. Tanks and trucks of the 2nd Armored Division pulled to the left side of the road to let him pass. When he saw a tank crew giving their food to a group of children, he pulled over, marched up to the men, and berated them for "feeding the enemy." He then chided them about the need to fight the enemy, not feed them. He had the men line up while one of his officers took down their names, ranks, serial numbers, and units, and informed them he was docking one-third of their pay for the next three months.[84]

Patton then ordered four tank crews to follow him. He continued up the costal road toward Marsala until a soldier with the 9th Infantry Division waved him down at a blown bridge over the Sossio River and told him the front was just ahead. Patton walked up to a lieutenant who was supervising a handful of Italian prisoners building a fjord. "Who's in charge here?" Patton barked. The lieutenant told him he was. When Patton asked him what he was doing, the lieutenant explained that his men had come under fire and he did not want to advance without armor and other support. "Well," Patton told him forcefully, "we're going to cross here. Let the armor through." While a soldier dug a foxhole for him, Patton watched as the tanks crossed the river to the right of the blown bridge. Bang! The Germans opened fire on the tank. Rounds flew everywhere. Patton took a step toward his foxhole before catching himself and looking at the lieutenant who was already in his. "Lieutenant," he beckoned, "go ahead and do what you were doing." With that, he turned and hurried back to his vehicle.[85]

That evening, Keyes sent Patton a message that 2nd Armored would attack the next morning at 6:00 a.m. Palermo was in sight, but Patton did not want to just take it, he wanted to capture it with tanks. On his map he drew a line around Palermo, declaring it his "Blue Line" and put out a directive that no infantry, except patrols, could cross the line. He even recorded in his diary that his infantry units had halted "so as not to interfere with the 2nd Armored Division." This was the point of the battle Patton relished. The infantry had prepared the battlefield, now the armor would exploit a breakthrough and charge the enemy. Where Benson Force had failed in Tunisia, the 2nd Armored would succeed in Sicily. There was only one problem: there was no real enemy for the armor to overrun. When Truscott told Keyes there was nothing in front of 2nd Armored except possibly land mines, Keyes agreed but explained it would be an important action for American armor. Truscott, who had done a masterful job of driving his unit up the island, was justifiably disappointed with Patton's decision.[86]

The next day, July 21, Patton launched the 2nd Armored against almost no resistance. Italians defending roadblocks readily surrendered to tank crews, some even pointing out the locations of their German allies. Truscott was right. Still, Patton drove to the front to motivate and lead his tankers. When he found tanks halted by a mine field, he raged. Soldiers from the 20th Engineer Battalion arrived in trucks to disarm the mines but Patton was too angry to understand. "Get those Goddamned fucking trucks out of here!" He cursed at the engineers. "This is a tank country now!" The engineer captain explained they were there to remove the mines and Patton calmed down enough to let them through.[87] Later, when he discovered that a tank commander had abandoned his tank because of enemy fire, he ordered the tank retrieved at all costs. Later, while passing another tank clanking up a mountain road, he shouted, "Go get those bastards!"[88] He kept up the pressure. When he came upon a tank crew eating lunch, he asked the men, "Are you gassed?" When they replied that they were, he exhorted, "Eat on the run, if at all. Sleep on the run, if at all. Mount up and continue. Don't stop except for gas. We have them on the run. Keep it that way."[89] Yet, he changed his tune with the infantry. When he came across an exhausted chemical mortar platoon on the advance, he asked the captain in charge, "Are these men or mules?" When the captain answered, "Men," Patton told him, "If they're men, have them put their dicks in their pants and fall out and rest."[90] That night he wrote in his diary, "I really feel like a great general today—all my plans have worked. I hope God stays with me."[91]

As Keyes's Provisional Corps, spearheaded by Truscott's infantry, neared Palermo on July 22, Keyes sent Patton a message: "Can we make a touchdown on our own initiative? Rush reply." Keyes had just received a civilian delegation from Palermo that begged Truscott's assistant division commander, Brigadier General William Eagles, to let the city surrender. Eagles refused but forwarded the request to Keyes. Patton replied within

CHAPTER EIGHT ★ FIGHTING FROM GELA TO PALERMO

thirty minutes: "You have the ball. Call the touchdown play."[92] Patton sent Gay to meet with Gaffey, to help lead the tanks into Palermo. Upon his arrival, Gaffey told him, "If you give me the authority, I'll break out of here and go clear up to the sea and I'll turn right and I'll be right behind the enemy and we'll end this whole damn thing." Gay gave him the nod and Gaffey headed off.[93]

Truscott's 3rd Infantry Division received no such encouragement. When Gay happened upon a patrol from the 3rd inside the city, he asked their commander, "Don't you know that you're not supposed to be beyond the Blue Line?" But the officer, Lieutenant Colonel John Heintges, explained that he was only patrolling and that his men had just captured the Italian commanding general of Sicilian forces. Gay wanted nothing to do with him or his infantry unit. He told Heintges to leave the city, but when he refused, Gay said, "Well, hold on what you've got here and don't move any further until you get orders." Patton would have his liberation by armor, despite the infantry beating them to it. The tanks of 2nd Armored Division were soon rolling down the narrow streets of Palermo, mixing with Truscott's soldiers.[94]

That afternoon, Patton took off for the front. His vehicle passed destroyed enemy artillery pieces and tanks, some of them, according to Patton, covered with blood. Whenever he passed 2nd Armored men, they saluted and waved. "It was quite cheering," said Patton of his old unit.[95] Local Sicilians crowded the streets to greet him. He was slightly bewildered by the reception. "They even threw flowers, lemons and watermelons," he chuckled to a correspondent. "But it should be emphasized all the fruit was tossed at us in a spirit of friendliness."[96]

Patton finally entered Palermo at 10:00 p.m., on July 22, at the head of an armored column.[97] The hills on either side of him were aflame, as was an enemy fuel dump. Civilians filled the streets, cheering, "Down with Mussolini!" and "Long live America!" He loved it. "It is a great thrill to be driving into a captured city in the dark," he confessed in his diary. Patton's jeep stopped only once, to pick up a British Special Air Service commando, Captain Philip Pinckney, who had parachuted into the area earlier to disrupt enemy supply lines. Patton's column made it to the Royal Palace, where Keyes and Gaffey had set up their respective headquarters. He congratulated them and passed a flask around to celebrate. Just then he received word from Alexander: "This is a great triumph. Heartiest congratulations to you and all your splendid soldiers." President Roosevelt wrote to congratulate him, "You are doing a grand job in the advance," and suggested that after the war he might be appointed the Marquis of Mount Etna.[98]

That night, a victorious Patton wrote in his diary, "I feel that future students of the Command and General Staff School will study the campaign of Palermo as a classic example of the use of tanks." Maybe not. While the tanks of the 2nd Armored helped repulse the Axis attacks on the Gela landings, they did not maneuver or even sweep the battlefield. For the push west and north, the fight was an infantryman's battle. The terrain was just too mountainous for tanks to maneuver; instead, they were relegated to the roads, just like any other vehicle. But to Patton, this was classic tank doctrine. "I held them [the tanks] back far enough so that the enemy could not tell where they were to be used; then[,] when the infantry had found the hole, the tanks went through and in large numbers and Fast." Was Patton trying to convince himself or his superiors that he had blitzkrieged his way to Palermo? He must have planned that his diary would eventually be published. "Such methods assure victory and reduce losses." His use of armor to exploit a battlefield would have to wait for the plains of France.[99]

Still, the capture of Palermo constituted a major victory. It was the largest city in Sicily and a major port. More important, the Americans, whom the British and the Germans scorned as inferior troops, had captured it and made it look effortless. *Time* magazine boasted that "this raw army was putting on an even better show than the II Corps had staged in Tunisia."[100] Patton called a press conference at his Agrigento headquarters. "We had about two hundred miles to go over crooked roads to get to Palermo," he told reporters. "Our drive was faster and over rougher ground than anything the Germans ever did. We didn't give them a chance to dig in." He then listed Seventh Army's booty: 44,000 prisoners captured (mostly Italian); 6,000 enemy killed and wounded; 190 enemy aircraft destroyed; and 67 big guns captured. "This was the greatest armored blitz in history," he exaggerated.[101]

Omar Bradley called Patton's drive on Palermo a public relations gesture and judged the city had no strategic significance. But he was wrong. With its harbor and airfields, Palermo would allow Patton to attack east in strength instead of on a shoestring.[102] Surprisingly, Patton could be humble about his success. He wrote his wife, praising the American fighting soldier and his country's amphibious capabilities. He also credited Keyes and Bradley for doing the yeoman's work thus far. He was merely along for the ride. The one exception being on July 11, when he first arrived on the island. "I think that I personally changed possible defeat into a positive victory," he wrote Beatrice. "I certainly love war."[103]

Two early decisions contributed to Patton reaching Palermo: promoting Lucian Truscott to command of the 3rd Infantry Division and insisting on having Terry Allen's 1st Infantry Division take part in the campaign. Allen had saved the amphibious assault three days after the initial landings when he launched his surprise night attack. Truscott bolted up the island, utilizing the "Truscott Trot," a method of his own invention consisting of quick marching combined with shorter breaks.[104] While Patton believed in the constant attack, his two division leaders adopted his vision and made it work in their own ways.

Patton occupied Palermo's royal palace, which he jokingly called his "little house," and put Italian prisoners to work cleaning both it and the surrounding streets. He also made them repair the docks. The palace appealed to Patton's love of history. It dated back to AD 1000 and contained oil paintings, a grand staircase, and gold furniture. "It is a very gorgeous and tawdry looking building on the inside," he wrote, "but very well constructed."[105] He slept in the king's bedroom on three mattresses. Seven anterooms separated the bedroom from the state dining room. His bathroom glass was etched with the Arms of Savoy. "I get quite a kick about using a toilet previously made malodorous by constipated royalty," he wrote Beatrice. The well-trained servants all gave him the fascist salute. He also won a bottle of gin from Air Marshal Wigglesworth for reaching Palermo twenty-four hours before the July 24 deadline—and bet him now that he would reach Messina by August 22.[106]

CHAPTER NINE

Victory at Messina

In only twelve days, Patton had pushed his Seventh Army some ninety-five miles north and cut Sicily in half, but his success left part of his army out of a job. Montgomery, with his left flank secured, could now drive for Messina. Patton, with four divisions in Palermo, planned to keep fighting and possibly win the campaign himself. On the morning of July 23, he admitted to Truscott, "Well, the Truscott Trot sure got us here in a damn hurry."[1] Middleton was not far behind. Later that day his 45th Infantry Division reached the north coast at Termini Imerese, twenty-four miles east of Palermo, putting Seventh Army that much closer to Messina.[2]

One of the first officials to greet the victorious Patton in Palermo was a bishop representing Cardinal Luigi Lavitrano, who worried that the Americans would interfere with the church. Patton explained that one of the fundamental rules of freedom was religion. He then expressed amazement at the Italian army's stupidity and gallantry: "Stupid because they were fighting for a lost cause, and gallant because they were Italian." He told the bishop that the Italian soldiers had fought magnificently but urged him to spread the word that further fighting would be a waste of blood.[3] Patton also drew up passes allowing the bishop and the local priests to visit Italian prisoners of war, adding that if the bishop found anything adverse to report it to him directly.[4]

The next day, July 24, marked the end of operations for Keyes's Provisional Corps. With Palermo taken, Keyes pointed the 82nd Airborne and the 2nd Armored west and sent them charging to the northern corner of the island. The airborne troops took the lead, encountering sporadic fire on the way to Trapani, the northwesternmost city. By the time the corps had completed its mission, it had suffered 272 casualties (57 killed, 170 wounded, 45 missing), having captured 53,000 prisoners, and killed

Figure 27. On the streets of Palermo, Patton enjoys a report from Major General Lucian Truscott (bottom, right) on how his infantrymen captured the city on July 23, 1943. Major General Geoffrey Keyes (center) listens. Catalog number: 11-SC 179717, National Archives and Records Administration.

and wounded 2,900 enemy troops. Keyes's men also captured 189 large guns, 359 vehicles, and 41 tanks. Patton may not have gotten his hoped-for armored breakthrough against an implacable foe, but his Provisional Corps had racked up an impressive score.[5]

Patton spent the rest of the day visiting three Greek temples, guided by Palermo's mayor. When the latter explained that a temple had suffered war damage, Patton asked him from which war, the mayor told him, "the Second Punic War."[6] One particular temple had more recent war damage: two soldiers' names from Kansas scratched on it. When Patton later learned he was to attend a meeting with Montgomery and Alexander at Montgomery's Syracuse headquarters, he grew concerned. "I fear the worst," he confessed to his diary, "but so far I have held my own with them."[7]

On July 25 Patton's C-47 arrived a half hour early to Syracuse. As the plane came in to land, Patton spotted a table laid out for lunch. Once

CHAPTER NINE ★ VICTORY AT MESSINA

Figure 28. Patton confers with Cardinal Luigi Lavitrano, the archbishop of Palermo shortly after Seventh Army captured the city. Catalog number: 208-PU-153H-41, National Archives and Records Administration.

the aircraft landed, he rushed off to shake hands with Montgomery. There were no bands, no honor guard, and no ceremony for the victor of Palermo, but Montgomery did offer Patton a cigar. Patton cursed himself for rushing. "I made an error by hurrying to meet him," he wrote. "He hurried a little too, but I started it." Montgomery then spread out a map on his car hood and the two generals discussed the boundaries between their armies, particularly in the town of Linguaglossa, northeast of Mount Etna. When Patton said he could use its road to head north to Messina, Montgomery said he wanted it too. Patton offered to share the roads west of the town, and Montgomery's reaction surprised him. "He agreed so readily that I felt something was wrong but have not found it yet." He could not believe Montgomery's cooperation.[8]

Alexander arrived with Beetle Smith and Major General Charles H. Miller, Alexander's logistics officer. Alexander, angry about Montgomery's aloofness in the campaign, ordered him to explain his attack plan. Montgomery said that he and Patton had already decided their next moves. Alexander, now even madder, asked again for his plan, with which Montgomery finally complied.[9] Alexander then asked Patton for his plan, which he delivered, not repeating Montgomery's mistake. Patton explained that he wanted to conduct a series of amphibious landings along the Sicilian north coast, for which he would need forty-five LSTs. Miller only wanted to give him thirty-five, but Patton held his ground until Miller reluctantly agreed, explaining that Admiral Cunningham would make the final decision. Smith spoke up, saying that the decision would be made at Eisenhower's headquarters, reprimanding Miller for forgetting that it existed. "So is [sic] everyone else," Patton later mused, "it never asserts itself."[10]

Patton requested naval cruisers to escort the LSTs, making no secret that he wanted a flotilla capable of landing a reinforced regiment. The British thought nothing of his idea, but he was already thinking about attacking off the map, much as he had done during the Louisiana maneuvers. As the meeting broke up, Alexander told Patton, "I want to assure you that 15th Army Group is completely Allied in mind and favors neither army." Patton agreed but later wrote in his diary, "I know this was a lie, but said I felt that he was right—God pardon me."[11] The meeting over, Montgomery bade everyone goodbye and headed off without asking anyone to lunch.[12] Patton flew back to Palermo, where an honor guard and band greeted him. It was a far cry from Montgomery's cigar.

Patton woke up the next morning, ready to set the stage for his eastern attack, but bigger news came to his attention: Benito Mussolini, the fascist leader of Italy, had stepped down. There had been peace rumbling out of Rome for a while already, as the war turned against Italy, encouraged by an American bombing of the capital city. With Mussolini failing to withdraw from the war, Italy's King Victor Emmanuel III acted, asking Mussolini on July 20 to step down, as the only impediment to saving the country. Mussolini refused, but, four days later, the Fascist Grand Counsel voted overwhelmingly for the king to take over the armed forces. When Mussolini reported to the king about the vote, Victor Emmanuel quickly told him he had to resign and that Marshal Pietro Badoglio would take his place. Mussolini was arrested. When news got out about Mussolini's overthrow, Italians in Rome danced in the streets, attacked Fascist party officials, and tore down Fascist symbols—as they had in Palermo. Still, although Mussolini may have exited the stage, Italy remained in the war, although clearly the Sicily campaign was showing strategic results.[13]

After absorbing the news about Mussolini, Patton spoke to Lucas about relieving Terry Allen and Teddy Roosevelt "without prejudice" and replacing them with Huebner and Brigadier General Norm Cota. He also jotted off a letter to Eisenhower requesting the replacement. This is the first written sign that Patton considered changing the leadership of the 1st Infantry Division. Historians have speculated on the reason for Allen's relief. After all, he had proved to be the Army's best division commander in theater, holding his unit together at Kasserine Pass, delivering victory at El Guettar, surviving the Axis onslaught on the first day in Sicily, and succeeding in a night attack against the Germans. Surely this was a commander worthy of promotion, not relief. Tom Ricks, in his book *The Generals*, theorized that Bradley and Eisenhower did not like Allen's type of personality.[14] General Bradley took credit for Allen's relief: "Responsibility for the relief of Terry Allen was mine and mine alone," he wrote in his memoir, "George did nothing more than concur in the recommendation." Bradley said he did it because Allen had become temperamental and disdainful of both regulations and his superiors, despite his brilliant combat record. At the same time, Bradley claimed to have relieved Roosevelt because of a supposed rivalry between Allen and Roosevelt.[15] But Bradley's claims and stories do not stand up to scrutiny

In fact, Eisenhower had proposed Allan's departure from 1st Division well before the invasion of Sicily. According to Hap Gay, in a hand-scrawled note on the back page of one of Patton's transcribed diary pages:

> [Sometime] in June 1943 [at least a week before Sicily], Gen. Eisenhower called Gen Patton on [the] phone—from Algiers (Patton at Mostaguem) and stated he planned on returning General Terry Allen to the U.S. to take a new command. Gen. P asked that this be delayed until after the landing in Sicily and promised that he (Gen P) would relieve Gen Allen from this duty as soon after the landing—as such could be done with out [sic] depreciating the efficiency of the 1st Div. Gen P further stated that such relief should be without prejudice.[16]

While Eisenhower never mentioned Allen's name to General Marshall, he did discuss sending experienced officers back to the United States to train recruits. On May 11, three months before HUSKY, he wrote Marshall, "without damaging ourselves, we can provide a few of these officers, some of whom will be recommended for promotion." Marshal wrote back, asking Eisenhower to submit a list generals and senior field officers.[17]

In addition, two officers in Sicily directly countered Bradley's story: Lieutenant Colonel Robert Porter, Allen's intelligence officer, and Colonel Oscar Koch, Patton's intelligence officer. Porter explained to a U.S. Army historian in 1961 that "[Major] General [Clarence] Huebner had been picked some months before by General Marshall to take over the division," adding, "Allen knew *at the time of the landing* [author's italics] that Huebner would take over the division within a short time." Koch reinforced Porter's version of events during a similar interview, saying, "I am personally familiar with General Allen's having been requested by General Marshall as Chief of Staff, to return to the states after Tunisia, to take command of a Corps in the States."[18] As further evidence, General Roosevelt showed up at Patton's headquarters on August 3, four days before his and Allen's official relief, to complain about it. Patton wrote in his diary that night, "I reassured him and also Allen."[19] So Allen's departure did not happen the way Bradley described it. Patton, for his part, considered Allen one of the "best damn officers in the U.S. Army" and would later consider bringing him back to fight under him.[20] As a result, Patton did more than concur with Bradley's recommendation, he oversaw and implemented it. Bradley simply relayed Patton's orders. However it happened, Major General Terry Allen would soon be going home.

That same day, Patton and Keyes drove to Cardinal Lavitrano's residence to garner goodwill with the civilian population. A press entourage followed Patton's command car and took pictures of him standing in his passenger seat with his ivory pistol visible. The troops seemed unimpressed with their victorious leader. Some soldiers had one arm draped over a local girl and a bottle of wine in the other. A chaplain thought Patton looked like a western outlaw. "To us," he snorted, "he looked ridiculous."[21] Upon arrival, Patton thought to kiss the Cardinal's ring, but Keyes recommended against it since he was not faithful enough. They then went into a church to pray together as cameras flashed. Patton later assured the cardinal that he would allow Sicilian POWs to return to their homes and that clergymen could visit them. "I feel that he is on our side," Patton wrote in his diary, "and this fact will have a good effect on the inhabitants."[22]

With the local populace subdued, Patton returned to his headquarters where his old friend, Colonel Harry "Paddy" Flint, appeared, looking for a role in the campaign. Patton had been pressing his division commanders for months to bring Flint into the fray, even suggesting that Gaffey and Harmon give him a command in one of their armored divisions, but they had begged off, not wanting a fifty-five-year-old officer in their ranks.[23] In Patton's headquarters, word arrived that the commander of the 39th Regimental Combat Team, a 9th Infantry Division unit supporting the 1st Infantry, had broken his leg. Patton sent Flint to take over. Flint soon arrived at regimental headquarters, telling the staff, "Georgie sent me." Patton had made a good call: Flint would flourish as a regimental commander. "He is in fine spirits and is delighted with the job," Patton wrote.[24]

Patton was ready to make his own lunge for Messina. Unfortunately, Middleton's 45th Infantry, the spearhead of the attack, had exhausted itself fighting up the center of the island and grinding east along the north coast road. Patton needed to replace it with a fresh division. That night he invited Truscott to the Royal Palace. Over drinks, he told Truscott how he "would certainly like to beat Montgomery to Messina." Truscott vowed that if Patton put the 3rd Infantry into the line, he would assure a win. Just like with Agrigento, Truscott promised exactly what Patton hoped for. Patton had his attack force. He would also soon have his own navy. Admiral Hewitt had scrapped together whatever ships he could find and organized them under Rear Admiral Lyal A. Davidson. Naval Task Force 88—better known as "General Patton's Navy"—consisted of two cruisers, fourteen destroyers, fourteen Motor Torpedo Boats, two LSTs, ten Landing Craft Infantry (LCIs), and seven Landing Craft Tanks (LCTs). It also included a number of small escort craft.[25] Still, the fleet was considerably smaller than the flotilla Patton requested—he could only land a battalion, not a regiment as he originally envisioned.

Two days later, on July 28, Montgomery arrived with his staff to work out the details for the drive on Messina. His personal B-17 bomber had a rough time on Patton's short runway. The pilot had to make a hairpin turn to avoid crashing into a hanger, collapsing the landing gear on one side. Patton made up for it with a reception that put Montgomery's to shame. A band played both the "Star Spangled Banner" and "God Save the King," and an honor guard stood attention while the two rivals inspected the ranks. Patton quietly told his British aide, Henriques, "I'll teach those bastards they've got allies."[26] Patton wanted Montgomery to know that these were not the same soldiers who had been overwhelmed at Kasserine Pass. Patton had another motive: "I hope Monty realized that I did this to show him up for doing nothing for me."[27] Obviously, Patton had not appreciated his cigar.

The men and their staffs lunched at Patton's palace, where the host delighted his guests with stories of the American campaign. Francis de Guingand enjoyed the atmosphere and Patton's humility, later writing, "One could sense his great love for the American fighting man." After lunch, the commanders adjourned to a planning room to figure out boundaries, maintenance routes, and air support. Montgomery presented his plan to capture Messina, highlighting the progress of each of his divisions, all of which were still south of Mount Etna. He repeatedly referred to Middleton's drive to the coast, calling it a significant action. "I can't decide whether he [Montgomery] is honest or wants me to lay off [route] 120," Patton later wrote. At this point in the campaign, they would have to be careful not to fire on each other as the two armies converged on Messina.[28]

The next day, Patton drove to the front near Nicosia, where he found a helmetless Roosevelt and some soldiers atop a hill, scanning for Germans. Dismounting his command car, Patton marched over to Roosevelt and barked, "General Roosevelt, you know what my orders are: Every man in this outfit will wear a helmet." Before Roosevelt could respond, he added,

CHAPTER NINE ★ VICTORY AT MESSINA

Figure 29. Patton escorts Field Marshal Bernard Montgomery to his Palermo headquarters to discuss the capture of Messina. National Archives and Records Administration.

"General, you are going to start wearing your helmet as of now. You are hereby fined forty dollars."[29] He then drove to Bradley's headquarters to discuss the following day's drive on Messina. Patton recommended committing the rest of the 9th Infantry Division, which had arrived via the port of Palermo, adding that he had replaced the 45th Infantry with the

3rd, possibly hinting at his desire that fresh troops lead the new offensive. The meeting over, Patton returned to Palermo to learn that Eisenhower had approved the reliefs of Allen and Roosevelt.

That night, Patton made special mention of Roosevelt in his diary. The day before, the 1st Infantry had captured the town of Nicosia. When Patton found out that an entire patrol, save one man, had been killed while responding to Germans who waved a white flag and then opened fire, he wrote, "This will mean the death of many more Germans, damn them."[30] As for Roosevelt, his organization and discipline impressed Patton, even if he sometimes removed his helmet: "he none the less, is a gallant fighting soldier who had fought well and incessantly for nearly nine months." Then Patton added a sentence which, in retrospect, says more about himself than his two ill-fated commanders: "Both he and Allen are now suffering from battle fatigue." So Patton was aware of battle fatigue and could see its effects on men. He could see the long-term effects of it on his friends at least, as opposed to nameless and seemingly uninjured soldiers sitting in hospital beds.[31]

On July 30 Patton began putting the pieces into place for Messina. He drove up to Middleton's headquarters and told him that Truscott's division would replace his. "I think I will give the 45th a rest and use the 3rd," he told Middleton, who proudly responded, "I would never ask for a rest." When Patton pressed that it would be in the best interest of the country, Middleton finally relented: "I think that is what you should do." Middleton's attitude impressed Patton: the man wanted to fight but did not want to ask for help. Wanting to ensure an orderly relief in place, and to make sure Middleton's men did not feel slighted, Patton drove to the front and visited a regimental command post. "I hope you all know how good you are, for everyone else does," he told all the men within earshot. "You are magnificent." On his way to visit some frontline engineers, Patton came across two soldiers rummaging through a captured German vehicle and asked, "You boys having fun?" The soldiers looked up and told him they were. He laughed and continued on.[32] Once he finished his tour, he climbed in a Cub plane and flew back to Palermo. It would be the 3rd Infantry Division's battle now. That night, Patton proudly recorded in his diary that the 45th spent the day attacking.[33]

To help Truscott, Patton met with General Ridgway and Colonel Gavin and proposed dropping paratroopers behind German lines while executing an amphibious landing to cut off German delaying forces. He picked

CHAPTER NINE ★ VICTORY AT MESSINA 191

a regiment from the 3rd Infantry, a battalion from the 82nd Airborne, and five Stuart tanks from his own headquarters to touch down somewhere between Falcone and Barcelona (some twenty-eight miles east of Sant'Agata, where Patton's forces would eventually land). After studying the proposal, the men agreed that the terrain was too restrictive for an airborne drop. So Patton would only use amphibious forces to ensnare the Germans.[34]

Eisenhower finally visited Patton on July 31. Patton greeted him with the usual band and honor guard, but as an extra salute to his commander, he chose the 15th Infantry Regiment's honor guard, the only unit Eisenhower ever directly commanded. Patton told Eisenhower that he had become a more moderate general, "which he thought was a compliment," Patton wrote, "but which I regret." The two generals reviewed the plan to attack Italy under Mark Clark's Fifth Army. Eisenhower explained that if Clark got into trouble, he would call on the Seventh Army to land near Florence, in northern Italy. If things went well, however, Patton would bring Seventh Army up to England for the cross-channel invasion. Patton thought his chances of ending up in Italy were better than England. "I have a feeling that the UK show will never materialize," he wrote in his diary. "The British don't want to have England bombed."[35]

Throughout the visit, Patton beamed with pride over his army's accomplishments and called it "the best group of fighting men in the world." He defended his slow but steady progress to Eisenhower, explaining that he beat the rugged territory by aligning artillery and mortars with infantry assaults. He also complimented his engineers, who were constantly rebuilding bridges along the coast road. Patton passed a letter to Eisenhower from the cardinal, which he wanted sent to the Pope. Captain Butcher asked Patton how Colonel Charles Poletti, the former lieutenant governor of New York, was doing and Patton joked, "Beautifully, but I think he is electioneering for Roosevelt among Sicilians."[36] Before he left, Eisenhower gave Patton permission to remove Allen and Roosevelt as part of a rotation of command. Patton telegraphed Bradley the news but also sent him a personal note to hold off until Eddy's 9th Infantry Division had taken over the line.

Eisenhower followed up his visit with a message to Patton that his and Montgomery's attacks "will have a profound influence on the future strategy of the whole world." He encouraged Patton to attack day and night and lauded praise on Seventh Army's accomplishments. Sensitive

Figure 30. Eisenhower visits General Patton at the Palermo airport on July 31, 1943, where he told Patton he would either fight in Italy or bring his Seventh Army to England for the liberation of France. Catalog number: 111-SC 185260, National Archives and Records Administration.

to how Patton felt when he was stationed in Morocco while the war continued in Tunisia, he ended the note with a promise: "I personally assure you that if we speedily finish off the German in Sicily, you need have no fear of being left there in the backwater of the war."[37]

While Patton planned his amphibious surprise, the Germans did all they could to stop it. Before sunrise on August 1, the Luftwaffe attacked the port of Palermo. American anti-aircraft gunners had difficulty hitting the swarming planes in the dark. A bomb explosion partially flooded the destroyer USS *Mayrant*, while another bomb killed an entire gun crew on a dock. The attack lasted more than two hours.[38] While enemy planes continued to swoop down and drop bombs, Patton inspected the damage with Keyes and Lucas. They were standing on a dock when a bomb exploded in the water no more than fifty yards away. Fortunately, no one was injured. One plane came under fire and crashed nearby, looking to Patton like "an inverted blazing cross."[39] As he left the area, reporters flagged him down and asked about the severity of the damage. "I couldn't

CHAPTER NINE ★ VICTORY AT MESSINA

get very close—too hot," he explained while anti-aircraft guns fired and bombs exploded. "There appear to be at least two ships burning. And they hit the freight yards. But fortunately," he added with a broad grin, "they missed the transports altogether."[40] Patton's primary tool to flank the Germans had survived.

The next morning the switchover began with the 3rd Infantry moving through the 45th at San Stefano while the 9th Infantry headed east to replace the 1st Infantry, which had closed in on the town of Troina. Patton lamented the mountainous terrain his soldiers had to fight over but knew it was the only way to keep pressure on the Germans. "The enemy simply can't stand it," he wrote in his diary, adding—for the first time—what really drove him: "Besides, we must beat Eighth Army to Messina."[41]

Patton's passion for capturing Messina was no secret. "Messina is our next stop!" he wrote in an order issued to all soldiers of Seventh Army and to the airmen of XII Air Support Command. He also wrote Lieutenant General Leslie McNair about his next goal: "We have been very fortunate in our operations so far, and I am betting we get to MESSINA first in the current horse race."[42] To Bradley, Patton implored, "I want you to get to Messina as fast as you can. I don't want you to waste time on these maneuvers, even if you've got to spend men to do it. I want to beat Monty to Messina." Patton's seeming disregard for his own soldiers left Bradley shocked and sickened.[43]

Patton began August 2 by visiting the 91st Evacuation Hospital, where he pinned Purple Hearts on forty wounded soldiers. He asked one soldier where he got hit. "In the chest," the man replied. "Well, it may interest you," Patton told him, "that the last German I saw didn't have a chest and no head either." He then extolled the lopsided numbers of enemy dead, suspecting it much larger than reports indicated. "Get well quickly," he told the soldier. "You want to be in on that final kill." When Patton asked an African American soldier where he had been hit, the man responded, "in the bivouac area, sir." Patton and his staff got a good laugh. Finally, he came to an unconscious soldier wearing an oxygen mask. Patton took off his helmet, knelt down and pinned the award on a man so close to death. "He seemed to understand," Patton wrote, "even though he could not speak." According to Codman, there wasn't a dry eye in the ward. Patton later wrote his wife that the man recovered.[44]

In the afternoon, Alexander visited to review the situation. Gay's little deceit at delaying the halt order had not fooled him. "I was very much amused at his statement that he was delighted with our ability to carry out his plans for the early capture of Palermo," Patton later wrote. Maybe Alexander was so used to Montgomery's insubordination that Patton's was only a mild slight. When Alexander's logistics officer, General Miller, asked Patton to surrender some of his boats for the upcoming invasion of Italy, he refused. "I told him there was no use starting a new war till we had won this one and that we needed the boats to win it." And Patton needed boats for his amphibious assault on the enemy's rear. That night he wrote to his wife, "We are going to pull a stunt on the enemy pretty soon—long before you get this that might become quite famous." To Leslie McNair he wrote, "I am betting that we get to MESSINA first in the current horse race."[45]

Patton's continual attacks, even while he switched out divisions, kept the opposing forces on their heels. That same day, the Hermann Goering Division's leaders were planning their retreat from the island. The following day, a German memo—which the Allies intercepted—went out explaining that everyone needed their weapon if they expected to cross over to Italy. Also, soldiers were ordered to blow up materials that could not be carried, since burning them would attract the attention of Allied pilots. Finally, no one should allow Italian soldiers to guard any bridges, or allow Italian soldiers or civilians to impede their retreat (read: kill anyone interfering). The order only pertained to the Italians: "Shoot all who fail to obey." Patton must have been pleased when he read the captured document.[46]

The next day, Patton spoke to Major General Huebner, who told him the ranks were getting thinner, partly because of men avoiding their duties by malingering in hospitals.[47] With those words in his ears, Patton stopped at the 15th Evacuation Hospital, filled with 350 wounded men. He had no medals to give out but chatted with the men. Some were missing arms and legs, and several had suffered their second battlefield injury. As Patton remembered it, "some of the wounded were in terrible, ghastly shape." The men's bravery and cheerfulness emboldened Patton, at least until he arrived at the bed of Private Charles H. Kuhl. Sitting on the edge of his cot, Private Kuhl, from Company L, 26th Infantry Regiment, 1st Infantry Division, wore no bandages and had no outward signs of injury. Patton asked him what was the matter. Kuhl replied, "I guess I can't take it." In a flash, Patton exploded. According to one report, "He called the man every kind of loathsome coward and then slapped him across the face with his gloves." When Kuhl fell back, Patton grabbed him by the scruff and physically kicked him out of the hospital.[48]

Kuhl had been admitted to the hospital three times previously for exhaustion. On his second visit, he had been administered sodium amytal (known today as amobarbital) to relax him. On the day Patton slapped him, a medic wrote on his Emergency Medical Tag: "He can't take it at the front evidently. He is repeatedly returned." Upon admission this time Kuhl, suffering with malaria, registered a temperature of 102.2 degrees Fahrenheit.

As Patton left the tent, a cheer went up from the surrounding tents. The wounded men had heard the scuffle and nurses had relayed what was going on before it had even ended. The men approved of Patton's action. In their eyes, they had seen too many slackers and felt the Army could not beat the Nazis without harsh discipline from the top.[49] Later, reflecting on the incident, Patton wrote in his diary, "Companies should deal with such men and if they shirk their duty they should be tried for cowardice and shot."[50] The encounter barely rattled Lucas. "Anyone who knows him [Patton] can realize what that would do to George," he wrote. "The weak sister [Kuhl] was really nervous when he got through."[51]

Later that night, the Kuhl incident bothered Patton so much that he wrote an order for the entire Seventh Army, calling any soldier who escaped battle in a hospital a coward who discredited the Army and disgraced their fellow soldiers. He ordered every soldier to "take measures to see that such cases are not sent to the hospital, but are dealt with in their units. Those who are not willing to fight will be tried by Court-Martial for cowardice in the face of the enemy."[52]

His chaotic hospital visit over, Patton arrived at Bradley's headquarters. After lunch Patton visited Allen to check on the 1st Infantry Division's progress toward Troina. It did not go particularly well. When Patton spotted an artilleryman wearing a wool cap, he knocked it off with his riding crop.[53] Patton then found Allen and, as they were speaking, a jeep raced down the mountain toward them, chased by successive enemy artillery explosions. The torn-up vehicle braked and a sergeant jumped out and reported that Troina was strongly defended. The news shattered Patton's plan to race through Troina to Messina. He bristled with anger as he and Allen sped away.[54]

Patton then drove north to the coast road, where he found Truscott outside of San Stefano; optimistically, Truscott assured Patton he could capture Sant'Agata, some twenty-miles miles away. Patton doubted it but kept quiet. Despite heavy artillery support and mule trains keeping his men supplied, Truscott had been stopped cold by the Germans defending the mountain tops. They had even mined the streams, making it difficult for the frontline soldiers to get water.[55] That night, after flying back to Palermo in a Cub plane, Patton finalized his amphibious attack plan. He sent Keyes to inform Truscott, who selected Lieutenant Colonel Lyle Bernard, of the 30th Infantry Regiment's 2nd Battalion, to lead the amphibious force.[56]

Figure 31. Patton talks to Lieutenant Colonel Lyne W. Bernard about his amphibious attack at Brolo. Bernard led two amphibious end runs behind German lines. Catalog number: 208-PU-153510, National Archives and Records Administration.

While Truscott worked on the amphibious plan, Patton tried to scratch together more ships and air support for an effective operation. The day before, Hewitt had sent him an order to surrender one of his LSTs in need of repair and replace it with local craft. Patton would have none of it and had Colonel Paul Harkins, his deputy chief of staff, send a refusal, stressing, "Attack of 7th Army to the east can only be a success."[57] To Patton, the Navy did not understand the importance of time and improvisation in combat. "If they can't get everything they want they say they can't move," he vented. He blamed the problem on the Navy's policy of court martialing captains who lost ships. Two destroyers had been hit by Luftwaffe bombs, "but we (the Army) have had many thousands of men hit."

Air support proved just as problematic. Bradley had reported two friendly fire incidents from the Army Air Forces: one on Allen's command post and another on a tank column that had popped yellow smoke to identify itself. Patton complained to Spaatz about the lack of close air support during the initial stages of an amphibious assault and asked for more planes in the sky. He also recommended using smoke to identify friend or foe, using artillery to fire a certain color on the enemy and a different color on friendly forces. In addition, he suggested planes drop colored smoke when they approach the front lines to identify themselves to the troops on the ground. "It would save a great deal of indiscriminate shooting at our planes," Patton explained.[58] Despite his difficulties, Patton was still confident that he would reach Messina by his designated date. When Everett Hughes contacted him about visiting, Patton wrote back, "If you don't get here by the 22nd August, this damned war mit [sic] be over."[59]

The next day, August 6, Truscott attacked the German line in a series of uncoordinated small attacks, something uncharacteristic of the 3rd Infantry's commander. All were repulsed. Around noon he decided to pull the trigger on the amphibious assault.[60] Patton moved his headquarters to San Stefano to better monitor Truscott's progress. He arrived late in the day and immediately visited a field hospital where he saw two soldiers suffering from battle fatigue. One man kept going through the motions of crawling. Patton understood battle fatigue if he saw the physical manifestation of the symptoms, but if he could not, he would inflict his wrath on the victim, just as he had with Kuhl. Before Patton left, he saw a soldier with most of his head blown off. The sight of so much blood shook him, and he worried it might make it hard to order men into battle. "That would be fatal for a General," he later confessed.[61]

Enemy fire rained on Patton's new headquarters as he arrived. He worried for a minute as the shells exploded but became disgusted with his fear and spent the rest of the time barking out orders while shells landed. "I have trained myself so that usually I can keep right on talking when an explosion occurs quite close," he later wrote. "I take a sly pleasure in seeing others bat their eyes or look around." Truscott's troops were also coming under heavy enemy fire as they struggled forward against Germans entrenched in the mountainous high ground. Worse, an enemy bomb had damaged one of Patton's LSTs, delaying the assault for one day while another LST was rushed from Palermo. Not all the news was bad: The 1st Infantry had finally captured Troina and the British had captured Catania, something Montgomery claimed he was about do twenty-three days earlier.[62]

The next morning Patton met with Truscott, who, after several failed attempts to crack the enemy line, assured Patton his men could support an amphibious landing behind enemy lines. The meeting may have been more contentious than either man reported. According to Dr. Gerald Kent, Truscott told him that Patton arrived at his headquarters the day before and ordered the 3rd Infantry Division to attack a certain hill by 5:30 the next morning (possibly Hill 171—which, according to division records, was attacked unsuccessfully at 4:00 a.m. on both August 4 and 5 by the 15th Infantry Regiment).[63] The next day, the hill had yet to be taken, so Patton set out to find Truscott. "Truscott!" he yelled upon seeing him, "I told you to attack at dawn and I see you sitting here in your tent." Truscott tried to respond, but Patton cut him off. "I don't want a word out of you: I told you to attack." Every time Truscott tried to explain, Patton shouted him down, accusing him of insubordination. Finally, Truscott stood up and said, "General, if you want my stars, here is my shoulder, but remember, you have no other officer who can do this job as well as I." With that, Patton raised his hand, stopped for a second and brought it down. "Alright, Truscott, I expect that mountain captured by tomorrow."[64]

Patton contacted Keyes back at his headquarters and told him to commence the amphibious assault. Patton was going off the map to foil the enemy. But he could not stay in his headquarters waiting on results. Instead, he headed for the front to push men forward. When he came upon some parked tanks from the 753rd Tank Battalion under fire, Patton got out of his vehicle and approached the tanks. "Lieutenant, what the hell are you doing here?" he asked the first officer he saw. When the lieutenant explained that he was supposed to be attacking but was waiting for more support, Patton became furious. "You're supposed to go and attack that area." Patton demanded incredulously. "Get your ass out of here and do it!" The men obeyed and rolled off, firing at anything they saw.[65]

On the way back from the front, Patton could hear bombing to the north, which he later learned was the Luftwaffe, making a second, unsuccessful attempt at his fleet.[66] The amphibious force now consisted of

CHAPTER NINE ★ VICTORY AT MESSINA

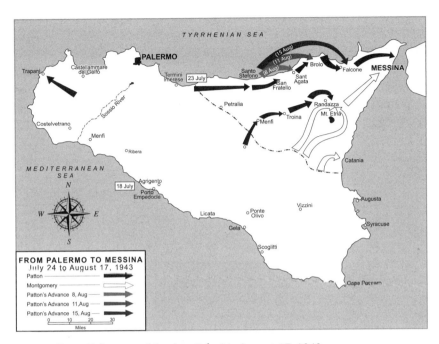

Map 6. From Palermo to Messina, July 24–August 17, 1943.

two LSTs, seven LCTs, and an LCI, carrying Bernard's battalion, plus a platoon of tanks and a battery of field artillery. Patton and Truscott took off again for an observation post atop a mountain to watch Truscott's attack on the town of San Fratello, only some four thousand yards away but separated from the Americans by several ridges.[67]

The Germans, however, were aware that an amphibious assault was on its way. German general Walter Fries, the commander of the 29th Panzer Grenadier Division facing Truscott, knew that a small fleet had assembled near Santo Stefano and that the Luftwaffe had bombed it. Truscott's artillery and American naval fire encouraged Fries to pull back just as the fleet set sail. Lieutenant Colonel Bernard's men touched down in the darkness at 3:15 a.m. on August 8, at the wrong spot: Sant'Agata, some nine miles behind the enemy lines, instead of at Terranova, two miles farther east. The soldiers quickly knocked out three enemy tanks and captured or killed 350 enemy troops and numerous tanks and vehicles, but the bulk of the German forces had withdrawn. Meanwhile, at Truscott's front, the Italians, realizing the Germans had abandoned them, surrendered. Truscott had no trouble linking up with Bernard's amphibious battalion by noon.[68]

Figure 32. Sant'Agata beach on the northern side of Sicily, where Patton sent an amphibious force behind enemy lines. Patton took this photograph himself while flying over the area. Library of Congress, OV 13, 70.

Although the landing had failed to outflank the enemy, Patton deemed it a complete success. Between this hammer and anvil, the 3rd Infantry had captured fifteen hundred prisoners. Alexander showed up to say he was very pleased with the operation.[69] Patton later told Codman, "I consider that yesterday was the first day of this war that I earned my pay as an Army commander."[70] While the ingenious maneuver had not cut off an entire German division, it had clipped its rear, unhinging part of the northern Axis defense line. The attack also had forced the enemy to retreat, and, more important, showed what the American military could do. It also gave elements of the 3rd Infantry more experience in amphibious landings. If the assault had occurred a day earlier, or landed at the correct location, Patton may have caught his quarry. Had the Navy provided him more ships, it might have guaranteed Patton the launch date he desired (perhaps even a few days earlier) and would have landed an entire regiment at the enemy's rear, opening the way to Messina that much faster. Patton knew the best way to keep casualties down was to go around the enemy and end the campaign as quickly as possible.

Meanwhile, with Troina taken, it was time to replace Allen and Roosevelt. Three telegrams arrived at Allen's headquarters on August 6. The first relieved Allen, the second relieved Roosevelt, and the third announced Huebner as the new commander. Huebner was present when the telegrams arrived, ready to take command. Even though he knew it was coming, Allen broke down. Roosevelt wrote his wife that they were both "thunderstruck." It was a blow to almost everyone in the division.[71] Allen and Roosevelt drove to Bradley's headquarters to get the official word. Bradley simply blamed the War Department's policy of rotation in command and said nothing further. They later visited Patton. Roosevelt asked him if the relief would be a blot on his professional record. Patton said no and explained that the War Department had wanted them out after Tunisia but that he had told Eisenhower that "he could not lose his most experienced amphibious and mountain fighters." He got a reprieve after Tunisia but that was it. He told Allen he would be assigned a corps once he returned to the United States, but first he would be attached to Eisenhower's headquarters and then Alexander's, to explain his combat methods and operations. "All of this was, of course, Patton's supposition," Allen wrote to his wife. Roosevelt was assigned to Mark Clark's Fifth Army. Patton did write a letter to Lieutenant General Leslie McNair, asking him to meet with Allen upon his return to the United States and that he (Patton) would be happy to have Allen serve under him again as a division commander.[72]

The next day, Patton and Alexander visited Bradley to learn about the capture of Troina. Patton called it "the hardest fight in which American troops have engaged in either Africa or Sicily." He was not exaggerating. The 1st and 9th Infantry Divisions had hammered away at the German defenses for six days, eventually flanking the town from two sides. Bradley had gotten two airstrikes from American A-36 fighter bombers to help crack the defenses. The Germans retreated and elements of Allen's division entered the smashed town to sporadic gunfire. During the fighting, Patton received a letter plucked off a dead German, in which the soldier claimed to his parents that the fighting in Sicily was worse than Stalingrad.[73] The briefing over, Patton escorted Alexander to his headquarters, where he found the Luftwaffe still trying to sink his fleet. "The Germans again bombed our landing craft," he wrote in his diary, "but had no luck."[74]

Patton began planning another amphibious attack for Bernard's battalion, this time aiming at the coastal town of Brolo, fifteen miles farther east. He wanted to launch it the night of August 9 but worried that Truscott's land forces could not be able to reach Brolo in time. Farther south, Eddy's 9th Infantry Division pushed forward, having reached the northern base of Mount Etna. Montgomery wanted the 9th and asked Patton when it would be available. "Not until we take Messina if I can help it," he confessed to his diary. That morning Bradley visited Patton, asking him to court-martial the two soldiers accused of shooting prisoners. He also told Patton that three American deserters of Italian descent had been captured wearing civilian clothes. "I shall try to have them shot," Patton wrote. "Desertion in the face of the enemy—the bastards."[75] The stress of spending so much time at the front was getting to him. He confessed in a letter to his wife that the noise of enemy guns scared him, yet his old habit of sticking his head out on the rifle range was still with him. Every time he heard a shell explode, he wanted to get up.[76]

On the morning of August 10, Keyes reported that the amphibious assault force was again ready, consisting of the same troops as the Sant'Agata operation. Next, Patton addressed another administrative matter. He explained to Brigadier General Frank McSherry, the military governor of Sicily, that he and Bradley wanted to give civilians cash awards for reporting Germans in civilian clothes, Italian Fascists posing as civil affairs officials, and Americans disguised as locals. Next, Patton met with General (possibly Leon) Johnson of the Air Forces to discuss the possibility of a third amphibious landing, this one incorporating the 509th Parachute Battalion. Patton sent the request to Alexander.[77] His administrative duties completed, he and Bradley drove to Truscott's headquarters, where they found the commander busy supervising mule-trains hauling artillery to the front. Confident that the stage was set for his next amphibious hammer-anvil attack, Patton departed.[78]

On the way back to his headquarters, Patton stopped off at the 93rd Field Hospital. As he had done five days earlier, he visited with the patients, telling them they had done a fine job and wishing them a speedy recovery. One soldier with a missing leg asked him, "Are you General Patton? I've read all about you." Another soldier, dying from a head wound, continuously shouted, "How about chow?" Patton worked his way down the aisle until he came to Private Paul G. Bennett, who was huddled up and shivering. When Patton asked him what was wrong, Bennett explained, "It's my nerves," and began sobbing. When Patton asked him again, Bennett repeated, "It's my nerves, I can't stand the shelling anymore." Like with Kuhl before, Patton exploded. "Your nerves Hell, you are just a Goddamn coward, you yellow son of a bitch." Patton then slapped Bennett. "Shut up that Goddamn crying!" he shouted. "I won't have these brave men here who have been shot seeing a yellow bastard sitting here crying." Patton then slapped him again, knocking the soldier's head so hard his helmet liner tumbled into the next tent.

Patton turned to the receiving officer and barked, "Don't admit this yellow bastard, there's nothing the matter with him! I won't have the hospitals cluttered up with these sons of bitches who haven't the guts to fight!" Patton then began to sob. "I can't help it," he told Colonel Donald Currier, the hospital's commanding officer. "It makes me break down to see brave boys and think of a yellow bastard being babied." Patton turned back to Bennett, who was now sitting at attention, although shaking from head to toe. "You're going back to the front lines," Patton told him. "And you might get shot and killed but you're going to fight. If you don't, I'll stand you up against a wall and have a firing squad kill you on purpose. In fact," Patton declared as he drew his ivory-handled pistol from its holster, "I ought to shoot you myself, you god damned whimpering coward."[79] Patton caught himself and stormed out of the hospital in a blind range, trailed by doctors and nurses pleading with him. "There's no such thing as shell shock!" he shouted, "It's an invention of the Jews!"[80]

Bennett, a four-year army veteran, had an excellent service record. His artillery unit had been attached to Bradley's II Corps, and he had been doing fine until his best friend was wounded near him. After that, Bennett had not slept for four days. He had been ordered to the hospital, although he begged not to go. He did not want to leave his unit. He arrived at the hospital the same day Patton walked in.[81] After Patton left the hospital, Bennett demanded to be returned to the front but was denied by the doctors. He felt his world had been dashed to pieces. "Don't tell my wife! Don't tell my wife!" he pleaded to anyone who spoke with him later. A talk with a chaplain finally calmed him.[82]

After leaving the hospital, Patton seemed to forget about the whole incident. Soon, he was back on the road, cajoling and cheering his soldiers. To a sergeant eating C-Rations on the side of the road, he shouted, "Great work sergeant—keep it up!" In his trail he left men amazed to see a general so close to the front.[83] Later, back at his headquarters, Bradley showed up to ask Patton to delay the amphibious assault, warning that Truscott's land forces were not in a position to relieve the amphibious force if it got in trouble. Patton denied the request, possibly because of his desire to capture Messina, or knowing that his last delay had let the Germans slip through his fingers, or perhaps because of his anger over perceived cowards in his army. Bradley repeated his request, only to be

Figure 33. Patton visits with wounded soldiers in Sicily awaiting evacuation at an airstrip. While he could recognize the signs of battle fatigue when he saw them, he questioned men who showed no outside signs of the affliction. Catalog number: 208-PU-153 E-1, National Archives and Records Administration.

denied again. An exasperated Bradley then marched out of the headquarters, knowing he had no alternative but to obey orders.[84]

That evening, as Patton wrote a letter to his wife, Truscott called to say the Germans were counterattacking. Patton could hear the increase in enemy fire from his headquarters, but told Truscott he was in the perfect position to defend since the Germans had to attack uphill. Patton returned to writing and noticed the firing had died down. Then Keyes called Patton to explain that Bradley and Truscott wanted to postpone the amphibious assault since the ground offensive had not progressed enough to make it work. "Dammit!" shouted Patton, "the operation will go on!"[85]

Now fully agitated, Patton arrived at Truscott's headquarters. He gave hell to everyone he saw, from the MPs guarding the headquarters to any soldier who crossed his path. The first officer to greet Patton was Captain Ransom Davis, Admiral Davidson's chief of staff, who told Patton the landings should be called off since the fleet had left port an hour late and would not land before 4:00 a.m. Patton snapped back that if it could land before 6:00 a.m. it should go on. According to Patton, he said to Truscott, "If your conscience will not let you conduct this operation, I will relieve you and put someone else in command who will." Truscott remembered it differently: in his recollection, a furious Patton yelled at him, "Goddammit, Lucien, what's the matter with you? Are you afraid to fight?"

Both men had somewhat conflicting views of what happened next. According to Truscott, he responded to Patton, "General, you know that's ridiculous and insulting. You have ordered the operation and it is now loading. If you don't think I can carry out orders, you can give the division to anyone else you please. But I will tell you one thing, you will not find anyone who can carry out orders which they do not approve as well as I can." Patton wrote in his diary that Truscott said, "General, it is your privilege to reduce me whenever you want to." According to Truscott, Patton then calmed down and threw his arm over Truscott's shoulder.[86]

But Patton recalled a more detailed exchange. He told Truscott that he did not want to relieve him, adding, "I got you the DSM (Distinguished Service Medal) and recommended you for Major General, but your own ability really gained both honors. You are too old an athlete to believe it is possible to postpone a match." To which Truscott replied, "You are an old-enough athlete to know that sometimes they are postponed." Patton said, "This one won't be. The ships have already started." Truscott replied, "This is a war of defile and there is a bottleneck delaying me in getting my guns up to support the infantry. They—the infantry—will be too far west to help the landing." Patton responded, "remember Frederick the Great: L'audace, L'audace, toujours l'audace [Audaciousness, audaciousness, always audaciousness]! I know you will win and if there's a bottleneck, you should be there and not here." Patton then told Truscott he had total confidence in him, and to prove it he departed. He would not interfere with Truscott's battle.[87]

That night, Patton worried about his order to Truscott, but he felt reassured when he thought of the risks and successes of Ulysses S. Grant and British admiral Horatio Nelson. "That is the true value of history," he wrote in his diary. Still concerned about the attack, he made a few calls to make sure there would be sufficient air cover for both the land and sea forces. He even marched into Major General Edwin House's tent an hour before midnight to get assurances about air cover. House commanded XII Air Support Group. The entire scene left Patton feeling anything but humble. "I may have been bull-headed," he wrote, "but I truly feel that I did my exact and full duty and under rather heavy pressure and demonstrated that I am a great leader."[88]

While Patton waxed about his greatness, the amphibious force touched down at Brolo fifteen minutes before 3:00 a.m. on August 11. The infantry captured a few Germans in a lemon grove, but the armor could not traverse the railroad embankment that paralleled the shore. Bernard's main objective was Mount Cipolla, a double-peaked mountain. His men ascended while the tanks and artillery found ways around the embankment. When the Americans opened fire on a German truck, Bernard lost the element of surprise. The battle was on. Bernard's force, split between the mountain and the town, drew heavy fire. The rough terrain disabled several tanks, but the artillery fired on the Germans, who had to turn their big guns east to try to break through this second set of Americans. The cruiser USS *Philadelphia* added to the American's firepower, smashing the German's attempts to counterattack. The Americans were winning the fight and threatening to split an entire German division in the hammer-anvil Patton had envisioned. But after seven hours of fighting, the captain of the *Philadelphia* headed back to Palermo.

Bernard called for fire from Truscott's 155-mm guns and Truscott obliged. Truscott also radioed Patton's headquarters that he needed naval

CHAPTER NINE ★ VICTORY AT MESSINA

support. The *Philadelphia* returned with two other cruisers and resumed bombarding the Germans. American fighter planes added to the barrage. Just as things seemed to go Patton's way, Bernard's radio went dead. The *Philadelphia*'s captain, unable to receive word from the beach forces, departed again at 3:00 p.m. Bernard's force continued to slug it out with the Germans until an errant strafing run by American planes knocked out his remaining artillery, killing and wounding nineteen men in his headquarters. With few options left, Bernard ordered all his men to the top of Mount Cipolla for a last stand. The *Philadelphia* returned a third time and laid down fires until the Luftwaffe attacked, forcing the captain to leave the area for good. The Germans, now in control of the coastal road, continued their retreat, content to leave Bernard's men alone and isolated.

While Bernard and his men battled with the retreating Germans, General Alexander visited Patton's headquarters, where Patton did not worry about the amphibious landing as much as he worried about the second slapping incident. He explained the matter to Alexander, who recommended Patton go to Eisenhower about it, advice Patton failed to heed. Alexander later made known his belief that if the incident had never occurred, Patton would have led the invasion of Italy.[89]

When Bernard's stand finally ended, Patton boarded a Piper Cub and took off for the beachhead. Sitting in the back seat, he studied his maps and communicated with the pilot through hand signals. The plane made a pass over the beach so he could see Truscott's supporting artillery, but a Luftwaffe pilot spotted the small plane and gave pursuit, machineguns blazing. The Cub pilot stalled the plane and put it into a dive, corkscrewing toward the sea and pulling out only a few feet above water. The enemy pilot, thinking he had damaged Patton's plane on his first run, did not try another. Patton's pilot, careful not to fly too close to the enemy-occupied coast, put the plane down back at Palermo. "Nice flight, lieutenant," was Patton's only comment.[90]

At dawn the next morning, elements of Truscott's ground forces reached the area and the men atop the hill passed the code word "Copacett," meaning everything was under control. Bernard led his party down the hill singing, "The cavalry, the artillery, the dirty engineers, They'll never beat the infantry in a hundred million years."[91] Patton's second amphibious assault had come close to trapping an entire enemy division and flanking the entire German line, but his force was too small, too late, and

Figure 34. Patton holds an informal conference with General Sir Harold Alexander in the backseat of a command car at Lucian Truscott's 3rd Infantry Division headquarters, on August 25, 1943. National Archives and Records Administration.

the naval and air support too sporadic. Patton, however, was learning and staying creative on a battlefield with few options for maneuver.[92]

When Patton received word about the linkup, he headed to the area with Senator Henry Cabot Lodge Jr. of Massachusetts. Lodge had been an officer in the 1st Armored Division, until President Roosevelt ordered all congressmen serving in the armed forces to choose between their office and their uniform. Lodge had asked Patton if he should stay in the Army or return to the Senate. Patton advised he should remain a senator unless he could get assurances from Secretary of War Stimson that he would get combat pay. With that, the two climbed into Patton's command car and headed to the battlefield. Dead Germans covered the ground for miles. The GIs refused to bury them, as the German habit of booby-trapping the dead had become all too common.[93]

West of Brolo they interviewed the men who had fought there. "They looked tired but were in good spirits," Patton later wrote. When he saw the soldiers from the amphibious force coming down the hill, he shouted

CHAPTER NINE ★ VICTORY AT MESSINA

to them, "All you men from Massachusetts fall in over here." The men obeyed, then stood quiet and motionless as Lodge spoke while Patton remained ramrod straight in his command car. Then Patton spoke: "The American soldier is the greatest soldier in the world," he then raised his hand and pointed at the mountain. "Only American soldiers can climb mountains like those."[94] Their visit over, the general and the senator departed. On their way back to Patton's headquarters three German bombers swooped down and attacked his caravan. Patton's driver hit the brakes and the bombs hit close, but no one was injured. Surprisingly, Truscott came up to Patton and reviewed the situation amid the action. Patton later wrote of Truscott, "I wish that there could have been more spectators present to see how officers conduct themselves in tight positions."[95] Meanwhile, that same day, Eddy's 9th Infantry Division captured the town of Randazzo, uniting with the British.

The anxiety over the amphibious landing and the stress from the bombing attack left Patton exhausted. In addition, he still suffered the effects of sand-fly fever.[96] Lucas passed him on the road and thought Patton looked "washed out."[97] Yet, he still visited the front and prepared for another amphibious operation, this time using the 45th Infantry Division's 157th Infantry regiment and five Stuart tanks from Patton's own headquarters. The objective would be Falcone, another coastal town eighteen road miles east of Brolo. Bradley and Truscott tried to call off the operation, arguing that elements of the 3rd had already passed Falcone. The 1st Infantry, in fact, was already near Messina, ten miles east of Falcone. But Patton would have none of it. He ordered the assault forward. Bradley told him his troops would be waiting to greet the amphibious force when it came ashore.[98] The operation went off successfully, save for sixteen heavily equipped soldiers who died when their landing craft accidentally dumped them into the water. It could have been worse. As the task force approached the beach, the lieutenant with the supporting tanks saw an American tank destroyer on a hill. To prevent a friendly fire incident, he radioed all his tank commanders to turn their turrets to the side so the tank destroyer crews ashore could see the white star on the side of their turrets. The task force landed and was greeted by the soldiers of the 3rd Infantry, just like Bradley had promised.[99]

With all that going on, Lucas arrived at Patton's headquarters with a message from Eisenhower telling him to stop wearing his ivory handled pistols and acting like a madman, or he was doomed. He also related that "correspondents have some stories on Geo[rge] they are dying to use."[100] Patton continued wearing his pistols. Without paying the letter much regard, Patton went about his duties until something odd caught his eye. Outside his headquarters, he came across Private Jack Copeland, who usually managed his top-secret maps, pulling guard duty. When Patton asked him what he was doing, Copeland explained that Lieutenant Colonel Codman had put him there. "By God," Patton roared. "My staff does not stand guard duty!" Patton chewed out Codman, threatening to send him to the front. "That private knows more where my troops are than I do," Patton yelled in his squeaky voice. "If the Boche ever get ahold of him they would have a field day!" Patton gave Copeland different duties. An angry Codman refused to speak to Copeland for almost two months.[101]

Around 2:00 a.m. on August 17, Patton received a message from Truscott that his troops had entered Messina two hours before midnight. Patton contacted Eisenhower, Alexander, and Bradley and told them the good news. He told Bradley they would be entering the city around 10:00 a.m. As the sun rose, he flew with Lucas and Gay to Falcone, where he picked up General Keyes and drove to the top of a hill overlooking the Messina. On the hilltop, Truscott greeted him. "What the hell are you all standing around for?" Patton asked. Truscott, who had arranged a motorcycle and scout car escort, assured Patton they were just waiting for him. They took the winding road into Messina, passing burning German tanks, self-propelled and anti-aircraft guns, and hordes of Germans, some dead, others waiting to head to POW camps. Civilians peeked out of the caves along the sides of the cliff where they had sheltered to escape the crossfire.

A woman in a red dress ran on to the road, trying to stop Patton's command car. The driver kept going, but immediately afterwards, German artillery, firing from across the straits, exploded in the streets behind him. One shell hit the second vehicle behind Patton, wounding everyone in it. The vehicle behind that one suffered four flat tires, but no injuries. "I wonder how she knew this was going to happen," General Gay later wrote, "and I was sure she was trying to protect us."[102] The air then rocked with return fire from American 155s. As the caravan advanced, the men noticed bomb craters, smashed buildings, and wrecked vehicles littering the city's empty streets. On a corner wall someone had written in big black letters, "Il Duce." Patton later confessed to his diary, "M[essina] is the worst mess I have seen."[103]

CHAPTER NINE ★ VICTORY AT MESSINA

Patton's command car rolled through the city until it came upon a column of British tanks, with commandos riding on top. As the column stopped, British brigadier John C. Currie climbed down from his tank and shook Patton's hand. "We got in around 10:00," said Currie. "It was a jolly good race. I congratulate you." Patton assumed this was Montgomery's last grasp at stealing the show from him. "I think the general was quite sore that we had got there first," Patton wrote in his diary, "but since we'd been in there for fourteen hours when he arrived, the race was clearly to us."[104]

Patton and Truscott made their way to city hall, where the mayor officially surrendered to Truscott. The civilians seemed pleased to see the Americans.[105] On the way out of town, Patton encountered Beetle Smith and Brigadier General Lyle Lemnitzer. He took Smith in his car and drove off to Truscott's headquarters for lunch. During the meal, Patton and Smith spoke about promotions for the Seventh Army staff. Patton thought they deserved promotions for the victorious campaign, not as a favor but as a right. Smith said it had been decided before the campaigns that there would be no promotions. Patton wrote him off as "a typical s.o.b."[106]

Soon after, Patton issued his congratulations to Seventh Army: "Born at sea, baptized in blood and crowned with victory in the course of 38 days in incessant battle and unceasing labor you have added a glorious chapter to the history of the war." Again, like his order issued when he left II Corps, Patton spread the thanks to support units and the Navy. But this time he issued solid numbers to support his army's success. "As a result of this combined effort, you have killed or captured 113,350 enemy troops. You have destroyed 256 of his tanks, 2,324 vehicles and 1,162 large guns and in addition have collected a mass of military booty running into hundreds of tons." He pointed out a more important achievement—"You have destroyed the prestige of the enemy"—and concluded, "your fame shall never die."[107]

But the victory was not complete. Despite his left-right punch with Truscott in the north and Allen in the center of Sicily, most of the Germans and many of Italians escaped the island. Since neither Patton nor Montgomery could effectively get behind the Axis forces, on August 4, the Germans had begun a phased withdraw from the island to the mainland. They developed five ferry routes across the Straits of Messina, the narrow waterway between Messina and Calabria, Italy, and gathered a flotilla of 134 small naval vessels, ferries, and barges to transport the men. While equipment was ferried during the day, troops were ferried at night. Flack batteries on both sides of the straits defended the crossing from air interdiction, while patrols of minesweepers, E-boats, and Italian mini submarines kept the Allied navies at bay. To maintain discipline and prevent panic, the German commander in charge of the evacuation, General Hans Valentin Hube, ordered that anyone interfering with the crossings would be immediately shot or clubbed to death. In one section, any soldier without his rifle was not to be allowed on a ferry. The Italian crossing plan was not as well organized and often threated to collapse, but unlike the Germans, the Italians also ferried men *to* Sicily, mostly native Sicilians who planned to surrender to the Allies once they reached home. Amazingly, the Allies had no plans to stop the evacuation. British naval commanders refused to duel with the German flack batteries, and with the navy refusing to commit to an attack, the air forces did not feel compelled to go it alone. While there were raids and bombing missions, there was no concentrated effort. The evacuation went on almost unhindered. When it was over, the Germans had evacuated almost forty thousand soldiers, along with tanks, vehicles, and other equipment, while the Italians evacuated around seventy thousand soldiers, as well as vehicles, heavy weapons, ammunition, and mules.[108]

The British war office described Sicily as a "strategic and tactical failure."[109] Most military historians label the Sicily campaign as a German victory, since German forces managed to escape to the mainland with much of their equipment, a far better showing than the British evacuation at Dunkirk. Yet, the campaign provided numerous strategic advantages to the Allies. By taking Sicily, the Allies reopened the Mediterranean Sea to supply ships headed to the Middle East, and, eventually, the Soviet Union. In addition, the campaign drew in German Luftwaffe units from Norway, where they had been attacking Atlantic convoys, making crossings easier. However, the campaign also showed the limitations of the Allied Air Forces and the Royal Navy. It added to Montgomery's image as a plodding commander who rarely risked extending his army for a knock-out blow against the enemy, especially if it risked his men.[110] Yet it was a victory for Patton, who had achieved his objectives and then some. He had raced up the island while Montgomery stalled on the east coast. He had captured Palermo and Messina and proved himself a superior general and the American soldier as good if not better than his British counterpart. In addition, Patton had led a successful amphibious landing and airborne operation and personally helped repel an enemy attack. He pushed his troops hard, driving Seventh Army to Palermo. During the race to Messina, he went off the map and flanked the German army twice. Through his personal influence on the battlefield, he had made sure that an American army entered Messina before the British. Through it all, he had defied and cajoled his superiors and combat lieutenants to accomplish victory. He had done much to erase the embarrassment of Kasserine Pass.

Accolades came pouring in. George Marshall wrote, "You have done a grand job of leadership and your corps and division commanders and their people have made Americans very proud of their army and confident of the future." From President Roosevelt: "All of us are thrilled over the Sicilian campaign now successfully concluded in accordance with the timing and planning of the Allies." From British King George VI: "On the final accomplishment of the occupation of Sicily I wish to send to you and to all members of the forces that you command with such distinction my heartfelt congratulations on a great achievement." Even Montgomery had positive words for the commander of Seventh Army: "The Eighth Army sends it warmest congratulations to you and your splendid army on the way you captured Messina." Other generals, admirals and airmen also chimed in with congratulatory notes.[111] But the record was not spotless. Patton learned that tragically large friendly fire incidents were a price to be paid on the modern battlefield, where technological advancements were no match for a man with an itchy trigger finger. And his mad obsession with a speedy advance made him a terror, whether pushing civilians over cliffs or slapping sick soldiers in hospitals.

The enemy took note of the battle for Sicily. In Berlin, the Japanese pressed German propaganda minister Joseph Goebbels to hold onto Sicily under any circumstances, urging extraordinary measures. They insisted that were they defending the island, they would use suicide torpedoes and suicide flyers to devastate the British Mediterranean fleet. Goebbels agreed, noting, "I, too, believe that it is necessary to do something beyond the normal."[112] In Sicily, German general Eberhard Rodt, who commanded the 15th Panzer Division, which Patton faced, admitted that his unit was "little troubled" by Montgomery's attacks, which the Germans fought to a standstill. The old Africa veterans were familiar with the enemy's style, "and we behaved accordingly." Patton was different: "The latter only advanced on the northern flank, where it proved particularly difficult to maintain contact with the 29th Division, fighting the rearguard action on the north coast road." The Germans took to calling the coast road to Messina "Death Alley." In addition, Rodt and his men constantly worried that an amphibious landing would "cut the division's line of retreat." The Germans faced an American commander who was both creative and aggressive.[113]

On the minus side of the ledger, Patton's rapid advance across Sicily also negated an Allied advantage. Sicilian-born OSS officers had planned to reach behind enemy lines and organize resistance against the Axis (without the aid of the Mafia), but their efforts came practically to naught in the dust of Patton's Seventh Army. "The speed of the Sicilian campaign has made our plans redundant and infiltrations are almost impossible," the agents radioed their superiors in Algiers. "Patton's troops are moving too fast for even our efficient intelligence techniques." Patton's rapid advance across France would have the same effect on airborne operations, forcing planners to scrap several planned airdrops because Patton's tanks were overrunning drop zones before the aircraft could even get in the air.[114]

The campaign had strategic consequences for the Axis. Not only did the Sicilian campaign topple Mussolini's regime in Italy, it also forced Hitler to pull three of his best armored divisions out of the Battle of Kursk—one of the largest tank battles of the war—surrendering the initiative to the Soviets. Although the Fuehrer did this more out of concern that Italy would pull out of its alliance with Germany than to shore up the Sicilian front, the result was the same, and that's exactly what Joseph Stalin had wanted: attacks from the western Allies to relieve pressure on Soviet forces. Patton's forceful leadership had repercussions more than fifteen hundred miles away. Not knowing where the next Allied attack in the Mediterranean might come, Hitler was also forced to divert more troops from the Russian front and post them in the Balkans and Greece. Patton would later play a role in hyping up those German anxieties.[115]

Despite the accolades and larger impact of the campaign, Patton's victory left him feeling low. "I feel let down," he recorded in his diary. This was caused by his constant pushing of commanders and troops, the battles with the Navy and Air Force for more support, the frustrations of stubborn enemy defenses, the aloofness of his British allies, and the strain of seeing his soldiers maimed and killed, while, in his mind, others who shirked their duty under the guise of battle fatigue. He also had a few battles with the press. For example, early in the campaign, he read a story in *Stars and Stripes* about soldiers under fire diving into foxholes and called a reporter for the paper to his headquarters. Patton ordered him to stop publishing lies, but when the reporter queried Patton about his order, he told him what he had read and demanded, "Americans are the bravest soldiers in the world. They stand upright and fight!" The reporter then related to Patton how he had hurt his knee in Gela when he jumped into a foxhole during a Luftwaffe attack and a two-star general jumped in on top of him.[116]

Patton retired to his bed the next day, August 17, still suffering the effects of sand-fly fever. Yet he regretted nothing. If given the same opportunity, he swore he would not have changed a thing. He saw himself as just a chip floating on the river of destiny, victim or beneficiary of wherever it took him. It was typical Patton, pushing himself as hard as possible and leaving it to a higher power to control things he could not. "I trust that the same fortune which has helped me before will continue to assist me." Events would prove he could not have been more wrong.[117]

PART III
Limbo

CHAPTER TEN

The Slapping Incidents and Italy

GENERAL GEORGE C. Marshall wanted nothing to do with Italy. He viewed the entire Mediterranean operation as nothing but a "suction pump" taking men and resources away from the invasion of France. With North Africa and Sicily secured, he wanted to quickly cross the English Channel and attack France, so his armies could sweep into Germany. Once Germany was defeated, he could shift the weight of the American military to the Pacific and crush Japan. The British, he felt, were too focused on the war in Europe and did not share his sense of urgency. Once the Sicily operation was completed, he did not want to continue west but would only consider an invasion of Corsica or Sardinia, east of Sicily, since either would be a good springboard into southern France. If the British wanted to plunge farther east in the Mediterranean, he told President Roosevelt, "they do it alone."[1]

But the British wanted to take advantage of Italy's teetering government to attack either Italy or the German-occupied Balkans. The twelve-day TRIDENT Conference in Washington in mid-May 1943 failed to break the stalemate between American and British planners. Finally, Winston Churchill and Marshall flew to Algiers to consult Eisenhower, who favored invading Italy, just so long as the Allies did not get bogged down there. Reluctantly, on July 16, while Patton was fighting his way to Agrigento, Marshall approved the invasion of Italy.[2]

General Alexander would again head 15th Army Group. The plan called for Montgomery to land the bulk of his Eighth Army at Calabria on Italy's toe, in a maneuver codenamed Operation BAYTOWN. Six days later, Mark Clark's Fifth Army would touch down on the west coast at Salerno, codenamed Operation AVALANCHE. The two forces would then race toward each other, cutting off Axis forces in the south. The attack on Calabria was scheduled for September 3, while the invasion of Salerno was scheduled for September 9. As Eisenhower had told Patton during the Messina campaign, his Seventh Army would land near Florence (where the German 16th Panzer Division was reported) in case things did not go as planned.[3]

But Patton's Italian campaign was not to be. On August 17, the day Patton entered Messina as a conquering hero, Eisenhower received a report prepared by Demaree Bess of the *Saturday Evening Post* and his associates from his chief surgeon, Brigadier General Fred Blesse, on the two slapping incidents. The severity of the allegations about Patton's personal conduct shocked Eisenhower, who told his aide Captain Butcher that he would have to give Patton a "jacking up" for his behavior. When Butcher reminded his boss that Patton had done a "swell job" in Sicily, Eisenhower, citing the same report, countered that many American soldiers had marched over Sicily's rough terrain until they had literally worn the skin off their feet. They deserved better.[4]

Meanwhile, on Sicily, the letdown after the campaign left Patton feeling gloomy. To him, the future of his army did " not look bright." He spent the day after his victory in Messina feeling shaky, which he blamed on his sand-fly fever.[5] The next day, on August 18, Eisenhower cabled Patton that his Seventh Army no longer had a role in Italy. Worse, Seventh Army would be broken up and fed to Clark's Fifth Army as needed. Patton's command would consist of nothing but anti-aircraft soldiers and mechanics, a harsh blow to the victor of Messina. "I feel awful to day [sic] and all let down," he wrote his wife. "I have no inkling what's going to happen to 7th Army." He speculated, however, that he might have a part in the eventual invasion of southern France.[6]

Patton got his first hint that he might be in trouble two days later, when Eisenhower cabled him that he was sending General Lucas to his headquarters and that Patton should personally greet him and give both Lucas and the message "your full attention."[7] But before Lucas arrived, General Blesse presented Patton with a confidence-shattering letter from Eisenhower, which detailed the report on the slapping incidents. While Eisenhower reassured Patton that he was proud of his accomplishments, calling his contributions to the Allied cause "incalculable," he left little doubt how he felt about the allegations. If they were true, "I must so seriously question your good judgment and your self-discipline as to raise serious doubt in my mind as to your future usefulness."

CHAPTER TEN ★ THE SLAPPING INCIDENTS AND ITALY   221

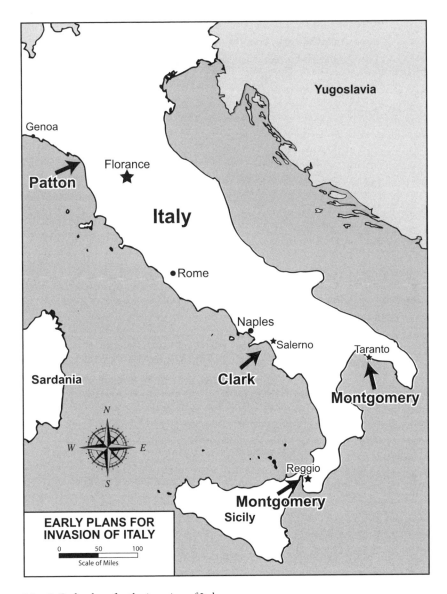

Map 7. Early plans for the invasion of Italy.

Eisenhower, although angered by Patton's actions, did not entirely close the door on his future. In fact, he added some advice, imploring Patton to give the matter his "instant and serious consideration, so that no incident of this character can be reported to me in the future, and I may continue to count upon your assistance in military tasks." He assured Patton that the only record of the incident resided in his secret files, and he wanted Patton to reply personally, and secretly, to him. Finally, he advised Patton to apologize to the "individuals concerned" before responding to his letter. Eisenhower's final line must have turned Patton's stomach: "No letter that I have been called upon to write in my military career has caused me the mental anguish of this one, not only because of my long and deep personal friendship for you, but because of my admiration of your military qualities; but I assure you that conduct such as described in the accompanying report will *not* be tolerated in this theater no matter who the offender may be."[8]

Eisenhower's reprimand surely surprised Patton. To him, the slapping incidents were simply military matters that he had addressed with his signature discipline. He later admitted he was wrong and, although working from insufficient knowledge, thought his motives were correct. "One cannot permit skulking to exist," he vented to his diary, comparing it to any communicable disease. He decided to fix the problem quickly, not only to clear his name, but, more important, to please Eisenhower. "I hate to make Ike mad when it is my earnest study to please him." General Lucas came over that night to tell him just how mad Eisenhower was, leaving Patton depressed. "I feel very low," he wrote. Lucas advised Patton to apologize to everyone: from the soldiers he slapped to every division in the Seventh Army. He also suggested that Patton promise to never do any like it again. Patton would follow his advice, and it was this act of contrition that helped him regain his standing in Eisenhower's eyes and probably prevented him from being sent home for the duration of the war.[9]

In a bitter irony, Eisenhower felt there would have been no outcry if Patton had slapped the two soldiers closer to the front. "No one would have even noted it," Eisenhower wrote after the war, "except with the passing thought that here was a leader who would not tolerate shirking."[10] Still, there may have been more to the Bennett slapping episode than recorded. In 1957, Lieutenant Colonel Currier, whom Patton spoke to during the incident, wrote to the *Boston Herald*'s William Cunningham that "considerably more took place than has ever appeared in print," adding, "If you had seen and heard what I did, you would feel as I do, that what happened to Patton was very much less than he deserved."[11]

In the event, Patton acted immediately. On August 21, the day following the reprimand, he met with Private Bennett and apologized,

CHAPTER TEN ★ THE SLAPPING INCIDENTS AND ITALY

explaining that he had hoped to restore his manhood in chewing him out. They shook hands and Bennett left. But any sympathy Patton may have felt towards Bennett evaporated later that day when Brigadier General John A. Crane, Bennett's artillery commander, told Patton that Bennett was absent without leave from his unit and had gone to the rear, falsely reporting his condition to the surgeons. "It is rather a commentary on justice when an Army Commander has to soft-soap a skulker to placate the timidity of those above," Cane wrote. Having to apologize to someone he felt had feigned illness just increased Patton's resentment toward Eisenhower. Nevertheless, on August 22, he met with Private Kuhl, the other soldier he slapped, and repeated the speech and handshake.[12]

Earlier that day, Patton had met with the doctors, nurses, and enlisted men who witnessed the slapping incidents. He told them about a friend from World War I who lost his nerve and, when no one tried to help him snap out of it, killed himself. Patton said he was trying to prevent that from happening again. Later, he spoke to reporters about the incidents, telling them, "When things are happening, a commanding general is under great nervous tension. He may do things he may afterwards regret. I know many people who regard me as an a--. But I have patted five soldiers on the back for every one I have spoken a harsh word to. I dealt harshly with a couple of soldiers and was wrong. I am going to apologize to them."[13]

Ironically, that same day, Lucas presented Patton with an oak leaf cluster to add to his Distinguished Service Cross. Standing in the Royal Palace's courtyard, Lucas pinned on the medal and presented Distinguished Service Crosses to Geoffrey Keyes and Hugh Gaffey. Patton had earned his award for his actions at Gela beach back on July 11. "When a breakthrough by the enemy threatened to split the American lines," the citation read, "General Patton promptly moved to the scene of action over a road that was being constantly bombed and strafed by enemy planes. Personally directing the movement of reinforcements, he closed the gap and repulsed all counter-attacks [sic]. His prompt action in the attack and his presence on the front line among his troops prevented the recapture of Gela by the enemy and made possible the establishment of a secure bridgehead." Patton did not believe he deserved the award, "but I won't say so," he wrote Beatrice.[14]

Deep down, Patton may have felt other than contrite. Speaking to one reporter about the incident with Kuhl, Patton explained, "Looking at the others in the tent, so many of them badly beaten up, I simply flew off the handle."[15] As for slapping Bennett, he only dedicated three lines to the incident in his diary. "Saw another alleged nervous patient—really a coward," he wrote that day. "I told the doctor to return him to his company and he began to cry so I cursed him well and he shut up. I may have saved his soul if he had one." Still, when asked a few days later about the Bennett incident, Patton told reporter Henry J. Taylor, "I felt ashamed of myself and I hoped the whole thing would die out."[16] Patton never wrote a report on either incident.

Bradley, for his part, believed that Patton felt no remorse. In his first memoir, Bradley mentioned that Patton had shown up at his headquarters back on August 10, apologizing for his lateness because of the slapping incident at the hospital. Bradley claimed that Patton told him, "There were a couple of malingerers there. I slapped one of them to make him mad and put some fight back in him." Bradley recalled that Patton spoke of the incident casually, without remorse or any feeling of wrongdoing.[17] Meanwhile, Everett Hughes detected irony in the whole incident. "Geo[rge] had to boot men off the bunk in Casa Blanca [sic] to get them into the fight and again at Gela. He gets the DSC [Distinguished Service Cross] for one type of slapping or booting, and jumped on for slapping them in the hospital."[18]

Unsurprisingly in these circumstances, Patton worried about his position. To Beatrice, he wrote cryptic messages, explaining that his "exuberant personality" had gotten him in trouble with Eisenhower, whom he referred to as "Divine Destiny": "I seem to have made divine destiny a little mad, but that will pass." But as word spread, he wrote, "Some of the damndest lies are being spread about me," and expressed worry that General Marshall would believe the worst about his actions. He waxed philosophically to his wife, calling himself "a passenger floating on the river of destiny."[19]

Seeking to find out how Patton's commanders viewed him, Eisenhower first asked Alexander if he wanted Patton replaced over the slapping incidents, but Alexander explained that Patton was too valuable a fighting commander to remove in the middle of a campaign in which he was performing so well. To Alexander, it was a "family matter" for the Americans and best left to Eisenhower to decide. Eisenhower's correspondence to Marshall repeated Alexander's view.[20]

Eisenhower first wrote Marshall about the situation on August 24. He spent most of the first half of his letter lauding Patton's accomplishments in Sicily, his energy, and drive. He even stressed that Patton never once said, "We will rest here and recuperate and bring up more strength." Eisenhower wrote that Patton had done so well as an army commander that Seventh Army's drive across Sicily would be taught in the War College and at Fort Leavenworth, noting, "This has stemmed mainly from Patton." He then addressed Patton's failings and his own measures to repair the damage. "If he is not cured now, there is no hope for him." But, once again, Eisenhower had confidence in his subordinate. "Personally, I believe he is cured—not only because of his great personal loyalty to you and to me but because fundamentally he is so avid for recognition as a great military commander that he will ruthlessly suppress any habit of his own that will tend to jeopardize it." Eisenhower felt that, save for Patton's temper, his fighting qualities were too valuable to lose, "unless he ruins himself." No matter the outcome of this latest incident, Eisenhower concluded, "he can be classed as an army commander that you can use with certainty."[21]

Yet, Patton's star had dimmed in Eisenhower's eyes. Three days after his first letter, Eisenhower wrote Marshall again, this time placing Bradley at the top of his list of battle commanders. "Bradley is a standout in any position and is running absolutely true to form." While he still considered Patton the preeminent combat commander, Eisenhower stressed that Patton's temper hampered his abilities and judgment. "He is a one-sided individual," he wrote, "and particularly in his handling of individual subordinates is apt at times to display exceedingly poor judgment and unjustified temper." Still, Eisenhower asked Marshall not to discount Patton when selecting future assignments for generals.[22]

Worse, however, soldiers who heard about the slapping incidents changed their attitudes toward Patton. Where once they admired, respected, and trusted him, now they questioned what they were fighting for. Patton tried to prevent the expression of discontent, preventing reporters from interviewing anyone from Seventh Army without his permission, under threat of court-martial.[23] Even doctors were stymied from speaking out. On August 27, Patton sent Hap Gay to see the psychological warfare branch chief and tell him that no reports were to be written about Seventh Army personnel without Patton seeing them, thus precluding doctors from interviewing soldiers without Patton's permission. Again, any violators were threatened with a court-martial.[24]

Despite the cloud looming over Patton, he still made time for entertainment. The same day he apologized to Bennett, he welcomed entertainers Bob Hope and Frances Langford, touring with the USO, to his headquarters. Patton was decorating two Native Americans with the 45th Infantry Division when the celebrities arrived. After saluting and shaking hands with the recipients, Patton called the two entertainers in and asked them how things were in California, his home state. He told them that many of the men they had entertained at his Desert Training Center in California were now with him in Sicily. Patton so impressed Hope that the entertainer later wrote, "as far as I'm concerned, a general can have war fatigue too."

Patton had such a good time with his guests that he invited them back for dinner. Afterward, he gave them a tour of the palace. He showed them his bedroom, where he pointed out the artwork, telling them, "All my life I've heard about things being done 'to the queen's taste.' If this is it, I'll take Macy's basement." Patton said that he had missed their show and talked them into repeating their performance for him and his staff. Once they finished, Patton told Hope that his men enjoyed anything in the way of entertainment. Hope asked Patton what he meant by anything and Patton responded, "Well, let's say *everything*." Everyone laughed that Patton's humor had topped Hope's.[25]

When not hosting visitors—or awaiting Eisenhower's final judgement—Patton focused his attention on Italy, which, despite Eisenhower's order that Seventh Army would have no role in the campaign, was the only active front. Besides, Patton knew that in war, nothing was ever set in stone and the situation could always change. After addressing the 2nd Armored Division on their performance, Patton met with British major general Francis Rennell Rodd, known as Lord Rennell, who told him that Winston Churchill "very much" opposed the cross-channel attack into France and that all the troops in North Africa and Sicily might head to Italy. With that information, Patton focused on landing Seventh Army north of Florence, discussing with Rennell the possibility of using the roads in northern Italy near the German border. Patton worried that Clark would be in charge of British divisions during the assault on Salerno and that the British would do the covering while the Americans did the fighting. When Alexander later asked Patton about Seventh Army's equipment, Patton worried that he would steal it and give it to Clark. Still stinging from Eisenhower's letter of reprimand, Patton felt cornered. "If I suggest to Ike that this is the case," he later wrote, "he will tell me I don't see the 'big picture.' I wish to God he was an American."[26] Compounding Patton's anger, he called Clark in North Africa, only to hear a woman operator come on the line. An enraged Patton yelled obscenities at her, asking "what the hell" was going on. The Woman's Auxiliary Corps radio operator cried and shook as she connected Patton's call.[27]

To prepare for the eventual fight in Italy, and to apologize for the slapping incidents, Patton visited his divisions. On August 25, in an open-air area in Bagheria, he told the men of the 45th Infantry Division that they were superior to the Germans, whom they would meet again on the continent. He warned them against Germans using armor at the point of their attacks and demanded, "By God, this point will not get through! When it strikes at you, you must be ready to strike first! Blunt it! Hit it from both sides! Knock the hell out of it! Take the initiative! Hit and hit again until there is no point and nothing behind the point to oppose you. Drive forward!" He also expressed his care for the men: "I love every bone in your heads, but be very careful. Do not go to sleep or someone is liable to slip up behind you and hit you over the head with a sock full of shit, and that's an embarrassing way to die." The men cheered their victorious commander. His words stuck. The men of the 45th started calling themselves "Boneheads."[28]

The following day Patton visited the 9th Infantry Division's 60th Infantry Regiment but only got off one word—"Men"—before the soldiers broke out in cheers. They tossed their helmets in the air and chanted, "Georgie! Georgie!" Patton pleaded for their attention but they continued cheering as he stood shaking his head with tears streaming down his cheeks. After a few sharp words he left the stage and headed for his vehicle. When an officer barked "Attention!" the men put on the nearest helmet, buttoned the chinstraps, and saluted as he roared away, standing in his vehicle, still with tears running down his cheeks. "We loved him," commented one officer. When Patton spoke to another 9th unit, men in the back rows, feeling no need for an apology, inflated condoms and poked the makeshift balloons forward. When Patton saw that, he turned red and left the stage.[29]

The 1st Infantry Division offered him no such reception. Patton arrived on August 27 to a hill in front of a natural bowl in which fifteen thousand soldiers waited. Two motorcycles escorted Patton's vehicle as sirens blared, but the soldiers were unimpressed. They were still angry over the relief of their beloved commanders, Terry Allen and Teddy Roosevelt. Even worse, Patton arrived two hours late, forcing the men to stand around without shade as they waited for him.[30] "You are part of the Seventh Army that was born at sea and baptized with the blood of our enemy," Patton began. "We have killed many more of them and will have the opportunity to kill more. That is what our job is. We are here to kill the enemy." He then explained that things he had done in the past were for the good of the army, and that now he was sorry for them. When he finished, he only heard silence. He turned and looked at the barren countryside behind him. Then he haltingly turned back to the troops, squinting at them in the bright sunshine. Not knowing what to do, he stomped back to his vehicle and drove off. The veterans did not know what he was talking about. Was this about sacking Allen and Roosevelt? They did not understand the speech was part of his penance for slapping two soldiers.[31] One soldier who witnessed the speech commented, "That fucking fucker of a general swears too fucking much." Yet, for all the hostility the 1st Infantry veterans showed him, few said a harsh word about him. When reporter John Marquand interviewed soldiers about what they thought of Sicily, they told him they hated the island, "but I did not speak to a single soldier," wrote Marquand, "who had a thing to say against the General."[32]

Three days later, Patton spoke to the 3rd Infantry Division, referring to the slapping incidents with only one sentence before launching into a rousing speech about the Division's success: "You have done a damn fine job. You have pissed on the despised Boche! You have beaten the shit out of every enemy force that resisted you. You have shown the God-damn Germans that they are no match for us. You have every right to be proud of yourselves as I am of you. Now you must prepare yourselves for the next attack so that we can get this fucking war over and all go home." He finished on a high note, declaring his war philosophy: "I love the smell of a dead Kraut!"[33]

After Patton had finished speaking to the 1st Infantry on August 27, he returned to Palermo to find that General Charles H. White and Brigadier General Russell Reynolds had been sent by Eisenhower to review the Sicily campaign with him. Patton dined with both men and stayed up late with Reynolds, articulating what had worked and what was needed on future battlefields. Patton boasted to Reynolds, "Our soldiers are the fightin'est sons of bitches on Earth and they know it." He complimented the M-1 rifle, stressed the success of night-time operations, and hailed bayonet charges. "The Jerry is scared as hell of the bayonet," he told Reynolds. "None of our men were killed with the bayonet in Sicily, but we have killed many." He credited the artillery for much of his army's success and said his troops needed more of it. He cited an infantry cannon

CHAPTER TEN ★ THE SLAPPING INCIDENTS AND ITALY   229

Figure 35. Patton addresses soldiers from the 82nd Airborne Division. After the slapping incidents, he apologized to every division under his command. Library of Congress, OV 15, 1.

company that captured nine enemy pack howitzers and, even though they had never used them before, loaded them and fired, destroying two enemy batteries. Patton explained that it proved that "the biggest lie in the world is that you have to be a fish to swim."

For improvements, Patton told Reynolds he wanted more discipline instilled in units. Soldiers who could not salute or wear proper uniforms could not be expected to fight. "It is murder to send units with poor discipline into battle." He wanted better leadership at all levels. "The only true specialist in this war is the infantry platoon leader," he said, and credited failure in battle to officers' "lack of moral courage," adding, "Lack of moral courage is [the] inability to force others to do the things they are paid to do." Since men ate less in combat and tended to only eat the candy and smoke the cigarettes in C-rations while throwing away the rest, he wanted smaller C-rations and the candy and cigarettes separated from the other foods.

Patton saved his most important comments for his divisions and corps. As he explained it to Reynolds, after the first week in combat, divisions increased in efficiency, at which level it remained for about another week, but by the third week it started to decline, due to casualties and fatigue. "Sensing this period is one of the most important functions of a senior commander," he explained. He suggested that corps be composed of three divisions, with one division in reserve to replace the most worn-out division, preventing this decline that so concerned him. He also recommended that an army comprise two corps with two armored divisions. Patton was finally getting away from the armored corps concept—an entire corps comprised of armored divisions—he had developed during the Louisiana maneuvers of 1941.[34]

On August 29 Patton flew to Catania with Bradley, Keyes, and Truscott to watch Eisenhower present Montgomery the Legion of Merit and to review plans for the invasion of Italy. Eisenhower ordered Patton to get an assessment of Fifth Army from Clark because if anything happened to both Bradley and Clark, Patton would take it over. "I seem to be third," Patton wrote in his diary, "but will end up on top." He had even more reason to be optimistic. He had received a letter from Lucas, explaining that Eisenhower had written Marshall a glowing account of him. Thinking again that the slapping incidents were behind him, Patton wrote in his diary that night, "Well, that was a near thing, but I feel much better."[35]

Before the meeting, Patton slipped Eisenhower a letter about his actions to rectify the slapping incidents. In it, he thanked Eisenhower for his graciousness. "I am at a loss to find the words with which to express my chagrin and grief at having given you," he wrote, "a man to whom I owe everything and for whom I would gladly lay down my life, cause for displeasure with me." He assured Eisenhower that he did not intend to be harsh or cruel to the two soldiers he accosted. He again used the story about his World War I friend who had succumbed to battle fatigue. He concluded by telling Eisenhower he said something to the doctors involved that had not been reported: "After each incident I stated to the officers with me that I felt I had probably saved an immortal soul."[36]

That same day, Eisenhower sent another message to Marshall regarding the invasion of Italy, mentioning Patton in the subtext. Eisenhower called Patton "preeminently a combat commander," who was unappreciated by others for his innate skills. In Patton he found a leader who never thought about caution, fatigue, or doubt. "Patton is not affected by these and, consequently, his troops are not affected." Eisenhower also saw the "Patton Effect" on his corps and division leaders: "If they had had an example of pessimism, caution and delay above them, they could not possibly have acted as they did." Eisenhower balanced his report in his summation. On the one hand, he repeated his view of Patton from the letter he sent Marshall three days earlier; on the other, he noted that

Patton's "outstanding qualities must not be discounted when you are determining future assignments of senior officers."[37] Eisenhower was not the only officer lobbying Marshall to keep Patton in the saddle. When Wedemeyer—now in India—learned about the incidents, he penned a letter to Marshall praising Patton's leadership in Sicily. British admiral Louis Mountbatten also wrote Marshall, to the same effect.[38]

While many questions have been raised about Patton's behavior in the slapping incidents and accusations made about his reprehensible behavior, no one has asked where Eisenhower was for the months leading up to this incident. If the slapping incident had occurred in a vacuum, then Patton, and Patton alone, could be labeled the villain. But Patton had been slapping, kicking, shaking, and throttling soldiers for almost a year, and none of his superiors had lifted a finger to stop his actions. During the three-day Operation TORCH campaign, Eisenhower never left his Gibraltar cave to visit Patton in Morocco, where he would have seen him hitting and kicking soldiers in their rear ends. Eisenhower never visited the Tunisian front where Patton resorted to draconian behavior while training his men. Once Patton started his drive east to Gabes, Eisenhower only visited him twice. During the Sicilian campaign, Eisenhower visited once while Patton drove to Messina. Eisenhower never checked on Patton's leadership and instead let him reign on the battlefield. A military officer is responsible for the men in his command and for steering them on the right path. If the men fail, it is considered a failure of leadership. In the Mediterranean theater, Eisenhower did not shine as a commander or leader. That would come later. Patton's outbursts and subsequent slapping incidents might have been prevented had Eisenhower been aware of his furious explosions on the battlefield and checked them with a threat of relief if they continued. Instead, Eisenhower kept his distance, only to be surprised when he learned that Patton had struck two sick men.

Despite the work on Italy, the slapping incidents never strayed far from Patton's mind. He showed Eisenhower's letter, and his reply to it, to reporter Henry J. Taylor of the Scripps-Howard newspapers, and asked him his thoughts. "It sounds to me like only half of the story," Taylor told him. Patton told Taylor that Eisenhower's letter had arrived "on the eve of a new attack in which I had been written in for a large part in the plans, already issued," referring to the Italy invasion. "Eisenhower's problem," he explained to Taylor, "was whether what I had done was sufficiently damaging to compel my relief on the eve of an attack, thus losing what he described as my unquestioned military value, or whether less drastic measures would be appropriate." Patton then reviewed everything he had done to correct the situation, from apologizing to the two soldiers, to apologizing to the doctors and nurses present, to apologizing to the entire Seventh Army. "Beyond that, except to leave the Army and get out of the war, I do not know what I could have done."[39]

As the slapping incidents continued to weigh down Patton, he watched the bigger events of the surrounding war. Back in Palermo, he and Truscott watched a large Italian bomber land and taxi onto the far side of an airfield. Patton told a confused Truscott that he had expected the arrival of the enemy aircraft and had ordered the anti-aircraft gunners to hold their fire. The plane contained Italian general Giuseppe Castellano and his staff, who were on their way to Syracuse to work out an armistice between Italy and the Allies before the invasion. It had to be kept secret lest the Germans find out the Italians were actively seeking peace.[40]

On August 31 Patton flew to his old North African headquarters in Mostaganem, where he attended General Clark's final meeting on Operation AVALANCHE. He did not like what he heard. Clark planned to use the Sele River as a boundary between his British and American corps, without specific orders to hug the riverbanks. Patton saw this as the perfect place for the Germans to launch a counterattack, splitting the two forces. Patton advised Clark to immediately seek the cooperation of a leading Italian, for example, the mayor or ex-mayor of any captured town, because these types of officials had been most helpful in Sicily. When British air marshal Tedder promised air support for the landings, Patton leaned over to Major General Fred Walker, the commander of the 36th Infantry Division, the spearhead unit, and said in a loud voice, "Don't believe every damn word he says. If you see any friendly planes before day three, you'll be doing well." Patton jokingly told Admiral Hewitt, who would now be bringing Clark to his battlefield, that if he wanted to get in good with Eisenhower, he should promote Eisenhower's naval aide, Captain Butcher, to commodore. After the meeting, Patton pulled Eisenhower aside and asked if he could take Butcher back to Sicily. When Eisenhower told Butcher about the offer, Butcher refused, explaining, "As I have no desire either to leave or, if I had one [allotted leave], to spend it in Sicily."[41]

The next day, General Alfred Gruenther, one of Clark's planners, asked Patton what he thought of AVALANCHE. "Just as sure as God lives," Patton told him, "the Germans will attack down that river." Gruenther explained that artillery would cover the river, but he failed to convince

Patton, who knew plans always broke down in combat, especially in amphibious operations. Patton fumed that no senior commanders sought his counsel about landings, especially since he had the most experience, particularly from Operation TORCH, the largest, and—by Patton's estimation—the most difficult landing operation so far in the war. "Whom the Gods wish to destroy," he penned in his diary, "they first make mad."[42]

With the Salerno landing plans complete, Eisenhower called Patton to Algiers on September 2 to finally receive his face-to-face reprimand for the slapping incidents. Earlier in the day, Eisenhower met with Ed Kennedy, a bureau chief for the Associated Press, who told him that thousands of GIs were talking about the slapping incident and it might be better for the correspondents to write the story before wounded soldiers returned to the United States and spread the word. Eisenhower disagreed, explaining how he had chastised Patton. Kennedy agreed with Eisenhower's handling of the situation, although Eisenhower admitted to being amazed at how the incident seemed to snowball toward the United States. He reiterated his confidence in Patton's leadership but called the latter's behavior "despicable" and contemplated ordering him to hold a press conference to state for the record just what had happened, adding another apology to Patton's growing list. While Eisenhower never technically imposed censorship on the story, he told reporters that the two incidents would be fodder for enemy propaganda. The reporters, for their part, never wrote about the incidents or included them in radio broadcasts.[43]

When Patton arrived, Eisenhower lectured him for almost two hours about his disgraceful behavior and then hit Patton right where it hurt him most. Although Patton had made the rounds apologizing to any American who cared to listen, Eisenhower now ordered him to apologize to Montgomery for his temper, an action he knew Patton would despise. Eisenhower then reprimanded him for entering Messina first, which—according to Eisenhower—ruined Montgomery's career. Also, he said he would send an Army Inspector General (IG) to Sicily to ask the soldiers their thoughts on Patton.[44] He told Patton that Seventh Army would be broken up and its units divided between Italy and England. Eisenhower reiterated that there would be no army-sized landings in Florence for Patton and no immediate chance to put the slapping incidents behind him. Eisenhower explained that Bradley would head to England to command the American forces and plan the invasion of France. Patton argued that he, too, was a "pretty good planner." Eisenhower disagreed, saying he—like Eisenhower himself—did not like to work on plans.[45] It was as if Eisenhower was plucking Patton's limbs, one by one, pulling apart everything he held dear. If Eisenhower's goal was to tear Patton down, he succeeded greatly.

For the next three days, a depressed Patton laid low, staying in bed, reading papers, and sailing a boat. He tried to reassure himself in his diary, writing about Eisenhower, "He likes me. Of course he should." Yet Patton dreaded his visits to Eisenhower's headquarters, which he called "a British headquarters commanded by an American." During his stay in Algiers, only three people complimented him on his Sicily victory. He considered the snub intentional, since while his army had made Montgomery's Eighth Army "look like thirty cents in Sicily." It would be Montgomery's forces that would hit the Italian shore, not his.[46]

On September 3, the same day that Montgomery launched his amphibious assault of southern Italy, General Castellano signed a short-term armistice ending Italy's alliance with Germany. It would be made public five days later. While the war advanced to Italy, on September 6, Patton received a message that knocked the wind out of him: Omar Bradley would command the new American First Army for the invasion of France. Although Eisenhower had already told him this, it still came as a shock. The news, as Patton recorded it in his diary, "ruined me." In his view, green troops under a green army headquarters would spearhead the war's most important invasion. Worse, there was now no mission for his Seventh Army, only a small hope that it would be the follow-up force in France. Hap Gay wrote in his own diary, "It is a definite plan to get rid of Patton and 7th Army." After wondering if Eisenhower had even seen the message, Gay concluded, "Probably sent by Smith." Patton considered the message more heartbreaking than when Clark got Fifth Army. He wrote to Beatrice, "I guess you're the only one who loves me," and admitted to his diary, "I feel like death, but will survive—I always do." Despite his defiance, with Seventh Army's future in such doubt, Patton offered his staff a chance to transfer to other units hoping to get into action. No one took him up on the offer.[47]

Patton was riding an emotional rollercoaster. He swayed from anger to depression to optimism. He often sat at his desk, cleared of the usual maps and papers, staring into space. "He was exceedingly lonely," observed the 1st Infantry's Colonel Stanhope Mason, who passed by Patton's office one day. Patton, seeing Mason, asked him in and spoke about the Sicily campaign. With no one around, Patton dropped the warrior persona and was gracious. "The ham actor side of his character was completely absent," wrote Mason.[48] But Patton could just as quickly flip to rage. He cursed an officer for wearing a sun helmet, calling him, "an S. O. B. in every way" for what Patton called "an Elephant Hat!"[49] When Bradley stopped in on his way to meet General Marshall in England, Patton tried to put on a brave face by greeting him with an honor guard and band, but Bradley saw through it, considering his former commander near suicidal. Patton said it was because Eisenhower had dissolved Seventh Army, but Bradley's plum assignment had just as much to do with it. "I feel like death," he told Bradley, but he just as quickly convinced himself he would bounce back. He pushed onto Bradley all the combat ideas he could conjure, hoping Bradley would share them with Marshall, showing that he was still ready for a combat role in the upcoming fight. Bradley found the entire experience awkward. "This great proud warrior, my former boss, had been brought to his knees," Bradley wrote in his memoir. Despite his jealousy, anger, and depression, Patton lent Bradley the use of his C-47 for the next leg of his journey.[50]

While Patton lamented the possible end of his career, Eisenhower still supported him. In a message to Marshall about permanent major general appointments, he stressed that any list had to include Patton's name, noting, "His job in rehabilitating the Second Corps in Tunisia was quickly and magnificently done. Beyond this, his leadership of the Seventh Army was close to the best of our classic examples." After reciting Patton's blunders and explaining that he had effectively cured some of his weaknesses, Eisenhower assured Marshall that the incident was an anomaly. "You have in him a truly aggressive commander and, moreover, one with sufficient brains to do his work in splendid fashion." Yet he also warned Marshall that Patton's future missteps "might cause you to regret his promotion." Eisenhower revealed how he controlled Patton: "His intense loyalty to you and to me makes it possible for me to treat him much more roughly than I could any other senior commander." He even hinted that Patton would be better suited to fight in France over Italy: "I think he will show up even better in an exclusively American theater than an allied one."[51]

Meanwhile, on September 8, as General Mark Clark's Fifth Army headed to Salerno, Eisenhower's headquarters announced the armistice with Italy. Italian general Pietro Badoglio, who replaced Mussolini as prime minister, made a similar broadcast from Italy. The messages signaled the Italian air force and navy to head for prearranged locations to surrender to the Allies. Patton told his commanders that the Italian air force would be flying to Sicilian airfields while the navy sailed to Allied ports. He then stationed troops around the airfields to make sure the Italians obeyed the Allied rules. While he obeyed his orders, Patton secretly felt it a bad idea to announce the armistice to Fifth Army before it landed on a possibly hostile shore. "Should they get resistance instead of friendship," he wrote that night, "it would have a very bad effect."[52] Patton was right. The combined American and British force landing at Salerno ran into strong German defenses and a gap formed between the British and American corps that Clark could not seal. The Germans made four strong counterattacks in an effort to push the Allies into the Mediterranean. The armistice made no difference to Germans on the battlefield.

Things were not going much better for the commander of Seventh Army. While Clark's forces struggled, Patton received a letter from Everett Hughes informing him his army had been accused of four war crimes during the Sicilian campaign: Using prisoners to unload ships; driving prisoners with whips; forcing prisoners to clear minefields; and shooting prisoners. Patton responded, addressing the letter point for point. He admitted to using prisoners to unload ships but claimed they were removed from the ships during enemy air raids. As for whipping prisoners, he explained that his guards had found a collection of Italian whips that they only carried as swagger sticks until General Keyes halted the practice. Patton could not believe that an American soldier would ever whip a prisoner. "The greatest criticism we have of our troops," he explained, "is that they fraternize too much with prisoners." As for the removal of mines, before the campaign Patton's judge advocate general had advised him it was legal. The two incidents of his soldiers shooting prisoners, he explained, were being addressed. The sergeant who shot prisoners had been tried and convicted, and Patton had requested the captain be transferred from Africa to stand trial. Patton noted that the Germans had been booby-trapping their dead and sniping at Americans in bypassed towns at the time of both shooting incidents.

Hughes thought out loud that it might be a good idea to send his provost marshal to Palermo to investigate the items, and Patton concurred. He wanted Hughes to know he had nothing to hide. Still, the whole incident left Patton unnerved. He saw it as the result of jealous officers working against him because of his victory in Sicily. "It is hard to be victimized for winning a campaign," he complained in his diary. Gay fed Patton's anxiety when he said the British were probably behind the smear campaign as payback for making Montgomery look foolish in Messina.[53] The provost marshal officer did indeed show up a few days later, asking Patton about the improper treatment of prisoners. Patton sent him to talk to Sicily's archbishop, who explained that Patton was like a father to his Italian prisoners. The officer returned fully satisfied that Patton's prisoners were being cared for and none of them were being whipped. "Well," Patton recorded in his diary, "that hurdle is past."[54]

Things did not go as smoothly with Eisenhower's inspector general. Colonel Herbert "Bertee" Clarkson soon arrived in Sicily and met with Patton before interviewing random men about their commander's leadership. He came away unimpressed with Patton, thinking him "a bum from every angle." Clarkson returned to Eisenhower's headquarters on September 18 to present his findings, but Hughes intercepted him. When Clarkson told Hughes he thought Patton was a bum, Hughes countered that Patton was "a bum as a gentleman but not as a commander." After some back and forth, Hughes finally got Clarkson to rework his report in a more favorable light. "B[ertee] never knew the difference [between a gentleman and a commander]," Hughes later wrote, "but he worked four years rating efficiency reports."[55] Hughes may have saved Patton's career.

Clarkson's revised report must have impressed Eisenhower, who soon after reading it asked Patton to advise General Alexander on how to command American troops. Patton flew to Alexander's Bizerte headquarters, where he watched the surrendering Italian fleet sail by on its way to Tunis. From witnessing this amazing symbol of Allied success, Alexander took Patton into his command post and showed him a map of the Salerno landings. It quickly quelled any feelings of envy Patton may have held. He could see the Allies only had only a toehold on the beach, "which is not good." Alexander considered the situation critical. Patton advised Alexander on American leadership, regretting aloud that he was not as calm as Alexander in battle, but Alexander retorted that the British were too calm and fought better when they were less so.[56]

Upon returning to Palermo, Patton learned he had a distinguished visitor: Norman Davis, chairman of the International Federation of the Red Cross and Red Crescent Societies and the president of the Council on Foreign Relations. The two men dined together and spent most of the time criticizing Eisenhower. Patton considered Davis "very pro-American."[57] The next day, September 11, Patton accompanied him on a tour of all the Red Cross facilities in the area. When it was over, Davis addressed several thousand soldiers while Patton stood nearby. Reporter

Quentin Reynolds later wrote that "fifty thousand of them would shoot Patton on site." When Davis finished, Patton stepped up to the microphone, without a prepared speech, and said, "I just thought I'd stand up here and let you soldiers see if I'm as big a s. o. b. as you think I am." The troops cheered madly. When Harry Butcher heard this, he penned in his diary, "You can't keep a fellow like that down."[58]

Patton spent the next two days visiting dignitaries, sailing, and flying until he received word from Alexander that Clark was having more problems in Italy. The Germans had counterattacked with five divisions down the Sele River, just as Patton had predicted, and driven a wedge between the American VI Corps and the British X Corps. Several American units had been decimated, with no reserves to throw into the fight. Fortunately, rapid fire from two U.S. artillery battalions prevented the Germans from a full-blown breakthrough. Clark had even radioed Admiral Hewitt, requesting plans to evacuate VI Corps and redeploy it closer to X Corps. Montgomery had promised to race to the Americans' aid with all possible haste. Alexander told Patton the situation was critical and to expedite all follow-up equipment and troops. "This is being done," Patton recorded as he tried to find enough boats to ship equipment to the far shore. Alexander later told Patton that Eisenhower made assisting Clark priority one, while priority two was assisting Montgomery.[59] News that General Ridgway would fly the 82nd Airborne as reinforcement to the beachhead greatly relieved Patton.[60]

The next day, September 14, as enemy tanks pushed dangerously close to the Salerno beach, Patton prepared to send Truscott's 3rd Infantry Division to help. Patton walked Truscott to the torpedo boat that would take him to Italy, encouraging him to shorten the front and have the British stand fast while the Americans go on the offensive. "We must attack," Patton told Truscott, "or it will be a second Gallipoli." Truscott told him that Eisenhower had said that Patton was the only general who could inspire men to conquer. "I wish he would give me a chance to do some more conquering," Patton later vented. He wanted to be in on the fight but bit his lip, hoping his silence would bring him a future battle command.[61]

Before Patton went to bed that night, he read a message that he interpreted as Clark saying he had redeployed. He had not. The decision to move VI Corps to a different part of the beach had been scrapped. In fact, by the time Patton received the message, the Germans had been halted, and the battlefield stabilized. Still, Patton thought the idea of a

CHAPTER TEN ★ THE SLAPPING INCIDENTS AND ITALY   239

commander pulling his headquarters backward, and even to a ship, fatal. "Think of the effect on the troops," he wrote in his diary. "A commander, once ashore, must conquer or die." In Morocco, Patton had departed the beach for Hewitt's ship, but at the time Patton's front was stable and he had not yet established his headquarters.⁶² On September 16 General Truscott returned to Sicily, where he found Patton studying maps of Italy. He related a story of two reporters who drove between Montgomery's Eighth Army and Clark's perimeter without encountering the enemy. Patton burst out laughing.⁶³

On September 17 Eisenhower stopped at Palermo on his way to Italy. Patton initially thought Eisenhower was relieving Clark, but "no such luck," Patton wrote that night. Instead, Major General Ernest J. Dawley, the VI Corps commander, was getting the axe. Patton recommended Geoffrey Keyes to replace Dawley. When Eisenhower said it would be Lucas, Patton stressed that Keyes should take over II Corps, since Bradley had left for England. Then Patton asked that he be given a corps, any corps, under Clark, whom he still despised. "I would serve under the devil to get a fight," he later wrote. To Patton, Clark was near to the devil himself, but Eisenhower knew it and refused the request, reminding him that the two "were not soul mates." Eisenhower repeated that Patton would command an army in England when the time came, but Patton doubted it, noting in his diary, "Destiny better get busy." The two spent the rest of the visit talking about replacements for Patton's diminished veteran units. Patton wanted to use soldiers from the 1st Infantry Division to make up for losses in the 9th Infantry. Eisenhower told him no. If the soldiers of the Big Red One ever found out about Patton's idea, they would resent it, giving them one more reason to hate him.⁶⁴

The meeting prompted Patton to write Eisenhower a personal letter about replacements, describing fighting soldiers as "men actuated by strong personal emotions" and claiming that the veterans of 1st and 9th infantry divisions "actually cried on being separated from their units." The letter did not seem to address any crisis in replacement policies, only offering that more soldiers could be packed into troop ships. It was as if Patton were pleading to remain with Seventh Army and that it still have a role in future combat.⁶⁵

The next day, Patton was pleased to learn that Lucas got VI Corps and Keyes would get II Corps. He sent Lucas a box of cigars and some notes on the Sicilian campaign. That night he entertained Brigadier General Arthur Wilson, a former staff officer in Morocco, who was writing an account of the U.S. Army in North Africa. They spent much of their dinner denigrating Clark. Wilson told Patton that Clark only got command of Fifth Army "due to the effort of Jews." Patton's Clark bashing was not over. The next day, when Dawley visited on his way back to the United States, Patton blamed Clark's interference and vacillations for the battlefield failures. When Dawley explained that the British X Corps commander, Lieutenant General Richard McCreery—the same General McCreery who called Americans in Tunisia timid—complained that Dawley did not keep him informed, Patton later wrote, "I forgot to ask if he kept Dawley informed—I doubt it." While Patton considered Dawley manly and restrained, he admitted that he lacked drive.[66]

Patton spent the rest of September keeping tabs on the war in Italy, sailing, entertaining guests, exploring Sicily, taking brisk walks, writing a report on the Sicilian campaign, and horseback riding. His palace had a private riding hall under his office. Against Army regulations, he sent two Arabian stud horses to a remount unit in Italy for castration. "Alone, alone all alone," he wrote to Beatrice. After a particular day of church and dancing with some locals, he wrote in his diary, "At least we killed off another day of uncertainty. I am getting awfully fed up."[67]

During this time Patton received a letter that Keyes had forwarded to him. It was written by Eisenhower in support of Keyes. Although it is not clear why Keyes forwarded the letter to Patton, reading it only added to the latter's funk. Eisenhower had never written one like it to Patton. "The letter was aimed at me too," he wrote. "I have immediately written every division during or immediately after a fight and praised people and always written letters of commendations to all commanders, even to Ryder after Tunisia. . . . I have never received a commendation or compliment from Ike since I have served under him except the DSM for Morocco."[68]

At a dinner for Frank Knox, the secretary of the Navy, Captain Butcher told Patton that General Marshall would take over in England and make Eisenhower the Army chief of staff, even though Eisenhower had requested to stay in North Africa. When Butcher said that Patton would be sent to England to command an army, Patton told him he already knew that and "can't see how he could have done otherwise. I have been very successful three times." Patton was pleased to learn that a British officer had said "George is such a pushing fellow that if we don't stop him he will have Monty surrounded." He later wrote, "I know I can outfight that little fart any time."[69]

CHAPTER TEN ★ THE SLAPPING INCIDENTS AND ITALY   241

Still, Patton doubted the validity of promises of a future command in England. "Things are just dull for me as they were in Rabat," he wrote Beatrice. He desired to be transferred elsewhere. "I am sure that it would be better for all concerned," he noted, complaining, "I am certainly fed up with idleness." A few days later he tried to be more optimistic with Beatrice. After admitting the uncertainty of his future, he enthused, "I am not as jealous of Wayne [Clark] as I was for I think that his party may well be an anti-climax."[70] Yet, his loneliness was getting the better of him. When Major General Jimmy Doolittle visited on his way to Italy in late September, Patton rushed to him as he climbed off his plane and threw his arms around him. With tears streaming down his cheeks, Patton said, "Jimmy, I'm glad to see you. I didn't think anyone would ever call on a mean old son-of-a-bitch like me."[71]

Seeking a way out, Patton kept trying to show himself useful to the war effort. On October 4 he wrote McNair, encouraging him to introduce frontal assaults in battalion training. He considered them necessary, even if they were "foolish and murderous." He also suggested doubling the number of troops in a unit engaging the enemy for the first time, writing, "After they have had their baptism of blood, these regulars can be withdrawn and their experience of battle used to great advantage in training." In addition, he asked McNair to expedite issuing Bronze Stars since his men were getting "fed up" at seeing replacements with medals similar to theirs. To drive home the point, he wrote that when he had decorated seventy-five men, he noticed their "change of facial expression, which the habit of looking death in the eye has caused these men. Their eyes and mouths are distinctly more forceful than they were a year ago, and it is certain that the future of our Country in the hands of men with such facial features is safe."[72]

While Patton struggled to stay relevant, more of his team departed Sicily. On October 6 Geoffrey Keyes brought his staff to Patton's headquarters for their last meal before heading to Italy. Patton worried for Keyes as he considered anyone serving under Clark in danger. "I told Geoff to be careful—never to mention Seventh Army and always win," he wrote in his diary, adding, "I wish something would happen to Clark." Not everyone left in such good graces. Engineer Colonel Charles H. Mason had been court-martialed for providing transportation for Sicilian prostitutes, reduced in rank to major, and forced to pay a $1,000 fine. Mason presented himself to Patton hoping for some leniency, since Patton had yet to sign off on his punishment. Patton, thinking that Mason should be kicked out of the Army, told him a story of a general who, after being discharged from the Army, reenlisted as a private, and ended up commanding a regiment. He told Mason he hoped the same for him. Alarmed by Patton's response, Mason asked for permission to present his case to Eisenhower. Patton approved.[73]

Patton had his own problems with prostitutes and brothels. To combat the rapid increase of venereal disease in Sicily, he ordered all soldiers on leave be given the names of approved brothels. A group of chaplains complained about this policy in a letter, which he ignored. The chaplains wrote again, this time threatening to go over his head to Eisenhower. Patton responded by modifying his orders to give men the locations of Seventh Army prophylactic stations in "specified brothels." It was not what the chaplains had hoped for, but it was better than nothing.[74]

October followed much like September. Patton kept tabs on the bitter fighting in Italy—and criticized all the theater commanders. He rehearsed theoretical landings, attended dinners, watched movies, pinned medals on soldiers, and visited historical sites and his old battlefields. He rode a horse as often as he could to stay in shape and stopped smoking. "Whenever I get into one of these yearns to be fit," he wrote, "it means war & has so far." But there was nothing for him.[75]

The Italian campaign continued with its slow grind. On October 6, a naval commander working with Fifth Army wrote General Gay, "I wished we had the 7th Army staff to work with," explaining, "we didn't appreciate you folks until we found ourselves working with the 5th. . . . It seemed to me that we were constantly being confronted with situations that your people long ago found the answers to, and which your staff would take in their stride."[76] General Lucas also wrote Patton about his difficulties with the British, explaining that he had to send messages twice to "my cousin" just to be understood.[77] That same day Patton received a wire from Eisenhower, informing him that he had been nominated for the promotion to the permanent rank of major general (his lieutenant general rank was a wartime, temporary promotion), although it would have to first be passed by the U.S. Senate. "You have lived up to each one of the expectations I have held for you during the past twenty-five years."[78]

On October 13 Patton flew to the Gela beach. Recalling the battle, he realized he was only a few hundred feet from the Germans when they attacked and that the fire he came under, which he thought was from an airplane, was actually from the ground. He decided it was only the discipline of the 1st Infantry and the stupidity of the Germans that had prevented his Army from being pushed off the beach. "God what a chance I took personally and as a commander," he later wrote. "But I would do it again."[79] Later, he drove over Montgomery's rout to Messina and was unimpressed. "When the history of this war is written fifty years hence," he wrote in his diary, "General Montgomery will catch hell for being so stupid and timid." That night his anxieties of being left out of the war returned. He wrote General McNair, "If you find out what is to become of me, please let me know because no one here has the vaguest idea, or if they have, they keep it to themselves."[80]

On October 16 Patton flew to Algiers to dine with Eisenhower. He was so nervous he had to take a sleeping pill the night before. After dinner, Eisenhower told Patton he was acting his part and then accused him of having an inferiority complex. Patton laughed and agreed, although he secretly believed he had too little of a complex. "In fact I look down my nose at the world and too often let them know it." If Patton had a complex, it was about being sent home. Later, Hughes, who attended the dinner, told Patton that it was Eisenhower who lacked humility since he could not criticize the British and, therefore, took it out on the Americans, adding that the better Eisenhower knew someone, the more he preached to him. Sixty-four-year-old Major General Kenyon Joyce, one of Eisenhower's deputies and Patton's former commander and mentor, told Patton that Eisenhower had praised him to Secretary of the Treasury Henry Morgenthau and Ambassador to Russia Averell Harriman and many British officers. Hughes laughed when Patton referred to Joyce, a two-star general, as "six," the title for a superior, out of respect for his former commander.[81]

Two days later, a delegation led by Treasury Secretary Henry Morgenthau visited Sicily. Patton gave them the royal treatment, including a cruise in Palermo's harbor. Morgenthau's concerns about the war's cost impressed Patton, and his less-than-enthusiastic talk about the British endeared him to the general. One of Morgenthau's advisors, Dr. Harry Dexter White, did not leave the same impression. Patton considered him a non-Aryan, and "damn near a communist." The second part of Patton's impression of White proved prescient. After the war, the Federal Bureau of Investigation discovered that White was passing secret documents to the Soviets during the Truman administration.[82]

Awards continued to come Patton's way for his work in Sicily. On October 21, the cardinal of Sicily presented him with a silver medallion, an honor usually reserved for cardinals or kings. Lieutenant Colonel Codman speculated his boss had become a papal prince. Paddy Flint told Patton he should run for Pope. While Patton lamented the time it took for him to become a permanent major general, he confessed to Beatrice, "I prefer ribbons."[83] To commemorate the Sicilian victory and cheer their boss, Patton's staff presented him with an elaborately decorated Sicilian cart, painted on one side with an image of Patton's landing at Gela and on the other with one of Patton shaking hands with Cardinal Lavitrano. Patton made no mention of it in his diary.[84]

In contrast, the 1st Infantry Division gave no effusive praise to Patton. On October 23, beribboned and impeccably dressed, he boarded a launch and sailed out to bid the soldiers of the Big Red One farewell. The men, headed for England, had been ordered to man their troopship's rails as Patton's launch circled their ships. The men followed the order, but when Patton's launch cruised by in the calm sea, with the general standing in full view of everyone, the men stood in complete silence. The incident highlighted Patton's distance from the men and his feelings of isolation and loneliness. Yet, for all Patton had endured in the last two months, things were about to get worse.[85]

CHAPTER ELEVEN

Spiraling Down and a Chance for Redemption

ON OCTOBER 25, after witnessing the 82nd Airborne Division conduct a practice jump and glider landing, Patton received a message from Eisenhower's headquarters for a new mission:

> Commander-in-Chief directs you to proceed initially to Algiers as soon as you can conveniently do so, accompanied by 3 or 4 senior staff officers of your selection, prepared for a tactical reconnaissance of four to five days in an area to be communicated to you on your arrival.

Patton saw this as a good omen, since most of his important assignments arrived through cryptic messages. "Here's hoping," he wrote in his diary.[1] But it was not a call to combat; instead, the message signaled George C. Marshall's idea to send Patton around the Mediterranean to keep the Germans off balance and expecting an attack anywhere and everywhere. With Clark's attack on the German Winter Line fortifications in Italy scheduled for November 5, Marshall had recommended Eisenhower send Patton to Corsica, since "Patton's movements are of great importance to German reactions and therefore should be carefully considered." Marshall also suggested Cairo and Cyprus but felt Corsica carried "much more of a threat" to the Germans.[2] Prior to the invasion of Sicily, the British had launched Operation ANIMALS, deceiving the Germans into believing the Allies were preparing to invade Greece and the Balkans by stepping up guerilla operations in those countries and creating a fake army in Egypt. Hitler responded by sending five divisions to Greece that could have tipped the scales in Sicily. Maybe Patton could achieve the same effect, and if not draw more forces away from Italy, at least pin down enemy divisions already in Greece, the Balkans, and even southern France.[3]

Two days later Patton flew to Algiers and lunched with Eisenhower, Beetle Smith, and Eisenhower's driver, Kay Summersby, to learn about the plan. Officially, he would take several French officers to Corsica to reconnoiter the island as a potential staging area. From there, he would stop in Tunis, hoping German spies would spot him and recommend that their forces remain dispersed. Finally, he was to visit Cairo in Egypt. To enliven Patton's waning spirits, Eisenhower reiterated he would eventually command an army in England. Smith added that he had informed Marshall that Patton was the greatest assault general in the world and should lead the cross-channel invasion. This must have bolstered Patton until Smith added that Marshall considered Patton's staff weak, citing supply problems at Gela. Patton responded that he would stick with his staff. Smith readily agreed and stressed how much he admired Patton. "He is such a liar," Patton later fumed in his diary. "I wonder if he ever said that to Marshall." The mission depressed Patton. Instead of fighting a battle, he was off on his own, decoying the enemy, a waste of his talents. "This is the end of my hopes for war," he groused.[4]

The next morning, Patton flew to Tunis and spent the night in a small villa—but instead of flying out for Corsica the next morning at the scheduled time of 9:00 a.m., he left an hour earlier. Aware that German spies might monitor his movements, his old battle sense told him to change plans. His entourage took off in a C-47 and missed its promised escort into Corsica, landing at 9:14 a.m. to be met by a single British officer. Patton's sense had been right. An hour after his arrival a German fighter-bomber circled the Corsican airfield. "Good thing I left at 0800," he later noted. Corsica, Napoleon Bonaparte's birthplace, boasted monuments and historical locations associated with the great marshal. Patton visited a statue of Napoleon and a cave in which the Corsican had once studied. He also toured the house where the French leader was born and touched the couch where baby Napoleon was delivered. Patton relished every minute. "It is quite a thrill to be in Napoleon's hometown," he wrote in his diary.

At the port town of Bastia, Patton asked a patrol boat crew why they were not attacking the Germans across the sea in Italy. The captain's explanation that they raided the Germans at night and slept during the day mollified Patton. "Oh, okay," he told the captain, "Give 'em hell."[5] For the rest of the tour, Patton's driver careened around the island through the narrow mountain passes and cliffsides with drops of several hundred feet, terrifying Patton. "The only brake that fellow used on the corners was his horn."[6] He visited the town of Calve, one of Christopher Columbus's reported birthplaces, and where, in 1794, shrapnel had injured British admiral Horatio Nelson's right eye when he bombarded the city. After watching French troops conduct a maneuver, Patton's staff was impressed at how similar they were to the Americans' until Patton explained, "we copied their methods in 1918."[7]

The first leg of his tour completed, Patton flew back to Palermo on November 1, to receive Major General Courtney Hodges, the commander of Third Army and a WWI veteran. "He apparently is less dumb than I had considered him," Patton later wrote, "and [he] talks very violently about his disciplinary actions." The next day they toured Patton's Sicilian battlefields. Hodges was most interested in German defenses, pointing out that whereas in the last war the Germans tended to defend lower slopes, they now defended ridges, making it easier to pull out after a delaying action, something that had never occurred to Patton. Overall, Patton enjoyed Hodges's visit and praised his keen eye for battlefield detail, commenting, "I had more satisfaction in taking him over the ground than anyone else I have met so far."[8]

During Hodges's visit, Patton learned that his chief engineer, Colonel Garrison H. "Gar" Davidson, was being transferred. Eisenhower and Lieutenant General Jacob Devers, who was taking command of the Mediterranean theater, were picking generals. Eisenhower wanted Patton in England, while Devers would keep the Seventh Army staff for the possible invasion of southern France. Devers specifically wanted Davidson to plan the invasion, even though Davidson wanted to stay with Patton. When Patton received orders to release Davidson that morning, he wired back one word, "NO," and jotted off a note to Hughes at Eisenhower's headquarters, pleading, "It is meaner to rob those who while dying are not dead. FOR GOD'S SAKE DON'T LET ALL THE STAFF OF THE LATE SEVENTH ARMY BE REMOVED UNTIL THE VOLLEY'S [sic] ARE FIRED." He concluded the note pleading, "Gar does not want to go and I don't want to lose him. HELP!!!" But the letter went out too late for Hughes to do anything about it. Davidson said his farewell to Patton later that day. By the time Eisenhower and Devers finished, Patton would keep only sixteen staff officers. The rest went to Devers.[9]

Meanwhile, Patton dealt with several rape cases. Of five cases, a white soldier committed one, and African Americans committed the others.

The white soldier received life imprisonment while the black soldiers were hung. This was not unusual. Of the seventy American soldiers executed in Europe between 1943 and 1946, almost all of them were African Americans in an army that was overwhelming white. Overall, African American soldiers, who made up 8.5 percent of the U.S. Army, were accused of committing 79 percent of all capital crimes. Black soldiers in the Mediterranean and Europe knew that dating a white woman carried the risk of being accused of rape by white soldiers and officers.[10] Patton considered the uneven verdicts a miscarriage of justice. When three more blacks were accused of rape, Patton added two black officers to the trial court. Despite the move, Patton still saw the court's decisions divided on racial lines. "Although the men were guilty as hell," he penned in his diary, "the colored officers would not vote death—a useless race."[11]

Finally, on November 3, Patton got his chance to see the war in Italy, but only as an observer. For as much as he hated Beetle Smith, Smith would not reciprocate the feeling. Instead, Smith had his personal plane stop at Palermo to fly Patton to Naples. Patton made no mention of gratitude in his diary, later writing that Smith was "an s. o. b. of the finest type, selfish, dishonest and very swell-headed." Upon landing, Patton examined the port of Naples, which the Germans had gutted but American salvage crews had restored. His only comment was that the salvage operators had learned their trade in Casablanca and Palermo. He first visited General Lucas, whom he found in great spirits. Next, he saw Clark, about whom he harbored many complaints: his headquarters was too far from the front; his battle maps showed too much detail of troop displacement; and his battle captains, particularly Truscott, wanted to leave him and fight with Patton. The last item might have been more a figment of Patton's imagination than Truscott's opinion.

A Luftwaffe attack on Naples infuriated Patton, but not because of the Germans' audacity in the action. As the bombers flew over, GIs stopped their vehicles and took cover. "Disgusting," Patton snapped. His driver wanted to stop but Patton ordered him on, knowing they had a better chance of surviving if they kept moving, despite driving over a shell crater. Al Stiller offered Patton his helmet since he was not wearing one—an oddity for Patton. When the Americans laid a smoke screen, Patton's vehicle had to stop and wait as anti-aircraft fragments clinked on the pavement "like fireflies," recalled Patton. The Naples trip intensified Patton's disdain for Clark. He thought the campaign an unnecessary waste of manpower. With the Italian government's surrender to the

Allies, the Germans had to occupy and defend the country. "Italy was a burden to the Germans which they should be left to bear," he complained to Lieutenant Colonel Charles Odom, his personal surgeon since the Sicily operation. But Patton did not make policy, he could only complain about it.[12]

Patton's restlessness and bitterness grew throughout November. He became contemplative, particularly when the first anniversary of Operation TORCH rolled around. His diary became a tome of complaints and rants—more so than usual. He regretted that he halted his drive after his breakthrough at El Guettar: "Live and learn," he wrote. His racism bubbled to the surface. He called the Sicilians a "bastard race" and condemned the British after hearing that a British general used a superior officer's stateroom. "They have no shame nor modesty and will take all they can get." He complained that soldiers in Italy were exhausted and too reliant on artillery fire, and he wondered why Eisenhower was not sending Clark more troops. He wrote that both Clark and Clark's chief of staff were jumpy, adding, "I hope that he or Gruenther or both break down, but I don't want the job myself." He even feared a Russian victory, which would further negate his chance to redeem himself on the battlefield. He complained to Odom that Eisenhower was looking for a reason to send him home, and only Marshall and Stimson were preventing it. He even worried about enemies he had created in 1940 when he proposed the formation of a tank corps during the Louisiana maneuvers. He criticized Montgomery as "too big for his britches," complaining that during the Sicily campaign he "had shown a complete lack of knowledge of how to exploit a breakthrough."[13]

Into Patton's angry and resentful world finally came some good news. A repatriated British POW named Ion Gallaway reported that Patton's son-in-law, John Waters, was doing well in captivity. Gallaway had been a prisoner at Oflag VIIB in Bavaria when he saw Waters arrive. Although the American was initially depressed about being a prisoner, "he got over that fast," said Gallaway. Waters soon took up classes taught by his fellow POWs to keep his mind busy. He, in turn, taught them softball. "We all agreed," said Gallaway, "he was a grand addition to the camp." Gallaway reported that Waters was athletic and healthy. Unfortunately, the Germans transferred him to prison near Poland once his camp became overwhelmed with prisoners.[14]

On November 11, Armistice Day and also Patton's birthday, the general lamented that, whereas a year ago he had entered Casablanca at the vanguard of a victorious task force, "now I command little more than my self-respect." When General McNair congratulated him on the one-year anniversary, writing, "You are the Seventh Army," Patton penned, "He was more right than he knew." A birthday telegram from Eisenhower did little to cheer him. That afternoon at a memorial service at a 2nd Armored Division cemetery, he laid a wreath and declared, "I consider it no sacrifice to die for my country" and thanked God for "men like these have lived rather than to regret that they have died." On the radio that night he heard his wife, backed by the boys and girls of Boston, singing the Armored Corps March, which Beatrice had written for her husband's II Armored Corps. The song had been adopted as the official march for all the armored divisions.[15]

Figure 36. Patton walks through a cemetery for tankers of the 2nd Armored Division in Sicily with Hap Gay and Paul Harkins on Armistice Day, his birthday, November 11, 1943. Library of Congress, OV 15, 46.

At a dinner celebrating his birthday and the capture of Casablanca, Patton asked reporter John P. Marquand what people back home thought about the victory in Sicily. When Marquand hesitated, Patton insisted he not "dress it up." Marquand told him newspapers reported that "American forces had knifed through token Italian resistance while the British faced the brunt of the fighting around Catania." Patton exploded, "By God, don't they know we took on the Hermann Goering Division? Don't they know about Troina? By God, we got moving instead of sitting on down, and we had to keep moving every minute to keep them off balance or we'd be fighting yet—and what were they doing in front of Catania?" Patton also defended his amphibious attacks as superior to British tactics: "They don't even know how to run around end. All they can do is make a frontal attack under the same barrage they used in [the World War I battle at] Ypres." After inviting Marquand to visit the battlefields, Patton calmed down. "These things make me emotional," he explained. "Maybe too emotional sometimes." He turned to Codman and asked him about an incident that might have revealed just how depressed he had become: "Do you remember the time I got emotional and drove the jeep right across the mine field?" Codman said he had. After his diatribe, the night improved when cooks brought out an enormous birthday cake for the general's fifty-eighth birthday.[16]

Figure 37. Patton cuts his birthday cake with Major General Geoffrey Keyes and Colonel Paddy Flint. He had turned fifty-eight years old. Catalog number: 208-PU 153 B-4, National Archives and Records Administration.

Worried that he had erred in criticizing Montgomery's troubles at Catania, Patton invited Marquand to his headquarters a few days later, but this time his frustration with Eisenhower and Smith boiled over. He showed Marquand letters of recommendation he had written for soldiers who had fought in Sicily and said he was happy to sign them. "You know why? Because usually in the Army you can expect loyalty from the bottom up, more than you can from the top down, and I ought to know." He told Marquand about the inspector general complaining that his Italian prisoners did not have enough latrines. "They never knew what a goddam latrine was until I showed them," he roared. Then he recalled his words about Montgomery: "I seem to be in a lot of hot water lately, and suppose we just forget the whole episode." Marquand agreed and kept his word.[17]

To distract from his troubles, Patton wrote his son, George, still struggling in his freshman year at West Point, warning him that if his father made headlines again, the ladies would run after the plebe, "so look out." He cautioned that women who run after men "are usually not worth having" and bad for cadet rank. He lectured that when he was a cadet, "the clap [gonorrhea] was a sure ticket home. Battle is nothing compared to it. For while clap can be cured, Syph[ilis] can't."[18]

He wrote Beatrice that he felt "lower than whale tracks" and sent a poem to Hughes.

> What makes a soldier swear so hard
> What makes him to Perspire
> It isn't getting up to rush
> Or Laying down to fire
> It's the everlasting waiting
> On the everlasting road

Soon Patton had another problem. Hunger riots broke out in Agrigento and spread throughout Sicily. Thieves were stealing flour from farmers making deliveries to towns or the Mafia-controlled black market. Rumors spread that communists backed the riots, which were stalling any kind of progress to a return to normal. Patton could not find his civilian matters expert, British Major General R. H. Clark, to deal with Agrigento's rioters so he sent sixty soldiers in half-tracks with one assault cannon. He blamed the uprising on Colonel Charles Poletti, the former lieutenant governor of New York and the senior civilian affairs officer who had appointed leading Mafia figures as local leaders. "He plays politics instead of commanding," Patton wrote. "He should be gotten rid of." The situation became so tense that Patton cancelled a trip to the opera for fear of a demonstration. He worried that civilians were getting less food than they had under the Italian administration. "They are comparing Democracy unfavorably with Fascism," he wrote. Cardinal Lavitrano had to dissuade Patton from hanging black marketers.[19] As tensions ratcheted, someone tried to assassinate him. As he left his headquarters one Sunday morning for church, someone threw a hand grenade at his command car, but the would-be-assassin missed, and the grenade exploded about five feet behind the moving vehicle. The perpetrator was never caught.[20]

A week later, on November 18, as the unrest continued, Patton called together his various chiefs and told them to prepare for combat. He wanted all of his officers and clerks armed. "We can put down anything the Italians start," he told them. When civil affairs officers asked Patton to take over the island, he refused to do so unless things got out of hand. He did, however, ask Eisenhower's headquarters for ten thousand tons of flour to cover acute shortages. A Sicilian had told Patton, "All Sicilians are crooks. The trouble with you Americans is that you think we are not and treat us as if we are not." The food unrest would continue until the beginning of 1944, after Patton left.[21]

On November 17 Patton hit a new low. The 2nd Armored Division had departed the island three days before, following the 1st and 9th Infantry Divisions, to England. Patton received notice that his Seventh Army was "not desired" in England. It finally hit him that he truly commanded nothing and was not wanted anywhere. "I have seldom passed a more miserable day," he wrote in his diary. "I have absolutely nothing to do and hours of time in which to do it." He wrote to his wife that he could not sleep at night. He resorted to taking sleeping pills and would wake up groaning, spending his daylight hours sleepy. Still, he tried to bolster himself, concluding in his diary, "Pretty soon I will hit rock bottom and then bounce, but I wish this descent would become more rapid." He got his wish four days later.[22]

The storm broke on November 21, when Eisenhower received notice that American reporter Drew Pearson had broadcast on his radio program that Patton had slapped two soldiers. Pearson added that Eisenhower had severely reprimanded Patton and that he thought Patton would not "be used in combat anymore."[23] For Eisenhower, the timing could not have been worse. President Roosevelt was in Tunisia, on his way to Tehran for the conference to decide the leader of the cross-channel invasion of

France: Eisenhower or Marshall. Now, he could lose his chance at the position, all because of Patton. Eisenhower, feeling he had pacified his one loose cannon, told Smith to speak to the press. Before he did, Smith issued a statement that no soldier had disobeyed Patton's orders and that Patton "had never on any occasion been reprimanded officially by the C-in-C [commander in chief]." But Eisenhower *had* punished Patton, just not officially and to the extent of sending him home. Now the incidents reflected poorly not only on Patton but on Eisenhower. The three-month-old incidents again took center stage, and this time everyone knew about them. The next day, Eisenhower had Smith order Patton not to speak to any reporters. Smith would later tell Patton, "I have been kissing the asses of a lot of correspondents on your account and some of them turned the other cheek." Everett Hughes claimed that the new incident wracked Eisenhower's nerves and called Pearson's actions a "dis-service" to the country.[24]

When Patton first heard about Pearson's broadcast and Smith's statement, he scoffed. "I had been expecting something like this for some time," he wrote. He knew Smith's statement had been a misstep. "It would have been much better to have admitted that whole thing to start with," he wrote in his diary, "particularly in view of the fact that I was right." But as the days passed, Patton continued to worry. His future was again in question. He fumed that a successful general could be brought down by "a discredited writer like Drew Pearson." On Thanksgiving Day, Patton wrote, "I had nothing to be thankful for so I did not give thanks." He penned a letter to Secretary of War Stimson, explaining the incidents— "my method was too forthright"—and sent a copy to Hughes to show Eisenhower. Hughes advised Patton not to send the letter since some of the wording was archaic, explaining that the World War I term "shell-shock" was outmoded.

As word spread around the United States, family members mailed newspaper clippings of the story to soldiers in Sicily. If Patton's troops had not learned of the slapping incidents in the chow lines and gambling circles, they were now reading about it. The *Stars and Stripes* editor in Sicily, Herbert Mitgang, refused to assign a reporter to cover the story, deciding instead to reprint a different newspaper's account of the slappings. One of his reporters warned him that "if we run the piece here in Seventh Army country, and General Patton reads it and throws up his breakfast, we'll both be on permanent KP for the rest of this war." Mitang brought the proposed article to an Army Public Affairs major, whose face dropped in fear. "Let Ike handle Georgie," the major demanded, asking, "Do you wise guys on *Stars and Stripes* want to make things worse for all of us here?" The article never ran in Sicily.[25]

Even so, things looked bad for Patton. A Gallup poll ran four to one in favor of his firing.[26] General McNair wrote him that "your temper has long threatened to undo you," even though he admitted that Patton had "done a mighty deed for the war effort."[27] Isolated and alone, Patton typed a letter to Hughes: "I get so bored I almost die but know if I protest too much I will get some sort of a supervising job and arrive nowhere. . . . I have been out of war so long now that I doubt if I know how to command any more." It had only been three months. "I certainly have forgotten how to type." He took to reading his Bible and ignoring the newspapers and radio. "There is no use in giving myself indigestion for nothing," he wrote in his diary. From that point on, he never spoke about the incident to the press.[28]

Even a letter from Smith, reiterating that he would go to England and ask that Patton receive a new command, could not revive the crestfallen general. Patton still desperately wanted to retain control of his beloved Seventh Army. "I will have to find a way of circumventing such a move." The anti-Patton fervor was nothing more than Army politics, he told himself, with other generals using it to jockey for position once Marshall took over in Europe. Patton could not believe either that Eisenhower would command the cross-channel attack or that his boss appreciated him, writing, "Ike and Beetle are not at all interested in me but simply saving their own faces." Like he did when the scandal first broke, Patton tried to lose himself in his work. He busied his staff with planning an invasion of Southern France from Corsica and wrote notes on his Sicilian campaign, crunching the numbers to determine that one American died for every 13.5 of the enemy. He filled his diary with pages and pages on the battle of Malta—better that than writing about the depressing things his future might hold.[29]

While Patton tried to ignore the aftershocks of Drew Pearson's exposé, his friends unloaded on the salacious reporter. Patton's friend and mentor, Major General Kenyon Joyce, called Pearson a swine. General Lucas called him an "SOB" who refused to help the war effort. Lieutenant Colonel Charles Odom blamed communists for the story having broken, claiming that Pearson's broadcast fired up "the pink press in the United States." Codman defended his boss to his wife, Theodora, praising Patton's "amazing capacity for instant rightness and lucid anger. It's a rare and invaluable quality. . . . For the individual who blunders, of course, it's hard—it is foudroyant [stunning]—but it has the inestimable virtue of making others fighting mad and God knows that's what we need." He pointed out some of his boss's tougher decisions as proof of his greatness, concluding, "Someday I am going to do a piece on the boss' modest, self-deprecating side."[30]

On November 23 Marshall asked Eisenhower for details of the infamous incidents. Eisenhower reviewed the slappings, stressing Patton's energetic and inspired battlefield leadership, but admitted that Patton had "momentarily lost his temper and upbraided the individuals in an unseemly and indefensible manner." He then laid out his actions to correct Patton, his investigation into Patton's standing with the troops in Sicily, and Patton's efforts to make amends. Eisenhower summed up the situation by saying that although Patton "was guilty of reprehensible conduct, I decided that the corrective action as described above was adequate and suitable in the circumstances. I believe that this decision was sound." He concluded by explaining that any time Patton presents himself before troops in Sicily, "He is greeted with thunderous applause." Eisenhower then fired off a message to Patton telling him that while the storm would soon blow over, he wanted him to keep quiet and not give in to "impulse." If the press asked him questions, "I insist that you stick to the facts and give a frank exposition of what occurred." A chastened Patton wrote back, "Regret trouble I am causing you. Will abide implicitly with your instructions."[31] Meanwhile, rumors flew around Sicily. Soldiers, with no fighting to keep them busy, gossiped wildly about Patton's fate. Word spread that Patton had been court-martialed or that he had been busted down to brigadier general, stripped of two of his stars. Almost everyone believed he would never hold an important command again.[32]

Back home, Pearson's broadcast shocked Beatrice. Her husband had never mentioned the incidents in his letters. A reporter called her and quoted her as saying, "I've always heard that some people like to spread gossip about others. This is the first time it has happened to me." When her quote ran the next day in the paper, she pasted it in her scrapbook and wrote on it. "I didn't think they'd print my comment, but they have. No shame. Anything for 'human interest.'" It would be her last entry into the scrapbooks. She gave the duty to their oldest daughter, Little Bea, for the rest of the war. But the family kept a running tab on who was for and against their patriarch. Five months later, at Patton's request, Beatrice sent her husband a thirteen-page list of Congressional leaders, broadcasters, correspondents, columnists and newspapers, all of whom were for or against him. The Pattons took such things personally.[33]

The news, having arrived on the eve of Thanksgiving, divided families in the United States. Newspapers editorialized about the incidents. One paper, the New York *PM Daily*, published a mail-in form letter to the War Department, demanding Patton be court-martialed. Edward Kennedy of the *St. Louis Post Dispatch*, who reported from Sicily, wrote, "While many soldiers under Patton's command may not have much affection for him, they respect him as a great general and have confidence in him as a commander." The *Times of London's* special correspondent in Algiers also defended Patton, arguing that he was "too great a commander to be anywhere but in the field of active service."[34]

Three days after Pearson's broadcast, the U.S. Senate Military Affairs Committee voted unanimously for a full report. Republican senator Edwin C. Johnson of Colorado said Patton's actions had shocked the nation, "and a slap on the wrist will not suffice." His colleague Styles Bridges of New Hampshire proposed that Patton also "might be a victim of battle fatigue without realizing it." Democratic senator Claude Pepper of Florida wanted Patton court-martialed.[35] Democratic senator Harry S Truman from Missouri, a National Guard officer who fought in World War I and a critic of the regular Army, used Smith's original press statement as proof of the Army's "highranking officer protective club," adding, "When soldier strikes officer he's shot. Officer strikes soldier tis denied."[36] In the House of Representatives, Democrat Jed Johnson of Oklahoma called for Patton's removal and wrote a letter to Marshall demanding the same. Countering this, Republican Robert A. Grant of Indiana, who claimed slapping victim Charles Kuhl as a member of his district, called for the Army to handle its own problems.

Even Patton's ally, Senator Henry Cabot Lodge Jr. of Massachusetts, whom Patton had hosted in Sicily during the Brolo landing, seemed to abandon him. Beatrice noted that although Lodge undoubtedly knew about the slapping incidents, since he was there, he treated her coolly about the situation. When she asked him to issue a statement about her husband's character, he responded he first had to see "how the wind was blowing." He never made a statement.[37]

The same day that the Senate committee requested the report, the *Boston Traveler* published a letter Private Charles Kuhl sent to his girlfriend. It read, in part, "General Patton slapped my face yesterday and kicked me and cussed me. This probably won't get through (referring to Army censorship), but I don't know. Just forget about it in your letters."[38] The press quoted Kuhl's father as saying, "I hold no personal feelings against Gen. Patton. If he is a good man, as they say, let's keep him. We need good men. We don't want to stand in the way of promotion for Gen. Patton." A poll of fifteen stateside enlisted soldiers found they supported Patton two to one. "The whole incident should have been forgotten a minute after it happened," said one.[39] Three days after the Senate committee made its request, it received Eisenhower's letter to Marshall, describing his unofficial reprimand to Patton. A week later, the committee dropped the case. The storm had passed in the United States, but Patton was far from sure it had blown over in Europe.

To buttress his relations with Eisenhower, Patton sent him his copy of *The Greatest Norman Conquest*, about the conquest of Sicily. Patton enjoyed the book so much he corresponded with the author, James van Wyck Osborne. Eisenhower graciously accepted it but complained he did not have time to read it as "I live in a rapidly revolving squirrel cage." Eisenhower also thought the furor back home was dying down but admitted, "we may yet have a lot of grief about it." He assured Patton he stood by his original actions. "You don't need to be afraid of me weakening on that proposition in spite of the fact that, at the moment, I was more than a little annoyed with you."[40]

While Patton stewed in Sicily, Roosevelt, Churchill, and Stalin met at the Tehran Conference in Iran, where Roosevelt picked Eisenhower to lead the invasion of northern France. In addition, Eisenhower would take over the invasion of southern France under Devers once the two forces united. Marshall would continue to direct the war from Washington. Patton learned of all this from John McCloy, the undersecretary of war, who visited him on December 7. Patton, naturally, asked about himself. McCloy said that he had spoken with General Marshall, who replied that Patton "will have an Army." Patton should have been pleased but instead·wanted an army group, "but that will come."[41] McCoy also told Patton he had within him certain chemicals that no other generals had, and although he did meet the magnitude of a German field marshal like Helmet von Moltke the Elder, he was a great leader and an inspiring soldier. "He also said that I look and act like a general and that no one else we have does." Before he left, McCloy asked about the slapping incidents and Patton read aloud the letter he had prepared for Stimson. When McCloy said he should have sent it, Patton handed it to him.[42]

The next day President Roosevelt arrived in Palermo on his way back from the conference, with generals and advisors in tow. Harry Hopkins, the president's special advisor, calmed Patton by saying, "Don't let what that SOB [Pearson] said about you worry you." Eisenhower again assured him he had a place in England. Patton apologized to his boss and Hughes for his desperate letter a week before about Gar Davidson. "God knows I have given both of you enough trouble," he later wrote Hughes. "Both you and DD [Eisenhower] are hard people to thank but I think at bottom you both know how truly grateful I am." He promised to never "pull that particular fool stunt again," and concluded with, "I am much better in a clean war than in regretting the past and fearing for the future." Despite the positive meeting, a troubled Patton requested of Beatrice, "Send me some more pink medecin [sic] this worry and inactivity has raised hell with my insides."[43]

With the Tehran Conference players having propped up his ego, Patton headed to Cairo, still part of Marshall's plan to keep moving him moving around the Mediterranean and keeping the Germans guessing. He called the week-long journey his Cairo farce, though he found it thrilling to fly over the pyramids. He visited a British tank school, which he thought worthless since the war had moved far from Egypt. Heading to Jerusalem on December 14, he took pictures of almost everything he saw. He visited Jesus Christ's tomb, the garden of Gethsemane, the Mount of Olives, and the spot where Mohamed ascended into heaven. Patton felt it funny that four secret servicemen constantly accompanied him through such a holy place. "Lack of faith?" he mused in his diary.[44] He spent the next few days in and around Cairo, visiting the land of the Pharaohs: the pyramids, the Valley of the Kings, King Tut's tomb, and Rameses II's palace and temple. The pyramids did not impress him (he thought they were smaller than the ones in Mexico), but he consoled himself by remembering that his hero, Napoleon, had once been there too. He also encountered Polish general Wladyslaw Anders, commander of the II Polish Corps, who had fought both the Germans and Russians back in 1939. He had been wounded seven times and tortured by the Soviets before being released when Germany invaded the Soviet Union. Anders told Patton that if his men found themselves between a German and Russian army, "they would have difficulty in deciding which they wanted to fight the most."

Patton, who considered Anders "very much a man," presented him with a Seventh Army patch, which brought a smile to the man's face.⁴⁵

Good news greeted Patton when he returned to Palermo. A Gallup poll in the United States found 77 percent support for him, 19 percent against him, and 4 percent abstaining. Out of thirty-eight letters received at his headquarters, only six contained foul language against him. He believed he would head the invasion of southern France and already knew the operation had been titled ANVIL. "I shall certainly be glad to fight again," he wrote in his diary, "and the place is the one which we have been studying and reporting on for six weeks." Christmas found him upbeat about his future. "My destiny is sure and I am a fool and a coward ever to have doubted it," he wrote. Secretary Stimson responded to his letter, praising his tact and ability to win on a battlefield and noting, "I am looking forward to even greater successes for you in the future."⁴⁶ Patton regretted that he had not sent it sooner, "but Ike was opposed to it," he wrote in his diary. In fact, he saw Eisenhower and Smith as the only two general officers against him. "I wish to God Ike would leave and take Smith with him. They cramp my style. Better to rule in Hell than serve in Heaven."⁴⁷ The slapping incidents still weighed him down, though. He wrote to Hughes, "After I win the next battle I will have a press conference of my own and tell the truth. What has been said in the states is mostly lies so far as I hear for I have not and will not read it, it gives me indigestion. After all[,] women and most men have spanked babies and regretted it." Regarding Drew Pearson, he added, "I hope you are with me when I meet D. P. or thare [sic] might be murder."⁴⁸

While Patton prepared for ANVIL, Eisenhower and Marshall tried to figure out where best to use him. On December 23 Eisenhower telegrammed Marshall, explaining that he wanted Bradley as the American army group commander, adding, "One of his Army commanders should probably be Patton." Marshall responded, "I was not and am not opposed to Patton with OVERLORD [the operational name for the cross-channel attack]." Eisenhower wrote back that "in no repeat no event will I ever advance Patton beyond army command," considering either Bradley or Courtney Hodges for army group command. He also considered giving Patton Fifth Army in Italy and sending Clark to England to prepare for the invasion of France. A few weeks later, Marshall and Eisenhower agreed to bring Patton to England and give him an army. Marshall toyed with the thought of sending Patton back to the United States temporarily but decided against it, because of the publicity surrounding the slapping incidents.⁴⁹

Still alternating between planning his next operation and worrying that the scandal had derailed it, Patton wrote McNair on December 29, "I was not as mad as people seem to think. I was putting on an act, which at the time I thought necessary. My mistake was picking the wrong locality for the act. However, I assure you that I shall not again, either in anger or due to histrionic talent, repeat my performance, and I deeply appreciate as always your honest and sincere backing of me and of what I have done." He then switched his tone, requesting an armored division and more artillery brigades, concluding, "I [can] also assure you that given the opportunity I will attack and attack successfully with anything from a platoon up."[50] To Hughes, he wrote about George C. Marshall's name: "Did it ever occur that those letters stand for General Court Martial—I wonder??"[51] He even spent some time collecting first-hand accounts of soldiers defending him and attacking Pearson. In accordance with Eisenhower and Devers's plans, Patton's staff traveled to Algiers to plan ANVIL on the last day of 1943, but Patton himself was not invited. He did not like the implication that if he went to London, it would be without his staff.[52]

In an effort to keep himself on the straight and narrow path, Patton composed a prayer, which he called "religious fiction," for a prayer book. It was as much a prayer for soldiers as it was his reaffirmation and a reflection on the slapping incidents.

A SOLDIER'S PRAYER
By Lieutenant General George S. Patton Jr.
God of our Fathers, who by land and sea has ever led us on to victory, please continue Your inspiring guidance in this the greatest of our conflicts.

Strengthen my soul so that the weakening instinct of self-preservation, which besets all of us in battle, shall not blind me, to my duty to my manhood, to the glory of my calling, and to my responsibility to my fellow soldiers.

Grant to our armed forces that disciplined valor and mutual confidence which insures [sic] success in war.

Let me not mourn for the men who have died fighting, but rather let me be glad that such heroes have lived.

If it be my lot to die, let me do so with courage and honor in a manner which will bring the greatest harm to the enemy, and please, oh Lord, protect and guide those I shall leave behind.

Give us victory, Lord.[53]

When Patton learned on January 1, 1944, that he was being relieved of command of Seventh Army and was to report to Eisenhower's headquarters, any hopefulness disappeared. "I feel very badly for myself but particularly for my staff and headquarters soldiers who have stood by me all the time in good weather and bad." Before meeting with Eisenhower, Patton stopped by Hughes's office. Hughes was not looking forward to the visit. "Patton lost his army and is arriving at 1:15 to cry on my shoulder," he wrote in his diary. "He gets an Army in UK but not a group of men [his staff]."[54] The visit burdened Hughes as much as it relieved Patton. Hughes told his wife, "His visits take as much out of me as I used to take out of you when I came home to cry on your shoulder."[55] Hughes did not exaggerate. After their visit, Patton fumed in his diary about losing Seventh Army, using such words as "unfair and insulting." He saw his transfer as foolish and damnable, and he wanted to hurt whoever had come up with the idea. To calm himself, he read a book on the Duke of Wellington. "He too had many adversaries," Patton wrote. "His staff was also changed several times. Fate."[56]

The meeting with Eisenhower went well, although Patton was too busy feeling sorry for himself to realize it. Eisenhower again told him he would have a role in Operation OVERLORD, commanding an army under Bradley, who would be Patton's army group commander. Eisenhower worried about the role reversal. Although he considering Patton "the outstanding soldier our country has produced," the humiliation of reporting to a former subordinate might be too much for the latter. He hoped Patton's loyalty to him might sway him to accept the assignment. Patton put Eisenhower's mind to rest when he told him he wanted no higher post.[57]

Instead of returning to Palermo, Patton took up an offer from New Zealand air marshal Keith Park to visit Malta. Although not one of Marshall's official locations for Patton to visit, it would serve his mission of traveling around the Mediterranean to deceive the Germans. He arrived in a L-5 and parked at a revetment in front of several fighter craft. When a flight officer asked Patton to move his plane, he snapped, "The hell I will! I'm General George S. Patton!" He then chewed out an enlisted man out for having his fatigues unbuttoned. Patton went into the operations shack and found it empty, to be greeted only by cigarettes smoking in ashtrays. The men had fled at the sight of him. Patton then found the American colonel in charge of the airstrip and chewed him out for his missing men.[58] Air marshal Park eventually showed up and gave Patton a tour of the island. Patton found Field Marshal Lord Gort, the military governor of the island who had been in charge at Dunkirk, charming yet quiet. He spent two days touring the island's ancient defenses and caves, used during the German air attacks in 1942. "The forts are of a different type from any I have ever examined," he wrote. He also saw a library and the relics of the Knights of Malta who defended the island from the Turks in the early 1500s. "The Knights had to vow poverty, chastity, and obedience," he wrote in his diary. "They only kept the last vow. They were not priests."[59]

Patton took off on January 4, 1944, and flew over his North African battlefields en route to Palermo. "It was quite thrilling to fly over Gafsa and El Guettar," he wrote, "hundreds of memories surged up and all were of success." In his mind's eye he could still see hundreds of tanks, guns, and tents, even though all evidence of fighting had been erased by the desert. He later wrote about it to Hughes. "It was interesting and a little sad to gaze down upon my scenes of departed greatness. I feel like an undertaker attending to the details of my own funeral."[60]

Upon his return to Palermo the next day, Patton had Hap Gay read out the order of his relief of Seventh Army to the staff. Thinking Clark would take over the Seventh, Patton told everyone to be as loyal to Clark as they had been to him. As he thanked his men for their service he broke into tears. It seemed like everyone was moving onto better commands but him. When Patton learned that Jimmy Doolittle had taken command of the Eighth Air Force in England, he wrote him, "Why the hell didn't you tell me you were going to England when I saw you the other day, so I could congratulate you?" Doolittle thanked Patton for his letter, addressing him as "General Patton." Patton shot back: "Why the goddam hell do you get so formal as to address me as General Patton? It would seem to me that two men of our low mental and moral characteristics should be more informal." That same day Jacob Devers told Hughes, "Patton's through."[61]

Visiting the theater of war again—either as part of Marshall's plan to keep Patton moving around the Mediterranean or out of his own curiosity—Patton flew to Italy and met with Clark and Gruenther. He still thought Clark kept his headquarters too far away from the front. "Both Gruenther and Clark are most condescending and treated me like an undertaker treats the family of the deceased." When a Signal Corps photographer went to take Patton's picture, he told him, "Make sure you see my ivory handled pistols."[62] He had a better time later touring the front with Geoffrey Keyes. After inspecting an artillery observation post atop a hill, Patton, Keyes, and party were making their way down when the American artillery fired a volley from the valley below. Patton stopped to take a picture. Just then, an enemy artillery barrage exploded where he was headed. Four shells blasted two craters into the ground and tore into the cliff wall and trees to their right. Metal and rock flew everywhere. A piece of shrapnel dented Codman's helmet while another piece ricocheted close to Patton's foot. Some shrapnel ignited ammunition boxes in a nearby cave. "I have never seen people move so fast in an evacuation," Patton mused. The incident revived his self-confidence. He later told Codman, "Proves my luck is still with me."[63]

Before he left Italy, Patton met separately with Lucas, Clark, and Truscott. Lucas seemed worried. He was planning an amphibious landing behind the Germans lines at Anzio named Operation SHINGLE. Patton hoped that it would succeed, "but I am concerned that he does not have sufficient drive." Patton later predicted about the operation, "If the thing is a success, Clark will get the credit. If it fails, Lucas will get the blame." Clark, too, was concerned about SHINGLE and kept changing its launch date—doing so three times in front of Patton, who noticed that the left corner of Clark's mouth seemed paralyzed. "He is quite jumpy," he later penned in his diary. He asked Clark what his role might be in the invasion of France, to which Clark said he would probably command an army that would follow the assault on the French beaches. "Well," Patton replied, "I think that would be a poor command for an officer who has had my experience. Anyways, unless I get some army command, I think that I'll retire."[64] When it came to Truscott, with whom Patton later discussed river crossings and heavy weapons, there was no worry about his experienced and confident infantrymen. Despite their squabbles, Patton judged Truscott to be a first-rate warrior.[65]

While Patton explored Italy, Eisenhower and Marshall decided his fate. On January 17 Marshal wrote Eisenhower about his commander for the invasion of southern France. "Anvil certainly requires an army commander with battle experience against the Germans," adding, "What do you think of Patton retaining command of Seventh Army and carrying out Anvil?" Eisenhower thought Patton was the best man to plan and lead the southern invasion, especially if the operation were reduced in scale. "Patton's reputation as an assault commander, which is respected by the enemy, would serve to increase the value of the threat." Eisenhower added that Patton knew the terrain and had kept most of his staff, two factors that favored him. But along with his praise, Eisenhower added a prescient worry. "It is my impression that Devers and Patton are not, repeat not, genial." Still, Eisenhower wanted Patton.[66]

Meanwhile, the slapping incidents faded from the public eye. The latest U.S. polling showed 89 percent were pro-Patton and only 11 percent against. But whatever the polls might have done to bolster him, other news brought him back down.[67] At breakfast on January 8, Sergeant Meeks, Patton's orderly, told Patton that he had heard on the radio that General Bradley had been named commander of all ground troops in England. A disappointed Patton vented in his diary about Bradley's mediocrity, listing all of his timid actions from North Africa to Sicily. He even blamed the friendly fire incident with the 82nd Airborne over Sicily on Bradley. Patton then, sarcastically, listed his attributes: "He wears glasses, has a strong jaw, talks profoundly and says little, and is a shooting companion of the Chief of Staff." Still, Patton concluded by admitting that "I consider him among our better generals" and told himself, "If I am predestined, as I feel that I am, this too will eventually be to my advantage." Yet he saw Bradley's promotion as a personal affront, "calculated so that I will say 'What the Hell! Stick it up your ass and I will go home,' but I won't." He spent the entire next day in bed.[68]

To calm his nerves and take his mind off Bradley's promotion, Patton spent two days exploring Greek ruins in the Sicilian cities of Himera and Selonius. Both dated back to 300 B.C. and boasted ancient temples, walls, and columns. On returning to Palermo, he received a telegram: "To: CG Seventh Army, for Patton, 22 January 44. George S. Patton, Jr. Lieut. General, 02605, U.S. Army, orders issued relieving you from assignment this theater and assigning you to duty in U.K. Request you proceed to NATOUSA, Algiers for orders. ---CG NATOUSA."

At last Patton had his invitation to get back in the war, but why, he wondered, had destiny taken so long? "Why have they been so slow about it and why have they taken all my staff?" He did not worry for long. He wired General Devers, who had taken over the North African Theater of Operation (NATOUSA), but Devers was busy. Operation SHINGLE, the assault on Anzio, kicked off that day.

The next day, Patton placed a bronze plaque, made from a Navy propeller, in the church he attended in Palermo. It read:

TO THE GLORY OF GOD
In memory of the heroic Americans of the Seventh Army and of the supporting units of the Navy and Air Force who gave their lives for the victory in the Sicilian Campaign, July 10–August 17, 1943. From their General.[69]

Patton spent the rest of the day packing. His departure from the Mediterranean involved a bit of subterfuge. The original plan was to depart on the U.S. Army Transport *James Parker*, but when German radio announcer Axis Sally found out the plans of "the pesky *Parker* and that pest Patton" and added that "we will let you have it every day in every way," he made other plans. Surprisingly, he showed up that evening at Palermo's harbor anyhow. A heavy cloud of dust hung in the air from a collapsed seawall. He raced up the *Parker*'s gangway and inspected the crew on the sport deck, where he told them a few history stories. He then crossed over to the other side of the ship, passing honor guard soldiers who had waited all day to greet him but were now sleeping on laundry bags in the alleyway. He opened a hatch and dropped down to a waiting small boat, which whisked him away through the cloud of dust.[70]

The next morning, Patton and two of his staff flew to Algiers but he could still not find Devers. He learned from Hughes that Devers had simply forwarded the orders to him, and there was no need for a meeting about his assignment. "This was very nice of Devers but was not instigated by me." That night, in a last effort to put the whole affair behind him, he wrote Beatrice an apology for the slapping incidents. "I am sure that the 'incident' was far harder on you than it was on me as I simply did the ostrich act and would neither see nor hear any evil though I did a hell of a lot of thinking."[71]

Patton flew out of Algiers for England on January 25, with 250 pounds of personal files and clothes. At a stopover at Marrakesh, he ran into Brigadier Dunphie, who had been wounded the day Dick Jenson was killed in Tunisia. Patton asked him why he was not wearing the Silver Star he had issued him, even though Patton had refused medals for anyone involved in the incident. When Dunphie said he never received it, Codman took off his own Silver Star ribbon and Patton did the honors.

It was the only award given for that day. The impromptu ceremony over, Patton reboarded his plane for the flight to Prestwick, Scotland, and his new command.[72]

CHAPTER TWELVE

A New Country, a New Army, and the Ghosts of Sicily

ON JANUARY 27, 1944, after a stop off in Prestwick, Scotland, to pick up Eisenhower's dog Caacie, Patton, along with Codman, touched down at Cheddington airfield, northwest of London. Only Major General John C. H. Lee, Eisenhower's supply officer, and Captain Butcher were there to greet him. Once he got settled in his flat, Patton called Eisenhower, who curtly reminded him to count to ten before issuing an order or taking an abrupt action. Eisenhower now commanded the Supreme Headquarters Allied Expeditionary Force (SHAEF), responsible for all forces heading into France. Having finished his reprimand, Eisenhower told Patton the big news: he would command Third Army. Patton was not enthused about the prospect. "All novices and in support of Bradley's First Army," he wrote. "Not such a good job but better than nothing." It would be Seventh Army supporting Montgomery's flank all over again. He wrote Hughes, "I have the same job I had last July only I may land on a wharf," meaning he would have no role in the initial beach assault and would probably come ashore at a coastal city.[1] Yet, just like he had in Sicily, Patton swore to himself to make the situation work. "I have an army and it is up to me."[2]

At dinner that night with Eisenhower, Butcher, Summersby, and a few other officers, Patton poured out compliments, telling Eisenhower that "anyone would be foolish to contest the rightness of the supreme commander" and calling him "the most powerful person in the world." But when Patton got back to his room, he recorded in his diary that Eisenhower acted very nasty and "show-offish." Patton promised Eisenhower that he would carefully choose the place to throw his next tantrum and that it would not be a hospital. Eisenhower could not have been reassured. Patton was under a press blackout, but Eisenhower thought it might be lifted in a few days, just as Bradley's name had already been announced to the press as the American invasion commander.³

In order to try to get a handle on Operation OVERLORD, Patton spent his second day in England visiting various commanders, many of whom he knew from the Mediterranean theater. At Bradley's headquarters he learned that Bradley's First Army and British lieutenant general Miles Dempsey's Second Army would assault the beaches of Normandy, followed by his Third Army after the capture of a suitable port. He would then march Third Army west into Brittany and liberate more ports while everyone else headed east toward Germany. Once he completed his mission in the west, he would join the drive east on Bradley's right flank. Patton did not like the plans for OVERLORD. He thought Bradley's forces were landing too close together. "An attack against one affects the whole thing," he wrote. Yet there was no other solution. Omaha Beach, sandwiched between two steep ridgelines, was the only place suitable to land troops.

When Patton learned of an alternative plan to OVERLORD, Operation RANKIN A, B, and C, which would be triggered by a complete German collapse, he proposed a third plan in case the initial landings became boxed in: a landing at Pas-de-Calais, the port city northeast of Normandy and the closest port to England. He did not know that British intelligence had been working feverously to convince the Germans that the actual invasion was coming to Calais to pin down as many German forces there as possible, assuring success in Normandy. He requested from Lieutenant General Spaatz, now the commander of U.S. Strategic Air Forces in Europe, a heavy air bombardment to prepare the battlefield. Spaatz agreed and promised to blast a hole five miles long and wide for Patton to safely land a force. When Patton learned the significance of the deception plan, he dropped his idea.⁴

Then there was the question of Patton's staff. While Beetle Smith approved fifteen of Patton's former staff members to stay with him, both he and Eisenhower balked at allowing Hap Gay to continue as Patton's chief of staff. Smith felt that Gay had gone rogue in Sicily, ordering Gaffey's 2nd Armored Division to break out of the Gela beachhead without informing Patton.⁵ Eisenhower wanted Gay replaced with General Everett Hughes, who would keep Patton in line, unlike Gay, who worshiped his boss. Hughes wanted nothing to do with the role, writing his wife, "You don't have to be told how difficult would be an assignment to keep Geo[rge] in line."⁶ Patton considered General Gaffey for the job but brought Gay up from Sicily anyway, to serve as his unofficial chief. Overall, Patton was pleased with his first full day in England. "Everyone including destiny [Eisenhower] its self [sic] seems glad I am here," he wrote Beatrice that night, "especially a couple of cousins [translation: British] whom I knew in Sicily."[7]

Patton set up headquarters at Peover Hall (pronounced Peever—or as his soldiers called it: Pee Over), an ancient red-brick manor house surrounded by gardens and horse stables in the British countryside south of Manchester. Patton's staff came to call the house the "Lucky Peel" estate, "Lucky" being the codename for Third Army.[8] Patton mused that the place had seen no repairs since 1627 and later complained it had too many creeks and was haunted by a "pink ghost." He set up his quarters across the hall from his war room, guarded by armed sentries. Here he held war councils with his corps and division commanders, planning Third Army's role on the Continent. He attended Sunday mass at a small chapel a short walk away from the house. Tombs of knights and their ladies, with life-sized statues, lined the interior. Despite the chapel's freezing January temperatures—Patton could see his breath—he enjoyed its austere sincerity.[9]

For exercise, Patton played badminton, tennis, and a rare game of golf. He also ran a mile a day and tried to walk four miles in less than an hour. While there were ample hunting grounds, he eschewed the sport, not wanting to risk injury with a campaign so close. He also bought himself a sun lamp for overcast days.[10] To relax, he and his staff dined at the Mainwaring, a local pub. He made two rules for the pub: no enlisted soldiers were allowed entrance, and a vase of fresh flowers had to be placed on his personal table, next to the fireplace.[11]

On January 28, Patton met his first contingent of Third Army headquarters personnel as they stepped off the *Queen Mary*. "Gentlemen," Patton said to the thirteen officers and thirty-five enlisted men, "welcome to the U.K., I'm George Patton, your new commander of the Third Army. Your baggage will be taken on a special train and we will meet in the club car where refreshments have been laid on. In the morning we will go to work at Peover Hall, our new headquarters, where you will wear many hats until the main body arrives. My presence and assignment here are secret, so don't talk or write about me. Thank you and good night." The men stood agape as Patton departed. This would be the first of many greeting speeches. He was just getting started.[12]

The next day, the staff filed out on to the front lawn where Patton waited. "I have been given command of the Third Army for reasons which will become clear later," he announced. "You made an outstanding reputation as an able and hard-working staff under my predecessor [Courtney Hodges]. I have no doubt that you will do the same for me. You are now in an active theater of war. Ahead of you lies battle. That means just one thing. You can't afford to be a damn fool, because in battle 'dammed fool' means dead men. It is inevitable for men to be killed and wounded in battle, and there is no reason why such losses should be increased by incompetence or carelessness. I never permit either on my staff." Then he listed the three reasons the United States was at war:

> The first is because we are determined to preserve our traditional liberties. The second is to defeat and crush the Nazis, who would destroy our liberties. The third is because men like to fight and always will fight. Some sophists and other crackpots deny that. They are goddamn fools or cowards or both. Men like to fight. They always have and always will. If you don't like to fight then I don't want you around here. You better get out now before I kick you out later. That's all gentlemen, and good luck.[13]

Patton would repeat the performance for the continued flow of staffers to his headquarters. Some said the experience left them "covered in goose pimples." Patton's message was always the same, but with different examples. To one group he explained that Third Army was the best in the world and would be in Berlin ahead of everyone. He stressed the importance of discipline, explaining that a pint of sweat was worth a gallon of blood. "We are going to kill German bastards," he told them, personally preferring to "skin them alive." When he finished speaking, a soldier in attendance wrote his family, "He was a man for whom you *would* go to hell and back."[14]

His greeting complete, Patton boarded a train to visit a club in London. When he stepped on board, unfortunately, a crowd of hundreds cheered him. He did not want his presence known, lest it give Eisenhower another reason to send him home. He had one of his staff members contact the censor's office in London to make sure there were no references to his presence. But he would not enjoy the same anonymity in England as Bradley did. He was too much of a celebrity.[15]

At Peover Hall, Patton enjoyed good meals and conversation with his staff, often reminiscing about the past. At one dinner, he lectured the staff

CHAPTER TWELVE ★ A NEW COUNTRY, A NEW ARMY, AND THE GHOSTS OF SICILY   273

about the importance of criticizing subordinates. He explained that, as the 2nd Armored Division commander at Fort Benning, he had visited the motor pool and found not a single operating vehicle. He called for the officer in charge, "a poor bastard, just out of school." Patton had chewed out the lieutenant and told him he would come back in twenty-four hours to see the young man drive each vehicle by him. Sure enough, "that son-of-a-bitching shavetail drove every one of those vehicles by me himself. He's probably somewhere in the Army, doing one hell of a job, just because I chewed his ass!" Suddenly, one of Patton's officers, Lieutenant Allison Wysong, burst out laughing. "What's so funny, Wysong?" Patton asked. "Yes sir, I was that poor bastard at Fort Benning." Patton leaned back, smirked, and said, "Guess I've made my point."[16] In another instance, one of his staff officers presented Patton with a detailed map of France. After reviewing it, Patton told the officer, "This is fine, but it only goes as far east as Paris. I'm going to Berlin."[17]

While Patton spent most of his time at Peover Hall, General Lee had found him a three-story flat in London down the street from Eisenhower's Grosvenor Square headquarters. When Patton first pulled up to it, he thought it fine, since it had an unobtrusive entrance. Upon entering he changed his mind. The second-floor landing's paneled walls were covered with exotic paintings. The thick carpet and soft lighting reminded Codman of a boudoir and Patton of a brothel. The flat even contained a library filled with pornographic materials. Patton's personal bedroom was worse. It contained a ceiling mirror, pink silk walls and curtains, and a white, bear-skin rug. When Patton caught his reflection in the ceiling, he blurted out, "JESUS!" He did not like the place. When Major General Alexander "Sandy" Patch visited a few hours later, Patton told him, "I'd rather be shot than spend the evening sitting around this Anglican bordello." Patton's staff, however, preferred the new residence to the average troop hotel, referring to it as the "passion pit."[18]

Patton and Patch attended the play *There Shall Be No Night*, about the Finns' heroic resistance against the Russian army in 1940, at Haymarket Square, put on by Patton's friends Alfred Lunt and his wife, Lynn Fontanne. Few people recognized Patton. Those who did could not place him. Patton considered the lack of recognition bad for his soul. Halfway through the second act, he snuck out to the cold, misty night, to smoke a cigarette, in violation of London's blackout rules. A young, chubby girl approached him and propositioned him for a fun night together, something common from Patton's World War I days in London when he was a young captain. "I'm sorry young lady," Patton smiled at her, "but you're one war too late."[19]

The next day, Patton met with the combat commanders who would help Third Army fight across the Continent. First was Major General John "P" Wood, commander of the 4th Armored Division. Originally an artilleryman, Wood earned the nickname "P" for "professor" as a West Point cadet for tutoring his classmates. Wood had a reputation for smart thinking, bold leadership, and an attachment to his men. Yet, he could act with bravado. During training in subzero temperatures, he impressed his men by taking off his shirt and dashing ice water and snow across his torso.[20] Wood was happy to see Patton and together they reviewed the troops, which Patton considered superior to any of his other units. To aid him in speaking to his men, Wood had obtained a mobile loudspeaker on a truck, "just like a candidate for election," he wrote.[21] A few months later, Patton returned to witness a live-fire exercise. He stressed careful planning and a violent execution of attack. During the practice, a fragment from an exploding shell hit a forward artillery observer who was walking with him. When the rest of the infantry dropped prone, Patton shouted and kicked them upright.

Demonstrations were Patton's first glimpse of the new armor division structure. The old formations were called "heavy" and comprised two regiments, called Combat Commands—Combat Command A and Combat Command B, usually referred to as CCA and CCB. Army planners based the divisions on cavalry divisions, with tanks replacing horses. The divisions contained 232 medium tanks and 158 light tanks. The 1st, 2nd, and 3rd Armored Divisions had been created as heavy divisions, but the disaster at Kasserine Pass proved the formation too unwieldy and sent Army planners back to the drawing boards to create divisions based on combined arms tactics and not cavalry tactics. The new, reorganized divisions used fewer tanks and more infantry and artillery. They consisted of three combat commands: CCA, CCB, and CCR (for "Combat Command Reserve.") In theory, CCA and CCB would draw from CCR as needed. Once in combat however, CCRs operated just like the other two combat commands. The new divisions contained only 168 medium tanks and 83 light tanks. Although the reorganized tank divisions were smaller, they were considered leaner and better balanced.[22]

Later, Patton met General Otto P. Weyland, who would command the fighter aircraft over Third Army, at the head of the XIX Tactical Air

Command. Weyland, a cool and quiet commander, did not look forward to his new assignment. "Nobody was just real anxious to do it [join Patton]. Nobody was *really envious of me*," he later said. Patton probably questioned Weyland's credentials, especially after his own bitter experiences in North Africa and Sicily. Still, although Weyland had no combat experience, having spent his entire military career in tactical operations, the two generals got along surprisingly well. Patton would come to count on Weyland, often asking his advice in staff meetings.[23]

Patton wrote Beatrice that he had the same job in England as he had in Sicily. "A rose by any other name." When he heard from friends at home that Beatrice was still stressed about the slapping incidents, he wrote her an apology but still defended his actions. "I know Damned well I did my duty and if more people did it the same way we would win a war instead of just fight one." He later wrote it might have been a good thing, for without it he would have ended up with Bradley's job, which was too high to be effective: "the altitude is too great," he mused.[24]

Meanwhile, Eisenhower, at a press conference, admitted to Patton's presence. When a reporter mentioned going to Italy to see Patton, Eisenhower explained, off the record, "Patton's here. He's still among my topdrawer generals and when the time comes, he'll have an important command. You'll be hearing a lot from him." Eisenhower's statement was no aside or fluke. There had been considerable debate between Beetle Smith and the Public Relations office whether to release Patton's name. Eisenhower made the final decision, reasoning it would be better to reveal his presence in England in case some "unscrupulous columnist [read Drew Pearson]" wrote that Eisenhower was deliberately hiding Patton from the American public and guarding the fact that he would have a part of the invasion of France. Time proved Eisenhower correct.[25]

On February 7 Patton flew to Northern Ireland to inspect Major General Walter Robertson's 2nd Infantry Division and Major General Leroy Irving's 5th Infantry Division. Both impressed him, although the 2nd would later only fight under him for a few days.[26] During his inspection, Patton passed a five-foot, three-inch tall first sergeant. He stopped and faced the NCO. "Who in the name of hell made you a first sergeant?" The soldier stood there, dumbstruck. "Sergeant, are you deaf? I asked you who in the name of hell made you a first sergeant." Snapping out of his fog, the sergeant responded, "With all due respect, the same that made you a general made me a first sergeant." Patton looked at the surrounding officers, then back at the sergeant. "Hummph," was his only response.[27]

Patton also visited the Major General William C. McMahon's 8th Infantry Division, where he ordered all the officers to have their rank insignia welded onto their helmets so he would not have to hunt for the man in charge.[28] To Colonel Edward M. Fickett's 6th Cavalry Group, he explained, "The only good Germans are dead Germans with one reservation: Hitler. I am going to shoot that son of a bitch right between the eyes."[29] To a group of truck drivers, he said, "Now, if ever you're in convoy, moving along, and enemy planes are overhead, strafing, if you get out into the ditch to hide, it isn't going to do you any good, because if I come along and see you in the ditch there, I'll kill you myself."[30]

On February 11 Patton attended his first invasion meeting. Montgomery hosted, with Bradley, Dempsey, and Canadian Lieutenant General Harry Crerar, the commander of the First Canadian Army, in attendance. Patton wore a newly fitted uniform and boots for the occasion, his first new uniform since leaving the United States. He still chaffed at being left out of the initial campaign but was pleased to be part of the Brittany campaign and cracking the German army. When he found out Third Army was scheduled to be in France twenty-five days after D-Day, he burst out into a tirade about what he would do to those "Goddamn sons of bitches!" The other generals delighted in their spirited colleague.[31]

To many people, Patton did not look well. While in Sicily, he had caught a tiny piece of shrapnel in his lip that would crack the skin every time he yawned. In England, a doctor sent him to a specialist, who burned the spot with an X-ray machine. It hurt and looked terrible, but the treatment worked. Rumors swirled that Patton was dying of lip cancer, until the burn mark healed and disappeared.[32]

On February 16 Eisenhower called Patton at 1:30 a.m., ordering him to his headquarters. He arrived before sunrise to hear Eisenhower tell him, "I am afraid you will have to eat crow again for a little while." A worried Patton asked what he had done this time. Instead, he was delighted to learn that the Anzio beachhead in Italy was in danger of being overrun and he was to fly down to Italy to restore order, much as he had done to II Corps in Tunisia. His skills were needed. He would replace General Lucas, whose VI Corps had floundered. Eisenhower showed Patton General Alexander's request, which read, "If you cannot send me a thruster like George Patton, I recommend putting a British officer in command." Eisenhower could only spare Patton for a month but fully expected him to resolve the crisis. Patton asked Eisenhower to support him, so he would not seem like a rogue general abandoning his Normandy

CHAPTER TWELVE ★ A NEW COUNTRY, A NEW ARMY, AND THE GHOSTS OF SICILY   277

assignment. Eisenhower agreed and put a transport plane and a bomber on standby. "I am tickled to death," Patton wrote, "and will make a go of it." To his wife he wrote, "I am skipping like a gazelle," even though he could not reveal why. Eisenhower told only Smith about Patton's new mission, and he fully expected Devers to quickly find a leader to inspire the troops on the beach. If he could not, "Patton is the man that can give it to them."³³ The next day, while Patton was having his lip X-rayed, one of Eisenhower's aides called and told him to head back to Knutsford. The aide provided no explanations. He later learned that Lucas's temporary replacement, Major General Truscott, had proved up to the job and the request was rescinded. The news deflated Patton.³⁴

Patton called Eisenhower the next day. When Eisenhower mentioned that he had requested Major General Charles Corlett to command XIX Corps because of his success in the Pacific at Kwajalein, Patton groused that his commanders had done pretty well in the Mediterranean. Eisenhower got angry and hung up, so Patton called Smith to "bootlick" Eisenhower. Patton's bruised ego received some buttressing when he spoke with Brigadier General J. E. Hull, an operations officer fresh from Marshall's office. He told Patton that when reports of the difficulties at Anzio reached Marshall's desk, the chief of staff said, "I wish Patton was commanding the beachhead." Hull also related that Major General Troy Middleton, who had returned to the United States with an arthritic knee, told him that Patton had pushed him further than he thought he could endure.³⁵

His Italian adventure over before it began, Patton returned to worrying about the Normandy invasion. He felt the wording for the OVERLORD plan was shortsighted: "secure a lodgment on the Continent from which further operations can be developed" implied there would be phase lines to be met. "We must keep driving, like we did in Sicily," he wrote.³⁶ He preferred to focus on his attack. On February 18 he pleaded with Bradley for an invasion of Calais. Bradley explained that if it came to that, he would trade one of his amphibiously trained divisions for one of Patton's. Bradley was unaware of Operation FORTITUDE. Bradley's solution brought Patton no relief. "I fear that, after we get landed in France, we will get boxed in a beachhead, due to timidity and lack of drive, which is latent in Montgomery," he wrote in his diary. "I hope I am wrong."³⁷

From time to time, the Germans reminded Patton that they were still in the fight. On February 18 German bombers raided London and fragments fell on Patton's roof. An inspection the next day revealed smashed windows and a few wrecked vehicles.[38] Patton knew the Germans had not singled him out because his presence in England remained secret. When he walked into a room of reporters at Eisenhower's headquarters, he told them he was only a ghost. They assured him that they would not say a word.[39]

On March 1 Patton met with Eisenhower to discuss his chief of staff issue. While Eisenhower would not order Patton to replace Gay, he believed the latter incapable of taking over a headquarters if something happened to Patton. Patton resented the order, feeling he had earned the right to pick his own chief of staff, but he saw the writing on the wall. He again considered Hugh Gaffey but was not yet convinced he should give up on Gay. Later, Smith offered Patton Brigadier General Robert McClure, in charge of Eisenhower's press relations, as his new chief. A week earlier McClure had told Eisenhower that Patton should not lead an army because of his reputation. "Good God!" Patton wrote, "I suppose that he [Smith] did not know what McClure had said about me to Ike." Bitter that he could not make his own choice, Patton commented in his diary that Eisenhower drank too much. "I really feel sorry for him," he added, noting, "I think that in his heart he knows that he is not really commanding anything." Patton could not have been more wrong. Eisenhower was deeply involved in the coming invasion, spending his days arguing with Churchill about the invasion of southern France, wrestling with his own Air Force about preparing the Normandy battlefield, and dealing with feuding British air marshals. Patton, upset with his commander, was simply looking for a chink in Eisenhower's armor.[40]

The situation with Gay stressed Patton. He called on Hughes and Smith, seeking their advice. Hughes urged him to follow Eisenhower's orders. Patton visited Smith to stay on Eisenhower's good side. Making the rounds exhausted Patton and left him bitter, as he worried about hurting Gay's feelings. "After all the ass kissing I have to do, no wonder I have a sore lip." He toyed with quitting over the matter but admitted to himself that he was not that big-hearted. Patton finally broke the news to Gay on March 6, telling him that Eisenhower had ordered him to do it. Gay was surprisingly upbeat about the news, probably knowing that in war, losing a staff job was not the worst thing in the world.[41]

Mired as he was in frustration over losing Gay, Patton's ugly side showed itself. He met with General Lee, who told Patton about his plans to integrate African American soldiers with white soldiers at training

CHAPTER TWELVE ★ A NEW COUNTRY, A NEW ARMY, AND THE GHOSTS OF SICILY   279

centers. Patton despised the idea and worried it would "cause a great deal of unnecessary suffering and killing when we get back to the States." He later wrote Beatrice that "the question of people like George Meeks [his African American aide] is going to be terrible after the war. The girls here—nice girls—prefer them. It is the damdest [sic] thing you ever saw."[42]

To cheer himself up, Patton bought a seventeen-month-old Scottish bull terrier named Punch. The dog's previous owner had been a Royal Air Force fighter pilot who failed to return from a mission. His wife, who worked during the day, had to sell the dog. Punch was already a combat veteran, having accompanied his master on a raid over Berlin. Patton soon renamed his dog Willie, after the chorus, "L'il Willie Whiffle" from a tune he heard an African American child singing at a 1934 barbeque in Virginia. Patton described his new best friend as "pure white except for a little lemin [sic] on his tail which to a cursory glance would seem to indicate that he had not used toilet paper."[43] Patton thought his squinty-eyed, short-haired dog "cute" and walked often with him, sometimes breaking into a run. Willie's previous owner taught him to ask for his food with a hearty "woof." He barked for his evening walk and would look at the clock around nine each night. The woman who gave Patton the dog wrote in a note, "I am sure that you will find him a very loyal friend."[44]

Patton threw a birthday party for his new pet, which included a dinner with the Third Army staff, followed by cake and singing "Happy Birthday to You."[45] He had his first scare with Willie ten days later when a car ran over the terrier's hind leg, tearing off the skin. Patton showed as much sympathy for his dog as he did for his soldiers. "He feels very sorry for himself but is not really hurt at all," Patton wrote.[46] During briefings, Willie would wander the room until Patton shouted, "damn you, get over here and lay down!" If Willie disobeyed, Patton would drag him by the collar to his chair. He loved his dog, even though Willie rarely stayed still, liked to eat letters off of Patton's desk, and once ate a box of thumbtacks and an eraser.[47] Whenever Willie heard George Meeks coming to fetch him in the morning, he would jump into Patton's bed and crawl under the covers. "Geo[rge] has Willie almost accustomed to cows, rabbits and country life," Hughes reported at the end of March.[48]

With Gay out and Willie on board, Patton finally settled on his new chief of staff on March 8. Middleton was no longer an option since Marshall had returned him to the European theater to command VIII

Figure 38. Patton's dog Willie resting in a jeep. National Archives and Records Administration.

Corps. That left Gaffey, who still commanded the 2nd Armored Division. Gaffey did not want to give up his command, but he owed Patton a lot and promised to do as asked. The pick pleased Patton, both because Gaffey had already been his chief of staff and because Gaffey and Gay were friends, making it easier for Patton to transfer responsibilities from Gay, whom he kept on the staff.

Patton and Bradley went to Eisenhower's recently established Widewing office outside of London in Bushy Park to tell him about Gaffey. They found Eisenhower sternly talking on the phone with Air Marshal Tedder, Eisenhower's new SHAEF deputy supreme commander, about the infighting among the American and British air forces and navies. "I'm tired of dealing with a bunch of prima donnas," he said into the phone and demanded they stop quarreling like children. If they couldn't get along, "I'll quit!" Eisenhower's words took Patton aback. He was impressed with his boss's directness, yet he could not help but find something to criticize. After approving Patton's new chief of staff, Eisenhower referenced using metal tracks for tanks. Patton assumed he did it "because Monty does." But Eisenhower was focusing on getting tanks off the Normandy beaches and into the farm fields, where there were few paved roads. While Eisenhower was thinking about the Normandy countryside, Patton was thinking about towns and cities well beyond the beaches where rubber tracks were more suitable.[49]

After the meeting, Patton issued lengthy orders to Third Army on his principles of command, combat procedures, and administration gleaned from lessons learned.[50] Most were from the Mediterranean theater, others were just plain Patton. For command and control, he stressed that his commanders should visit the front daily to see conditions with their own eyes, but not interfere. "Remember that praise is more valuable than blame." He stressed the importance of rest periods and keeping command posts at least a half hour's drive from division headquarters and all other lower units correspondingly shorter. The closer a headquarters was to the front, the less time it would take to visit other units and the less communication wire used. As for monitoring the enemy, "You can never have too much reconnaissance," he wrote, concluding, "information is like eggs: the fresher the better."

For operations and resupply, he wanted orders issued promptly, because the lower engineer and ordnance officers needed time to perform their tasks. "They too have plans to make and units to move." For supplies, he put the onus on both the supplier and the receiver. The forward units had to anticipate their needs and make timely requests, while the suppliers had to get things to the right place at the right time. "The DESPERATE DETERMINATION to succeed is just as vital to supply as it is the firing line." He called replacements the "spare parts" of the Army. "A company without riflemen is just as useless as a tank without gas." He wanted all his hospitals close to the front and for his commanders to visit the wounded personally and issue awards promptly, since their main value was in "raising the fighting value of the troops." To keep up morale, he wanted every commander to have a staff officer proficient in writing up medals.

He also wanted only one kind of discipline in Third Army: "PERFECT DISCIPLINE. If you do not enforce and maintain discipline, you are potential murderers." He did not want his commanders to blindly trust night reconnaissance and certainly not information given by the walking wounded or stragglers. "These latter seek to justify themselves by painting an alarming picture." Finally, he wanted his men at peak physical toughness. "Fatigue makes cowards of us all. Men in condition do not tire." He concluded with one sentence about courage: "DO NOT TAKE COUNSEL OF YOUR FEARS."⁵¹

With his orders issued, Patton returned to inspecting his army. Major General Lunsford P. Oliver's 5th Armored Division did not impress him. The men looked disheveled and their kitchens, latrines, and quarters were not up to Patton's standards. "In a word, it lacks a good leader." In contrast, General Robert Grow's 6th Armored Division pleased him. He knew Grow from the Louisiana maneuvers, during which Grow had angered him by dining on a fine meal while his men were in the field. Grow, however, had been one of the pioneers of tank doctrine when the idea of an American blitzkrieg was in its infancy. Grow's work impressed Patton, who considered the division in "superior shape."⁵²

On March 24 Patton had his headquarters troops, now numbering more than one thousand men, fall out in front of Peover Hall. Many of them had recently arrived from the States. Patton announced he was as concerned about their well-being as Courtney Hodges had been, telling them, "Despite some similarities in speech, English and Americans are not the same. English are foreigners to us, and we to them. General Montgomery told me that once himself."⁵³ He emphasized that men like to fight and there was a short distance between a pat on the back and a kick in the pants. He concluded his remarks by having the men look to their right and left. "One of you won't be here at the end of the war."⁵⁴ Among the new staffers was Robert S. Allen, an intelligence officer, who had been a reporter with Patton's nemesis, Drew Pearson. Nevertheless, Patton hoped for the best from him.⁵⁵

Patton never hesitated to administer discipline to his staff. One day, he passed through a basement room where several officers were talking. Most stood up when he passed through, but one lieutenant colonel remained seated. Patton walked through the room three more times and, on the third time, suddenly wheeled, walked over to the sitting officer and said, "I should think that an officer who has been in the Army long enough to be a lieutenant colonel would know enough to get to his feet when his commanding officer enters a room." With that he turned on a heel and walked away.⁵⁶

On March 26 Patton took formal command of Third Army.⁵⁷ The next day, the British honored him and his staff for their work in North Africa by presenting him the Commander of the Bath (COB) medal, while his staff received lesser medals. Bradley and Eddy also received the COB medals. Field Marshal Allen Brooke pinned the medal on a beaming

Patton. "Don't wince, Patton," said Brooke, "I shan't kiss you," and added that he had earned the decoration more than any other American.[58] Despite the attention, Patton still chaffed at the secrecy surrounding his presence in England. "This secrecy thing is rather annoying," he had earlier written Beatrice, "particularly as I doubt if it fools anyone. Every time I make a speech I have to say now remember you have not seen me—a voice crying in the wilderness."[59]

As days drew near to the invasion date, Patton remained busy. He took German language lessons and wrote a paper on close tank support for infantry, something he had written about earlier, during World War I. He accepted a new command car, complete with a steel bottom to defend against landmines, a horn, and a lamp for reading maps at night.[60] He wrote to Leslie McNair that "I would prefer to be in the shooting war sooner, but I have been so fortunate in all assignments that I am sure that the way things are set up will work for the best. Certainly, I will do my damndest!"[61] One day, while driving with Bradley, Patton told him, "Wouldn't it be a shame, after all we've been through, if we died in a car accident?"[62]

Patton continued to address arriving troops who would serve in his army. When he visited a hospital staff, he laced his speech with profanity, despite the presence of women nurses. To another medical group he boomed, "Gentlemen, we will make every effort to get our men to you, but if we can't, I expect you to go to them. If need be, you are expendable. I expect the Third Army to have the finest medical service in the entire U.S. Army."[63] To a third medical group he said, "Your helmet can save your life, soldier." During one speech, as women nurses and WACs sat in the front row, he mentioned something about how much skin he could skewer with all his medals. Then an aide ran up and whispered in his ear. "Oh, sorry ladies," he apologized, "but, oh, what the hell, you know what I'm talking about anyhow."[64] He acted out the elation soldiers should feel from plunging a bayonet into the bowels of a German soldier. "This is the enemy. Why are we fighting? Because we like a good fight."[65]

Patton worried about his men's fighting spirit and their battlefield intellect. "I wish we had more of a killer instinct in our men," he wrote to Beatrice.

They are too damned complacent—willing to die but not anxious to kill. I tell them that it is fine to be willing to die for their country but a damned sight better to make the German die for it. No one ever told them that. The British have suffered and are mad but our men are not. Roman Civilization fell out due to the loss of the will to conquer, satisfaction of the status quo and high taxes which destroyed trade and private enterprise and eventually forced people out of cities. The cycle is returning.

He also worried that his infantry units were failing to utilize their tank battalions. "There is a tendency to park them in the rear and forget about them," he complained to McNair.[66] He addressed his concern by constantly talking about fighting and killing to his combat units.[67]

As Patton visited his combat units around the United Kingdom from February to June 1944, he honed his speech to both educate and motivate the troops. It was the third variation of the Patton speech. The first, delivered to green troops before TORCH, was from a commander who had not seen combat for twenty-four years. The theme was victory or death, since Patton knew there would be no reinforcements if his men ran into trouble on the Moroccan beaches. Before the Sicily invasion, he toned it down for his veteran units, since both he and they were now bloodied by combat. To the inexperienced units he emphasized killing. In England, he was now an experienced veteran speaking to completely green troops. He was also an iconic figure, a hero the men had seen in movie newsreels, read about in newspapers and magazines, or had heard about from radio profiles. His words carried weight. When Lieutenant General William Simpson introduced Patton to the soldiers of XII Corps before one of his speeches, he told the men that Patton was a "great man" who would lead them with "heroism, ability, and foresight" and who had "proved himself amid shot and shell."[68]

While Patton never wrote his speech down, the context remained the same. He often gave it flanked by other officers and accompanied by an honor guard. He often paused several times during the speech as soldiers cheered, laughed, or applauded. He filled it with tips for surviving the battlefield, the need for teamwork, killing the enemy, and the importance of constantly pressing ahead. And, of course, he seeded it with foul language to fire up the young soldiers. There's nothing like hearing an old person cuss.[69]

Patton often began the speech by mentioning the men's patriotism and love of competition:

Men, this stuff we hear about America wanting to stay out of the war—not wanting to fight—is a lot of bullshit. Americans love to fight, traditionally! All real Americans love the sting and clash of battle. When you were kids, you all admired the champion marble player, the fastest runner, the big league ball players, the toughest boxers. Americans love a winner and will not tolerate a loser . . . Americans play to win all the time. I wouldn't give a hoot in hell for a man who lost and laughed. That's why Americans have never lost nor will ever lose a war, for the very thought of losing is hateful to Americans.[70]

He built on the theme of victory by emphasizing America's material advantages, as well as teamwork: "We have the finest food, the finest equipment, and the finest spirited men in the world. Why, by God, I actually pity those sons-of-bitches we're going up against—by God I do. An Army is a team. It lives, sleeps, eats, and fights as a team. This individual heroic stuff is a lot of crap."[71] Then he got visceral: "The bilious bastards who wrote that kind of, kind of stuff for the *Saturday Evening Post* don't know any more about real fighting under fire than they know about fucking! We're not just going to shoot the bastards, we're going to rip out their goddammed guts and use them to grease the treads of our tanks. We're going to murder those lousy Hun bastards by the bushel basket."[72]

He then addressed the men's fears but quicky shifted to praising the attack:

Some of you men are wondering whether or not you'll chicken out under fire. Don't worry about it. I can assure you that you'll do all do your duty. The Nazis are the enemy. Wade into them. Spill their blood. Shoot them in the belly. When you put your hand into a bunch of goo that a moment before was your best friend's face, you'll know what to do. There's another thing I want you to remember. I don't want to get any messages saying we're holding our position. We're advancing constantly and we are not interested in holding onto anything, except the enemy. We're going to hold onto him by his balls and kick the hell out of him all the time. We are going to go through him like crap through a goose![73]

He implored the men to be constantly alert, and not let down their buddies.

A man must be alert at all times if he expects to stay alive. If you're not alert, sometime, a German son-of-a-bitch is going to sneak up behind you and beat you to death with a sockful of shit! There are four hundred neatly marked graves somewhere in Sicily, all because one man went to sleep on the job. But they are German graves, because we caught the bastard asleep and before they did.[74]

He wanted his men to know that everyone in uniform had an important job, not just the frontline infantry or the tankers, and for that, they had to be brave:

All the real heroes are not storybook combat fighters either. Every single man in the Army plays a vital part. What if every truck driver suddenly decided that he didn't like the whine of those shells and turned yellow and jumped headlong into a ditch? He could say to himself, "They won't miss me—just one guy in thousands." What if every man said that? Where the hell would we be now? No, thank God, Americans don't say that. Every man does his job. Every man serves the whole. Every department, every unit, is important to the vast scheme of things. The Ordnance is needed to supply the guns, the Quartermaster is needed to bring up the food and clothes for us—for where we are going there isn't a hell of a lot to steal! Every last damn man in the mess hall, even the one who heats up the water to keep us from getting diarrhea, has a job to do. Even the Chaplain is important, for if we get killed and he is not there to bury us, we would all go to hell. Each man must not only think of himself but think of his buddy fighting alongside him. We don't want yellow cowards in the Army. They should be killed off like flies. If not, they will go back home after the war, god-damn cowards, and breed more cowards. The brave men will breed more brave men.[75]

He would often recall soldiers he considered real men: An American lieutenant in North Africa, who, with a Lugar against his chest, jerked off his helmet and hit the German with it while simultaneously sweeping the gun aside with his other hand. The German shot the lieutenant in the chest, yet the American jumped on the gun and killed another German; next was a man atop a telephone pole in Sicily, repairing wires while enemy fighters strafed the area; finally, there were the truck drivers in Tunisia, who drove for more than forty consecutive hours, braving enemy artillery barrages to resupply the frontlines.[76]

Ever mindful of his role in Operation FORTITUDE, Patton reminded the men that he was not in England, and that they had not seen him. "Let the first bastards to find out be the goddamned Germans. Someday, I want to see them raise up on their piss-soaked hind legs and howl, 'Jesus Christ, it's the Goddammed Third Army again and that son-of-a-bitch Patton again!!'" And once he routed the Germans, he wanted another fight: "We want to get the hell over there. The quicker we clean up this goddammed mess, the quicker we can take a little jaunt against the purple pissing Japs and clean out their nest too. Before the goddammed Marines get all of the credit." He knew, however, that he commanded citizen soldiers who did not want to make the military their profession. For that, too, he had assurances:

> Sure, we want to go home. We want this thing over with, but you don't win a war lying down. The quicker way they are whipped the quicker we go home. The shortest way home is through Berlin. Why, if a man is lying down in a shell-hole, if he just stays there all the day the Boche will get to him eventually, and probably get him first! There is no such thing as a foxhole war anymore. Foxholes only slow up an offensive. Keep moving! We will win this war, but we will win it only by fighting and by showing guts.[77]

Patton would conclude the speech by peering into the future.

> There is one great thing that you will be able to say when you go home. You may all thank God for it. Thank God that at least thirty years from now, when you are sitting around the fireside with your brat on your knee, and he asks you what you did in the great World War II, you won't have to say, that you shoveled shit in Louisiana. No, sir, you can look him straight in the eye and say, "Son, your granddaddy rode with the great Third Army and a son-of-a-bitch named Georgie Patton!"[78]

To an infantry division Patton addressed in April, he exhorted the troops to "kill, kill, kill—or be killed!" He explained to them that the German was no superman, but he was tough, well trained, and equipped.[79] A witness to the speech compared his conclusion to a modern-day version of the St. Crispin's Day speech from Shakespeare's *Henry the Fifth*. One soldier reacted, "you wanted to go out with your bare hands and kill the Germans."[80] After one speech, Patton turned to an officer on the stand and asked, "Well chaplain, did I make that rough enough for them?"[81] To a collection of British officers, he hammered the importance of keeping moving across an open beach, concluding, "Of course, you British have had experience in landing on beaches, in the last war, at Gallipoli. The trouble is, most of you are still there!" The British got the point and thoroughly enjoyed it.[82]

Still, Patton could not escape trouble. An Associated Press story exposed Patton's Mediterranean trips to distract the Germans the previous year. It quoted a letter from Major General Alexander D. Surles, the Army public relations director, to Roy A. Roberts, the president of the American Society of Newspaper Editors, which explained that the Army had delayed news of Patton's slapping incident because he "was to be used in a cover plan following operations in Sicily. In lieu of that, the Theater Commander was extremely desirous that his reputation should not be impaired by a wide discussion of the soldier-slapping incident." In one fell swoop, an Army official had revealed Patton's subterfuge trips. Marshall immediately wrote to Roberts, demanding that he take care of the matter since the American public was "not aware of what war means as is the public in England where thousands have died and many more thousands have been injured.[83]

The ghosts of Sicily continued to haunt Patton. On April 5 he was called to London to meet with a special investigator for the Army inspector general, a Lieutenant Colonel Williams, who was looking into Patton's role in the killing of prisoners in Sicily. The two incidents of Captain John T. Compton and Sergeant Horace West had both been tried by military courts in October and September 1943, respectively. West had been found guilty, stripped of his rank, and sentenced to life imprisonment. Compton was acquitted and returned to the division, with a different regiment, and died in action in Italy on November 8, 1943. "In my opinion," Patton wrote, "both men were crazy." Either way, the investigator's

CHAPTER TWELVE ★ A NEW COUNTRY, A NEW ARMY, AND THE GHOSTS OF SICILY 289

Figure 39. Patton addresses his troops in England, using a combination of anecdotes and foul language. National Archives and Records Administration.

presence in London angered many in the Army high command as they prepared for D-Day.[84]

In Captain Compton's case, thirty-six Italian soldiers, some in civilian clothing, had surrendered to his men under a white flag. A soldier brought them to his sergeant, who reported to Compton. The captain ordered them shot. The men formed a firing squad and dispatched the prisoners. West's case was similar. He had been given forty-six prisoners to deliver from Biscari airport to the rear by the battalion's executive officer. Three prisoners were Germans, the rest Italians. All had had their shirts and shoes removed. West, and several guards, marched them about four hundred yards when he stopped the column and separated a small group to be taken to the intelligence officer. He then moved the prisoners off the road, telling the other guards he was "going to shoot these sons of bitches." He asked another sergeant for his Tommy Gun and several clips of ammunition. When the sergeant asked why, West told him "this is orders." West then inserted a clip into the machine gun and warned the guards that if they did not want to witness what he was doing, they should walk away. He then walked to the front of the column of twos and began firing the machine gun. The prisoners begged for mercy. By the time he finished with the first clip there were only three Italians left standing, who took off running. When someone shouted to stop them, the other guards opened fire, knocking at least one down. West reloaded and then, walking among the bodies, fired into anyone he thought was still alive.[85]

Four doctors of a five-doctor panel found West sane at the time of the killings; one judged him temporarily insane, basing his conclusion on West having been under almost constant fire for three days and without any sleep. At his trial, West admitted that the day of the killings he had witnessed Germans capturing two American soldiers and forcing them into a blockhouse. When he reached the blockhouse, he found the Americans dead and the Germans going through captured documents. He tossed a grenade into the house and pulled the American bodies out. "I knew they killed them after taking them prisoner," he confessed. "One thing it seemed to me was to take apart every living soul up there." It was after he described his feelings that West claimed that Patton's order guided his actions.[86]

The two cases, known as the Biscari Massacre for the airfield the 45th was trying to capture, had become somewhat of a scandal. General McNarney considered it highly secret since Patton's name was attached and had taken extreme measures to cover it up, as McNarney explained it, "to safeguard it in the United States, although there might be considerable knowledge of it in the United States." Both West and Compton had claimed that they were following Patton's orders not to take prisoners from a speech he had given the division before it debarked for Sicily. Brigadier General Philip E. Brown, with the inspector general's office, recommended an interim report be written about both cases, which would include "testimony of two officers [probably Patton and Bradley] and the comments of the theater commander [Eisenhower]."[87]

Williams asked Patton if he would testify and if he knew his rights. Patton had prepared for the meeting. That morning he had sought out General Middleton, who commanded the 45th Infantry Division in Sicily, and reviewed what he had said to the troops. There were never any orders to kill prisoners. He told the men if the enemy kept firing until they were right on top of him, "you can't stop shooting when he tries to surrender." He added that "if he wants to surrender he must do it in time, or do it with his hands up. If he snipes at you from the rear, you must kill him if you can."

Middleton had already told investigators on February 19, 1944, that he did not interpret Patton's order as an order to shoot prisoners. Patton, he told the court, "is very emotional"; he further explained that while Patton extolled his soldiers to kill any enemy who continued to fire at him at close range. "I never interpreted any statement he made to indicate you would shoot a man with his hands up, and certainly not after he had surrendered." When questioned directly about Patton's use of the term "he shall not live" during the speech, Middleton had told the court, "He was building up a brave sprit, of course." Both Stiller and Codman, who were with Patton when he gave the speech, agreed that that was all Patton had said.[88]

The whole incident shook Patton. Was this another attempt to get rid of him? The next day Hughes visited Patton to see if he was okay. "Geo[rge] is crying on my shoulder again," he wrote. The two sat down and wrote an account of Patton's dealings during the incidents. Hughes went one extra: He penned a letter to his friend Major General E. L. "Pete" Peterson, the Army inspector general, defending Patton and imploring his importance to the war effort. "I am firmly convinced that Patton never at any moment advocated the destruction of prisoners of war under any circumstances. I am convinced that Patton is a fighter for he looks at war realistically and does what few men in our army have yet dared to do—talk openly about killing." He concluded, "I am so concerned over the success of this war and the need for fighting men and fighting leaders and I am so convinced that Patton is one of the men we need that I have written the above to you as an old friend and also the Inspector General to tell you what I must tell someone."[89] Patton wrote Beatrice about the investigators, calling them "fair haired boys," "friends of freedom," and "fools." He complained that if the men had killed Japanese prisoners, people would cheer and not condemn him. "I think I will quit and join a monastery." He reasoned that all he had to do was survive until he could get back into combat, then he would be okay. He liked Beatrice's idea of shooting his wrongdoers as spies, just like General Sherman had done in the Civil War.[90]

Then Patton and Hughes visited Bradley, but Bradley said he was too busy to discuss the matter. Bradley may have been avoiding Patton. Indeed, he seethed about the investigation. As he saw it, if word of the court-martial got out, that American generals encouraged their men to kill prisoners, it would put the lives of all American POWs at risk. Bradley later angrily wrote about the incident, "Patton's big mouth had us dancing on yet another griddle." To take Patton's mind off his troubles, Hughes took him to see a play, which featured "pretty girls with pretty legs."[91]

The next day, Patton's latest crisis was put on hold for a briefing on Operation OVERLORD. General Montgomery hosted at St. Paul's School in Kensington—Montgomery's headquarters and alma mater—with all the major players present, including Churchill. Standing with a pointer in hand, Montgomery described the landings in a two-hour lecture in front of a giant scale model of the Normandy coast, tilted up so the other generals, in their tiered seats, could see. He explained the initial invasion, with British troops capturing Caen and pushing south to Falaise on D-Day. Once ashore, American forces would target the Cotentin Peninsula, cutting it off from the Germans. He explained that the breakout would occur once Patton arrived on the continent. Patton would then head west and capture the Brittany ports while protecting the southern flank so the British and Canadian forces, as well as the American First Army, could drive east toward Paris. Patton later took pride in being the only army commander Montgomery mentioned specifically by name. "Saying P's army will do this and that," he wrote Beatrice. Montgomery referred to the other armies by numbers. Churchill concluded the meeting. Patton was unimpressed with the prime minister's speech, although he allowed that "he had the idea."[92]

When it was all over, Patton discovered no one had forgotten his latest failing. At dinner that night with Eisenhower, Bradley, Lieutenant

General Joe McNarney, General Marshall's assistant chief of staff, and Assistant Secretary of War John J. McCloy, a furious Eisenhower accused Patton of talking too much. "If you order me not to, I will stop," Patton responded. "Otherwise, I will continue to influence troops the only way I know, a way which so far has produced results." Eisenhower, realizing the value of Patton's speeches to the troops, relented. "Go ahead," he told Patton, "but watch yourself."[93] No action was taken against Patton. The memory of the massacres, or atrocities, would dissipate once the fighting in France commenced, as the war took on a larger and more brutal nature.

On April 11 Patton received notice that Third Army units would serve under Bradley's First Army until Patton and his headquarters arrived on the continent, and that once activated, he would serve under Montgomery's 21st Army Group, "until such time as the Supreme Commander assigns command of U.S. Forces to First United States Army Group (FUSAG)." Patton assuredly hoped the time would be short, although he did not relish the thought of serving under either Bradley or Montgomery. He also felt that neither of them wanted to oversee George S. Patton. "If they knew what little respect I had for the fighting ability of either of them they would be even less anxious for me to show them up." He still considered Montgomery too cautious and averse to calculated risks.[94]

Major Generals Wade W. Haislip and Middleton, the commanders of the XV and VIII Corps, respectively, briefed Patton on their conditions and readiness. A pleased Patton told them, "I have won in battle and I'm going to win again. But I've won because I've had good commanders and staff officers, and today's presentations are further evidence of that." He then reminded everyone that he did not want Graves Registration to bury any bodies along the roads, because "those not buried had a lot of grave markers to look at."[95] Middleton reported about his difficulties deploying tanks in Sicily and Italy and Patton made him write a report on it. Middleton did so and concluded that the terrain in both places did not support a large number of tanks. Patton responded three days later by issuing "Tactical Use of Separate Tank Battalions," a letter of instruction to his army, incorporating Middleton's ideas and crediting him for it.[96]

On April 18 Generals McNarney and Lee, with Assistant Secretary of War McCloy, visited Peover to review Patton's plans for the upcoming campaign. Patton stressed his need for replacements. When the briefing ended, they warned Patton about his mouth. He pushed back that his words produced fighting men and he would be untrue to himself if he did not use them. McCloy warned that if he got in trouble again, the Senate would demand his recall. His words were prophetic. He also said that Patton would command an army despite hell. McNarney took a different view. He wanted Patton to stay out of trouble so he could command men in the field. As they prepared to leave, McNarney asked Patton, "If I were God, what besides replacements would you ask me for?" Patton responded: "To fight this Army in France!" Patton later suspected that McNarney would instead ask to have his major general rank made permanent. Patton likened his limbo situation to fishing in a pond full of fish. "You know the fish are there," he wrote Bea, "but you trail your hook for a long time between strikes."[97] The feeling that he was missing out on the war weighed on him. That night he dreamed of fighting with Beatrice over her giving away a pair of his pants. He also heard his old West Point friend Hugh McGee call out his name, "just as distinctly as I ever heard any thing." Maybe Patton wished for simpler times.[98]

On April 20 Patton visited the 90th Infantry Division in Cheltenham. The officers' appearance and discipline impressed him (that would change when he reached France). At the division's headquarters he told the staff a secret to his battlefield success. After each battle he visited small units and gathered the men around him to hear how they seized hills or attacked bunkers. According to one staffer, "He constantly wanted to find out more and more." From there he headed to Major General Walton Walker's XX Corps at Marlboro. Although Walker tried to emulate Patton in dress and bombastic talk, and despite his organized leadership, Patton distrusted him. "Walker tries hard but is fat and short," two things Patton could not tolerate. He never explained how Walker could get taller.[99]

Patton spent the rest of the day watching a tank platoon from the 4th Armored Division support an infantry unit. Major General Wood oversaw the exercise, even though he was still recovering from a jeep accident. When it was over, Patton mounted a platform and announced to the men, "I know you guys don't know why you came three thousand miles from home" to fight the war in Europe, "but I'll give you a good reason: what American boy doesn't like a good fight? As long as we're here let's kill every son-of-a-bitch that we can!" The men cheered wildly.[100] Patton was less impressed with Major General Grow's 6th Armored Division, which was in the middle of firing exercises. "The bazooka was bad as they were firing at long ranges," he wrote. "The tactical dispositions were bad but the use of weapons good. It was also apparent that they took too long to get on targets of opportunity." The men failed to use their superior numbers of light tanks to attack a few medium tanks, which disappointed him.[101] Either way, Patton was in his element.

CHAPTER THIRTEEN

FORTITUDE and Knutsford

THE GERMANS KNEW that the Western Allies were planning an invasion of France, but they did not know where it would come ashore. As far back as July 1943, while Patton battled across Sicily, the British chiefs of staff finalized Normandy as their target, under Operation OVERLORD. To keep the Germans guessing, the British organized the London Controlling Section (LCS), an innocuous-sounding group charged with misleading the Germans about where and when the Allies would storm ashore. The LCS soon launched Operation FORTITUDE, disseminating false information that the invasion was coming to Pas de Calais, more than two hundred miles to the east of Normandy and the closest port city to southern England.

To help sell the ruse, the British created fake army divisions, corps, armies, and army groups. They relayed the information through a German spy who was actually a Spaniard working for the British, named Joan Pujol Garcia. The Germans referred to him by the codename "Arabel," while the British called him "Garbo." Over time, Garbo "recruited" twenty-four spies. British agents conjured them to make the Germans feel they had a window into British intelligence and the Allies' command and control. By the time Patton arrived in England, the Germans believed the Allies had fifty-five divisions preparing for the invasion when they only had thirty-seven.[1]

Yet, the Germans did not always decipher British "leaks" the way the LCS hoped. Even though they put out information on American units and an entire army, the conjured Fourth, none of this was recorded by the Germans on their December 1943 maps. The Germans knew Montgomery and Bradley had prominent roles in the upcoming invasion. On January 17, 1944, Reuters reported that Bradley had been picked as the commander of all forces in Europe. The Germans soon placed Montgomery as the commander of 21st Army Group. Two months later they tallied two American armies in England, the First and the Ninth, adding, "It is possible that General Patton, hitherto commander of the Seventh Army in the Mediterranean, will command one of the American armies." The Germans believed that Bradley had been placed in charge of the fictitious First US Army Group (FUSAG). They had not understood the clues.[2]

It is unclear when Patton learned about his role in FORTITUDE. He never wrote about it in his diary or letters. His presence in England was secret, as he told every unit he visited, but, at some point, the word had to have come out. He possibly learned about it in late February 1944, when he hinted to Colonel Joe Aleshire, "At the moment I am not supposed to exist, so when the proper moment arrives I can be used as a shock to the Boche." He also wrote to Beatrice, "I may break cover any day now with the result that there will probably be a flare up at home but it won't do any harm." Patton was prescient in one sense and totally off the mark in another.[3]

By April 24, the Germans had still failed to take the bait of Patton assuming command of FUSAG. While they believed armies were concentrating in southern England, they could not agree if those concentrations were in the east or the west. The LCS had to convince them the troops were gathering in the east, closer to Calais. It also became harder to relay information to the Germans. For security reasons, the British had imposed military censorship and banned travel to Ireland, followed by a ban on all travel to and from England. On April 24 they imposed censorship on all diplomatic mail.[4]

While the British struggled to get word to the Germans about the Calais invasion, Patton, unknowingly helped them out. The day after diplomatic mail censorship went into effect, on April 25, he attended the opening of a British Welcome Club in a building in downtown Knutsford called the Ruskin Rooms, hosted by Mrs. Constantine Smith of the Women's Voluntary Service. The women hoped American servicemen would meet British women at the club and eventually visit their homes for meals, something that had worked out well in other parts of England. To prevent attracting attention, Patton arrived late, only to discover a crowd of about sixty people waiting for him. As he headed into the building, a British photographer snapped his picture. Patton told him he could report his name but not his job. Everyone then filed up to the second floor, where a hostess declared the club open and turned to Patton, asking him to say a few words.

Figure 40. Patton speaks to British women at Knutsford Hall on April 25, 1944. Newspaper accounts of the speech almost led to Eisenhower sending Patton home. National Archives and Records Administration.

Caught a little off guard, Patton stood up behind a table festooned with flowers, his hands clasped together. He did his best to be careful:

Until today, my only experience in welcoming had been to welcome Germans and Italians to the "Infernal Regions." In this I have been quite successful, as the troops whom I have had the honor to command have killed or captured some one hundred seventy thousand of our enemies. I feel that such clubs as this are a very real value, because I believe with [Irish playwright] Mr. Bernard Shaw, I think it was he, that the British and Americans are two people separated by a common language, and since it is the evident destiny of the British and Americans, and, of course, the Russians, to rule the world, the better we know each other, the better job we will do. A club like this is an ideal place for making such acquaintances and for promoting mutual understanding. Also, as soon as our soldiers meet and know the English ladies and write home and tell our women how truly lovely you are, the sooner the American ladies will get jealous and force this war to a quick termination, and I will get a chance to go and kill Japanese.

As he spoke, the photographer took his picture, capturing a smiling Patton. His comments concluded, the small crowd proposed a vote of thanks to the Americans, then the British. The band played "God Save the King" and "The Star-Spangled Banner." People urged Patton to stay for dinner, but he begged off and went back to Peover Hall.

The storm broke the next day while Patton and his staff briefed Generals Gilbert "Doc" Cook and Walton Walker, two of his corps commanders, as part of a three-day Third Army exercise. "I've won a battle before and I'm going to win again," he told his staff. When he finished, a public relations officer from Eisenhower's office called Hap Gay to ask about Patton's wording at Knutsford, specifically, what he said about the British and the Americans ruling the world.[5] Patton recited his lines about England, the United States, and the Russians. It was then that Gay related that some newspapers failed to carry the mention of the Russians. A furious Patton took Willie for a walk to cool his nerves. He debated whether to become a hermit or an owl—quiet and observant.[6]

Later that day, he fired off a letter to Everett Hughes, explaining that he deliberately arrived late and was unaware of any reporters present, "because the meeting was so small that I had no idea that anybody would even mention it." He recited his entire speech in the letter, adding "it appears to me a most innocuous statement of the policy of the three great powers as I understand it," and he included affidavits from Constantine Smith and Colonels N. W. Campanole and T. Blatherwick, confirming that he had included the Russians in this speech.[7]

Despite the growing storm clouds, on April 28 Patton met with French general Philippe Leclerc, the commander of the French 2nd Armored Division, the only foreign unit in Third Army. Patton considered him intelligent and "a good type French soldier." Leclerc had fought aggressively in North Africa but now worried that his division lacked replacements and asked for Patton's help. After the visit, Patton told his staff he needed to "get out that French pronunciation record and brush up on my accent."[8] He had already moved on from the flap.

If the Knutsford incident seemed behind him, it was about to be front and center. While most newspapers made the correction in a day or two, the damage was done. Beetle Smith called and told Patton never to talk in public without first submitting prepared words to Eisenhower personally for review and censorship, adding that Patton's "unfortunate remarks" had stalled both his and Smith's promotions to the permanent rank of lieutenant general. Patton was furious that no one from Eisenhower's office had defended him against the British and compared Eisenhower, Smith, and Lee, to Benedict Arnold. He worried that the gag order would prevent him from addressing his green troops, resulting in higher casualties. The next day, he refused to accept the salute at a military parade and watched from a private car on a side street as Gay took the salute for him. The fear of being relieved crept into Patton's head as he hunkered down and waited for the axe to fall.[9] He did not have to wait long.

Eisenhower himself, who was returning from a two-day amphibious landing operation, Exercise TIGER, in Slapton Sands in southern England, had missed the latest crisis until Smith called him and read a cable from Marshall about its effects in the United States. Eisenhower immediately considered sending Patton home. The Allied commander was in a foul mood. Not only did TIGER go poorly, but German E-boats attacked a convoy of LSTs, sinking two and damaging one. Approximately 750 Americans were killed, another 300 wounded. American officers with top-secret knowledge of the landings were missing, and the exercise may have tipped off the Germans to where the Allies were planning to land. Having to deal with Patton's troublesome nature in the midst of this disaster strained Eisenhower. "I'm getting sick and tired of having to protect him," he told Bradley.[10]

Marshall's cable mentioned that newspapers carried "glaring reports of General Patton's statements" and stressed his concern that Patton's words had jeopardized a list of general promotions (of which Patton's was one) awaiting Senate approval. "This I fear has killed them all," noted Marshall. When Eisenhower returned to his headquarters, he wrote back that "I have grown weary of the trouble he causes you and the War Department to say nothing of myself, that I am seriously considering the most drastic action." Yet, he deferred the ultimate decision until he heard from Marshall to see if Patton's latest flap might dissipate in a few days. He asked Marshall two important questions: if Patton's statement would prevent approval of the promotions; and if keeping Patton could wreck, or even hurt, the public or the government's confidence in the War Department. "If the answer to either of the above is in the affirmative then I am convinced that stern disciplinary action must be taken so as to restore the situation."

Ever the pragmatic thinker, Marshall weighed Patton's combat values against the effects of his actions on the troops, on Eisenhower, and the public's confidence in Eisenhower. "Patton is the only available Army Commander for his present assignment who has actual experience in fighting Rommel [he didn't] and in extensive landing operations followed by a rapid campaign of exploitation." Yet, Marshall cabled Eisenhower that it was purely his decision to make. "If you feel that the operation can be carried out with the same assurance of success with Hodges in command, for example, instead of Patton, all well and good. If you doubt it, then between us we can bear the burden of the present unfortunate reaction. I fear the harm has already been fatal to the confirmation of the permanent list."[11] While Marshall's cable could be considered hands-off, he was really asking for a nondecision from Eisenhower: Select a green commander who had not seen combat since World War I, or go with the loose-lipped leader who had dueled with the enemy's best general and was relatively fresh from battle. The promotion list was not an issue, as Eisenhower could not make it better or worse from this point on. It boiled down to who was qualified to command Third Army.

If things were bad for Patton in England, they were worse back in the United States. Reacting to the misinformation that he had left the Russians out of his speech, congressmen sounded off. In the House of Representatives, Republicans castigated Patton, with Hamilton Fish III of New York calling his speech "detrimental to the war effort.... Patton is not reflecting the opinion of even a small percentage of Americans when he says so." Harold Knutson from Minnesota declared, "Such statements served only one purpose, and that is to prolong the war." Karl E. Mundt of South Dakota harkened back to Patton's last embarrassment in Sicily, observing that Patton "succeeded in slapping the face of every one of the United Nations except Great Britain." From the other side of the aisle, the Democrats were split. While Democrat Hatton Sumners of Texas said, "the general has been shooting off his head again," John Costello, from Patton's home state of California, defended Patton, saying his speech would encourage American women to work harder "to get the war over so our boys can get home sooner."[12]

In the Senate, Republicans kept up the attack. Robert Taft of Ohio called the speech "an irresponsible incident." Both senators Ralph Brewster of Maine and Kenneth Wherry of Nebraska said that it was Secretary of State Cordell Hull who dictated foreign policy and that Patton "should be taken off the stump."[13] Patton, infuriated by the words coming from the Senate floor, wrote to General Joyce about his enemies list: "I have to revise my card index by adding the names of certain descendants of female dogs."[14]

On Sunday, April 30, while Patton attended mass, he received word that Eisenhower wanted to see him the next day. Patton's mind raced. He feared it meant a reprimand or a reduction in rank and even entertained thoughts that it meant an alternative plan for the coming campaign. If he got sent home, he reasoned, he would run for political office, where his honesty and straightforwardness would make him either "a great success or a dismal failure." He wrote Beatrice that he would soon have free time to go sailing, "the Chesapeake in the spring is said to be lovely."[15] He found some relief when he learned Hughes had brought his statements on the incident to Eisenhower, who was preparing a cable to Marshall that he would no longer protect Patton; however, upon reading the statements Eisenhower said, "Oh hell!" and ripped up the cable (he actually send the cable to Marshall). "Hughes is still worried about me," Patton wrote, "so am I." He immediately wrote Hughes, calling the incident a frame-up. He offered to have his name removed from the promotion list, "if in your judgment you consider it wise." He concluded, "Of course you know what my ambition is—and that is to kill Germans and Japanese in the command of an army. I cannot believe that anything I have done has in any way reduced my efficiency in this particular line of action."[16]

On May 1 Patton reported to Eisenhower for what he thought was a likely execution. "George, you have gotten yourself in a very serious fix," Eisenhower greeted him. Eisenhower was mad, not as much from Patton's statement but from Patton having defied his early warning to avoid the press. Patton was immediately reticent. "Before you go any further," he blurted out, "I want to say that your job is far more important than mine, so if in trying to save me you are hurting yourself, throw me out." Eisenhower would have none of it. "It's not a question of hurting me but of hurting yourself and depriving me of a fighting army commander."

Eisenhower then brought up Marshall's cable about how Patton's actions had shaken the American public's confidence. In an almost passive-aggressive move, Eisenhower told Patton that if he were sent home, he would not be demoted to colonel; nor could he look forward to a permanent promotion. He then added that leaders back home had said that even if Patton was the best tactician and strategist in the Army, he had showed a lack of judgment that made him unfit for command. At times, Eisenhower raised his voice so loudly that sentries down the hall could hear him. The verbal tongue lashing brought Patton to tears. He put his head on Eisenhower's shoulder, causing his helmet to fall off.[17]

Patton addressed his greatest fear to Eisenhower: being sent home. He argued that if he were reduced to a colonel, he would demand the right to command one of the assault regiments. Eisenhower turned him down, explaining that he would need him as an Army commander (did Patton not pick up on this hint?). Patton tried to sidestep the entire issue by shifting the conversation to the coming invasion, complaining that it was not big enough to succeed. Eisenhower, however, stayed on message, explaining that he had written Patton a savage letter, and that public opinion back home would force his hand on it. Patton teared up again and apologized for criticizing his old friend behind his back. Eisenhower laughed it off, telling Patton, "You owe us some victories; pay off, and the world will deem me a wise man."[18] A contrite Patton picked up his helmet, put it on and asked Eisenhower, "Sir, could I now go back to my headquarters?" Eisenhower, feeling odd from what he called a "ridiculous situation," granted the order.[19]

When Patton exited Eisenhower's headquarters, he felt like his career had been killed. "I feel like death," he admitted in his diary, "but I am not out yet." He spent the five-hour ride back to his headquarters reciting poetry to himself, particularly Rudyard Kipling's "If"—with its imagery of risk and reward. Back at Peover Hall, he refused to eat (he had not eaten since the affair erupted) and kept breaking out into a sweat every time the phone rang. Knowing that Marshall would have a hand in deciding his fate, he prematurely blamed the chief of staff for sending him home. Later that day, Patton gathered enough energy to visit a nearby Army hospital to have his teeth cleaned. Once finished, a doctor asked Patton to inspect the staff and he obliged, later writing a letter to the doctor's superior that he should be promoted. Maybe Patton felt someone should get promoted if it was no longer in the cards for himself.

That night, he vented in his diary that the coming invasion would be another Anzio, reminding himself that the plan had been hatched back in 1943 and that it would fail, using only five divisions. Here Patton misled himself. He knew well the invasion would include nine divisions, ten if he included the 90th Infantry Division, which would land later in the day. It didn't matter. He almost wanted it to fail were he left out. He closed out his dairy, lamenting that even if the entire Knutsford incident was "so trivial in its nature and so terrible in its effect," it had been the hand of God, testing his destiny to achieve greatness. "His will be done."[20]

For his part, Eisenhower worried that this time he might not be able save his intemperate commander and pondered what he should do with Patton. Marshall cabled the day after Eisenhower dressed down the general. After first reminding the Supreme Allied Commander that the decision on Patton was his alone to make, Marshall went on to promote Patton, if in a back-handed way. "My view, and it is merely that, is that you should not weaken your hand for OVERLORD. If you think that Patton's removal does not weaken your prospect, you should continue with him in command." Whether Eisenhower decided to send Patton home or keep him in country, either as Third Army commander or a reserve commander, Marshall told him not to worry about Patton's rank. He did not want Eisenhower burdened with that responsibility. Worried that an editorial he had sent Eisenhower might encourage him to send Patton home, Marshall acknowledged that it did not demand for Patton's relief. "Do not consider the War Department position in this matter," he added. He wanted Eisenhower to focus exclusively on OVERLORD. "Everything else is of minor importance."[21]

While Eisenhower and Marshall exchanged missives, the press in the United States exploded. Tom Trainor of the *Los Angeles Times*, who had spent time at the battlefront, told readers that Patton's men did not like him.[22] A *Washington Post* editorial accused Patton of lacking balance and suffering from "glaring defects as a leader of men." It also accused the War Department of cronyism, of having "set up a clique or club" through permanent promotions for generals during war. "All thought of such promotion should now be abandoned." Patton's gaffe not only threatened his promotion but those of all officers awaiting Senate confirmation.[23]

Making matters worse, *Time* magazine's May 1 issue featured a cover story on Bradley's command of First Army for the coming invasion. The article praised Bradley as discreet and compassionate, contrasting him to Patton. Using anonymous interviews with Seventh Army soldiers, the story painted Patton as contemptuous of Sicily's helpless civilians, adding that the Knutsford incident proved that he was "tolerated as an eccentric genius solely because he was considered indispensable." The article probably did nothing for his ego.[24]

As the storm raged around him, Patton waited to hear from Eisenhower. He stewed the next day, doing little and feeling like a Thanksgiving Day turkey, "waiting for the axe to fall." Had Eisenhower reached his limit? He had saved Patton after the slapping incidents, placed him at the head of a second army only to be repaid by legal officers looking into a massacre, and now this security breach only three weeks after he had warned Patton to stay quiet. Still, Eisenhower may have been sympathetic to Patton's plight, having experienced something similar. A month earlier, several newspaper articles had quoted personal letters that Eisenhower had mailed to friends and family back in the United States. To a friend he wrote, "Nothing I detest more than to have my private letters made public." Eisenhower knew how it felt to have a bright light shined on his private life.

Eisenhower was not the only one who wanted Patton to keep a low profile. When Patton visited Major General John Wood at his Chippenham headquarters, a messenger arrived with a letter from Secretary of War Stimson, Patton's old friend. He read the letter grim-faced, then passed it to Wood. "What do you think of that?" he asked. Wood read the letter, in which Stimson explained that he had done all he could do to cover Patton's foot-in-mouth disease and that he could do it no more. Wood recommended that Patton limit his public statements to subjects like patriotism and motherhood.[25]

When Patton got back to his headquarters, General Gay handed him a letter from Eisenhower, who had finally decided on the Third Army commander's fate. "I am once again more taking the responsibility of retaining you in command in spite of damaging repercussions resulting from personal indiscretion," Eisenhower wrote, emphasizing the only reason for his decision: "I do this solely because of my faith in you as a battle leader and from no other motives." He explained that his original letter to Patton about the incident would be placed in the official files, and no further action taken. "I expect you to plunge into the task of preparing your army with undiminished vigor." But he wanted Patton to disappear from the public eye and warned him again not to put himself in a position to "cause any further embarrassment to your superiors or yourself."[26]

Eisenhower had decided that Patton, despite all the headaches, was worth keeping for the coming campaign. In his 1948 memoir, *Crusade in Europe*, Eisenhower explained two points that helped him in his choice: that Patton had refused to speak at Knustford until his hosts insisted, and that he had been assured there would be no press covering his remarks.[27] To make sure Patton got the message, Eisenhower sent his public relations officer, Colonel Justus "Jock" Lawrence, to Patton's headquarters with a message that he was not to make any more public statements "until further notice from him personally." Patton laughingly asked, "Come on, Jock, what did Ike really say?" Lawrence confessed, "He said that you were not to open your goddamned mouth again publicly until he said you could." Patton broke out in laughter.[28]

"The war is over!" Patton called out to Gay in Peover Hall, his code phrase when a crisis had passed. Other staff officers thought it meant that Patton had been relieved. When he took a celebratory drink with Gaffey, Gay, Codman, and Stiller, those officers thought him callous, but he now felt thirty years younger. Patton fired off a thank-you note to Eisenhower, who called later that day and was cordial. "Sometimes I am very fond of him," Patton wrote, "and this is one of the times."[29] Two days later, Eisenhower wrote Marshall, "There is no question that the relief of Patton would lose to us his experience as commander of an Army in battle, and his demonstrated ability in getting the utmost out of soldiers in offensive operations." Everett Hughes still worried about Patton, feeling that he had finally used up all his favor with Eisenhower and that one more embarrassment would lead to Patton's demotion to colonel. For Hughes knew the decision had to come from Eisenhower, without undue pressure from Marshall. "The people in the US put the final decision up to the man over here," he wrote his wife. "I think it was a good one."[30]

If learning he could stay in Europe and command his army weren't enough, later that day Patton received something he could really enjoy: gossip about Mark Clark's poor performance in Italy. Brigadier General Raymond McLain, who had served under Patton with the 45th Infantry Division in Sicily and later under Clark in Italy, called to tell Patton that the German counterattack at Salerno had terrified Clark, even though it was not as bad as the counterattack Patton faced at Gela. Thus, the battle cry for Anzio became: "No more Salernos!" The Anzio attack had also bogged down because of timid leadership. McLain said that the Americans could easily have taken the high ground on the first or second day but had moved so slowly that the Germans quickly rallied their forces and captured it. Patton praised his messenger, who provided him this chance to relish some schadenfreude. "McLain is a National Guard officer of great courage and efficiency," Patton wrote. Still, the past week's roller-coaster ride left Patton on edge.

Amid the whirlwind Patton had just put himself through, his staff had finalized Third Army's attack plan on May 3, and he sent it off to Eisenhower for approval. The idea of his boss rejecting it after deciding to keep him was just too much to bear. He took some pills with a Bromide (a stomach sedative), to no effect. The next day he stayed in and wrote a paper on the use of armored divisions. He felt much better despite the day's rain, writing Beatrice that he looked forward to calling himself "Mr. Patton" after the war and spending his time sailing and fox hunting. That same day, back in the States, Beatrice saw a newspaper headline "INVASION FEINTS," and wrote, "Thank God George is no longer on Page 1."[31]

For all of Patton's grief, the FORTITUDE planners used the Knutsford speech to their advantage. The day after the speech, April 26, an agent codenamed Freak reported to the Germans that the Third Army headquarters were near Knutsford.[32] By the end of the month, according to historian Carlo D'Este, "the secret decrypts of German message traffic clearly showed that the Germans were convinced that Patton would lead the invasion."[33] By May 9, British agents began putting out the word that units were moving to East Anglia, a perfect place from which to assault Calais. By May 15, the Germans reported that "the main concentration is showing itself even more clearly to be in the South and South-east of the Island." By the end of the month, the Germans believed seventy-nine divisions were in England when in fact there were only fifty-two. On the last day of May, an agent codenamed Brutus reported that Patton had taken command of FUSAG from Bradley, yet the Germans greeted this news with skepticism. It took a direct message from Garbo to convince them. He told them that Bradley had taken a command under Montgomery, and when he asked one of his (nonexistent) agents who had replaced him at FUSAG, he was told, "he replied that it was General Patton who had taken over command which had temporarily been held by Bradley during the first phase of the formation. In the conversation held, I was able to find out that the headquarters of General Patton, that is

CHAPTER THIRTEEN ★ FORTITUDE AND KNUTSFORD   309

to say FUSAG . . . is situated near Ascot [west of London]." The Germans bought it. They began moving their unit pins farther east on their maps of England. Despite Patton's agony, the plan was working.[34]

Is it possible that the FORTITUDE planners deliberately put Patton's name in the newspapers to convince the Germans he was in England, preparing for the invasion of Calais? The April 26 message confirms that the LCS turned Patton's speech around pretty quickly, getting word of Patton's presence in England to the Germans in about twenty-four hours, something odd for the meticulous planners of FORTITUDE. If true, it meant the British outed Patton as part of their deception plan without notifying Eisenhower, almost leaving him to invade Europe without his best battlefield commander, and that Patton's career was almost sacrificed by short-sighted FORTITUDE planners who did not appreciate the consequence of their actions.

Meanwhile, with the invasion of France only a month away, Patton returned to training his army. On May 6 he took part in multiple flyovers of the infantry so they could identify friendly fighter planes. P-38 Lightnings, Spitfires, Mosquitos, and P-51 Mustangs took turns circling above units four times before diving. Patton went aloft in a Mosquito, a British double-engine fighter-bomber, and appreciated the effects of gravity while pulling out of a three-hundred-mile-an-hour dive: "You are actually pushed down uncomfortably on the seat and have difficulty moving your arms and legs," he wrote. He felt the same thing through high-speed turns. Although he had difficulty seeing ground objects, he could see the soldiers' faces looking up.[35]

Three days later, he observed two 4th Armored Division rehearsals. During the morning demonstration, tanks rolled forward, accompanied by armored infantry. Patton noticed that the infantry advanced in rushes and failed to fire their weapons. He called together the officers, explaining their mistakes in fiery language. He then watched the afternoon rehearsal from a half-track and, again, did not like what he saw. This time the tankers did well but the supporting infantry and reserves lagged too far behind. He considered the anti-tank gun employment poor and the infantry-occupied positions disappointing. Officers and noncommissioned officers "just went along as members of the chorus," he wrote. Again, he chewed out the officers.

The next day, May 10, Patton put on a marching-fire demonstration. Soldiers, with tank support, lined up and advanced while firing from the hip. The tanks joined in, firing their machine guns, while mortar teams leap-frogged forward. The idea was to keep the enemy's head down until the Americans were right on top of them, maybe even killing a few Germans. It was a relatively new concept, since previous armies did not possess semiautomatic weapons such as the M1 Garand or carbine rifles. It also went against what soldiers learned back in the States, which was mainly to aim and shoot at targets, not spray an area with ammunition. The exercise pleased Patton, even though he had to take over and lead the second demonstration himself because none of his green commanders truly understood the concept. "Our officers do not realize the necessity of utilizing all the means at hand, all weapons, to accomplish victory," he wrote that night.[36]

That evening, Patton took a train to London to meet with Eisenhower and other officers for a luncheon the next day celebrating the anniversary of their victory in North Africa. He arrived early enough to take in a show with Hughes. He may have regretted it. As he stepped out of his car, three photographers snapped his picture with lightbulbs flashing. He pushed them aside and headed in. No sooner had he sat down in his box than a reporter knocked on the door, insisting on getting a statement. He refused. Later in the production, the manager entered the box and invited Patton to some refreshments with the leading lady after the show. He declined.

Patton tried to put the whole incident behind him by visiting Colonel Walter Leyman, Eisenhower's head of soldier replacements. Accompanied again by Hughes, Patton argued for beefing up platoons with more soldiers and lieutenants to offset immediate casualties. He used the Duke of York's casualties in the late 1700s as an example of failing to get replacements to the front—resulting in the rise of Napoleon. The next day he showed up at the luncheon, which was attended by more than thirty other generals who had been a part of the North African campaign. Surprisingly, Eisenhower gave a speech that validated Patton's marching fire concept. He suggested that if every general and admiral in the room had fired a machine gun for half an hour in North Africa, they would have won a greater victory. Then he turned serious and asked everyone to stand for a silent toast to those who died in the campaign. Patton turned to Air Marshal Coningham, with whom he had clashed in Tunisia over air cover, and told him he hoped neither of them would be the subject of a similar toast. When it was over, Eisenhower asked to speak alone with Patton. It was a pleasant visit. "No lecture at all," Patton later wrote. This may have been Eisenhower showing Patton that the Knutsford incident was behind him and it was time to get back to war preparations.[37]

But Patton's quiet respite did not last long. He and Hughes walked to a local saddle shop where they chatted with the patrons until Patton introduced himself by name. "The whole scene changed at once," wrote Hughes, "and from then on he couldn't say or do anything without being in the limelight." The two men walked five blocks away where they entered a gun shop. Again, Patton identified himself by name and again a ruckus ensued. People offered him drinks and other items free of charge. "He may escape getting his name in the papers again," Hughes wrote his wife, "but I doubt it."[38]

On May 15, all the senior commanders connected to Operation OVERLORD and their staffs gathered again at the London St. Paul's School for a final review of the invasion plan. The dark room was cold enough that everyone wore coats. The key players sat in armchairs in the front row; everyone else sat on wooden rows arranged in a crescent, looking down on a huge floor map depicting the D-Day invasion beaches. This would be the last major review, a final opportunity to smooth out any wrinkles, the last time all the major players gathered in one room before the invasion. Adding to the gravity of the meeting was the attendance not only of Churchill but of King George VI. The rehearsal started promptly at 9:00 a.m., when Montgomery ordered the doors shut to begin his presentation. Patton arrived late and encountered two MPs guarding the door. Undeterred, he banged on the door until a frustrated Montgomery ordered it opened. In marched Patton, wearing his newest uniform and all the medals he knew his British colleague detested.[39]

During the meeting, an optimistic Montgomery claimed that his tanks would reach the city of Caen and head south to Falaise and "knock about a bit down there," on D-Day itself—a distance of some thirty-two miles from the beaches. To his credit, Montgomery changed his plan when he later learned there was more German armor in his sector than originally expected. Still, Patton and the other American officers would hold the Caen-on-D-Day statement around Montgomery's neck for the rest of the war.[40]

After Montgomery's introduction came Eisenhower, who emphasized that the air, ground, and sea commanders had to iron out all their disagreements before they left the room. Following Eisenhower, each service commander made presentations on preparations and operations. Patton approved of both Bradley's and Spaatz's speeches, but he interrupted Air Marshal Arthur Harris, the head of Bomber Command, as he spoke about the strategic air bombardment. Patton interjected that they needed to be more concerned with bombarding the enemy instead of just attacking him. His words landed like lead balloon. A commander not directly involved in the coming invasion was telling those who had been working on it ceaselessly for months how to do their jobs, and at the last minute. Even Patton realized his mistake, calling it an "ill-timed argument."[41]

Patton redeemed himself somewhat when one of the Canadian generals got long winded. Frustrated at the man's droning on, he whispered in a loud enough voice for those around him to hear: "If that [vulgar words] doesn't shut up, I'm going to [vulgar words]." Everyone around Patton either quietly snickered or tried to hold in their laughter, including General Henry Crerar, the commander of Canadian forces. Freddy Guingand rushed up the speaker and whispered in his ear, and the man immediately ended his speech.[42]

The morning meeting concluded with a speech by King George, but his stutter took the punch out of any inspiring words he tried to deliver. "It was rather painful to watch the efforts he made," Patton recalled. At lunch, Patton ended up sitting across from Churchill. When he told the prime minister he remembered him from their last meeting, Churchill treated him to a glass of whiskey. The meeting resumed, focusing on the cross-channel attack. Churchill spoke last, delivering a typically stirring combat oratory, encouraging everyone to worry less about governing France and more about capturing the country. Patton considered the speech the best of the day.[43]

While in London, Patton kept up appearances. When he came across Brigadier General James Gavin, now the deputy commander of the 82nd Airborne Division, in the lobby of the Claridge's Hotel, he asked him, "Gavin, do you think machine-gun ammunition should be loaded, in belts with one round of tracer to every five or six rounds, or do you believe we should not have tracer mixed in with ball?" This was Patton's way of chatting with the troops, engaging them in a professional conversation that would put them at ease and let them get to know their general. Once the conversation concluded, Patton headed to the door, but before walking through, he turned and shouted, "See you in Pas-de-Calais, Gavin!" Gavin, who had no idea Patton was displaying the FORTITUDE ruse, cringed at the perceived breach of security.[44]

CHAPTER THIRTEEN ★ FORTITUDE AND KNUTSFORD 313

On May 27 Patton made his only trip associated with FORTITUDE. He flew to East Anglia, on the British southeast coast, to speak to a fighter group of P-51 Mustang pilots. His appearance, so far from the actual invasion fleet gathering in the southwest harbors, gave credence to the fiction that he was leading the attack on Calais. Patton poked around various air stations, spoke to pilots and crews, and watched a wing of P-51s take off to bomb a bridge at Rouen. He even let airmen take his picture. This time, any publicity associated with his visit was a net positive.[45]

Possibly to curry favor with Eisenhower, Patton issued a letter to all his commanders, in which he heavily quoted Eisenhower, stressing the need to crush Nazi Germany, the importance of training, and how Third Army's fighting spirit "will crown our efforts with final victory." He also issued a letter to his corps and division commanders about the use of armored divisions, stressing that "*haste* and *speed* are not synonymous," the importance of firing while advancing or when covered by smoke, and that tanks should never enter villages. Although he filled the memo with technical advice about tanks, armored infantry, and weapons, he squeezed in a few Patton-esque maxims: "The quickest way to get to heaven is to advance across open ground swept by effective enemy anti-tank fire," "Battles are won by a few brave men who refuse to fear and who push on," and "Any gun that is not firing is not doing its job."[46]

But not all was well with Patton's armor forces. Beetle Smith called to say that someone told Eisenhower that Major General Lunsford Oliver's 5th Armored Division's morale and discipline were wanting and that numerous men were AWOL. The call infuriated Patton. The last thing he wanted was for Eisenhower to think there were problems in Third Army, especially since he prided himself on bolstering unit confidence. "Damn these people who listen to rumors, and double damn those who spread them," he wrote to his diary. He dispatched Middleton and Colonel Halley Maddox, his operations chief, to look into it. The 5th had been assigned to the marshalling yards for two months to cook meals and perform general housekeeping for the assault forces practicing amphibious landings. The men called it "K. P. in England," where they qualified as cooks—a serious worry to trained combat tankers. On May 24 General Oliver reported to Patton that he spoke to every man in the division, explaining the importance of their task, no matter how mundane. In April, forty men had gone AWOL and thirty-nine came back, every case the result of the difficulty in moving the division. The next day, Patton wrote Smith of the division's high morale and low AWOL rate. Smith appreciatively responded by telling him that Eisenhower was completely reassured. To prevent any other surprises, Oliver invited so many officers to inspect his unit that one tank officer wrote training memorandums on "How to Conduct Inspecting Officers through Kitchens." Oliver need not have worried. Patton thought he and his division were doing an excellent job.[47]

As the date of the invasion approached, Patton openly spoke about his worry about being left out of the war. His words made it back to Eisenhower, who sent Assistant Secretary of War John McCloy to Peover Hall to tell Patton he would get him into the war as soon as possible, but until then, to "keep his goddamn mouth shut!" Patton accused McCloy of destroying his confidence, to which McCloy responded that if he wanted to do that, he would tell Eisenhower to send him home. Patton complied.[48] Chastened, Patton focused his anxiety, fear, and anger at Beetle Smith. He blamed him for pulling men from Third Army while simultaneously denying him needed equipment. When Smith denied Patton a command post closer to the embarkation area, he accused him of short-sightedness. "People who lack both imagination and experience are a menace in war," he thundered. When he learned Smith was trading a specialized shotgun priced around $2,000 for a $20 model electric train, he called it the cheapest swindle he had ever seen. When Smith sent Patton a photograph of himself dated April 28, at the height of the Knutsford controversy, Patton called him Judas. And when he heard a story that in Sicily, Smith had leapt from his car into a ditch at the sound of friendly artillery outside of Messina and had refused to get out despite the pleas from the surrounding officers, Patton copied it into his diary. Patton may have been referring to Smith when he wrote Beatrice on May 24 that "I know a lot of people I could use the knife on, only they have nothing to remove."[49]

Patton received another blow on May 25 when he learned that the Senate Military Affairs Committee had tabled his name for permanent promotion to major general. All fourteen other generals on the list had been approved. It was a cruel stab to be singled out. Democratic senator Albert "Happy" Chandler of Kentucky, the committee chairman, said he kept Patton off the list specifically because of the slapping incidents, adding that Patton had not been voted down, "just passed over for the time being." Some members of the committee were more disturbed by Patton's dig at American women, in which he portrayed them as jealous of British women. An unnamed committee senator twisted the knife when he told reporters, "If he does something gallant in the field, if he makes a good record in the invasion, he'll probably come through all right. But he'll have to keep his mouth shut and control his temper." Patton considered himself a failure if he made it through the war without reaching that permanent rank. In response, he put together a list of British and American generals and admirals who congratulated him for capturing Messina. Whom he sent it to is unknown. His brother-in-law, Frederick Ayer, wrote a letter to Republican senator Sinclair Weeks of Massachusetts, listing Patton's accomplishments and urging the Senate to promote him.[50]

To relieve his stress, and for his enjoyment, Patton outlined his army's route of attack on a map of Northern France, using a black pen to circle cities. It proved highly prescient. He circled such towns as Fougères, Rennes, Laval, Angers, Tours, Bourges, Nevers, and Dijon (he also circled Troyes, Reims, Nancy and Metz, but these seem to be circled in pencil). He may have still clung to the belief that he would be advancing from Calais, because he also circled Abbeville, St. Pol-sur-Ternoise, and Arras, all south of Calais. Later, during the campaign in France, he used the map again to trace his advances with a green grease pencil. "I was right," he would proudly write on the map. He also began a tradition that he would carry through for the rest of the war: writing letters and poems to his grandchildren that he claimed were dictated by his dog Willie. They were light and clever, and a nice break for Patton from his daily stresses.[51]

Patton spent the rest of May inspecting units and hosting his commanders to dinner. When Ninth Army commander, Lieutenant General William Simpson, and his chief of staff came over for dinner on May 30, Patton treated the two to a briefing, with Patton serving as his own operations officer. He had worried that Simpson trusted his staff too much and wanted to show that he also could be his own operations officer, as well as other staff positions. The presentation had the desired effect. When Simpson expressed that Patton was ready to take on the operations role himself, Patton responded, "Of course, I always am."[52] The next day, Patton and Codman drove to Bradley's Bristol headquarters, where the two generals spent two days going over First Army's final war plan. He found Bradley quite cheerful, which depressed him. If Bradley's plan succeeded, he thought, there would be nothing for him to do.

On June 1, as the clock wound down to D-Day—set for June 5— Patton and Bradley flew to Montgomery's headquarters in Portsmouth for a final meeting with the four army commanders. Patton still felt slighted for not being in the campaign's kickoff and vented, questioning the quality of his fellow generals. His first target was the British general Dempsey, who, Patton noted, had failed to capture Catania as a corps commander in Sicily. "He is not impressive looking and I take him to be a yes-man." The second was Canadian General Harry Crerar, who was better, "but not impressive." Patton even critiqued Freddy de Guingand, Montgomery's chief of staff, whom he considered "very clever but [who] is extremely nervous and continuously twists his long, black oily hair into little pigtails about the size of a match." Patton took notice that twice Montgomery told Bradley, "Patton should take over for the Brittany, and possibly the Rennes Operation."[53] At that moment, Patton may have actually liked Montgomery, or at least agreed with him.

Montgomery stressed that he wanted to know where each commander's headquarters would be on D-Day and the succession of commands almost down to battalion level. At dinner later, Montgomery introduced Patton to one of his favorite traditions—gentleman's gambling. A staffer produced Montgomery's betting book, and the British general asked Patton if Great Britain would be at war again in ten years. Montgomery said it would not, so Patton took the opposite side. The bet was written into the book and both men signed their names. (It's debatable who won. The Korean War, which both Great Britain and the United States took part in, ended in 1953, although it ended in a truce, not peace. In 1954, however, the Irish Republican Army attacked the British Gough Barracks in Armagh on June 12, signaling a renewal of IRA activity. While the Irish might have considered it war, the British did not.)

Drinks were poured and Patton raised his glass: "As the oldest Army commander present, I would like to propose a toast to the health of General Montgomery and express our satisfaction in serving under him." Everyone drank. Later, Patton confessed to his diary, "The lightning did not strike me [for the lie]." Then they gambled at what was called a "racing card game." By Patton's admission, he won too much early on but finished a slight loser. Still, he came down to breakfast the next morning grinning from ear to ear, telling everyone he had taken their money. The entire experience bolstered Patton's view of Montgomery.[54]

Patton spent the next day watching artillery demonstrations and tracking the movements of Hodges, Bradley, and Montgomery, noting down which ship they would be on as they waited to go ashore in France, and observing that Montgomery would soon set up his headquarters at Grande Camp in Normandy. Patton could imagine each of them directing operations on the beach while he remained back in England. He had a hard time sleeping that night and admitted to his diary, "I wish I were leading the assault." He longed to be on the far shore. One of Patton's staff officers wrote that day, "George is champing at the bit."[55]

Patton spent the scheduled morning of D-Day, June 5, listening to the radio for reports of the invasion. There was no news. Eisenhower had postponed the invasion at the last minute to wait for a gap in the storms passing over the channel. Without knowing about Eisenhower's delay, Patton spent the morning glued to the radio, taking a break only to call Hughes to send a congratulations message to the commanders in Italy who had just taken Rome. When he received a report from Eisenhower explaining that landing craft were still in their harbors, Patton deduced that the invasion had been put off a day, something Bradley had mentioned that he preferred. The night before, he had written Beatrice, "Don't be excited when the whistle blows, I am not in the opening kick off."[56] Despite the years of planning, the rehearsals, the deception and the preparatory bombings, Patton still had his own feelings about the Normandy invasion: "I still believe in night attacks."[57]

CHAPTER FOURTEEN

D-Day and the Dawn of Third Army

ON D-DAY, JUNE 6, Patton listened to a 7:00 a.m. BBC broadcast announcing the airborne and amphibious landings in Normandy. "I wish I were in it now," he wrote his son George at West Point. "I am fed up with just sitting." He expressed the same sentiment to Beatrice: "It is Hell to be on the sidelines and see all the glory eluding me but I guess there will be enough for all." The suddenness of the invasion brought home to Patton the realities of combat and his own mortality. He admitted to his son he did not plan on being killed, but if it did happen, "don't worry but set yourself to do better than I have." He stressed boldness, but thoughts of death again came through: "No dead general has ever been criticized so you have that way out always."[1]

So the American general with the most combat experience, amphibious experience, airborne experience, who had tramped around the towns of Normandy as a young man—the only American general who had done so—sat out one of the most pivotal battles of World War II. Had Patton commanded First Army's assault on Normandy, he may have done things differently, based on his own experience, to ensure success. Too much preparation had gone into the false attack at Pas de Calais—Operation FORTITUDE—to allow Patton to attack there, but he certainly would have changed the attack elements for the American beaches.

The Americans were responsible for three coastal locations: Omaha Beach, Pointe du Hoc, and Utah Beach, all of which were assaulted at dawn during low tide to allow for the exposure of mines and obstacles on the beaches. Elements of the 1st and 29th infantry divisions assaulted Omaha, charging off landing craft, crossing the beach, ascending the bluffs, and pushing inland. Army Rangers assaulted Pointe du Hoc by scaling the sheer cliff wall at the water's edge. Once on top, they accomplished two missions: knocking out artillery cannons capable of raining fire on both beaches while also cutting the road connecting Utah and Omaha. The Utah Beach assault was more complex. Two airborne divisions, the 82nd and 101st, dropped into the near-flooded countryside, capturing the town of Sainte-Mère-Église and the causeways leading off the beach. The 4th Infantry Division landed to light resistance and tentatively linked up with the airborne elements. The airborne assaults commenced at midnight on June 6, while beach assaults followed at dawn. The attack relied on the light of a full moon for the airborne troops to maneuver.

Omaha Beach was a slaughter. The assaulting infantry ran directly into German kill zones and were cut down by the score. Most of the amphibious tanks that were supposed to support the infantry sank in the English Channel. Heavy smoke from burning grasses along the hills reduced visibility for the Navy's big guns and confused the captains commanding the follow-up landing craft. Hours into the battle, Omar Bradley closed part of the beach to additional troops, basically marooning the men at the Vierville Draw.[2]

While it is impossible to know how Patton would have changed OVERLORD, it is possible to speculate, based on his experience from the Mediterranean campaign. Patton disliked daylight amphibious assaults. His landings in Morocco, southern Sicily, and the three amphibious end runs along Sicily's northern coast all occurred under the cover of night. He would have insisted on the same for Normandy, trading the danger of beach obstacles for the protection of darkness. He was not alone. Major General Clarence Huebner, the new 1st Infantry Division commander, Brigadier General Norm Cota, the 29th Infantry Division's assistant division commander, and Admiral John Leslie Hall, who commanded the naval force at Omaha Beach, all argued for changing the assault to predawn. Direct fire from well-ensconced Germans caused most of the casualties at Omaha Beach. At Utah Beach, a nighttime beach assault would have also improved the chances for a strong linkup with the airborne troops. Whereas Eisenhower and Bradley passed assault problems down to their ground commanders to solve, the combat-experienced Patton would have interjected himself into all phases of planning, just as he had done before and would continue to do.[3]

There was little Patton could have done to improve the situation on Omaha in the daylight, but photographs of the initial landings shocked him, prompting him to say, "The outstanding mistake was again the overloading of enlisted men with too much equipment."[4] He said "again"

CHAPTER FOURTEEN ★ D-DAY AND THE DAWN OF THIRD ARMY   321

because he had learned that troops had a better chance of surviving the transfer from landing craft to the shore with less equipment on their backs. He would have doubled the number of radios with the landing troops, for the Brolo assault had taught him the importance of backup communications. As for decision making during the battle, he would have never closed a beach during a fight. He knew the fog of war affected both sides and that bad news at the beginning of a battle was normal. He also saw mistakes that a veteran commander would not have allowed.

Patton would have put short shrift to some of the advice commanders gave their men about Omaha Beach. In the days leading up to the assault, generals, colonels, and other officers told their men that the Air Force bombing would crater Omaha Beach, providing the assault troops ready-made foxholes. Leaders also stressed that Allied aircraft would fill the skies. On D-Day, there were no ready-made foxholes on Omaha Beach, nor was there any plan to create them. Omar Bradley had specifically requested for light bombs from the air forces, so as not to crater the beach, thus allowing tanks, trucks, and other vehicles to quickly move off the beach without falling into a crater. Yet, somehow, word went out about the craters, and it was taken as doctrine that the men would have their ready-made foxholes. Patton would have stopped such talk. As for the mass of aircraft, the skies over Omaha seemed empty to the men fighting on the ground. Patton knew that direct air support rarely showed up at the initial stage of a planned amphibious attack, something he experienced and had even warned General Fred Walker about before the Salerno landing, when he told him that he wouldn't see air support until three days after his assault. Patton knew the limits of American airpower, and he would have refused to give his men false hope.[5]

At Pointe du Hoc, where the Rangers scaled the cliffs to take out the guns and cut the road, Patton would have probably again added more radios. Part of the Pointe du Hoc plan called for reinforcements to switch to Omaha Beach if they were not needed. Those reinforcements ended up attacking at Omaha and helped turn the tide by seizing the strategic high-ground at Vierville Draw and securing the assault's right flank. Patton would have insisted on reinforcing the Rangers even if they did not request it. The Germans were notorious for their counterattacks, and Patton would have wanted the Rangers to resist. Also, if the beaches had been attacked at night, Omaha might not have needed the Rangers to help.

Behind Utah Beach, German ground fire downed many transport planes before the paratroopers could leap into the night. Once on the ground, many troops found themselves far from their objectives and spent most of the six hours before sunrise walking to their goal. Patton was no fan of division-sized airborne assaults. Although he admired the airborne commanders and respected the fighting spirit of the men as an elite force, he felt airborne troops should drop only in regimental sizes at most. He also had smarted from the friendly fire incident in Sicily and would not have wanted to employ such a chancy tactic again.[6]

On Utah's beach line, the initial landings went well, but one unit failed in its D-Day mission. Veteran paratrooper Colonel Edson Raff commanded an amalgamated task force of glidermen riding the tanks from an independent tank battalion, supported by armored scout cars. Raff's two missions after racing off Utah Beach were to defend a glider landing zone and reach Ste.-Mère-Église, where it would defend against any armored German counterattacks. Not only did Raff not reach the town until the next day, he also failed to reach the landing zone. Thus, glider pilots misinterpreted his burning tanks as landing beacons. They met deadly German crossfire.[7]

Patton would not have allowed an airborne commander to lead an armored force. Nor would he have utilized such a mixed task force for a precision operation. Independent tank battalions supported the infantry and traveled at the speed of foot soldiers, cavalry vehicles were lightly armored and not designed to fight toe-to-toe with enemy armor, and glider troops were light infantry, trained for assaulting from a glider, not clinging to the side of a tank. Patton would have probably assigned elements of an armored division for the mission. Armored divisions were designed to throttle to their objective without stopping to engage other units—in their words: "Haul ass and bypass!" They also possessed armored infantry, men specifically trained to support tank operations. Patton could have picked from at least seven armored divisions in England and chosen a tank battalion or combat command that had already trained (or fought—in the case of the 2nd Armored Division) together since its formation back in the States. Altogether, reflecting on the battle for the beaches three months later, Patton concluded that D-Day had been, "quite a failure."[8]

Patton's one significant contribution to June 6 worked perfectly, however, and it would continue to do so. On D-Day, believing the Normandy landings were just a feint, nineteen German Divisions stood idle in Calais, waiting for Patton's "real" invasion. Five panzer divisions in reserve were

CHAPTER FOURTEEN ★ D-DAY AND THE DAWN OF THIRD ARMY

also frozen out of the Normandy fight. They remained in place for weeks after D-Day while the Allies built up their beachhead. After D-Day, the Germans continued to believe Patton was still preparing to attack Calais. Two days after the invasion they were losing faith in the belief that Montgomery might attack west to Brittany and that he and Patton would use the Seine River as a border between their two armies. Stories of Patton's whereabouts became less of a secret. On June 14, a week after the D-Day landings, a short-wave radio message went out across the western hemisphere, asking "Where is Patton's Army?" When Patton's wife learned about it, she wrote a friend, "I am content to be in the dark so long as the Germans are there with us."[9] And they were. As late as June 22, the Germans contemplated that "still available army group Patton" may or may not assault the port of Brest by sea. Two days later they saw Montgomery pointing his army toward Paris, with "a corresponding attack by Patton's Army Group in the Seine-Somme area." By the end of June, they believed that one of Montgomery's divisions was encroaching on "Patton's formations."[10] The Germans had no idea the object of their anxiety was not even in France.

Back in England, at 11:00 a.m. on D-Day, Patton walked into his staff meeting and declared, "Congratulations, gentlemen, the war is finally on." He promised they would soon be in the fighting, and that "Third Army will either make glorious history or we won't be around to alibi why we didn't." He stressed the importance of secrecy surrounding the invasion and the subsequent campaign, concluding, "The Germans do not know that Third Army is in England and it is vital this be kept from them until they find it out when we kick them in the teeth."[11] He spent the rest of the day listening to news updates and radio addresses by Churchill and the king. He liked the speeches but questioned the on-the-ground updates: "I know that were I on the beach I would not know a damn thing . . ., so how can the commentators know anything?" He wore his shoulder holster to get into a fighting spirit and started packing up his belongings, hoping "that someone will get killed and I will have to go." He then read his Bible.[12]

To prepare for life on the battlefield, Patton started sleeping in his new headquarters truck, which included a bed, desk, sink, and map board. It also sported an outside shower—a bucket with a showerhead. A generator lit the cabin at night so Patton could keep updating his maps. Once on the Continent, the truck served as Patton's home for most of the war—if he wasn't occupying a castle or another residence. He preferred it to some of the insufficiently warm castles he occupied. It also served as Willie's headquarters.[13]

By the next day, Patton was restless. "This is the longest day I have ever spent," he wrote Beatrice. "We are doing nothing but waiting." He cleared out his desk, hoping to cross the Channel soon. It was not to be. For the next twelve days, he attended morning briefings, read fan mail (it surprised him that after ten months of inaction people still remembered him), and listened to the radio for news, never getting an accurate picture of what was happening. One day, Omaha Beach was in trouble, the next day it was Utah.[14]

As the picture became clear in Normandy, Patton lamented the high casualties and lack of progress. He reviewed reports from France and Italy that the Americans were suffering twice the casualties as the British. He decided that First Army lacked leadership. With Bradley relieving and losing a number of his colonels, Patton sent over some of his to fill the gaps. When he learned that Bradley had relieved two division commanders, he wrote, "I doubt the expediency or the justice of such wholesale beheading. It creates fear and a lack of self-confidence." One commander had asked to be relieved, the other failed to move his division despite direct orders.[15]

But Patton, too, was forced to relieve a commander. The tankers of the 10th Armored Division's 712 Tank Battalion despised their leader, Lieutenant Colonel Whitside Miller, calling him crazy. Miller had lectured his men on the dangers of alcohol, before personally taking a swig in front of them. He yelled at tankers for interrupting his meals or waking him up at the time he requested, and he once punished his executive officer for not responding to a command fast enough by having him run past of a group of enlisted men. The situation peaked when Miller misinterpreted a directive to put blackout lights on wheeled vehicles and ordered them put on his tanks. He repeatedly yelled at his maintenance officer who kept trying to explain the directive. After reading the inspector general's report, Patton concluded that Miller was a fool. Even though the unit was scheduled to land in Normandy in only three weeks, Patton reluctantly pulled Miller from command.[16] He also chewed out Miller's commander, Colonel Fay Smith, for mishandling the situation and lacking command of his troops. Patton told Smith that if it happened again, he would be out of a job.[17]

Patton went on five-mile walks, with some running in between, "in case of the need to run after the Germans—not from them." He reviewed an OSS film of the landings and had his staff conduct a dry-run battle briefing on the seizure of Brittany's ports. Most people assumed he had left England. It chagrined him that his friends and "most of the Germans—seem to think I'm in France," he wrote to his old West Point classmate Colonel Hugh McGee, without giving away his location. When he attended a play and the leading man pointed him out in the audience during a curtain call, he worked to suppress press coverage of the event. "Such is fame," he wrote his son.[18]

Time dragged. It sounded like the Allies were happy to be holding the beachhead, not advancing inland. "I am full of gloom," he lamented to Beatrice.[19] He killed time by test driving a M-29 Weasel—a light, tracked vehicle that would be used as an ambulance, attending a weapons demonstration by wounded British soldiers, and riding in a tank with a new high-velocity 76mm tank cannon on the Salisbury Plain, where most armored divisions trained. Tankers of Grow's 6th Armored Division were putting on a demonstration of the new weapon when Patton climbed into a tank and fired seven rounds while the tank drove through the range. After about a mile, the tank clanked to an abrupt halt. The driver tried to restart it while Patton cursed. The tank was out of gas. Recalled the tank's bow gunner, "Patton really chewed everyone out."[20]

The 76mm cannon demonstration would lead to wild rumors that Patton had delayed the deployment of heavy tanks to the battlefield. He acknowledged the armor-piercing superiority of the new weapon compared to the 75mm cannon but worried about its complexity and the fact that it had not been combat tested. While he did not elaborate on which complexities concerned him, the heavier gun caused the tank to consume too much gas and reduced the tank's speed, something the former cavalryman detested. Afterward, he accepted enough 76mm tanks to equip three separate battalions but held off on getting more until they could prove themselves on the battlefield. This decision affected only his Third Army. Any other decisions about the deployment of new weapons would been made by either Bradley or Hodges in First Army.[21]

When Patton learned that Manton Eddy's 9th Infantry Division had reached the west coast of the Cotentin Peninsula, cutting off Cherbourg on June 18, he had a dream that he and Paddy Flint were mending a flagpole on a roof, then enjoying some cooked duck out of a basket.

His mind was on his old friend in Eddy's division. Three weeks earlier, Patton had written Flint predicting he would be promoted to brigadier general, but it was not in the cards. "The star you spoke about will never come," Flint wrote, "but 'hit don't make no difference, all we can do is drive on."[22]

Patton visited his London headquarters, where he inspected the damage done by a V-1 rocket, called a Buzz Bomb for its sputtering engine that cut off seconds before exploding. Patton described it as a normal plane with a cold. The bomb's blast had blown leaves off trees for at least an acre, shattered windows in the surrounding blocks, and destroyed a monastery. He wrote that the one that passed over him looked like a British Spitfire. He heard numerous Buzz Bombs that night. "I think these planes will get on people's nerves in time," he wrote, probably referring to himself.[23]

Being left out of the action continued to gnaw at Patton. "I can't tell you how much I hate this sitting around," he wrote Beatrice on June 20, followed two days later with a repeat of the message, calling it the "longest day," and concluding, "Lord how long?" By the end of the month he told her, "I wish I were fighting."[24] He may have been projecting his own feelings when he warned his staff not to look depressed. "Don't go around looking gloomy," he stressed. "The worse things get, the more cheerful you must look." He also warned them against rumormongering. "By the time the story gets to the third toilet, it sounds like doom was about to descend on all of us." He then grinned, "Well gentlemen, we are one day nearer to getting into it!"[25]

To keep everyone in a fighting mood Patton visited the troops. He told the men of the 5th Infantry Division that they were not going in on D-Day, "but you'll think it's D-Day."[26] To French general Jacques-Philippe Leclerc's 2nd Armored Division, he walked up and down the ranks asking individual soldiers their weapon of choice and heard responses like gun or carbine. He stopped and declared these were not the answers he expected from French soldiers. He claimed the bayonet his favorite weapon and suddenly lunged forward like he was stabbing someone, "because when you finish using it, your target *Boche* was right in front of you!" The Frenchmen laughed at his pantomime. While he enjoyed the French spirit, their kitchens appalled him. To remedy the situation he sent a captain, lieutenant, and some enlisted men to instruct them on managing their mess halls, a true insult to any Frenchman.[27]

On June 26 Patton and Eisenhower attended a 35th Infantry Division training exercise. They watched a tactical demonstration from a hilltop, but when Patton noticed a squad of men crouched low as they ran along a ten-foot swale, he charged from the reviewing stand, down to the soldiers, who were now laying prone in firing positions, and stood over one, shaking his fist in the air and calling out: "You have no need to stoop when you are under cover! Save your energy! You show you have no knowledge of the art of war!" He then swaggered up the hill and rejoined Eisenhower's party.[28]

When the two generals inspected the troops after their demonstration, Patton felt the first inkling of a suspicion that Eisenhower had his eyes on the presidency. He noticed that Eisenhower found common points of interest with the soldiers and had photographers snap pictures to send to the soldier's hometown newspaper. When Eisenhower finished chatting with the men they applauded. To Patton, this leadership style was less of a general officer and more of an office seeker. "A commander cannot command and be on the same level [as the men],' he complained in his diary. "I try to arouse fighting emotion—he tries to get votes—for what?"[29]

Patton also told Eisenhower, "When we finish licking these bastards, I want you to make me the Heinrich Himmler for the occupation." Then, rubbing his hands together and slightly grinning, he added, "I'll show them a reign of terror like they have never imagined." Eisenhower did not reply: he was resigned to Patton's over-the-top declarations, yet appreciated his zeal. He rated Patton "superior" on his efficiency report and rated him second, out of the twenty-six lieutenant generals he knew, as an army commander, and number eight in a general rating. Eisenhower had in Patton, he wrote, "a brilliant fighter and leader, impulsive and quick-tempered, likely to speak in public in an ill-considered fashion."[30]

At the end of June, Patton officially left Peover Hall. As he had done in Morocco and Palermo, before departing, he placed a bronze plaque on the Peover chapel's wall that read, "Presented by headquarters, Third U.S. Army, January–June 1944." Patton asked the vicar to keep the ceremony secret until after his army had departed.[31] He also stopped by the Mainwaring pub, where he had often lunched, and donated enough money to keep flowers at his table for a year.[32] He traveled to southern England, where he took up residence in a huge manor called the Breamore House in Hampshire. While overseeing the waterproofing of vehicles, he accidentally dropped a blackout screen on his toe, almost taking off his toenail and producing a painful blood blister under the nail that had to be drained. To keep pressure off his toe, he borrowed one of George Meeks's boots, which was slightly larger than his own.[33]

As Bradley's army continued to grind away in Normandy's hedgerow country with little to show for its high casualties, Eisenhower lamented, "Sometimes I wish I had George Patton there."[34] Hughes visited Patton and found him in a "fine feddle" over his prospects, boasting that he had learned to keep quiet in several languages.[35] Patton handed Hughes a battle plan to give to Eisenhower, which showed how to flank the Germans by landing two infantry divisions and one armored division in the Brittany Peninsula, one hundred miles west of the Cherbourg Peninsula. The new force would then drive east for Alençon and then Argentan. Patton included names like Clausewitz and Moltke in the plan to catch Eisenhower's eye. Although Eisenhower appreciated the plan, he never approved it, considering a second amphibious landing a sideshow, especially since Bradley was working on his own breakout plan. Patton admitted it was too bold, but it would roughly match the path his Army blazed through Normandy a month later.

As an alternative, Patton proposed lining up two armored divisions next to each other and driving them south, under airbursts, to crack the German line. "While probably expensive in tanks," he admitted, "it would insure [sic] our breaking through to Avranches." He predicted that his risky plan would reach Avranches in two days. This is exactly what General Troy Middleton did at the end of the month to begin the breakout, although it took him three days to capture Avranches. To Patton, Bradley only wanted to play it safe, attacking on articulated lines and failing to move boldly. At Bradley's rate, Patton calculated, "we will die of old age before we finish." In any case, at this point the Normandy campaign was little better than a stalemate.[36]

FORTITUDE, however, was still working its magic. The Germans could not decide if Patton was preparing an attack or already in France. On July 3 they reported that his army group "is being made ready in London and in Southern England for the next landing." Despite all the speculation as to where he would land, it had become obvious to the Allies that, at some point, Patton would have to be removed from his exalted-yet-fake post to become an army commander again. The British developed a cover story back on June 26, in which Patton would be placed in command of Third

CHAPTER FOURTEEN ★ D-DAY AND THE DAWN OF THIRD ARMY 329

Army because he complained too much to Eisenhower about the loss of his FUSAG divisions to the 12th Army Group. The British could have easily made it about the Knutsford incident.[37]

On July 4 Patton finally arrived in London for his flight to Normandy. He visited a frustrated Eisenhower, who was following the slow progress in Normandy. The supreme commander was weighing heading over to France to take personal command from Montgomery, but "he cannot bring himself to take the plunge," Patton wrote. The two then reviewed the buildup plan on the continent. Four American armies would eventually land in France: The First Army, which was already fighting under Bradley, Patton's Third, Bill Simpson's Ninth, and Sandy Patch's Seventh, Patton's old army, landing in southern France (in early 1945 Fifteenth Army under Lieutenant General Gerow became operational on the continent). Bradley would command three armies, "with me on the southern flank," Patton wrote. Since the British were at their limit for men with fourteen divisions, Eisenhower would give a small army, Simpson's, to Montgomery, which Patton hated and saw only as a token gesture "to save the face of the little monkey."[38] Patton still chaffed over Eisenhower's lack of recognition of his accomplishments so far. When Eisenhower's headquarters sent out a request for all army commanders' list of military medals, foreign and domestic, Patton sarcastically listed five foreign medals and zero American medals from November 1942 to January 1944. To drive the point home, he listed all his commands since the Louisiana maneuvers, including his posting as commander of Seventh and Third Armies.[39]

On the night of July 4, Patton attended another meeting, one which he did not record in his diary. He met with Jean Gordon, his niece on his wife's side. But she was more than a niece, she had been his mistress. In 1932, when Patton and his family were stationed in Hawai'i, Gordon showed up on her way to Asia. Patton was forty-seven at the time and Jean was seventeen, the same age as Patton's second daughter, Ruth Ellen. Despite Ruth Ellen's efforts to set Gordon up with other men, she had her sights set on Patton, and he returned her attention. They consummated their relationship on a trip to one of Hawai'i's islands and kept it to going for the length of Gordon's stay. Beatrice was fully aware of her husband's infidelity but stayed with him. Now Gordon was in London, assigned to her uncle's Army as a Red Cross doughnut server—a "donut dollie." Five days after their secret reunion, Patton boasted to Everett Hughes, "She's been mine for twelve years." She would be a constant presence throughout the European campaign.[40]

To prepare himself for the battles ahead, or to just relieve feelings of guilt from his infidelity, Patton wrote a prayer. It reflected not only his desire for victory but his desire to succeed and awareness of his own mortality:

> God of our Fathers, who by land and sea who has ever led us onto victory, please continue Your inspiring guidance in this the greatest of our conflicts. Strengthen my soul so that the weakening instinct of self-preservation, which besets all of us in battle, shall not blind me to my duty, to my manhood, or the glory of my calling, and to my responsibility to my fellow soldiers. Grant to our armed forces that discipline and valor and mutual confidence which ensures success in war. Let me not mourn for the men who have died fighting, but rather let me be glad that such heroes have lived. If it be my lot to die, let me so with courage and honor in a manner which will bring the greatest harm to the enemy, and please, oh Lord, protect and guide those I shall leave behind. Give us the victory, Lord.[41]

While Patton was happy to be closer to combat, the war in London made him uneasy. Buzz Bombs, which he had taken to calling "Flying Dutchmen," after the famed ghost ship, pounded the city. One had already killed one of his staff officers. At one point, he counted six explosions in two hours, close enough to shake his residence. Then, on July 6, exactly one month after the D-Day assault, he boarded his C-47 to Normandy. "I was glad to leave London," he admitted.[42]

Patton's flight across the Channel made sense. July 6 through 9 represented the last moon-and-tide combination necessary for any landings in Calais. The Germans might deduce that if the Allies did not deliver their main punch between those four days, the Calais invasion was a ruse. Patton would no longer be needed in England. Sure enough, the Germans soon planned an armored attack using their Fifteenth Army, which had been waiting for Patton in Calais.[43] Accompanying Patton in his aircraft were Al Stiller, Charles Codman, and George Meeks. Willie followed Patton onboard and curled up on the seat of the general's jeep, which had been lashed down. Patton's aircraft took off exactly at 10:25 a.m., the exact same time, he noted, that he left Algiers for Sicily. "This time I doubt if we get our feet as wet," said Stiller. "I know," Patton responded gloomily. "A hell of a way to make an amphibious landing." Two other C-47s flew with Patton's aircraft. Four P-47 Thunderbolt fighter planes soon joined them. Patton was finally returning to the fight.[44]

The plane flew over scores of ships headed for Normandy and touched down on a temporary airfield off Omaha Beach. "Well come on," he told his staff, "let's see if there's still a war going on." As he stepped off the plane, men clamored around him to take pictures. One sailor likened the scene to "seeing Babe Ruth stride up the plate." Patton stood up in his jeep and declared, "Men, I am proud to be here fighting beside you." Then he roared, "Now let's cut the guts out of these krauts and get the hell to Berlin!" The men cheered. "And when we get to Berlin, I'm going to personally shoot the Goddamn eyes out of that paper-hanging son-of-a-bitch! Just like I'd shoot a snake!" The men loved it. Back in the United States, newspapers erroneously reported that Patton landed on the beach waving a $1,000 bill and betting that he would beat Bradley and Montgomery to Paris. When Patton saw the article, he sent it to General Marshall, assuring him he had done no such thing and that he had never even seen a $1,000 bill.[45]

Patton then drove the four-mile length of Omaha Beach, examining the wrecked landing craft from the assault and from a storm that had wreaked havoc on the beaches. When he saw the German defenses, he considered them a testament that "good American troops can capture anything." He then headed to Bradley's headquarters, south of Isigny, where the two generals reviewed the situation at the front, including timed artillery barrages and bomber schedules. Bradley was uneasy about having Patton under him and worried about their role reversal, especially since Patton was six years older than him. He also worried about Patton's "impetuous habits." Nevertheless, he realized that Patton knew what he was doing and would need no prodding or encouragement to attack the enemy.[46]

Bradley told Patton that Montgomery was still held up north of Caen, with no indication of cracking the German line. While Bradley had cleared the Cherbourg Peninsula to the west, the Germans were frustrating his infantry in the hedgerows five miles north of St. Lo and Périers. When Bradley said that Montgomery demanded that he send him daily updates on his battalions' positions (which numbered more than one hundred), Patton agreed, "that is pretty stupid."[47]

Bradley had tried to break out of the beachhead on July 3, hoping to reach Avranches. He attacked with all four of his corps, composed of nine infantry divisions and only a part of an armored division. The attack lasted five days and brought few results. Stalemate threatened. General Hodges showed up and briefed Patton on German small-unit tactics he had gleaned from watching them for hours with a high-powered telescope. He told Patton that the Germans would fire machine guns to make the Americans take to the ground, then drop mortar rounds on them while the Americans responded with artillery. If the fire became too intense, the Germans would just pull back to the next hedgerow. Patton had a simple solution to this: "A violent tank attack, covered by air bursts, would certainly break up this form of defense." Despite heavy and loud German shelling that night, Patton and Bradley had drinks in Bradley's trailer. Patton then retreated to a tent but could not sleep. American counterfire continually shook the tent walls, reminding him what it was like to be in a war zone. Several times Willie left the tent to see about the noise, sometimes followed by his master.[48]

The next day, Patton visited Montgomery at his Bayeux headquarters. He found him pinning medals on American soldiers. Cameramen took pictures while Montgomery spoke into a microphone attached to a loudspeaker on a pole, "so his priceless words would not be lost," Patton mocked. Montgomery had already earned the ire of his American colleagues by failing to capture Caen, having explained to Eisenhower and Bradley on the last day of June that he intended to hold the left flank, while expecting Bradley to break through on the right. Eisenhower and Bradley agreed that if there were to be a breakout, it would have to come from the Americans.[49] Patton refused to let cameramen film him at the event, not wanting the Germans to know his whereabouts. Bradley joined them and the three sat down in Montgomery's war tent to discuss the situation. Patton took sly pride in Montgomery's inability to capture Caen. "Montgomery went to great length[s] explaining why the British had done nothing," he wrote in his diary. Montgomery hinted that Patton's army would not become operational until Bradley's forces had captured Avranches, almost fifty miles south of the American lines, but Bradley, eager to become an army group commander equal to Montgomery, refused to consent. Bradley reiterated to Patton that once Third Army came on line, he would head west to capture the port cities in the Brest Peninsula, then head east to attack the German's southern left flank. Bradley promised him ten infantry divisions but said nothing about tanks.⁵⁰

Patton spent the next two weeks visiting V-1 launch sites, talking to war correspondents (after telling them not to write about him until after Third Army had become operational), driving along Omaha Beach, and exploring the German defenses around Cherbourg. He also attended open-air church services while planes flew overhead and artillery boomed. On one visit to Omaha Beach, he spotted Army trucks bunched up in the open along a road. He marched up to a nervous lieutenant and demanded, "Who the hell is in charge of this Goddamn mess? One Jerry coming down here with a plane could wipe out that highway."⁵¹

On another visit to Omaha Beach, Patton recognized his forward observers debarking from their ships. "I need several missions done," he told them. "I was told that I could not order anybody to do them because of the danger, only ask for volunteers. Those assigned to these missions will be required to operate independently. You will not get routine services, including Army rations. Instead, you will have to do it the old-fashioned way—live off the land." He wanted the men to penetrate the German lines and report back daily. When he asked for a French-speaking volunteer to work as a liaison with the French resistance, one man raised his hand. In French, Patton asked the man his favorite food, and the man answered in French.⁵²

Patton also passed the time by visiting his commanders. Troy Middleton, commanding VIII Corps, told him his 90th, 83rd, and 8th infantry divisions were fighting poorly. Paddy Flint, on the other hand, showed Patton his regiment's tactic for taking hedgerows: firing machine-guns and mortars at the corners, then advancing using marching fire to capture the field. Flint called his tactic "a clip for each field." Huebner, commanding the 1st Infantry Division, used Flint's tactics, which pleased Patton, but he was surprised to find Huebner in a dugout. "I don't like the idea of hanging out in a dugout," he wrote, but at least Patton didn't urinate in it.⁵³

To prepare for Third Army's activation, Patton set up headquarters in an apple orchard outside the town of Néhou, south of Valognes. From his campsite, he could just see the local church with its shot-away steeple.⁵⁴ It was there that he finally had his toenail pulled off from his broken toe. He had been walking with a limp and still using Meeks's boot. He entertained himself and his staff by playing with Willie. He would pull an apple tree branch down so Willie could grasp it with his teeth. Then he would lift Willie and swing him in a circular motion. The branch would twist around the tree, spinning the dog. The soldiers cheered while Patton repeated the trick.[55] But Willie was not always the apple of his master's eye, such as when he dug up a recently buried enemy soldier, "to the shame and disgrace of the military service," Patton wrote.[56] Néhou buzzed with military activity as Patton's men went about their headquarters duties. His doctors and dentists treated soldiers and the occasional French civilian.[57] Through it all, Patton still chafed to get into action, worried that the war would end before he could get into it.[58] Codman noted that "he is not going to be happy until Third Army becomes operational." The XX Corps historian reported that an angry Patton declared (using four-letter words) that he was tired of the delay and that in eighteen days he could be in Paris, and that he would drive his men, leaving little time for food or rest. To Beatrice, Patton wrote, "I will go mad waiting when I know I could do a better job."[59]

Patton found any excuse to criticize Eisenhower's leadership. When he learned that Eisenhower had refused to turn Bradley's rear area over to General John Lee's recently established 9th Communications Zone because it would hurt Bradley's feelings, he lamented, "That is a hell of a way to run a war." When he heard about the confusion on the beaches and back in southern England's ports, he blamed Eisenhower, calling him a fool who lacked inspired leadership. "We actually have no Supreme Commander—no one who can take hold and say that this shall be done and that shall be done," he wrote in his diary. "It is a very unfortunate situation to which I see no solution."

Patton's feelings toward Montgomery were not much better. He constantly felt the British commander was delaying the activation of his army so he could remain the sole army group commander, when it was actually Eisenhower who delayed Patton's activation in an effort to sidestep command problems with Montgomery. Eisenhower knew that activating Patton's army would immediately shrink British prestige, an inevitability.[60] When Patton heard a rumor that he and the rest of his Third Army staff were to remove their shoulder patches and paint over their vehicles' unit markings, he blamed Montgomery. Montgomery's written order that Third Army would become operational only after the capture of Avranches confirmed it. Patton also accused Montgomery of fearing to put him into the fight because he would steal the show,

CHAPTER FOURTEEN ★ D-DAY AND THE DAWN OF THIRD ARMY

"which I will," he admitted. Secretary of War Stimson wrote Patton that the British were not pulling their weight, which delighted him, but the secretary also warned Patton to keep his mouth shut and "let my actions speak for me."[61] Patton became so worried about never taking command in Europe, he wrote Stimson a few days later, asking for a posting in the Pacific to fight the Japanese.[62]

Bradley did not escape Patton's wrath either. He saw his new boss as a big nothing who did nothing and lacked "the stuff." When Bradley tried to assure Patton that he would be put into the fight as soon as possible, Patton blew it off, complaining that Bradley could do it immediately, "if he had any backbone." Patton saw Bradley as pushing all along his front, not leading an armored breakthrough. "All that is necessary now is to take chances," he wrote.[63]

But Bradley was doing just that. Since July 11, he had been formulating a new plan to break out of the hedgerows—Operation COBRA. Instead of sending forth all his forces, with COBRA he would focus on just one corps, clearing a path to drive a wedge in the German lines. But how could he assure a single corps would penetrate the German line? The risky and unconventional answer was airpower. He planned to have the Eighth and Ninth Air Forces bomb a four-mile stretch of ground between the towns of Périers and St. Lo, after which Major General Joe Collins would drive his VII Corps ten miles south to the town of Coutances, only thirty-three miles north of Avranches.

The air bombardment would comprise eighteen hundred heavy bombers striking a four-mile-by-one-mile rectangular target south of the Périers-St. Lo highway for one hour, followed by 350 fighter-bombers strafing and bombing for another twenty minutes. After that, 396 medium bombers would attack the southern section of the target for an additional forty-five minutes. During the entire attack, 500 fighters would fly cover over the air fleet. Bradley asked the air chiefs to use only light bombs with instantaneous fuse settings to prevent cratering that would impede his troops' progress. To prevent friendly fire incidents, he would pull ground troops back twelve hundred yards, not too far to be unsafe but close enough to advance immediately following the bombardment. As a last measure of safety, he asked that the bombers fly parallel to the road, not perpendicular to it, so that the planes would not be flying over the heads of his troops, putting them in mortal danger as well as dropping bombs short of their target. To make the ground penetration,

Collins would use two infantry divisions to hold open the sides of the breach, followed by two armored divisions driving south and pivoting to the right to capture Coutances. Bradley believed Collins would reach Avranches in ten days.[64]

Bradley briefed Patton and his staff on COBRA—and came to regret it. On July 17 Bradley learned that a Third Army staffer, Colonel C. C. Blakeney, had prematurely briefed the press on Operation COBRA. Patton acted immediately. He met with the correspondents and admonished them for breaking his trust, telling them he was both shocked and disgusted by the incident, especially since one reporter had shared the information with a colleague in First Army. He had them all sign a statement of regret.[65] He then confronted Blakeney, who admitted to the slip but defended it, telling Patton he had done it out of loyalty to him. "I think he is honest, but stupid," Patton wrote in his diary. He decided to fire Blakeney but would wait until after COBRA so as not to draw attention. To make matters worse, Patton's Civil Affairs section published two papers without his knowledge, containing disparaging remarks about Bradley's First Army. They also commented on segregated African American troops, a sensitive topic to Patton. He had both papers recalled.[66]

While Patton treaded lightly among these slights, Eisenhower had been working back in England to ensure that the Germans still expected Patton to attack Calais. Amazingly, the Germans still clung to the belief that he was preparing his First Army Group, an idea fully encouraged by their "spies" in England. On June 28 Eisenhower had learned that the visitors' ban was about to be lifted in the country, which threatened to reveal that there was no American army in East Anglia. The British had already lifted their diplomatic ban. If the visitors' ban were also lifted it could convince the Germans that no follow-up attack would ensue. Eisenhower asked the British war cabinet to keep the ban in place until the end of July, right about the time Patton was expected to take command of Third Army on the Continent. Eisenhower reinforced his request by adding that Montgomery make a special appeal "for the retention of the ban as essential for the success of his future operations."[67]

On the day Patton arrived in France, Eisenhower asked Marshall to send him Lieutenant Generals Lesley McNair, John L. DeWitt, or someone of equal reputation to replace Patton as the commander of the First Army Group, since, according to Eisenhower, "the enemy will soon learn

CHAPTER FOURTEEN ★ D-DAY AND THE DAWN OF THIRD ARMY

of the presence in the lodgment areas of 1st U.S. Army Group and Patton with his Third Army." McNair would get the fake assignment. Three days later, Beetle Smith recommended that it was time to leak a story that Patton had been relieved of his army group command "because of displeasure at some of his indiscretions, and that he is reduced to Army command." It was a story easily believed by both sides.[68] On July 19 an agent codenamed Brutus communicated to the Germans that General Leslie McNair had replaced Patton as head of FUSAG. "I suppose that Eisenhower and Patton were not in agreement on the change in Order of Battle," he reported. A German newspaper in Paris claimed that Patton was on the Continent and at the head of an army group. More than a week later, an OKH intelligence summary documented that "according to captured documents confirmed credible, Abwehr reports the American Third Army had now transferred to France."[69]

As Patton waited, one of his friends passed away, but not from enemy fire. General Teddy Roosevelt died on July 12 of a heart attack in his sleep. After being sent home during the Sicily campaign, he had gotten himself assigned to the 4th Infantry Division and had landed with the first waves on D-Day, where his leadership inspired the men and tankers to push inland, despite having landed in the wrong location. Bradley had given him command of the troublesome 90th Infantry Division because of his courageous performance, but Roosevelt died before Eisenhower signed the order. Patton regretted that Roosevelt had not died in battle. At the evening funeral two days later, Patton served as a pallbearer, though he positioned himself at the rear of the coffin to hide from the cameras. While Patton considered the ceremony "a flop," with uninspired chaplains and a mispositioned honor guard, the firing of nearby anti-aircraft guns "gave an appropriate requiem to the funeral of a really gallant man."[70]

The morning before Roosevelt's funeral, Patton had driven to Utah Beach to see one of his engineer commanders. On the way, he stood in his jeep as it drove through two columns of soldiers marching inland on either side of the road. He waved to the men, wet from having just waded ashore. Suddenly, a German Me-109 fighter strafed the road. The men dove into ditches, but Patton just kept on waving as tracer bullets exploded under his jeep, never touching him.[71]

On July 20 news raced through the Allied ranks that Adolf Hitler had survived an assassination attempt by German army officers. While almost everyone cheered the news of the Fuehrer's near demise, Patton raced to Bradley's headquarters and pleaded to be given command of Third Army at once. "For God's sake Brad," he begged, "you've got to get me into this fight before the war is over. I'm in the doghouse here and I'm apt to die there unless I pull something spectacular to get me out." Yet, Bradley did not shift the plan.[72]

Two days later, Patton attended a demonstration of a new weapon, an M5 light tank with 10- to 12-inch metal spikes welded to its front hull. The concept behind this bizarre-looking tank was to drive into the dreaded hedgerows and rip open a hole, like "a spoon through warm butter."[73] The test went flawlessly, plowing through the natural obstacle without even stopping. An impressed Patton nodded his approval. The hedgerow cutter would give him endless maneuver possibilities.[74]

The troops who would soon come under Patton's command, however, did not impress him. Brigadier General Jay MacKelvie's 90th Infantry Division had performed poorly since it landed on Utah Breach on D-Day. Because of this, Bradley replaced MacKelvie with Major General Eugene Landrum, who did not do much better. During a July 22 attack, a German platoon wiped out an entire battalion. When Patton learned about the situation, he replaced Landrum with Brigadier General Raymond S. McLain, the former 45th Infantry Division's artillery commander. Things were not much better with Grow's 6th Armor Division, which was waiting to go into action. A company commander he spoke with was more concerned about what the Germans would do to his company than what he was going to do with Germans. Patton addressed the company to help the men overcome their fear. "This will be no God Dam [sic] Sunday school picnic," he told them. "Tighten your belts, from now on its C or K rations."[75]

Meanwhile, Bradley had scheduled COBRA for July 24 but called it off due to clouds. Not all the Eighth Air Force pilots got the word and bombed the road, killing approximately twenty-five Americans and wounding fifty. Patton, who knew something about friendly fire disasters, shook his head at the news. "All in the spirit of good fun," he lamented. The bombers had not come in parallel to the St. Lo/Périers Road, but perpendicular to it. Air commanders worried that a parallel route would expose their bombers to too much enemy ground fire. A furious Bradley launched an immediate investigation and found the air generals had flat-out lied to him. Worse, they refused a second attack unless Bradley agreed to a perpendicular attack. Bradley relented.[76]

CHAPTER FOURTEEN ★ D-DAY AND THE DAWN OF THIRD ARMY

The success of COBRA became paramount for both Bradley and Eisenhower. A week before, Montgomery had launched his own attempt to break out using a COBRA-like carpet bombing—Operation GOODWOOD. He had boasted to Eisenhower that "my whole eastern flank will burst into flames" and assured him of far-reaching results. The plan excited Eisenhower, who viewed the attack with "most tremendous optimism and enthusiasm." He felt it would be a decisive blow against the enemy. It was not. After Montgomery's forces penetrated only three miles, the Germans blunted the assault and counterattacked, leaving the British front stalemated. GOODWOOD left Eisenhower furious with Montgomery. He had believed the British general's hype and had begun to see daylight at the end of the tunnel, only to have it snuffed out. Now he looked to Bradley to save the front.[77]

The next day, at about four in the afternoon, the bombers came again. This time eighteen hundred of them filled the sky. To the shock and horror of the generals and the infantry, the bombers did not come in parallel to the Périers-St. Lo road; they bombed perpendicular to it, as Bradley had reluctantly agreed. As the first set of bombs exploded south of the road, clouds of dirt and debris obscured the road for follow-on bombers, resulting in bombs dropped on American troops. No less than three hundred men were killed by their own forces. This time, Patton made no judgement on the tragedy. No use in criticizing Bradley while he conducted a bold maneuver.[78]

While the bombs dropped, Patton took ill. He thought it was from too much chlorine in his drinking water. Willie suffered from the chemicals too. Despite feeling sick, he visited Bradley's headquarters, still worried that the war would pass him by. He repeated his plea, "I must get in and do something spectacularly successful," he told Bradley, "if I am to make good." Eisenhower showed up and tried to cool Patton by telling him he would receive $1,000 for each week he got ahead of schedule.[79] Patton spent the rest of the day finalizing plans for his Third Army. Once activated, he would command Middleton's VIII Corps, Haislip's XV Corp, and Walker's XX Corps. Middleton and Haislip would head west to capture the Brittany ports and Quiberon Bay, respectively, while Walker would push south to Rennes, protecting the army's left flank. Each corps contained at least one armored division along with two infantry divisions. Patton planned to put his tanks in the van, followed by armored infantry and timed artillery fire. He placed a lot of confidence in his tanks equipped

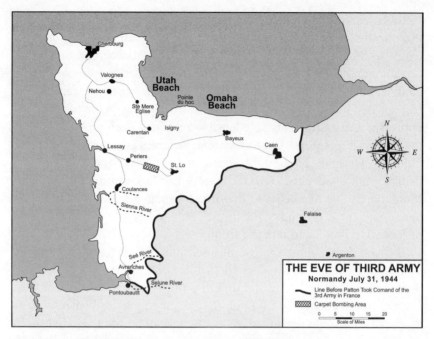

Map 8. The eve of Third Army, Normandy, July 31, 1944.

with hedgerow-cutting spades. "My plan is very simple and discreet," he wrote in his diary. Of his three corps commanders, only Middleton had any combat experience. But Middleton had never commanded tanks in the assault role Patton foresaw. Would he be able to adjust to this new form of warfare?[80]

COBRA cost Patton two friends. The first was Paddy Flint, who had taken a bullet to the helmet while leading his regiment from the front, directing a single tank and firing his own weapon at the enemy. "Paddy was a gallant soldier and a great friend," Patton lamented in his diary. "He died as he would have like to, in battle." Patton hoped to be as fortunate when the gods of war stopped smiling on him. While Flint had died from an enemy bullet, Lieutenant General Leslie McNair had been killed by COBRA bombs. He had been occupying a foxhole near the front when bombs exploded around him. "A sad ending to a useless sacrifice," Patton wrote. "He was a great friend."[81] While Flint was an excellent fighter, McNair's death had more impact on the Allied strategy. Operation FORTITUDE agents quickly reported his death to the Germans, knowing the information would get out anyway. Lieutenant

General William Simpson temporarily took on the mantle of FUSAG's chief until Lieutenant General John L. DeWitt could be flown in.[82]

Once the bombing ended, COBRA's ground attack initially failed to break through. Collins's infantry divisions, which were to rush into the gap, ran into stubborn German resistance. Eisenhower, who had flown to France to witness the breakthrough, flew back to England visibly depressed. Once again, troops under his command seemed to have died needlessly. But the operation was not over. The bombing had given the Germans a tremendous beating: killing scores of enemy infantry and commanders; burying tanks and artillery pieces; and disrupting communications. The German resistance was a last-stand effort with no backup.[83]

The next day, Collins continued to push his infantry. Middleton also attacked with his infantry divisions, making incremental progress. After two full days of indecisive combat, Middleton replaced his two infantry divisions with Wood's 4th and Grow's 6th Armored Division, which had been transferred to his command the day before.[84] On July 28 Wood kicked off at 9:00 a.m., and Grow followed a few hours later. The result was electric. Waves of tanks pushed through the hedgerow country, filling the air with the deafening roar of engines and the smell of gasoline. Half-tracks followed, packed with soldiers. Bringing up the rear were mobile artillery, tank retrievers, and supply trucks. The war for maneuver had begun. The armored spearheads sliced through the battered German defenses and raced south. Wood's tankers reached Coutances, ten miles south, before noon, where they fought street-to-street against the Germans, sometimes led by Wood himself on foot. The tankers spent the rest of the day clearing the city, later greeting Collins's 3rd Armored Division, the unit that was supposed to take the town.[85]

About the same time Wood captured Coutances, Bradley ordered Patton to assume temporary command of Middleton's VIII Corps and to put Haislip's XV Corps into action on Middleton's left. Although still feeling ill, Patton departed for Middleton's headquarters ready to take charge, but when he arrived around 7:00 p.m. he kept a low profile. He did not stay long, but what he saw fired his imagination. Returning to his own headquarters, he called Bradley and recommended dropping paratroopers on the Selune River dams, south of Avranches. Bradley shied off, explaining that airborne troops took too long. "Feel much happier over war," he wrote in his diary that night. "May get in it yet." Patton had reason to be happy. The day before a correspondent relayed that General Marshall had called Bradley a limited-objective general, but "when we get moving, Patton is the man with the drive and the imagination to do the dangerous things fast." Although Patton took the story with a grain of salt, he no doubt appreciated the sentiment.[86]

The next morning, Wood and Grow continued pushing their tanks south. Middleton ordered Grow to capture Avranches, thirty-three miles south, so Patton headed out to check out his armor divisions' progress. He drove up to the front just north of Coutances, where he could see its impressive cathedral, dating back to 1056.[87] Along the road, the advance guard for the 4th Armored Division's CCA roared south past Patton's vehicle as hundreds of German prisoners headed north. Whatever pleasure he may have taken from the scene, what he saw next soured his mood.[88] He came across a group of tankers from the 6th Armored Division standing around. His command car came to a screeching halt and he charged up to the officer in charge. "Who are you?" he demanded. "Sir," the saluting officer responded, "Colonel Lagrew, 15th Tank Battalion." Patton got to the point. "What in the goddammed hell are you doing stopped in this road?" The colonel explained that he was in reserve but was traveling as fast as he could. "Reserve hell! There is no reserve in the Third Army! Everybody that's here is supposed to fight." Patton built himself into a lather. "Boy," he called the colonel, "if you don't get up and get going after these guys, if I ever see you stopped on the road again, I'm going to personally kick your ass." "Yes sir," was the colonel's only response.[89]

Patton's mood did not improve when he found General Grow just south of Coutances, stopped at the Seine River. Grow was studying a map with Brigadier General James Taylor, CCA's commander. Patton asked Grow what he was doing and Grow explained he was looking for a place to cross. Thinking Patton may need him for something, he added that he was not doing anything. Patton, stifling his temper, asked Grow if he had been down to look at the river. Grow responded "no" and Patton exploded, telling him that unless he did something he would be out of job. Patton then walked down to the river, finding it just a foot in depth, with only a few Germans on the far bank. He ordered Grow to cross right there and immediately departed. Grow did as ordered, and within minutes his tanks rolled across the river.[90]

Patton did not fire Grow for being slow, but he did relieve him from capturing Avranches, passing it onto Wood, whose tanks were driving south so quickly that his artillery battalions had to leapfrog each other just to keep up. By evening, the 4th Armored had reached the outskirts of Avranches, but the Germans, realizing entire divisions in the Brittainy peninsula would be cut off if the Americans captured the mountain-top city, stopped and fought. For two days, Wood's tankers and infantry fought in and around Avranches. Sometimes, his tankers dueled with German tanks from point-blank ranges across hedgerows and around building corners. By 1:00 p.m. on July 30, the 4th Armored declared Avranches cleared of Germans. Three hours later, Wood's tanks secured the bridges over the Selune River, particularly the ancient Pontoubault bridge. The doorway to the Brittany ports had been opened.[91]

While many historians give Patton credit for the armor breakout following the COBRA bombing, it was actually Middleton who put two armored divisions in the fore on the morning of July 28. Patton did not show up to his headquarters until after 5:00 p.m. that night. While Wood and Grow plowed south that day, Patton spent his time attending a mass, visiting units, and flying over bombed-out fields of Operation COBRA with Bradley. Although Middleton knew Patton's plan once Third Army was activated, it was he who made the change to armor after he realized his infantry's limits in the hedgerows. At no time did Patton make any decisions that effected the next days' actions, save ordering Grow to cross the Seine River. General Wood later wrote, "We were supposed to have been inspired by George Patton to go through Coutances and Avranches and Rennes when in fact I never saw him or had any contact with him from the time he came to see me at my headquarters in England until I went by his headquarters north of Laval on my way out of Brittany in the middle of August."[92] Without urging or input from Patton, Middleton made the call, changing the tenor of the battlefield.

On the last day of July, with the birth of Third Army only hours away, Patton rose at a staff meeting and addressed his soldiers. "We go operational at noon tomorrow," he told them. "Doubtless, there will be some complaining about pushing people too hard, but I believe in the old axiom that an ounce of sweat is worth a gallon of blood. One thing we must remember: The harder we push, the more Germans we kill and the sooner the war will be over. And we must forget this business of always worrying about our flanks. We have to guard our flanks, but not to the extent that we don't do anything else. Some Goddamned fool once said you have to protect your flanks and some son-of-a-bitch since has been going crazy guarding his flanks."

Then he drew on the speeches he had been giving all over England. "I don't want to get any messages 'I am holding my position.' We are not holding anything. Let the Germans do that. We are advancing constantly and not interested in holding anything, except the enemy. We're going to hold on to him and kick the hell out of him all the time. We have to push to keep advancing and we are going to advance. Frederick the Great said 'Audacious, audacious, always audacious.' That's what we want to be, always audacious. Remember that. From here on out, until we win or die in the attempt, we will always be audacious." Then, amused, he concluded, "I want to thank you for your work. You performed well doing nothing. I want you to do just as good doing something."[93] Later, Patton received an encouraging note from Eisenhower: "The best good luck to you," the commander wrote, "I don't have to urge you to keep them fighting—that is one thing I know you will do." The note was a far cry from the dressing down Eisenhower gave Patton before he sailed for Sicily.[94]

That evening, Patton drove to Middleton's headquarters to learn his tanks had reached the Selune River south of Avranches. When Middleton asked what he should do next, Patton told him that throughout history, wars had been lost by armies not crossing rivers, and ordered Middleton to cross immediately. While they discussed where exactly to cross, someone from Wood's 4th Armored Division called to report the ancient bridge at Pontaubault was damaged but still intact. Also, Wood had seized several dams east of the bridge and had captured two thousand Germans. "Now that's my kind of fighting," Patton told his staff. "Those troops know their business. We'll keep right on going, full speed ahead." The prospects looked good for Third Army's debut.[95]

Patton did not fall asleep until after midnight. It had been a long journey from the beaches of North Africa in November 1942, to Sicily, to England, to France. He had started his war one year, nine months, three weeks, and two days earlier. During that time, he only spent ten weeks and three days in combat. Now, at the head of Third Army, he would fight continually for more than ten months until final victory. Unlike Morocco, he was now an experienced commander. Unlike Tunisia, his troops would not be recovering from a defeat. Unlike Sicily, he faced a much more challenging foe. He had accumulated more combat experience than any of his contemporaries, he had survived his errors and misjudgments, and he had garnered a reputation among friend and foe alike as a warrior—someone to be feared on the battlefield. As the sun rose over France on August 1, 1944, Patton was ready to put himself to the test on a new battlefield.

Acknowledgments

ALTHOUGH WRITING A book can sometimes seem like lonely work, so many people helped me complete this project that I can honestly say that no author is an island.

I spent countless hours over the years pouring over General Patton's papers at the Library of Congress Manuscripts Division. As far back as 1996, the team there helped me access the papers when I first discovered the general's photographs. Bruce Kirby, in particular, answered all my questions and helped me provide context to some of Patton's more archaic entries. Plus, he's a nice guy I have come to call my friend. The rest of the staff also helped, in too many ways to count. Those professionals include Jennifer Brathovde, Jeff Flannery, Joseph Jackson, Lia Kerwin, Patrick Kerwin, and Lewis Wyman. The staff in the Main Reading Room got me everything I needed on my Saturday visits for years, and the team at the Veterans History Project, especially Robert Patrick, helped me access the endless soldiers' stories they had collected.

Having done research at the National Archives and Records Administration for the past thirty years, I can attest that everyone there always greeted me with a smile, especially Holly Reed, who knew I thought I knew more about the collections than she did. But seriously, everyone there has helped me in some capacity. Besides Holly in Still Pictures, Tim Nenninger, the branch chief for Modern Military Records, offered advice and wisdom to my research. He would often show up at my research desk with a box of papers, telling me he had stumbled over some documents that were relevant to Patton. You can't put a price on that. Mitch Yokelson is not only an expert on twentieth-century warfare, he is also a great European tour guide and an even better friend. He's always good for a history chat in the Archives cafeteria or a café somewhere in

England. Other people who helped me include Robin Cookson, Mike Dolan, Sue Strange, Sim Smiley, and Nathan Patch.

Other people and research facilities gave this book the color and layers needed to provide a better understanding of Patton. They include the staff of the University of Tennessee's Special Collections: Justin Eastwood, Nick Wyman, Elizabeth Dunham, and William Eigelsbach. Also helpful was my friend and research assistant Keith Buchanan. Dr. Jessica Sheets at the U.S. Army Heritage and Education Center, in Carlisle, Pennsylvania, not only let me review newly acquired materials that had not yet been logged in but also jumpstarted my car when I had left my lights on. Again, you can't put a price on that. The staff at the Patton Museum at Fort Knox, Kentucky, helped me with extant texts and veteran interviews. Especially helpful were my friends Chris Kolakowski and Candice Fuller.

Several professional soldiers/historians at the U.S. Army Combat Studies Institute at Fort Leavenworth, Kansas, where I worked for three years, helped me with my research and writing, making me a better historian. They include Don Wright, Rod Cox, Thomas Hanson, Carl Fischer, Kevin Kennedy, and Ryan Wadle. Kevin wore two hats as editor and running partner in numerous races and obstacle courses. Additionally, Fort Leavenworth's Combined Arms Research Library helped me with endless research assistance. Those helpers include Edwin Burgess, Mallory Owens, Theresa Taylor, Michael Browne, Russell Rafferty, and Joanne Knight.

The staff and fellow historians at Stephen Ambrose Historical Tours have enabled me to visit numerous battlefields in Europe and share my stories with tourists. Back in 2003, my friend Chris Anderson asked me to be a tour guide, to which I replied, "I don't know anything about being a tour guide." I've been a historian/tour guide for the company for the last sixteen years and counting. The company's president, Yakir Katz, is a trusted friend and has been a troubleshooter too many times to count. The office staff have done the yeoman's work to make my tours go as smoothly as humanly possible. They include Claire Heller Aubrey, Mark Bielski, Olga Degtjarewsky, Cheryl DalPozzal, Jenni DeLong, Terry Sercovich, and Carrie Williamson. I have shared a lot of laughs (and drinks) with my fellow guides, tour managers, and bus drivers. They have made me look good and broadened my historical horizons. They include Matt Beroggie, Rick Beyer, Steve Bourque, Charles Bower, Hank de Jong, Alex Eversman, Eric Flint, Connie Kennedy, Richard Latture, John

ACKNOWLEDGMENTS 349

Mountcastle, Marty Morgan, Koop Steenbergen, Bryan Perissutti, and the late Steve Weiss. My friend Brigadier General Raymond Bell Jr. (AUS, Ret.) gets a special shout out. We met when I worked at *ARMY* magazine and he encouraged me to create the Patton tour, which we led together. He has been a constant source of inspiration and has let me use his home when I've researched at the U.S. Military Academy at West Point. I've seen Ray keep his cool under some of the most stressful situations. I would follow him anywhere. When it came to pick my own assistant, I chose one of my former clients, and good friend, Keith Buchanan (you get two shoutouts, Keith). Keith takes a lot of burden off my shoulders and makes my tours enjoyable. Keith has also helped me in my research. If only he didn't love bagpipes.

My boss at Arlington National Cemetery, Dr. Steve Carney, the command historian, deserves special acknowledgement, if anything, for simply approving my vacation time so I could finish this book. My fellow historians at Arlington are always good for a chat about history or the play *Hamilton:* Allison Finkelstein, Tim Frank, Rod Gainer, and Jenifer Van Vleck. In addition, the gang at Sovereign Media have worked with me, and I with them, for decades. They published my articles in *WWII History* and *WWII Quarterly* magazines, and I worked off-and-on as their photo and art director, finding hard-to-find images to go into the magazines. I loved that work. The team includes Carl Gnam, Mark Hintz, Samantha Detulleo, and Laura Cleveland, Mike Haskew, and Flint Whitlock.

I owe a special thanks to certain individuals. U.S. Army Major Alex Schade escorted me around Morocco to see Patton's Operation TORCH battlefields in 2015. Alex, then a captain and a Foreign Area Officer assigned to U.S. Embassy Rabat Office of Security Cooperation, spent two days with me, driving me around Morocco and helping me explore the invasion beaches, battlefields, and ports. We had a lot of fun in the process. Alex, I could not have done it without you. Another special thanks goes to the Brothers family, Alan, Joan, Lindsey, and Zach, for letting me use their vacation house on St. Helena Island in South Carolina, twice. The uncluttered atmosphere, free of television and telephones, enabled me to concentrate and get this ball rolling and then to refocus when I needed to. Luke Sprague at the Wisconsin Veterans Museum provided me with some excellent oral histories from soldiers who served under Patton. Finally, Bobby Wright provided the excellent maps in these pages.

Bobby, you were a pleasure to work with. I hope we can do it again soon (there will be a volume 2, you know).

The team at the University of Missouri Press did the yeoman's work on this book. Technically, they were there at the inception. It all started in 2004, when my new friend, Dr. John McManus, curators' distinguished professor of U.S. military history at the Missouri University of Science and Technology (Missouri S&T), challenged me to write a magnum opus on Patton. I dove in and churned out a stack of chapters, but when no one seemed to want my rough manuscript, I began to challenge John whenever he pressed me to complete it. I eventually asked him what the University of Missouri Press would do for me. He immediately agreed to strive to publish my work as a volume in his series with UMP, The American Military Experience, if I ever got it done. John, and his wife Nancy, have been great friends for the last fifteen years. I look forward to their visits now that I'm back in D.C. When I lived in Kansas, visiting them in St. Louis was something I always looked forward to. In addition, Andrew Davidson, editor in chief at the University of Missouri Press, walked me through the opening stages of the publication process and read my first-draft manuscript, and Associate Acquisitions Editor Mary Conley graciously showed me how to properly format endnotes, as well as took care of a list of problems I was having with my documents. Dr. Irina du Quenoy did a great job of editing the manuscript and she did something some editors fail to do: She let me keep my voice. Drew Griffith oversaw the editing process and put up with my prima donna ways.

Other friends who helped me out along the way include Bruce, Nancy, Jacqueline, and Hannah Hall, Dave and Amanda Rudolph, Lynn and Susan Berg, Kevin Biscoe, Kay and Camille Casey, Christian and Erin Chae, Lucio Corsini, Mike and Stephanie Delaune, Joël Denis, Raymond Denkhaus, Scott Devine, Don Fox, Geoff Emeigh, Liz Fraser, Adi Frimark, Harry Gilbert, Elisabeth Gozzo, Denny Hair, Vince Hodge, George Hofmann, Jennifer Holik, Mike and Kate Hudson, Charles Ingram, Lena King, Cole Kingseed, Bob Knutsen, Renee and Rian Lambert, Richard Latture, Tim Lawson, Barbara Lewandrowski, Kerry Lynn, David Mansburger, John Marchetti, Don McKeown, Paul Minus, Pete Murphy, Mike Nadonley, Jonathan Neumann, Ward Nickdish, Les Owen, Helen Patton, David Peterson, Carlton Philpot, Clint Poole, Bob Quackenbush, Mark Reardon, Mike Riha, Steve and Denise Schaick, Rodney Scully,

ACKNOWLEDGMENTS

Ken Stewart, Matt Seelinger, Mary Soule, Koop Steenbergen, Brooke Stoddard, Monika Stoy, Judy Taylor, Sheryl and Helen Tiseth, Ashley Topolosky, Jeff Trammell, Rob and Penka Trimble, Cyd Upson, Barbara Venske, Paul Woodage, Mike Yarborough, Dave Zabecki, and Jim Zwit.

My buddy Tony Carlson proved himself invaluable through this whole process. As a fellow historian with the U.S. Army Combat Studies Institute's Afghan Study Team back in 2011, Tony and I hung out a lot together at work, the gym, running races, drinking beers at a gas station (which we entitled The Gentlemen's Club), and attending a few Kansas City Royals games. We constantly talked history, philosophy, literature, and, occasionally, some sophomoric topic of the day. These days, we edit each other's work, be it for chapters, articles, or books. Although we are half a country apart, I can always count on my phone ringing sometime after work and hearing the question "What are you doing?" on the other end. Tony has served as a sounding board, source advisor, editor, and frustration valve throughout this project.

Three other editors greatly improved my writing: Annette McDermott, Claire Noble, and Joe Balkoski. Annette wrote for the History Channel as well as other companies. Claire has worked for several publishers. Both honed my text and simply broke my habit of using useless adverbs. Joe Balkoski, America's leading D-Day expert, edited the chapter on D-Day and made it more professional.

Certain members of my family were also instrumental in the completion of this book. My brother Greg Hymel, and his wife, Rachel Manning, invited me into their home when I was between jobs (translation: unemployed). I worked on the book in their basement and had the opportunity to better acquaint myself with my nephew and nieces. Thank you both for your generosity. My sisters also deserve a shout out: Amy Moorer, Beth Hymel, Joy Hymel, Madeline Fleischmann, Peggy Hymel, and Judi Jacobs.

Finally, my Pop, Gary G. Hymel, gave me the important first edit. Pop worked for the *New Orleans States-Item* newspaper for about thirteen years before he and my mom packed up my six sisters and one brother and moved to Washington, D.C., where I was born. He worked on Capitol Hill for representatives Hale Boggs (D-La.) and Tip O'Neill (D-Ma.) before becoming a lobbyist. He's retired now and lives with my sister Joy in Atlanta. He shares my fascination with American history and edits just about all my freelance writings. Thanks Pop!

Notes

Introduction

1. *Army Leadership and the Profession*, Army Doctrine Publication 6-22 (Washington, D.C.: Department of the Army, 2019), vii.

2. Thomas E. Ricks, *The Generals: American Military Command from World War II to Today* (New York: Penguin, 2012), 9.

3. Martin Blumenson, *Patton: The Man behind the Legend, 1885-1945* (New York: Morrow, 1985), 55.

4. Robert H. Patton, *The Pattons: A Personal History of an American Family* (New York: Crown Publishers, 1994), 39, 63, 67, 122.

5. Martin Blumenson, ed., *The Patton Papers*, vol. 1, *1885-1940* (Boston: Houghton Mifflin, 1972), 428.

6. Carlo D'Este, *Patton: A Genius for War* (New York: HarperCollins, 1995), 171, 172; GSP to BAP, June 26, 1943, box 11, file 2, George S. Patton Collection, Manuscript Division, LOC (henceforth the GSP Collection); Patton, *The Pattons*, 125.

7. Blumenson, *Man behind the Legend*, 33, 34, 54, 123; D'Este, *Genius for War*, 90-91.

8. Ruth Ellen Patton Totten, *The Button Box: A Daughter's Loving Memoir of Mrs. George S. Patton* (Columbia, MO: University of Missouri Pres, 2005), 74.

9. D'Este, 132-34.

10. Blumenson, *Patton Papers*, vol. 1, 262, 263; idem., *Man behind the Legend*, 74, 75; D'Este, 133.

11. Blumenson, *Man behind the Legend*, 86, 87.

12. D'Este, 213-17.

13. Blumenson, *Man behind the Legend*, 109-11.

14. Blumenson, *Patton Papers*, vol. 1, 969.

15. Blumenson, *Patton Papers*, vol. 1, 969; Patton, *The Pattons*, 212, 213.

16. Blumenson, *Patton Papers*, vol. 1, 969; Totten, *Button Box*, 260-61.

17. Blumenson, *Man behind the Legend*, 137-40.

18. Blumenson, *Patton Papers*, vol. 1, 969; D'Este, 366-27.

Chapter One

1. Robert Henriques, *From a Biography of Myself: A Posthumous Selection of the Autobiographical Writings of Robert Henriques* (London: Secker and Warburg, 1969), 114.

2. Milton F. Perry and Barbara W. Parke, *Patton and His Pistols: The Favorite Side Arms of General George S. Patton, Jr.* (Harrisburg, PA: Stackpole, 1957), 111, 115; Kevin M. Hymel, *Patton's Photographs: War as He Saw It* (Dulles, VA: Potomac Books, 2006), 8.

3. Hymel, *Patton's Photographs*, 117.

4. Patton's diaries, November 7-8, 1943, box 2, file 13, George S. Patton Collection, Manuscripts Division, Library of Congress. (Hereafter cited as GSP diary).

5. Samuel Eliot Morison, *Operations in North African Waters, History of United States Naval Operations in World War II*, vol. 2, 3–42; James Wellard, *General George S. Patton Jr.: Man Under Mars* (New York: Dodd, Mead, 1946), 57.

6. Barrie Pitt and Frances Pitt, *The Month-by-Month Atlas of World War II* (New York: Summit Books, 1989), 4–29.

7. Henriques, *From a Biography of Myself*, 78.

8. GSP diary, October 25–November 8, 1942, box 2, file 13; Rick Atkinson, *Army at Dawn: The War in North Africa, 1942–1943* (New York: Henry Holt, 2002), 104.

9. "Attack and Attack!" unknown source and date, Patton Scrapbooks, reel 1, and transcript of Patton speech, reel 3, GSP Collection.

10. Perry and Parke, *Patton and His Pistols*, 4.

11. GSP to BAP, November 6, 1942, box 10, file 11, GSP Collection; GSP to Guy V. Henry, November 6, 1942, box 10, file 11, GSP Collection.

12. Ladislas Farago, *Patton: Ordeal and Triumph* (New York: Ivan Obolensky, 1964), 13, 14.

13. Atkinson, *Army at Dawn*, 106, 107.

14. GSP diary, November 8, 1942, box 2, file 3.

15. Morison, *History*, vol. 2, 41–42; Mark Clark, *Calculated Risk* (New York: Harper, 1950), 100.

16. Ed Sullivan, "Little Old New York," unknown source, December 12, 1942, Patton Scrapbooks, reel 3, GSP Collection.

17. GSP diary, November 8, 1942; Richard W. Belt Jr., "On Board the 'AUGIE' at Casablanca," *Naval History* 29, no. 5 (October 2015): 33, https://www.usni.org/magazines/naval-history-magazine/2015/october/board-augie-casablanca; Norman Gelb, *Desperate Venture: The Story of Operation Torch, the Allied Invasion of North Africa* (New York: W. Morrow, 1992), 169.

18. Perry and Parke, 1, 2, 4, 40; Carlo D'Este, *Patton: Genius for War* (New York: HarperCollins, 1995), 174.

19. Newspapers back home erroneously reported that Patton's landing craft had been destroyed by enemy fire just as he was about to step onboard.

20. Richard Nelms Jones, unpublished memoir, 39, Veterans History Project, LOC.

21. GSP diary, November 8, 1942.

22. David Zabecki, ed., *Chief of Staff: The Principal Officers Behind History's Great Commanders* (Annapolis, MD: Naval Institute Press, 2008), vol. 2, 131–33; Paul

Harkins photo albums, vol. 2, U.S. Army Heritage and Education Center (henceforth USAHEC).

23. Harold V. Boyle, "Patton Weeps at Death of Pasadena Aide," *AP*, April 1, 1943, Patton Scrapbooks, reel 3, GSP Collection.

24. George Forty, *The Armies of George S. Patton* (New York: Arms and Armour, 1996), 84.

25. Ruth Ellen Patton Totten, *The Button Box: A Daughter's Loving Memory of Mrs. George S. Patton* (Columbia: University of Missouri Press, 2005), 288–90; Larry Newman, "General George S. Patton, Jr., Soldier and American," *INS New York*, December 26, 1945, Patton Scrapbooks, reel 1, GSP Collection.

26. Gelb, *Desperate Venture*, 132.

27. Charles Codman, *Drive* (Boston: Little, Brown, 1957), 20, 21.

28. Henriques, 114.

29. Henriques, 114; Codman, *Drive*, 22; BAP to GSP, December 2, 1942, box 10, file 12, GSP Collection. Oddly enough, when Patton's wife visited wounded soldiers from the Western Task Force at Walter Reed Army Medical Center, in Washington, D.C., she encountered a soldier who had been strafed after laying down on the beach. "Maybe if you stood up and kept going ahead you wouldn't have gotten hit," she told him. The other men in the ward burst out laughing.

30. GSP diary, November 8, 1942.

31. Henriques, 115–17.

32. John A. Moroso, "Snipers Kept Busy in Morocco," *AP*, November 17, 1942, Patton Scrapbooks, reel 3, GSP Collection.

33. Dwight D. Eisenhower, *Crusade in Europe* (Garden City, NY: Doubleday), 104; Gelb, 232.

34. Harry Butcher, *My Three Years with Eisenhower: The Personal Diary of Captain Harry C. Butcher, USNR, Naval Aide to General Eisenhower* (New York: Simon and Schuster, 1946), 185–88.

35. Carlo D'Este, *Eisenhower: A Soldier's Life* (New York: Henry Holt, 2002), 355.

Chapter Two

1. Kevin M. Hymel, "Profiles: Twice General Joseph Stilwell Landed Two of the United States' Most Coveted Commands, and Twice He Lost Them," *WWII History* 1, no. 5 (September 2002): 18, 19.

2. Dwight D. Eisenhower, *Crusade in Europe* (Garden City, NY: Doubleday, 1948), 82.

3. Norman Gelb, *Desperate Venture: The Story of Operation Torch, the Allied Invasion of North Africa* (New York: W. Morrow, 1992), 84, 85, 110; Martin Blumenson, ed., *The Patton Papers*, vol. 1, *1885-1940* (Boston: Houghton Mifflin, 1972), 941.

4. James Kelly Morningstar, *Patton's Way: A Radical Theory of War* (Annapolis, MD: Naval Institute Press, 2017), 68.

5. Kevin M. Hymel, "Red River Kids at War," *America in World War II* 13, no. 2 (August 2017): 23. Many historians have written that this meeting took place in the basement of a local high school. This is not possible since no major buildings had basements in Louisiana. Also, historians do not identify Bolton as the high school. It

was one of only two high schools in Alexandria, Louisiana, the other being a segregated school for African American teens.

6. Blumenson, *Patton Papers*, vol. 1, 970; George F. Hoffmann, *Through Mobility We Conquer: The Mechanization of U.S. Cavalry* (Lexington: University Press of Kentucky, 2006), 157.

7. Martin Blumenson, ed., *The Patton Papers*, vol. 2, *1940–1945* (Boston: Houghton Mifflin, 1974), 14, 15.

8. Blumenson, *Patton Papers*, vol. 2, 35.

9. Carlo D'Este, *Patton: Genius For War* (New York: HarperCollins, 1995), 395–98.

10. Stanley P. Hirshson, *General Patton: A Soldier's Life* (New York: HarperCollins, 2002), 252–53.

11. Porter B. Williamson, *I Remember General Patton's Principles* (Tucson: Management and Systems Consultants, 1979), 95.

12. Douglas Porch, *The Path to Victory: The Mediterranean Theater in World War II* (Old Saybrook, CT: Konecky and Konecky, 2004), 273–76.

13. Eisenhower, *Crusade in Europe*, 40, 41.

14. Blumenson, *Patton Papers*, vol. 2, 62–72.

15. Porch, *Path to Victory*, 59–60.

16. David Schoenbrun, *Soldiers of the Night: The Story of the French Resistance* (New York: E. P. Dutton, 1980), 205, 214.

17. Blumenson, *Patton Papers*, vol. 2, 86, 87.

18. D'Este, *Genius for War*, 421; Gelb, *Desperate Venture*, 132.

19. B. J. McQuaid, "Rundstedt's Big Problem," *New York Post*, 1945, Patton Scrapbooks, reel 1, GSP Collection; Blumenson, *Patton Papers*, vol. 2, 86.

20. Lida Mayo, *The Ordnance Department: On Beachhead and Battlefront* (Washington, D.C.: Office of the Chief of Military History, 1968), 165; Gelb, 138.

21. GSP diary, October 17, 1942, GSP Collection.

22. Marvin Jensen, *Strike Swiftly! The 70th Tank Battalion from North Africa to Normandy to Germany* (Novato, CA: Presidio, 1997), 19.

23. Katherine Marshall to GSP, August 22, 1943, box 11, file 6, GSP Collection; D'Este, 423; Blumenson, *Patton Papers*, vol. 2, 91–93.

24. GSP diaries, October 21, 1942, box 2, file 13; Charles Codman, *Drive* (Boston: Little, Brown, 1957), 146.

25. Robert Allen, *In Memoriam: George S. Patton Jr., General, U.S. Army* (pamphlet), 11, 12, the Center for the Study of War and Society, University of Tennessee; *Time* magazine, April 12, 1943, 31.

26. Clifford Kingston, interviewed by Sandra Stewart Holyoak, Shaun Illingsorth, and Bojan Stefanovic, November 3, 2000, Rutgers University Oral History Archives; D. K. R. Crosswell, *Beetle: The Life of General Walter Bedell Smith* (Lexington: University Press of Kentucky, 2010), 338.

27. Oral History, Hobart R. Gay Papers, USAHEC.

28. John C. McManus, *American Courage, American Carnage: 7th Infantry Chronicles: The 7th Infantry Regiment's Combat Experience, 1812 through World War II* (New York: Forge, 2009), 312–13.

29. Kent Hewitt, *The Memoirs of Admiral Kent Hewitt*, ed. Evelyn M. Cherpak (Newport, RI: Naval War College Press, 2004), 164.

30. GSP to BAP, November 11, 1942, box 10, file 11, GSP Collection; Orr Kelly, *Meeting the Fox: The Allied Invasion of Africa, from Operation Torch to Kasserine Pass to Victory in Tunisia* (New York: John Wiley and Sons, 2002), 37.

31. Samuel Eliot Morison, *History of the United States Naval Operations in World War II: Operations in North African Waters*, vol. 2 (Boston: Little, Brown, 1975), 158; Joseph Watters, WWII Veterans Survey, 3rd Infantry Division, USAHEC; "Yanks Four Miles From Casablanca," *AP*, November 9, 1942, Patton Scrapbooks, reel 3, GSP Collection.

32. D'Este, 437; Robert W. Boven, *Most Decorated Soldier in World War II: Matt Urban* (Victoria, B.C.: Trafford, 2000), 44–48.

33. GSP to Sultan of Morocco, November 10, 1942, box 10, file 11, GSP Collection; Gelb, 130.

34. Robert Henriques, *From a Biography of Myself: A Posthumous Selection of the Autobiographical Writings of Robert Henriques* (London: Western Printing Services, 1969), 118–25.

35. Boven, *Most Decorated Soldier*, 44–48.

36. GSP diary, box 2, file 13; GSP to BAP, November 11, 1942; Codman, *Drive*, 40–42.

37. Hugh A. Scott, *The Blue and White Devils: A Personal Memoir and History of the Third Infantry Division in World War II* (Nashville: Battery Press, 1984), 11–13.

38. GSP to BAP, November 11, 1942.

39. Ernest Harmon, *Combat Commander: Autobiography of a Soldier* (Englewood Cliffs, NJ: Prentice Hall, 1970), 93–98.

40. "U.S. General Packs 3 Guns," *U. P.*, November 14, 1942, Patton Scrapbooks, reel 3, GSP Collection; GSP to BAP, November 11, 1942. Admiral Hewitt has also been credited to having the exact same conversation with Michelier.

41. Codman, 46.

42. George F. Howe, *Northwest Africa: Seizing the Initiative in the West* (Washington, D.C.: U.S. Government Printing Office, 1957), 173.

43. Codman, 46–47.

44. Richard W. Belt Jr., "On Board the 'AUGIE' at Casablanca," *Naval History* 29, no. 5 (October 2015): 36.

45. John A. Moroso, "Snipers Kept Busy in Morocco," *AP*, November 17, 1942, Patton Scrapbooks, reel 3, GSP Collection.

46. Untitled transcript of press release, Patton Scrapbooks, reel 3, GSP Collection.

47. Martin Blumenson, *Patton: The Man behind the Legend, 1885–1945* (New York: Morrow, 1985), 173.

Chapter Three

1. GSP to BAP, November 14, 1942, box 10, file 11, GSP Collection.

2. GSP to BAP, November 14, 1942; Description of Visit by the CG and Staff to Gen. Noguès and the Sultan of Morocco, November 16, 1942, box 10, file 11, GSP Collection.

3. James Wellard, *General George S. Patton Jr.: Man Under Mars* (New York: Dodd, Mead, 1946), 62.

4. Samuel Eliot Morison, *History of the United States Naval Operations in World War II: Operations in North African Waters*, vol. 2 (Boston: Little, Brown, 1975), 175; Robert Henriques, *From a Biography of Myself: A Posthumous Selection of the Autobiographical Writings of Robert Henriques* (London: Western Printing Services, 1969), 134–35.

5. Steve Vogel, *The Pentagon: A History: The Untold Story of the Wartime Race to Build the Pentagon—and to Restore It Sixty Years Later* (New York: Random House, 2007), 285; Edwin P. Hoyt, *The GI's War: The Story of the American Soldier in Europe in World War II* (New York: McGraw-Hill, 1988), 130; Wellard, *General George S. Patton Jr.*, 68.

6. D. K. R. Crosswell, *Beetle: The Life of General Walter Bedell Smith* (Lexington: University of Kentucky, 2010), 346–50.

7. David Schoenbrun, *Soldiers of the Night: The Story of the French Resistance* (New York: E. P. Dutton, 1980), 228.

8. Harry C. Butcher, *My Three Years with Eisenhower: The Personal Diary of Captain Harry C. Butcher, USNR, Naval Aide to General Eisenhower* (New York: Simon and Schuster, 1946), 275.

9. Kenneth Pendar, *Adventure in Diplomacy: Our French Dilemma* (New York: DaCapo, 1976), 122–24; Crosswell, *Beetle*, 371.

10. Carleton S. Coon, *A North Africa Story: An Anthropologist as OSS Agent, 1941–1943* (Ipswich, MA: Gambit, 1980), 54–55.

11. Alfred D. Chandler Jr., ed., *The Papers of Dwight David Eisenhower: The War Years*, vol. 2 (Baltimore: Johns Hopkins University Press, 1970), 857.

12. R. Harris Smith, *OSS: The Secret History of America's First Central Intelligence Agency* (Berkeley: University of California Press, 1972), 71.

13. Wellard, *General George S. Patton Jr.*, 64, 65.

14. Dwight D. Eisenhower, *Crusade in Europe* (Garden City, NY: Doubleday, 1948), 126.

15. Description of Visit by the CG and Staff to Gen. Noguès and the Sultan of Morocco, November 16, 1942.

16. Eisenhower, *Crusade in Europe*, 100.

17. GSP to BAP, November 14, 1942; GSP to BAP, November 19, 1942, box 10, file 11, GSP Collection; Douglas Porch, *The Path to Victory: The Mediterranean Theater in World War II* (Old Saybrook, CT: Konecky and Konecky, 2004), 341.

18. Kevin Hymel, *Patton's Photographs: War as He Saw It* (Dulles, VA: Potomac Books, 2006), 16.

19. GSP to DDE, November 19, 1942, box 2, file 14, GSP Collection.

20. GSP to BAP, November 19, 1942.

21. GSP diary, November 18, 1942, box 2, file 13.

22. Eisenhower, 127, 128, 130.

23. Pendar, *Adventures in Diplomacy*, 124–25; GSP to BAP, November 24, 1942, box 10, file 11, GSP Collection.

24. GSP to BAP, November 24, 1942.

25. Pendar, 132.
26. James McLaughlin Jr., interview, the National World War II Museum, Charleston, WV, no date.
27. Zachary B. Friedenberg, *Hospital at War: The 95th Evacuation Hospital in World War II* (College Station: Texas A&M University Press, 2004), 17.
28. Robert Allen Collection, unpublished diary, page 10, The Patton Museum.
29. GSP to BAP, December 26, 1942, box 10, file 12, GSP Collection.
30. Ernest Harmon, *Combat Commander: Autobiography of a Soldier* (Englewood Cliffs, NJ: Prentice Hall, 1970), 106.
31. Chandler, *Papers of Dwight David Eisenhower*, vol. 2, 770.
32. GSP to BAP, November 19, 1942.
33. GSP diary, November 24, 1942, box 2, file 13.
34. Special Order 15, November 25, 1942, Patton Scrapbooks, reel 3, GSP Collection.
35. Michael J. McKeogh and Richard Lockridge, *Sgt. Mickey and General Ike* (New York: G. P. Putnam Sons, 1946), 55; GSP to BAP, December 2, 1942, box 10, file 12, GSP Collection.
36. GSP diary, December 6, 1942, box 2, file 13.
37. Norman Gelb, *Desperate Venture: The Story of Operation Torch, the Allied Invasion of North Africa* (New York: W. Morrow, 1992), 270; Rick Atkinson, *An Army at Dawn: The War in North Africa, 1942-1943* (New York: Henry Holt, 2002), 219-29.
38. Carlo D'Este, *Eisenhower: A Soldier's Life* (New York: Henry Holt, 2002), 370.
39. Paul McDonald Robinett, *Armor Command: The Personal Story of a Commander of the 13th Armored Regiment, of the CCB, 1st Armored Division, and of the Armored School during World War II* (Washington, D.C.: McGregor and Weener, 1958), 110.
40. Mark Clark, *Calculated Risk* (New York: Harper, 1950), 139.
41. Account of General Patton's Visit to the Tunisian Front, box 2, file 13, GSP Collection; Eisenhower, *Crusade in Europe*, 141.
42. GSP to BAP, December 20, 1942, box 10, file 12, GSP Collection.
43. Robert Allen collection, unpublished diary, 8, the George S. Patton Museum; GSP diary, December 23, 1942, box 2, file 13.
44. D'Este, *Eisenhower*, 372.
45. George S. Patton Jr., *War as I Knew It* (New York: Great Commanders, 1975), 20-21.
46. GSP diary, January 4, 1943, box 2, file 13.
47. DDE to GCM, January 17, 1943, Eisenhower Papers, page 908, Dwight D. Eisenhower Presidential Library and Museum.
48. Charles Codman, *Drive* (Boston: Little, Brown, 1957), 67; GSP to Everett Hughes, January 26, 1943, box II-1, file 11, Everett S. Hughes Collection, LOC.
49. Eisenhower, 135.
50. Crosswell, 368, 374.
51. Butcher, *My Three Years with Eisenhower*, 237-38; Devers to BAP, February 12, 1943, box 10, file 14, GSP Collection.
52. GSP diary, January 16-17, 1943, box 2, file 13.

53. Butcher, 283.
54. GSP diary, January 15–18, 1943, box 2, file 13; GSP to BAP, January 11, 1943, box 10, file 13, GSP Collection.
55. GSP diary, January 16, 1943, box 2, file 13.
56. GSP diary, January 28, 1943, box 2, file 14.
57. Clark, *Calculated Risk*, 145; Carlo D'Este, *Patton: A Genius for War* (New York: HarperCollins, 1995), 452.
58. GSP diary, February 2, 1943, box 2, file 14.
59. DDE to GSP, February 4, Eisenhower Papers, page 938–39; GSP to BAP, February 23, 1943, box 10, file 14, GSP Collection.
60. Francis De Guingand, *Operation Victory* (New York: Charles Scribner's Sons, 1947), 234.
61. Rupert Clarke, *With Alex at War: From the Irrawaddy to the Po, 1941–1945* (London: L. Cooper, 2000), 102–3.
62. GSP to BAP, December 20, 1942, box 10, file 12, GSP Collection; GSP diary, March 1, 1942, box 2, file 14, GSP Collection.
63. Citation by Col. Peter C. Hains, March 12, 1943, box 10, file 14, GSP Collection; GSP diary, March 2, 1943, box 2, file 14.

Chapter Four

1. Carlo D'Este, *Eisenhower: A Soldier's Life* (New York: Henry Holt, 2002), 397.
2. Christopher Rein, "Fredendall Failure: A Reexamination of the II Corps at the Battle of Kaserine Pass," *Army History*, PB 20-18-3, no. 108 (Summer 2018): 11.
3. Steven Thomas Barry, *Battalion Commanders at War: U.S. Army Tactical Leadership in the Mediterranean Theater, 1942–1943* (Lawrence: University Press of Kansas, 2013), 76.
4. Steven L. Ossad, "Command Failures: Lessons Learned from Lloyd R. Fredendall," *Army* 53, no. 3 (March 2003): 45–51.
5. Douglas Porch, *The Path to Victory: The Mediterranean Theater in World War II* (Old Saybrook, CT: Konecky and Konecky, 2004), 373.
6. Martin Blumenson, *Kasserine Pass: Rommel's Bloody, Climactic Battle for Tunisia* (New York: Cooper's Square, 2000), 303-4; Paul Kennedy, *Engineers of Victory: The Problem Solvers Who Turned the Tide in the Second World War* (New York: Random House, 2013), 147; D'Este, *Eisenhower*, 360, 393; Porch, *Path to Victory*, 372.
7. Rupert Clarke, *With Alex at War: From the Irrawaddy to the Po, 1941–1945* (London: L. Cooper, 2000), 84.
8. Rein, "Fredendall Failure," 12, 13; D'Este, *Eisenhower*, 396–97.
9. GSP diary, March 2–12, 1943, box 2, file 14.
10. GSP diary, March 2, 1943, box 2, file 14.
11. Paul Harkins photo album, Album 1, USAHEC; Martin Blumenson, ed., *The Patton Papers*, vol. 2, *1940–1945* (Boston: Houghton Mifflin, 1974) 182; Leo Barron, *Patton's First Victory: How General George S. Patton Turned the Tide in North Africa and Defeated the Afrika Korps at El Guettar* (Guilford, CT: Stackpole, 2018), 2.
12. GSP diary, March 5, 1943, box 2, file 14.
13. Harry C. Butcher, *My Three Years with Eisenhower: The Personal Diary of*

Captain Harry C. Butcher, USNR, Naval Aide to General Eisenhower (New York: Simon and Schuster, 1946), 273.

14. Robert St. John, "People," NBC, March 3, 1943, box 10, file 15, GSP Collection.

15. D. K. R. Crosswell, *Beetle: The Life of General Walter Bedell Smith* (Lexington: University Press of Kentucky, 2010), 374.

16. Omar N. Bradley, *A Soldier's Story* (New York: Modern Library, 1999), 43.

17. GSP to BAP, March 13 and 15, 1943, box 10, file 15, GSP Collection; James Wellard, *General George S. Patton Jr.: Man Under Mars* (New York: Dodd, Mead, 1946), 78.

18. Bradley, *A Soldier's Story*, 45.

19. Barron, *Patton's First Victory*, xxviii.

20. Jack Copeland, WWII Veterans Surveys, Numbered Armies, box 1, USAHEC; GSP diary, March 6, 1943, box 2, file 14.

21. "8th Armored Unit Plans Bring Promotions to 5," *Courier Journal*, March 13, 1942, 4; Gerald Astor, *Terrible Terry Allen: Combat General of World War II: The Life of an American Soldier* (New York: Ballantine, 2003), 14, 20, 122; Orr Kelly, *Meeting the Fox: The Allied Invasion of Africa, from Operation Torch to Kasserine Pass to Victory in Tunisia* (New York: John Wiley and Sons, 2002), 47; William Frye, "Gen. Terrible Terry Alen, Not So Hot in Peacetime, but a Fireball in a War," *Fort Worth Star-Telegram*, June 2, 1943, 12.

22. Memorandum to all Units, 1st Infantry Division, March 9, 1943, RG 407, Records of the Adjutant general's Office, WWII Operational Reports, 1940-48, 1st Infantry Division, box 5002, folder 301-0.3, NARA.

23. Teddy Roosevelt Jr. to Elenor Roosevelt, March 6, 1943, box 10, file 1, Theodore Roosevelt, Jr. Papers, Manuscripts Division, LOC.

24. Robert C. Weed, *In Time of War* (Tucson: Wheatmark, 2006), 146–47.

25. Martin Blumenson, *Patton: The Man behind the Legend, 1885-1945* (New York: Morrow, 1985), 183; Carlo D'Este, *Patton: Genius for War* (New York: HarperCollins, 1995), 465; General Order #6, II Corps Headquarters, March 12, 1943, box 10, file 15, GSP Collection.

26. Anna Marjorie Taylor, *The Language of World War II: Abbreviations, Captions, Quotations, Slogans, Titles and Other Terms and Phrases* (New York: H. W. Wilson, 1948), 94.

27. Albert E. Cowdrey, *Fighting for Life: American Military Medicine in World War II* (New York: Free Press), 118.

28. Arthur L. Kelly, "Andrew Kiddey," October 31, 1986, Louie B. Nunn Center for Oral History, University of Kentucky.

29. Stanley Silverman, WWII Veterans Survey, 1st Armored Division, box 6, USAHEC.

30. Alfred De Grazia, *A Taste of War: Soldiering in World War II* (Princeton, NJ: Quiddity, 1992), 146.

31. William C. Westmoreland, *A Soldier Reports* (Garden City, NY: Doubleday, 1976), 25; Weed, *In Time of War*, 143–44.

32. Harry Semmes, *Portrait of Patton* (New York: Appleton-Century-Crofts, 1955), 146.

33. Monty Boinott, interviewed by Tommy Lofton the National World War II Museum, Iowa, June 30, 2008.

34. Ralph Ingersoll, *The Battle Is the Pay-Off* (Washington, D.C.: Infantry Journal, 1943), 26; Flint Whitlock, *The Fighting First: The Untold Story of the Big Red One on D-Day* (Boulder: Westview, 2004), 15–16; Bradley, 44.

35. Astor, *Terrible Terry Allen*, 180–81.

36. John "Jack" Vessey, interview, the National World War II Museum, New Orleans, LA, no date.

37. Copeland, WWII Veterans Surveys.

38. Whitlock, *Fighting First*, 16; Stanhope Mason Papers, box 7, folder 30, page 33, McCormick Research Center, First Infantry Division Museum.

39. Max Arthur, *Forgotten Voices of World War II: A New History of World War II in the Words of the Men and Women Who Were There* (Guilford, CT: Lyons Press, 2004), 208–9.

40. Ernest D. Whitehead, *World War II: An Ex-Sergeant Remembers* (Kearney, NE: Morris, 1996), 38.

41. Homer R. Ankrum, *Dogfaces Who Smiled through Tears* (Lake Mills, IA: Graphic Publishing, 1987), 233.

42. Evelyn M. Monahan and Rosemary Neidel-Greenlee, *And If I Perish: Frontline U.S. Army Nurses in World War II* (New York: Knopf, 2003), 93.

43. Robert Henriques, *From a Biography of Myself: A Posthumous Selection of the Autobiographical Writings of Robert Henriques* (London: Western Printing Services, 1969), 115.

44. Copeland; Westmoreland, *A Soldier Reports*, 24, 25.

45. "Patton Rides Through Nazi Fire to Visit Front," AP, March 24, 1943, Patton Scrapbooks, reel 3, GSP Collection; GSP to BAP, March 11, 1943, box 10, file 15, GSP Collection.

46. F. W. Winterbotham, *The Ultra Secret* (New York: Dell, 1974), 134.

47. Alfred D. Chandler Jr., ed., *The Papers of Dwight David Eisenhower: The War Years*, vol. 2 (Baltimore: Johns Hopkins University Press, 1970), 1014; GSP diary, March 8, 1943, box 2, file 14.

48. Robert Patton, *The Pattons: A Personal History of an American Family* (New York: Crown Publishers, 1994), 261.

49. Ankrum, *Dogfaces*, 194; Rick Atkinson, *An Army at Dawn: The War in North Africa, 1942–1943* (New York: Henry Holt, 2002), 354, 476.

50. GSP diary, March 14, 1943, box 2, folder 14.

51. James M. McPherson, *Battle Cry of Freedom: The Civil War Era* (Oxford: Oxford University Press), 529, 531.

52. Dwight D. Eisenhower, *Crusade in Europe* (Garden City, NY: Doubleday, 1948), 144.

53. Barron, 117.

54. Report on Operation Conducted by II Corps United States Army Tunisia, March 15–April 10, 1943, page 2, box 10, file 17, GSP Collection.

55. GSP to BAP, March 11, 1943; Clarke, *With Alex at War*, 87.

56. GSP diary, March 12, 1943, box 2, file 14; Bradley, 46.

57. Michael J. McKeogh and Richard Lockridge, *Sgt. Mickey and General Ike* (New York: G. P. Putnam Sons, 1946), 77.
58. Ingersoll, *Battle Is the Pay-Off*, 34.
59. "Eisenhower Puts General Patton in Command," untitled and undated article, Patton Scrapbooks, reel 3, GSP Collection.
60. Weed, 130–31.

Chapter Five

1. David Irving, *The Trail of the Fox* (New York: Avon Books, 1977), 332, 334, 339.
2. GSP to BAP, March 15, 1943, box 10, file 15, GSP Collection; Norman Gelb, *Desperate Venture: The Story of Operation Torch, the Allied Invasion of North Africa* (New York: W. Morrow, 1992), 270.
3. Correlli Barnett, ed., *Hitler's Generals* (New York: Grove Weidenfeld, 1989), 349.
4. John MacVane, *Journey into War: War and Diplomacy in North Africa* (New York: D. Appleton-Century, 1943), 26–27.
5. GSP diary, March 13, 15, and 16, box 2, folder 14; Orr Kelly, *Meeting the Fox: The Allied Invasion of Africa, from Operation Torch to Kasserine Pass to Victory in Tunisia* (New York: John Wiley and Sons, 2002), 262.
6. Omar N. Bradley, *A Soldier's Story* (New York: Modern Library, 1999), 52; James Wellard, *General George S. Patton Jr.: Man Under Mars* (New York: Dodd, Mead, 1946), 88.
7. Leo Barron, *Patton's First Victory: How General George S. Patton Turned the Tide in North Africa and Defeated the Afrika Korps at El Guettar* (Guilford, CT: Stackpole, 2018), 16.
8. Barnett, *Hitler's Generals*, 350; Kelly, *Meeting the Fox*, 261.
9. Alfred D. Chandler Jr., ed., *The Papers of Dwight David Eisenhower: The War Years*, vol. 2 (Baltimore: Johns Hopkins University Press, 1970), 1059.
10. Robert C. Weed, *In Time of War* (Tucson: Wheatmark, 2006), 140–43; GSP diary, March 16, 1943, box 2, file 14; Ralph Ingersoll, *The Battle Is the Pay-Off* (Washington, D.C.: Infantry Journal, 1943), 35–36; RG 338 Records of US army Operational, Tactical and Support Operations (World War II and Thereafter), II Corps, Historical Section, Subject Files, 1943–1945, box 12, Entry P 42890, Report on Operations Conducted by II Corps, United States Army, Tunisia, March 15–April 10, 3, NARA.
11. R. J. Rogers, "*A Study of Leadership in the First Infantry Division During World War II: Terry de la Mesa Allen and Clarence Ralph Huebner*" (MA thesis, U.S. Army Command and General Staff College, 1965), 23, 24.
12. Alan Moorehead, *The End in Africa* (New York: Harper and Brothers, 1943), 165.
13. MacVane, *Journey into War*, 231–32; GSP diary, March 17, 1943, box 2, folder 14.
14. GSP to BAP, March 15, 1943, box 10, file 16, GSP Collection.
15. Barnett, 350.
16. Chandler, *Papers of Dwight David Eisenhower*, vol. 2, 1042.
17. GSP to BAP, March 15, 1943, box 10, file 16, GSP Collection.

18. GSP diary, March 17, 1943, box 2, file 14.
19. GSP to BAP, March 19, 1943, box 10, file 16, GSP Collection.
20. Paul McDonald Robinett, *Armor Command: The Personal Story of a Commander of the 13th Armored Regiment, of the CCB, 1st Armored Division, and of the Armored School during World War II* (Washington, D.C.: McGregor and Weener, 1958), 204.
21. Chandler, vol. 2., 1048, 1049.
22. GSP diary, March 17, 1943.
23. Captain Richard Jenson to BAP, March 20, 1943, box 10, file 16, GSP Collection.
24. 338 Records of US army Operational, Tactical and Support Operations (World War II and Thereafter), II Corps, Historical Section, Subject Files, 1943–1945, box 12, Entry P 42890, Report on Operations Conducted by II Corps, United States Army, Tunisia, March 15–April 15, 3, NARA.
25. Bradley, *A Soldier's Story* 60; Chandler, vol. 2, 1056.
26. Paul O. Huber, interview by Winston P. Erickson, July 14, 2000, tapes nos. 69 and 70, "Saving the Legacy: An Oral History of Utah's World War II Veterans," Special Collections department, University of Utah.
27. GSP diary, March 21, 1943, box 2, file 14; GSP to General Malin Craig, March 22, 1943, box 10, file 16, GSP Collection; Barron, *Patton's First Victory*, 25, 26.
28. Rick Atkinson, *An Army at Dawn: The War in North Africa, 1942–1943* (New York: Henry Holt, 2002), 446.
29. Kelly, 265.
30. GSP diary, March 22, 1943, box 2, file 14.
31. Barron, 56, 66.
32. Wellard, *General George S. Patton Jr.*, 64, 96; Barron, xi, 105, 162; Atkinson, *An Army at Dawn*, 441.
33. Clift Andrus, "Notes on Bradley's Memoirs," 51-1, 51-2, McCormick Research Center, First Division Museum at Cantigny.
34. William O. Darby, *Darby's Rangers: We Led the Way* (San Rafael, CA: Presidio), 77.
35. Gerald Astor, *Terrible Terry Allen: Combat General of World War II: The Life of an American Soldier* (New York: Ballantine, 2003), 164, 166, 168, 169.
36. Barron, 130, 159.
37. Atkinson, 444.
38. GSP diary, March 22, 1943, box 2, file 14.
39. Edward Opal, WWII Veterans Survey, 1st Infantry Division, 18th IN regiment, box 1, USAHEC.
40. Atkinson, 443.
41. Rogers, "Study of Leadership," 28; GSP diary, March 24, 1943, box 2, file 14.
42. "Patton Stickler for Rules Even during Battle," *AP*, March 30, 1942, Patton Scrapbooks, reel 4, GSP Collection.
43. MacVane, 260.
44. "Patton Rides through Nazi Fire to Visit Front," *AP*, March 24, 1943, Patton Scrapbooks, reel 3, GSP Collection.

45. Christopher M. Rein, *The North African Air Campaign: U.S. Army Air Forces from El Alamien to Salerno* (Lawrence: University Press of Kansas, 2012), 122.
46. GSP to BAP, June 1, 1943, box 11, file 2, GSP Collection.
47. Evelyn M. Monahan and Rosemary Neidel-Greenlee, *And If I Perish: Frontline U.S. Army Nurses in World War II* (New York: Knopf, 2003), 95.
48. Wellard, 18.
49. Interview with Philip Cochran, October 21, 1975, Air Force Oral History Interview (#K239.0512-876) Nimitz Education and Research Center, The National Museum of the Pacific War, Fredericksburg, Texas, 24.
50. Bradley, 64.
51. GSP diary, March 24, 1943, box 2, file 14.
52. Atkinson, 450; GSP diary, March 24, 1943.
53. Barron, 173, 181.
54. GSP diary, March 25, 1943, box 2, file 14.
55. Douglas Porch, *The Path to Victory: The Mediterranean Theater in World War II* (Old Saybrook, CT: Konecky and Konecky, 2004), 401–2; Edwin P. Hoyt, *The GI's War: American Soldiers in Europe during World War II* (New York: Cooper Square, 2000), 182.
56. GSP diary, March 26, 1943, box 2, file 14.
57. Kevin M. Hymel, "Commanding Patton's Personal Tanks," *WWII Quarterly* 9, no. 2 (Fall 2017): 22; Chandler, vol. 2, 1055–57, 1059; Adele Ulman to Landon Morris, August 22, 1944, box 12, file 7, GSP Collection.
58. GSP diary, March 26, 1943; George F. Howe, *Northwest Africa: Seizing the Initiative in the West* (Washington, D.C.: U.S. Government Printing Office, 1957), 582.
59. Henry Gerard Phillips, *El Guettar: Crucible of Leadership* (Penn Valley, CA: Henry Gerard Phillips, 1991), 5.
60. GSP diary, March 27, 1943, box 2, file 14.
61. GSP diary, March 28, 1943, box 2, folder 14.
62. Hamilton H. Howze, *A Cavalryman's Story: Memoirs of a Twentieth-Century Army General* (Washington, D.C.: Smithsonian Institution, 1996), 164, 165.
63. Howe, *Northwest Africa*, 568, 569.
64. Phillips, *El Guettar*, 38.
65. GSP diary, March 28, 1943.
66. Frederick Ayer, *Before the Colors Fade: Portrait of a Soldier: George S. Patton, Jr.* (Atlanta: Cherokee, 1964), 151. Patton, of course, did not command an army at the time. Either he meant to say "corps," or the incident occurred in Sicily but Patton misplaced it in telling the story to Ayer. GSP diary, March 29, 1943, box 2, file 14.
67. Hymel, "Commanding Patton's Personal Tanks," 22.
68. GSP diary, March 29, 1943; Barron, 185.
69. Interview with Ben Franklin by G. Kurt Piehler, John B. Romeiser, and Braum Lincoln Denton, November 19, 2004, Veteran Oral History Project, University of Tennessee.
70. Phillips, 55.

71. "Yanks Gain Ground," *Stars and Stripes*, European Theater of Operations, March 31, 1943, page 1.
72. GSP diary, March 30, 1943, box 2, file 14.
73. GSP to BAP, March 30, 1943, box 10, file 16, GSP Collection.
74. Phillips, 55; GSP diary, March 31, 1943, box 2, file 14.

Chapter Six

1. Jack W. Copeland, *Secrets of an Army Private*, unpublished memoir, WWII Veterans Survey Collection, Numbered Armies, box 1 of 2, folder: Copeland, Jack, USAHEC, 47, 49.
2. Copeland, *Secrets*, 48.
3. Copeland, 48.
4. Copeland, 48.
5. Copeland, 48.
6. Copeland, 48.
7. Kevin Hymel, "Commanding Patton's Personal Tanks," *WWII Quarterly* 9, no. 2 (Fall 2017): 23. Craig remembered the attack not coming from the Luftwaffe but from German artillery.
8. Copeland, 49.
9. Copeland, 49.
10. GSP to Echo Jenson, box 4, George S. Patton Papers, USAHEC.
11. Hansen War Diary, April 1, 1943, box 4, folder 1, series II, Chester Hansen Collection, USAHEC (henceforth Hansen War Diary); Bradley, *Soldier's*, 17.
12. Copeland, 49.
13. Alfred D. Chandler Jr., ed., *The Papers of Dwight David Eisenhower: The War Years*, vol. 2 (Baltimore: Johns Hopkins University Press, 1970), 1011.
14. GSP to BAP, March 6, 1943, box 10, file 15, GSP Collection.
15. Copeland, 49.
16. Chandler, *Papers of Dwight David Eisenhower*, vol. 2, 1011; Copeland, 49.
17.17 Dwight D. Eisenhower, *Crusade in Europe* (Garden City, NY: Doubleday, 1948), 150.
18. GSP to BAP, April 1, 1943, box 10, file 17, GSP Collection.
19. GSP to Echo Jenson, box 4, George S. Patton Jr. Papers, USAHEC.
20. Hansen War Diary, April 2, 1943, box 4, folder 1, series II. There are no records of II Corps for the month of April 1943 at the National Archives at College Park, Maryland, to corroborate or deny any of the versions of Jenson's death. As Copeland prepared his memoir, he wrote a letter to then-retired Lieutenant Colonel Chester Hansen in 1995, asking if he remembered the same story. Hansen wrote Copeland back on August 28, 1995. He maintained the Benson Force story but admitted the following: "I frequently recall how Dick Jenson was killed. While you were firing that '50, I headed into a slit trench along with Dick, General Bradley and Lou Bridge. Indeed, you may have been one of the guys to lift Dick's body into my jeep." So while Hansen's letter does not place Patton at the scene, it does place Copeland there, firing the .50 caliber machine gun, just as Copeland claimed.
21. Hymel, "Commanding Patton's Personal Tanks," 23.

22. Oversized 14, GSP Collection.
23. GSP diary, April 2, 1943, box 2, file 13.
24. Copeland, 50.
25. Copeland, 49.
26. GSP diary, April 1, 1943, box 2, file 13.
27. Max Arthur, "Obituary: Maj-Gen Sir Charles Dunphie," *Independent Sunday*, February 24, 1999, http://www.independent.co.uk/arts-entertainment/obituary-majgen-sir-charles-dunphie-1072843.html.
28. Omar N. Bradley, *A Soldier's Story* (New York: Modern Library, 1999), 61, 62.
29. Copeland; GSP to BAP, February 20, 1944, box 11, file 15, GSP Collection. Codman eventually did, when his wife published his letters after his death, for the book, *Drive*.
30. George F. Howe, *Northwest Africa: Seizing the Initiative in the West* (Washington, D.C.: U.S. Government Printing Office, 1957), 572].
31. GSP diary, April 2, 1943; Eisenhower, *Crusade in Europe*, 118.
32. Henry Gerard Phillips, *El Guettar: Crucible of Leadership* (Penn Valley, CA: Henry Gerard Phillips), 57.
33. Phillips, *El Guettar*, 58.
34. Christopher M. Rein, *The North African Air Campaign: U.S. Army Air Forces from El Alamien to Salerno* (Lawrence: University Press of Kansas, 2012), 123.
35. Chandler, vol. 2, 1073, 1074.
36. D. K. R. Crosswell, *Beetle: The Life of General Walter Bedell Smith* (Lexington, University Press of Kentucky, 2010), 394.
37. GSP diary, April 3, 1943, box 2, file 14; Arthur Tedder, *With Prejudice: The World War II Memoirs of Marshal of the Royal Air Force Lord Tedder, Deputy Supreme Commander of the Allied Expeditionary Force* (Boston: Little, Brown, 1966), 411; Bradley, *A Soldier's Story*, 64; Chester Hansen Diary, April 3, 1943, USAHAC; Hymel, 22.
38. GSP diary, April 3, 1943; GSP to BAP, April 8, 1943, box 10, file 17, GSP Collection.
39. GSP diary, April 3, 1943; GSP to BAP, April 8, 1943.
40. Chandler, vol. 2, 1073, 1074.
41. Bradley, 65.
42. Ernest Harmon, *Combat Commander: Autobiography of a Soldier* (Englewood Cliffs, NJ: Prentice Hall, 1970), 123–24.
43. William C. Westmoreland, *A Soldier Reports* (Garden City, NY: Doubleday, 1976), 25; GSP to BAP, June 1, 1943, box 11, file 2, GSP Collection.
44. Harmon, *Combat Commander*, 125.
45. GSP diary, January 18, 1944, box 3, file 4; GSP diary, April 6, 1943, box 2, file 14; Oversized, 12, 60, GSP Collection; GSP to BAP, April 17, 1943, box 10, file 15, GSP Collection.
46. GSP diary, April 7, 1943, box 2, file 14; Phillips, 64.
47. GSP diary, April 7, 1943; Hansen War Diary, April 7, 1943.
48. Orr Kelly, *Meeting the Fox: The Allied Invasion of Africa, from Operation Torch to Kasserine Pass to Victory in Tunisia* (New York: John Wiley and Sons, 2002), 283.

49. Eugene Wington, WWII Veterans Survey, 1st Armored Division, box 1, USAHEC.
50. Walter S. Andariese, *World War II thru Korea* (Hastings, NE: Snell, 1974), 21–22.
51. GSP diary, April 7, 1943.
52. "Patton Lauds Corps for Winning Battle," *Washington Post*, April 13, 1943, Patton Scrapbooks, reel 4, GSP Collection.
53. GSP diary, April 9, 1943, box 2, file 15.
54. Barrett McGurn, *YANK, the Army Weekly: Reporting the Greatest Generation* (Golden, CO: Fulcrum, 2004), 150–51.
55. GSP diary, April 10, 1943, box 2, file 15; GSP to BAP, April 13, 1943, box 10, file 17, GSP Collection; GSP to Henry Cabot Lodge, April 21, 1943, box 10, file 17, GSP Collection.
56. GSP diary, April 10, 1943; Harmon, 126.
57. Robert Marsh, WWII Veterans Survey, 1st Armored Division, box 4, USAHEC.
58. Crosswell, *Beetle*, 398.
59. Bradley, 67; Kelly, *Meeting the Fox*, 304.
60. Rick Atkinson, *An Army at Dawn: The War in North Africa, 1942-1943* (New York: Henry Holt, 2002), 477; GSP to General Alexander, GSP diary, April 11, 1943, box 2, file 14.
61. GSP diary, April 11–12, 1943, box 2, file 15.
62. Harmon, 128.
63. GSP to BAP, April 13, 1943.
64. James M. McPherson, *Battle Cry of Freedom: The Civil War Era* (Oxford: Oxford University Press, 1988), 528, 530; GSP diary, April 15–16, 1943, box 2, file 15.
65. Earl Harold Alexander of Tunis, *The Alexander Memoirs: 1940–1945* (London: Frontline Books, 2010), 44.
66. DDE to GSP, April 14, 1943, box 10, file 17, GSP Collection.
67. Paul D. Harkins, *When the Third Cracked Europe: The Story of Patton's Incredible Army* (Harrisburg, PA: Stackpole, 1969), 15.
68. GSP diary, April 15, 1943, box 2, file 15,; Oversized 14, 17, GSP Collection.

Chapter Seven

1. Interview with Philip Cochran, October 21, 1975, Air Force Oral History Interview (#K239.0512-876), Nimitz Education and Research Center, The National Museum of the Pacific War, Fredericksburg, Texas, 89, 90.
2. Carlo D'Este, *Eisenhower: A Soldier's Life* (New York: Henry Holt, 2002), 377.
3. GSP diary, April 16, 1943, box 2, file 15.
4. GSP diary, April 16, 1943.
5. Harry C. Butcher, *My Three Years with Eisenhower: The Personal Diary of Captain Harry C. Butcher, USNR, Naval Aide to General Eisenhower* (New York: Simon and Schuster, 1946), 287–88.
6. Everett Hughes diary, April 17, 1943, box I-2, file 3, Everett Hughes Papers, Manuscript Division, LOC (hereafter Hughes Papers).

NOTES TO CHAPTER SEVEN

7. Everett S. Hughes to Theresa Hughes, May 2, 1943, box II-1, file 15, Hughes Papers.
8. Hugh Pond, *Sicily* (London: W. Kimber, 1962), 11, 29, 30, 44.
9. Albert N. Garland and Howard McGaw Smyth, *Sicily and the Surrender of Italy* (Washington, D.C.: U.S. Government Printing Office, 1965), 34.
10. Alfred D. Chandler Jr. ed., *The Papers of Dwight David Eisenhower: The War Years*, vol. 2 (Baltimore: Johns Hopkins University Press), 1046.
11. GSP diary, April 21, 1943, box 2, file 15.
12. *Time* magazine, April 12, 1943, page 31; GSP to BAP, May 10, 1943, box 11, file 1, GSP Collection.
13. James M. Gavin, *On to Berlin: Battles of an Airborne Commander, 1943–1946* (New York: Viking, 1978), 17.
14. Jack Copeland, WWII Veterans Survey, Numbered Armies, box 1, USAHEC.
15. Copeland.
16. Ronald Lewin, *Ultra Goes to War: The First Account of World War II's Greatest Secret Based on Official Documents* (New York: McGraw-Hill, 1978), 280.
17. Gerald Astor, *Terrible Terry Allen: Combat General of World War II: The Life of an American Soldier* (New York: Ballantine, 2003), 189; Martin Blumenson, ed., *The Patton Papers*, vol. 2, *1940–1945* (Boston: Houghton Mifflin, 1974), 257.
18. Samuel Eliot Morison, *History of the United States Naval Operations in World War II: Sicily—Salerno—Anzio*, vol. 9 (Boston: Little, Brown, 1975), 21–22.
19. GSP diary, April 29, 1943, box 2, file 15.
20. GSP diary, April 29, 1943.
21. Nigel Hamilton, *Monty: The Battles of Field Marshal Bernard Montgomery* (New York: Random House, 1994), 179, 180; Bernard Montgomery, *The Memoirs of Field Marshal the Viscount Montgomery of Alamein, K.G.* (Cleveland: World Publishing, 1958), 158.
22. GSP diary, May 3, 1943, box 2, file 15; Herbert Mitgang, *Newsmen in Khaki: Tales of a World War II Soldier Correspondent* (Lanham, MD: Taylor Trade, 2004), 82.
23. Morison, *History*, vol. 9, 20; GSP diary, May 3, 1943.
24. GSP to BAP, May 7, 1943, box 11, file 1, GSP Collection.
25. Everett Hughes diary notes, May 7-8, 1943, box I-2, file 3, Hughes Papers.
26. GSP diary, May 7, 1943, box 2, file 15.
27. Garland and Smyth, *Sicily and the Surrender of Italy*, 89, 91.
28. GSP to BAP, June 26, 1943, box 11, file 2, GSP Collection.
29. GSP diary, May 16 and 17, 1943, box 2, file 15,.
30. GSP diary, May 8, 1943, box 2, file 15.
31. GSP diary, May 11, 1943, box 2, file 15.
32. GSP diary, June 25, 1943, box 2, file 15; Robert Winkel, unpublished memoir, page 12, Veterans History Project, LOC.
33. GSP diary, June 9, 1943, box 2, file 15.
34. GSP diary, May 6, 13, and 18, 1943, box 2, file 15; Harry Semmes, *Portrait of Patton* (New York: Appleton-Century, 1955), 155.
35. Winkel, unpublished memoir.

36. Homer R. Ankrum, *Dogfaces Who Smiled through Tears* (Lake Mills, IA: Graphic Publishing, 1987), 293.
37. Charles Codman, *Drive* (Boston: Little, Brown, 1957), 94.
38. GSP diary, June 20, 1943, box 2, file 15; GSP to BAP, May 21, 1943, box 11, file 1.
39. Chandler, *Papers of Dwight David Eisenhower*, vol. 2, 1141, 1142; GSP diary, May 5 and 17, 1943, box 2, file 15; Omar N. Bradley, *A Soldier's Story* (New York: Modern Libaray, 1999), 106.
40. Copeland.
41. GSP diary, May 16 and 20, 1943, box 2, file 15; GSP to BAP, May 21, 1943.
42. GSP diary, June 1 and 2, 1943, box 2, file 15.
43. Bradley, *A Soldier's Story*, 119.
44. Notes on the Arab, GSP diary, June 1943, box 2, file 15.
45. GSP to BAP, June 26, 1943, box 11, file 2, GSP Collection.
46. Letter of Instruction, GSP diary, June 5, 1943, box 2, file 15.
47. GSP to General Leslie McNair, June 8, 1943, RG 337, HQS, Commanding General, General Corres, file 1940-44, box 10, NARA.
48. GSP diary, June 14, 1943, box 2, file 15.
49. Louis P. Lochner, ed., *The Goebbels Diaries 1942-1943* (Garden City, NY: Doubleday, 1948), 311.
50. Albert C. Wedemeyer, *Wedemeyer Reports!* (New York: Henry Holt, 1958), 222.
51. A. C. Wedemeyer, Memorandum for the Chief of Staff, July 23, 1943, Papers of Everett S. Hughes, box 6, file 4, LOC.
52. GSP diary, June 21, 1943, box 2, file 15.
53. George S. Patton, Jr., *War as I Knew It* (New York: Great Commanders, 1975), 34-35.
54. Garland and Smyth, 101.
55. Garland and Smyth, 93, 94, 95.
56. Earl Harold Alexander of Tunis, *The Alexander Memoirs: 1940-1945* (London: Frontline, 2010), 46.
57. Chandler, vol. 2, 1167.
58. Flint Whitlock, *The Rock of Anzio: From Sicily to Dachau: A History of the 45th Infantry Division* (Boulder: Westview, 1998), 29.
59. James M. Gavin, "Two Fighting Generals: Patton and MacArthur" *ARMY* 15, no. 4 (April 1965): 32-33; Ed Ruggero, *Combat Jump: The Young Men Who Led the Assault into Fortress Europe, July 1943* (New York: HarperCollins, 2003), 120-21.
60. John M. Taylor, *General Maxwell Taylor: The Sword and the Pen* (New York: Doubleday, 1989), 47.
61. Paul Carter, interview, the National World War II Museum, no date.
62. Whitlock, *Rock of Anzio*, 34.
63. Testimony of Colonel Forrest E. Cookson, February 16,1944, RG 159, Entry 26F, Office of the Inspector General, General Correspondence, 1939-1947, folder

333.9, box 67, NARA; James J. Weingartner, "Massacre at Biscari: Patton and an American War Crime," 30; GSP diary, April 4, 1944, box 3, file 4. One account has him saying "That bastard will die!"

64. Interview, Bob Bosser with author, April 16, 2010.

65. GSP diary, June 21, 1943, box 2, file 15; GSP to BAP, June 16, 1943, box 11, file 2, GSP Collection; interview with Mr. Charles Scheffel, by Barry Basten, Admiral Nimitz National Museum of the Pacific War, Fredericksburg, Texas, May 10, 2000, 23.

66. John A. Heintges Papers, Oral History, vols. 1–3, USAHEC, 157.

67. Hugh A. Scott, *The Blue and White Devils: A Personal Memoir and History of the Third Infantry Division in World War II* (Nashville: Battery, 1984), 37.

68. Franklyn Johnson, *One More Hill* (New York: Funk & Wagnalls, 1949), 78–79.

69. Ben Macintyre, *Operation Mincemeat: How a Dead Man and a Bizarre Plan Fooled the Nazis and Assured an Allied Victory* (New York: Broadway Books, 2010), 270.

70. "Notes on Planning and Assault Phases of the Sicilian Campaign" by A Military Observer (later identified as Robert Henriques), COHQ Bulletin No. Y/1, II Corps, Historical Section, Subject Files 1943–1945, RG 338, box 12, NARA.

71. "Rough Tough Warrior Patton Is a Poet; His prayer to 'God of Battles' Acclaimed," *New York Times*, August 22, 1943, Patton Scrapbooks, reel 4, GSP Collection.

72. Morison, vol. 9, 61.

73. GSP diary, June 21, 1943, box 2, file 15.

74. John Lucas diary, June 5, 1943, box 4, John P. Lucas Papers, USAHEC.

75. John Lucas diary, June 5, 1943; GSP diary, July 6, 1943, box 3, file 1.

76. GSP diary, June 30, 1943, box 2, file 15.

77. Douglas Porch, *The Path to Victory: The Mediterranean Theater in World War II* (Old Saybrook, CT: Konecky and Konecky, 2004), 426.

78. GSP diary, July 6, 1943, box 2, file 15; Morison, *History*, vol. 9, 64.

79. Philip Gerard, *Secret Soldiers: The Story of World War II's Heroic Army of Deception* (New York: Penguin, 2002), 78.

80. Untitled article by Alexander Clifford, AP, July 6, 1943, Patton Scrapbooks, reel 5, GSP Collection; GSP diary, July 7, 1943, box 2, file 15,.

81. Semmes, *Portrait of Patton*, 161.

82. GSP to Everett Hughes, June 25 and July 8, 1943, box II-1, file 17, Hughes Papers.

83. GSP to BAP, July 5, 1943, box 11, file 3, GSP Collection.

84. Hansen War Diary, July 10, 1943, box 4, file 2, Chester B. Hansen Collection, USAHEC.

85. Garland and Smyth, 111.

86. Hobart R. Gay Papers, diary, July–September 1943, May–December 1944, box 2, page 97, USAHEC.

Chapter Eight

1. Albert N. Garland and Howard McGaw Smyth, *Sicily and the Surrender of Italy* (Washington, D.C.: U.S. Government Printing Office, 1965), 117, 118, 119; William Breuer, *Drop Zone Sicily: Allied Airborne Strike, July 1943* (Novato, CA: Presidio, 1983), 56, 57.

2. General Albert Weydemeyer, postwar interview, Albert Weydemeyer Papers, box 6, folder 3, Hoover Institution Archives, Stamford University.

3. Untitled article by Alexander Clifford, *AP*, July 6, 1943, Patton Scrapbooks, reel 5, GSP Collection.

4. Donald E. Houston, *Hell on Wheels: The 2d Armored Division* (San Rafael, CA: Presidio, 1977), 162; Garland and Smyth, *Sicily and the Surrender of Italy*, 158; Hugh Pond, *Sicily* (London: W. Kimber, 1962), 88, 89.

5. "Notes on Planning and Assault Phases of the Sicilian Campaign" by a Military Observer (later identified as Robert Henriques), COHQ Bulletin No. Y/1, II Corps, Historical Section, Subject Files 1943–1945, RG 338, box 12, NARA.

6. GSP diary, July 10, 1943, box 3, file 1.

7. Carlyle Holt, "How General Patton, A Timid Soul, Was Saved by Bone-Handled Pistols off Casablanca," unknown publisher, May 25, 1946, Patton Scrapbooks, reel 1, GPS Collection.

8. Garland and Smyth, *Sicily and the Surrender of Italy*, 176.

9. Ladislas Farago, *Patton: Ordeal and Triumph* (New York: Ivan Obolensky, 1964), 298.

10. Noel Monks, *Eyewitness* (London: Frederick Muller, 1955), 187.

11. Pond, *Sicily*, 90, 92.

12. William O. Darby, *Darby's Rangers: We Led the Way* (San Rafael, CA: Presidio, 1980), 90.

13. "Comments on General Patton" by Russel B. Reynolds, Army Retired File, box 1, Russel B. Reynolds Papers, USAHEC; GSP to McNair, August 2, 1943, box 11, file 5, GSP Collection.

14. Blythe Foote Finke, *No Mission Too Difficult!: Old Buddies of the 1st Division Tell All about World War II* (Chicago: Contemporary Books, 1995), 130; Edward L. Trey, interview by author, December 27, 2010; and Robert W. Black, *Rangers in World War II* (New York: Ivy Books, 1992), 94.

15. Charles B. Odom, *General George S. Patton and Eisenhower* (New Orleans: World Picture Productions, 1985), 9.

16. Samuel W. Mitcham Jr. and Friedrich von Stauffenberg, *The Battle of Sicily: How the Allies Lost Their Chance for Total Victory* (Mechanicsburg, PA: Stackpole, 2007), 125, 126.

17. James Altieri, *The Spearheaders* (New York: Bobbs-Merrill, 1960), 283; GSP diary, July 11, 1943, box 3, file 1.

18. Malcolm S. MacLean, "Adventures in Occupied Areas" (unpublished memoir, U.S. Army War College, 1975), no pages; GSP diary, December 1, 1943, box 3, file 4; Adrian R. Lewis, *Omaha Beach: A Flawed Victory* (Chapel Hill: University of North Carolina Press, 2001), 59.

19. Pond, 97, 98.
20. Omar N. Bradley, *A Soldier's Story* (New York: Modern Library, 1999), 130.
21. GSP diary, July 11, 1943; Gerald Astor, *Terrible Terry Allen: Combat General of World War II: The Life of an American Soldier* (New York: Ballantine, 2003), 199.
22. Omar N. Bradley and Clay Blair, *A General's Life: An Autobiography by General of the Army Omar N. Bradley* (New York: Simon and Schuster, 1983), 183.
23. Paul Harkins photo album, Album 1, USAHEC; GSP diary, July 11, 1943; Hobart R. Gay Papers, Diary, July–September 1943, May–December 1944, box 2, USAHEC, 100; Odom, *Patton and Eisenhower*, 9.
24. John Lucas diary, June 12, 1943, box 4, John P. Lucas Papers, USAHEC.
25. GSP diary, July 11, 1943.
26. Garland and Smyth, 177, 180, 181, 182.
27. R. J. Rogers, "A Study of Leadership in the First Infantry Division during World War II: Terry de la Mesa Allen and Clarence Ralph Huebner" (MA thesis, U.S. Army Command and General Staff College, 1965), 44, 45.
28. GSP diary, July 12, 1943, box 3, file 1; Harry C. Butcher, *My Three Years with Eisenhower: The Personal Diary of Captain Harry C. Butcher, USNR, Naval Aide to General Eisenhower* (New York: Simon and Schuster, 1946), 360; and John Gunther, *D Day* (New York: Harper and Brothers, 1943), 69.
29. John Lucas diary, July 13, 1943, box 4, John P. Lucas Papers, USAHEC.
30. GSP diary, July 12, 1943; Butcher, *My Three Years with Eisenhower*, 360.
31. "Notes on Planning and Assault Phases of the Sicilian Campaign."
32. John Lucas diary, June 13, 1943, box 4, John P. Lucas Papers, USAHEC; Jack Copeland, WWII Veterans Survey, Numbered Armies, box 1, USAHEC; Garland and Smyth, 200; Mitcham and von Stauffenberg, *Battle of Sicily*, 195, 196; GSP diary, July 12, 1943; Pond, 115.
33. Rupert Clarke, *With Alex at War: From the Irrawaddy to the Po, 1941–1945* (London: L. Cooper, 2000), 113; James M. Gavin, "Two Fighting Generals: Patton and MacArthur," *ARMY* 15, no. 4 (April 1965): 32; idem., *On to Berlin: Battles of an Airborne Commander, 1943-1946* (New York: Viking, 1978), 43; William David Laird, unpublished memoir, 10–11, Veterans History Project, LOC.
34. Astor, *Terrible Terry Allen*, 207.
35. Charles M. Province, *The Unknown Patton* (New York: Bonanza Books, 1983), 16.
36. Altieri, *The Spearheaders*, 293.
37. Noel Monks, "Gen. Patton Wades Ashore to Battle," *London Daily Mail*, July 13, 1943, Patton Scrapbooks, reel 5, GSP Collection.
38. Alfred D. Chandler Jr., *The Papers of Dwight David Eisenhower: The War Years*, vol. 2 (Baltimore: Johns Hopkins University Press, 1970), 1255; GSP diary, July 13, 1943, box 3, file 1.
39. Christopher M. Rein, *The North African Air Campaign: U.S. Army Air Forces from El Alamein to Salerno* (Lawrence: University Press of Kansas, 2012), 152.
40. Garland and Smyth, 208, 209; John Lucas diary, July 14, 1943, box 4, John P. Lucas Papers, USAHEC; Clarke, *With Alex at War*, 113; GSP diary, July 13, 1943.

41. Mitcham and von Stauffenberg, 180.
42. GSP letter, July 12, 1943, box 11, file 3, GSP Collection; GSP letter, July 24, 1943, box 11, file 3.
43. Pond, 206.
44. Garland and Smyth, 210; GSP diary, July 14, 1943, box 3, file 1.
45. John Lucas diary, July 15, 1943, box 4, John P. Lucas Papers, USAHEC.
46. Bradley and Blair, *A General's Life*, 188; GSP to BAP, August 18, 1943, box 11, file 6, GSP Collection.
47. Oscar Koch to BG James A. Norell, December 15, 1960, RG319 Records of the Chief of Military History, Background Files: Sicily and the Surrender of Italy 1937–1967, Critique of Manuscript, Copy 2 to Progress Reports and Orders of Continuation, box 18, ARC ID 2216436 P Entry 103, NARA.
48. Lucian K. Truscott Jr., *Command Missions: A Personal Story* (Novato, CA: Presidio, 1990), 217–18.
49. GSP diary, July 14, 1943.
50. Peter Deeb, interviewed by Robert Van Hassel, June 23, 2015, New York State Military Museum, accessed 29 May 2021, https://www.youtube.com/watch?v=EErht8ctJbg&t=3743s
51. Anthony Cave Brown, *The Last Hero: Wild Bill Donovan: The Biography and Political Experience of Major General William J. Donovan* (New York: Times Books, 1982), 352.
52. GSP diary, July 15, 1943, box 3, file 1; Kevin Hymel, *Patton's Photographs: War as He Saw It* (Dulles, VA: Potomac Books, 2006).
53. Testimony of MG Troy Middleton, Office of the Inspector General, February 19, 1944, RG 159, Entry 26F, Office of the Inspector General, General Correspondence, 1939–1947, folder 333.9, box 67, NARA; GSP diary, April 5, 1944, box 3, file 5, LOC.
54. Mitcham and von Stauffenberg, 196.
55. GSP diary, July 24, 1943, box 3, file 1.
56. Mitcham and von Stauffenberg, 196; GSP diary, July 17, 1943, box 3, file 1.
57. John Lucas diary, July 20, 1943, box 4, John P. Lucas Papers, USAHEC.
58. John Lucas diary, July 21, 1943, box 4, John P. Lucas Papers, USAHEC.
59. GSP to BAP, July 16, 1943, box 11, file 3, GSP Collection.
60. GSP diary, July 15, 1943, box 3, file 1.
61. GSP to Hugh McGee, July 16, 1945, box 28, file 15, GSP Collection.
62. GSP diary, July 17, 1943, box 3, file 1.
63. General Alexander to GSP, July 16, 1943, box 3, file 1, GSP Collection.
64. "Interview with Charles Scheffel," May 10, 2000, Nimitz Education and Research Center, The National Museum of the Pacific War, Fredericksburg, Texas, 25.
65. Bradley, 140.
66. GSP diary, July 15, 1943; GSP diary, "Summary of Events," July 18, 1943, box 3, file 1.
67. Clifford Duncan, interview, Fall 2004, MS-0871, Center for Archival Collections, University Libraries, Bowling Green State University.

68. Hobart R. Gay Papers, diary, July–September 1943, May–December 1944, box 2, USAHEC, 105a.
69. GSP to BAP, July 18, 1943, box 11, file 4, GSP Collection; GSP to BAP, August 15, 1943, box 11, file 5, GSP Collection.
70. GSP diary, July 19, 1943, box 3, file 1.
71. James Holland, *Sicily '43: The First Assault on Fortress Europe* (New York: Atlantic Monthly, 2020), 374; Pond, 162.
72. Stephen Brooks, ed., *Montgomery and the Eighth Army: A Selection from the Diaries, Correspondence and Other Papers of Field Marshal the Viscount Montgomery of Alamein, August 1942 to December 1943* (London: Bodley Head for the Army Records Society, 1991), 249.
73. Nigel Hamilton, *Monty: The Battles of Field Marshal Bernard Montgomery* (New York: Random House, 1994), 180; Harry Semmes, *Portrait of Patton* (New York: Appleton-Century-Crofts, 1955), 168. Semmes interviewed Gay for his book; Gay claimed the incident took place on July 16, but Montgomery's letter is dated July 19. This makes more sense, because by the nineteenth, Truscott had captured Agrigento and the Provisional Corps had been formed.
74. GSP to BAP, July 20, 1943, box 11, file 4, GSP Collection, LOC.
75. Truscott to BG James A. Norell, January 10, 1961, RG 319 Records of the Army Staff, Office of the Chief of Military History, Background Files: Sicily and the Surrender of Italy 1937–1967, box 18, NARA.
76. Garland and Smyth, 251; Kevin M. Hymel, "The Real Fury" *WWII Quarterly* 8, no. 1 (Fall 2016): 76.
77. GSP diary, July 20, 1943, box 3, file 1.
78. Kevin M. Hymel, "Patton and the Tiger," *Supply Line* 36, no. 2 (April/May 2017): 23–25; Holland, *Sicily '43*, 204, 266, 281, 282; Hymel, *Patton's Photographs*, 35.
79. GSP to BAP, July 20, 1943, box 11, file 5, GSP Collection.
80. Robert G. Eiland, *In Some Ways It Was a Fascinating War* (Philadelphia: Xlibris, 2008), 38–39.
81. Bruce N. Monkman, *Act 2: WWII: The Adventures of Bruce N. Monkman, 1941–1945* (Los Angeles: B. N. Monkman, 2006), 48.
82. Eiland, *In Some Ways It Was a Fascinating War*, 45.
83. GSP to BAP, March 5, 19, and 23, 1944, box 11, file 16, GSP Collection; Eiland, 87; Seymore Korman, "Patton's Apology Recalls Other Tales of the General," *Fort Worth Star Telegram*, November 24, 1943, 1, 8.
84. Anders Arnbal, *The Barrel-Land Dance Hall Rangers: World War II, June 1942–February 1944* (New York: Vantage, 1993), 122–23.
85. "Charles Scheffel," by Barry Basten, Admiral Nimitz National Museum of the Pacific War, Fredericksburg, Texas, May 10, 2000, 26.
86. Truscott, *Command Missions*, 224.
87. George Griffenhagen, interview with the National World War II Museum, New Orleans, LA, May 8, 2009.
88. George E. Crago, "McCartney Remembers Well Patton's Welcome Wink," Dominion News, James R. McCartney collection, Veterans History Project, LOC; John

T. Waters, interviewed by Shaun Illingsworth, June 16, 2003, Rutgers University Oral History Archive of WWII.

89. Gordon A. Blaker, *Iron Knights: The United States 66th Armored Regiment* (Shippensburg, PA: Burd Street, 1999), 184.

90. Interview with Edward L. Trey.

91. GSP diary, July 21, 1943, box 3, file 1.

92. Garland and Smyth, 254; "Palermo a Touchdown," *AP*, July 22, 1943, Patton Scrapbooks, reel 4, GSP Collection.

93. Hobart R. Gay Papers, Oral History, box 1, USAHEC.

94. John A. Heintges Papers, Oral History, vols. 1–3, 153, 154, USAHEC.

95. GSP diary, July 22, 1943, box 3, file 1.

96. Don Whitehead, *Combat Reporter: Don Whitehead's World War II Diary and Memoirs*, edited by John B. Romeiser (New York: Fordham University Press, 2006), 173.

97. Truscott, 227.

98. GSP diary, July 22, 1943; FDR to GSP, August 4, 1943, box 11, file 5, GSP Collection; Pond, 193.

99. GSP diary, July 22, 1943.

100. "Patton's Men," *Time*, August 2, 1943, page 67.

101. Whitehead, *Combat Reporter*, 178; Richard Tregaskis, *Invasion Diary* (New York: Random House, 1944), 24.

102. Bradley and Blair, 191, 192.

103. GSP to BAP, August 9, 1943, box 11, file 5, GSP Collection.

104. John McManus, *American Courage, American Carnage: 7th Infantry Chronicles: The 7th Infantry Regiment's Combat Experience, 1812 through World War II* (New York: Forge, 2009), 338.

105. GSP diary, July 25, 1943, box 3, file 2.

106. GSP to Brigadier General Wedemeyer, August 1, 1943, box 11, file 5, GSP Collection; Hymel, *Patton's Photographs*, 37.

Chapter Nine

1. Lucian K. Truscott Jr., *Command Missions: A Personal Story* (Novato, CA: Presidio, 1990), 227.

2. Flint Whitlock, *The Rock of Anzio: From Sicily to Dachau: A History of the 45th Infantry Division* (Boulder: Westview, 1998), 53.

3. Raymond Clapper, "Palermo's Fall," unknown source, August 26, 1943, Patton Scrapbooks, reel 4, GSP Collection; GSP diary, July 23, 1943, box 3, file 2.

4. GSP diary, September 13, 1943, box 3, file 3.

5. Albert N. Garland and Howard McGaw Smyth, *Sicily and the Surrender of Italy* (Washington, D.C.: U.S. Government Printing Office, 1965), 255.

6. GSP diary, July 24, 1943, box 3, file 2.

7. John Lucas diary, June 25, 1943, box 4, John P. Lucas Papers, USAHEC; GSP diary, July 24, 1943.

8. GSP diary, July 25, 1943, box 3, file 2.
9. Rupert Clarke, *With Alex at War: From the Irrawaddy to the Po, 1941–1945* (London: L. Cooper, 2000), 119.
10. GSP diary, July 25, 1943; Hobart R. Gay Papers, diary, July 25, 1943, box 2, USAHEC.
11. GSP diary, July 25, 1943.
12. Hugh Pond, *Sicily* (London: W. Kimber, 1962), 206.
13. Garland and Smyth, *Sicily and the Surrender of Italy*, 266–68.
14. Thomas E. Ricks, *The Generals: American Military Command from World War II to Today* (New York: Penguin, 2012), 78.
15. Omar N. Bradley, *A Soldier's Story* (New York: Modern Library, 1999), 155, 156.
16. GSP diary, July 25, 1943 (reverse side of page).
17. Alfred D. Chandler Jr. ed., *The Papers of Dwight David Eisenhower: The War Years*, vol. 2 (Baltimore, Johns Hopkins University Press, 1970), 1123, 1124.
18. RG319 Records of the Chief of Military History, Background Files: Sicily and the Surrender of Italy 1937–1967, Critique of Manuscript, Copy 2 to Progress Reports and Orders of Continuation, box 18, ARC ID 2216436 P Entry 103, NARA. It should be noted that Porter told the historian Major Albert Garland on February 8, 1961, that "General Porter does not wish this to be printed." Oscar Koch's interview was conducted by Brigadier General James A. Norell, the U.S. Army's chief of military history, on December 15, 1960.
19. GSP diary, May 3, 1943, box 2, file 15.
20. Gerald Astor, *Terrible Terry Allen: Combat General of World War II: The Life of an American Soldier* (New York: Ballantine, 2003), 161; GSP diary, December 20, 1943, box 2, file 15.
21. Anton Earl Carpenter and A. Anne Eiland, *Chappie: World War II Diary of a Combat Chaplain* (Mesa, AZ: Mead, 2007), 71, 72.
22. GSP to Cardinal Lavitrano, July 26, 1943, GSP Collection; GSP diary, July 26, 1943, box 2, file 15.
23. GSP diary, May 26, 1943, box 2, file 15.
24. Kevin M. Hymel, *Patton's Photographs: War as He Saw It* (Dulles, VA: Potomac Books, 2006), 39, 40; GSP diary, May 26, 1943.
25. Garland and Smyth, 320.
26. James Holland, *Sicily '43: The First Assault on Fortress Europe* (New York: Atlantic Monthly, 2020), 428; Pond, *Sicily*, 206.
27. GSP diary, July 28, 1943, box 2, file 15.
28. Francis De Guingand, *Operation Victory* (New York: Charles Scribner's Sons, 1947), 301.
29. Franklyn A. Johnson, interview by Shaun Illingworth and Sandra Stewart Holyoak, September 13, 2001, Rutgers Oral History Archives.
30. GSP diary, July 28, 1943.
31. GSP diary, July 29, 1943, box 2, file 15.
32. Interview, Bob Blosser with the author, April 16, 2010.

33. GSP diary, July 30, 1943, box 2, file 15.
34. James M. Gavin, *On to Berlin: Battles of an Airborne Commander, 1943–1946* (New York: Viking, 1978), 46; Seventh Army Headquarters Directive, August 12, 1943, box 11, file 5, GSP Collection.
35. GSP diary, July 31, 1943, box 2, file 15.
36. Harry C. Butcher, *My Three Years with Eisenhower: The Personal Diary of Captain Harry C. Butcher, USNR, Naval Aide to General Eisenhower* (New York: Simon and Schuster, 1946), 377.
37. Chandler, *Papers of Dwight David Eisenhower*, vol. 2, 1307–8.
38. Carpenter and Eiland, *Chappie*, 73.
39. GSP to BAP, August 1, 1943, box 11, file 5, GSP Collection.
40. Richard Tregaskis, *Invasion Diary* (New York: Random House, 1944), 57.
41. GSP diary, August 1, 1943, box 2, file 15.
42. General Order #10, August 1, 1943, box 11, file 5, GSP Collection; GSP to Leslie McNair, August 2, 1943, box 11, file 5, GSP Collection.
43. Omar N. Bradley and Clay Blair, *A General's Life: An Autobiography by General of the Army Omar N. Bradley* (New York: Simon and Schuster, 1983), 199.
44. GSP to BAP, July 1943, box 11, file 4, GSP Collection; Charles Codman, *Drive* (Boston: Little, Brown, 1957), 111.
45. GSP diary, August 2, 1943, box 2, file 15; GSP to BAP, August 2, 1943, box 11, file 5, GSP Collection; GSP to Leslie McNair, August 2, 1943, RG 337, HQs, Commanding General, General Corres, file, box 10, NARA.
46. Oscar Koch to GSP, August 11, 1943, box 11, file 5, GSP Collection.
47. Martin Blumenson, ed., *The Patton Papers*, vol. 2, *1940–1945* (Boston: Houghton Mifflin, 1974), 333.
48. Members of the Overseas Press Club of America, *Deadline Delayed* (New York: E. P. Dutton, 1947), 151.
49. Donald V. Bennett, *Honor Untarnished: A West Point Graduate's Memoir of World War II* (New York: Forge, 2003), 146–50.
50. GSP diary, August 3, 1943, box 2, file 15.
51. John Lucas diary, August 3, 1943, box 4, John P. Lucas Papers, USAHEC.
52. Overseas Press Club of America, *Deadline Delayed*, 151.
53. Clift Andrus, "Notes on Bradley's Memoirs," 44–160, McCormick Research Center, First Division Museum at Cantigny.
54. Fred H. Salter, *Recon Scout* (New York: Ballantine, 2001), 143–44.
55. Samuel W. Mitcham Jr., and Friedrich von Stauffenberg, *The Battle of Sicily: How the Allies Lost Their Chance for Total Victory* (Mechanicsburg, PA: Stackpole, 2007), 266, 267.
56. Truscott, *Command Missions*, 231.
57. Hobart R. Gay Papers, diary, August 3, 1943, box 2, USAHEC.
58. GSP diary, August 5, 1943, box 2, file 15; Christopher M. Rein, *The North African Air Campaign: U.S. Army Air Forces from El Alamein to Salerno* (Lawrence: University Press of Kansas, 2012), 158; Bradley, *A Soldier's Story*, 151.
59. Everett Hughes diary, August 5, 1943, box I-2, file 1, Hughes Papers.
60. Mitcham and von Stauffenberg, *Battle of Sicily*, 269.

61. GSP diary, August 6, 1943, box 2, file 15.
62. GSP diary, August 6, 1943; Pond, 115.
63. "Report of Operations of Third Infantry Division in Sicily, July 19–23, July 31–Aug. 7, 1943," RG 407, WWII Operations Reports, 1940–48, 3rd Infantry Division, file 303-0.3, pages 7–9, NARA.
64. Gerald T. Kent, *A Doctor's Memoirs of World War II* (Cleveland: Cobham and Hatherton, 1989), 125.
65. Interview with Peter Havale by the author, July 15, 2013.
66. GSP diary, August 7, 1943, box 2, file 15.
67. Samuel Elliot Morison, *History of the United States Naval Operations in World War II: Sicily-Salerno-Anzio*, vol. 9 (Boston: Little, Brown, 1975), 198.
68. Mitcham and von Stauffenberg, 270.
69. GSP diary, August 7, 1943, box 2, file 15.
70. Codman, *Drive*, 125.
71. R. J. Rogers, "A Study of Leadership in the First Infantry Division during World War II: Terry de la Mesa Allen and Clarence Ralph Huebner" (MA thesis, U.S. Army Command and General Staff College, 1965), 49; Rick Atkinson, *Day of Battle: The War in Sicily and Italy, 1943–1944* (New York: Henry Holt, 2007), 159.
72. GSP to Lieutenant General Leslie McNair, August 10, 1943, box 11, file 5, GSP Collection; Astor, *Terrible Terry Allen*, 240; Teddy Roosevelt Jr. to Elenor Roosevelt, [n.d.], box 10, file 1, Theodore Roosevelt, Jr. Papers, Manuscripts Division, LOC.
73. GSP to BAP, August 9, 1943, box 11, file 5, GSP Collection.
74. Garland and Smyth, 342–47; GSP diary, August 8, 1943, box 2, file 15.
75. GSP diary, August 9, 1943, box 2, file 15.
76. GSP to BAP, August 9, 1943.
77. Hobart R. Gay Papers, diary, August 10, 1943, box 2, USAHEC.
78. GSP to LTG Leslie McNair, August 10, 1943, box 11, file 5, GSP Collection; GSP diary, August 10, 1943, box 2, file 15.
79. Overseas Press Club of America, 153; Colonel Donald E. Currier to Colonel Richard Arnest, August 12, 1943, Donald E. Currier Papers, USAHEC.
80. Noel Monks, *Eyewitness* (London: Frederick Muller, 1955), 195.
81. Overseas Press Club of America, 152.
82. Louis L. Snyder, ed., *Masterpieces of War Reporting: The Great Moments of World War II* (New York: Julian Messner, 1962), 287.
83. Sherman W. Pratt, *Autobahn to Berchtesgaden: A Combat Soldier's View of His Role in World War II as Seen from the Lower Ranks Looking Up* (Baltimore: Gateway, 1992), 278–79.
84. Bradley, 158.
85. GSP to BAP, August 11, 1943, box 11, file 5.
86. Truscott, 235.
87. GSP diary, August 10, 1943.
88. GSP diary, August 10, 1943; Hobart R. Gay Papers, diary, August 10, 1943.
89. Earl Harold Alexander of Tunis, *The Alexander Memoirs: 1940–1945* (London: Frontline, 2010), 45.

90. Alfred W. Schultz, *Janey: A Little Plane in a Big War* (Middletown, CT: Southfarm, 1998), 63–64.
91. Tom Treanor, "The Home Front," *Los Angeles Times*, September 5, 1943, Patton Scrapbooks, reel 4 (microfilm), GSP Collection.
92. Garland and Smyth, 391–405.
93. John Lucas diary, August 12, 1943, box 4, John P. Lucas Papers, USAHEC.
94. Don Whitehead, *Combat Reporter: Don Whitehead's World War II Diary and Memoir*, ed. John B. Romeiser (New York: Fordham University Press, 2006), 206.
95. GSP diary, August 12, 1943, box 2, file 15.
96. Charles B. Odom, *General George S. Patton and Eisenhower* (New Orleans: World Picture Productions, 1985), 12.
97. John Lucas diary, August 16, 1943, box 4, John P. Lucas Papers, USAHEC.
98. Bradley,
99. Whitlock, *Rock of Anzio*, 61; Kevin M. Hymel, "Commanding Patton's Personal Tanks" *WWII Quarterly* 9, no. 2 (Fall 2017): 24.
100. Everett Hughes diary notes, August 16, 1943, box I-2, file 3, Hughes Papers.
101. Jack Copeland, WWII Veterans Survey, Numbered Armies, box 1, USAHEC.
102. Hobart R. Gay Papers, diary, August 17, 1943, box 2, USAHEC.
103. GSP diary, August 17, 1943, box 2, file 15; Truscott, 243; Pratt, *Autobahn*, 281; GSP to BAP, August 18, 1943, box 11, file 6, GSP Collection.
104. Tregaskis, *Invasion Diary*, 89; GSP diary, August 17, 1943.
105. Hobart R. Gay Papers, diary, August 17, 1943, box 2, USAHEC.
106. GSP diary, August 17, 1943.
107. "'Fame Is Yours,' Patton tells Men," *AP*, August 25, 1943, Patton Scrapbooks, reel 4, GSP Collection.
108. Mitcham and von Stauffenberg, 286, 287, 289, 291, 294, 307.
109. Pond, 220.
110. Douglas Porch, *The Path to Victory: The Mediterranean Theater in World War II* (Old Saybrook, CT: Konecky and Konecky, 2004), 417, 445.
111. Larry I. Bland, ed., *The Papers of George Catlett Marshall*, vol. 4 (Baltimore: Johns Hopkins University Press, 1996), 92; Seventh Army Memorandum, August 19, 1943, box 11, file 6, GSP Collection; Seventh Army Memorandum, August 25, 1943, box 11, file 6, GSP Collection.
112. Louis P. Lochner, ed., *The Goebbels Diaries, 1942–1943* (Garden City, NY: Doubleday, 1948), 421.
113. Harry Yeide, *Fighting Patton: George S. Patton Jr. Through the Eyes of His Enemies* (Minneapolis, MN: Zenith, 2011), 214; Pond, 210, 211.
114. Holland, *Sicily '43*, 100, 457.
115. Stephen J. Zaloga, *Sicily 1943: The Debut of Allied Joint Operations* (Long Island City, NY: Osprey, 2013), 90; Porch, *Path to Victory*, 447.
116. Seymore Korman, "Patton's Apology Recalls Other Tales of the General," *Fort Worth Star Telegram*, November 24, 1943, 1, 8.
117. GSP diary, August 17–18, 1943, box 2, file 15.

Chapter Ten

1. Ed Cray, *General of the Army: George C. Marshall, Soldier and Statesman* (New York: Norton, 1990), 386, 387; Carlo D'Este, *Eisenhower: A Soldier's Life* (New York: Henry Holt, 2002), 427.

2. Cray, *General of the Army*, 406.

3. The Situation in Italy, 1 July, 1943, RG 218, box 103, file 6, Records of the U.S. Joint chiefs of Staff, NARA.

4. Harry C. Butcher, *My Three Years with Eisenhower: The Personal Diary of Captain Harry C. Butcher, USNR, Naval Aide to General Eisenhower* (New York: Simon and Schuster, 1946), 390–91.

5. GSP diary, August 18-19, 1943, box 3, file 2.

6. BIGOT Message to GSP, August 18, 1943, box 11, file 6, GSP Collection; GSP to BAP, August 18, 1943, box 11, file 6, GSP Collection.

7. Alfred D. Chandler Jr., ed., *The Papers of Dwight David Eisenhower: The War Years*, vol. 2 (Baltimore: Johns Hopkins University Press, 1970), 1350.

8. Chandler, *Papers of Dwight David Eisenhower*, vol. 2, 1340–41.

9. GSP diary, August 20, 1943, box 3, file 2; D'Este, *A Soldier's Life*, 440.

10. Dwight D. Eisenhower, *Crusade in Europe* (Garden City, NY: Doubleday, 1948), 180, 181.

11. Donald E. Currier to William Cunningham, June 10, 1957, Donald E. Currier Papers, USAHEC.

12. GSP diary, August 21, 1943, box 3, file 2.

13. Louis L. Snyder, ed., *Masterpieces of War Reporting: Great Moments of World War II* (New York: Julian Messner, 1962), 278.

14. GSP to BAP, August 18 and 22, 1943, box 11, file 6, GSP Collection; Gaffey diary, August 21, 1943, USAHEC.

15. Members of the Overseas Press Club of America, *Deadline Delayed* (New York: E. P. Dutton, 1947), 151.

16. GSP diary, August 10, 1943, box 2, file 15; Overseas Press Club of America, *Deadline Delayed*, 153.

17. Omar N. Bradley, *A Soldier's Story* (New York: Modern Library, 1999), 160.

18. Everett S. Hughes to Theresa Hughes, August 17, 1943, box II-2, file 1, -Hughes Papers.

19. GSP to BAP, August 22 and 23 and September 4, 1943, box 11, file 6, GSP Collection.

20. Rupert Clarke, *With Alex at War: From the Irrawaddy to the Po, 1941–1945* (London: L. Cooper, 2000), 119.

21. Chandler, vol. 2, 1353.

22. Chandler, vol. 2, 1357.

23. Noel Monks, *Eyewitness* (London: Frederick Muller, 1955), 187; Hap Gay diary, August 27, 1943, USAHEC.

24. Hap Gay diary, August 27, 1943.

25. Bob Hope, *I Never Left Home: Bob Hope's Own Story of His Trip Abroad* (New York: Simon and Schuster, 1944), 73–75; Charles Codman, *Drive* (Boston: Little, Brown, 1957), 115.

26. GSP diary, August 24–25, 1943, box 3, file 2.
27. Dorothy Millard Weirick, *WAC Days of WWII: A Personal Story* (Laguna Niguel, CA: Royal Literary, 1992), 30.
28. Edward L. Trey, interview with author, December 27, 2010; Flint Whitlock, *The Rock of Anzio: From Sicily to Dachau: A History of the 45th Infantry Division* (Boulder: Westview, 1998), 67.
29. Carlo D'Este, *Patton: Genius for War* (New York: HarperCollins, 1995), 542–43.
30. Paul O. Huber, interview by Winston P. Erickson, July 14, 2000, tapes nos. 69 and 70, Saving the Legacy: An Oral History of Utah's World War II Veterans, Special Collections department, University of Utah.
31. Flint Whitlock, *The Fighting First: The Untold Story of the Big Red One on D-Day* (Boulder: Westview, 2004), 37–38.
32. Franklyn Johnson, *One More Hill* (New York: Funk and Wagnalls, 1949), 122; Blyth Foote Finke, *No Mission Too Difficult!: Old Buddies of the 1st Division Tell All about World War II* (Chicago: Contemporary Books, 1995), 172; William Faust, WWII Veterans Survey, 1st Infantry Division, Division Artillery, box 1, USAHEC; Codman, *Drive*, xiii.
33. Hugh A. Scott, *The Blue and White Devils: A Personal Memoir and History of the Third Infantry Division in World War II* (Nashville: Battery, 1984), 68–69 and Sherman W. Pratt, *Autobahn to Berchtesgaden: A Combat Soldier's View of His Role in World War II as Seen from the Lower Ranks Looking Up* (Baltimore: Gateway, 1992), 284.
34. Russel B. Reynolds, "Comments of General Patton," Army Retied File, box 1, Russel B. Reynolds Papers, USAHEC.
35. GSP diary, August 29, 1943, box 3, file 3.
36. Martin Blumenson, ed. *The Patton Papers*, vol. 2, *1940 – 1945* (Boston: Houghton Mifflin, 1974), 341. [DREW: FORMATTING HERE IS OFF, BUT I COULDN'T FIX IT]
37. Chandler, vol. 2, 1357.
38. GSP diary, February 17, 1944, box 3, file 5.
39. GSP diary, August 10, 1943, box 2, file 15; Overseas Press Club of America, 154, 155.
40. Lucian K. Truscott, *Command Missions: A Personal Story* (Novato, CA: Presidio, 1990), 246.
41. Butcher, *My Three Years with Eisenhower*, 404; Des Hickey and Gus Smith, *Operation Avalanche: The Salerno Landings, 1943* (London: W. Heinemann, 1983), 54.
42. GSP diary, September 1, 1943, box 3, file 3.
43. Snyder, *Masterpieces of War Reporting*, 279.
44. ESH diary, September 2, 1943, box I-2, file 1, Hughes Papers.
45. GSP diary, September 2, 1943, box 3, file 3.
46. GSP diary, September 2, 1943.
47. GSP diary, September 6, 1943, box 3, file 3; GSP to BAP, September 10, 1943, box 11, file 7, GSP Collection; Gay diary, September 6, 1943, USAHEC; Eisenhower, *Crusade in Europe*, 184.

48. Stanhope Mason Papers, box 7, folder 30, page 51, McCormick Research Center, First Infantry Division Museum.
49. Bernard Carter to Louise Carter, Bernard Shirley Carter Papers, September 6, 1943, box 2, folder 2, Manuscripts Division, USMA Library.
50. GSP diary, September 7, 1943, box 3, file 3; Omar N. Bradley and Clay Blair, *A General's Life: An Autobiography by General of the Army Omar N. Bradley* (New York: Simon and Schuster, 1983), 208; Bradley, *A Soldier's Story*, 165.
51. Chandler, vol. 2, 1387–88.
52. Truscott, *Command Missions*, 247; GSP diary, September 8, 1943, box 3, file 3.
53. GSP diary, September 10, 1943, box 3, file 3.
54. GSP diary, September 13, 1943, box 3, file 3; Gay diary, September 13, 1943, USAHEC.
55. Everett Hughes to Theresa Hughes, February 15, 1945, box II-4, file 12, Hughes Papers.
56. GSP diary, September 10–11, 1943, box 3, file 3.
57. GSP diary, September 10, 1943.
58. Butcher, 417; GSP diary, September 11, 1943, box 3, file 3.
59. Bernard Carter to Louise Carter, Bernard Shirley Carter Papers, September 14, 1943, box 2, folder 2, Manuscripts Division, USMA Library; GSP to BAP, October 15, 1943, box 11, file 9, GSP Collection; Gay diary, September 6, 1943, Hap Gay Papers, USAHEC.
60. Samuel Eliot Morison, *History of the United States Naval Operations in World War II: Sicily—Salerno—Anzio*, vol. 9 (Boston: Little, Brown, 1975), 286–90; GSP diary, September 10, 1943.
61. GSP diary, September 14-15, 1943, box 3, file 3.
62. GSP diary, September 15, 1943, box 3, file 3.
63. Gay diary, September 16, 1943, Hap Gay Papers, USAHEC.
64. GSP diary, September 17, 1943, box 3, file 3; Gay diary, September 20, 1943, Hap Gay Papers, USAHEC.
65. GSP to DDE, September 19, 1943, box 11, file 7, GSP Collection.
66. GSP diary, September 22, 1943, box 3, file 3; Lucas to GSP, October 17, 1943, box 11, file 9, GSP Collection.
67. GSP to BAP, September 19, 1943, box 11, file 7, GSP Collection; GSP to George Patton IV, November 14, 1943, box 11, file 10, GSP Collection, LOC; Ralph D. Whitcomb, unpublished memoir, Veterans History Project, LOC.
68. Dwight D. Eisenhower to Geoffrey Keyes, September 27, 1943, box 11, file 7, GSP Collection.
69. GSP diary, September 21-29, 1943, box 3, file 3.
70. GSP to BAP, September 29, 1943, box 11, file 7, GSP Collection; GSP to BAP, October 3, 1943, box 11, file 8, GSP Collection.
71. Gen. James H. "Jimmy" Doolittle, *I Could Never Be So Lucky Again: An Autobiography* (New York: Bantam, 1991), 363.
72. GSP to General McNair, October 4, 1943, RG 337, HQs, Commanding General, General Corres, file, box 10, NARA.

73. GSP diary, September 28 and October 6, 1943, box 3, file 3; Gay diary, September 28, 1943, Hap Gay Papers, USAHEC.
74. Anton Earl Carpenter and A. Anne Eiland, *Chappie: World War II Diary of a Combat Chaplain* (Mesa, AZ: Mead, 2007), 80.
75. GSP to BAP, October 14, 1943, box 11, file 9, GSP Collection; Bernard Carter to Louise Carter, October 9, 1943, box 2, folder 2, Bernard Shirley Carter Papers, Manuscripts Division, USMA Library.
76. Bob English to Hap Gay, October 8, 1943, box 11, file 8, Bernard Shirley Carter Papers, Manuscript Division, LOC.
77. J. C. Lucas to GSP, October 17, 1943, box 11, file 9, Bernard Shirley Carter Papers, Manuscript Division, LOC.
78. Frederick Ayer to Sinclaire Weeks, June 1, 1944, box 12, file 12, Bernard Shirley Carter Papers, Manuscript Division, LOC.
79. GSP to BAP, October 14–15, 1943, box 11, file 9, Bernard Shirley Carter Papers, Manuscript Division, LOC.
80. GSP diary, October 21, 1943, box 3, file 3, Bernard Shirley Carter Papers, Manuscript Division, LOC; GSP to Leslie McNair, October 13, 1943, RG 337, HQs, Commanding General, General Corres, file, box 10, NARA.
81. GSP diary, October 16, 1943, box 3, file 3; Everett S. Hughes to Theresa Hughes, October 16, 1943, box II-2, file 3, Hughes Papers.
82. GSP diary, October 19, 1943, box 3, file 3; David M. Oshinsky, *A Conspiracy So Immense: The World of Joe McCarthy* (New York: Free Press, 1983), 98, 347.
83. GSP to BAP, October 22, 1943, box 11, file 9, GSP Collection.
84. Kevin M. Hymel, *Patton's Photographs: War As He Saw It* (Dulles, VA: Potomac Books, 2006), 36.
85. Whitlock, *The Fighting First*, 43–44.

Chapter Eleven

1. GSP diary, October 25, 1943, box 3, file 3.
2. Larry I. Bland, ed., *The Papers of George Catlett Marshall*, vol. 4 (Baltimore: Johns Hopkins University Press, 1996), 163; Norman Polmar and Thomas B. Allen, *World War II: America at War 1941–1945* (New York: Random House), 34.
3. Douglas Porch, *The Path to Victory: The Mediterranean Theater in World War II* (Old Saybrook, CT: Konecky and Konecky, 2004), 484.
4. GSP diary, October 27, 1943, box 3, file 3.
5. Interview with Edwin Dubois, February 21, 1997, Nimitz Education and Research Center, the National Museum of the Pacific War, Fredericksburg, Texas, 32, 33.
6. Carlyle Holt, "Number 4 of a Series," unknown publisher, May 31, 1946, Patton Scrapbooks, reel 1, GSP Collection.
7. GSP diary, October 29–31, 1943, box 3, file 3.
8. GSP diary, November 1–2, 1943, box 3, file 3.
9. Stanley P. Hirshson, *General Patton: A Soldier's Life* (New York: HarperCollins, 2002), 431–32; GSP to Everett S. Hughes, November 2, 1943, box II-2, file 5, Hughes

Papers; Robert S. Allen, *Lucky Forward: The History of Patton's Third U.S. Army* (New York: Vanguard, 1947), 47.

10. Alice Kaplan, *The Interpreter* (New York: Free Press, 2005), 156, 157. In the book, the author calls the disproportionate numbers of African Americans accused of rape "patently absurd."

11. GSP diary, November 8, 1943, box 3, file 3; Christopher Paul Moore, *Fighting for America: Black Soldiers—The Unsung Heroes of World War II* (New York: Ballantine, 2005), 212–13.

12. GSP diary, November 3–5, 1943, box 3, file 3; GSP to BAP, November 11, 1943, box 11, file 10, GSP Collection; Charles Odom, *General George S. Patton and Eisenhower* (New Orleans: World Picture Productions, 1985), 21.

13. Odom, *Patton and Eisenhower*, 17, 20.

14. Percy to BAP, November 10, 1943, box 11, file 10, GSP Collection. There is no further information who this Percy was, only that he served in the G-3, Force Headquarters in England.

15. Eisenhower to GSP, November 11, 1943, box 11, file 10, GSP Collection; Doroty G. Wayman, "Gen. Patton Greeted by Wife's Song on His 58th Birthday," *Boston Daily Globe*, November 17, 1943, Patton Scrapbooks, reel 4, GSP Collection; GSP diary, November 11, 1943, box 3, file 3.

16. Charles Codman, *Drive* (Boston: Little, Brown, 1957), xvi–xvii.

17. Codman, *Drive*, xx.

18. GSP to GSP IV, November 17, 1943, box 11, file 10, GSP Collection.

19. James Holland, *Sicily '43: The First Assault on Fortress Europe* (New York: Atlantic Monthly, 2020), 458; GSP diary, 12–16 November 12–16, 1943, box 3, file 3.

20. Holt, "Number 4 of a Series."

21. GSP diary, November 18, 1943, box 3, file 3; Harry L. Coles and Albert Weinberg, *The United States Army in World War II: Special Studies: Civil Affairs: Soldiers Become Governors* (Washington, D.C.: Center for Military History, 1986), 315.

22. GSP diary, November 5–20, 1943, box 3, file 3; GSP to BAP, November 20, 1943, box 11, file 11, GSP Collection; GSP to BAP, December 21, 1943, box 11, file 13, GSP Collection.

23. Louis L. Snyder, ed., *Masterpieces of War Reporting: The Great Moments of World War II* (New York: Julian Messner, 1962), 276.

24. Everett S. Hughes to Theresa Hughes, November 25, 1943, box II-2, file 4, Hughes Papers; GSP to Everett S. Hughes, December 9, 1943, box II-2, file 5, Hughes Papers; D. K. R. Crosswell, *Beetle: The Life of General Walter Bedell Smith* (Lexington: University Press of Kentucky, 2010), 533.

25. Herbert Mitgang, *Newsmen in Khaki: Tales of a World War II Soldier Correspondent* (Lanham, MD: Taylor Trade, 2004), 70–71.

26. Everett Hughes diary notes, December 11, 1943, box I-2, file 3, Hughes Papers; GSP to Everett S. Hughes, November 1943, box II-2, file 4, Hughes Papers; Everett S. Hughes to Theresa Hughes, November 30, 1943, box II-2, file 4, Hughes Papers.

27. Leslie McNair to GSP, November 27, 1943, RG 337, HQS, Commanding General, General Corres., box 10, NARA.

28. GSP to Stimson, November 27, 1943, box 11, file 11, GSP Collection; GSP diary, November 21–28, 1943, box 3, file 3; Codman, 130.
29. GSP diary, November 29–December 1, 1943, box 3, file 3.
30. Kenyon Joyce to BAP, December 1, 1943, box 11, file 12, GSP Collection; John Lucas to GSP, December 1, 1943, box 11, file 12, GSP Collection; Odom, 13; Codman, 124–25.
31. Alfred D. Chandler Jr., ed., *The Papers of Dwight David Eisenhower: The War Years*, vol. 2 (Baltimore: Johns Hopkins University Press, 1970), 1572–74.
32. Seymore Korman, "Patton's Apology Recalls Other Tales of the General," *Fort Worth Star Telegram*, November 24, 1943, 1, 8.
33. "Report Gen. Patton Disciplined for Mistreating Sick Soldier," unknown source and date, copy of digest sent to GSP, April 10, 1944, Patton Scrapbooks, reels 4 and 5, GSP Collection; GSP to BAP, March 23, 1944, box 11, file 16, GSP Collection.
34. "PM Believes: Gen. Patton Should be Court-Martialed," *PM Daily*, November 24, 1943, Patton Scrapbooks, reel 5, GSP Collection; Snyder, *Masterpieces of War Reporting*, 280.
35. "Patton Case Stirs Congress," *Times Herald*, November 24, 1943, Patton Scrapbooks, reel 5, GSP Collection.
36. Crosswell, *Beetle*, 535.
37. GSP diary, August 11, 1943, box 2, file 15.
38. Hal Boyle, "War Department Wants Patton Forgiven," *Boston Traveler*, November 24, 1943, Patton Scrapbooks, reel 5, GSP Collection.
39. "Removal of Gen. Patton Urged as Congress Debates Issue," AP, no date, and Jimmy Jemail, "The Intriguing Photographer," *News*, December 1, 1943, Patton Scrapbooks, reel 5, GSP Collection.
40. DDE to GSP, December 1, 1943, box 11, file 12, GSP Collection; James Kelly Morningstar, *Patton's Way: A Radical Theory of War* (Annapolis: Naval Institute Press, 2017), 160.
41. GSP diary, December 7, 1943, box 3, file 4.
42. GSP diary, December 7, 1943.
43. GSP to Everett S. Hughes, December 9, 1943, box II-2, file 5, Hughes Papers; GSP to BAP, December 10, 1943, box 11, file 12, GSP Collection.
44. GSP diary, December 14, 1943, box 3, file 4.
45. GSP diary, December 13–20, 1943, box 3, file 4; Kevin M. Hymel, *Patton's Photographs: War as He Saw It* (Dulles, VA: Potomac Books, 2006), 47; Martin Blumenson, ed., *The Patton Papers*, vol. 2, *1940–1945* (Boston: Houghton Mifflin, 1974), 389.
46. Stimson to GSP, December 18, 1943, box 11, file 12, GSP Collection.
47. GSP diary, December 20–30, 1943, box 3, file 4.
48. GSP to Everett Hughes, December 21, 1943, box II-2, file 6, Hughes Papers.
49. Bland, *Papers of George Catlett Marshall*, vol. 4, 210–11, 239; Dwight D. Eisenhower, *Crusade in Europe* (Garden City, NY: Doubleday, 1948), 215.
50. GSP to Leslie McNair, December 29, 1943, RG 337, HQS, Commanding General, General Corres., box 10, NARA.
51. GSP to Everett Hughes, December 30, 1943, box II-2, file 6, Hughes Papers.

52. GSP diary, December 31, 1943, box 3, file 4; GSP to BAP, December 29, 1943, box 11, file 12, GSP Collection.
53. GSP to Everett Hughes, December 31, 1943, box II-2, file 6, Hughes Papers.
54. Everett Hughes diary, January 2, 1944, box I-2, file 1, Hughes Papers.
55. Everett Hughes to Theresa Hughes, January 4, 1944, box II-2, file 6, Hughes Papers; GSP diary, January 1, 1944, box 3, file 4.
56. GSP diary, January 3, 1944, box 3, file 4.
57. Eisenhower, *Crusade in Europe*, 215, 216.
58. Alvin Callender, interviewed by Thomas Snockin, the National World War II Museum, no date.
59. GSP diary, January 4–5, 1944, box 3, file 4; George S. Patton Jr., *War as I Knew It* (New York: Great Commanders, 1975), 57.
60. Patton, *War as I Knew It*, 57; GSP diary, January 5, 1944, box 3, file 4; GSP to Everett Hughes, January 7, 1944, box II-2, file 6, Hughes Papers.
61. Everett Hughes diary, January 7, 1944, box I-2, file 1, -Hughes Papers; Gen. James H. "Jimmy" Doolittle, *I Could Never Be So Lucky Again: An Autobiography* (New York: Bantam, 1991), 374.
62. Interview, Frank S. Errigo with the author, July 22, 2010.
63. GSP diary, January 9, 1944, box 3, file 4; Codman, 134.
64. Mark Clark, *Calculated Risk* (New York: Harper, 1950), 257.
65. GSP diary, January 10–20, 1944, box 3, file 4.
66. Andrew Rawson, *Eyes Only: The Top Secret Correspondence Between Marshall and Eisenhower, 1943–45* (Gloucestershire, UK: Spellmount, 2012), 22.
67. Codman, 134.
68. GSP diary, January 18, 1944, box 3, file 4; GSP to BAP, January 19, 1944, box 11, file 14, GSP Collection.
69. GSP diary, March 16, 1944, box 3, file 4.
70. Edwin F. Boettger, interview by Mark Ven Ells, 1997 (OH 493), pages 25, 26, Wisconsin Veterans Museum Research Center.
71. GSP diary, January 9–22, 1944, box 3, file 4; GSP to BAP, January 23, 1944, box 11, file 14, GSP Collection.
72. GSP diary, January 19–22, 1944, box 3, file 4.

Chapter Twelve

1. GSP to Everett Hughes, date unknown, box II-2, file 6, Hughes Papers.
2. GSP diary, January 26, 1944, box 3, file 4.
3. Harry C. Butcher, *My Three Years with Eisenhower: The Personal Diary of Captain Harry C. Butcher, USNR, Naval Aide to General Eisenhower* (New York: Simon and Schuster, 1946), 481.
4. GSP diary, February 2, 1944, box 3, file 4.
5. Hobart R. Gay, Senior Officers Oral History Program Interview, Hobart R. Gay Papers, box 1, page 28–29, USAHEC.
6. Everett Hughes to Theresa Hughes, February 28, 1944, box II-2, file 7, Hughes Papers.

7. GSP to BAP, January 28, 1944, box 11, file 14, GSP Collection.
8. Harkin's Photo Albums, vol. 2, USAHEC.
9. Brenton G. Wallace, *Patton and His Third Army* (Harrisburg, PA: Military Service Publishing, 1946), 213–14; GSP to BAP, February 3, 1944, box 11, file 15, GSP Collection; GSP to BAP, March 5 and 16, 1944, box 11, file 16, GSP Collection; GSP to BAP, June 4, 1944, box 12, file 2, GSP Collection; Robert S. Allen, *Lucky Forward: The History of Patton's Third Army* (New York: Vanguard, 1947), 17.
10. GSP to BAP, February 5 and 26, 1944, box 11, file 15, GSP Collection; GSP to BAP, February 15, 1944, box 11, file 15, GSP Collection; GSP to BAP, April 9, 1944, box 11, file 17, GSP Collection; GSP to George H. MacNish, February 24, 1944, box 28, file 15, GSP Collection.
11. From author's personal notes and photographs. As of 2020, the pub has been renamed the Whipping Stocks Inn.
12. Ken Scharnberg, *Voices: Letters from World War II* (Nashville: Premium Press America, 1993), 265.
13. Robert Allen, *In Memoriam: George S. Patton Jr., General, U.S. Army* (pamphlet), page 15, the Center for the Study of War and Society, University of Tennessee.
14. Burch to Family, August 16, 1944, box 12, file 5, GSP Collection.
15. GSP diary, January 29, 1944, box 3, file 4.
16. Allison Wysong, unpublished memoir, pages 4, 14–15, Veterans History Project, LOC.
17. Oscar W. Koch, *G-2: Intelligence for Patton* (Atglen, PA: Schiffer Military History, 1999), 75.
18. Charles Codman, *Drive* (Boston: Little, Brown, 1957), 137–39; Wysong, memoir, 15.
19. Ladislas Farago, *The Last Days of Patton* (New York: Berkley Books, 1984), 15–18.
20. Lt. Col. Kenneth W. Hechler to Charles B. MacDonald, June 22, 1956, RG 319, Records of the Army Staff, Center of Military History, Breakout and Pursuit, Correspondence, Memorandum, Notes Relating to Seine, the Drive to-Chapter 26, Entry 93, box 9, NARA.
21. GSP to BAP, February 23, 1944, box 11, file 15, GSP Collection.
22. Steven J. Zaloga, *US Armored Divisions: The European Theater of Operations, 1944–45* (Oxford: Osprey, 2004), 10–15.
23. Wallace, *Patton and His Third Army*, 197; David N. Spires, *Patton's Air Force: Forging a Legendary Air-Ground Team* (Washington, D.C.: Smithsonian Institution, 2005), 27, 45.
24. GSP to BAP, February 3, 1944; GSP to BAP, February 15, 1944.
25. GSP to BAP, February 5, 1944, box 11, file 15, GSP Collection; "Belated Orchids to Gen. George S. Patton," unknown author and source, January 3, 1945, Patton's Scrapbooks, reel 1, GSP Collection; Andrew Rawson, *Eyes Only: The Top Secret Correspondence Between Marshall and Eisenhower, 1943–45* (Goucestershire, UK: Spellmount, 2012), 71.
26. GSP diary, February 7, 1944, box 3, file 4.

27. Harold A. Rodriguez, "Dispatches," 8; George Ross Wren, *Normandy to Czechoslovakia in World War II: A G.I.'s Memoirs* (St. Louis: Morris, 1998), 136.
28. Durward M. Kelton, undated and unpublished memoir, New York State Military Museum.
29. Larue Harper Barnes, *They Were There: Texas Veterans Remember World War II* (Hillsboro, TX: Hill College Press, 2006), 131.
30. John H. Cook, April 23, 1998, interviewed by G. Kurt Piehler and Richard Boniface for Rutgers University Oral Archives of WWII.
31. Francis De Guingand, *Operation Victory* (New York: Charles Scribner's Sons, 1947), 350; GSP to BAP, February 5, 1944; GSP diary, February 17, 1944, box 3, file 5.
32. GSP to BAP, March 5 and 19, 1944, box 11, file 16, GSP Collection.
33. GSP to BAP, February 16, 1944, box 11, file 15, GSP Collection.
34. Rupert Clarke, *With Alex at War: From the Irrawaddy to the Po, 1941–1945* (London: L. Cooper, 2000), 134; GSP diary, February 16, 1944, box 3, file 4; Alfred D. Chandler Jr., ed., *The Papers of Dwight David Eisenhower: The War Years*, vol. 3 (Baltimore: Johns Hopkins University Press, 1970), 1731.
35. GSP diary, February 18, 1944, box 3, file 5.
36. GSP diary, March 14, 1944, box 3, file 5.
37. GSP diary, February 18–26, 1944, box 3, file 5.
38. GSP to BAP, February 19, 1944, box 11, file 15, GSP Collection.
39. GSP to BAP, February 20, 1944, box 11, file 15, GSP Collection.
40. GSP diary, March 1–2, 1944, box 3, file 4; David Eisenhower, *Eisenhower at War, 1943–1945* (New York: Random House, 1986), 152–54.
41. GSP diary, March 2–6, 1944, box 3, file 4.
42. GSP to BAP, March 23, 1944, box 11, file 16, GSP Collection.
43. Ruth Ellen Patton Totten, *The Button Box: A Daughter's Loving Memory of Mrs. George S. Patton* (Columbia: University of Missouri Press, 2005), 244; GSP to BAP, March 6, 1944, box 11, file 16, GSP Collection.
44. Unknown writer to GSP, March 4, 1944, box 11, file 16, GSP Collection.
45. Richard J. Stillman and Mary F. Riggs, *General Patton's Best Friend: The Story of General George Smith Patton, Jr. and His Beloved Dog, Willie* (New Orleans: R. J. Stillman, 2001), 28.
46. GSP diary, March 10, 1944, box 3, file 5.
47. GSP to BAP, March 5 and 19, 1944, box 11, file 16, GSP Collection; GSP to BAP, April 16, 1944, box 11, file 17, GSP Collection.
48. Everett Hughes to Theresa Hughes, March 30, 1944, box II-2, file 8, Hughes Papers; GSP to BAP, April 16, 1944.
49. GSP diary, March 7–8, 1944, box 3, file 5.
50. Robert Meade Parker, "Recollections of the Second World War," page 4, WWII Survey Collection, 4th Armored Division, box 20, USAHEC.
51. Letter of Instruction, March 6, 1944, box 11, file 16, GSP Collection.
52. GSP diary, March 10, 1944; Kevin M. Hymel, "Armored Blitz in Avranches," *WWII History* 10, no. 1 (December 2010): 42, 43.
53. Robert Allen diary, April 1, 1944, Robert Allen Collection, box 1, folder 6, GSP Museum.

54. C. Cabanne Smith, *My War Years: 1940–1946: Service on Gen. Patton's Third Army Staff* (Houston: Rosenlaui, 1989), 33–34; Stillman and Riggs, *General Patton's Best Friend*, 22.
55. GSP to BAP, March 24, 1944, box 11, file 16, GSP Collection.
56. Robert Allen diary, March 31, 1944, Robert Allen Collection, box 1, folder 6, GSP Museum.
57. General Orders, Number 16, March 26, 1944, box 11, file 16, GSP Collection.
58. GSP to BAP, March 28, 1944, box 11, file 16, GSP Collection; GSP diary, March 28, 1944, box 3, file 4.
59. GSP to BAP, March 6, 1944.
60. GSP to BAP, April 11, 1944, box 11, file 17, GSP Collection; GSP to BAP, April 14, 1944, box 11, file 17, GSP Collection.
61. GSP to Leslie McNair, March 11, 1944, RG 337, HQS, Commanding General, General Corres., box 10, NARA.
62. Barnes, *They Were There*, 63.
63. Vincent P. Marran, *The Major Looks Over His Shoulder: A Medical Memoir of World War II* (Santa Rosa, CA: Manor House, 1989), 9.
64. Thomas J. Evans, *Reluctant Valor* (Latrobe, PA: St Vincent College Center for Northern Appalachian Studies, 1995), 19.
65. B. J. Olewiler, *A Woman in a Man's War* (Philadelphia: Xlibris, 2003), 93.
66. GSP to Leslie McNair, April 10, 1944, RG 337, HQS, Commanding General, General Corres., box 10, NARA.
67. GSP to BAP, March 24, 1944.
68. Stanley P. Hirshson, *General Patton: A Soldier's Life* (New York: HarperCollins, 2002), 474.
69. Charles M. Province, *The Unknown Patton* (New York: Bonanza, 1983), 29.
70. Carlo D'Este, *Patton: Genius for War* (New York: HarperCollins, 1995), 602.
71. Hirshson, *General Patton*, 475; D'Este, *Genius for War*, 603.
72. George Forty, *The Armies of George S. Patton* (New York: Arms and Armour, 1996), 61.
73. Forty, *Armies of George S. Patton*, 61.
74. Province, *Unknown Patton*, 31.
75. D'Este, 603.
76. Province, 33.
77. D'Este, 604.
78. Hirshson, 476; Province, 37.
79. Harry M. Kemp, *The Regiment: Let the Citizens Bear Arms!: A Narrative History of an American Infantry Regiment in World War II* (Austin: Nortex, 1990), 65.
80. Aaron Elson, *Tanks for the Memories: The 712th Tank Battalion During World War II* (Hackensack, NJ: Chi Chi, 2001), 304.
81. Lt. Col. George Dyer, *XII Corps: Spearhead of Patton's Third Army* (N.p.: XII History Association, 1947), 100.
82. Wallace, 204.
83. George C. Marshall, *The Papers of George Catlett Marshall*, ed. Larry I. Bland, vol. 4 (Baltimore: Johns Hopkins University Press, 1996), 391–92.

84. GSP diary, April 5, 1944, box 3, file 5; Omar N. Bradley and Clay Blair, *A General's Life: An Autobiography by General of the Army Omar N. Bradley* (New York: Simon and Schuster, 1983), 221.

85. United States v. Sergeant Horace T. West, RG 159, Entry 26F, Office of the Inspector General, General Correspondence, 1939–1947, folder 333.9, box 67, NARA.

86. United States v. Sergeant Horace T. West.

87. Memorandum for the Record, RG 159, Entry 26F, Office of the Inspector General, General Correspondence, 1939–1947, folder 333.9, box 67, NARA.

88. Testimony of Major General Troy H. Middleton, RG 159, Entry 26F, Office of the Inspector General, General Correspondence, 1939–1947, folder 333.9, box 67, NARA.

89. Evert Hughes to E.L. Peterson, RG 159, Entry 26F, Office of the Inspector General, General Correspondence, 1939–1947, folder 333.9, box 67, NARA

90. GSP to BAP, April 4, 1944, box 11, file 17, GSP Collection; GSP to BAP, April 12, 1944, box 11, file 17, GSP Collection.

91. Everett Hughes to Theresa Hughes, April 6 and 7, 1944, box II-3, file 1, Hughes Papers; Bradley and Blair, *A General's Life*, 221.

92. GSP to BAP, April 9, 1944; Bradley and Blair, 232, 233.

93. Bradley and Blair, 221.

94. Third Army Plans for "Operation OVERLORD," RG 407, Records of the Adjutant General's Office, WWII Operations Reports, 1941–48, Preinvasion Plans, 195 to 201, folder 201, box 19244, NARA; GSP diary, April 13, 1944, box 3, file 5.

95. Robert Allen diary, pages 25 and 26, GSP Museum.

96. James Kelly Morningstar, *Patton's Way: A Radical Theory of War* (Annapolis: Naval Institute Press, 2017), 83, 84.

97. GSP to BAP, April 16, 1944; GSP to BAP, April 19, 1944, box 11, file 17, GSP Collection; GSP diary, April 19, 1944, box 3, file 5.

98. GSP to BAP, April 19, 1944.

99. William G. Weaver, *Yankee Doodle Went to Town*, 33; GSP diary, April 20, 1944, box 3, file 5.

100. Alexander Bohen, interviewed by Marlene Zecca, May 22, 2015, New York State Military Museum, accessed May 29, 2021, https://www.youtube.com/watch?v=Mr_65M4LIfs&t=3883s.

101. GSP diary, April 20, 1944.

Chapter Thirteen

1. Roger Hesketh, *Fortitude: The D-Day Deception Campaign* (Woodstock, NY: Overlook, 2000), 169.

2. Hesketh, *Fortitude*, 172.

3. GSP to J. P. Alcshire, February 22, 1944, box 28, file 2, GSP Collection; GSP to BAP, February 20, 1944, box 11, file 15, GSP Collection.

4. Hesketh, 213.

5. Robert S. Allen, *Lucky Forward: The History of Patton's Third U.S. Army* (New York: Vanguard, 1947), 67.

6. GSP diary, April 27, 1944, box 3, file 5; GSP to BAP, April 27, 1944, box 11, file 17, GSP Collection.

7. GSP to Everett Hughes, April 26, 1944, box II-3, file 1, Hughes Papers; affidavit by N. W. Campanole, April 27, 1944, box 12, file 1, GSP Collection.

8. Robert Allen diary, page 30, Robert Allen Collection, GSP Museum; GSP diary, April 28, 1944, box 3, file 5.

9. GSP diary, April 30, 1944, box 3, file 5.

10. David Eisenhower, *Eisenhower at War, 1943–1945* (New York: Random House, 1986), 219, 220; Joseph Balkoski, *Utah Beach: The Amphibious Landing and Airborne Operations on D-Day, June 6, 1944* (Mechanicsburg, PA: Stackpole, 2005), 61; Carlo D'Este, *Eisenhower: A Soldier's Life* (New York: Henry Holt, 2002), 507.

11. Andrew Rawson, *Eyes Only: The Top Secret Correspondence between Marshall and Eisenhower, 1943–45* (Gloucestershire, UK: Spellmount, 2012), 73.

12. "Patton says America and Britain are 'Destined to Rule the World,'" AP, April 25, 1944, and "U.S. England and Russia to Rule World, Gen. Patton Tells British," AP, April 26, 1944, Patton Scrapbooks, reel 5, GSP Collection; Rawson, *Eyes Only*, 72.

13. "Patton Stirs Demands for More Silence," *Miami News*, April 27, 1944, 16.

14. GSP to Kenyon Joyce, June 12, 1944, box 28, file 11, GSP Collection.

15. GSP to BAP, April 30, 1944, box 11, file 17, GSP Collection.

16. GSP to Everett Hughes, April 30, 1944, box II-3, file 2, Hughes Papers; D'Este, *Eisenhower*, 507.

17. GSP diary, May 1, 1944, box 3, file 5; Dwight D. Eisenhower, *Crusade in Europe* (Garden City, NY: Doubleday, 1948), 224; Eisenhower, *Eisenhower at War*, 221; D'Este, *Eisenhower*, 508.

18. Eisenhower, *Crusade in Europe*, 180.

19. D'Este, *Eisenhower*, 508.

20. GSP diary, May 1, 1944; GSP to BAP, May 1–2, 1944, box 12, file 1, GSP Collection.

21. Eisenhower, *Crusade in Europe*, 225.

22. Ann W. Patton to GSP, August 19, 1944, box 14, file 20, GSP Collection.

23. Rawson, *Eyes Only*, 73.

24. Eisenhower, *Eisenhower at War*, 222.

25. John S. Wood, *Memories and Reflections*, unpublished memoir, 1956–1966, the Jack Hixson collection, 76.

26. GSP diary, May 1, 1944.

27. Alfred D. Chandler Jr., ed., *The Papers of Dwight David Eisenhower: The War Years*, vol. 3 (Baltimore: Johns Hopkins University Press, 1970), 1801; Eisenhower, *Crusade in Europe*, 224.

28. D'Este, *Eisenhower*, 589.

29. GSP diary, May 2–3, 1944, box 3, file 5; GSP to BAP, May 3, 1944, box 12, file 1, GSP Collection.

30. Everett Hughes to Theresa Hughes, May 7, 1944, box II-3, file 2, Hughes Papers.

31. GSP diary, May 3, 1944, box 3, file 5; BAP to Everett Hughes, May 4, 1944, box II-3, file 2, Hughes Papers; GSP to BAP, May 5, 1944, box 12, file 1, GSP Collection.

NOTES TO CHAPTER THIRTEEN   393

32. Hesketh, 176.
33. D'Este, 505.
34. Hesketh, 178, 181–84.
35. GSP diary, May 6, 1944, box 3, file 5.
36. GSP diary, May 9–10, 1944, box 3, file 5.
37. GSP diary, May 12, 1944, box 3, file 5.
38. Everett Hughes to Theresa Hughes, May 12, 1944, box II-3, file 2, Hughes Papers.
39. Carlo D'Este, *Decision in Normandy* (New York: Harper Perrenial, 1994), 83.
40. Omar N. Bradley, *A Soldier's Story* (New York: Modern Library, 1999), 235, 241.
41. GSP diary, May 15, 1944, box 3, file 5.
42. Stanley P. Hirshson, *General Patton: A Soldier's Life* (New York: HarperCollins, 2002), 468-69.
43. GSP diary, May 15, 1944.
44. William B. Breuer, *Hoodwinking Hitler: The Normandy Deception* (Westport, CT: Praeger, 1993), 159.
45. GSP diary, May 27, 1944, box 3, file 5.
46. Third Army Headquarters memo to "All Officer and Enlisted Men of My Command," May 19, 1944, box 12, file 1, Patton Papers, Manuscript Division, LOC.
47. GSP diary, May 18–24, 1944, box 3, file 5; Vic Hillery and Emerson Hurley, *Paths of Armor: The Fifth Armored Division in World War II* (Nashville: Battery Press, 1993), 40; GSP to Beetle Smith, May 25, 1944, box 3, file 5, GSP Collection; Beetle Smith to GSP, May 29, 1944, box 3, file 5, GSP Collection.
48. D'Este, *Eisenhower*, 517.
49. GSP diary, May 12–22, 1944, box 3, file 5; GSP to BAP, May 1–2, 1944; GSP to BAP, May 24, 1944, box 12, file 1, GSP Collection.
50. GSP to Hugh H. McGee, June 16, 1944, box 28, file 15, GSP Collection; GSP diary, May 25, 1944, box 3, file 5; "General Patton Is Passed Over," *Daily Mail*, May 25, 1944, box 12, file 1, GSP Collection; Frederick Ayer to Sinclair Weeks, June 1, 1944, box 12, file 2, GSP Collection; Drew Pearson, "Washington Merry-Go-Round," *Capital Times*, May 5, 1944, 18.
51. Map of France, Oversized 8, GSP Collection; GSP to BAP, May 22, 1944, box 12, file 1, GSP Collection.
52. GSP diary, May 30, 1944, box 3, file 5.
53. GSP diary, June 1, 1944, box 3, file 5.
54. Francis De Guingand, *Operation Victory* (New York: Charles Scribner's Sons, 1947), 369–72.
55. Bernard Carter to Louise Carter, Bernard Shirley Carter Papers, June 7, 1944, box 2, folder 4, Manuscripts Division, USMA Library; GSP diary, June 2–4, 1944, box 3, file 5, GSP Collection.
56. GSP to BAP, June 4, 1944, box 12, file 2, GSP Collection.
57. GSP diary, June 5, 1944, box 3, file 5.

Chapter Fourteen

1. GSP to GSP IV, June 6, 1944, box 12, file 2, GSP Collection; GSP to BAP, June 6, 1944, box 12, file 2, GSP Collection; Robert S. Allen, *Lucky Forward: The History of Patton's Third U.S. Army* (New York: Vanguard, 1947), 67.

2. Joseph Balkoski, *Omaha Beach: D-Day, June 6, 1944* (Mechanicsburg, PA: Stackpole, 2004), 157–59.

3. Adrian R. Lewis, *Omaha Beach: A Flawed Victory* (Chapel Hill: University of North Carolina Press, 2001), 5.

4. Hobart Gay Papers, diary, June 15, 1944, box 2, USAHEC.

5. Balkoski, *Omaha Beach*, 78, 85, 86; Kevin M. Hymel, "The Last Man in Hell," *WWII History* 15, no. 1 (December 2015): 50, 51.

6. Joseph Balkoski, *Utah Beach: The Amphibious Landing and Airborne Operations on D-Day, June 6, 1944* (Mechanicsburg, PA: Stackpole, 2005), 145–46.

7. Balkoski, *Utah Beach*, 278–80.

8. Kevin M. Hymel, "D-Day Dilemma," *WWII History* 7, no. 6 (August/September 2008): 52–59; GSP diary, September 23, 1944, box 3, file 5.

9. BAP to Everett Hughes, June 16, 1944, box II-3, file 3, Hughes Papers.

10. Roger Hesketh, *Fortitude: The D-Day Deception Campaign* (Woodstock, NY: Overlook, 2000), 200, 228, 230; Omar N. Bradley and Clay Blair, *A General's Life: An Autobiography by General of the Army Omar N. Bradley* (New York: Simon and Schuster, 1983), 255.

11. Allen, *Lucky Forward*, 73.

12. Robert Allen diary, Robert Allen Collection, GSP Museum; GSP diary, June 6, 1944, box 3, file 7.

13. GSP to BAP, June 10, 1944, box 12, file 2, GSP Collection.

14. GSP to BAP, June 9, 1944, box 12, file 2, GSP Collection.

15. GSP diary, June 17, 1944, box 3, file 5; Bradley and Blair, *A General's Life*, 269, 270.

16. GSP diary, June 9, 1944, box 3, file 5; Aaron Elson, *The Armored Fist: The 712 Tank Battalion in the Second World War* (Charleston, SC: Fonthill Media, 2015) 69, 70.

17. Hobart Gay Papers, diary, June 9, 1944, box 2, USAHEC.

18. GSP to Hugh H. McGee, June 16, 1944, box 28, file 15, GSP Collection; GSP to BAP, June 7–9, 1944, box 12, file 2, GSP Collection; GSP to George Patton IV, June 17, 1944, box 12, file 2, GSP Collection.

19. GSP to BAP, June 17, 1944, box 12, file 2, GSP Collection.

20. George F. Hofmann, *The Super Sixth: History of the 6th Armored Division in World War II* (Nashville: Battery Press, 2000), 48.

21. Hobart Gay Papers, diary, June 12, 1944, box 2, USAHEC; *Trip to London by Chief of Staff, 10–12 June 1944*, Hobart Gay Papers, diary, June 9, 1944. In 1998, 3rd Armored Division veteran Belton Cooper, in his memoir *Death Traps: The Survival of an American Armored Division in World War II* (Novato, CA: Presidio, 1998), accused Patton of downgrading production of the heavy M-26 Pershing tank. Cooper claimed that Patton convened a January 27 meeting at Tidworth Downs, where he

watched a demonstration of the Pershing and made his decision to downgrade it. Actually, Patton arrived in England on January 27 and made no mention of any such meeting for the last four days of January. The June 12 armor demonstration was the only one mentioned in Patton's memoirs or the Third Army daily diary. In addition, there were no Pershing tanks in Europe in 1944.

22. GSP to Paddy Flint, May 25, 1944, box 12, file 2, GSP Collection; GSP diary, June 9, 1944.
23. GSP diary, June 18, 1944, box 3, file 5.
24. GSP to BAP, June 20-22, 1944, box 12, file 2, GSP Collection.
25. Robert Allen diary, file 2, page 2, Robert Allen Collection, GSP Museum.
26. Mary Pat Kelly, *Home Away from Home: The Yanks in Ireland* (Belfast: Appletree Press, 1994), 102.
27. Ellen Hampton, *Women of Valor: The Rochambelles on the WWII Front* (New York: Palgrave MacMillan, 2006), 47-49; Hobart Gay Papers, diary, June 14, 1944, box 2, USAHEC.
28. John S. D. Eisenhower, *General Ike: A Personal Reminiscence* (New York: Free Press, 2003), 59-61.
29. GSP diary, June 26, 1944, box 3, file 5.
30. Martin Blumenson, ed., *The Patton Papers*, vol. 1, *1885-1940*, (Boston: Houghton Mifflin, 1972), 469-70.
31. Brenton G. Wallace, *Patton and His Third Army* (Harrisburg, PA: Military Service Publishing, 1946), 213-14; Hobart R. Gay Papers, diary, June 11, 1944, box 2, USAHEC.
32. The tradition continues to this day. If there are no fresh flowers, the staff of the Whipping Stocks places a small vase of fake flowers on Patton's table. Plaques of the general decorate the walls. From author's notes and photographs.
33. GSP to BAP, July 3, 1944, box 12, file 3, GSP Collection.
34. Carlo D'Este, *Eisenhower: A Soldier's Life* (New York: Henry Holt, 2002), 545.
35. Everett Hughes to Theresa Hughes, July 3, 1944, box II-3, file 4, Hughes Papers.
36. GSP diary, July 2, 1944, box 3, file 5.
37. Hesketh, *Fortitude*, 237, 242.
38. GSP diary, July 4, 1944, box 3, file 6.
39. R. B. Lovett to GSP, July 6, 1944, box 12, file 3, GSP Collection.
40. Robert Patton, *The Pattons: A Personal History of an American Family* (New York: Crown Publishers, 1994), 234; Martin Blumenson, *Patton: The Man behind the Legend, 1885-1945* (New York: Morrow, 1985), 228; Hughes diary, July 4-9, 1944, Box I: 1-2, Hughes Papers.
41. GSP diary, July 5, 1944, box 3, file 6.
42. GSP diary, July 5, 1944; Hobart Gay Papers, diary, June 19, 1944, box 2, USAHEC.
43. David Eisenhower, *Eisenhower at War, 1943-1945* (New York: Random House, 1986), 351.
44. Charles R. Codman, *Drive* (Boston: Little, Brown, 1957), 152; GSP diary, July 6, 1944, box 3, file 6.

45. Codman, *Drive*, 153; "Why Did Eisenhower Defy Public Opinion," Colliers, January 13, 1945, Patton's Scrapbooks, reel 1, GSP Collection; Larry I. Bland, ed., *The Papers of George Catlett Marshall*, vol. 4 (Baltimore: Johns Hopkins University Press, 1996), 635–36.

46. Omar N. Bradley, *A Soldier's Story* (New York: Modern Library, 1999), 355.

47. GSP diary, July 5, 1944.

48. GSP diary, July 6, 1944; William C. Sylvan and Francis G. Smith, Jr., *Normandy to Victory: The War Diary of General Courtney H. Hodges and the First U.S. Army*, ed. John T. Greenwood (Lexington: University Press of Kentucky, 2008), 43; Bradley and Blair, 272; "Notes on France," n.d., box 12, file 3, GSP Collection; GSP to BAP, July 8, 1944, box 12, file 3, GSP Collection.

49. Alfred D. Chandler Jr., ed., *The Papers of Dwight David Eisenhower: The War Years:*, vol. 3 (Baltimore: Johns Hopkins Universty Press, 1970), 1968, 1969.

50. GSP diary, July 7, 1944, box 3, file 6.

51. David P. Colley, *The Road to Victory: The Untold Story of World War II's Red Ball Express* (Washington, D.C.: Brassey's, 2000), 64.

52. Frank Wayne Martin, *Patton's Lucky Scout: The Adventures of a Forward Observer for General Patton and the Third Army in Europe* (Milwaukee: Crickhollow, 2009), 48.

53. GSP diary, July 9, 1944, box 3, file 6.

54. Bernard Carter to Louise Carter, Bernard Shirley Carter Papers, July 7, 1944, box 2, folder 5, Manuscripts Division, USMA Library.

55. Richard J. Stillman and Mary F. Riggs, *General Patton's Best Friend: The Story of General George Smith Patton, Jr. and His Beloved Dog, Willie* (New Orleans: R. J. Stillman, 2001), 46; GSP to BAP, July 10, 1944, box 12, file 3, GSP Collection.

56. George S. Patton, Jr., *War as I Knew It* (New York: Great Commanders, 1975), 69.

57. Hugh A. Harter, *Return to Patton's France: 1944's Odyssey Retraced* (London: Janus, 1999), x.

58. Patton, *War as I Knew It*, 67.

59. Forrest C. Pogue, *Pogue's War: Diaries of a WWII Combat Historian* (Lexington: University Press of Kentucky, 2001), 178; Codman, 153; GSP to BAP, July 15, 1944, box 12, file 4, GSP Collection.

60. Eisenhower, *Eisenhower at War*, 344.

61. GSP diary, July 14 and 17, 1944, box 3, folder 6.

62. GSP to Stimson, July 25, 1944, box 12, file 4, GSP Collection.

63. GSP diary, July 14, 1944, box 3, folder 6.

64. Martin Blumenson, *Breakout and Pursuit: The United States Army in World War II, the European Theater of Operations* (Washington, D.C.: Office of the Chief of Military History, 1961), 213–23.

65. Notes on the Meeting Between General Patton and the Correspondents, Including the P & PW Officer at 2200, July 17, 1944, box 12, file 4, GSP Collection.

66. GSP diary, July 17, 18, and 20, 1944, box 3, file 6.

67. Chandler, *Papers of Dwight David Eisenhower*, vol. 3, 1957, 1958.

68. Chandler, vol. 3, 1978, 1979, 1991.

69. Hesketh, 266, 267.
70. GSP diary, July 14, 1944.
71. John B. McBurney, *The 13th: A Private's Eye View* (Jennings, LA: J. B. McBurney, 1999), 69.
72. Bradley, 357.
73. Patton, *War as I Knew It*, 68.
74. Cooper, *Death Traps*, 45–46.
75. GSP diary, July 23, 1944, box 3, file 6; William C. Butz, *World War II as I Saw It* (Albany, NY: SpectraGraphics, 2005), 13; Blumenson, *Breakout and Pursuit*, 202, 203.
76. GSP diary, July 24, 1944, box 3, folder 6; Bradley and Blair, 279, 280.
77. Bradley and Blair, 273–78; Chandler, vol. 3, 2002–4.
78. GSP diary, July 25, 1944, box 3, file 6.
79. Chet Hansen diaries, box 4, file 11, Chester B. Hansen Collection, USAHEC.
80. Kevin M. Hymel, "Armored Blitz into Avranches," *WWII History* 10, no. 1 (December 2010): 41; GSP diary, July 25, 1944.
81. GSP diary, July 25 and 26, 1944, box 3, file 6.
82. Hesketh, 269, 270.
83. Blumenson, *Breakout and Pursuit*, 242–46.
84. Frank James Price, *Troy H. Middleton: A Biography* (Baton Rouge: Louisiana State University Press, 1974), 186; Hobart Gay Papers, diary, July 27, 1944, box 2, USAHEC.
85. RG 407, WWII Operations Reports, 1941–48, 4th Armored Division, 604-3.3, box 12395, NARA; RG 407, WWII Operations Reports, 1941–48, 6th Armored Division, 606-3.1, box 12552, NARA.
86. GSP to BAP, July 27, 1944, box 12, file 4, GSP Collection; GSP diary, July 27–29, 1944, box 3, file 6. Ladislas Farago's book, *Patton: Ordeal and Triumph*, credits Patton as telling Middleton, "I want Wood and Grow to lead the advance" (New York: Berkley Books, 1984), 455. But according to records, Middleton had already put them in the van. In addition, Frank James Price's *Troy Middleton: A Biography* (186) relates that Patton directed the two armored divisions be put in the van, but the transcripts of Price's interviews with Middleton, at the Manuscripts Division of the LSU Library at Louisiana State University, reveal no such evidence. Middleton never clarified if he ordered the armor forward or if Patton did.
87. Martin Blumenson, ed., *The Patton Papers*, vol. 2, *1940–1945* (Boston: Houghton Mifflin, 1974), 500.
88. Thomas J. Evans, *Reluctant Valor* (Latrobe, PA: St. Vincent College Center for Northern Appalachian Studies, 1995), 73.
89. Interview, Embry D. Lagrew by Richard Bean, May 21, 1986, Louie B. Nunn Center for Oral History, University of Kentucky.
90. Hymel, "Armored Blitz into Avranches," 44.
91. Allen, *Lucky Forward*, 86.
92. John S. Wood, *Memories and Reflections*, unpublished memoir, 1956–1966, the Jack Hixson collection, 74.

93. Robert Allen diary, 15, Robert Allen Collection, GSP Museum; Allen, 86.
94. DDE to GSP, July 30, 1944, box 12, file 4, GSP Collection.
95. Allen, 89; DDE to GSP, July 30, 1944; Patton, *War as I Knew It*, 69.

Bibliography

Archives and Manuscript and Collections

The American West Center, University of Utah
    Paul O. Huber
Center for Archival Collections, Bowling Green State University
    Clifford Duncan
The Center for the Study of War and Society, University of Tennessee
    Robert Allen, *In Memoriam: George S. Patton Jr., General, U.S. Army*
Dwight D. Eisenhower Presidential Library and Museum.
    Eisenhower Papers
Jack Hixson Collection, Leavenworth, Kansas
    John S. Wood, *Memories and Reflections,* unpublished memoir, 1956–1966.
Library of Congress
    Bernard Shirley Carter Papers
    Everett S. Hughes Collection
    George S. Patton Collection
Veterans History Project
    George E. Crago
    Richard Nelms Jones
    William David Laird
    James R. McCartney
    Ralph D. Whitcomb
    Robert Winkel
    Allison Wysong
Louie B. Nunn Center for Oral History, University of Kentucky.
    Andrew Kiddey
    Embry D. Lagrew
McCormick Research Center, First Division Museum at Cantigny
    Clift Andrus, "Notes on Bradley's Memoirs"
    Stanhope Mason Papers

New York State Military Museum, Saratoga Springs, New York
  Malcolm Atkinson
  Alexander Joseph Bohen
  Peter Deeb
  Durward M. Kelton
The Patton Museum, Fort Knox, Kentucky
  Robert Allen Collection
National Archives and Records Administration
  GSP to Leslie McNair, August 2, 1943, RG 337, HQs, Commanding General, General Corres. file, box 10.
  Report of Operations of Third Infantry Division in Sicily, July 19-23, July 31-Aug. 7, 1943, RG 407, WWII Operations Reports, 1940-48, 3rd Infantry Division, file 303-0.3, pages 7-9.
  GSP to General Leslie McNair, June 8, 1943, RG 337, HQS, Commanding General, General Corres. file 1940-44, box 10.
  Testimony of Colonel Forrest E. Cookson, February 16, 1944, Lt. Col. Kenneth W. Hechler to Charles B. MacDonald, June 22, 1956, RG 319, Records of the Army Staff, Center of Military History, Breakout and Pursuit, Correspondence, Memorandum, Notes Relating to Seine, the Drive to-Chapter 26, entry 93, box 9.
  "Notes on Planning and Assault Phases of the Sicilian Campaign," by A Military Observer (later identified as Robert Henriques), COHQ Bulletin No. Y/1, II Corps, Historical Section, Subject Files 1943-1945, RG 338, box 12.
  Oscar Koch to BG James A. Norell, December 15, 1960, RG319 Records of the Chief of Military History, Background Files: Sicily and the Surrender of Italy 1937-1967, Critique of Manuscript, Copy 2 to Progress Reports and Orders of Continuation, box 18, ARC ID 2216436 P Entry 103.
  RG 159, Entry 26F, Office of the Inspector General, General Correspondence, 1939-1947, folder 333.9, box 67.
  RG 319 Records of the Chief of Military History, Background Files: Sicily and the Surrender of Italy 1937-1967, Critique of Manuscript, Copy 2 to Progress Reports and Orders of Continuation, box 18, ARC ID 2216436 P, entry 103.
  RG 338, Records of US army Operational, Tactical and Support Operations (World War II and Thereafter), II Corps, Historical Section, Subject Files, 1943-1945, box 12, entry P 42890, Report on Operations Conducted by II Corps, United States Army, Tunisia, March 15-April 10, 3.
  RG 407, Records of the Adjutant general's Office, WWII Operational Reports, 1940-48, 1st Infantry Division, Box 5002, folder 301-0.3.
  RG 407, WWII Operations Reports, 1941-48, 4th Armored Division, 604-3.3, box 12395.
  RG 407, WWII Operations Reports, 1941-48, 6th Armored Division, 606-3.1, box 12552.
  The Situation in Italy, July 1, 1943, RG 218, box 103, file 6, Records of the U.S. Joint chiefs of Staff.

BIBLIOGRAPHY 401

Testimony of MG Troy Middleton, Office of the Inspector General, February 19, 1944, RG 159, entry 26F, Office of the Inspector General, General Correspondence, 1939–1947, folder 333.9, box 67.
Third Army Plans for "Operation OVERLORD," RG 407, Records of the Adjutant General's Office, WWII Operations Reports, 1941–48, Preinvasion Plans, 195 to 201, folder 201, box 19244.
Truscott to BG James A. Norell, January 10, 1961, RG 319 Records of the Army Staff, Office of the Chief of Military History, Background Files: Sicily and the Surrender of Italy 1937-1967, box 18.
United States v. Sergeant Horace T. West, RG 159, entry 26F, Office of the Inspector General, General Correspondence, 1939–1947, folder 333.9, box 67.
The National Museum of the Pacific War, Nimitz Education and Research Center, Fredericksburg, Texas
    Philip Cochran
    Edwin Dubois
    Charles Scheffel
National World War II Museum, Oral Interviews, New Orleans, LA
    Monty Boinott
    Alvin Callender
    George Griffenhagen
    James McLaughlin, Jr.
    John "Jack" Vessey
Rutgers University Oral History Archives
    John H. Cook
    Franklyn A. Johnson
    Clifford Kingston
    John T. Waters
Stanford University, Hoover Institution Archives
    Albert Wedemeyer Papers
University of Tennessee, Veteran Oral History Project
    Ben Franklin
U.S. Army Heritage and Education Center
    Donald E. Currier Papers
    Hobart R. Gay Papers
    Chester B. Hansen Collection
    Paul Harkins photo albums
    John A. Heintges Papers
    John P. Lucas Papers
    George S. Patton Papers
    Russel B. Reynolds Papers
    WWII Veteran Surveys
    Paul Carter
    Jack Copeland

William Faust
Robert Marsh
Edward Opal
Robert Meade Parker
Stanley Silverman
Eugene Wington
U.S. Military Academy Library, Manuscripts Division, West Point, New York
Bernard Shirley Carter Papers
Wisconsin Veterans Museum Research Center, Madison, Wisconsin
Edsin F. Boettger

Books

Alexander of Tunis, Harold, Earl. *The Alexander Memoirs: 1940–1945*. London: Frontline, 2010.

Allen, Robert S. *Lucky Forward: The History of Patton's Third U.S. Army*. New York: Vanguard, 1947.

Altieri, James. *The Spearheaders*. New York: Bobbs-Merrill, 1960.

Andariese, Walter S. *World War II thru Korea*. Hastings, NE: Snell, 1974.

Ankrum, Homer R. *Dogfaces Who Smiled through Tears*. Lake Mills, IA: Graphic Publishing, 1987.

Army Doctrine Publication 6-22. *Army Leadership and the Profession*. Washington, D.C.: Department of the Army, 2019.

Arnbal, Anders. *The Barrel-Land Dance Hall Rangers: World War II, June 1942-February 1944*. New York: Vantage, 1993.

Arthur, Max. *Forgotten Voices of World War II: A New History of World War II in the Words of the Men and Women Who Were There*. Guilford, CT: Lyons Press, 2004.

Astor, Gerald. *Terrible Terry Allen: Combat General of World War II: The Life of an American Soldier*. New York: Ballantine, 2003.

Atkinson, Rick. *An Army at Dawn: The War in North Africa, 1942-1943*. New York: Henry Holt, 2002.

———. *Day of Battle: The War in Sicily and Italy, 1943–1944* (New York: Henry Holt and Company, 2007), 159.

Ayer, Frederick. *Before the Colors Fade: Portrait of a Soldier: George S. Patton, Jr*. Atlanta, GA: Cherokee, 1964.

Balkoski, Joseph. *Omaha Beach: D-Day, June 6, 1944*. Mechanicsburg, PA: Stackpole, 2004.

———. *Utah Beach: The Amphibious Landing and Airborne Operations on D-Day, June 6, 1944*. Mechanicsburg, PA: Stackpole, 2005.

Barnes, Larue Harper. *They Were There: Texas Veterans Remember World War II*. Hillsboro, TX: Hill College Press, 2006.

Barnett, Correlli, ed. *Hitler's Generals*. New York: Grove Weidenfeld, 1989.

Barron, Leo. *Patton's First Victory: How General George Patton Turned the Tide in North Africa and Defeated the Afrika Korps at El Guettar*. Guilford, CT: Stackpole, 2018.

Barry, Steven Thomas. *Battalion Commanders at War: U.S. Army Tactical Leadership in the Mediterranean Theater, 1942-1943.* Lawrence: University Press of Kansas, 2013.
Bennett, Donald V. *Honor Untarnished: A West Point Graduate's Memoir of World War II.* New York: Forge, 2003.
Black, Robert W. *Rangers in World War II.* New York: Ivy Books, 1992.
Blaker, Gordon A. *Iron Knights: The United States 66th Armored Regiment.* Shippensburg, PA: Burd Street, 1999.
Bland, Larry I., ed. *The Papers of George Catlett Marshall.* Volume 4. Baltimore: Johns Hopkins University Press, 1996.
Blumenson, Martin. *Breakout and Pursuit: The United States Army in World War II, the European Theater of Operations.* Washington, D.C.: Office of the Chief of Military History, 1961.
———. *Kasserine Pass: Rommel's Bloody, Climactic Battle for Tunisia.* New York: Cooper's Square, 2000.
———. *Patton: The Man behind the Legend, 1885-1945.* New York: Morrow, 1985.
Blumenson, Martin, ed. *The Patton Papers.* Vol. 1, *1885 1940.* Boston: Houghton Mifflin, 1972.
———. *The Patton Papers.* Vol. 2, *1940-1945.* Boston: Houghton Mifflin, 1974.
Boven, Robert W. *Most Decorated Soldier in World War II: Matt Urban.* Victoria, B.C.: Trafford, 2000.
Bradley, Omar N. *A Soldier's Story.* New York: Modern Library, 1999.
Bradley, Omar N., and Clay Blair. *A General's Life: An Autobiography by General of the Army Omar N. Bradley.* New York: Simon and Schuster, 1983.
Breuer, William B. *Drop Zone Sicily: Allied Airborne Strike, July 1943.* Novato, CA: Presidio, 1983.
———. *Hoodwinking Hitler: The Normandy Deception.* Westport, CT: Praeger, 1993.
Brooks, Stephen, ed. *Montgomery and the Eighth Army: A Selection from the Diaries, Correspondence and Other Papers of Field Marshal the Viscount Montgomery of Alamein, August 1942 to December 1943.* London: Bodley Head for the Army Records Society, 1991.
Brown, Anthony Cave. *The Last Hero: Wild Bill Donovan: The Biography and Political Experience of Major General William J. Donovan.* New York: Times Books, 1982.
Butcher, Harry C. *My Three Years with Eisenhower: The Personal Diary of Captain Harry C. Butcher, USNR, Naval Aide to General Eisenhower.* New York: Simon and Schuster, 1946.
Butz, William C. *World War II as I Saw It.* Albany, NY: SpectraGraphics, 2005.
Carpenter, Anton Earl, and A. Anne Eiland. *Chappie: World War II Diary of a Combat Chaplain.* Mesa, AZ: Mead, 2007.
Chandler, Alfred D., Jr., ed. *The Papers of Dwight David Eisenhower: The War Years,* vols. 2 and 3. Baltimore: Johns Hopkins University Press, 1970.
Clark, Mark. *Calculated Risk.* New York: Harper and Brothers, 1950.
Clarke, Rupert. *With Alex at War: From the Irrawaddy to the Po, 1941-1945.* London: L. Cooper, 2000.
Codman, Charles. *Drive.* Boston: Little, Brown, 1957.

Colley, David P. *The Road to Victory: The Untold Story of World War II's Red Ball Express*. Washington, D.C.: Brassey's, 2000.
Coon, Carleton S. *A North Africa Story: An Anthropologist as OSS Agent, 1941–1943*. Ipswich, MA: Gambit, 1980.
Cooper, Belton Y. *Death Traps: The Survival of an American Armored Division in World War II*. Novato, CA: Presidio, 1998.
Cowdrey, Albert E. *Fighting for Life: American Military Medicine in World War II*. New York: Free Press, 1994.
Cray, Ed. *General of the Army: George C. Marshall, Soldier and Statesman*. New York: Norton, 1990.
Crosswell, D. K. R. *Beetle: The Life of General Walter Bedell Smith*. Lexington: University Press of Kentucky, 2010.
Darby, William O. *Darby's Rangers: We Led the Way*. With William H. Baumer. San Rafael, CA: Presidio, 1980.
De Grazia, Alfred. *A Taste of War: Soldiering in World War II*. Princeton, NJ: Quiddity, 1992.
D'Este, Carlo. *Decision in Normandy*. New York: Harper Perrenial, 1994.
———. *Eisenhower: A Soldier's Life*. New York: Henry Holt, 2002.
———. *Patton: Genius for War*. New York: HarperCollins, 1995.
De Guingand, Francis. *Operation Victory*. New York: Charles Scribner's Sons, 1947.
Doolittle, Gen. James H. "Jimmy." *I Could Never Be So Lucky Again: An Autobiography*. With Carroll V. Glines. New York: Bantam, 1991.
Dyer, Lt. Col. George. *XII Corps: Spearhead of Patton's Third Army*. N.p: XII Corps History Association, 1947.
Eiland, Robert G. *In Some Ways It Was a Fascinating War*. Philadelphia: Xlibris, 2008.
Eisenhower, David. *Eisenhower at War, 1943–1945*. New York: Random House, 1986.
Eisenhower, Dwight D. *Crusade in Europe*. Garden City, NY: Doubleday, 1948.
Eisenhower, John S. D. *General Ike: A Personal Reminiscence*. New York: Free Press, 2003.
Elson, Aaron. *The Armored Fist: The 712 Tank Battalion in the Second World War*. Charleston, SC: Fonthill Media, 2015.
———. *Tanks for the Memories: The 712th Tank Battalion during World War II*. Hackensack, NJ: Chi Chi, 2001.
Evans, Thomas J. *Reluctant Valor*. Latrobe, PA: St. Vincent College Center for Northern Appalachian Studies, 1995.
Farago, Ladislas. *The Last Days of Patton*. New York: Berkley Books, 1984.
———. *Patton: Ordeal and Triumph*. New York: Ivan Obolensky, 1964.
Finke, Blythe Foote. *No Mission Too Difficult!: Old Buddies of the 1st Division Tell All about World War II*. Chicago: Contemporary Books, 1995.
Forty, George. *The Armies of George S. Patton*. New York: Arms and Armour, 1996.
Friedenberg, Zachary B. *Hospital at War: The 95th Evacuation Hospital in World War II*. College Station: Texas A&M University Press, 2004.
Garland, Albert N., and Howard McGaw Smyth. *Sicily and the Surrender of Italy*. Washington, D.C.: U.S. Government Printing Office, 1965.
Gavin, James M. *On to Berlin: Battles of an Airborne Commander, 1943–1946*. New York: Viking, 1978.

Gelb, Norman. *Desperate Venture: The Story of Operation Torch, the Allied Invasion of North Africa*. New York: W. Morrow, 1992.
Gerard, Philip. *Secret Soldiers: The Story of World War II's Heroic Army of Deception*. New York: Penguin, 2002.
Gunther, John. *D Day*. New York: Harper and Brothers, 1943.
Hamilton, Nigel. *Monty: The Battles of Field Marshal Bernard Montgomery*. New York: Random House, 1994.
Hampton, Ellen. *Women of Valor: The Rochambelles on the WWII Front*. New York: Palgrave MacMillan, 2006.
Harkins, Paul D. *When the Third Cracked Europe: The Story of Patton's Incredible Army*. Harrisburg, PA: Stackpole, 1969.
Harmon, Ernest. *Combat Commander: Autobiography of a Soldier*. Englewood Cliffs, NJ: Prentice Hall, 1970.
Harter, Hugh A. *Return to Patton's France: 1944's Odyssey Retraced*. London: Janus, 1999.
Henriques, Robert. *From a Biography of Myself: A Posthumous Selection of the Autobiographical Writings of Robert Henriques*. London: Western Printing Services, 1969.
Hesketh, Roger. *Fortitude: The D-Day Deception Campaign*. Woodstock, NY: Overlook, 2000.
Hewitt, H. Kent. *The Memoirs of Admiral H. Kent Hewitt*. Edited by Evelyn M. Cherpak. Newport, RI: Naval War College Press, 2004.
Hickey, Des, and Gus Smith. *Operation Avalanche: The Salerno Landings, 1943*. London: W. Heinemann, 1983.
Hillery, Vic, and Emerson Hurley. *Paths of Armor: The Fifth Armored Division in World War II*. Nashville: Battery Press, 1993.
Hirshson, Stanley P. *General Patton: A Soldier's Life*. New York: HarperCollins, 2002.
Hofmann, George F. *The Super Sixth: History of the 6th Armored Division in World War II*. Nashville: Battery Press, 2000.
———. *Through Mobility We Conquer: The Mechanization of U.S. Cavalry*. Lexington: University Press of Kentucky, 2006.
Holland, James. *Sicily '43: The First Assault on Fortress Europe*. New York: Atlantic Monthly, 2020.
Hope, Bob. *I Never Left Home: Bob Hope's Own Story of His Trip Abroad*. New York: Simon and Schuster, 1944.
Houston, Donald E. *Hell on Wheels: The 2d Armored Division*. San Rafael, CA: Presidio, 1977.
Howe, George F. *Northwest Africa: Seizing the Initiative in the West*. Washington, D.C.: U.S. Government Printing Office, 1957.
Howze, Hamilton H. *A Cavalryman's Story: Memoirs of a Twentieth-Century Army General*. Washington, D.C.: Smithsonian Institution, 1996.
Hoyt, Edwin P. *The GI's War: American Soldiers in Europe during World War II*. New York: Cooper Square, 2000.
———. *The GI's War: The Story of the American Soldier in Europe in World War II*. New York: McGraw-Hill, 1988.

Hymel, Kevin M. *Patton's Photographs: War as He Saw It*. Dulles, VA: Potomac Books, 2006.
Ingersoll, Ralph. *The Battle Is the Pay-Off*. Washington, D.C.: Infantry Journal, 1943.
Irving, David. *The Trail of the Fox*. New York: Avon, 1977.
Jensen, Marvin. *Strike Swiftly!: The 70th Tank Battalion from North Africa to Normandy to Germany*. Novato, CA: Presidio, 1997.
Johnson, Franklyn A. *One More Hill*. New York: Funk and Wagnalls, 1949.
Kaplan, Alice. *The Interpreter*. New York: Free Press, 2005.
Kelly, Mary Pat. *Home Away from Home: The Yanks in Ireland*. Belfast: Appletree Press, 1994.
Kelly, Orr. *Meeting the Fox: The Allied Invasion of Africa, from Operation Torch to Kasserine Pass to Victory in Tunisia*. New York: John Wiley and Sons, 2002.
Kemp, Harry M. *The Regiment: Let the Citizens Bear Arms!: A Narrative History of an American Infantry Regiment in World War II*. Austin: Nortex, 1990.
Kennedy, Paul. *Engineers of Victory: The Problem Solvers Who Turned the Tide in the Second World War*. New York: Random House, 2013.
Kent, Gerald T. *A Doctor's Memoirs of World War II*. Cleveland: Cobham and Hatherton, 1989.
Koch, Oscar W. *G-2: Intelligence for Patton*. Atglen, PA: Schiffer Military History, 1999.
Lewin, Ronald. *Ultra Goes to War: The First Account of World War II's Greatest Secret Based on Official Documents*. New York: McGraw-Hill, 1978.
Lewis, Adrian R. *Omaha Beach: A Flawed Victory*. Chapel Hill: University of North Carolina Press, 2001.
Lochner, Louis P., ed. *The Goebbels Diaries, 1942–1943*. Garden City, NY: Doubleday, 1948.
Macintyre, Ben. *Operation Mincemeat: How a Dead Man and a Bizarre Plan Fooled the Nazis and Assured an Allied Victory*. New York: Oxford University Press, 2010.
MacLean, Malcolm S. "Adventures in Occupied Areas." Unpublished memoir, U.S. Army War College, 1975.
MacVane, John. *Journey into War: War and Diplomacy in North Africa*. New York: D. Appleton-Century, 1943.
Marran, Vincent P. *The Major Looks Over His Shoulder: A Medical Memoir of World War II*. Santa Rosa, CA: Manor House, 1989.
Martin, Frank Wayne. *Patton's Lucky Scout: The Adventures of a Forward Observer for General Patton and the Third Army in Europe*. Milwaukee: Crickhollow, 2009.
Mayo, Lida. *The Ordnance Department: On Beachhead and Battlefront*. Washington, D.C.: Office of the Chief of Military History, 1968.
McBurney, John B. *The 13th: A Private's Eye View*. Jennings, LA: J. B. McBurney, 1999.
McGurn, Barrett. *YANK, the Army Weekly: Reporting the Greatest Generation*. Golden, CO: Fulcrum, 2004.
McKeogh, Michael J., and Richard Lockridge. *Sgt. Mickey and General Ike*. New York: G. P. Putnam Sons, 1946.

McManus, John C. *American Courage, American Carnage: 7th Infantry Chronicles: The 7th Infantry Regiment's Combat Experience, 1812 through World War II.* New York: Forge, 2009.
McPherson, James M. *Battle Cry of Freedom: The Civil War Era.* Oxford: Oxford University Press, 1988.
Members of the Overseas Press Club of America. *Deadline Delayed.* New York: E. P. Dutton, 1947.
Mitcham, Samuel W., Jr., and Friedrich von Stauffenberg. *The Battle of Sicily: How the Allies Lost Their Chance for Total Victory.* Mechanicsburg, PA: Stackpole, 2007.
Mitgang, Herbert. *Newsmen in Khaki: Tales of a World War II Soldier Correspondent.* Lanham, MD: Taylor Trade, 2004.
Monahan, Evelyn M., and Rosemary Neidel-Greenlee. *And If I Perish: Frontline U.S. Army Nurses in World War II.* New York: Knopf, 2003.
Monkman, Bruce N. *Act 2: WWII: The Adventures of Bruce N. Monkman, 1941–1945.* Los Angeles: B. N. Monkman, 2006.
Monks, Noel. *Eyewitness.* London: Frederick Muller, 1955.
Montgomery, Bernard. *The Memoirs of Field Marshal the Viscount Montgomery of Alamein, K.G.* Cleveland: World Publishing, 1958.
Moore, Christopher Paul. *Fighting for America: Black Soldier—The Unsung Heroes of World War II.* New York: Ballantine, 2005.
Moorehead, Alan. *The End in Africa.* New York: Harper and Brothers, 1943.
Morison, Samuel Eliot. *History of the United States Naval Operations in World War II: Operations in North African Waters.* Vol. 2. Boston: Little, Brown, 1975.
———. *History of the United States Naval Operations in World War II: Sicily-Salerno-Anzio*, vol. 9. Boston: Little, Brown, 1975.
Morningstar, James Kelly. *Patton's Way: A Radical Theory of War.* Annapolis: Naval Institute Press, 2017.
Odom, Charles B. *General George S. Patton and Eisenhower.* New Orleans: World Picture Productions, 1985.
Olewiler, B. J. *A Woman in a Man's War.* Philadelphia: Xlibris, 2003.
Oshinsky, David M. *A Conspiracy So Immense: The World of Joe McCarthy.* New York: Free Press, 1983.
Patton, George S., Jr. *War as I Knew It.* New York: Great Commanders, 1975.
Patton, Robert H. *The Pattons: A Personal History of an American Family.* New York: Crown Publishers, 1994.
Pendar, Kenneth. *Adventure in Diplomacy: Our French Dilemma.* New York: DaCapo, 1976.
Perry, Milton F., and Barbara W. Parke. *Patton and His Pistols: The Favorite Side Arms of General George S. Patton, Jr.* Harrisburg, PA: Stackpole, 1957.
Phillips, Henry Gerard. *El Guettar: Crucible of Leadership.* Penn Valley, CA: Henry Gerard Phillips, 1991.
Pitt, Barrie, and Frances Pitt. *The Month-by-Month Atlas of World War II.* New York: Summit, 1989.
Pogue, Forrest C. *Pogue's War: Diaries of a WWII Combat Historian.* Lexington: University Press of Kentucky, 2001.

Polmar, Norman, and Thomas B. Allen. *World War II: America at War, 1941–1945.* New York: Random House, 1991.
Pond, Hugh. *Sicily.* London: W. Kimber, 1962.
Porch, Douglas. *The Path to Victory: The Mediterranean Theater in World War II.* Old Saybrook, CT: Konecky and Konecky, 2004.
Pratt, Sherman W. *Autobahn to Berchtesgaden: A Combat Soldier's View of His Role in World War II as Seen from the Lower Ranks Looking Up.* Baltimore: Gateway, 1992.
Price, Frank James. *Troy H. Middleton: A Biography.* Baton Rouge: Louisiana State University Press, 1974.
Province, Charles M. *The Unknown Patton.* New York: Bonanza, 1983.
Rawson, Andrew. *Eyes Only: The Top Secret Correspondence Between Marshall and Eisenhower, 1943–45.* Gloucestershire, UK: Spellmount, 2012.
Rein, Christopher M. *The North African Air Campaign: U.S. Army Air Forces from El Alamien to Salerno.* Lawrence: University Press of Kansas, 2012.
Ricks, Thomas E. *The Generals: American Military Command from World War II to Today.* New York: Penguin, 2012.
Robinett, Paul McDonald. *Armor Command: The Personal Story of a Commander of the 13th Armored Regiment, of the CCB, 1st Armored Division, and of the Armored School during World War II.* Washington, D.C.: McGregor and Weener, 1958.
Rogers, R. J. "A Study of Leadership in the First Infantry Division During World War II: Terry de la Mesa Allen and Clarence Ralph Huebner." MA thesis, U.S. Army Command and General Staff College, 1965.
Ruggero, Ed. *Combat Jump: The Yong Men Who Led the Assault into Fortress Europe, July 1943.* New York: HarperCollins, 2003.
Salter, Fred H. *Recon Scout.* New York: Ballantine, 2001.
Scharnberg, Ken. *Voices: Letters from World War II.* Nashville, TN: Premium Press America, 1993.
Schoenbrun, David. *Soldiers of the Night: The Story of the French Resistance.* New York: E. P. Dutton, 1980.
Schultz, Alfred W. *Janey: A Little Plane in a Big War.* Middletown, CT: Southfarm, 1998.
Scott, Hugh A. *The Blue and White Devils: A Personal Memoir and History of the Third Infantry Division in World War II.* Nashville: Battery Press, 1984.
Semmes, Harry. *Portrait of Patton.* New York: Appleton-Century-Crofts, 1955.
Smith, C. Cabanne. *My War Years, 1940–1946: Service on Gen. Patton's Third Army Staff.* Houston: Rosenlaui, 1989.
Smith, R. Harris. *OSS: The Secret History of America's First Central Intelligence Agency.* Berkeley: University of California Press, 1972.
Snyder, Louis L., ed. *Masterpieces of War Reporting: The Great Moments of World War II.* New York: Julian Messner, 1962.
Spires, David N. *Patton's Air Force: Forging a Legendary Air-Ground Team.* Washington, D.C.: Smithsonian Institution, 2005.

Stillman, Richard J., and Mary F. Riggs. *General Patton's Best Friend: The Story of General George S. Patton, Jr. and His Beloved Dog, Willie.* New Orleans: R. J. Stillman, 2001.
Sylvan, William C., and Francis G. Smith Jr. *Normandy to Victory: The War Diary of General Courtney H. Hodges and the First U.S. Army.* Edited by John T. Greenwood. Lexington: University Press of Kentucky, 2008.
Taylor, Anna Marjorie. *The Language of World War II: Abbreviations, Captions, Quotations, Slogans, Titles and Other Terms and Phrases.* New York: H. W. Wilson, 1948.
Taylor, John M. *General Maxwell Taylor: The Sword and the Pen.* New York: Doubleday, 1989.
Tedder, Arthur. *With Prejudice: The War Memoirs of Marshal of the Royal Air Force, Lord Tedder, Deputy Supreme Commander of the Allied Expeditionary Force.* Boston: Little, Brown, 1966.
Totten, Ruth Ellen Patton. *The Button Box: A Daughter's Loving Memoir of Mrs. George S. Patton.* Columbia: University of Missouri Press, 2005.
Tregaskis, Richard. *Invasion Diary.* New York: Random House, 1944.
Truscott, Lucian K., Jr. *Command Missions: A Personal Story.* Novato, CA: Presidio, 1990.
Vogel, Steve. *The Pentagon: A History: The Untold Story of the Wartime Race to Build the Pentagon—and to Restore It Sixty Years Later.* New York: Random House, 2007.
Wallace, Brenton G. *Patton and His Third Army.* Harrisburg, PA: Military Service Publishing, 1946.
Wedemeyer, Albert C. *Wedemeyer Reports!* New York: Henry Holt, 1958.
Weed, Robert C. *In Time of War.* Tucson: Wheatmark, 2006.
Weirick, Dorothy Millard. *WAC Days of WWII: A Personal Story.* Laguna Niguel, CA: Royal Literary, 1992.
Wellard, James. *General George S. Patton, Jr.: Man Under Mars.* New York: Dodd, Mead, 1946.
West Point Military History Series. *The Second World War: Military Campaign Atlas.* Wayne, NJ: Avery, 1989.
Westmoreland, William C. *A Soldier Reports.* Garden City, NY: Doubleday, 1976.
Whitehead, Don. *Combat Reporter: Don Whitehead's World War II Diary and Memoirs.* Edited by John B. Romeiser. New York: Fordham University Press, 2006.
Whitehead, Ernest D., Sr. *World War II: An Ex-Sergeant Remembers.* Kearney, NE: Morris, 1996.
Whitlock, Flint. *The Fighting First: The Untold Story of the Big Red One on D-Day.* Boulder: Westview, 2004.
———. *The Rock of Anzio: From Sicily to Dachau: A History of the 45th Infantry Division.* Boulder: Westview, 1998.
Williamson, Porter B. *I Remember General Patton's Principles.* Tucson: Management and Systems Consultants, 1979.
Winterbotham, F. W. *The Ultra Secret.* New York: Dell Books, 1974.

Wren, George Ross. *Normandy to Czechoslovakia in World War II: A G.I.'s Memoirs.* St. Louis, MO: Morris Publishing, 1998.

Yeide, Harry. *Fighting Patton: George S. Patton Jr. through the Eyes of His Enemies.* Minneapolis: Zenith, 2011.

Zabecki, David T., ed. *Chief of Staff: The Principal Officers Behind History's Great Commanders.* Vol. 2. Annapolis: Naval Institute Press, 2008.

Zaloga, Steven J. *Sicily 1943: The Debut of Allied Joint Operations.* Long Island City, NY: Osprey, 2013.

———. *US Armored Divisions: The European Theater of Operations, 1944–45.* Oxford: Osprey, 2004.

Articles

Belt, Richard W., Jr. "On Board the 'AUGIE' at Casablanca." *Naval History* 29, no. 5 (October 2015): 37. https://www.usni.org/magazines/naval-history-magazine/2015/october/board-augie-casablanca.

Gavin, James M. "Two Fighting Generals: Patton and MacArthur." *ARMY* 15, no. 4 (April 1965): 32–38.

Hymel, Kevin M. "Armored Blitz to Avranches." *WWII History* 10, no. 1 (December 2010): 41–47.

———. "Commanding Patton's Personal Tanks." *WWII Quarterly* 9, no. 2 (Fall 2017): 22–24.

———. "D-Day Dilemma." *WWII History* 7, no. 6 (August/September 2008): 52–55.

———. "The Last Man in Hell." *WWII History* 15, no. 1 (December 2015): 46–53.

———. "Patton and the Tiger." *Supply Line* 36, no. 2 (April/May 2017): 30–32.

———. "Profiles: Twice General Joseph Stilwell Landed Two of the United States' Most Coveted Commands, and Twice He Lost Them." *WWII History* 1, no. 5 (September 2002): 18–20.

———. "The Real Fury." *WWII Quarterly* 8, no. 1 (Fall 2016): 76–77.

———. "Red River Kids at War." *America in World War II* 13, no. 2 (August 2017): 20.

Ossad, Steven L. "Command Failures: Lessons Learned from Lloyd R. Fredendall." *Army* 53, no. 3 (March 2003): 45–52.

Rein, Christopher. "Fredendall Failure: A Reexamination of the II Corps at the Battle of Kasserine Pass." *Army History* no. 108 (Summer 2018): 6–21.

Rodriquez, Harold A. "Dispatches." *WWII History* (June/July 2008).

Weingartner, James J. "Massacre at Biscari: Patton and an American War Crime." *Historian* 52, no. 1 (November 1989): 24–39.

Author Interviews

Bob Bosser
Frank S. Errigo
Peter Havale
Edward L. Trey

Newspapers

Capital Times
Courier Journal
Fort Worth Star-Telegram
Independent Sunday
Los Angeles Times
Miami News
Stars and Stripes
Washington Post

Index

Page numbers in *italics* refer to illustrations.

1 Armored Corps: Fifth U.S. Army, 64; Hobart "Hap" Gay, 22; Keyes, 70; Palermo, 129; Patton, 15, 34, 129, 250; Seventh Army, 137, 152; Western Task Force, 35, 60. *See also* Seventh Army
101st Airborne, Operation OVERLORD, D-Day, Sainte-Mère-Église, 320
10th Panzer Division, 68, 82, 94, 99
157th Infantry Regiment, Operation HUSKY, Falcone landing, 209
15th Army Group, 184, 219
15th Infantry Regiment, 41, 191, 198
15th Panzer Division, 131, 165, 213
16th Panzer Division, 220
16th Infantry Regiment, Gafsa, 90
180th Infantry Regiment, Operation HUSKY, German prisoners, 168
18th Army Group, 15th Army Group, 72, 83, 121, 129, 137. *See also* 15th Army Group
1st Armored Division: Bizerte, 117–20; Combat Command B, 58; drive to the coast, 100–105; Fredendall, 63, 67, 69; Harmon, 116; Kasserine Pass, 81, 88; Henry Cabot Lodge, Jr., 208; Maknassy Pass, 82, 88; Maknassy, heights east of town, 93–95, 98; new formation of, 274; Patton, encounter, 58; Patton, fuel, 55; Patton, visit to, 76, 91; Patton's assessment of, 88; 21st Panzer Division, 113; Sened Station, capture of, 92–93; Sidi Bou Zid, 68; slow moving of, 93; Orlando Ward 93, 93. *See also* John Waters

1st Infantry Division: Allen, relief of, 185; Big Red One, 75; drive to the coast, 100, 102; El Guettar, 82, 94, 98; England, departure for, 253; Enna, 171, 173; Gafsa, 88, 89, 93; Gela, 154, 157, 159; German attack on, 94, 170, 113; *LIFE* magazine, 149; Nicosia, 190; Palermo, 131, 179; Patton, assessment of, 88, 239; Patton, farewell to, 244; Patton, shaming of, 163; Patton, visit to, 113, 147, 227–28; Ponte Olivo, 161; practice landing, 139; Seventh Army, initial assault plan, 144; Sicily, preparation for, 119; tank attack on, 154, 158–59; Troina, 193, 194, 195, 198, 201; Huebner, 320, 333. *See also* Allen, Terry de la Masa
20th Engineer Battalion, Operation HUSKY, 176
21st Panzer Division: 1st Armored Division, repulsion of, 113; Fredendall's II Corps, 68; Gafsa, 88–89
29th Infantry Division, Operation OVERLORD, D-Day, Omaha Beach, 319–20
29th Panzer Grenadier Division: Operation HUSKY, 199; Patton, difficulties with, 214
2nd Armored Division (French), 300
2nd Armored Division: Bradley, II Corps, 137, 166; D-Day, 322; England, departure for, 253; Fort Benning, 32; Gaffey, 144, 154, 270, 280; Gay, 22; Gela, 154; Harmon, 116; Jenson, 23; Licata, 144; new division structure of, 274; Patton, 32, 33, 36, 38,

413

2nd Armored Division (continued)
39, 226, 250, 322; Roosevelt (president), parade for, 62; Seventh Army, 137,167, 175, 273; Seventh Army, initial assault plan, 144–45; Southern Attack Group, 16; Tennessee, 33; Western Task Force, 16. *See also* Operation HUSKY

34th Infantry Division: anti-tank demonstration, 78; Bizerte, 119; John Crocker, 121; drive to the coast, 100, 103; Fondouk Pass, 121; helmets, 78–80; Robert Moore, 81; passes, defense of, 88; Patton's assessment of, 88; Tunis, victory parade in, 139; Tunisian front, French corps, 63

36th Infantry Division, 131, 159, 232

39th Regimental Combat Team, Flint, 187

3rd Armored Division, 274, 341

3rd Cavalry Regiment, 11, 31

3rd Infantry Division: Patton visit to, 56, 70, 147, 228; Roosevelt (president), parade, 62; Seventh Army, 137, 144, 162, 177, 179, 190, 198, 208, 238; Sicily, 161, 163, 165, 168, 291, 307; training exercises, 65; Western Task Force, 16, 26, 39. *See also* Operation AVALANCHE, Operation HUSKY, *and* Operation TORCH

45th Infantry Division: "Boneheads," 227; Native Americans, 226; Palermo, 131, 181; Patton visit to, 146, 227; Seventh Army, initial assault plan, 144–45. *See also* Operation HUSKY

47th Infantry Regiment, drive to coast, support to, 117

4th Armored Division, 274, 294, 309, 342, 343, 344. *See also* Operation OVERLORD

4th Infantry Division: Operation OVERLORD, D-Day, Sainte-Mère-Église, 320; Teddy Roosevelt (general), 337

4th Moroccan Tabor of Goums, Seventh Army, initial assault plan, 145, 174.

504th Parachute Infantry Regiment: 144, 155, 161. *See* Operation HUSKY, 504th Parachute Infantry Regiment

505th Parachute Infantry Regiment, 143–44, 163

509th Parachute Battalion, Operation HUSKY, Messina, Brolo landing, 202

5th Cavalry Regiment, 11

601st Tank Destroyer Battalion, 88, 94

60th Infantry Regiment, Patton visit to, 16, 227

70th Tank Battalion, 16

753rd Tank Battalion, Operation HUSKY, Messina, attack on, 198

78th "Batttleaxe" Infantry Division, Operation HUSKY, 172

7th Field Artillery Battalion, El Guettar, German attack on, 94–95

82nd Airborne Division: 312, 320; friendly fire incident, 161, 265; Italy, 238; large-scale airborne assault, Army's first, 143, 144, 145, 155, 158, 137; Patton's visit to, 245, *229*; Seventh Army, 137, 165, 173, 181, 191. *See also* Operation AVALANCH, Operation HUSKY, *and* Operation OVERLORD

83rd Infantry Division, Operation OVERLORD, 333

8th Infantry Division, Operation OVERLORD, 276, 333

90th Infantry Division. *See* Operation OVERLORD, 90th Infantry Division

91st Evacuation Hospital, 193

9th Cavalry Regiment, 11

9th Infantry Division, 16, 38, 76, 88, 92, 95, 98, 100, 102, 103, 104, 113, 145, 146, 147, 165, 169, 173, 175, 187, 189, 191, 193, 201, 202, 209, 227, 239, 253, 325. *See* Operation HUSKY, Operation OVERLORD, *and* Operation TORCH

II Corps: Harold Alexander, orders from, 72; Bizerte, 119–20, 135; Bradley command, 122, 137, 203; First Army, part of, 72; Fredendall, 56, 63, 64, 165; Kasserine Pass defeat, 68–69; Operation AVALANCHE, Keyes, 239; Operation HUSKY, 154; Enna, 171; Patton, Eisenhower, Bradley's recommendations to, 92; Patton, 70, 71, 72, 73, 74, 76, 77, 78, 83, 85, 87, 88, 91, 92, 95, 98, 100, 101, 109, 112, 113, 114, 115,

II Corps (continued)
116, 117, 119, 120, 121, 122, 123, 127, 128, 150, 178, 211, 276; under Seventh Army, 137
II Polish Corps, 259
VI Corps, Operation AVALANCHE, 238–39, 276
Vichy France, 16, 20, 49, 50
Victor Emmanuel III, 185
VII Corps, 333, 335
X Corps (British), 238, 240
XII Air Support Command, 97, 193, 206
XII Corps, Operation OVERLORD, Patton speech, 284
XIX Tactical Air Command, Operation OVERLORD, 274–75
XX Corps, Operation OVERLORD, Patton's visit to, 294, 334, 339

African American soldiers: executions of, 248; Gela beach, AWOL soldier, 156, 156; integration of, 278; Lee, 278; 91st Evacuation Hospital, soldier at, 193; Patton's Civil Affairs paper, 336; Patton and 8, 21, 279, 356; rape cases, 247–48; *See also* Meeks, George
Alexander, Harold, 5, 63, 72, 82, 83, 88, 89, 91, 92, 93, 98, 103, 113, 114, 115, 116, 167, 169, 170, 171, 172, 172, 177, 182, 184, 193, 194, 200, 201, 202, *208*, 210, 219, 226, 237, 238; 18th changed to 15th, 137; Bizerte meeting, 120; Eighth Army, under command of, 72; Fredendall, 67, 69; Patton, faith in, 100, 276; Patton, forces in El Guettar, 99; Patton, opinion of, 132, 134; Patton, slapping incident, 207, 224. *See also* Operation AVALANCHE, Operation BAYTOWN, Operation HUSKY, Operation TORCH, *and* Operation WOP
Algiers, attack on, 16, 19, 41, 57, 58, 71, 127, 132, 134, 135, 148, 149, 186, 214, 219, 233, 234, 243, 245, 246, 257, 281, 265, 266, 330
Allen, Robert S., 282
Allen, Terry de la Masa, 5, 74, 75, *97*, 113, 130; background of, 75; fighting spirit

of, 96; El Guettar, 94-98, Fredendall, 67; Gafsa, 89; Gela beach, 159–61, 179; Patton, accusations, 130; Patton, re-embarkation plans, 159; Patton, visit, 79, 88, 93; relief of command, 185–87, 190, 191, 201, 227, 228; Troina, 195, 211; Knute Rockne, 89; wool uniforms, 78. *See also* 1st Infantry Division
American First Army, 234, 292
Anders, Wladyslaw, 259–60
Anderson, Jonathan W., 16; French surrender, 26; offensive, trouble with, 57; Operation TORCH, second day, morning of, 39; Patton's birthday present, 43; relief of command, 65
Anderson, Kenneth, 52, 56, 57, 63, 69, 83, 121
Andrus, Clift, 95
Anfa Conference, 61, 63, 64
Anzio: battle cry for, 307; leadership, 308; Operation SHINGLE, 264, 265; Patton, 276, 277, 305
armor division structure of, 230, 274
Armored Corps March, 250
Army Ground Forces, 142
Army Group Afrika, Arnim command of, 87
Army Rangers: El Guettar, 95, Operation HUSKY, landing, 154, 157, 158, 162, 163; Operation HUSKY, Seventh Army, initial assault plan, 144; Sicily, 167, Operation OVERLORD, D-Day, Pointe du Hoc, 319–21; Patton, 98
Army War College, 10, 111, 143, 225
Arnim, Hans-Jürgen Von, 63, 68, 82, 87, 91
automobiles, in combat, 9–10
Avranches, 328, 332, 334-36, 341-44
Axis Sally, 266
Ayer, Frederick, 315

Badoglio, Pietro, 185, 235–36
Bangalore torpedoes, 136
Battle of El Guettar, 80, 82, 94–105, 119, 135, 185, 249,
Battle of St.-Mihiel, 10
Bennett, Paul G., slapping incident, 202-3, 222–25

Benson, Clarence C. "Chauncy," 103, 104, 105, 117-19
Benson Force, 110, 111-13, 176, 366n. See Tunisia, Benson Force
Berber Goumiers, 145, 174
Bernard, Lyle, *196*, 206, 207. See also Operation HUSKY
Bess, Demaree, 220
Big Red One. See 1st Infantry Division
Biscari Massacre, 290-93, 306
Bizerte, 92, 119, 121, 135-36, 237
Blakeney, C.C., Operation COBRA, 336
Blatherwick, T., 300
Blesse, Fred, 220
Blumenson, Martin, 46, 140-41
Bonus Army, 10-11
Boston Traveler, slapping incidents, Kuhl letter, 257-58
Bradley, Omar N., 5, 7, 145, 169, 230, 272, 280, 283, 292, 301, 325, 332, 337; air support, friendly fire, 197; Alexander, II Corps, argument for, 92; American First Army, 233-235, 239, 265, 297, 329, 331-333, 335, 338, 341, 342; Army group command, 260, 262, 293, 329, 331; Biscari Massacre, 202; Bizerte, II Corps capture of, 135; Bradley, Eisenhower, II Corps recommendations to, 92; Calais, 277; Chester "Chet" Hansen, photo, *138*; Commander of the Bath medal, 282; deputy commander, II Corps, 74, 78, 83, 91, 116, 117; 2ème Règiment de Marche Tirailleurs Algèriens, 143; Enna, 171; First US Army Group (FUSAG), 297-98; Lloyd Fredendall, opinion of, 68; Italy invasion, 230; Richard "Dick" Jensen, 107-8, 111, 112; Legion of Honor, 143; Operation COBRA, 328, 335-36, 338, 339, 343; Operation FORTITUDE, 277, 297-98, 308; Operation OVERLORD, 276, 277, 315-317, 320, 321, 324, 331; Patton, Biscari Massacre, 168, 202, 291, 292; Patton, killing of prisoners, 168, 202; Patton, resentment of, 113, 160, 166, 178, 193; Patton, 7th Army, dissolution of, 235; Patton, slapping incidents, 224, 225; II

Corps commander, 122, 135, 137, 140, 159, 166, 170, 171-73, 179, 201-5, 209, 210; *A Soldier's Story*, 112; Terry Allen, 185-187, 191, 201; *Time*, 305-6; Tunis, victory parade, 139. See also Operation HUSKY, *and* Operation OVERLORD
Brewster, Ralph, Knutsford incident, 303
Bridges, Styles, Patton, slapping incidents, 257
Britain, American army, lack of confidence in, 69
British Welcome Club, 298-300
Brittany American Cemetery, curator's story, 3
Brooke, Alan, 69, 165, 282-83
Brooklyn, 170
Brown, Philip E., 291
Browning, Frederick, Gulf of Gela, operations review, 143
Bull, Harold Pink, 111, 112, 140
Butcher, Harry, 28, 71, 72, 127, 128, 191; Cheddington airfield, Patton, 269; Fedala beach, Patton's silence, 28; Operation HUSKY, Eisenhower's visit on *Monrovia*, 162; Patton and Sicily, 232; Patton, Cheddington airfield, 269; Patton, slapping incidents, 220, 238; Patton, to England, 240-41
Butera, 167
Buzz Bomb, 326, 330

Caacie, 269
Calabria, 211; Operation BAYTOWN, 219, 220
Calais. See Operation FORTITUDE
Campanole, N. W., 300
Cardenas, Julio, 9-10, 21
Casablanca, 5, 16, 18, *24*, 26, 39-41, 43-44, 46-48, *48*, 49, 55, 57, 58, 60, 62, 73, 109, 130, 248-250
Casablanca Conference. See Anfa Conference
Castellano, Giuseppe, 232, 234
Catania, 129, 131, 132, 165, 171, 230, 251, 252, 316; capture of, 198
Centauro Division (Italian), Gafsa, 88-89

Chandler, Albert "Happy," Patton's promotion tabled, 314–15
Charlie (Hawai'ian war statue), 18, 25, *25*
Chauvin, 143
Churchill, Winston, 129, 278; Anfa Conference, 61, 62; Dunkirk, 17; Eisenhower, invasion of Italy, 219; France invasion, view on, 226; on Montgomery, 133, 134; on Patton, 134; Operation OVERLORD, 292, 311, 312, 232; Patton, telegram to, 100; Tehran Conference, 258
Clark, Mark, 35, 57, 58, 63, 64, 70, 139, 191, 226, 249, 264; Fifth Army, 56, 230, 248, 260; Medal of Honor, 55; Naples, Patton visit, 248, 263; Operation AVALANCHE, final meeting on, 232; Salerno, performance in, 236, 238, 239, 240, 241, 307
Clark, R. H., 252
Clarkson, Herbert "Bertee," 237
Cochran, Philip, 127
Codman, Charles, 193, 200, 251, 264, 269, 273, 315, 330, 334: background of, 113; Biscari Massacre, 291; Jack Copeland, 210; Dunphie, 266; Knutsford incident, 291, 307; Normandy, departure for, 330; Patton, Grand Cross Order of the Ouissam Alaouite, 61; Patton, silver medallion, 244; Patton, slapping incidents, 255–56; Patton, speech thirty-three, 137
Collins, Joe, Operation COBRA, 335–36, 341
Columbus, Christopher, 247
Command and General Staff College, 10, 178
Compton, John T., killing of prisoners, 168, 288–90
Coningham, Arthur: 310; Bizerte meeting, 120; Gulf of Gela, operations review, 143; Montgomery, HUSKY planning, 132; Patton, Bizerte meeting, 120; Patton, criticism of, 114; Patton, meeting with, 115, 116; Spaatz, criticism of, 114
Cook, Gilbert "Doc," Operation OVERLORD, Third Army exercise, 300
Coon, Carelton S., 50–51

Copeland, Jack, 107–13, 210
Corlett, Charles, Operation OVERLORD, XIX Corps, 277
Costello, John, Knutsford incident, 302–3
Cota, Norm, 185, 320
Council on Foreign Relations, 237
Coutances, Operation COBRA, 335–36, 341-342
Craig, Richard, Jenson's death, 108, 110
Crane, John A., Jenson's death, 111, 112; Patton, slapping incident, 223
Crerar, Henry, 276, 311, 312, 316
Crocker, John, 34th Infantry Division, 121
Crusade in Europe (Eisenhower), 307
Cunningham, Andrew, 184; HUSKY planning meeting, 131
Currie, John C., Operation HUSKY, Messina, 211
Currier, Patton, slapping incident, 203, 222

Dakar, Operation TORCH, 31
Darby, William O.: Butera, 167; Distinguished Service Cross, 163; Gela, 154, 157, 159; helmet, 95; promotion, refusal of, 163–64
Darlan, François, 49, 60
Davidson, Garrison H. "Gar," 247, 259
Davidson, Lyal A., Operation HUSKY, Naval Task Force, 188
Davis, Norman, 237–38
Davis, Ransom, 205
Dawley, Ernest J., VI Corps, relief of, 239–240
"Death Alley," 214
de Gaulle, Charles, 49, 60, 63
Dempsey, Miles, Operation OVERLORD, 270, 276, 316
Devers, Jacob: 277; ANVIL, 261; France, invasion of, 247, 258; Patton, 62, 263, 265, 266
DeWitt, John L., Operation FORTITUDE, 336, 341
Djebel Berta, 94, 98
Djebel Kouif, 69; Patton's headquarters, 73, 83
Dj El Hamra, 68

Donovan, "Wild" Bill, 168
"donut dollie," 329
Doolittle, James, 35, 74, 241, 263
Drum, Hugh, 34
Dunkirk, 17, 212, 263
Dunphie, 111, 112, 266

E'Este, Carlo, xv, 308
Eagles, William, Operation HUSKY, attack on Palermo, 176
Eddy, Manton: 146, 147; Battle of El Guettar, 100–5; Commander of the Bath (COB) medal, 282; headquarters, Patton visit to, 117; Patton on, 88. *See* 9th Infantry Division
Eddy, William, 36
Eighth Air Force, 263, 335
Eighth Army (British): 34, 63, 64, 81, 82, 116, 119, 129, 148, 150, 165, 168-70, 193, 213, 219, 234, 239; Calabria, 219; German squeeze, 71–77; making contact with II Corps, 118; Mareth Line, 72
Eisenhower, Dwight D., 48, 57, 58, 65, 92, 100, 127, 128, 275, 310, 313–314; background, 31-34; "Patton Effect," 230; Harold Alexander, 67, 92, 169, 224; Algiers meeting, Patton's diversionary tour, 246; Terry Allen, 185, 186, 190-191, 201; Allies, view of, 128–29; Anfa Conference, 61, 62, 63; Demaree Bess, 220; Fred Blesse, 220; Bradley, 74, 92, 185, 225, 235, 328, 332; Caacie, 269; Mark Clark, 64, 70; Arthur Coningham, 114, 116; *Crusade in Europe*, 307; François Darlan, North Africa, 49, 60; dog, 269; Fedala beach, Patton, failure to contact, 28; Lloyd Fredendall, 67, 69, 70; Gay, 270, 278; Gibraltar, Patton, meeting with, 52–53, 54; Gulf of Gela, operations review, 143; Hotel St.-George, 127; Italy, 219, 220, 230, 238, 239, 249, 276, 277; Ed Kennedy, 233; Richard Jenson, 109; Knutsford incident, letter to Patton, 306; *LIFE* magazine, 149; Marshall, 219, 224–25, 231, 235, 240, 245, 249, 256, 260, 264, 265, 305; Montgomery, 230, 339, 258; Operation COBRA, 328, 339, 341; Operation HUSKY, 129, 130-132, 135, 137, 140, 145, 149, 150, 169, 191, *192*, 210; Operation TORCH, 20, 28, 30, 31, 35, 36, 38, 41, 44; Operation OVERLORD, 258, 259, 278, 280, 281, 311, 317, 320, 329, 336; Patton, Biscari Massacre, 293; Patton, criticism of British, 64; Patton, difficult relationship with, 6–7, 51, 65, 116, 121, 128, 129, 166, 231, 272, 277, 314, 334; Patton, dinner with in Algiers, 243; Patton, dressing down, 65, 161, 164, 209–10; Patton, exile of, 5; Patton, first-wave landing, prevention of, 149; Patton, France invasion, 260; Patton, Fredendall's command, 70, 71, 73; Patton, Knutsford incident, 6, 301–7, 309, 311; Patton, letter of appreciation, 122–23; Patton, letter on replacements, 239; Patton, letter to Marshall on, 230–31; Patton, meeting on Operation OVERLORD, 239, 262; Patton, memorandum to, 109; Patton, North Africa command, 34–35; Patton, permanent major general rank, 242; Patton, pistols, 209–10; Patton, presence in England, 275; Patton, rating of, 327; Patton, II Corps, 72, 77, 80, 83, *84*, 88, 89, 91, 96, 122; Patton, slapping incidents, 207, 220–22, 224, 230-31, 233–34, 250, 253–55; Patton, tanks, 33; Patton, Third Army, 269, 344; Drew Pearson, slapping incidents, 220-224, 237, 243, 252–56, 259, 260, 262, 292; presidency, eye on, 327; *Saturday Evening Post*, 220; Supreme Headquarters Allied Expeditionary Force (SHAEF), 269; tanks, 33; Tunis, victory parade, 139; John Waters, 87
El Alamein, 17–18, 64
El Guettar, 80, 82, 87–105, 107, 119, 135, 185, 249, 263
Ely, L., Fedala beach, Patton's landing craft, 22
Exercise TIGER, 301

Faïd Pass, 81, 119
Fairbanks, Douglas, Jr., 150

Fedala beach, attack on, xvii, 11, 15–30, 27, 29
Fickett, Edward M., Operation OVERLORD, 6th Cavalry Group, Northern Ireland, 276
Fifth Army, 57, 137, 201, 230, 234, 240, 260; Seventh Army staff, 220, 242. *See also* Operation AVALANCHE, Fifth Army
Fifth Panzer Army, 63, 68
First Army (American), 63, 234, 269, 270, 325, 336
First Army (British), 52, 57, 71, 72, 83, 172
Fish, Hamilton, III, Knutsford incident, 302
Flint, Harry "Paddy," *251*; death of, 340; hedgerow tactics, 333; Patton, 136, 244, 325–26; 39th Regimental Combat Team, 187
"Flying Dutchmen," 330
Fondouk Pass, 121
Fontanne, Lynn, 273
Fredendall, Lloyd, 31, *69*; British, criticism of, 64; defeat at Kasserine Pass, 65, 68; leadership of, 67–69, 73-74, 76; Oran, Patton visit, 56; relief of command, 70
Frederick the Great, 143, 206, 344
Free French, 63
French Dewointine fighter plane, 26
Fries, Walter, 199
Frye, William, Terry Allen, 75
FUSAG, 293, 298, 308–9, 329, 337, 341

Gaffey, Hugh, 70, *71,* 93, 108, 110, 307; 2ème Règiment de Marche Tirailleurs Algèriens, 143; 2nd Armored Division, 144, 145, 154, 159, 173, 175, 177, 187, 270; Distinguished Service Cross, 223; Legion of Honor, 143; Operation HUSKY, attack on Palermo, 177; Operation OVERLORD, Patton chief of staff, 270, 278, 280; Seventh Army, initial assault plan, 144–45
Gairdner, Charles, HUSKY planning, 134
Gallaway, Ion, 249
Garcia, Joan Pujol, 297
Gavin, James, 143–44, 163, 190–91, 312
Gay, Hobart "Hap," *24,* 149, 234, 236, *250,* 300, 307; Operation HUSKY, 155, 160;

Operation HUSKY, Alexander's coded message, 172, 193; Operation HUSKY, Allen's relief, 185–86; Operation HUSKY, attack on Palermo, 177; Operation HUSKY, Messina, entrance into, 210–11; Operation TORCH, 22-23, 26, 40; relief of, 270, 278, 280; Patton, chief of staff, 270; Patton, 7th Army, 152, 234, 242, 263; Patton, slapping incidents, 225; Patton, war crimes, 236–37; return from Casablanca, 40; Seventh Army flag, *150*
Gela beach, 242; Seventh Army, initial assault plan, 129, 131, 132, 134, 143, 144; taking of, 154, *156*-160, 162, 174, 178, 215, 223, 224, 244, 246, 270, 307
"General Patton's Navy." *See* Naval Task Force 88
Generals, The (Ricks), 185
"Gentleman's Club prejudices," 140–41
George VI, 142, 213, 311, 312, 323
Germany, 6, 11, 20, 128, 129, 214, 219, 234, 259, 270, 313; Naples, attack on, 248; Operation FORTITUDE, 297–98; Operation HUSKY, Sicily, 213; study, American combat readiness, 142
Gerow, Operation OVERLORD, France, Fifteenth Army, 329
Giraud, Henri, Charles de Gaulle, 63
"God of Battles" (Patton poem), 148
Goebbels, Joseph, 142, 213
Gordon, Jean, 11, 329–30
Gort (lord), 263
Grant, Robert A., Patton, slapping incident, 257
Grant, Ulysses S., 135, 206
grappling hook, 135–36
Greatest Norman Conquest, The (Osborne), 258
Grigg, Percy James, 142
Grow, Robert W., Operation OVERLORD, 6th Armored Division, 282, 294–95, 325, 338, 341 43
Gruenther, Alfred, 232–33, 249, 263
Guingand, Francis "Freddie" de, 134, 169, 188, 312, 316
Gulf of Gela, operations review, 132, 143

Hall, John Leslie, 320
Hansen, Chester "Chet," 107–10, 112, *138*
Harkins, Paul, 160, 196, 250
Harmon, Earnest (Ernie), 120, 187; "Batter up," 20; Bizerte, 119–20; Casablanca, 43–44; Fredendall, assessment of, 69–70; French battalion, capture of, 22; fuel, 55; German breakthrough, 65; Safi, 20, 39–41; Southern Attack Group, 16; sultan of Morocco, 51; Ward replacement, 116–17; John Waters, 65; Orgaz Yoldi, 49. *See also* 1ˢᵗ Armored
Harriman, Averell, 243
Harris, Arthur, Operation OVERLORD, invasion plan review, 312
Heintges, John, Operation HUSKY, attack on Palermo, 177
Henriques, Robert: Fedala beach, 25, *25*; German safe, 48; Highway 124, 165; Montgomery liaison, 162, 168–69, 188; Operation HUSKY, Patton's re-embark message, 159; Patton on his uniform, 27–28; prisoner release, 42; transports, 147–48
Henry the Fifth (Shakespeare), 288
Hermann Goering Division, 131, 157, 165, 251, 194
Hewitt, Kent, *22, 23, 24, 45*; Casablanca, 41, 43, 48; landing craft, 22, *24*; Naval Task Force 88, 188; Operation AVALANCHE, 232, 238; Operation HUSKY, 239, 157; Operation HUSKY, Messina, planning for, 196; Operation HUSKY, planning, 131, 132, 142–43, 154; Operation TORCH, 28, 48; Patton, first meeting with 23, 36–37; Patton, help getting on board, 40; Patton, relationship with, 23; Patton, Seventh Army flag, 149
Hitler, Adolf, 16, 17, 20, 35, 36, 47, 49, 68, 87, 214, 245, 276, 337–38
HMS *Seraph*, 147
HMS *Welshman*, 28
Hodges, Courtney, 272, 282, 316; Eisenhower, army command, 260; German small-unit tactics, 332; Marshall, 302; new weapons, deployment of, 325; Palermo, visit to Patton, 247
Hope, Bob, 225–26
Hopkins, Harry, 63, 259
House, Edwin, 206
Howell, Reese, 95
Howze, Hamilton "Ham," 102
Hube, Hans Valentin, Operation HUSKY, 212
Huebner, Clarence, 174, 185, 186, 194, 201, 320, 333
Hughes, Everett, 130, 134, 151, 197, 236, 255, 261, 263, 266, 269, 270, 279; Biscari Massacre, 291–92; Herbert "Bertee" Clarkson, 237; Davidson, 247; Eisenhower, 62, 128, 149, 243, 247, 259, 278; Gordon, 329; Operation OVERLORD, 270, 317 328; Patton, "cry on my shoulder," 262; Patton, first-wave landing, 149; Patton, Grand Cross Order of the Ouissam Alaouite, 61; Patton, Knutsford incident, 300, 303, 307, 310, 311; Patton, letter on war crimes, 236; Patton, opinion of, 128; Patton, slapping incidents, 224, 252, 254, 260; Pearson, 254
Hull, Cordell, 303
Hull, J. E., Patton, 277

"If" (Kipling), 304
Ingersoll, Royal, 37–38
International Federation of the Red Cross, 237, 329
Irving, Leroy, 275
Italian Centauro Division, 88-89
Italy, armistice, 232, 234 –36
Italy, early invasion plans, map of, *221*

James Parker, 266
Japanese, 11, 68, 137, 292, 300, 303, 335; Operation HUSKY, Sicily, 213; Pearl Harbor 16, 32, 34
Jean Bart, 39, 62
Jenson, Richard "Dick," 23, 83, *111*; death of, 107–13, 123; 2ème Règiment de Marche

Jenson, Richard "Dick" (continued)
    Tirailleurs Algèriens, 143; Gafsa, 89;
    landing craft, 22-23, *24;* Legion of Honor,
    143; Mrs. Patton, letter to, 92
Jewell, Norman, Seventh Army, initial
    assault plan, 147
Johnson (general), Operation HUSKY,
    Messina, Brolo landing, 202
Johnson, E., landing craft, 22, *24*
Johnson, Edwin C., Patton, slapping
    incidents, 257
Johnson, Jed, Patton, slapping incident, 257
Joyce, Kenyon, 243, 255, 303

Kasserine Pass, 59, 68-69, 73-76, 78, 81, 82,
    84, 87-88, 91, 99, 112, 119, 122, 139, 185,
    188, 213, 274
Kennedy, Edward, 233, 257
Kent, Gerald, 198
Keyes, Geoffrey, 36, 41, 70, 143, 160,
    162, 173, 131, 160, 162, *182,* 187, 192,
    196, 198, 202, 205, 210, 230, 236, *251;*
    Distinguished Service Cross, 223; Gulf
    of Gela, operations review, 143; II Corps
    flag, *150;* Italy invasion, meeting on, 230;
    Operation AVALANCHE, II Corps, 239,
    240, 264; Patton, meal before Italy, 241;
    provisional corps, 165, 170, 173, 175-78,
    181-82; Wedemeyer on, 143. *See also*
    Operation HUSKY, Geoffrey Keyes
Kilpatrick John Reed, 37
Kipling, 304
Kirk, Alan, 148-149
Knights of Malta, 263
Knox, Frank, 240
Knutsford Incident, 6, 298-308, 311, 314,
    329
Knutson, Harold, 302
Koch, Oscar, 8, 70, 166, 186
Kuhl, Charles H., 194-95, 203, 223, 257-258
Kuter, Laurence, Coningham problem,
    meeting on, 115

Lagrew (colonel), Operation COBRA, 342
Lambert, Kent, 70

Landing Ship Tanks (LSTs), 135
Landrum, Eugene, 338
Langford, Frances, 225
Lavitrano, Luigi, 181, *183,* 187, 191, 244, 253
Lawrence, Justus "Jock," Patton, Knutsford
    incident, 307
LCS. *See* London Controlling Section
leader, army definition of, 3-4
Leclerc, Jacques-Philippe, 300, 326
Lee, John C. H., 269, 273, 278, 293, 301, 334
Leese, Oliver, 65
Lemnitzer, Lyle, 211
Leyman, Walter, 310
LIFE magazine, 33, 149
Lodge, Henry Cabot, Jr., 208-9, 257
London, 35-36, 53, 129, 139, 261, 269, 272-
    274, 277, 280, 288-289, 297, 309-12, 326,
    328-330
London Controlling Section (LCS), 297-98,
    309
Los Angeles Times, Patton, 305
Louisiana maneuvers, 32, 131, 184, 230, 249,
    282, 329
Lucas, John P.: Alexander, Palermo,
    169-70; British, 170, 242; Eisenhower's
    visit on *Monrovia,* 162; Hugh Gaffey,
    Distinguished Service Cross, 223;
    Geoffrey Keyes, Distinguished Service
    Cross, 223; Naples, Patton visit, 248;
    Operation AVALANCHE, VI Corps,
    239, 242, ; Operation HUSKY, 149,
    166, 169, 170, 185, 209; Operation
    HUSKY, Messina, entrance into, 210-11;
    Operation HUSKY, Palermo, Luftwaffe
    bombing of, 192; Operation SHINGLE,
    242, 248, 264, 270, 276; Patton, chaperone
    for, 149; Patton, oak leaf cluster, 223;
    Patton, slapping incidents, 195, 220-22,
    255, 230; Patton, return to *Monrovia,*
    160-61; Pearson, 255; USS *Mayrant,* 192
"Lucky Peel," 271
Luftwaffe, 48, 80, 105, 107, 113, 154, 163,
    197, 248; Brolo, 201, 207; Casablanca, 137;
    Friendly fire incident, 154-55, 171; Gela,
    160-61, 215; Naples, 248; Palermo,

Luftwaffe (continued)
    192; Patton's headquarters, 105; Patton's
    Piper Cub, 207; *Robert Rowan*, 160; Santo
    Stefano, 198, 199; Sicily, 152, 212; USS
    Maddox, 154
Lunt, Alfred, 273

MacKelvie, Jay, 338
Mainwaring, 271, 327
Maknassy, 119, 88, 92-94; Alexander, 98-99;
    German retreat from, 118; Harmon, 116;
    Patton's primary mission, 81-82; Ward,
    93-94, 98
marching-fire demonstration, 309-10
Mareth Line, 68, 72, 87, 91, 93, 99
Marquand, John P., 228, 250-52
Marshall, George C., 11, 35, 62, 135,
    139, 153, 279, 331; Allen, 75, 131, 186;
    Bradley, 235, 342; Eisenhower, 61, 91,
    114, 230-231, 2235, 254, 256, 264, 336;
    1st Infantry Division practice landing,
    140-41; Fredendall, 67, 70; Italy,
    invasion of, 219; "Marshall's Boys," 67;
    Mediterranean, "suction pump," 219;
    officers, relief of, 186-87, 249; Operation
    HUSKY, Patton, congratulations to, 213;
    Operation TORCH, 35, 37; Operation
    TORCH, Dwight D. Eisenhower, 31,
    34; Pacific, 219; Patton, ANVIL, 260,
    264; Patton, Carolina maneuvers, 34;
    Patton, diversionary tour, 245, 259,
    262-263, 288; Patton, HUSKY briefing,
    139; Patton, Knutsford incident, 301-5;
    Patton, OVERLORD, 255, 260; Patton,
    praise for, 61, 128, 213, 246, 277, 341, 342;
    Patton, roommate, 31, 38; Patton, slapping
    incidents, 224-25, 230, 235, 256-58, 261;
    Patton, staff, opinion of, 246; Seventh
    Army, 137; Sicily, concerns about, 129;
    Washington, 258
"Marshall's Boys," 67
Mason, Charles H., 241-42
Mason, Stanhope, 234-35
McCloy, John, 258-59, 293-94, 314
McClure, Robert, Patton, opinion of, 278
McCreery, Richard, 103, 117, 119, 240

McGee, Hugh, 294, 325
McKeogh, Michael, 83
McLain, Raymond S., 307-308, 338
McMahon, William C., 276
McNair, Lesley, 142, 193, 194, 201, 241, 243,
    250, 255, 261, 283-84, 336-37, 340
McNarney, Joe, 290, 293-94
McQuillan, Raymond E., 120
McSherry, Frank, 202
Mediterranean Air Command, 115, 131, 169
Meeks, George, 174, 265, 279; background,
    23; Algiers, bombing of, 137; boots, for
    Patton, 328; Bradley, 265; Casablanca,
    bombing of, 60; Fedala beach, landing
    craft to, 21-23, *24*; Hotel Miramar, 28;
    Jenson, grave of, 123; Normandy, flight to,
    330; Patton, relationship with, 8; Willie,
    279
Mehdia, 16, 21, 40
Meuse-Argonne offensive, 10
Mexico, 4, 9, 21, 38, 74, 145, 259
M5 light tank, 338
Michelier, François, 26, 44, *45*
Middleton, Troy: Avranches, 328, 342;
    background of, 145; 5th Armored
    Division, 313; Operation COBRA, ground
    attack of, 340, 341, 343; Operation
    HUSKY, 165, 181, 187-88, 190; Operation
    OVERLORD, VIII Corps, 279-80, 293,
    313, 333, 339, 341; Patton, 146, 277;
    prisoners, killing of, 168, 291; Selune
    River, 344; Seventh Army, initial assault
    plan, 144, 161; tanks in Sicily, 293. *See also*
    VII Corps *and* 45th Infantry Division
Miller, Charles H., 184, 194
Miller, Whiteside, 324
Mitgang, Herbert, 254-55
Moltke, Helmet von, the Elder, 258, 328
Monrovia, 150, 155, 109, 160; Casablanca,
    109; Eisenhower, 161; embarkation, 149;
    invasion, 153-54, 162; Kirk, bet with, 148;
    radios, 161
Montgomery, Bernard Law, *133, 189,* 233,
    237; Alexander, 131, 165, 172, 182;
    Churchill on, 134; El Alamein, 17, 64;
    Italy invasion, 230, 234; Legion of Merit,

INDEX

Montgomery, Bernard Law (continued) 230; Messina, 170, 172, 181, 187–88, 211, 243; Operation BAYTOWN, Calabria, 219, 234, 238; Normandy, 329, 331–32; Operation FORTITUDE, 297-298, 308, 323; Operation GOODWOOD, 339; Operation HUSKY, planning, 129, 131-134, 148; Operation HUSKY, 162, 165, 168, 172, 198; Operation OVERLORD, invasion planning, 276–77, 292-293, 311, 316; Operation TORCH, 17–18; Patton, in Sicily, 5, 202, 212, 249; Patton, misquote, 64-65; Patton, relationship with, 7, 150, 184, 213, 252, 282, 334; Tunisia, 68, 72, 87, 91-93, 100, 118-119, 122. *See also* Operation HUSKY

Moore, Robert, 81
Morgenthau, Henry, 243
M-29 Weasel, 325
Muhammad V: Anfa Conference, 61; anniversary of coronation, 53; Festival of Id el Kabir, *52*; Patton and Noguès, meeting with, 51–52, *54*; Patton, apology from, 60; Patton, letter from, 42; Patton, time with, 59, 61, 64; Roosevelt, 49, 62
Muller, Walter J., 37
Mundt, Karl E., Knutsford incident, 302
Mussolini, Benito: arrest of, 185, 235; Palermo, 177; portraits, Shell Building, 47; Sicily, 129, 214

Napoleon, 132, 143, 246, 259, 310
Native Americans, 226
NATOUSA. *See* North African Theater of Operations, U.S. Army
Naval Task Force 88, Operation HUSKY, 188
Nelson, Horatio, 206, 247
Ninth Air Force, Operation COBRA, 335
Ninth Army, 298, 315, 329
Nixon, Thomas, 135–36
Noguès, August, 44, 49–54, 60, 62
North African Theater of Operations, U.S. Army (NATOUSA), 61
Northern Attack Group, 16, 37

Odom, Charles, 249, 255

Oliver, Lunsford P., 282, 313-314
Operation ANIMALS, 245
Operation ANVIL, 260, 261, 264–65
Operation AVALANCHE: air support, 321; Anzio battle cry, 307; Harold Alexander, Salerno, 237–38; Clark's final meeting on, 232–33; Dawley, relief of command, 239; 82nd Airborne Division, 238; Fifth Army, embarkation, 235; Fifth Army, armistice, 235–36; Fifth Army, attack review, 191; Fifth Army, Salerno, 219, 235–36; Fifth Army, Seventh Army addition to, 220; German defenses at, 236; German counterattack, 238; Italy, armistice with, 235; Keyes, II Corps, 239; Lucas, 239; Mark Clark, Salerno, 219; McCreery, complaint about Dawley, 240; Patton, worries of, 226, 232; Salerno, 219, 236; II Corps, Keyes, 239; VI Corps, 239; 3rd Division, German counterattack, 238; Truscott, 238
Operation BAYTOWN, 219
Operation COBRA: Avranches, 342–43; C. C. Blakeney, 336; Bradley, air commanders, 338–39; Brittany ports, 339; Joe Collins, 335–36; Collins, VII Corps, ground attack, 341; Coutances, capture of, 341; Eighth Air Force, 335; Eisenhower, ground attack of, 341; 15th Tank Battalion, 342; Paddy Flint, 340; 4th Armored Division, 341–43; friendly fire, 338–39; ground attack of, 341; Grow, review crossing, 342; Grow, 6th Armored Division, ground attack of, 341–42; Haislip, Third Army, XV Corps, 339, 341; Lagrew, 342; Middleton, ground attack of, 341; Middleton, Selune River, 344; Middleton, Third Army, VIII Corps, 339–44; Ninth Air Force, 335; Patton, 15th Tank Battalion, 342; Patton, briefing, 336; Patton, Civil Affairs of, 336; Patton, VIII Corps, temporary command of, 341; Patton, Grow (general), river crossing, 342; Patton, James Taylor, river crossing, 342; Patton, Selune River, 344; Patton, 6th Armored Division, 15th Tank Battalion,

Operation COBRA (continued)
  342; Patton, Third Army, 339–45; Patton, Wood, Avranches, 342–43; Quiberon Bay, 339; Rennes, 339; 6th Armored Division, ground attack, 341–42; success of, 343; James Taylor, river crossing, 342; 3rd Armored Division, ground attack, 341; Third Army, 339–45; VII Corps, 335; VIII Corps, 339–44; Walker, Third Army, XX Corps, 339; Wood, 341–43; XV Corps, 339, 341; XX Corps, 339
Operation FORTITUDE, 297–98; Arabel, 297; Bradley, 277; Abwehr, 337; Beetle Smith, Patton, relief of, 337; Brutus, 308, 337; D-Day, 322-323; John L. DeWitt, FUSAG, 336, 341; end of, 330; Freak, 308; FUSAG, 293, 298, 308–9, 329, 336–37, 341; Garbo, 297, 308; Joan Pujol Garcia, 297; German Fifteenth Army, 330; Knutsford incident, 308–9; Lesley McNair, 336–37, 340–41; OKH intelligence, 337; Patton, cover story on, 328–29; Patton, East Anglia, 313; Patton, in England, 287; Patton, James Gavin, 312; Patton, German intelligence on, 328; Patton, German search for, 322-323; Patton, outing of, 309; Patton, role in, 298; visitors ban, 336; William Simpson, 341
Operation GOODWOOD, 339
Operation HUSKY: Agrigento, 162, 164, 166-167, 170, 174, 178, 219; airborne disaster, 164, 171, 213, 265, 322, 338; Terry Allen, 159-161, 179, 185–87, 190, 191, 195, 201, 227; amphibious battalion, Brolo, 201-202, 206–8, 321; amphibious battalion, Messina, 196, *196*; amphibious battalion, Sant'Agata, landing at, 198–99, 200; Army Rangers, 144, 154, 157–58, 162, 163, 167; Battle of Kursk, 214; Bernard, amphibious force to Messina, 196, *196*, 199, 206; Biscari Massacre, 290–93; Bradley, Falcone landing, 209; Bradley, on Allen's relief, 185–87; Bradley, Patton's fixation on Messina, 193; Bradley, Troina, 201; Brolo, 201–2, 205–8; campaign assessment, 212–14; Catania, capture of, 198; Codman, Jack Copeland, 210; Norm Cota, 185; John C. Currie, Messina, 211; Darby, 154, 157, 159, 163, 167; "Death Alley," 214; Eddy, Mount Etna, 202; Edwin House, 206; Falcone, amphibious landing, 191, 209; 15th Infantry Regiment, Eisenhower visit to Patton, 191; 15th Panzer Grenadier Division, exposed, 165; 504th Parachute Infantry Regiment, 144, 155, 161; 509th Parachute Battalion, Messina, Brolo landing, 202; Flint, 39th Regimental Combat Team, 187; Walter Fries, 199; Gaffrey, attack on Palermo, 177; Gay, Alexander's coded message, 172; Gay, Messina, 210–11; Gay, Palermo, 177; Gela, 154–59; "General Patton's Navy," 188; George VI, congratulations to Patton, 213; German evacuation of, 194, 211–12; Joseph Goebbels, 213; Harkins, Messina planning, 196; Hermann Goering Division, 131, 157, 165, 194, 251; Hans Valentin Hube, 212; Clarence Huebner, 174, 185–86, 194, 201; Hewitt, 131, 143, 149, 157, 188, 196; Italy, plan of attack, 191; Japanese thoughts on, 213; Johnson, Messina, Brolo landing, 202; 157th Infantry regiment, Falcone landing, 209; Oscar Koch, Allen's relief of command, 186; Kuhn incident, 195; Luigi Lavitrano, 181, *183*, 187, 191; Lyle Lemnitzer, Messina, 211; Henry Cabot Lodge, Jr., 208–9; Lucas, 149, 160–62, 166, 169, 170, 185, 192, 195, 209; Frank McSherry, 202; Middleton, 45th Infantry relief, 190; Miller, Meeting at Montgomery's Syracuse headquarters, 184; Mussolini, 185, 214; Naval Task Force 88, 188; Nicosia, helmetless Roosevelt, 188–189; 91st Evacuation Hospital, 193; OSS officers, 214; Palermo, 5, 129, 132, 164-179, 181-182, 189, 192; paratroopers, 153-154, 161; Piano Lupo, 144, 154; Ponte Olivo, 144, 160, 161; Port Empedocle, capture of, 164, 170; Robert Porter, Allen's relief of command, 186; Provisional Corp, 165, 173-174, 176, 181–82; Randazzo, 209;

INDEX

Operation HUSKY (continued)
Ransom Davis, 205; review of, 228–30; Eberhard Rodt, 213–14; Roosevelt (Teddy, Jr.), 185–90, 201; San Stefano, 172, 193, 195, 197; Sant'Agata, 199, *200*, 202; II Corps, Enna, 171; 753rd Tank Battalion, Messina, attack on, 198; Seventh Army, 143–45, 152, 159, 162, 165, 170, 172; 181; 193; 78th "Battleaxe" Infantry Division, 172; Beetle Smith, 184, 211; *Stars and Stripes*, foxhole jumping, 215; strategic consequences for, 214; 39th Regimental Combat Team, 187; Troina, 193, 195, 198, 201, 251, 172; "Truscott Trot," 179, 181; XII Air Support Group, 206; 29th Panzer Grenadier Division, 199, 214; USS *Philadelphia*, 170, 206–7

Operation HUSKY, 1st Infantry Division: Enna, 171, 173; Gela, 144–45, 154, 157–59, 163; German counter-attack on, 170, 179; Ponte Olivo, 161; relief of Allen and Roosevelt, 185, 190; Troina, 193, 195, 198, 201

Operation HUSKY, 2nd Armored Division: Butera, 167; Gela, landing at, 137, 144–145, 154; Palermo, attack on, 173, 175–78; Patton's provisional corps, 165; Trapani, 181

Operation HUSKY, 3rd Infantry Division: Agrigento, attack on, 162, 166, 170; Brolo, 201-02, 206, 208; Falcone, 209; 1st division, 170; 45th Infantry replacement, 189–93; Gela, tanks to, 157–58; landing, 144, 147, 154; Messina, 187, 190; Palermo, 131, 167, 173, 177; Patton's provisional corps, 165; San Fratello, 199; Sant'Agata, 199, 200

Operation HUSKY, 45th Infantry Division: Biscari Massacre, 168, 290–91; 3rd Infantry replacement of, 190, 193; exhaustion of, 187; Falcone landing, 209; landing, 146, 154; Highway 124, 165, 166; relief of, 189–90; Termini Imerese, 181

Operation HUSKY, 82nd Airborne Division: Axis attack, 158; Gela, invasion drop, 153, 155, 158; Gela, operations review, 143–45;

Palermo, 173; Patton's provisional corps, 165; Trapani, 181

Operation HUSKY, 9th Infantry Division: 1st Infantry replacement, 193; Paddy Flint, 187; Messina, 189–90; Mount Etna, 202; Palermo, 169, 173, 189; Patton, provisional corps, 165; Patton, visit to, 146–47; Randazzo, 209; Seventh Army, initial assault plan, 145; 39th Regimental Combat Team, 187; Sossio River, 175; Troina, 201

Operation HUSKY, Alexander: Gela, 150; Highway 124, 165; Montgomery, orders to split island, 165; Montgomery's Syracuse headquarters, meeting at, 182–84; Oder delayed, 172, 193-94; Palermo, 164, 169–71, 193–94; Patton's criticism of, 166, 166, 169, 170; Patton, congratulations to, 177–78; Patton, shift to, 172; Patton visit, 207; planning of, 129–34, 145; Troina, 201

Operation HUSKY, Bradley: Allen's relief, 185–87, 191, 201; Biscari Massacre, 168, 202; Brolo landing, 202-05; Falcone landing, 209; Highway 124, 165–66; Palermo, significance of, 178; Patton contradicting his command, 160; Patton's fixation on Messina, 193; Patton, meeting with, 171, 173; Patton's use of 1st Infantry Division, 159; planning and training, 135, 140; poor health, 160; Troina, 201

Operation HUSKY, Eisenhower: airborne disaster, 164; Alexander's decision on Palermo, 169; Allen's relief, 185–87, 190–91; Italy, plan of attack, 191; *Monrovia*, visiting Patton on, 161–62; Montgomery's Syracuse headquarters, meeting at, 184; Patton, worried about, 149; Patton, visit to in Palermo, 191, *192*; Patton, final word to before, 149; planning of, 129–32, 145; slapping incidents, 207, 220

Operation HUSKY, Keyes: Agrigento, 162; amphibious assaults, 196, 198, 202, 205; bet, days to capture Sicily, 160; Cardinal Lavitrano, 187; Messina, 210–11; Palermo, 176, 192; planning, 131, 143; Provisional Corps, 165, 177, 181–82

Operation HUSKY, Messina: air support, 197; attack on, 198–99; campaign objective, 129, 134; map, *199*; fall of, 210; Gavin planning, 190; Hewitt, 196; Montgomery, 5, 184, 188; Patton planning for, 164, 166, 172, 190, 193–97, 202; Patton's entrance, 210-11, 213; Ridgway planning for 190; Beetle Smith, 211; woman in red dress, 210

Operation HUSKY, Montgomery: Catania, 129, 198; Highway 124, 165; Palermo, condescending to Patton, 162, 168–69; Palermo, meeting with Patton at, 188, *189*; Patton, congratulations to, 213; Patton's criticism of, 148; planning, 131–34; Beetle Smith, 132–34; stymied, 172, 212; Syracuse 131, 182–84

Operation HUSKY, Patton: Agrigento, 164, 166, 170, 178; Alexander, 162, 164–66, 169-70, 172, 177–78, 184, 201; Allen, 159–60, 185-87, 190–91, 201; Paul G. Bennett, 202–3, 207; Biscari massacre, 168; Bradley, 159–60, 166, 168, 201, 203; Brolo, 201–2, 208; campaign assessment, 212–13; Darby, 157, 163–64, 167; deserters, 202; Eisenhower, *Monrovia*, 161-62; Eisenhower visit in Palermo, 191, *192*; Falcone landing, 209; 15th Evacuation Hospital, visit to, 194–95; Flint, 187; friendly-fire incidents, 161, 164, 171, 197; Gela, 154–58, 160; George VI's congratulations to, 213; Highway 124, 165; Kuhn incident, 194-95; Luigi Lavirtrano, 181, *183*, 187, 191; Henry Cabot Lodge, Jr., 208–9; Luftwaffe attack on fleet, 154; Marshall's congratulations to, 213; Messina, entrance into, 210–11; Messina, fixation on, 193–94; Messina, woman in red dress, 210; *Monrovia*, 148–49, 153, *155*, 160-62; Montgomery, 162, 168–69, 172, 182–84; 91st Evacuation Hospital, visit to, 193; 93rd Field Hospital, 202; Palermo, attack on, 175–79, 194; Palermo, meeting with Alexander on, 170–71; Palermo, Montgomery meeting at, 188, *189*; Palermo, royal palace, 179; planning and training, 127-128, 130-36, 139-42, 144, 147; re-embarkation message, 159; Roosevelt, 188, 190–91, 213, 201; San Stefano headquarters, 197; sand-fly fever, 171, 209; Seventh Army, congratulations, to, 211; Tiger tanks, 173; Troina, 195; Truscott, Brolo, 205–6; Truscott, Hill 171, 198; wounded soldiers, photo, *204*

Operation HUSKY, Truscott: Agrigento, attack on, 162, 166-67, 170; Brolo landing, 205–9; Falcone landing, 209; Hill 171, 198; Messina, 187, 210-11; Palermo, 176, 179, 181, *182*; Patton's praise of, 167; San Fratello, 199; San Stefano, 195–96; Sant'Agata, 196, *200*

Operation OVERLORD: "a clip for each field," 333; Robert S. Allen, 282; American armies landing in, 329; Army Rangers, D-Day, Pointe du Hoc, 319–21; Avranches, 328; briefing, 292; British intelligence, Calais, 270, 322; British planning of, 297; Charles Codman, Normandy, departure for, 330; Charles Corlett, XIX Corps, 277; Churchill, 292, 311–12, 323; Norm Cota, D-Day, predawn assault argument, 320; Crerar, 276, 312, 316; Dempsey, 270, 276, 316; Manton Eddy, 9th Infantry Division, 325; VIII Corps, 279–80, 293, 333, 341; 8TH Infantry Division, 276, 333; 83rd Infantry Division, 333; 82nd Airborne Division, D-Day, Sainte-Mère-Église, 320; Exercise TIGER, 301; Edward M. Fickett, 6th Cavalry Group, Northern Ireland, 276; Fifteenth Army, 330; XV Corps, 293, 341; 5th Armored Division, 282, 313-14; 5th Infantry Division, 275, 326; final meeting for, 315–16; First Army, 234, 239, 269, 270 292, 293; 1st Infantry Division, 319–20, 333; First United States Army Group (FUSAG), 293, 298, 329; Paddy Flint, 325–26, 333; fly-over training, 309; 4th Armored Division, 274, 294, 309, 342–44; Gaffey, Patton chief of staff, 280; James Gavin, London, Claridge's Hotel, 312; Gay, relief of, 278-80; George VI, invasion plan

INDEX

Operation OVERLORD (continued) review, 311–12; German small-unit tactics, 332; Gerow, Fifteenth Army, France, 329; Graves Registration, 293; Grow, 6th Armored Division, 282, 294–95, 325, 338; Freddie de Guingand, 311-12, 316; Wade W. Haislip, 293; John Leslie Hall, 320; Arthur Harris, invasion plan review, 312; Hodges, German small-unit tactics, 332; Clarence Huebner, 320, 333; invasion meeting, 276; Leroy Irving, 5th Infantry Division, Northern Ireland, 275; Eugene Landrum, 90th infantry Division, 338; Jacques-Philippe Leclerc, 2nd Armored Division, 326, 300; John C.H. Lee, 269, 273, 278, 293, 301, 334; Jay MacKelvie, 338; marching-fire demonstration, 309–10; Marshall, Patton, 260, 305; John McCloy, Patton griping, 314; McCloy, review of Patton's plans for, 293–94; Raymond S. McLain, 90th Infantry Division, 338; William C. McMahon, Northern Ireland, 276; McNarney, review of Patton's plans for, 293–94; George Meeks, Normandy, departure for, 330; Troy Middleton, VIII Corps, 279–80, 293, 313, 333, 328; Troy Middleton, "Tactical Use of Separate Tank Battalions," 293; Whitside Miller, relief of, 324; Montgomery, invasion meeting, 276; XIX Corps, Charles Corlett, 277; XIX Tactical Air Command, Third Army, 274–75; 90th Infantry Division, 294, 305, 333, 337-38; Ninth Army, 298, 315, 329; 9th Communications Zone, 334; 9th Infantry Division, 253, 325; Normandy, Third Army, map, 340; Lunsford Oliver, 282, 313–14; Omaha Beach, 319–21, 324, 331, 333; 101st Airborne Division, D-Day, Sainte-Mère-Église, 320; Patch, Alexander "Sandy," 273, 329; Pointe du Hoc, 319–21; Edson Raff, D-Day, Utah Beach, 322; Walter Robertson, 2nd Infantry Division, Northern Ireland, 275; Teddy Roosevelt (general), D-Day, 337; Sainte-Mère-Église, 320; 2nd Armored Division (French),

Patton's visit to, 326; Second Army, 270; 2nd Infantry Division, Northern Ireland, 275; William Simpson, 284, 315, 329, 341; 6th Armored Division, 294–95, 325; 6th Cavalry Group, Northern Ireland, 276; Beetle Smith, 313–14, 337; Fay Smith, 324; Spaatz, 270, 312; Al Stiller, Normandy, departure for, 330–31; Stimson, letter to Patton, 335; Tedder, phone call with Eisenhower, 280; Third Army, 329; 35TH Infantry Division, 327; XII, Patton speech, 284; XX Corps, Patton's visit to, 294; 29TH Infantry Division, D-Day, Omaha Beach, 319–20; Utah Beach, D-Day, 319–22; Vierville Draw, 320, 321; Walton Walker, XX Corps, 294, 334; Otto P. Weyland, 274–75, John "P" Wood, 274, 294; Allison Wysong, 273

Operation OVERLORD, 4TH Armored Division: Avranches, 341, 342–44; Patton, 274, 294, 309; rehearsals, 309

Operation OVERLORD, Bradley: D-Day, commanders, relief of, 324; final operation meeting, 315–16; First Army, 260, 262, 270, 305; invasion meeting, 276, 312, 315–16; Isigny headquarters, meeting with Patton, 331; leaders, 324; Normandy, 324, 328; Omaha Beach, 320-21; Patton, as superior of, 293, 331; Third Army 293

Operation OVERLORD, D-Day, 316–17, 319–23; Army Rangers, Pointe du Hoc, 319–21; Bradley, relief of commanders, 324; Raff Edson, 322; 101st Airborne Division, Sainte-Mère-Église, 320; 1st Infantry Division, 319–20; Jay MacKelvie, 338; Patton, 317, 319, 323; 29th Infantry Division, Omaha Beach, 319–20; 4th Infantry Division, 320, 337; 82nd Airborne Division, Sainte-Mère-Église, 320; 90th Infantry Division, Utah Beach, 338; Teddy Roosevelt, 337; Utah Beach, 319–21

Operation OVERLORD, Eisenhower: Bradley, 334; Exercise TIGER, 301; 9th Communications Zone, 334; Patton, 260, 262, 328; planning of, 278; tank tracks, 280–81; Tedder, 280; Third Army

428 INDEX

Operation OVERLORD, Eisenhower (cont.)
activation, 334; 35th Infantry Division,
training exercise, 327
Operation OVERLORD, Montgomery:
Bayeux headquarters, meeting with
Patton, 331–32; briefing, 292; Caen-on-
D-Day, 311; final operation meeting,
316; gentleman's gambling, 316; invasion
meeting, 276; invasion plan review, 311;
Third Army, 293, 334
Operation OVERLORD, Patton: alternate
landing site, 270; Avranches, plan for,
328; Bradley, Brest Peninsula, 332–33;
Bradley, criticism of, 335; Bradley's
Isigny headquarters, meeting at, 331;
Breamore House, 327; briefing, 292,
315-16; England, celebrity in , 272; Crerar,
criticism of , 316; Dempsey, criticism of ,
316; Guingand, criticism of , 316; D-Day,
319–23; Eisenhower, battle plan for,
328; final operation meeting, 315–16; 5th
Armored Division, morale and discipline
of, 313–14; 5th Infantry Division visit
to, 326; Paddy Flint, 325–326, 333; 4th
Armored Division rehearsals, 294, 309;
James Gavin, London, Claridge's Hotel,
312; gentleman's gambling, 316; George
(son), letter to, 319; grandchildren, letters
and poems to, 315; headquarters, London,
V-1 rocket, 326; headquarters, Néhou,
333–34; headquarters, Peover Hall,
271–73, 327, 282, 304, 327; headquarters,
personnel, meeting , 271–72;
headquarters truck, 323–24; Hodges,
332; invasion meeting, 276; invasion
plan review, 311–12; Philippe Leclerc,
300; letter quoting Eisenhower, 313;
Walter Leyman, 310; London flat, 273;
Mainwaring pub, 271, 327; marching-fire
demonstration, 309–10; Troy Middleton,
293, 313, 328, 333; Montgomery,
Bayeux headquarters, meeting at, 332;
Montgomery, opinion of at final operation
meeting, 316; Montgomery, Third Army
activation, 334; Mosquito, 309; M-29
Weasel, 325; 90th Infantry Division, visit
to, 294, 333; Normandy, departure for,
330; Lunsford Oliver, 313–14; Omaha
Beach, speech on, 331; Omaha Beach,
volunteer missions, 333; "passion pit," 273;
Patton speech, 282–88, 289; preparation
for, 270; principles of command, 281–282;
route of attack, map of, 315; 2nd Armored
Division (French) visit, 326; 6th Armored
Division, visit to, 294–95; 76mm cannon
demonstration, 325; Fay Smith, 324;
Beetle Smith, conflict with, 314; staff
of, 270; Stimson, 335; "Tactical Use of
Separate Tank Battalions," 293; tank
tracks, 280–81; Third Army, 270, 334,
339–40; 35th Infantry Division, training
exercise, 327; XX Corps, visit to, 294;
United States at war, reasons for, 272; V-1
launch site, 333; war, being left out of,
314; Weyland relationship, 275; Whitside
Miller, relief of, 324; Allison Wysong, 273
Operation OVERLORD, Third Army, 270,
274, 276, 281, 293, 313, 323; exercise, 300;
"Lucky," 271; map, 340; XIX Tactical Air
Command, 274–75; Patton letter quoting
Eisenhower, 313
Operation RANKIN A, B, C, 270
Operation SHINGLE, Lucas, 264
Operation TORCH, 16; amphibious
assault, problems with, 37–38; Jonathan
Anderson, 16, 39, 43; British concerns,
18, 35; Casablanca, 26, 41, 43–44, 48, 48;
Dakar, 31; Eisenhower, 28, 30, 31, 36, 41;
Lloyd Fredendall, 31, 67; French army in
Morocco, surrender of, 44–46; Harmon,
16, 20, 22, 39–41, 43-4; initial concept
of, 31; map, 17; Montgomery, 17–18;
Patton, mine-laying ship, 37–38; Patton,
second day rampage, 39–40; Patton, staff
review, 47; Patton, task force commander,
appointment, 31; planning sessions, 18;
political crisis, 49; Erwin Rommel, 31, 34,
39; Charles Ryder, task force commander,
appointment, 31; second day, 39–40;
third day, 40–41; 3rd Infantry Division,
Casablanca, 39–40, 43; Lucien Truscott,
Mehdia beach, 16, 21, 40, 42, 53

INDEX

Operation WOP, 88–92
Oran: Allen, 75; attack on, 16, 19, 67, 41; Fredendall, 56, 67; George VI visit to, 142; Patton, final staff meeting in, 148; Patton, headquarters, 130; Roosevelt, 19
Osborne, James van Wyck, 258

Panzerkampfwagen IV Tiger Ausf. Es, 173
Park, Keith, 262
Pas-de-Calais. *See* Operation FORTITUDE
Patch, Alexander "Sandy," 273, 329
Patton, Beatrice (wife): 9, 56, 59, 97, 110, 121, 134, 136, 141, 151, 224, 234, 241, 250, 283; African Americans, 279; boar's teeth, 64; "Charlie," 25; Jean Gordon, 329, Patton's dreams of, 294 171; Patton leaving the army, 292, 303, 308; Patton missing D-Day, 317, 319; slapping incidents, 256-57, 259, 266, 275; Patton waiting to get into combat, 324-26, 334
Patton, Beatrice, Little Bea (daughter), 9, 58, 171, 256
Patton, George: Allen, assessment of, 186; American forces, British command, 63; American soldiers, 142; amphibious landings, fourteen points, 141; Wladyslaw Anders, 259-60; Anderson, evaluation of, 26, 65; Anfa Conference, 61-63; anti-aircraft fragments, "like fireflies," 248; anti-Semitism, 8, 50, 203; Anzio, 264, 276-77, 305; appearance, Fedala beach, 15, 16, 23-26; "The Arab," 140; Arch of Trajan, 123, *123*; Armistice Day, 249-50; Army shoulder patch, 137-39; Army War College, 10, 111, 143, 225; artillery resupply ideas, 95; background of, 9-11; bayonets, 38, 100, 136, 139-40, 146, 228, 283, 326; birth, 7; birthday, 10, 43, 249-51, *251*; Bizerte, 92, 119-20, 135; boar hunting, 57, 64; bomb crater, Jenson's death, photo, *112*; bomber's jacket, 74; Bonus Army, 11; Bradley, 7, 265, 335; "brains and guts," 39; Styles Bridges, 257; British Welcome Club, 298-300, *299*; bronze plaque, 266, 327; cardinal of Sicily, silver medallion, 244; cars in combat, 9-10; cart, 174-75, 244; character as young officer, 7; "Charlie," 18, 25, *25*; Casablanca, 5, 18, 26, 41, 43, 46, 47, 53–55, 57, 60, 62, 130; Chauvin, 143; Cheddington airfield, 269; Chief of Cavalry Office, 10; chin strap order, 77, 79-80, 108; Churchill telegram, 100; Civil Affairs of, African American troops, 336; Civil War analogies, 64, 82, 135, 292; Mark Clark, 35, 57, 139, 263-64; Herbert "Bertee" Clarkson, 237; Codman, 264, 291; Command and General Staff College, 10; Commander of the Bath (COB) medal, 282; Arthur Coningham 114–16, 120, 310; "corpses don't eat," 37; Corsica, 219, 245–47, 255; Norman Davis, 237–38; Desert Training Center, 34, 226; 2ème Règiment de Marche Tirailleurs Algèriens, 143; Jacob Devers, 247, 263, 265-66; discipline, 5, 10, 32, 73, 77–78, 85, 141–42, 195, 229, 272, 281–82, 330; diversionary tour, 245–47, 259, 262–63, 288; dog, 269, 279, *280*, 315, 334; Jimmy Doolittle, 35, 74, 241; Manton Eddy, 76, 88, 100–102, 117, 147; William Eddy, 36; 82nd Airborne Division, 145, *229*; Eisenhower's rating of, 327; El Alamein after-action conference, 64; "an Elephant Hat," 235; El Guettar, 94-5, *97*, 97–98, 119; emotional, 4; Faïd Pass, 119; Douglas Fairbanks Jr., 150; Fedala beach, 11, 15, 19, 21, 24–26, 28, *29*; fencing, 9, 74; 5th Cavalry Regiment, 11; I Armored Corps, 15, 34, 60, 137; 1st Armored Division, speech to, 76; 1st Infantry Division, farewell to, 244; 1st Infantry Division, Gafsa, entrance into, 89; 1st Infantry Division, visit to, 147, 227–28; "fish to swim," 229; Paddy Flint, 187, 244, *251*, 325–26, 340; 45th Infantry Division, 145, 146, 165, 190, 227; .45 caliber automatic Colt "Peacemaker," 21; France, invasion from Corsica, 255; Fredendall's staff, 74; French (language), 9; French allies, dinner with, photo, *45*; Hugh Gaffey, photo of, *71*; Gafsa, 72, 81–82, 88–91; Gallup poll, 255, 260; Gela beach, 132, 134, 156,

Patton, George (continued)
156-60; General Court Martial, 26, 202, 225, 261; George S. (father), 7; story of foxhole soldier, 3; "God of Battles," 148; "going off the map," 33, 198; Jean Gordon, 11, 329–30; Goums, 145, 174; grandchildren, letters and poems to, 315; Grand Cross Order of the Ouissam Alaouite, 61; Robert A. Grant, slapping incidents, 257; Percy James Grigg, troop inspection, 142; Gruenther, 232, 263; Gulf of Gela, operations review, 143; Hawai'i, tours of, 10–11; helmet order, rank on, 78; Robert Henriques, 25, *25*, 27–28, 42, 147–48, 165, 168–69; Kent Hewitt, *22*, 23, 36–37, 40, 149, *150*, 232; history, knowledge of, 4; Courtney Hodges, 247, 332; Bob Hope, 225–26; horse kick, 11; Hotel Miramar, 27; Hughes, 62, 134, 151, 236, 243, 252, 254, 255, 262, 269, 291, 303, 311, 328–29; J.E. Hull, 277; hunting, 64; Italian campaign, disdain for, 248–49; Italian front, visit to, 263–64; Italy invasion, meeting on, 230; "I wish I was a corporal," 25, 27; Dick Jensen, 23, 107–111, 123; Norman Jewell, 147; Edwin C. Johnson, 257; Jed Johnson, slapping incident, 257; Kasserine Pass, 75–76, 81–82, 139, 213; Keyes, 36, 241, *251*, 264; Kipling, 304; Alan Kirk, bet with, 148–49; Knutsford incident, 6, 298–307; Oscar Koch, 8; landing craft, photo, *24*; Legion of Honor, 143; letter to son, 252, 319; lieutenant general, promotion to, 83–84, *84*; *LIFE* magazine, Tennessee maneuvers, 33; Henry Cabot Lodge Jr., 208, 257; *Los Angeles Times*, 305; Louisiana maneuvers, 32, 184, 249, 282, 329; Magnum "killing gun," 15, 21; John P. Marquand, 250–52; Hugh McGee, 294, 325; major general, permanent rank, 242; Malta, 255, 262–63; march, Columbus to Panama City, 32; Marrakech, 55, 59, 266; George C. Marshall, 11, 31, 34–35, 128, 135, 139, 213, 245, 261, 331, 342; Mas de la Tree, 9; Leslie McNair, 142, 193, 241, 243, 250, 255, 261, 284, 340–41; medals, 283, 311, 329; Meuse-Argonne offensive, 10; Mexico, 4, 9, 74, 21; M5 light tank, 338; François Michelier, 44; Troy Middleton, 146, 190, 277, 293, 333, 343–44; military writing, 141–42; mistakes, Richard Jenson, 5; M1913 Patton Saber, 9; M-1 rifle, 228; Robert Moore, 81; Morgenthau, 243; Morocco, 5, 7, 15, 18, 50–51, 53, 61, 73; Muhammad V, 42; Walter J. Muller, logistics, 37; Naples, 248; naval officer, photo with, 26; naval warfare, 21; Navy landings, 20; Navy peers, 36, 196; 1912 summer Olympics, 9; 9th Cavalry Regiment, 11; 9th infantry Division, 16, 38, 76, 88, 104, 113, 146, 175, 227; Nita, 8; August Noguès, 44, 50-51, 53–54, 60; North Africa fly over, 263; North Africa victory, anniversary luncheon, 310–11; Northern Attack Group, 16; Operation AVALANCHE, 232, 238–39; Operation COBRA, 336, 339, 341; Operation WOP, 88–92; Oran headquarters, 130; Palermo, photo, 182; Pancho Villa, 9; paratroopers, speech to, 145–46; Keith Park, 262; Patton speech, variations of, 284; Claude Pepper, 257; John J. Pershing, 9, 10, 38; pistols, "Banker's Special," 54; pistols, Rommel, 34; poem, *A Soldier's Prayer*, 261; prayer, 330; press uproar, 6; prisoners of war, killing of, 5–6; prostitutes, 242, 273–74; *Punch*, 279, *280*; Rabat, Thanksgiving, 56; racism of, 140–41, 174–75, 203, 247–49, 278–79; Rangers chaplain, 95; rape cases, 247–48; reincarnation, 7; Francis Rennell Rodd, 226; return to war, Third Army, 6, 265, 269; Russell Reynolds, Operation HUSKY review, 228–30; Rommel, 34, 39, 81-82, 87, 91, 130, 173, 302; "Rommel duel," 72; Franklin D. Roosevelt, 19, 49–50, 62–63; Teddy Roosevelt, Jr., death of, 337; Ruth Ellen (daughter), 9, 329; sand-fly fever, 171, 209, 215, 220; Saumur, 9; 2nd Armored Division, 16, 32–33, 38, 116, 167, 175, 177, 226, 249 *250*, 273; II Corps, 71–85, 122; semi-exile of, 5; Senate

INDEX

431

Patton, George (continued)
Military Affairs Committee, promotion tabled, 314–15; Sened Station, 93; "Seven Steps to Hell," 139; Seventh Army, 137, 149, 262–63; 70th Tank Battalion, 16; shrapnel, 136, 159, 264, 276; silver medallion, cardinal of Sicily, 244; 60th Infantry Regiment, visit to, 227; Walter Bedell "Beetle" Smith, 36, 65, 74, 211, 234, 246, 248, 252, 254, 260, 277–78, 301, 314; social beliefs, 8; speech thirty-three, 137; Stephen Sprindis, 53; staff meeting, criticism of British, 64; *Stars and Stripes*, "Blood-and-Thunder," 104; St.-Mihiel, 10; Stimson, 254, 260, 306, 335; sultan of Morocco, 51 52, 52, 53, 54, 59, 61, 64; Tank Corps, 4, 10, 32; tanks, 32–34, 58, 173–74, 325; *There Shall Be No Night*, 273; Third Army, 6–7, 269, 276, 281-82, 302, 323, 333-34, 336, 342, 344; 3rd Cavalry Regiment, 11, 31; 3rd Infantry Division, 16, 27, 56, 147, 179, 198, 228; Tiger tanks, assessment of, 173; *Time*, 122, 130, 305–6; Harry S. Truman, slapping incidents, 257; Truscott, 53, 166-67, 181, 187, 195, 198, 205-06, 209-11, 232, 238, 264; Tunis, 84, 139, 246; Twelfth Air Support Command, 97, 119; Ultra, 80–81, 130–31; USS *Augusta*, 15–30, 40; Utah Beach, German fighter, trip strafed by, 337; Vichy France, North Africa, treatment of locals, 50; Vichy policies, anti-Semitism, 50; VMI, 8; Fred Walker, air support, 321; Walter Reed Army Hospital, 38; Ward, 74, 91, 93, 98, 101–2, 105, 116; warrior example, 4; *Washington Post*, 305; John Waters, 58, 59, 81, 87, 92, 249; Wedemeyer visit, 142–43; Western Task Force, 16, 60, 73, 139; West Point, 8–9; Weyland, relationship with, 275; Charles H. White, review, 228–30; Wigglesworth, bet with, 179; Willie, 279, 280, 315, 330, 332, 334, 339; Arthur Wilson, 239–40; Woman's Auxiliary Corps, 226–27; John Wood, Knutsford incident, 306; World War I, 4, 10; wounded soldiers, no responsibility for, 122; *YANK* magazine, 119; Luis Orgaz Yoldi, 49, 60; youth, 7–8

Patton, George, Alexander: Bizerte headquarters, visit to, 237; dislike of, 134; 18th Army Group, chain of command, 83; Feriana headquarters, 88–89, 91; half-track, 99–100; Italy, 237, 238; letter to, 121; Operation HUSKY, 132, 145, 164–65, 170, 172, 177, 184, 193-94, 201, 210; opinion of, 82, II Corps, 91–92, 98, 100, 103, 113, 115, 121; slapping incidents, 207, 224

Patton, George, Beatrice: Armored Corps March, 250; background, 9; "Charlie," 25; Henry Cabot Lodge Jr., 257; media, 256, 308; General Sherman, 292; slapping incidents, 256–57, 266

Patton, George, Eisenhower: Biscari Massacre, 293; Britishness, 128; compliment, 135; criticism of, 116, 121; difficult relationship with, 6–7; dinner with in Algiers, 243; dressing down, 209–10; Gilbralter, meeting with, 52–53; *The Greatest Norman Conquest*, 258; helmet, 83; lack of praise from, 240; letter to on replacements, 239; London, criticism of, 269; meeting of Operation OVERLORD, 262; memorandum on being reckless, 109; nickname for, 224; North Africa command, 34–35; North Africa victory, praise for, 135; pistols, 209–10

Patton, George, Meeks: background, 23; Algiers, bombing of, 137; as a representative of race, 174, 279; boots, for Patton, 328; Bradley, 265; Casablanca, bombing of, 60; Fedala beach, landing craft to, 22–23, 24; Hotel Miramar, 28; Jenson, grave of, 123; Normandy, flight to, 330; Patton, relationship with, 8; pistols, 21; Willie, 279

Patton, George, Montgomery: criticism of, 132; dislike of, 134; lectures, cigarettes, 65; map of Sicily, 133; misunderstanding, 65; opinion of, 64; Palermo meeting, 188; relationship with, 7; support for, 82; Syracuse meeting, 182–84; view of, 240

Patton, George, Operation HUSKY: aftermath, 220–21; Agrigento, as headquarters, 174, 178; air support, 169; Alexander, criticism of, 132; Allen, 160, 186, 190, 195, 201; assault troops, message to, 150–51; Paul G. Bennett, 202–3; bet, days to capture Sicily, 160; Bradley, contradicting his command, 160; Brolo, 201–2, 206-09; Darby, Distinguished Service Cross, 163; deserters, 202; Eisenhower, 149, 161–62, 164, 169, 186, 191, *192*; Falcone landing, 209; 15th Evacuation Hospital, 194–95; final staff meeting, 148; 1st Infantry Division, use of, 159; Gavin, drink with, 163; Gela, 156–59, *158*, 160, 162; Germans, dead, pictures of, 168; Goum, hanging of, 174; grappling hook, 135–36; Keyes, 160, 162, 165, 175-76, 178, *182*, 187, 192, 205, 210; Kuhl incident, 195; Luigi Lavitrano, 181, *183*, 187, 191, 244, 253; Henry Cabot Lodge, Jr., 208–9; Messina, entrance into, 210–11; Middleton, 168, 190; *Monrovia*, 148-49, *155*, 153–54, 160–62; Montgomery, 134, 162, 168-69, 182–84, 188; Nicosia, helmetless Roosevelt, 188–89; 91st Evacuation Hospital, 193; 93rd Field Hospital, 202; on Roosevelt, 190; Palermo, 166, 167, 169–72, 175–79, *182*, 188, *189*, 192; planning, 130–34; Ponte Olivo, 160-61; Porto Empedocle, 164; preparation for, 135–37; provisional corps, 165; re-embark message, 159; review of, 228–30; Roosevelt, relief of, 201; sand-fly fever, 171, 209, 215; San Stefano, 195–97; Seventh Army, 143–45, 152, 161, 181, 211; Sicily, cash to civilians, 202; *Stars and Stripes*, foxhole jumping, 215; Stiller (major), 163; Troina, visit to, 195; Truscott, 166-67, 171, 181, 187, 195–96, 198-99, 205–6, 210-11; Ultra, 131; USS *Biscayne*, 166; war crimes, 236; Wigglesworth, 169; wounded soldiers, photo, *204*

Patton, George, Operation OVERLORD: chief of staff, 278; England, celebrity in, 272; England, secretly in, 283; 5th Infantry Division, Northern Ireland, 275; flight to Normandy, 329; Graves Registration, 293; headquarters personnel, meeting of, 271–72; invasion meetings, 276, 311; London flat, 273; Mainwaring, 271, 327; XIX Corps, 277; Pas-de-Calais, alternate landing at , 270; "passion pit," 273; Patton speech, 283–88, *289*; preparation for, 270, 323; 2nd Infantry Division, Northern Ireland, 275; short first sergeant, 275; Spaatz, 270; "Tactical Use of Separate Tank Battalions," 293; toe injury, 328; United States, reasons at war, 272; Allison Wysong, 273

Patton, George, Operation TORCH: assignment, 35; Casablanca, attack on, 43–44; Casablanca, clean up, 48; "Charlie," 25; French army in Morocco, surrender of, 44–46; Geoffrey Keyes, appointment of, 36; mine-laying ship, 37–38; preparation, 2nd Armored, 38, 39; preparation, 3rd Infantry Division, 39; preparation, 9th Infantry Division, diatribe, 38; second day, French bombers, 39; second day, morning of, 39; second day, rampage, 39–40; shooting and Arab, 15; staff review, 47; task force commander, appointment as, 31

Patton, George, Sicily: assassination attempt, 253; departure from, 266–67; hunger riots, 252–53; killing of prisoners, 288; loneliness in, 240, 253; restlessness during, 249; revisiting battlefields, 242–43

Patton, George, slapping incident, 220–28; anti-Semitism, 203; Beatrice, 256–57, 266; Paul G. Bennet, 202-03, 222–24; *Boston Traveler*, Kuhl letter, 257–58; Eisenhower, 224-25, 230–31, 233–35; Robert A. Grant, 257; Hughes, letter to, 255, 260; Edwin C. Johnson, 257; Jed Johnson, 257; Charles H. Kuhl, 194-95, 223; list of for and against, 256–57; Henry Cabot Lodge Jr., 257; Marshall, 224–25, 230–31, 235; John McCloy, 258–59; Claude Pepper, 257; Drew Pearson, 253–55, 260; press, 257; Stimson, 254; Styles Bridges, 257; Harry S. Truman, 257; U.S. Senate Military Affairs Committee, 257–58

INDEX

Patton, George, Tunisia: accomplishments in, 5; Allen, anti-tank support, 88; Allen's trenches, 79; Omar Bradley, 74; corps hospital visit, 76–77; discipline, 77–80; drive to the coast, 100; Feriana headquarters, 84, 88; frontline inspections, 80; Gafsa attack, planning of, 88; Jenson's death, 5, 107-113; Luftwaffe, 80; opinion on, 73; ruins, 73; scout car, photo, *101*; "the $25 derby," 77–78; II Corps, assessment of, 88; watching tanks, photo, *104*; wool uniforms, 78
Patton, George IV (son), 9, 38, 252, 319, 325
Patton, Ruth Ellen (daughter), 9, 329
"Patton Effect," 230
Pearson, Drew, 253–55, 259–61, 275, 282
Pendar, Kenneth, Roosevelt letter to sultan, 49–50
"penny packets," 67, 74
Pepper, Claude, Patton, slapping incidents, 257
Périers, 331, 335, 338, 339
Pershing, John, 9–10, 38, 56, 63, 116, 121, 128
Peterson, E. L. "Pete," 291
P-51 Mustang, 309, 313
P-47 Thunderbolt, 331
Philadelphia, 170, 206–7
phosphorous shells, 113, 117, 157
Pinckney, Philip, Operation HUSKY, attack on Palermo, 177
PM Daily, Patton, slapping incidents, 257
Poletti, Charles, 191, 252–53
Pontoubault bridge, 343
Port Lyautey, 16, 38, 53
Porter, Robert, Operation HUSKY, Allen's relief of command, 186
Provisional Corp, 165, 173–74, 176, 181–82
Punitive Expedition, 9, 75, 145
"Purple Heart Box," 100

Queen Mary, 271

Raff, Edson, Operation OVERLORD, D-Day, Utah Beach, 322
Rangers: El Guettar, 95, 98; Sicily, 144, 154, 157–58, 162-63, 167; Pointe du Hoc, 319, 321
Ratay, John, 43
Red Crescent Society, 237, 329
Red Cross, 237,
Reynolds, Quentin, 238
Reynolds, Russell, Operation HUSKY, review of, 228–30
Ricks, Tom, 185
Ridgway, Matthew: background of, 145; drive to Messina, 190; Eisenhower, 149; Gela, 155–56; Piano Lupo, 144–45, 153; Palermo, 173; Salerno, 238
Robert Rowan, sinking of, 160
Roberts, Roy A., 288
Robertson, Walter, Operation OVERLORD, 2nd Infantry Division, Northern Ireland, 275
Robinett, Paul, Patton's visit, 91
Rockne, Knute, 89
Rodd, Francis Rennell, 226
Rodt, Eberhard, 213–14
Rommel, Erwin, 17; Kasserine Pass, 68, 69; Marshall, 302; Montgomery, 64, 68, 82; North Africa, departure from, 87; Operation TORCH, 31; Patton, on fighting him, 34, 39, 72, 81–82, 87, 91, 130; Sbiba, 68; Tobruk, 34. See also Mareth Line
Roosevelt, Franklin D.: Anfa Conference, 61-62; BBC broadcast to North Africa, 19; congressmen, 208; cousin to Teddy Roosevelt, Jr., 75; Palermo, 259; Patton, congratulations to, 117, 213; Patton, escort, 62; Patton, promotion, 83–84, *84*; slapping incidents, Drew Pearson, 253; sultan of Morocco, letter to, 49–50, 52; Tehran Conference, 253–54, 258-59; war, American entrance into, 35
Roosevelt, Teddy, Jr., 5; death of, 337; El Guettar Battlefield, 96, 97; Franklin Roosevelt's cousin, 75; helmet, 188–89; Nicosia, 188–89; on Patton, 75; Patton's assessment of, 190; relief of command, 185–87, 190-91, 201, 227; son of President Teddy Roosevelt, 75
Royal Navy, 31, 147, 212

Rubio Ranch, 9, 21
Ryder, Chares "Doc": Crocker on, 121; El Guettar, Battle of, 88; helmets, ranks on, 78; Operation Torch, 31; Patton's assessment of, 88; push to coast, 100, 103; Ward, 105

"Second Manassas," 82, 96, 122
"Seven Steps to Hell," 139
submarines: Operation HUSKY, aircraft carriers, anti-submarine duty, 131; Operation HUSKY, Italian mini, Axis retreat, 212; Operation HUSKY, s-class as surface markers, 147; Operation TORCH, 19
Salerno. See Operation AVALANCHE
Sant'Agata, 196, 199, *200*, 202
Saturday Evening Post, 220, 285
Sbiba, Rommel attack, 68
Semmes, Harry, 40–41, 136
Seventh Army: bronze plaque, 266; brothels, 242; creation, 137; congratulations from Patton, 211, 227; Devers, 247; dissolution of, 220, 233, 235; Eisenhower, 225; flag, 149, *150*, 152; Goums, 145, 174; initial assault plan, 143–45, 147, 162; Italy, 191, 220, 226; make-up of, 137; Messina, 193; "not desired," 253; Palermo, 178, 213; Patton relieved, 262, 263; Patton, wanting to keep, 239, 255, 264; secondary role in Sicily, 170, 269; shoulder patch, 137-38, 260; slapping incidents, 222, 232; Termini Imerese, 181
SHAEF. *See* Supreme Headquarters Allied Expeditionary Force
Shakespeare, *Henry the Fifth*, 288
Sicily: hunger riots, 252–53; maps, *144*, *167*. See also Operation HUSKY
Sidi Bou Zid, 68, 87
Simpson, William, 284, 315, 329, 341
Smith Walter "Beetle": Algiers meeting, Patton's diversionary tour, 246; Bradley under Patton, 74; Arthur Coningham problem, 114; William Eddy, 36; Fifth Armored Division, 313–14; Fredendall, 70; Hap Gay, 270; Gulf of Gela, 132;

Montgomery, 133; Montgomery's lecture, 65; Operation FORTITUDE, 337; Operation HUSKY, Messina, 211, 314; Operation HUSKY, Montgomery's Syracuse headquarters, meeting at, 184; Operation HUSKY, planning, 132; Patton, flying to Naples, 248; Patton, Knutsford incident, 301; Patton, opinion of, 246, 248; Patton's opinion of, 211, 248, 260, 314; Patton, presence in England, 275; Patton, slapping incidents, 254–55; Patton, 3rd Infantry Division request, 105; Seventh Army promotions, 211; ulcers, 73
Smith, Constantine, 298, 300
Smith, Fay, Operation OVERLORD, relief of, 324
Soldier's Prayer, A (Patton), 261
Soldier's Story, A (Bradley), 112
Spaatz, Carl "Tooey," 64, 114–15, 131, 197, 270, 312
Spain, 11, 20, 25-6, 36, 49
Spanish Morocco, 44, 47, 49, 60-1
Sprindis, Stephen, 53
St. John, Robert, 72
St. Lo, Operation COBRA, 331, 335, 338–39
St. Louis Post Dispatch, 257
Stalin, Joseph, 17, 214, 258
Stalingrad, 201
Stars and Stripes, 104, 215, 254–55
Stiller, Al: bomb crater, Jenson's death, 110, *112*; Fedala beach, Patton's landing craft, 22–23; helmet, 248; Hotel Miramar, 27; knutsford, 307; Operation HUSKY, Biscari Massacre, 291; Operation OVERLORD, Normandy, departure for, 330–31; Patton, shoot prisoners speech, 291; Patton, shooting at Arab, 80; prostitute, 59; shooting down Messerschmitt, 163
Stillwell, Joseph, Operation TORCH, initial concept, 31
Stimson, Henry L.; Patton, 208, 249, 254, 259–60, 306, 335; Spain, 48
sultan of Morocco: Anfa Conference, 61; anniversary of coronation, 53; Festival of Id el Kabir, *52*; Patton and Noguès, meeting with, 51–52, *54*; Patton, apology

sultan of Morocco (continued) from, 60; Patton, letter from, 42; Patton, time with, 59, 61, 64; Roosevelt, 49, 62
Summersby, Kay, 246, 269
Sumners, Hatton, Knutsford incident, 302
Surles, Alexander D., 288
"Symbol," 61

Taft, Robert, Knutsford incident, 303
Taylor, Henry J., 224, 231
Taylor, James, 342
Tedder, Arthur, 115, 131-32, 143, 232, 280
Tehran Conference, 253, 258
Thala, 68
There Shall Be No Night, 273
"the $25 derby," 77-78
Third Army, 269, 272, 274, 276, 279, 281-83, 287, 293, 300, 302, 305, 313-14, 323, 325, 332-34, 336-39, 342-44
Tiger tank, 72, 157, 173
Time: Bradley, 305-6; Palermo, 178, 122, 130, 305-6
Times of London, 257
Timgad, 123
torpedoes, 213
Trajan's Arch, 123, *123*
TRIDENT Conference, 219
Troina, 172, 193, 195, 198, 201, 251
Truman, Harry S., Patton, slapping incidents, 257
Truscott, Lucian, 16; Agrigento, attack on, 162, 166; Anzio, 277; Brolo landing, 205-8; Falcone landing, 209; Hill 171, 198; Italy invasion, meeting on, 230; Lyautey battlefield, Patton visit to, 53; Mehdia, 16, 21, 40; Messina, *182*, 187, 190, 209-10; Naples, Patton visit, 248; Operation AVALANCHE, German counterattack, 238; Palermo, photo, 182; Patton's praise of, 167; Patton's visit to San Stefano, 195-98; Seventh Army, initial assault plan, 144
"Truscott Trot," 179
Tucker, Reuben, 504th, Seventh Army's initial assault plan, 144
Tunisia, 59, *90, 101, 104*; Kenneth Anderson, 52, 56-57, 69, 83, 121; Jürgen von Arnim, 68, 82, 87, 91; Benson Force, 110, 111-113, 176, 366n; Bizerte, 92, 119, 121, 135-36; Coningham, 114-16, 120, 310; Eisenhower, 57-58, 62-3, 67, 60-74, 80, 83, 87-89, 91-92, 100, 109, 114, 116,.121; Fifth Panzer Army, 68; front, new arrangement on, 63; Goumiers, 145; Richard McCreery, 103, 117, 119, 240; George Patton, 3, 5, *71, 84, 97, 101, 104*, 122, 139, 192, 231, 235, 240; II Corps, under Fredendall, 56, 63, 65, 68-9; II Corps, under Patton, 70-3, 76-8, 83, 85, 87-9, 91-92, 95, 98, 100, 109, 112-17, 119-21, 127; II Corps, under Bradley, 122, 135; soldier in foxhole, 3; weather of, 57, 73, 75, 78
Twelfth Air Support Command, 119

Ultra, 80-81, 130, 131
USS *Augusta*, 15, 18, 21, 23, 28, 40
USS *Biscayne*, 166
USS *Boise*, 154
USS *Maddox*, sinking of, 154
USS *Mayrant*, 192
USS *Philadelphia*, 170, 206-7
USS *Savanna*, 157

V-1 rocket, 326, 333
Villa, Pancho, 9, 21, 145
Virginia Military Institute (VMI), 8

Walker, Fred, 232, 321
Walker, Walton, 294, 300, 339
War Plans Division, 142, 145
Ward, Orlando, 75, *99*; El Guettar, 98-105; Fredendall, 67; Gafsa, 88, 91; Kasserine Pass, 74-75; Maknassy, 82, 93-94, 98; Patton, opinion of, 101-2; relief of command, 116-17; Sened Station, 92-93; Silver Star, 101
Washington Post, 305
Waters, John, 58, *59*, 65, 67-68, 81, 87, 92, 249
Wedemeyer, Albert, 142-43, 153, 231
West, Horace T., 168, 288-90
Western Task Force, 15, 16, 18, 23, 28, 35, 44, 60, 73, 139

Weyland, Otto P., 274–75
Wherry, Kenneth, Knutsford incident, 303
White, Charles H., Operation HUSKY, review of, 228–30
White, Harry Dexter, 243
Wigglesworth, 169–70, 179
Wilbur, William, 26, 40, 43
Williams (lieutenant colonel), 288–89, 291
Willie, 279–80, 300, 315, 324, 330–34, 339
Wilson, Arthur, Patton, 239–40
Winterbotham, Frederick, Ultra briefing, 80–81

Woman's Auxiliary Corps, 227
Women's Voluntary Service, 298
Wood, John "P.," 274, 294; Avranches, 342–43; Coutances, 341; Patton, 306, 343; Selune River, 342, 344
Wysong, Allison, Operation OVERLORD, 273

YANK magazine, 119
Yoldi, Luis Orgaz, 49, 60